DIAMONDS

Foremost of all amongst the glittering race
Far India is the *Diamond's* native place;
Produced and found within the crystal mines,
Its native source in its pure lustre shines:
Yet though it flashes with the brilliant's rays
A steely tint the crystal still displays.
Hardness invincible which nought can tame,
Untouched by steel, unconquered by the flame;
But steeped in blood of goats it yields at length,
Yet tries the anvil's and the smiter's strength.

With these keen splinters armed, the artist's skill
Subdues all gems and graves them at his will.

Part of a poem probably composed by the Abbott Marbodus (Marboeuf) when master of the Cathedrel School of Anjou from 1067 to 1081.

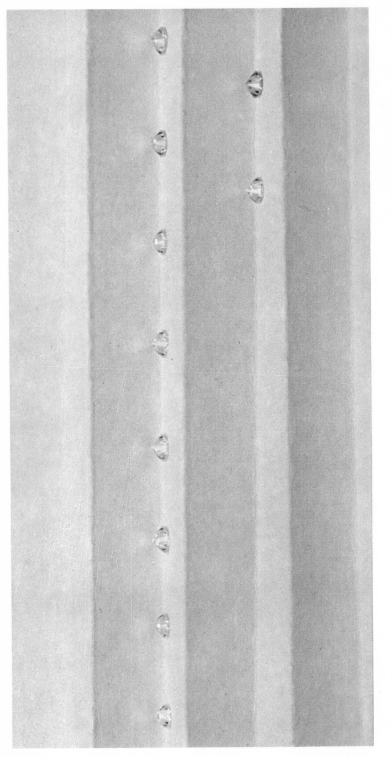

*It is impossible to show on the printed page an accurate range of polished diamonds graded for colour and the object of this plate is to give some idea of the narrowness of the range of colour in "white" stones. The stones in the top row are Cape Series stones and range from about Crystal to Yellow or Dark Cape (**see page 270**). There are several grades whiter than the stone on the left. The two stones on the lower row are Brown Series. The stones are shown on a corrugated piece of white paper in a white light at about the angle that they should be graded by eye. The difficulties in reproducing the colours accurately are in the different colour values caused by the camera lighting, the film stock, the ink used in reproduction and finally the paper on which the reproduction is printed, since that also has a tint which is several grades below that of the finest white diamond. Photograph by Peter Parkinson, F.I.I.P., London.*

DIAMONDS

Second Edition

Eric Bruton F.G.A.

CHILTON BOOK COMPANY
Radnor, Pennsylvania

ISBN: 0—8019—6789—9
Library of Congress Number: 78—66362

2 3 4 5 6 7 8 9 0   9 8 7 6 5 4 3 2 1 0

Contents

CONTENTS

vii

FOREWORD

by Professor S. Tolansky, Department of Physics, Royal Holloway College (University of London)

Diamonds have attracted man's attention for thousands of years. The striking exceptional hardness of the stone called adamas (diamond) was recognized almost in prehistorical times and remarkably enough this unique hardness today plays a formidable part in modern industrial technology.

There has always been an exceptional dichotomy in the evolution of the use and exploitation of diamond. It started off being worn as a talisman, inducing strength and courage by virtue of its hardness, whilst at the same time, even in Biblical times, it was used as a hard tool for engraving and maybe for drilling too. Then as time progressed, by the early Middle Ages it began to be used by the wealthy and the great as a decorative gem, whilst at the same time its uses for glass engraving and glass cutting were developed side by side. By the early nineteenth century the use of diamond as a fiery decorative gem was widespread amongst those who could afford it, yet again its employ as a hard technical material was gathering momentum. Indeed it was certainly being used for rock drilling early in the eighteenth century, if not before this.

The twentieth century saw a great upsurge in this dichotomous use of diamond. Primarily this came about through the discovery of the great new mining sources on the African Continent. To this has been added the invention some fifteen years ago of the manufacture of a true synthetic diamond material suited for grinding wheels.

Now many millions of men and women wear diamonds, mainly, but not exclusively, in rings, brooches and watches and likewise almost the whole of engineering and electrical industries, light and heavy, use considerable numbers of diamond machine tools, somewhere along the production line; from the making of fine lamp bulb filaments, to the smoothing of airplane runways, from manufacture of watches to building of bridges, from making a tiny screw to the building of a mighty oil tanker.

All this fundamental dichotomy is gone into in a most thorough and scholarly manner by Mr. Bruton in this book on diamond which we most heartily welcome. The author is in a rare and strong position for surveying this dual function of diamond in modern society. He has had long experience in the editorial chair, of the production of two journals, the one devoted to diamond as a gem, the other devoted to diamond as an industrial weapon. He has long been familiar with the formidable bibliography in both fields. He has also acquired special knowledge of the extensive diamond mining industry and, to crown it all, he has a most lively interest in the historical evolution and development of the use, the extraction and the exploitation of that king of stones, the diamond. I have enjoyed reading this most attractively written yet very complete general account about diamond and I am convinced that any other reader will equally respond to the infectious enthusiasm of the author.

This book does not set out to deal with the admitted formidable technical complexities of current scientific research on atomic diamond structure, such researches as are concerned, amongst other things with crystal lattices, light absorption and emission, thermal and electrical conductivity, chemical and physical impurities, etching and so on. It will not frighten off the lay reader with any overload of scientific technologies. On the contrary to the student of gemmology and mineralogy, to the practising diamond cutter and polisher, indeed to the non-technically minded diamond merchant, this book should prove to be a boon and something to whet the appetite.

September 1970   S. TOLANSKY

PREFACE TO SECOND EDITION

The world-wide acceptance of the first edition of *Diamonds* has made this second, extensively revised and extended, edition necessary, after several reprintings of the first edition in the U.K. and the U.S.A. The book was of value to people of widely ranging interests, to judge from the letters received from diamond dealers, cutters and polishers, gemmologists, jewellers, mining engineers, investment advisers, research workers, museum staff, other authors, amateur lapidarists, teachers, and others with information and suggestions, seeking information, or pointing out something with which they did not agree. Some just wrote a note of thanks. One American amateur actually built a cutting and polishing workshop from the information contained in Chapter Eleven and bought himself about five carats of diamonds to practise upon.

For help with the second edition, I am pleased to thank again almost all of those who helped me with the first and are mentioned in the other preface or in the list on page xiv, to which I have added more names. There are several whose assistance has been particularly valuable: Mr. Barry Mortimer, Group Public Relations Consultant in Johannesburg to the Anglo-American Corporation and De Beers, who made it possible for me to revisit or visit for the first time a number of mines; Mr. Richard Dickson and Mr. J. E. Roux both of De Beers Consolidated Mines, for generous help with information and checking proofs – also Mr. Howard Vaughan for great assistance when he was in Johannesburg – and, as before, to Mr. Arthur Monnickendam, and indeed the whole Monnickendam family, for providing facts and figures so freely and lending me goods to examine.

Two old friends have died since the first edition, Mr. Robert Webster, and Professor S. Tolansky. Mr. Lionel Burke, Group Public Relations Consultant in London to De Beers and the Anglo-American Corporation has retired; Mr. Harry Wheeler has become Secretary of the Gemmological Association and of the National Association of Goldsmiths, following Mr. Gordon Andrews; and I have relinquished the Editorship of *Retail Jeweller* to Mr. John Goodall, but continue as Publisher.

Again Mr. Alan Jobbins, of the Geological Museum, has put himself to much trouble checking selected galley proofs, as has Dr. F. A. Raal, Director, Diamond Research Laboratory in South Africa, who managed to return a set of proofs and his comments in five days from 5700 miles away in Johannesburg. Miss Diana Briscoe, Northwood Books, has also played a vital part in bringing the whole together.

Widmer End, Buckinghamshire.   ERIC BRUTON
1978

PREFACE TO FIRST EDITION

This book is the result of an interest in diamonds that began with a course in gemmology many years ago at the old Chelsea Polytechnic where the first lecturers were Mr. Basil Anderson, director of the London Gemmological Laboratory, and Mr. Robert Webster, long a senior member of the laboratory staff.

It happened that in the 1950s I became Editor of *The Gemmologist*, now alas defunct, and also *Industrial Diamond Review*, which today flourishes under the umbrella of De Beers. Much later, through the urging of Mr. Norman Harper, chairman of the Gemmological Association of Great Britain, who had started in Birmingham the first course in gem diamonds in Europe, I found myself running a parallel course at Sir John Cass College in London and in 1970 helped found a similar course at Barcelona University. Examinations for a diploma are held by the Gemmological Association of Great Britain and Professor S. Tolansky is the chief examiner.

Although some excellent books have been written on diamond with approaches ranging from very popular to very technical, there was still no single book that covered all or most of the aspects of gem diamonds, spanning the history of diamond digging and cutting, mining and recovery, cutting methods, grading and valuation, and identification of diamond and its simulants. The object of this book was to amend this omission in a style that could readily be understood by the layman as well as the serious student, as I have found on my 'diamond travels' that the diamond scene tends to be in an organized series of fairly tight compartments, so that, for example, the mining engineer has little information about the precious stones he is responsible for recovering, the geologist is hazy about the market-place, the retailer does not appreciate cutting and grading problems, and most of all, members of the general public do not appreciate that the possession of a diamond today, which is easy, has taken 4,000 years of endeavour – blood, toil, sweat and tears – to produce the modern brilliant-cut gem diamond.

There are very many people in addition to those already named who provided help and information. Of them my greatest thanks are due to Mr. Lionel Burke of De Beers Consolidated Mines in London, who made it possible for me to visit the principal diamond mines in the southern part of Africa to see and to ask my questions, a remarkable experience. Everywhere everyone was uninhibited with information. It is impossible to mention all by name but I must express particular thanks to Mr. Michael Grantham, who represents De Beers in Johannesburg, for his superb organization of visits to mines in four different countries.

In my present capacity of Editor and Publisher of *Retail Jeweller*, I have been fortunate in meeting many other people, too numerous unfortunately to mention by name, who have helped towards the eventual publication of this book.

Finally, my thanks are gratefully given to those who undertook the tiresome task of reading and criticizing the manuscript: Mr. Gordon Andrews, Secretary of the Gemmological Association of Great Britain, and various chapters in galley proof: Mr. Robert Webster, of the London Gemmological Laboratory; Mr. A. Monnickendam, Snr., principal of the cutters and polishers, A. Monnickendam Ltd.; Mr. Alan Jobbins, Chief Geologist, the Geological Museum; Mr. Howard Vaughan, of De Beers; Sir Samuel Fisher, Executive Vice-president of the London Diamond Bourse, Mr. Edmund Goldstein, Chairman of the London Diamond Club; and Mr. Herbert Tillander, Crown Jeweller, Helsinki, Finland, who is also Chairman of the Scandinavian Diamond Nomenclature Committee.

Finally my appreciation is especially due to Professor S. Tolansky for the difficult task he undertook of writing a foreword.

Great Bookham,   ERIC BRUTON
1970

ACKNOWLEDGMENTS FOR PHOTOGRAPHS
AND RELATED INFORMATION

Grateful thanks are due for pictures to:
De Beers Consolidated Mines – the publicity and photographic staff; Mr. Frank Beresford and Consolidated Diamond Mines of South-West Africa; the Anglo-American Corporation; the Diamond Research Laboratory, Johannesburg; Mr. R. Webster of the London Gemmological Laboratory; Dr. E. Gübelin, of Lucerne; Mr. R. Liddicoat, Director of the G.I.A. Los Angeles Gemological Laboratory; Mr. R. Crowningshield, Director of the New York Gemological Laboratory; Mr. H. Tillander, of Helsinki; Mr. J. T. McNish, of Cape Town; A. Monnickendam Ltd.; Mr. D. McNeil, Editor of *Jeweler's Circular-Keystone*, U.S.A.; the Editor of *Retail Jeweller*, U.K.; the Editor of *Watchmaker, Jeweller and Silversmith*, U.K.; the Editor of *Industrial Diamond Review*, U.K.; the Secretary of the Gemmological Association of Great Britain; the Industrial Diamond Information Bureau, London.

My thanks must also be extended to the following for the loan and sight of diamonds, without which this book could not have been written.
De Beers Consolidated Mines; the Diamond Trading Company; Diamond Research Laboratory; Consolidated Diamond Mines of South-West Africa; Mr. D. Whitehead, of Industrial Diamond Co. (Sales) Ltd.; Mr. Gordon Andrews, of the Gemmological Association of Great Britain; Mr. Albert Monnickendam, senior, and Mr. Arthur Monnickendam; Mr. B. W. Anderson, of the London Gemmological Laboratory; Mr. A. R. Emerson, of Sir John Cass College; Mr. D. Clark, of D. and P. Clark (Diamonds) Ltd.; Messrs D. Bucks and P. Propper of Polished Diamond Distributors, and many others.

My thanks as well to the following, who, with many from the lists above, assisted with pictures and/or information for the second edition:
Mr. Alan Hodgkinson, Gemmologist, Glasgow; Mr. Alexander Pickett, Star Diamonds, London; The Hon. Ian Balfour, I. Hennig and Co., London; Mr. Paul Daniel, Managing Editor, *Industrial Diamond Review*; Dr. J. B. Hawthorne, Chief Geologist, De Beers, Kimberley; Dr. J W. Harris, Grant Institute of Geology, University of Edinburgh; Dr. D. Elwell, Stanford University, California, U.S.A.; Dr. Robert Gaal, Gemological Institute of America, Santa Monica; Mr. W. J. Lear, De Beers Consolidated Mines, Dr. Judith Milledge, Dept. of Crystallography, University of London; Dr. Godehard Lenzen, Idar Oberstein, W. Germany; Mr. R. Huddlestone, Diamond Grading Laboratories Ltd., Mr. P. Reed, formerly of De Beers Consolidated Mines, London; Herr M. Eickhorst, System Eickhorst, Hamburg, W. Germany; Mrs. Niekerk, Chief Librarian, Kimberley Library, South Africa; Mr. and Mrs. J. Sinkankas, Peri-Lithon Books, San Diego, U.S.A.; Mr. P. Kaplan, Lazare Kaplan and Sons, New York, U.S.A.; Miss Rosemary May, De Beers Consolidated Mines, London; Mr. A. N. Wilson, former Editor, *International Diamond Annual*, S. Africa; Mr. Theodore Loevy, Editor, *Diamond World Review*, Tel. Aviv, Israel; the Editor, *Diamant*, Antwerp, Belgium; Mr. Joseph Gill M.G.S.S. J., and S. S. DeYoung Inc, Mass; Miss Marion Stern, W. Stern, London; Mr. P. G. Read, gemmologist, Bournemouth.
In addition, I would like to thank the General Mines Managers of every mine I have visited, who were unfailingly friendly and helpful. More recently they have been Mr. W. K. 'Kidger' Hartley (whom I first met at Consolidated Diamond Mines in South West Africa) of the Kimberley Mines Division; Mr. John Martens of Orapa Mines, Botswana; Mr. Andrew Brittz of the Namaqualand Mines Division; and Mr. Keith Whitelock of De Beers Lesotho Mining Co. Mr. Hubert J. Wright, Mines Manager, Kimberley Division, was particularly generous in having a special model of the block caving method of mining made and sent to me in the U.K. for use in teaching.

CHAPTER ONE

Diamonds in History

Introduction

As long as about three thousand years ago, man bent down to pick up a glistening pebble and by some chance found it to be different from other stones. From that time, diamond began to acquire magical powers and to be regarded with awe, worship and avarice. More recently it has become an object of extreme scientific curiosity.

Man began to collect diamonds, treasure them, build legends around them, trade in them, use them as tools, treat them as gems, raise loans with them, fight over them, and eventually to give them as symbols of love and trust. His early instinct to treat diamond as unique was true, because today probably more effort goes into discovering the nature of diamond than into research on any other material.

The desire for diamond because of its beauty as a gem, apart from its scientific and industrial uses, has not dimmed over the years but has become much more widespread. A century ago, the possession of a diamond was the prerogative of the rich alone. Since the discovery of huge deposits in Africa, and more recently diamond pipes in Russia, intensive mining and marketing of diamonds has brought them within reach of large sections of the populations of industrial countries, both as gems and as parts of working tools.

Diamond is the hardest substance man has ever discovered and the purest that occurs in Nature. Although very highly prized as a gem, however, it is composed of one of the commonest substances on earth, ordinary carbon. Carbon is found in all living things, plants as well as animals, and in many rocks.

Diamond can be broken with the blow of a hammer, yet will penetrate steel by pressure. It is extremely durable, being able to withstand attack by the strongest acids and alkalis, yet is an unstable form of carbon and will burn or oxidize on the surface if dropped in a fire for a short time. It has a very high melting-point and will cut steel for long periods at near red heat. Yet heated to bright red it will catch fire and convert to carbon dioxide gas.

Origin of the Name

Adamas and *adamant* were words implying extreme hardness, derived from the Greek *adamao* meaning 'I tame' or 'I subdue'. They were used in classical times to describe sapphire (corundum), which was sometimes confused with diamond. In the Bible, God tells the prophet Ezekiel (Chap. 3, verse 9), 'As an adamant harder than flint have I made thy forehead.'

Adimantum, a common Greek variation of *adamant*, is probably the root word of the old French *diamant* and the English *dyamaund* and *adamaund*, used at the beginning of the fifteenth century, as well as the poetic *dimaund*. The modern spelling originated in the mid-sixteenth century.

Fig. 1.1. *Jean Baptiste Tavernier, the French jeweller and traveller who made six trips of several years to the Orient buying and selling. Many famous Indian diamonds passed through his hands. His first trip was made in 1631 in his twenties.*

For many centuries, *adamant* referred to lodestone as well as hard materials such as diamond and corundum, owing to confusion with the Latin word *adamare*, 'to attract'. William Shakespeare used it in this sense at the beginning of the sixteenth century in *Troilus and Cressida* with the words, 'as a turtle to her mat ,/'As iron to adamant', but about sixty years later, John Milton was employing it in its original sense in *Paradise Lost*: 'Three folds were brass,/ Three iron, three of adamantine rock.' Adamantine, as used today, refers to the quality of impenetrable hardness, as in 'the adamantine lustre of a diamond's polished surface'.

The Hardness of Diamond

The Roman philosopher, Pliny the Elder, wrote: 'These stones are tested upon the anvil, and will resist the blow to such an extent as to make the iron rebound and the very anvil split asunder.'

The belief persisted for centuries. In the year 1476, Swiss mercenaries found diamonds belonging to Charles the Bold, Duke of Burgundy, after the battle of Morat, and struck them with hammers and hatchets to discover whether they were genuine, with the result that they powdered.

Many fine diamond crystals were broken in the same belief by miners of the

Indian mines from the fifteenth century to those of the early diamond diggings of South Africa in the last quarter of the nineteenth. It was said by Jean Baptiste Tavernier (1605–89) who was a French jeweller and one of the first 'globe-trotters' (Fig. 1.1), after he visited the Indian mines in the seventeenth century, that some merchants knew the true facts. They persuaded miners that stones they found were not diamond by breaking them with a hammer, then picked up the pieces after the disappointed miners had left.

'Diamond cut Diamond'

The truth is that, because diamond is the hardest known substance, it has relative brittleness. The two properties are different. Other materials are also brittle because they are hard, such as sewing needles and metal files. The eminent scientist Sir William Crookes used to demonstrate the hardness of diamond by placing a crystal between the jaws of a vice and tightening the vice. Diamond cannot be deformed plastically by normal forces, so the crystal penetrated the hardened steel jaws and did not break – an experiment that had been previously reported by Ibn Mansur in the thirteenth century.

One aspect of the hardness of diamond is, then, its extreme resistance to being deformed. Another is that it cannot be scratched except by other diamonds. But it resists scratching by another diamond in some directions more than in others. A diamond used in one of the harder directions will therefore cut another diamond in one of the 'softer' directions. That, and how to find the hard and 'soft' directions, was a secret kept for centuries by diamond cutters and engravers.

King Charles I of England was aware of the fact that powered diamond could be used to abrade a diamond (in a 'soft' direction). The night before his execution, in 1649, he wrote:

> 'With my own power my majesty they wound
> In the King's name the King's himself uncrowned
> So doth the dust destroy the diamond.'

Diamonds in Social History

The wearing of jewellery is as ancient a custom as any on record and appeared in early societies to be of primary importance after the seeking of food and shelter. It has been conjectured that the wearing of pretty stones was originally motivated by a desire to remember the spring with its promise of food and warmth, and later became the personal adornment or the symbol of rank or wealth that it is today.

Large diamonds were badges of rank worn by rulers and also convenient portable wealth in the early days of India. Most of the historical diamonds that still exist are Indian, and all have had eventful and sometimes bloody histories. Tavernier brought a number of them to Europe.

The Koh-i-Nûr, or Mountain of Light, has the longest history of all famous diamonds as it was known to be in the possession of the Rajahs of Malwa as long ago as 1304 and was facetted no later than 1530 (Fig. 1.2). It is believed to have been set by the Mogul emperors in the famous Peacock Throne as one of the peacock's eyes. The other eye was the Akbar Shah diamond. The Persian Shah took the diamond when he invaded India and later it came into the hands of the 'Lion of the Punjab' who accepted it in return for military help that he never gave. Eventually it was taken by the East India Company against losses and presented to Queen Victoria.

The 410 carat Regent Diamond (Fig. 1.3) played a part in the French Revolution. It was one of the last big diamonds to be found in India, in 1701. It came to England and was named 'the Pitt', and the major part after recutting was resold to the Regent of France, when it acquired its current name. Later Marie Antoinette wore it and on 17th September 1792, it was among the French Crown jewels that were stolen during the early stages of the French Revolution. Most of the treasures were quickly recovered but the Regent diamond did not come to light until fifteen months later when it was found in a hole in a beam of a Paris garret.

During the Directoire period, the Regent and other diamonds were pawned to a Berlin banker for 4,000,000 francs to keep fourteen French armies in the field. It was redeemed and then used as guarantee for a loan from a Dutchman. After it was again recovered, Napoleon Bonaparte had it set in the hilt of a sword he carried when being proclaimed Emperor of France.

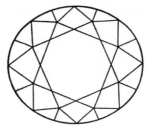

Fig. 1.2. The Koh-i-Nûr diamond, as it was first cut about 1530, and (centre) was recut in 1862 in Amsterdam. The present weight is 108.93 carats, and it is set in the British State Crown.

In the great Indian epic, the Mahabharata, which refers to events happening about 2000 B.C., one of the heroes wears the Koh-i-Nûr.

Fig. 1.4. The Hope diamond, which is thought to be part of the Blue Tavernier from the Kollur mine in India, brought to Europe by Tavernier after he had bought it in 1642. The Hope is now in the Smithsonian Institution Museum in Washington, D.C., U.S.A.

Fig. 1.3. The Regent diamond, from the Indian Partial mine. It was once in England and was known as the Pitt. Now in the Louvre, in Paris, it was one of the last big diamonds to be found in India, in 1701.

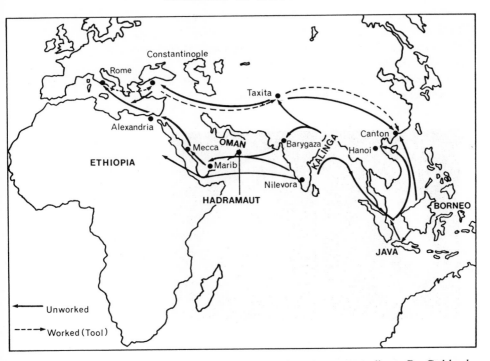

Fig. 1.5.   *Diamond trade routes from the first to the third century* B.C. *according to Dr. Godehard Lenzen.*

The Hope diamond, to which stories of tragedy have become attached, is supposed to have been part of the famous Blue Tavernier diamond brought to Europe by Tavernier. It was also stolen during the French Revolution, but never recovered. The 44½-carat Hope diamond (Fig. 1.4) is perhaps the largest of three parts into which the Blue Tavernier was cut. Hope's son lost his fortune after inheriting the stone. It was sold and eventually came into the hands of Mrs. Edward B. McLean, who lost her child in an accident, saw her family break up, lost her fortune, then committed suicide.

Diamonds' effect on social history has been mainly because they are possibly the greatest concentrated form of wealth which is negotiable almost anywhere. They have played a part in many upheavals and during recent world wars paid the way for the escape of refugees from totalitarian tyrannies.

From at least the fourth century B.C., India traded in diamonds, taxed them and exported them. There had long been trade between India and Babylon, Mesopotamia, Syria, Israel, Egypt, Ceylon, and Arabian countries. Diamonds that reached the western part of the Roman Empire were prized for their magical powers, but Rome also re-exported them to China as tool bits set in iron holders for cutting jade and drilling pearls during the first five centuries A.D. There were no superstitions in China to deny this use and, even as tools, they were still regarded as presents fit for kings, according to the Chinese philosopher Lao-tse in the first century A.D. The earliest known trade routes are shown in Fig. 1.5.

The Arabs and Persians monopolized trade between the Roman Empire and East Asia and, during the Middle Ages, between Europe and East Asia, until the sea route to India was discovered. It appears that they retained for themselves many of the finest diamonds from India and sold the poorer and smaller ones. The earliest price list of diamonds that has been discovered was issued in the twelfth century by the Arab, Teifaschius.

Fig. 1.6. *An Indian engraved diamond, the Jahangir, which is supposed to have been suspended from the beak of the jewelled peacock of the Mogul Emperor's Peacock Throne.*

Diamonds in Literature

It is difficult to isolate references to diamond in early literature because it is not known positively what certain names referred to. The word *jahalom* in the Bible, Exodus, Chap. 28, verse 18, instructing Moses to make a breastplate of judgement set with four rows of stones, is translated in the revised edition as diamond, but had it been one it would have been bigger that the Koh-i-Nûr. A reference in Jeremiah, Chap. 17, verse 1, thought to have been written about 600 years later, in 600 B.C., describes an iron pen with a point of a hard mineral. These early materials could have been diamond, but were more likely corundum. By 300 B.C., however, the Indians had certainly learned how to engrave with diamond and perhaps on diamond. An engraved Indian diamond is shown in Fig. 1.6.

The Roman, Pliny the Elder, who was born in A.D. 23 and died investigating the eruption of Vesuvius in A.D. 79, devoted a volume of his *Historia Naturalis* to precious stones, in which many rational statements are tangled with legend and myth. He wrote of diamonds: '. . . they resist blows to such an extent that an iron hammer may be split in two and even the anvil itself may be displaced . . . this invincible force, which defies Nature's two most violent forces, iron and fire, can be broken by ram's blood. But it must be steeped in blood that is fresh and warm and, even so, many blows are needed . . .'

'Valley of Diamonds'

Pliny also recorded that diamonds were found in a Valley of Diamonds, a belief that was based on an earlier legend of how Alexander the Great, during his campaign through India about 350 B.C., retrieved diamonds from a pit guarded by snakes whose gaze would kill a man. The snakes were killed by Alexander's soldiers using mirrors so that the snakes' gaze fell on themselves.

Sheeps' carcasses were then thrown into the pit. The diamonds adhered to the fat and vultures lured by the meat picked it up with the diamonds attached. The soldiers followed the vultures to their roosts and recovered the diamonds from nests and droppings. The Valley of Diamonds legend seems to have originated in writings of the Bishop of Constantia, Cyprus (c. 315–403) and was later repeated by Marco Polo.

The story has survived until today in the fable of Sinbad the Sailor, who was thrown into a diamond valley to die. He saved himself when he saw merchants throwing flesh into the valley. Wrapping some diamond-studded flesh round his body, he allowed a vulture to carry him to safety.

Professor Samuel Tolansky, an authority on diamond, suggested that the Valley of Diamonds legend was deliberately encouraged by Indian diamond merchants in Golconda, the trading centre, to disguise the true sources in river-beds of the surrounding country. He also suggests that the ram's or goat's blood legend may have had a similar purpose, to camouflage the art of cleaving, by which a diamond may be split to divide it by a single blow on certain places on the crystal.

Diamond Cutting

Early descriptions of facetting diamonds refer to polishing and it is presumed that octahedral crystals were left in their natural shape or the angles of the faces were altered by cutting, since they were called point-cut stones (Figs. 1.7 and 1.8). An octahedral face is in fact impossible to polish. Moreover, the process of cleaving produces pointed stones without the necessity for polishing. Grinding to

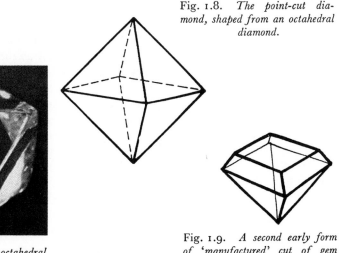

Fig. 1.8. *The point-cut diamond, shaped from an octahedral diamond.*

Fig. 1.7. *A natural octahedral diamond crystal of the type called a glassie which was sometimes set in jewellery.*

Fig. 1.9. *A second early form of 'manufactured' cut of gem diamond, the table-cut or table stone, made from a natural octahedron.*

7

remove the top point of the octahedral crystal to produce what was called the table stone (Fig. 1.9) presumably came later.

The history of cutting and polishing is poorly documented and the art remained a trade secret for many centuries. It is uncertain where cutting originated, whether in Europe or India, as well as which process came first. The origin in Europe was probably in the fourteenth century and in India possibly about the same time because there was an earlier ban for superstitious reasons on shaping diamonds. Superstition probably delayed the development in Europe, too, because the alteration of a diamond was supposed to destroy its magical properties.

Tavernier noted in the seventeenth century that there were considerable differences in the techniques of European and Indian cutters. He also surmised that the Indians used facets to hide flaws.

Mysticism and Diamond

Powerful material and spiritual powers have been attributed to gemstones from the earliest days until comparatively recent times. They were believed able to cure diseases, avert calamity, and to be able to ward off evil spirits. It was thought that the arbiter of a man's fate could be carried by him in his purse in the shape of a precious stone.

For many centuries before the spread of monotheism, man was believed to be a microcosm of the universe. He was its counterpart and for every part of his body there was a corresponding part of the universe. At the moment of dissolution of his body in death, his soul, if pure, united with the great universal soul – the Buddhist's *karma*. If his soul were impure, it passed through a number of transmigrations during which it animated animals, plants, and even some minerals, until it was purified and was absorbed into the universal soul. That is why gemstones were thought to have life.

These beliefs from ancient India spread through the East, then came to Egypt and to Greece and were influential in Europe in the Middle Ages, particularly through the activities of the alchemists.

Plato, the Greek philosopher, believed that precious stones were truly living beings and were produced by a sort of fermentation as the result of vivifying spirits descending from the stars. Distinguishing diamond from other stones as a kind of kernel formed in gold, he supposed it to be the purest and noblest part of the metal that had condensed into a transparent mass.

Later, Theophrastus, a pupil of Aristotle, divided precious stones into male and female specimens. It was a logical development of the belief in them as living beings. It followed that diamonds could reproduce themselves and, in 1566, Francisci Rueus referred in his work *De Gemma Tigur* to two diamonds belonging to a nobleman that did so. There were reports in the seventeenth century of diamonds recurring after three or four years in previously worked-out deposits both in Borneo and India; and in the same century, Johannes Bustamantius called attention to two diamonds that were 'married' and produced offspring!

Precious Stones

In 1501, on the threshold of the Renaissance, Jerome Cardan was born. He deserves a special place in gemmology, for he first defined a precious stone, and as a result, centuries later, led us to the absurdity of the semi-precious stone. Cardan classified all brilliant-appearing stones as gems. He reserved the expression 'precious stones' for those that were not only brilliant but rare and of small dimensions. Precious stones were still further divided into firstly, being brilliant and transparent like the diamond; secondly, those that were opaque like onyx; and thirdly, those 'formed by the conjunction of the two other kinds', an example being jasper. Onyx and jasper are actually similar material.

Cardan's beliefs were influenced by the animism of the previous centuries. He assumed precious stones to be living beings, that were 'engendered', in the same manner as the infant from the 'maternal blood', by juices distilled from precious minerals in the cavities of rocks. The diamond, emerald, and opal, he wrote, were distilled from gold. He added, 'And not only do precious stones live, but they suffer illness, old age, and death.' Even as late as 1876, Indians were told, 'Like men, diamonds are divided into Brahmins, Kshatriyas, Vaisyas and Sudras.' The divisions into caste were made by colour.

As a Medicine

Probably the earliest medicines were herbal and animal, but mineral substances were undoubtedly employed at an early date. Many pharmacopoeias acclaimed precious stones as among the most valuable remedies.

Diamond was not among the 'Five Precious Fragments' – the ruby, topaz, emerald, sapphire, and hyacinth (probably the orange-red zircon or hessonite garnet) – but was reckoned to have the power of resisting all poisons. If taken internally, however, it was supposed to reveal itself as a deadly poison. One belief was that a diamond grew dark in the presence of poison because particles emanating from the poison gathered on the surface of the stone, being unable to penetrate it.

Diamond has held this contradictory position in the view of several ancient authors. St. Hildegard (1098?–1179), a nun, maintained that a precious stone would only heal a person if held in his hand while making the sign of the cross. It would also heal if taken to bed and warmed by one's body, or if held in the mouth, especially when fasting, if breathed upon, or if worn next to the skin. She added that a diamond held in the mouth of a liar or scold would cure his spiritual defects.

The Hindus believed that only the powder of a flawed diamond was poisonous, causing various ailments and diseases such as lameness, jaundice, pleurisy and leprosy. Powder from diamonds of different colours, they said, had different flavours, from sweet to sour or salty. (There were also reports of the scent of powdered gems.) The powder of the highest quality diamonds, when swallowed, had the opposite effect to that of flawed ones, for it imparted energy, strength, beauty, happiness, and long life.

Alphonse X of Castile (1226?–84), in his *Lapidario*, declared that diamond was only to be used for chronic cases of bladder disease.

As a Poison

Emperor Frederick II (1194–1250) died, according to legend, through a fatal dose of powdered diamond. The Turkish Sultan Bajazet (1447–1513) is said to have been poisoned to death by his son, who mixed a large amount of pulverized diamond in his father's food. In 1532, Pope Clement VII was ailing and was prescribed doses of powdered precious stones, including diamond, by his physicians. Apparently he failed to survive the fourteenth spoonful, by which time the bill was 40,000 ducats.

There are other records of the death of prominent people by diamond poisoning. Catherine de Medici's powder tipped into food or drink – the famous *poudre de succession* – is supposed to have been powdered diamond. If it was, there was probably another secret ingredient, possibly arsenic. Catherine (1519–89) was the dominating wife of Henry II of France.

The celebrated Italian goldsmith, Benvenuto Cellini (1500–71), wrote at length about an attempt on his life by his enemy, P. L. Farnese, son of Paul III, who attempted to poison him by causing powered diamond to be mixed with his salad. Cellini attributed his escape to the fact that the lapidary who was employed to pulverize the stone kept it for himself and substituted powdered glass for the diamond powder.

It is possible that the belief that diamonds were poisonous was fostered to reduce the risk of stealing, particularly from the mines, by swallowing the stone and recovering it later.

Magic Powers

Precious stones were significant in astrology. In a table of planets given in the seventeenth century, diamond is equated with the sun thus: Planet: *Sun.* Metal: *gold.* Precious stones: *diamond, sapphire, jacinth, lodestone.*

A curious belief about the diamond was that, if held in the mouth, it caused the teeth to drop out. Jewellers today often advise the owner of a valuable diamond ring to hold it with her teeth while washing her hands, to eliminate the risk of leaving the ring behind.

Diamond was supposed to be of service to lunatics and those possessed of devils. It also repelled the attacks of phantoms and made the sleep of the wearer free from nightmares. It was worn in battle because it dispelled vain fears and made the wearer courageous as well as magnanimous and virtuous.

Another benefit of diamond was its ability to baffle the magic arts and to cause lawsuits to be settled in favour of the wearer. It was not explained what happened when both parties wore diamonds. If a house, orchard, or vineyard were touched at each corner with a diamond, it was thought to be protected from lightning, storms and blight.

A property of some diamonds, known in Roman times, if not earlier, and regarded as proof of diamonds' magic, was their ability to glow in the dark after being subjected to strong sunlight for a time; that is their phosphorescence after exposure to ultra-violet light.

The ancients declared that the magic powers of diamond were so superior that a lodestone would lose its magnetism in the presence of diamond. It is easily proved that a diamond, when rubbed, will pick up small pieces of paper and other light objects because of the static electrical charge induced. (When rubbed on wool it becomes electrically positive.) Probably it was this fact that lively imaginations developed into superior magnetic powers. No one thought of experimenting to discover whether the fact was true. Intellectual theory was supposedly vastly superior to practical experiment, particularly in Greek times. The value of experiment was not appreciated until the eighteenth century.

Diamond as a Gem

Diamonds have not always been regarded as dominant gemstones. In early times the Persians certainly preferred pearls, which could be perfect and very beautiful when taken from the oyster, whereas the diamond crystal was insignificant in appearance, relying on its invincible properties for its value. In the Middle Ages, diamond was rated below ruby and emerald and had slipped to seventeenth place in importance in medieval lapidaries as its powers became less credible. Cutting and polishing, as the techniques improved, restored diamond to a high place in the list of gems, but for different reasons.

Attributes of Gems

All gems have three attributes in common. They are beautiful; they are durable; and they are rare. Beauty in some gems relies on colour alone. In others it comes from a display of light, as in the iridescence of opals and pearls, the schiller of moonstone and bronzite – and the fire of diamond. Beauty is also affected by the lustre of the surface. The lustre of diamond is unique and for that reason has been given its own name – adamantine.

Durability is an obvious necessity for a valuable gem. It usually relates to hardness, but not always, for pearls are quite soft, yet endure for thousands of years. Diamond is again unique in durability. Few well-known diamonds have been lost for ever. They usually turn up again, even after centuries.

Diamond is the only colourless and transparent gemstone that has great beauty. Colourless zircon is poor by comparison. The man-made strontium titanate, that has been appropriately named Fabulite by the trade, compares with it in appearance, although it is too 'flashy' and too soft. Another man-made mineral, yttrium aluminate (Y.A.G.), is also a good simulant which is hard but has less fire than diamond. The most deceptive is probably zirconium oxide (Djevalite).

Rarity is a term that must be qualified in relation to value. Rubasse is a rare rock crystal with red spangles in it, but it is not valuable. About seven tons of diamond are mined every year, yet diamond is valuable. By rarity, one means how far the supply fulfils the demand. For example, the demand for good coloured emerald outstrips the supply, with the result that emerald prices are always rising. The supply of diamond is related to the demand and average prices keep roughly in step with world inflation.

Despite new finds of gem diamond sources, ultimately the supply of natural diamonds must fail. Nature does not provide endless reserves, so prices will tend to climb. This has happened already with diamonds over a carat in weight, which are becoming harder to come by. Even if diamonds are discovered on other planets, the cost of recovery will keep prices high.

Synthetic Diamonds

What about synthetic diamond, made in the factory; surely that will reduce the value of natural diamonds? The question is frequently asked. Diamonds have been made synthetically in commercial quantities since 1954 and today many tons are manufactured, although no commercial gem diamonds have appeared yet. Gem diamond was first made in 1970 on a laboratory scale by a long and very costly process, by General Electric of America.

When commercial gem diamonds appear on the market they will be expensive. If the price later falls, will this cause the prices of natural gem diamonds to plummet? Definitely not. Thousands of tons of synthetic rubies and sapphires are made yearly, mainly for industrial uses, but also as gems. The huge numbers of synthetic rubies and sapphires on the market at under £1 each have not reduced the high prices of the natural stones. The same is true of synthetic emeralds. In fact, the shortage of fine natural emerald has kept the price of synthetic emeralds much higher than the prices of many other attractive natural stones.

Therefore synthetic gem diamonds are not a threat to natural gem diamonds, but might well expand the market and the demand for natural stones and push up prices.

A synthetic stone is exactly the same material as a natural one. A synthetic diamond is like a natural one, a unique structure of carbon atoms. A synthetic ruby, like a natural one, is a particular structure of aluminium oxide. The differences that exist between the natural and synthetic are often extremely small. Often the synthetic is too perfect for Nature to have made.

While it remains possible to identify a natural from a synthetic stone, a price difference will exist. It is often necessary to call in the services of a specialist laboratory to determine whether a stone is natural or synthetic. This is particularly true of synthetic emerald, and may be so of synthetic gem diamond.

Synthetics and Simulants

It should at this point be made clear that in gemmology the expression synthetic applies only to a man-made replica of a natural material, so synthetic diamond is real diamond. A copy, which looks identical or very similar but is not the same material, is called an imitation or a simulant. The high-density glass, known as strass or paste, used to copy diamond, is therefore a diamond simulant, or an imitation diamond. It is *not* a synthetic diamond. Strontium titanate, zirconium oxide, lithium niobate and yttrium aluminate (Y.A.G.), one trade name of which is Diamonair,* are oddities. Having no counterparts in Nature, they are not strictly speaking synthetic stones, although for convenience they are called synthetic. When either is used to imitate a diamond, it is used as a diamond simulant.

Diamonds in Jewellery

After diamonds were discovered, they were not worn in jewellery if they were worn at all, as they were regarded as talismans. At some point they acquired value in exchange for other goods or for services and therefore became a means of acquiring wealth in a conveniently portable and durable form. Perhaps the first wearers were the princes of India seeking magical protection and then

---

* The trade name Diamonair has been condemned by some European gemmologists because of its likeness to diamond.

displaying their power and wealth. The diamond had become a badge of rank.

It has been suggested that diamonds were known to the ancient Greeks but this seems unlikely as they also used the word *adamas* for iron and for sapphire. A small bronze statuette in the British Museum in the Greek style of about 500 B.C. has been cited as evidence because the eyes are set with small diamonds. The Museum, however, places the statue among Roman bronzes of the first century B.C. or A.D. Moreover, the diamonds were examined by several specialists, including B. W. Anderson, director of the London gem laboratory, in 1953, who came to the conclusion that the diamonds had a form of rose cut similar to the diamond endstones used in the late eighteenth century in watches and chronometers. The diamonds were crudely set and foiled and must have been added at a relatively recent date.

In the first and second centuries A.D., Romans wore diamond crystals set in gold rings, but for superstitious reasons of protection rather than as jewellery. The early history of the diamond in jewellery still has many mysteries.

One of the earliest pieces, if not the earliest, set with diamonds (uncut) must been a queen's crown – the Holy Crown of Hungary, or Crown of St. Stephen, shown in Fig. 1.10. Figures on it of the Emperor of the Romans (Michael Dukas) and the King of Hungary (Geza I) indicate that it was a gift from Byzantium to the Hungarian Royal Court between the year 1074, when Geza became king, and 1078, when Dukas lost his throne. After World War II, it was taken to the U.S.A. and was returned to Hungary in 1978 by President Carter.

It was unusual for a king to have his own picture on a crown and the crown itself has the characteristics of one for a queen, therefore the crown may have been intended for Queen Synadene, who came from a Byzantine noble family and was the wife of King Bela I, Geza's father. The diamonds are set, with pearls, in the arches over the crown.

One of the earliest places where diamonds were worn must have been Paris, because it was a centre of goldsmiths as long ago as the seventh century, when three jewellers, Eloi, Alban de Fleury, and Theau, were canonized. Only the monasteries had workshops and made pieces for the priests for a long period, but by the twelfth and thirteenth centuries, secular jewellers had become well established. The earliest reference to diamonds seems to be in 1319, however, about a diamond necklace said to have been worn by the French Queen Clemence, Hungarian wife of King Louis X the Quarreler (1289–1316).

Edward, Prince of Wales (1330–76), the eldest son of Edward III and later known as the Black Prince, was very fond of jewels to judge from records that still exist. In 1355, for instance, among his jewel purchases were twenty-seven rings, some set with rubies, some with diamonds, and some with pearls. A crown of gold set with diamonds, rubies, sapphires 'and other great pearls' fell into his hands when the owner, King John II of France, was taken prisoner at Poitiers in 1356.

The Duke of Burgundy gave his mother a ruby brooch surrounded by diamonds and pearls in 1369. In 1396, when King Richard II of England married his second wife Isabella of France (who was seven years old at the time), he gave her a number of presents, one being a collar of diamonds, rubies, and large pearls. There are many other records of Royal gifts of diamonds from these early times to the present day, but it is difficult to determine from them whether or not the diamonds were faceted or not, that is, when faceting was invented.

A well-publicized gift of diamond jewellery was that of Jacques Coeur, a French diamond merchant of the mid-fifteenth century, to Agnes Sorel, mistress of King Charles VII of France (Fig. 1.11). Jacques Coeur was firstly a coin maker who, when young, was exiled for competing with the Royal Mint. He was reinstated after fighting for the Pope, and became a powerful trader with the

Fig. 1.10. *The Crown of St. Stephen, which is perhaps the earliest jewelled piece in existence set with (uncut) diamonds. It is in the Hungarian Crown jewels and is dated between 1074 and 1078.*

14

Fig. 1.11. *Agnes Sorel (1422?–50) popularized the wearing of diamond jewellery in the French court.*

East. Agnes Sorel persuaded Jacques Coeur to finance the king's battle against the English and subsequently arranged for him to become the king's financial adviser and later master of the Royal Mint.

Coeur imported stones from India and diamond cutters from Venice and Constantinople. He made diamond necklaces, brooches, and buckles for Agnes Sorel to wear, and she became famed for her jewels.

In the reign of Queen Elizabeth I of England, from 1558 to 1603, it was for some time fashionable among the wealthier to wear rings set with octahedral crystals of diamond with the point of a four-sided pyramid to the front. At one time they became known as scribbling rings after the craze for using them to scribble love messages on glass window-panes. Even the Virgin Queen herself, it is said, exchanged rhymes with Sir Walter Raleigh on a window-pane.

Over the centuries, diamond jewellery has become more and more widespread until today in Britain, three women in four own diamond rings.

Where Diamonds are Found

Pliny remarked that the diamond accompanied gold. Diamonds *are* found with gold, but we know now that they arrive together through the actions of winds and rain over millions of years gradually shaking and sifting them and other heavy minerals together. Diamond does not occur in its original sources with

Fig. 1.12. *A natural diamond of rounded octahedral shape in blue ground, the rock that brings it to the surface from over 120 miles deep in the Earth where it was formed. Diamonds are completely enclosed in the blue ground and 'spring out' when the rock is crushed. Occasionally one is held, as shown here, after the rock has been crushed. Millions of years ago, the forces of nature broke up the exposed blue ground to release any diamonds; these were then carried away by rivers and eventually trapped in what are now alluvial deposits.*

gold. Pliny referred to six types of diamond, but from his descriptions some of the types were sapphires, which are very heavy and are also found with gold.

As far as is known, all early sources of diamond were in the beds of active or dried up rivers, despite the legends. India was the only known source for over 2,000 years, except for Borneo where diamonds were probably first mined in the sixteenth century. The Brazilian diamond fields were discovered in the gold-mining area of Minas Gerais in 1725.

New discoveries always seem to have been regarded with scepticism. The genuineness of the Brazilian stones was questioned on the London market and as late as 1740 a jeweller declared in print that it was a 'false idea that the (gold) mines of Brazil furnish diamonds'. Even a century later, Portuguese merchants used to take the Brazilian diamonds to Goa, a Portuguese possession in India, to sell them. Mining was carried out so intensively that main areas were almost exhausted in twenty years.

By an extraordinary coincidence, the South African diamond fields were discovered in 1866, by the time that the Brazilian fields were exhausted. When the news arrived in Brazil, history repeated itself. The Brazilian merchants refused to believe the fact, and many were ruined. Professor J. R. Gregory, a London University mineralogist, actually spent three weeks in the South African diamond fields and subsequently wrote an article for the *Geological Magazine* in 1868 declaring the story of South African diamonds was false and 'simply a scheme for trying to promote the employment and expenditure of capital in searching for the precious stone in that country'.

Major diamond deposits were found in the arctic areas of Yakutia in Russia from 1954. Again there was disbelief in some quarters before the diamonds came on to the market in the West, but now the Russian mines have an output comparable with that of South Africa.

World Production

It has been estimated that only about 200 tons (204 tonnes) of diamonds have been mined since they were first discovered thousands of years ago. That may seem to many readers to be a large amount of diamond in relation to a half-carat stone in a ring, which weighs about 0·0035 oz (0·1 g). The reward of 200 tons (204 tonnes) of diamond is very small against the effort of discovering the source and mining it. Finding a needle in a haystack is an easy task by comparison.

The present yearly production of diamond is about 11·8 tons (12 tonnes). This amount sells for about U.S. $3,750,000,000 as raw material. About 20 per cent only is useful as gem material, yet accounts for at least $3,000,000,000 of the value. The remaining 80 per cent, plus much more that that amount of synthetic diamond, is consumed by industry.

Jewellers Subsidize Industry

The value of the gem is thus about five times as much as the very much larger quantity of industrial diamonds. If there were not such a strong demand for gem diamonds, the whole cost of mining would be born by scientific and industrial users. The jeweller and the members of the public who buy diamond jewellery are doing industry and their country a considerable service by subsidizing mining. Modern industry would come to a halt without industrial diamond. Diamond is used for all high-precision machining and for drilling oil wells and has a million other uses. But for the young man who buys a diamond ring for his girl, industry would have to pay very much more for its diamonds.

Nearly all diamond sources are in the more remote places of the world and the crystals are usually extremely difficult to recover from old river-beds or beaches beneath the deep sands of the desert, from thousands of feet down in 'volcanic' pipes, some deep under permanent arctic ice, or from under the treacherous ocean waves off the 'forbidden' coast of South West Africa (Figs. 1.12 and 1.13). The amount of sand, earth, rocks, gravels, and other material that has to be removed to recover a diamond varies in different places, but can be in the order of a hundred million to one. Mining and recovery means finding and sorting of 200,000,000 tons of diamondiferous ore in remote places to discover a year's supply of diamond. A carat is a fifth of a metric gramme. There are about 142 in an ounce avoirdupois.

Unwettable but Grease-attracting
A clean diamond cannot be wetted by water. The water just forms into drops and rolls off. On the other hand, grease very easily sticks to it. The discovery of this fact led to the method of extracting diamonds from the rest of the heavy residue from diamond mines and diggings by passing it over a layer of grease to which the diamonds stuck while the rest was washed away by a stream of water.

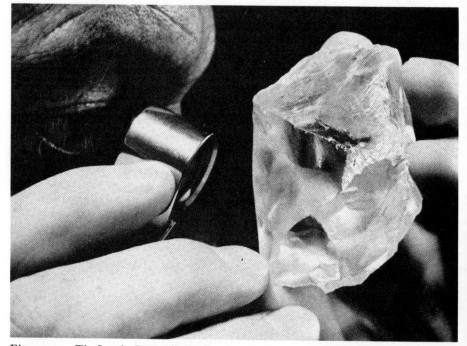

Fig. 1.13. *The Lesotho Brown diamond, a 601·25 ct. stone of faint brownish tinge, was found in the Letseng-le-Terai diggings in Lesotho (formerly Basutoland) in 1967. Shown here larger than actual size, it has now been cut into a number of gemstones by Harry Winston of New York.*

Fig. 1.14. *The 968·9 ct. Star of Sierra Leone, found on 14th February, 1972, about actual size.* (below) *Models of the three largest diamonds ever found: the Cullinan (3106 ct.), the Star of Sierra Leone, and the Excelsior (995·2 ct.).*

Fig. 1.15. *The biggest diamonds found were irregular in shape. This exception, a 616 ct. octahedron, was found in the Dutoitspan mine, Kimberley, on 17th April 1974, where many relatively large yellow octahedra have been recovered. It is the ninth largest stone ever found and is shown beside a 1 ct. stone.*

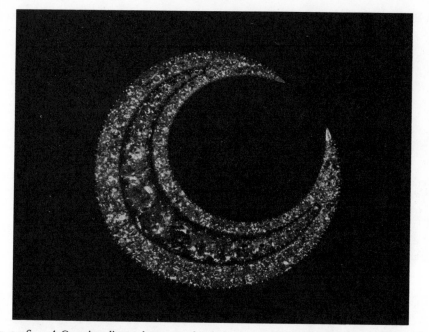

Fig. 1.16. *A Georgian diamond crescent, dated about 1790. It is shown here actual size. The diamonds are brilliant cut but with higher and smaller tables, and deeper pavilions than modern stones. This cut provides more weight but less light and fire.*

The affinity of diamond for grease also means that diamond jewellery will pick up grease and oils from the skin of the wearer and should be cleaned regularly in a diamond cleaner or a detergent. It is more important to clean the back than it is the front, not just because that is where the grease is trapped, but because the back facets will not reflect if they are coated with grease.

The Brilliant Cut

The shape of the modern brilliant-cut stone is derived from the shape of the most common form of crystal, the octahedron. For about two centuries, one point was ground or polished off to produce the square table-cut diamond. From around mid-seventeenth century, more facets were added and the shape made rounder. In the later eighteenth century, the shape was like the modern stone (Fig.1.16). The modern round brilliant-cut gem (Fig. 1.17), with fifty-eight accurately-placed facets, was the result of a book of theory written in 1919. The author worked out the angles that produced the maximum display of light and flashing colour and gave us the modern brilliant-cut stone, which was shallower than the earlier polished diamonds and consequently threw more light back to the person looking at the stone by reducing the leakage of light through the back. He formulated what cutters, particularly in New York, were discovering by practice.

Smaller Diamonds

As a gemstone, diamond is now relatively common. The big South African discoveries, followed by the Russian ones, and the development of modern mining methods are responsible. Diamonds are bound to become more common because the average size of crystals being mined is gradually getting smaller. Most gem diamonds are found along the desert coast of South West Africa, trapped in potholes in the rock under 60 ft (18·3 m.) of sand, parallel to the long rolling breakers of the sea. Consolidated Diamond Mines of South West Africa find as many as 90 per cent of gems among the crystals they recover. But the average size fell from 0·90 carat in 1967 to 0·84 carat in 1968.

When a full or brilliant-cut diamond is fashioned out of a natural crystal, much weight is lost. Diamonds weighing a carat are often the biggest that can be cut from a crystal weighing 2 carats. If the crystal is mis-shapen or faulty the recovery will be lower, even as low as a fifth of a carat or less.

Price Stability

It is inevitable therefore that smaller diamonds will be appearing in jewellery and designers will be swinging away from single stone rings and featuring more smaller diamonds. A number of small diamonds is more economical in price for the same area of diamond since diamond prices rise rapidly as weight increases. Very roughly, a diamond twice as heavy and of the same quality as another will cost four times as much, but the area of the top will only increase by about a fifth.

The production of smaller stones from the mines will bring diamond jewellery into reach of many more people.

Fig. 1.17.   *A modern brilliant, cut to angles that provide maximum fire (brilliance), is shown on the left with pear and marquise (boat-shaped) brilliant-cut stones. The 'emerald-cut' diamond on the right recovers most weight from a long stone but reduces its brilliance.*

Fig. 1.18. *One of the few black famous diamonds in existence, the Black Orloff, weighing 67.50 carats. It is believed to have come from India and to have been known as the Eye of Brahma.*

Trust in Trading

Diamond is the only mineral that still has to be sorted by hand as a last stage in the mining process, however automatic and sophisticated it may be. There is no substitute for the human hand, eye, and brain, in gauging quality and estimating value. There is no other mineral, except perhaps among the very rare earths, that has such a high intrinsic value when mined. Diamond crystals are therefore kept under guard from the moment they are discovered. They remain so through the stages of sorting, cutting, and setting in jewellery, yet they are commonly transmitted from place to place through the ordinary post.

Extreme security precautions have to be taken to protect both crystals and polished stones from crooks. Yet within the trade itself, diamonds of great value pass from hand to hand on a signature and often without even that formality. Anyone unconnected with the diamond trade is amazed at the extent of the trust placed in each other by buyer and seller. This trust is the keystone that keeps the entire trade in being.

In the rest of the chapters of the book many of the subjects referred to in this preliminary chapter are explored in more detail, but much has to be left unsaid because the subject of this one material is so vast, so much as yet unrelated work has been done on it and so much unrelated history written about it, that a lifetime could profitably be spent on the study of diamond alone.

REFERENCES

Historia Naturalis, Book 37, by Pliny the Elder (A.D. 77).
Gemmarum et Lapidum Historia, by Anselmus Boetius de Boot. (Lyons, France, 1636).
Antique Gems: their origin, uses and value, by Rev. C. W. King M.A. (London, 1866).
The History of Diamond Production and the Diamond Trade, by Godehard Lenzen (London, 1970).
Mani-Mala, or a Treatise on Gems, by Sourindro Mohun Tagore (Bengal, 1876).
Diamond Design, by Marcel Tolkowsky (London, 1919).
The History and Use of Diamond, by S. Tolansky, F.R.S. (London, 1962).
A History of the Crown Jewels of Europe, by Lord Twining (London, 1960).

CHAPTER TWO

Where Diamonds are Found

All early 'diamond mines' were the alluvial gravels in the banks or beds of active or dried-up rivers in which diamonds and other heavy and hard crystals had been concentrated by the action of flooding water. Alluvial deposits near active rivers were later called river diggings or wet diggings.

Some alluvial gravels containing diamonds were found under the surface in desert regions where rivers had dried up many thousands of years ago. They were called dry diggings. In the second half of the last century, a few dry diggings in Africa were found to be the tops of great columns of a special kind of rock that had diamonds trapped in it, apparently having carried them from their source of origin deep in the earth. These diggings were renamed pipes or pipe mines.

The Indian Mines

Alluvial diamonds were known in India as early as about 800 B.C. The diamonds were found in compact sandstones and conglomerates and in the same materials after they had weathered, as well as in the sands and gravels of river-beds and terraces. Indian diamonds were exported through the port of Alexandria at an early time and there is a reference in the writings of the Alexandrian astronomer Ptolemy (90?–168?) to a diamond river in India. It is likely that diamonds were first found in India while mining for gold because the two minerals are found together in alluvial deposits.

Tavernier visited a number of mines between 1630 and 1668, and most of our knowledge about them comes from his writings. The most famous workings were at Kollur in the great gorge cut by the river Krishna in the south of the former kingdom of Golconda, now part of the State of Hyderabad. Kollur was where several historical diamonds, including the Koh-i-Nûr, the Regent, the Great Mogul, and the Tavernier Blue were found. Tavernier reported that there were 60,000 men, women and children at work at the diggings on the south bank of the river, which are said to have been discovered by the find of a 25 carat stone there about 1560.

Headquarters of the many diamond merchants were at the fortress town of Hyderabad to the north of the river workings. Diamonds from the scattered diggings were faceted if necessary at the village of Karwan outside the city walls.

The mines were divided into claims operated by local merchants who paid a levy to the local ruler plus a percentage of the value of stones discovered. The miners worked to a strict religious ritual. Having decided on the place to be worked, they levelled off an area beside it and surrounded this by a 2 ft (60 cm) wall, with holes or gates in it at intervals around the vase. The gates were

23

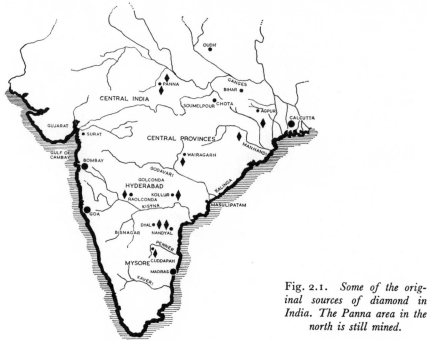

Fig. 2.1. *Some of the original sources of diamond in India. The Panna area in the north is still mined.*

blocked and earth and gravel from the mining area was dumped in the walled enclosure by women and children. When the mining area had been excavated, usually to a depth of about 14 ft (4·3 m), water seepage prevented further mining. The water was taken in pitchers and tipped into the walled area to bring the earth and gravel to a consistency of soup, which it reached after one or two days.

The gates were then opened to draw off the water and mud. Sometimes two or three washings were necessary until the hot sun dried off the remaining moisture and left only sand containing diamonds.

The smaller material was winnowed like grain in baskets to allow the lighter elements to be blown away by the wind. The remainder was raked over, which exposed many lumps. The miners broke up the lumps by pounding the whole area with large wooden pestles or rams before winnowing once more. Finally the miners ranged themselves on one side and worked across the sand to pick out any diamonds by hand.

The best stones at Kollur, Tavernier reported, had a green crust on the surface, 'because when cut they proved to be white and of very beautiful water'. Nearly all the world's finest historical diamonds came from the Indian mines which were situated in an area of quite different geological formation from those in Africa and Siberia where most diamonds have been found subsequently.

On the north bank downstream of the Krishna were more diggings called the Parteal that were worked until as late as 1850. Two mines were also exploited in the Golconda area from the 1960s. Some of India's old and modern mining areas are shown in Fig. 2.1.

Fig. 2.2. *How some early mines in Panna, India, were worked in pits in the sandstone. Note the armed guards on the right.*

West of Kollur were the Ramulkolta mines, worked in the nineteenth century, which are believed to have been the lost workings referred to by Tavernier as at Raolconda. Originally the miners dug deep pits in the sandstone and used iron rods, crooked at one end, to extract diamond-bearing gravels from veins in the rocks.

To the south-east were more mines at Karnul, Nandyal and Wajrah Karur, which became famous later in Indian diamond mining history for the many large stones of around 60 carats found there. Diamonds were at one time found on the surface in a deposit washed out during the monsoons in a district known as Baraganpilly, after the name given to the diamondiferous stratum of gravel bound with stiff clay about 3 ft (1 m) thick and from about 3 ft to 16 ft (1–5 m) deep under a sand and rubbed layer. Diamonds from the deeper level were almost round because of long attrition in water.

The most southerly mines were by the Penner or Pannar river in the Cuddapah district north of Madras, where the river cuts through the Eastern Ghats. The gravels here were of the Baraganpilly type.

North of the Golconda area were alluvial workings at Wairagah on the banks of the river Wairagah in what became the Chanda district of Nagpur. They were called the Beiragahr mines by Tavernier. The diamonds occurred in a yellowish sandy soil.

Other diamond deposits were found near rivers west of Calcutta. The most northerly deposits were in the Panna area of the small state of Madhya by the Jumna and some tributaries of the Ganges river. The gravels are very thin and are from $19\frac{1}{2}$ to 26 ft (6–8 m) below the surface overlaid in some parts by clay, sandstone and laterite although there were areas where the diamondiferous deposit was on the surface. Near the town of Panna itself the old miners had to dig pits about 33 ft (10 m) deep and more than that across in the wet sandstone to extract diamonds (Fig. 2.2).

Current Mining

The Panna area (apparently unknown to Tavernier) has three types of deposit: Primary – pipes; Secondary – conglomerates, that is ancient alluvial deposits now lying deeply under later strata; and alluvial. Of three pipes known, Majhgawan, Hinota, and Angore, only the first is being worked commercially. One other area being worked in 1976 was the Ramkheria alluvial deposit. Of many alluvial deposits, only this and others on the Baghain River and in the Udesna area are large enough for exploitation. The conglomerates were extensively worked in the past but today a few individuals dig in the shallow areas. The two areas in production are being developed by the National Mineral Development Corporation, which took control of production in 1960.

Apparently in early days, the Indians believed that diamonds possessed the magical power of growing like seeds, so old dumps and tailings were worked over many times to see if any new diamonds had been generated in them. In fact, conglomerate and sandstone in which diamonds were trapped broke up after a time on exposure to the weather to release the stones.

Fig. 2.3. *Some of the earlier mining areas in Brazil, which was the main source of supply in the eighteenth century and first half of the nineteenth century.*

Mining in Brazil

Diamonds were first discovered in Brazil at the beginning of the eighteenth century. Crystals had been found by gold miners in gravels of river workings near Tejuco in Minas Gerais, which has since become famous for many other gems too. Gold miners apparently used them as counters while playing cards until an official who had seen diamond crystals in India recognized their nature and sent some to Lisbon. Some of the samples were cut in Amsterdam and found to be as fine diamonds as those found in India.

Tejuco is about 300 miles (480 km) north of Rio de Janeiro and 250 miles (400 km) west of the Atlantic coast and is now called Diamantina. The country is very rough, being a plateau about 4,000 ft (1,220 m) above sea level that is crossed by gorges and valleys and terminates in sudden mountainous walls.

The official discovery of diamonds in Brazil by the Portuguese, who then occupied the country, is recorded as in 1725. Many other deposits were found and production was increased so much that prices tumbled and the Portuguese Government restricted production almost to a trickle. They made mining a Royal monopoly in 1772. Diamonds in Minas Gerais are found only in rivers that flow through strata composed of itacolumite (flexible sandstone).

Another big discovery occurred in 1844, in Bahia, twenty-two years after Brazil had gained its independence. Unfortunately the deposits were again worked so intensively that they were more or less exhausted in twenty years. Tough, black, impure diamond was found in the Chapida Diamantina area of Bahia. It was often in large lumps of several ounces, was called carbonado, or 'carbons' and was of no commercial value at the time but was afterwards discovered to be valuable as an industrial abrasive.

Diamonds usually occur in Brazil in a gravel of rounded quartz pebbles and light coloured sand, known locally as *cascalho*. All the diggings are alluvial, situated in or near river-beds. Sources are shown in Fig. 2.3.

The method of recovery when Brazil was the world's biggest supplier of diamonds, was to dig down to the diamondiferous gravels, which were usually about ten feet deep, and to pile the gravel in heaps near washing huts. The huts were occupied by overseers sitting on high seats. In front were washing troughs, where labourers washed away the finer sands and soil and picked out the diamonds. During the dry season, the waters of rivers were diverted through canals to the troughs, which are shown in Fig. 2.4.

A different method was used in the Paraguassu, one of the Bahia fields. Diamonds were found trapped in the river bed and divers worked in movable caissons, crude diving bells, gathering cascalho into sacks which were lowered from the surface. Two men worked in alternate three hour shifts in the caissons.

There are still some independent diamond diggers called *garimpeiros* (snipers) in Brazil and in the 1960s the rivers that were still diamondiferous were mined by dredger, using modern placer methods, but Brazil's main contribution to world supply lasted only until three-quarters through the nineteenth century. During 250 years of diamond mining it produced about 15,000,000 carats, compared with about 60,000,000 carats *a year* from current world mines.

It seems fortuitous, but probably is a result of economic forces, that as India's supply of diamonds was running out, deposits were found in Brazil, and just as Brazil's were nearly exhausted, huge supplies were found in Africa.

Diamonds in Africa
Diamonds were first discovered in the interior of South Africa in the land of the Griquas, who were descended from the original Hottentots of Cape Colony. The Griquas had been driven from the Cape by European colonists and had emigrated north, in turn driving away the Bushmen from the area formed by the junction of the Vaal River with the Orange River. See Figs. 2.5, 2.15 and 2.16.

European hunters gradually found their way northwards and were followed

Fig. 2.4. *Diamond diggers in Brazil at work collecting gravel and washing it under the eyes of overseers. The man on the right will swirl his pan in water to cause any diamonds to settle to the centre at the bottom.*

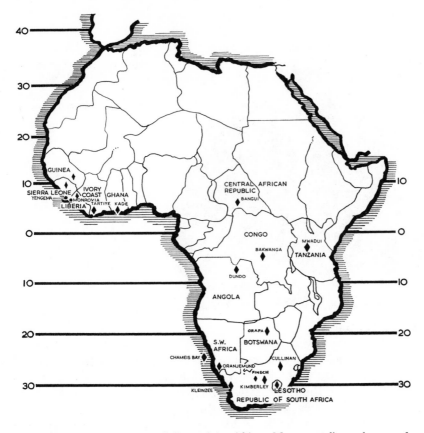

Fig. 2.5. *Main current sources of diamond in Africa. Most gem diamonds come from the coastal deposits in South West Africa. The Congo (Zaire) and Angola fields are largest but almost all the diamonds there are of industrial quality.*

by Dutch farmers, the Boers, trekking with herds of cattle and sheep in search of places suitable to settle. The few Boers who settled in the lands of the Griquas were joined by hundreds more after the Great Trek from the Cape in 1836, incensed by the British decision to free slaves in the middle of a harvest which led to ruination of the crops.

These Voortrekkers crossed the Orange River and tried to claim all the land in the fork of it and the Vaal to form the Orange Free State. Some continued across the Vaal to the north-east and established an independent South African Republic in the Transvaal. This left the Griquas with lands in the central area bordered by Cape Colony to the south and the Kalahari Desert to the north. In the east they had indefinite and disputed borders with the Boers. The captain or chief of Griqualand West was Nicholas Waterboer (Fig. 2.6) and the land was sometimes called 'Waterboer's land'.

Waterboer had a white agent, David Arnot, who negotiated land and border settlements as well as concessions. It was on the farms on the borders of the Cape, Orange Free State, and Griqualand, that diamonds were found.

Fig. 2.6. *Captain Nicholas Waterboer, Chief of the Griquas of Griqualand West, who controlled some of the state borderlands where diamonds were found.*

The First Diamond

Early pioneers were driven by strong religious convictions and the intention to convert coloured people to their own beliefs. The Berlin Mission Society set up missions on the banks of the River Vaal (Fig. 2.7), at Pniel and at Platberg. In the daily diary of the Pniel station is a record of a 5-carat diamond being found in 1859 on the river bank near Platberg by a native and its purchase by a priest for £5. Even today the Berlin Mission sells diamonds found on its concession to licensed buyers in Kimberley.

First Authenticated Diamond

The first authenticated discovery of a diamond was in December 1866 or most likely in February 1867,* at a time when the colony was suffering from the after-effects of the American Civil War of 1861–5, worsened by drought and plagues of locusts. It was made on a farm named De Kalk (Fig. 2.11) just south of the Orange River in Cape Province, owned by two Boer farmers, Schalk Van Niekerk (Fig. 2.8) and Siewert Wiid, his step-father. On 10th November 1866, Van Niekerk had agreed verbally to sell his share of the farm to another farmer, Daniel Jacobs. The Jacobs family moved into the farmhouse and Van Niekerk and his family to a small house some distance away on the same farm.

The stone was picked up by 15-year-old Erasmus Jacobs who had been sent by his father to clear the outlet pipe from a dam. He cut a stick to do so and sat down in the shade of a tree when he noticed a glittering pebble lying between some limestone and ironstone. The place was some distance from the Jacobs homestead but only about 200 yds (180 m) from the river. Erasmus picked up the stone, took it home, and gave it to his youngest sister to play with. A month

* A photograph of the stone has a note on the back in the writing of W. B. Chalmers, Civil Commissioner of Hopetown, giving the later date (Fig. 2.10). In his old age, the finder Erasmus Jacobs gave the earlier date.

Fig. 2.7. *The Vaal river in earlier days with Barkly in the distance. The diamond rushes began on the banks of this river.*

or two later, Erasmus and his brother and two sisters were playing 'five stones' with the diamond and other river stones when Van Niekerk arrived. He saw the stone and, thinking it might be of some value, asked Mrs. Jacobs to sell it to him. She laughed at the idea of selling the stone and told him he could have it for nothing. Erasmus Jacobs is shown in Fig. 2.8.

Van Niekerk was in the habit of collecting pebbles and it was reported that von Ludwig, the government surveyor, discovering this interest, had encouraged him by the gift of a book on precious stones and a suggestion that the area could be diamondiferous. Thinking the Jacobs children's stone might possibly be a diamond, Van Nierkerk entrusted it to a hunter, trader and part-time farmer, John Robert O'Reilly (Fig. 2.8) who had some property on the Orange River, across which he tried to run a ferry to Waterboer's country. O'Reilly was probably passing Van Niekerk's house on his way from a trip to the Zambezi to trade guns and ammunition (which was illegal) for ivory, ostrich feathers and animal skins, and he may have been asked to show the stone to W. B. Chalmers, Civil Commissioner of Hopetown. Chalmers had run foul of authority and has been posted to Hopetown, which he described as 'the least known, most insignificant and the most outlandish and expensive District in the Colony'. He was very active trying to bring the English and Boer communities together and had become friendly with Van Niekerk, whom he described as 'a very

Fig. 2.8. *Schalk Jacobus van Niekerk with John Robert O'Reilly. Van Niekerk who recognized the Eureka, the first stone, as a diamond, is here holding the second significant find – the Star of South Africa. Erasmus Jacobs, as an old man, is shown above.*

observant man, and more intelligent than the rest of his countrymen in this district'.

According to Chalmers, O'Reilly showed the stone to everyone in Hopetown saying he thought it was a diamond but 'we only laughed at him (I among the number), so much so that he nearly threw it away. He then took it to Colesberg; some there half believed it to be a diamond, but most ridiculed the idea, so much so that he himself became doubtful of its being a diamond.'

The Clerk to the Civil Commissioner in Colesberg, Lorenzo Boyes, described later what happened there. 'In 1867, a trader named John O'Reilly came into Colesberg, and had in his possession a Stone which was supposed to be a Diamond. O'Reilly had shown the Stone to several Jews in Hoptown who declared it to be no Diamond but a "Topaz", and of no value. Mr. Lorenzo Boyes, then Acting Civil Commissioner, met O'Reilly in the Billiard Room, and asked to see the Stone, and having tried it, and found it made distinct cuts in the bottom of a tumbler, declared it to be a Diamond. O'Reilly said; "You are the only man who says it is worth anything, and whatever it is worth you shall have a share of it." One Dr. Kisch, a Jew, who was present, said *he* was an expert in Diamonds, and also declared it to be a Topaz, and made a bet of a new hat against its being a Diamond . . . .'

Dr. T. B. Kisch was an apothecary whose hobbies were geology and mineralogy and who claimed to be the first diamond prospector in South Africa, before 1867. The stone, although described in early accounts as white, was yellowish to the experienced eye, which probably suggested the idea of topaz. One of the most knowledgeable men in the colony on minerals and many other subjects at this time was a Dr. William Guybon Atherstone of Grahamstown (Fig. 2.9), so with O'Reilly's permission, Boyes sent the stone to him, with this covering letter: 'My Dear Sir, – I enclose a stone which has been handed to me by Mr. John O'Reilly as having been picked up on a farm in the Hopetown district, and as he thinks it is of some value I sent the same to you to examine, which you must please return to me. Yours very sincerely, L. Boyes.'

The letter was simply fastened by gum and not registered. The diamond was quite loose inside it and Dr. Atherstone's granddaughter subsequently described the scene. He was seated under a large pear tree in front of his house in Beaufort Street and casually opening the envelope he subconsciously noticed that something small fell on the lawn. On reading the letter he realized its import and calling his daughter to his aid, both searched among the grass until they found the pebble. Atherstone had never seen a rough diamond before, but 'upon taking its specific gravity and hardness, examining it by polarised light and so on, I at once decided that it was a genuine diamond of considerable value'.

Atherstone took the stone to show his neighbours and friend, the Right Rev. Dr. Ricardo, who cut his initials and the date on one of the panes of glass in Dr. Ricardo's sitting-room. The pane was subsequently removed and is preserved today in Grahamstown. He wrote at once to Boyes: 'I congratulate you on the stone you sent me; it is a veritable diamond, weighs 12¼ carats, is worth £500; has spoilt all the jewellers' files* in Grahamstown; *where* that came from are lots *more*; can I send it to Mr. Southey, Colonial Secretary?' Boyes received the letter on 8th April 1867, and the local newspaper, the *Colesberg Advertiser*, must have been exceptionally alert to be able to publish the news the next day under the heading:

THE WONDERFUL SOUTH AFRICAN DIAMOND

'There is a story this morning afoot in the village. It has been told to us by a lady and we will give it just as we have heard it.' (A brief account of O'Reilly's find 'in the North Country' and Dr. Atherstone's identification of it followed. The value was given as £800.) The newspaper's informant may well have been Mrs. Boyes.

Both Boyes and Atherstone wrote about the stone to Richard Southey,

* A file may be used on a crystal but *never* on a polished diamond.

Fig. 2.9. *Dr. William Guybon Atherstone of Grahamstown, about 1880. He contributed much to the early colony and authenticated the first significant diamond, discovered in 1867.*

33

probably on the same day. Atherstone's reference to it was casual despite his apparent excitement in identifying it. The first paragraph of his letter dealt with the title to a property, the second to some matters of botany and in the third he wrote, 'I have received a fine diamond from Hope Town District, its value in its rough state is £800 being 20 carats. . . . I tried to scratch it with a glazier's diamond but unsuccessfully and the latter was useless for glass cutting afterwards, its sp. gravity is 3·5343 (that of the diamond being 3·5295 to 3·6). Its index of refraction which is the crucial test I have not been able to try. I have for years suspected that precious gems would be found in the neighbour-hood, as I had previously received rubies, amethysts, heliotropes of large size, opals, etc. Galpins' working jeweller Wilcox feels certain it is a diamond, having seen several rough diamonds in England of exactly similar shape, colour, etc. What a pity it could not be sent to the French Exhibition. . . .'

When Southey received the stone he showed it to Ernest Heritte, the French consul, who was known to have a good knowledge of, and interest in, precious stones, and whose office was only a few doors away. It was also examined by Louis Hond, a diamond polisher for twenty-two years who described himself as a lapidary, by Jacob Leoni, 'another Hollander' and diamond cutter who had turned to dealing in curios, and by C. Schmieterloew, a chemist and apothecary, who provided a list of tests for diamond which included among the more usual, such as crystal shape and insolubility in acid, the following:

> 'Diamonds when rubbed (on woollen stuff) get electric. The electricity is posatif and when electrified and isolated (placed on a piece of thick dry glass) show a phosphorescent light (in the dark).
> 'Diamonds when heated do not get electric like Topaz.'

Hond valued the stone at £500 in the rough and £800 polished. He offered £400 for it. Heritte was also anxious to purchase and made repeated offers of £500. It is interesting that up to this time O'Reilly had apparently not disclosed the fact that the stone was found on the De Kalk farm. There were clearly good reasons for keeping the location secret. He did tell Boyes that he got the stone from a Boer. Van Niekerk's part in the find did not appear until quite late in the story. The first letters mentioning him were written on 1st June 1867.

Permission being granted, the stone was sent to England to be tested by Messrs. Hunt and Roskell, the Crown Jewellers, in London, with the intention of sending it on for exhibition on the Colony's stand at the Paris Exhibition, which was to be opened on 1st April by the Emperor Napoleon III. The Crown Jewellers declared it to be a diamond and John Blades Curry, Clerk of the Peace, in Cape Town, organized its exhibition in Paris. Curry was the man who later chose the name of Kimberley for the diamond fields.

Southey had, of course, kept the Cape Governor, Sir Philip Wodehouse, informed. Sir Philip also became interested in buying diamonds and made an offer to O'Reilly through Southey and Boyes of £500 for the $21 \cdot \frac{3}{16}$-carat stone and £150 for a second stone of $8 \cdot \frac{3}{16}$-carat picked up by Jan Duvenhage on his father's farm Paardekloof by the Orange River near Hopetown and sold to O'Reilly. He said he would give £670 for the two stones.

At about this time, de Wiid, who still owned part of the farm De Kalk,

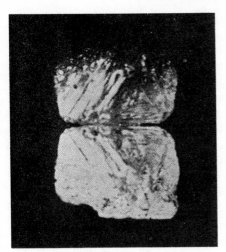

Fig. 2.10. *The Eureka diamond, 10·73 ct. after cutting, was the first authenticated find in South Africa.* (left) *A photograph of the rough stone, sent by Richard Southey to W. B. Chalmers in 1867.* (below) *Chalmers' note on the back of the photo indicates the stone was found in 1867. The photograph is now in the archives of Kimberley Public Library.*

Photograph of the First Cape Diamond found in Feb. 7 1867 *on the Farm of Schalk Van Niekerk. on the Orange River* Weight 21¼ Carats. *The Dimensions are fully about true actual size.*

claimed that the first diamond had been found on his part of the farm, so the Governor withdrew his offer for this stone fearing he might be drawn into litigation over its ownership. Later de Wiid signed an affidavit withdrawing his claim at the instigation of Van Niekerk and, after protracted negotiations, Sir Philip's offer of £500 was accepted by O'Reilly, who stuck out for £200 for the other stone. Eventually Sir Philip bought that as well.

The £500 was sent to the Civil Commissioner in Colesberg, Henry Green, Boyes's superior, and was probably given to O'Reilly by Boyes who certainly went with him to cash the cheque and received his commission of £25 plus a 'good-for for £25' which was never honoured by O'Reilly. Incidently, Boyes had hinted at commission for Southey in his letters but had been ignored. O'Reilly announced that he had given half the £500 to Van Niekerk.

What the Jacobs family received is not recorded although, when in his eighties Erasmus Jacobs declared that his father had had nothing from the deal. This is unlikely, however, from what is known of Van Niekerk. As the negotiations for the sale of the farm were incomplete, a consideration for the stone was probably included.

O'Reilly's pronouncements that were reported are often contradictory. At different times he said the stone was found by a Bushman, a Griqua, and a Hottentot, although he did not see him. Erasmus Jacobs in his old age declared that, when he found the pebble, a Hottentot who was employed by his father mainly to look after sheep was standing near by.

Both O'Reilly and Boyes petitioned parliament later when diamonds were realized to be a huge asset to the colony. Both wanted some reward. Dr. Atherstone, the remarkable man who contributed so much to the colony – he introduced anaesthetics and even contributed ideas to the railway system – was poorly recognized at the time for his part in the history of diamond discovery, although in 1888 the mining companies clubbed together to present him with a 4-carat diamond in recognition of his services.

Boyes caught 'diamond fever' and obtained permission from Southey to prospect in the area which by then he knew was the De Kalk farm. Southey wrote on 8th June 1867 to Boyes's superior, Green, 'I am sorry Mr. Boyes did not stumble upon any Diamonds but I am told he must not expect to find them on the surface but under the soil. If the exact spot where the one was found is known, an attempt might be made by digging there, and washing the soil turned up through fine sieves, which would leave the stones behind and among them Diamonds might be discovered.

'The Government, however, is not prepared at present to incur any expense.

'If the stone sent to England is pronounced there to be a valuable diamond, which I have no doubt about, something might be done.

'I have had a good many other stones sent to me since, but all are quartz.'

Mining Rights
The would-be diamond seekers were nervous of the government's intentions even if the government itself was adopting a *laissez-faire* attitude. The British, had introduced perpetual quitrent – a lease for an indefinite period – for land in 1813 and some freeholds from the 1840s, but all land titles gave mineral rights to the Crown. Southey wrote to Boyes to reassure O'Reilly that he 'need not be afraid that the Government will interfere with him, if he discovers more, for the present'. Green also wrote to Southey asking if the Government would rigidly impose quitrent rights to mines of precious stones. He pointed out that the right was to mines and wanted a definition of a mine. He suggested that if the right were abolished, it would stimulate discovery of diamonds. In the event, this incentive was not needed.

The first authenticated diamond was named the Eureka (Fig. 2.10) and changed hands several times over the years until purchased in 1966 by De Beers Consolidated Mines and presented to the people of South Africa. It is kept in Parliament in Cape Town.

In *The Cape Standard and Mail* of May 1867, a correspondent reported that Van Niekerk had found two diamonds before the Eureka. The first was much bigger and Van Niekerk came across it several years earlier. He gave it to some children to play with and they lost it. Then he discovered another and a friend

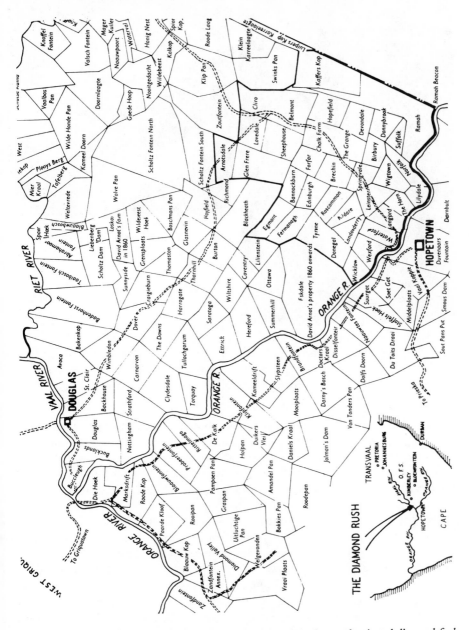

Fig. 2.11. *Farms around the Orange River at the time of the first authenticated diamond finds. The De Kalk farm was where the Eureka diamond was picked up. The Star of South Africa was claimed, by the purchasers, to have been found on the Zandfontein farm, although the finder said he picked it up north of the river in West Griqua territory. The first big diamond rushes occurred farther up the Vaal River, see Fig. 2.16. The Zandfontein farm, from which the Star of South Africa was taken to the De Kalk farm, is on the left of the map and the two are linked by the dotted track shown. Scale about 11 miles to 1 inch.*

37

Fig. 2.12. *The 83·5 ct. Star of South Africa in the rough, from a photograph in the Kimberley Public Library.* (left) *The Star, cut as a 47·96 ct. pear-shaped pendant, in a necklace. This was sold by Christies of London in Geneva in 1974 for 1,600,000 Swiss francs.*

'tested' it by placing it on an anvil and dealing it 'a tremendous blow with a sledgehammer, which smashed it to atoms'. This story might be dismissed except for the fact that the correspondent was probably David Arnot, the agent for Nicholas Waterboer, who was well informed and knew a lot of what went on.

The First Big Find

There are records of two other early finds, but it was an $83\frac{1}{2}$-carat crystal that really started the world-wide rush of fortune seekers to Griqua country. Up to that time, a small population of diggers worked the wet diggings along the Vaal, Orange, and Hartz Rivers, and later the Riet and Modder Rivers. The diggers discovered that many Griquas and some of the Bushmen who were left knew of the stones, but not of course that they were diamonds.

The $83\frac{1}{2}$-carat crystal that eventually became known as the Star of South Africa, (Fig. 2.12) was picked up by a shepherd known as Swartboy, or Zwartbooi (Fig. 2.13), or similar name, working for the owner of the Zandfontein Farm (Fig. 2.11), situated on the Orange River well to the west of the De Kalk Farm where the first big diamond had been found. According to a statement he made later, Swartboy found the stone 'and recognized it as a diamond' on the opposite side of the river (northern side) before he joined the Zandfontein Farm, which therefore must have been before 12th November 1868. He had hidden the stone, thinking it would be confiscated by Waterboer, as it was found on his territory and he was a Waterboer subject. He told some friends and members of his family and a friend, Willem Piet, was entrusted with its sale. Piet followed the Orange River upstream until he reached the De Kalk Farm, where he sold the stone, which weighed $83\frac{1}{2}$ carats, to Van Niekerk for 500 sheep, ten head of cattle and one horse.

Fig. 2.13. *The finder of the Star of South Africa. He was known as Swartboy and similar names, and was a subject of Captain Waterboer who ruled West Griqualand.*

News of the find soon spread after the sale and James Wykeham offered £11,100 for it, but Van Niekerk sold it to the Lilienfeld brothers for £11,200, much to Wykeham's disgust as he and his partner had apparently been prepared to go to £13,000. The Lilienfelds, aided by the Amsterdam diamond cutter, Louis Hond, seem to have cast some doubt on Wykeham's ability to pay. Wykeham responded by obtaining a temporary injunction restraining the Lilienfelds from selling the stone on the grounds that it had been found on Waterboer's territory and he had given no authority for its sale. Wykeham was a Justice of the Peace and a Deputy Sheriff.

A legal battle followed with no holds barred. Swartboy was virtually kidnapped twice by the defending side in order to persuade him to change his story and say he found the stone on the Zandfontein Farm. There were even claims that it was found on the De Kalk Farm. Swartboy did change his story and many other witnesses swore to obvious lies in their affidavits. One letter still extant suggests there was only one way to solve the problem, to 'get possession of Swartboy and bring him "kindly" over to your side or else "fix" a 50 lb. Wgt. to his neck and drop him in a fish Pond.'

When the interdict came before the Supreme Court in Cape Town to show whether or not it should be made absolute, the Chief Justice remarked that the affidavits were merely based on hearsay evidence. Swartboy had admitted he was a liar, but one judge commented that some people might consider a man had a moral right to tell a lie if asked an impertinent question upon a matter he wished to keep secret.

The application was refused, however, partly on the grounds that Waterboer was not a party to it; the Lilienfelds were also awarded costs. The diamond was sent to London on M. V. *Celt* after being exhibited at Port Elizabeth. The cargo was listed as wool, feathers, hides, sheep and goat skin, oil, wine, raisins, ivory, a box of diamonds from Adler and Co. of Port Elizabeth, and five live zebras.

Fig. 2.14. *There is a small monument today at Canteen Kopje, formerly called Klipdrift, where the first diggings were begun. Around the obelisk, the ground is still like an area that has been shelled in wartime.*

En route, it was exhibited in Cape Town on behalf of the Ladies' Benevolent Society, and eventually reached London, where it sold for £25,000 by Hunt and Roskell to the Earl of Dudley. It became known as the Dudley Diamond, although it had been referred to as the Star of South Africa in the court case.

After 'disappearing' for some years, it turned up again as the Star of South Africa in a sale held by Christie, Manson and Wood in Geneva in 1974, where it fetched 1,600,000 Swiss francs, worth at the time £225,000.

There is a story that, before its despatch from South Africa, it was placed on the table of Parliament and the Colonial Secretary declared, 'This diamond, gentlemen, is the rock on which the future success of South Africa will be built.' It is a good story; unfortunately the diamond had left for London by the time the South African Parliament was convened on 23rd June 1869.

First Diggings

The first diggings in South Africa, apart from isolated finds, were at Klipdrift (now called Canteen Kopje) on the banks of the Vaal river not far from Barkly West. On the edge of the pock-marked ground, reminiscent today of a World War One battlefield, a small flint obelisk (Fig. 2.14) has been erected to commemorate the event. The early days were well described by J. L. Babe in a now very rare book *The South African Diamond Fields*, published in New York in 1872. Babe was rifle salesman, digger, inventor, and special correspondent of the *New York World*. He described the Vaal as a 'beautiful stream lined nearly all its length with fine trees . . . 200 feet wide opposite the great camps' (diggings). He explained that the river alternated between stretches of smooth water like this, hardly ever more than a mile in length, and rapids. Immense tracts of water-worn pebbles were to be seen; around the undulating country which was about 5,000 ft (1,500 m) above sea level were dotted here and there hills covered with immense boulders of ironstone. During the months of June, July, and August, the river became very low.

Diamonds were at first located by long lines of natives who joined hands and walked slowly over the ground, especially after rain. These were offered to traders at exorbitant prices according to Babe, who cites one of which the starting price was £2,500 – in the 1870s! It was sold after three days for £150. It was not until 1870, he wrote, that someone thought of organizing a prospecting company. King William's Town provided one party that was sent to the Vaal under the leadership of Mr. McIntosh. There were eight partners, four to prospect and four to mine. A similar party started from Natal under Capt. Rolliston. The parties met at Hebron and, after early suspicions of each other were dispelled, agreed to work together on the west bank of the river. The local natives would not allow them to touch the ground with pick and shovel, however. After three months of prospecting with sharp sticks only, the parties became dispirited and parted company, but agreed to inform each other of any finds.

After another month, the McIntosh party was taken to a drift or ford by a native where they found a half-carat stone in soil at the roots of a thorn tree. They were forbidden from digging and sent for the Natal party, who, despite objections, used pick and shovel to remove a load of ground which was washed in an Australian cradle at the river bank about a thousand yards away. They found diamonds and continued to do so. One day a native seized a 9-carat stone that the diggers had found. The diggers compelled him to return it and he complained to his chief who, surprisingly, backed the diggers. The parties tried to keep the news of their finds to themselves, but one day someone saw a 5-carat stone roll out of a pack. A trader named Stafford Parker became interested and wrote letters to the papers about the finds. Also a young man named Slater wrote to his father in Port Elizabeth confirming the finds and urging his friends to come at once. These announcements started the rush.

According to Babe, most of the newcomers went to Klipdrift and the Old Kopje. The two parties, who had started at the Old Kopje, were working a triangular area here. Old Kopje was soon taken up with 20 ft (6·1 m) claims. The diggers then moved on to the Second or Town Kopje, down river, and to the Third or Colesburg Kopje, after the party that had found diamonds on it.

According to the *Grahamstown Journal* of 12th August 1870, 'Every town in the colony has sent its contingent to the army of workers at the Vaal fields. In May there were about one hundred men at the diggings. Before the end of June there were seven hundred, at the close of July there were over 1,000, and at present it is estimated that there are at the Klipdrift, Pniel, Hebron, and Kuskamana Fields no less than 2,000 men.' This news was reprinted in London and New York which attracted more fortune hunters so that by April 1871, there were about 5,000 diggers working along the Vaal, Modder and Orange rivers.

Transport to the diamond fields was long and difficult. Some of the routes are shown in Fig. 2.15, a map which has been partly redrawn from one that appeared in 1872 in *The South African Diamond Fields* by Jerome Babe, inventor of the Baby, a sieve used by diggers. Although the route from Port Elizabeth was the shortest, it was the most difficult. The only public transport was the ox-wagon and the journey over the passes took 30 to 60 days. By 1870, the

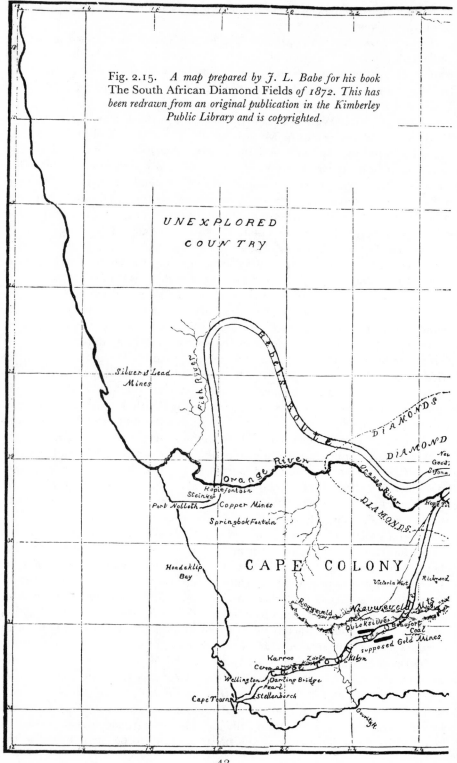

Fig. 2.15.   A map prepared by J. L. Babe for his book
The South African Diamond Fields of 1872. This has
been redrawn from an original publication in the Kimberley
Public Library and is copyrighted.

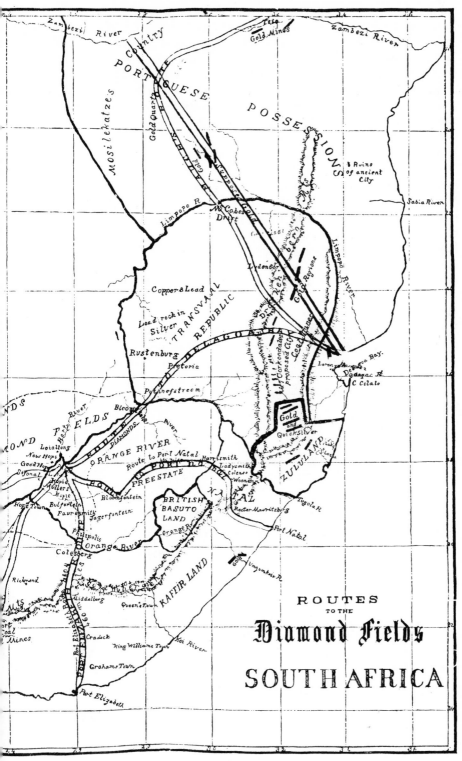

ROUTES
TO THE

𝔇𝔦𝔞𝔪𝔬𝔫𝔡 𝔉𝔦𝔢𝔩𝔡𝔰

SOUTH AFRICA

Inland Transport Company was running express weekly wagons from Cape Town to Klipdrift at a charge of £12 a person, taking from 7 to 10 days. Passengers, wagon and the eight horses or ten mules used to pull it, were taken by sail to Wellington and took the Karoo Poort, a pass through the mountains from there to the desolate, mountain-ringed Karoo Plains. The journey was then to Beaufort West, Victoria West, Hopetown and across the Orange river to Pniel. When diamonds were discovered, the only railway in South Africa was about 30 miles long, in the Cape. Within a few years, Kimberley was connected to all the Cape ports by rail.

Adventurers of all kinds, gold miners from Canada and Australia, Europeans in every walk of life, deserting seamen, honest men and riff-raff began to pour into South Africa on every ship. Many had then to earn enough money to make the long trek at about ten miles a day. A very small sprinkling of men had some diamond experience in India, Borneo, or Brazil, but most knew nothing of mining. Soon they abandoned their normal clothes and adopted the rough breeches and wide-brimmed hats of the Boers. They even grew whiskers, like the Boers, to protect their faces from the sun and from the biting sand in the wind, and those who could afford it carried revolvers at their waists.

Hope Town

It was usual to make at first for Hope Town, which had become a rough and bustling frontier town where would-be miners could buy picks, buckets, spades, and sieves. From there, not far off the river, they went out into the semi-desert

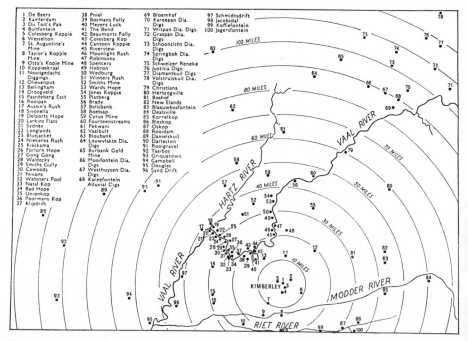

Fig. 2.16. *Some of the many claims around the Vaal river in the 1870s and 80s (as shown by McNish). The pipe mines in the Kimberley area, became by far the most productive.*

and the farms to prospect. Many thousands of diggers became scattered over a huge territory, working haphazardly and digging holes that were in many cases much too shallow to penetrate to any diamondiferous gravels even if they existed. There was constant trouble with farmers over prospecting rights and because sheep fell into prospect holes and were crippled or died. There were battles, too, over the livestock that disappeared into diggers' cooking-pots and continuous squabbles and fights over the very few sources of water.

The dry diggings were being worked fairly extensively at this time, and the newcomers had little luck owing largely to their inexperience and the size of the territory over which they were spread. This led to a movement back towards the river diggings, which became so jammed that there was utter chaos in the better areas, where there were diggers' camps, and thousands of sheep, oxen, horses, donkeys, cattle, wagons and equipment among the piles of discarded gravels.

Fine diamonds were being found in some areas, but others were barren. The invasion of newcomers brought crooks who paid a few pounds for useless claims, salted them with a few stones, and resold them at large profits. The lack of policing resulted in much thieving of poultry, cattle and other goods. The demand for timber for shacks and fires was so great that trees everywhere were cut down and stolen from the farms until not a tree existed for miles around.

As many as 10,000 claims were being worked along the Vaal by 1870. The various camps and claims had their own names, sometimes referring to the digger's name or fortune, such as Forlorn Hope, Waldeck's Plant, Poorman's Kopje, Webster's Pool, and the rich Gong Gong, which is still being worked. Many are shown in the plan in Fig. 2.16.

On the opposite side of the river from Klipdrift, on what Babe called the

Fig. 2.17.   *Sorting gravel at the early river diggings. The gravel does not seem to have been washed or concentrated with much skill or care.*

45

Fig. 2.18. *The Scotch cart played a big part in transport in early diamond days in South Africa. Its merit lay in its tipping body. This example is in the Open Mine Museum at the Big Hole, Kimberley.*

'Free State side', a stretch of 15 miles (24 km) was owned by the Berlin Mission at Pniel, some 3 miles (4·8 km) up river, under the Rev. M. Kallenburg. This was where the first recorded diamond was found. During the activities on the opposite bank a Dutchman found a half-carat stone and received permission to mine from the Rev. Kallenberg in return for a quarter of the finds. The news soon got out and in less than a month 300 families, mostly Dutch, had moved there. Parties from the Klipdrift side were refused permission to cross under an agreement with Stafford Parker, spokesman for the diggers on this bank, but about 500 diggers crossed and occupied every available claim. Many dodged payment of a quarter of their proceeds so later a tax of 10 shillings (50p) a month was applied by the Mission which netted about £2,500 a month.

J. L. Babe gave a graphic description of how he left Colesburg on 29th June 1870 for Pniel. 'Everything ready to start for diamond fields, 170 miles (272 km) in north-west direction. There are three partners in the concern, Messrs Rawstorne, Plewman and myself. Messrs Rawstorne and Plewman are merchants at Colesburg. We take two coloured boys with us. We have sent on a Scotch cart (Fig. 2.18) drawn by four oxen in charge of two other boys. This cart contains our washing machine, pump, hose, and mining tools. We expect to come up with them about half-way to the fields.

'Rawstorne and I travel in a six-mule spring wagon, which will also contain our provisions, carpenter's tools, bedding and clothing; we have very few of the latter but they are substantial. . . . We hired the wagon and mules for three months. The balance of our outfit, including the Scotch cart and four oxen, cost us £100.' The party arrived at Pniel Mission Station at 12 noon on 5 July and took a claim of 20 ft (6·1 m) square 'which seems to have been overlooked'.

Pniel had about 3,000 inhabitants then, in 1870, and the place was gradually growing although many had left for new rushes. 'There are new stores, auction marts, saloons, billiard tables, bakers, butchers, doctors, lawyers, but no undertakers yet. But an enterprising acquaintance of mine had just started up with a nest of coffins on speculation, so that intending emigrants need have no fears of not being decently buried, in case they should want to remain there. A post office has been established and a newspaper *Diamond News* is successfully under way, and has six pages of news and advertisements; it is issued weekly (on

Fig. 2.19. *Stafford Parker, first President of the short-lived Diggers' Republic.*

Saturdays). You can safely ship diamonds by post from here if you register them. . . .'

The Standard Bank helped to provide security for diamonds and money when they set up a branch with a safe at Klipdrift, opposite Pniel, in 1870. In the same year a judge with the forbidding name of Lynch arrived in Pniel Camp.

The Diggers' Republic

Before this time, many Boers had crossed the Vaal River and annexed much of the Griqua lands to found another independent state, the Transvaal. The lands along the river had remained in the hands of Griqua chiefs, however, some of whom had granted concessions to diggers. President Pretorius and the Transvaal Government began to cast envious eyes on the riches in the earth and in 1870 claimed all the diamondiferous areas along the northern bank of the Vaal down to the junction with the Hartz River. The Orange Free State also laid claim to lands along the rivers.

The Transvaal Government made the incredibly naïve move of not only claiming the area but of giving the concession for mining it to a group of local men. The diggers' reaction was to refer the Transvaal Government to an agreement made between one of their original number, Stafford Parker, and the Griqua chief, Jan Bloem, at Nooitgedacht. A Mutual Protection Committee was formed at a big meeting of river diggers and at a subsequent meeting at Klipdrift, it was decided to found a Diggers' Republic in the same way as the Boers had formed their two independent farmers' republics. Stafford Parker, who was a claim owner, ex-policeman, ex-seaman, one-time gold-miner, father of eighteen children, and local dance-hall owner, was elected first President (Fig. 2.19).

Stafford Parker took his duties seriously. He wore a top-hat and frock-coat he had purchased on impulse while in London. He appointed an ex-butcher as State Punisher and introduced flogging for theft of stock and diamonds. Card cheats were ducked in the river and petty thieves had to parade through the camps ringing bells and carrying cards labelled 'thief'. Another punishment was to be hauled across the river by a rope tied round the wrists and attached to the stern of a boat, similarly to keel-hauling. Parker also made it compulsory for diggers to train for military service. The flag of the Diggers' Republic showed a horse, with a Union Jack in one corner.

President Pretorius of the Transvaal, with a small armed force and the three concessionaries, travelled to the diggings to claim the land, but had to turn tail when Parker's 'army' advanced on them. Pretorius then tried to make a deal with Parker but was unsuccessful. In the meantime, the British Government in Cape Province ordered its agent on the spot to disarm the diggers, which was another ingenuous directive. The British had earlier annexed the territories taken by the Boers – the Orange Free State and the Transvaal – but had abandoned them because of the expense involved. They, too, had become interested again when diamonds were found in quantity.

President Brand of the Orange Free State claimed the Vaal River diggings from the Griqua chief, Nicholas Waterboer, including the land of the Berlin Mission Society on the southern bank. Diggers refused his demands too, so he sent a unit of commandos to Waldeck's Plant, downstream of Pniel. Within a short time the commandos were confronted by thousands of armed diggers. Stafford Parker arrived to consult the commando leaders. In the meantime the men of the commando unit began talking to the diggers and finished the Free State's attempt at annexation in a drinking spree that lasted several days.

Waterboer had lawful claims to the territory and had granted concessions to the diggers. There were many confusing manœuvres and eventually legal action. A Court of Arbitration was set up which included a referee, a representative of the British Government and one of the Transvaal.

The decision was in favour of the Griqua chief, which angered not only President Brand, but President Pretorius in the Transvaal, who tried again to make an agreement with the diggers. His failure cost him the presidency, as he was forced on this issue to resign. Waterboer asked the British to take over his country, a manœuvre it now became obvious was planned, for the Griqua chief received a large pension and his territory became a Crown Colony in October, 1871, being renamed Griqualand West.

Many diggers wanted to fight even the British Government to retain their republic, but Stafford Parker declared, 'You cannot fight your own Queen', and the Diggers' Republic ended.

The First Pipe Mines

The first source of diamonds in the Orange Free State was discovered in July 1870, on the farm Koffiefontein, on a bank of the Riet River, north-west of Fauresmith (Figs. 2.20 and 2.21). One day a transport driver named Bam, while camped close to the river, picked up a stone which he thought might be a diamond. Bam continued on his journey to the Vaal, where the stone was positively identified, but the river diggers were sceptical about his having found it so far away. Bam gathered together some friends and they returned to Koffiefontein and dug successfully for a number of years almost undisturbed. The workings of one of the party was so deep by 1874 that he had installed a horse-driven whim

Fig. 2.20.   *Koffiefontein, the first pipe found, as it was when abandoned after earlier working was finished. It was reopened in 1971.*

Fig. 2.21.   *Koffiefontein today. Underground working began in 1977–8 by a long-hole chambering method. By 1981, open-cast operation will be phased out.*

to raise buckets of ground. Up to this time only relatively shallow sources had been found.

The diggings turned out to be an original source of diamonds, the first known pipe of blue ground from deep in the earth, which was weathered to yellow ground at the top, and was covered with overburden to the surface. The diggers at this time knew little or nothing about the origin of diamonds, but the finding later of other deep mines brought in the financiers, who realized that to exploit such rich sources of diamond, money and organization were essential. When the Koffiefontein pipe became too deep for individual diggers to mine successfully, they sold the rights to Alfred Mosely, who formed a company to exploit it in 1891. In the same year, a 136-carat stone was found there, which made many more people aware of its existence. Eventually it was purchased by the De Beers Mining Company and worked until 1931. It was reopened in 1971, forty years later, to replace the Jagersfontein mine, the discovery of which is described in the next paragraph. It yielded well over 333,000 carats in 1975, when a second main rock shaft was sunk to its final depth of 2,300 ft (702 m) in preparation for underground mining.

One man who heard about the Koffiefontein finds was de Kerk, foreman of the farm Jagersfontein about 6 miles (9·6 km) from Fauresmith. The farm was in a valley through which ran a stream, which was dried out for most of the year. Having learned the rudiments of diamond recovery from Vaal river men passing through, de Kerk decided to try his luck in the river bed. He dug down several feet to the river bedrock and concentrated the gravels he found there with an ordinary garden seive and a tank of water. In August 1870, he found a 50-carat diamond.

A few Vaal river diggers heard about the find and tried the area, but the occurrence was patchy. The owner of the farm, Miss Visser, charged what was at the time the high fee of £2 a month for a claim, which discouraged more extensive searching. Some diggers remained, however, and found themselves being drawn towards one area. Around 1878, it became evident that the diggings were not alluvial, as was naturally assumed, but the relatively small area with higher yields of good-quality stones was the mouth of a pipe.

The open cast working of the Jagersfontein pipe was easier than others at first because the hard basalt rock around it eliminated most of the problem of surrounding reef falling into the hole as it was worked deeper.

The Excelsior Diamond

J. T. McNish tells the story of an agreement for the owners of the Jagersfontein mine to sell to Wernher, Beit and Co., all diamonds found between July 1892, and midnight 30th June 1893. Before the time ran out, an overseer had become suspicious of one of the coloured labourers, but had been unable to find anything positively wrong. Half an hour before midnight, the labourer took fright and gave himself up to the mine overseer. He produced a top quality carat diamond that measured 2½ by 2 in. (64 × 51 mm) and was 1 in. (25 mm) thick! It was at that time the largest ever found. It weighed 972 carats and was subsequently named the Excelsior (Fig. 2.22).

Despite the earlier suspicions of him, the labourer was rewarded with £500, a

Fig. 2.22. *The Excelsior diamond, that weighed 972 carats in the rough, when found in the Jagersfontein mine. For a time it was the largest known.*

horse and equipment, and released from his contract. Wernher, Beit and Co. gained the crystal for a fraction of its worth because the contract specified a relatively low price per carat for all stones found. The Excelsior lay in their safe for thirty-three years awaiting a buyer.

In 1910, a 1,020 ft (311 m) shaft was sunk beside the pipe and another added later, for underground working. The pipe was closed for a time during the world depression of 1930 and was not worked during the Second World Waar when the buildings were used as an internment camp. It was worked again for a number of years, however, but was closed once more in 1971.

More Pipe Mines Discovered

In 1867, a Yorkshireman named William Anderson went to Durban to prospect in Africa for gold as an employee of the London and Limpopo Gold Mining Co. Although he found traces of gold, his interest turned to diamonds and he went to the Vaal diggings. A short time there, however, persuaded him that their future was limited, so, having heard of the stones bought by Van Niekerk which had been found on the open veld, he decided to leave the river diggings and try his luck elsewhere. He began by examining the prospecting pits of other diggers and eventually came to the farm, Dorstfontein, owned by Adrian J. van Wyk. It had been bought by van Wyk from another farmer, Abraham du Toit, who himself had purchased it from the Free State Government in 1860.

Van Wyk had built himself a mud-walled hut on the edge of a pan (pond) which was filled with brackish water in the wet season and was an area of cracked mud in the dry season. Anderson asked for permission to dig, but was refused, as van Wyk had no wish to see the place overrun by diggers. Nevertheless, Anderson became friendly with the Boer farmer, whose children one day showed him some stones in the mud walls of the hut. He recognized with excitement that they were diamonds and asked the children to point out the place from which the mud had been dug.

This convinced him that there was an important source of diamonds on the farm, but he kept the knowledge to himself and made a visit to a neighbouring farm, Bultfontein, where he persuaded the owner, Cornelius du Plooy, with whom he had become acquainted, to let him dig. There, too, he found diamonds in the mud of the farm's pan.

Anderson's next move was to find friends who would back him in a venture to exploit both Bultfontein and the pan on the Dorstfontein farm, which eventually became known as Du Toit's Pan (Figs. 2.23 and 2.24). If Anderson had succeeded in his plans, he would have owned two of the richest diamond pipes in what was later named Kimberley. They are still being mined intensively today. He would have become a millionaire many times over. Unfortunately, as so often happens, one of his friends was unable to keep the secret and the news spread throughout the Vaal diggings, causing a rush of diggers to Du Toit's Pan in 1870. Anderson was able to make a stake, but as far as is known, his ground was not particularly profitable.

Biggest Rush to the Dry Diggings

News of the dry diggings spread not only through the diggers' communities but throughout the world and very soon there were thousands more adventurers from most of the European countries and from Australia, America, Canada, and New Zealand on the way to the new dry diggings in South Africa. Soon after the end of 1870, the river camps, including Pniel and Klipdrift, were practically deserted.

Chaos reigned wherever there were diamonds in the veld. Farming became impossible. Trees, livestock, vegetation all disappeared. Van Wyk was so distressed that he sold his land for £2,000 to the London and South African Exploration Co., which was represented locally by Henry Webb and Martin Lilienfeld, one of the people who had bought the Star of South Africa from Van Niekerk in 1869.

At this time, the farm was seething with diggers and would-be diggers pegging claims, fighting over them and working them. When Webb told diggers to leave because the company he represented had bought the land, he found a revolt on his hands despite his threats to call in the police. He soon realized the situation was uncontrollable. The diggers wanted the area to be declared a public diggings. Webb was asked to attend a meeting of the Diggers' Mutual Protection Association Committee, which he managed to delay until the directors of his company arrived. The result was an agreement that diggers could stake claims anywhere except in the immediate area of Webb's house. Webb declared later that he only signed because he was threatened. It was at this meeting that the mine was named Du Toit's Pan.

Meanwhile, on the neighbouring farm of Bultfontein, the owner du Plooy had been to the Vaal River to see the diggings for himself and had tried searching for diamonds on his own land, but without much success. Very soon after Du Toit's Pan was overrun, there were approaches to du Plooy to allow claims on his land and late in 1870 diggers began prospecting without permission. Du Plooy knew that he would soon be faced with the same problem as his neighbour, unable to farm the land, and he began to look for a buyer.

Du Toits Pan Camp. Late 1871.

Fig. 2.23.   *The diggers' camp on the Dutoitspan farm in late 1871.*

He was offered £2,000 by a land speculator and when Martin Lilienfeld, now representing the Hope Town Diamond Mining Co., heard about the offer he went to du Plooy and persuaded the religious farmer that as the offer had been made on a Sunday, it was illegal. He offered £2,600 for the land, with an indemnity against court action. Legal action was in fact taken by the first buyer, who won £500 and costs but lost one of the world's biggest diamond pipes.

The Hope Town Diamond Co. began mining Bultfontein themselves, employing a large number of native Africans. When the Du Toit's Pan Diggers Committee heard about this, they decided it was unfair because it eliminated claim pegging. The two companies approached each other for self-protection and amalgamated under the London and South African Exploration Co., with Henry Webb in charge to work both mines. Unable to clear the diggers from Du Toit's Pan, they concentrated on Bultfontein (Fig. 2.25).

The Government Steps In

In the meantime, unsuspected by the company, the government in Bloemfontein was putting the finishing touches to a law that was to explode like a land mine among owners of diamondiferous land. In 1871, the government decreed that owners of property where diamonds were found had to declare the areas as public diggings. If they did not, the ground would be confiscated at the compensation of £1 per morgen.* All finds of diamonds had to be reported to government

* A morgen is 2·1165 acres (0·86 ha).

53

inspectors who would be appointed to control both diggings and diggers. The government would then take half of what owners of land earned in issuing claim licences. Certain conditions were imposed on, and protection granted to diggers.

One result was that the Exploration Co. lost all their digging rights, half of what revenue they could get from allowing claims, and in addition had to pay 10 per cent of what was left to the Diggers' Committee. Another result was that as soon as the news was known, there was a mad rush to Bultfontein.

In effect, the Cape government annexed the diamondiferous farms Vooruitzicht, Bultfontein, Du Toit's Pan (Dorstfontein), Kenilworth, and Wesselton (Benaaudheidsfontein), but not Koffiefontein and Jagersfontein which lay outside the limits of the government's land survey.

Into Yellow Ground

At this time, only the surfaces of the dry diggings which were on pipes were being scratched. It was not until the end of 1871 that a digger went through the over-burden of limestone to the decomposed yellow ground where the diamond concentration was much higher. About 6,000 diggers were active on the two farms at this time. Diamonds of over 100 carats were frequently found in 'The Pan'. Claims changed hands for high prices but not all were rich or even payable. Some were given away when they turned out apparently to be barren, and the following day the new owner would find a fortune.

Rough hotels, canteens, shops, and bars were set up for the multitude of diggers who lived in tents and shacks. Prices of goods were high and sometimes outrageous when transport was difficult and supplies short. Most of the time a haze of dust hung over the diggings but when the rains came the diggings became flooded and all work had to stop. When people died they were buried in a cemetery near the Bultfontein diggings. Some strange customs originated in communities of diggers. Apparently, it was the practice of some Vaal river diggers to build cairns of stones surmounted by a black flag on a stick along the river banks for their dead.

The de Beer's Farm

On a neighbouring farm to Bultfontein, known as Vooruitzicht, a lone Dutch digger called Corneilsa had been allowed to work a claim on condition that he paid 25 per cent of all he received to the owners of the farm, the de Beers* brothers (Fig. 2.26). News of this seeped to a Vaal river digger, Richard Jackson, who eventually decided to form a party of four to investigate. The party found Corneilsa, who innocently welcomed them and introduced them to the farmers.

Jackson's party returned to the Vaal and suggested to several friends that they form a larger party, but the news got out and the biggest rush to date started to the de Beer's farm. Horses and wagons and mules were literally raced neck and neck across the veld and apparently Jackson and his friends only beat the main body of the rush by a hundred yards or so to hammer in their pegs. Within hours, the whole area was pegged out beyond the Vooruitzicht farm border, regardless

* The original family name was de Beer.

Dutoitspan Mine H.B. Webbs Claim. 1880.

Fig. 2.24.   *The Dutoitspan mine in 1880, showing the claims worked to different levels.*

Bulfontein Mine. Hope & Hadden 1879.

Fig. 2.25.   *Claims in the Bultfontein pipe mine, on the next farm to Dutoitspan, in 1879.*

Fig. 2.26. *Johannes Nico-las, as one of the de Beer brothers who bought the Voor-uitzicht farm for £50 and sold it for £6,300. About £590 million worth of dia-monds have been found there.*

of what might have been the owners' wishes, and into parts of the neighbouring Kaufersdam and Dorstfontein farms.

Jackson found his own six claims worthless as they were just outside the circle of what was a new pipe mine, and he abandoned them with nothing left but his pick and shovel.

Corneilsa took fright at the ruthless rush for land and sold his claim for £110. The de Beer brothers, bewildered by the madness around them, on 19th October 1871, sold the farm to a syndicate for £6,300, which was a large sum compared with the £50 they had paid for the farm eleven years earlier. After-wards they complained that they had been tricked and should have received a new wagon and equipment as well! Later, the syndicate sold the farm to the Cape Government for £100,000. To date, about £1,000,000,000 worth of diamonds have been recovered from the farm, which later came into the ownership of De Beers Consolidated Mines.

The 'Big Hole' of Kimberley

Among the men who arrived at the de Beer farm was a man named Fleetwood Rawstone, who led a group known as the Colesberg Party after the place from which they had originally come. The party had been late arrivals, but Raw-stone had bought a claim that they had worked with success, until Rawstone lost it gambling (Fig. 2.27).

Dispirited, the party set off again and camped on the edge of a depression not very far from the de Beer diggings to the west. They were so unlucky there, that some members returned to find employment on other diggings. Rawstone had a cook-boy called Damon who had grown up with his family. Damon was reliable, even in bad times, except when he managed to get hold of alcohol.

At the time that the party, who had begun to call themselves the 'Red Cap Company' because they wore red bags on their heads, were testing this ground and finding nothing, Damon came across a friend with whom he got drunk and became more obstreperous than usual. Rawstone dismissed him, but relented when Damon pleaded for his job and sent him to start a prospect pit in a previously abandoned area.

A few days later, on the Saturday evening of 15th July 1871, according to the story recorded by one of the Red Cap survivors years later, Damon came to the tent where Fleetwood Rawstone and some of the others were playing bridge and said quietly, 'Fleet, I want to see you.' Irritably, Rawstone told him to come in and Damon opened his hand to disclose three diamonds.

The effect was electric. The card table was overthrown and the players rushed for their pegs and hammers. Claims were marked out for all members of the party, including those who had left, around Damon's pit, which was under a camelthorn tree in the knee-high grass. The next day, Sunday, Rawstone reported the discovery officially to the government surveyor, but already the

Fig. 2.27. *The Red Cap Company, under Fleetwood Rawstone, who found what became the Kimberley mine – now called the Big Hole. Rawstone made a bad claim and gained nothing from the £50 millions' worth of diamonds found there. Damon is on the left.*

Fig. 2.28. *Prospecting at the Kimberley mine in 1871. This is the oldest known picture of Kimberley and was painted by A. F. White after J. W. George. The painting by A. F. White now hangs in the Kimberley Club.*

Fig. 2.29. *At Nooitgedacht, on the banks of the Vaal river, independent licensed diggers still work by the traditional methods, except for using trucks. Pegs in the foreground show staked claims.*

news had spread and a big new rush was on. On the Monday the government surveyor was already recording and checking claims. (Fig. 2.28.)

The mine was first called the 'New Rush' and afterwards became known as the Kimberley Mine, and finally the 'Big Hole' of Kimberley. It was worked until 1914. Before then, the 38 acre (15.4 ha) hole had become about 1 mile (1.6 km) round the edge and about 440 yd (402 m) deep. Shafts were sunk to mine it from underground to a depth of 3,601 ft (1098 m). The story of its mining is told in Chapter Four. About 25,000,000 tons (25,400,000 tonnes) of ground were dug out to recover about three tons of diamond (14,500,000 carats) worth about £50,000,000 (Fig. 3.6).

Rawstone was unlucky to the last. Of his four claims, two were inside the area of the pipe and two outside, but even the diamondiferous ones were very poor and he hardly paid his way from them. Others in the party were more fortunate. All members of the Red Cap Party were awarded claims although some had not been present when the find was made. One, T. B. Kisch, was mentioned earlier as the first known European to prospect for diamonds in Africa.

Present Small Diggings

Most of the inland alluvial diggings, dry diggings in dried-out river beds and banks in South Africa, which were the most numerous of all, are today exhausted, but some diamonds are still found in the most productive of them at Barkly West, Bloemhof, and Lichtenburg. A handful of individual diggers still work about 6 square miles (15.5 sq. km) of bushland called Nooitgedacht on the Vaal River near Kimberley which is owned by De Beers Consolidated Mines. No new diggers' licences have been issued since 1945 and the prospectors and their labourers still live and work in the conditions of the early frontier (Fig 2.29).

River claims were first 20 ft (6.1 m) square. Later they were made 30 Cape ft square, and eventually 30 by 60 ft (9 × 18·3 m). Claims at the dry diggings,

59

Fig. 2.31 (above). *A digger's grave at Nooitge-dacht, where a few diggers still work. His mug, knife, spoon and fork are on the grave with an old torch. Wire netting around his bedstead keeps the jackals away.*

Fig. 2.30 (left). *A tattered Union flag, symbol of the law that came to the diggings in the 1890s, was still flying at Bosmansfontein, near Bloemhof, when a rush for claims was organized there in 1947.*

i.e. the pipe mines, were always 30 ft (9 m) square, but the English foot was used at Dutoitspan and Bultfontein, and the Cape foot at the De Beers, Kimberley, and Jagersfontein mines, which made the claims there 31 English ft (9·5 m) square.

The Diggers' Press

One of the earliest arrivals on the original Vaal fields was R. W. Murray, co-founder of the *Cape Argus* newspaper in 1857. In August 1870, he produced the first diggers' publication, *The Diamond Field*, at Pniel. On the following day, a rival appeared, *The Diamond News*, published by Richards, Glanville and Co., who were publishers of the old *Grahamstown Journal*. The company's printing press was carted after the diggers to Du Toits Pan, and then to the New Rush. The name was changed to *The Diamond and Vaal Advertiser*, and again on a change of ownership in the 1870s to *The Diamond Fields Advertiser*. It is still published under the last name as a daily newspaper from Kimberley. *The Diamond News* is now a trade paper, also published from Kimberley.

REFERENCES

The South African Diamond Fields, by J. L. Babe (New York, 1872).
Reminiscences of Kimberley, by Louis Cohen (London, 1911).
Diamonds and Precious Stones, by Louis Dieulafait (London, 1874).
Early Diamond Days, by Oswald Doughty (London, 1963).
Incwadi Yami, by J. W. Matthews (*c.* 1792).
The Road to El Dorado, by J. T. McNish (Cape Town, 1968).
The Glittering Road, by J. T. McNish (Cape Town, 1970).
Diamond Fever 1866–1869, by Marian Robertson (Cape Town, 1974).
The Diamond Fields Advertiser, Kimberley. Various issues.
The Diamond News, Kimberley. Various issues.

CHAPTER THREE

The Big Mining Companies

Cecil Rhodes at Kimberley

The last twenty years of the nineteenth century saw the rise of the big mining companies and gradual elimination of individual diggers in South Africa. The man who had most influence on the course of African history and on the diamond industry in particular, and gave his name to Rhodesia, sailed into Durban in a small barque after a seventy days' journey from England. The date was 1st September, 1870, two and a half months after the New Rush. Cecil Rhodes (Fig. 3.1) had been sent to a better climate at the age of 17 because of his poor health and intended to join his elder brother Herbert, who was farming in Natal, but arrived to find that Herbert had caught 'diamond fever' and had left for the river diggings, where he had made a rich strike.

Cecil stayed on the farm, got to know a number of important people, and lived off an income he made by selling gold shares on commission. In 1871, Herbert returned to find that his younger brother had leased a farm called Lion's Kloof. The two brothers cleared the area for cotton growing, but Herbert was drawn again to the diamond fields as more news came through of big fortunes being made. He departed at short notice leaving behind the advice to wind up the farm and follow him. This Cecil Rhodes did, and arrived on the fields himself in May, 1871. He tried unsuccessfully to buy a claim at the de Beers' diggings and then moved to an area near Fleetwood Rawstone's camp, where he employed some Zulus to dig for him. He was unlucky, however, and had to resort to selling ice-cream, and then water, in order to survive.

As the 1870s continued, the difficulties for individual diggers in the pipe mines became enormous. At first one person was allowed officially to work two claims 30 ft (or 31 ft) square (9 m or 9·5 m). Then, in 1874 the number of claims permitted was increased to ten. In 1876, the restriction was removed altogether, mainly because of the difficulties of working separate claims in a concentrated area of yellow ground which reduced in diameter as the diggings became deeper. Removal of the restriction made amalgamations possible.

Cecil Rhodes went into partnership with two Englishmen, Charles D. Rudd and Wallace Anderson, and raised £900 to buy a pump in Port Elizabeth which they hired to diggers whose claims were flooded, earning a considerable sum of money. Rhodes again had serious health problems and this time he returned to England to recover. He was 21 years old. During visits to England, he borrowed money from his aunt to take a degree in law at Oxford University.

While in South Africa in 1873, he managed to buy one claim in the de Beer mine. His profits from the pump venture went to further claims and to enter into partnership with owners who did not want to sell out entirely, until by 1880, he was one of the largest owners.

Fig. 3.1.   *Cecil J. Rhodes, visionary, pioneer, and financier, who formulated diamond marketing policy.*

In 1880 and 1881 there was a period of reckless company promotion and share rigging, combined with great difficulties in working claims, that led to more amalgamations. Most active still in buying claims was Rhodes, who in 1880 had formed the De Beers Mining Co. Ltd., working with two other groups. It took him until 1887 to gain complete control, as some small companies held on to their shares to the end.

Barney Barnato

The same year that Rhodes returned to South Africa, 1873, another man who was to have a considerable influence on the course of events also arrived at the diamond fields. His name was Barney Barnato (Fig. 3.2) and he was the opposite of Rhodes in almost every respect. Rhodes was delicate in health, tall and fair in appearance, and cold and scholarly in manner. Barnato was almost the same age, but robust in health, short and dark, uneducated, and rumbustious in manner.

Barnato also came out to join his elder brother, Harry. Their real surname was Isaacs, but they had changed it when Barney, at the age of 14, had partnered his brother in a variety act. His prompt to come on stage were the words 'And Barney, too'. This became a nickname Barnato, which both brothers adopted as their surname.

Fig. 3.2. *Barney Barnato, photographed after he had formed Barnato Diamond Mining, his first company, with a capital of £300,000.*

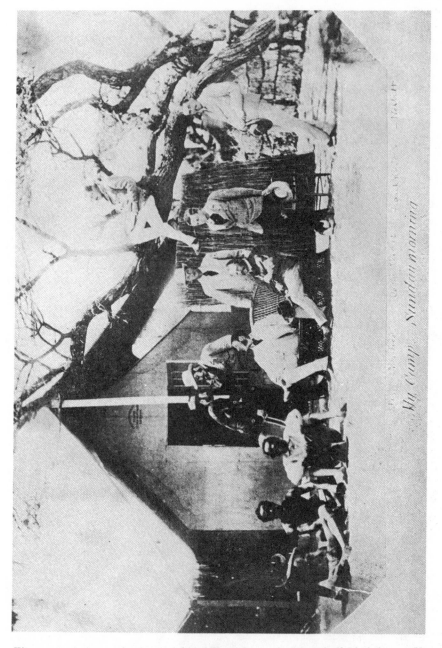

Fig. 3.3. *A picture taken in 1871 during Dr. Atherstone's visit to Cecil Rhodes' camp. He had not been able to go earlier because he was so busy as a medical practitioner in Grahamstown. Standing centre facing the camera is Cecil Rhodes with (Colonel) Frank Rhodes on his left. Herbert Rhodes and Dr. Atherstone are seated.*

Barney arrived on the fields at the age of 18, with sixty boxes of doubtful cigars as capital, in the middle of a slump in prices to find his brother almost destitute. He had to turn his hand to selling anything he could get hold of. He also set up a boxing ring to make a little money taking on allcomers for bets. The original booth is now set up in the extensive museum maintained by De Beers on the edge of the Big Hole in Kimberley. He managed to save £30 and with this amount of capital he set up in business as a kopje walloper, as diamond dealers were called, in partnership with a man named Louis Cohen.

Cohen described Barney as a 'decidedly unscrupulous character, who had, nevertheless, a grain of gold in his nature'. Cohen put up £60 and Barney added 'forty boxes of the best cigars that ever came from Havana' to his smaller capital, saying that he had acquired them 'through the acumen and sharpness of his brother-in-law – the famous connoiseur, Joel Joel'. Cohen wrote later, 'Cornydon, the lawyer, drew up an agreement, and one fine morning we entered into possession of an iron shanty about eight feet by six. The cigars duly arrived and were piled in a corner of the office. I tested a sample. . . . I felt sick, but the man's wonderful earnestness (of course, it was all acting) convinced me that it must be my own fault and not that of the "Havanas". But those cigars cost me dear.'

The joint cash capital was deposited in the bank in Cohen's name and he alone had the power to sign cheques. Barney's post, he wrote, 'was to be out all day walloping on the Kopje while I sat in the shanty – a much more comfortable job, I need not explain. You can hardly realize what it is, as wet with perspiration one minute and the pores of the skin clogged with deadly dust from the next, you toil around from mound to mound under a glaring sun. And this to a man with rather defective sight. . . . The establishment closed, we too would sit in the front office discussing the mess (nearly always curry and rice) with two empty Bass bottles having candles stuck in them for lights. Neither of us drank alcoholic liquor, and seldom smoked – and *never* our own cigars. After dinner we undressed a little, arranged on our blankets, and slept comfortably' on the earthern floor.

One day one of their best customers, a Dutchman, was given a cigar after a deal and rushed back with his mouth inflamed saying it was the cigar which was made of gunpowder or something worse. Barney insisted the cigars were Havana and they lost the incensed Dutch digger's business. A number of other clients never came back after having been given a cigar. This led, wrote Cohen, 'to a bit of bother between me and Barney, but I insisted on selling the Havanas by auction and sacrificing them at half-cost'.

When the diggers were abandoning their claims in the Kimberley Mine because they thought that the diamonds were running out at the end of the yellow ground, Barney gave up buying stones and rejoined his brother as Barnato Brothers. Having heard the arguments of the geologists who thought the hard blue ground under the yellow ground should also contain diamonds, and the opposing views of many diggers who said it was hard bedrock like they had found under gravel and sand in alluvial diggings and was barren, Barnato Brothers decided to take a chance and buy up claims as near as possible to the centre of the diggings. In 1880, they formed the Barnato Mining Co., which

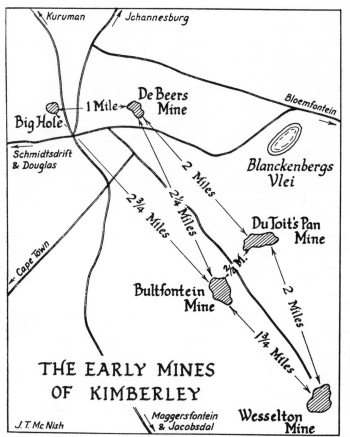

Kuruman   Johannesburg

De Beers Mine
Bloemfontein
Big Hole — 1 Mile —
Schmidtsdrift & Douglas
Blanckenbergs Vlei
2 Miles
2¾ Miles
2¼ Miles
Du Toit's Pan Mine
Cape Town
⅔ M.
Bultfontein Mine
2 Miles
THE EARLY MINES
OF KIMBERLEY
1¾ Miles
J. T. McNish
Maggersfontein & Jacobsdal
Wesselton Mine

Fig. 3.4. *The pipe mines that became the town of Kimberley.*

later merged with the Kimberley Central Mining Co., and bought out the remaining six claims in the centre of the mine from a man named Stewart. In 1883–4, Kimberley Central, under Barney Barnato's control, was the first to sink shafts into the centre of the mine.

By 1887 the mining operations in Kimberley – the town that had grown from the original mining camps around the group of four pipe mines, Kimberley, De Beers, Dutoitspan, and Bultfontein – were concentrated in the hands of three main groups (Fig. 3.4). Rhodes was the chairman of De Beers Mines and Barnato was the most influential figure in the Kimberley Mine. The third group, the Compagnie Française des Mines de Diamant du Cap de Bon Espèrance, had the next most important holding in the Kimberley Mine (Fig. 3.5 to 8).

Rhodes, with financial backing from his friend Alfred Beit and from Rothschilds in London, made an offer of £1,400,000 for the French company. When Barnato heard of this, he immediately thought Rhodes was poaching on this territory and made a counter offer of £1,750,000.

Rhodes, typically, did not compete, but went to Barnato with the suggestion that they co-operate. If he were allowed to buy at the lower price, he said, he would sell the French company to Barnato for a fifth interest in Kimberley

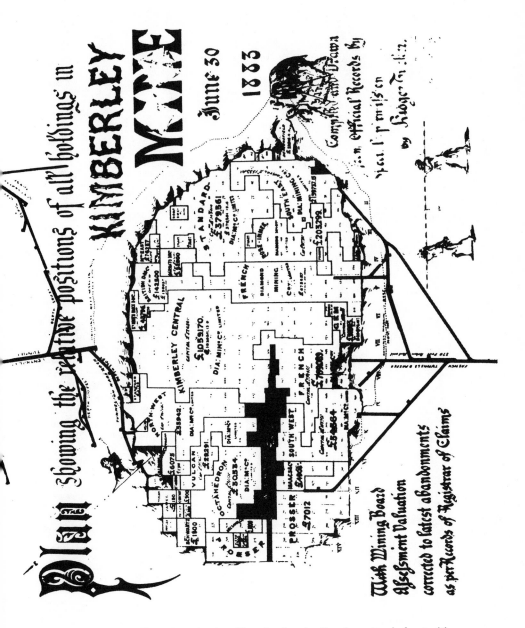

Fig. 3.5. *Claims in the Kimberley mine in 1883, showing the French company's key position next to Barnato's Kimberley Central.*

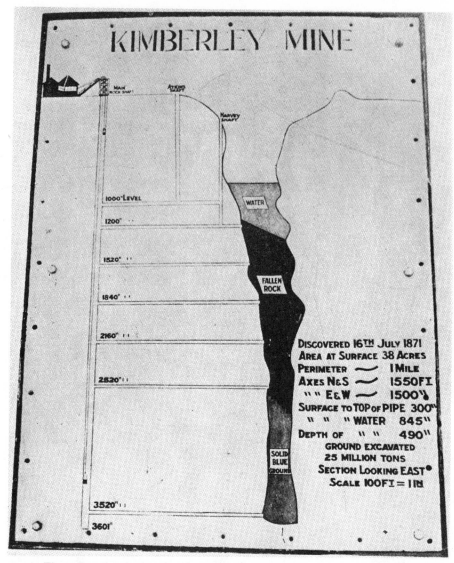

Fig. 3.6. *A notice board at the Big Hole today giving details of the workings.*

Central and £300,000 in cash. Barnato agreed, sure that the minority holding Rhodes would gain could easily be contained.

Barnato grossly underrated Rhodes. A financial battle for control of Kimberley Central developed between them with rival bids being made for the remaining holdings. As the prices of shares in the mining companies shot up, the prices of diamonds were dropping owing to a slump in sales at the same time as high production from Africa. At one time top grade stones were as low as 10*s*. (50p) a carat.

De Beers Consolidated Mines

This was at about the time when the incident of Barney's bucket (related in

Fig. 3.7. *The Big Hole, or Kimberley Mine, today. The town of Kimberley reaches almost to its edge. It was probably the biggest man-made hole until recent times.*

Chapter Seven) occurred. Although tricked, Barney admired Rhode's *chutzpah** in keeping a large quantity of stones off the market for some time although he had sold them. Relationship between them improved for a time, but Barney lost control of the Kimberley Mine and continued to resist Rhodes's attempts at amalgamations.

Cecil Rhodes broke the deadlock in typical fashion. Instead of attempting to hold a meeting at Barnato Brothers' or his own office, he proposed a lunch at the Kimberley Club, which had been founded by the English-speaking social

* Yiddish for cheek.

elite, many of whom disliked and despised the Jewish cockney 'upstart'. It tickled Barney Barnato's fancy to be asked. He accepted and behaved deliberately so outrageously at that and many subsequent meetings, that members tried to get him banned, a resolution that Rhodes vetoed and countered by putting him up for membership. Members were incensed. At least one of Rhodes's co-directors threatened to leave the Board if Rhodes was successful in his amalgamation plans, the case for which he continuously promoted to Barney. He also promised to nominate Barney for the Cape Assembly, which later he did.

Rhodes' methods of persuasion were successful and Barney Barnato eventually capitulated at a meeting in Dr. Jameson's bungalow, which Jameson was sharing with Rhodes. Also present on Barney's side was Woolf Joel, his nephew and partner. Although Barney would become the biggest shareholder of the new company, De Beers Consolidated Mines Ltd, that Rhodes proposed to control both pipes, consolidate all the diamond mining interests and control the output, he was still suspicious because Rhodes would be chairman and there was no guarantee that Barney would remain on the board. He therefore proposed that there should be life governors to oversee the company board. To this Rhodes eventually agreed. The life governors were to be Rhodes, Barnato, Beit, and

Fig. 3.8.   *Another view of the Big Hole in recent times. There is now a magnificent museum on the edge of it, created by Basil Humphries, with the backing of Ken Loftus (then general manager at Kimberley). Now run and developed by Frank Beresford; it is a re-creation of old Kimberley and its diamond mining history.*

Fig. 3.9.   *De Beers mine in 1872, after it had become so deep that cables and buckets had to be used to bring up the ground. A man winding up a bucket can be seen on the left.*

F. S. Philipson-Stow, one of those who pooled their shares to form the original De Beers Mining Company and the man who had threatened he would resign rather than serve with Barney. He then nearly wrecked the new concord with Barney Barnato, but was talked round by Rhodes and Beit.

De Beers Consolidated Mines Ltd, was incorporated on 13th March 1888, with a nominal capital of £100,000 in £5 shares, over 6,000 of which were held by Barney and about 4,000 each by the other three life governors. Rhodes had gained his objective, however, which was contained not in the distribution of shares but in the powers set out in the Deed of Trust to which Barney and his nephew had agreed.

Some shareholders in Kimberley Central were so dissatisfied with the agreement that they took the matter to court on the grounds that the Kimberley Central charter provided that it should merge only with a similar mining company and that De Beers Consolidated was not similar as its charter was to build an empire and even permitted it to 'take steps for good government of any territory, raise and maintain a standing army, and undertake warlike operations'.

The court decided in favour of the dissident shareholders, but without altering the outcome, because Rhodes and Barnato liquidated Kimberley Central and sold the assets to De Beers. Then they handed to the liquidators for distribution to the shareholders in Kimberley Central a cheque for £5,338,650. The cancelled cheque was framed and still hangs in the De Beers boardroom at Kimberley.

Two years before the formation of De Beers Consolidated Mines, Rhodes had visited the Rand by ox wagon to investigate the goldfields, but had returned to Kimberley on hearing of a friend who was dying. He considered and turned down the chance of buying a farm for £250 that was worth £2,000,000 only two years later. He became Prime Minister of Cape Colony at the age of 37. Barnato, who was a year older, took a big part in developing the Rand gold fields, but gradually broke down in mental health under the strain of running his huge

Fig. 3.10. *The site of Kimberley before diggers arrived from all over the world.*

Fig. 3.11. *The big mining camp that grew up between the Kimberley (Big Hole) and De Beers mines and the Bultfontein and Dutoitspan mines; shown here in about 1876.*

financial empire and at the age of 44 jumped overboard from the ship on which he was travelling to England.

Rhodes was responsible for the British annexation of Bechuanaland (now the independent Botswana) and the Matabele territory that became known as Southern Rhodesia. He resigned as Premier in 1896 after being censored in the British Houses of Parliament for his part in the Jameson Raid which was launched from Bechuanaland to the Transvaal with the aim of helping topple President Kruger. The worsening of Anglo-Boer relations that followed helped to precipitate the Boer War.

In 1899, the Boers of the two independent states under Kruger, the Transvaal president, declared war on Britain and besieged Mafeking, Ladysmith and Kimberley; the last was under siege from 1899 to 1900. What Rhodes called the 'Imperial pop guns' were so ineffective at Kimberley that George Labram, an American who was chief engineer for De Beers, designed a 28-pounder which was named 'Long Cecil' after Rhodes and was made in the De Beers' workshops. The Boers retaliated by bringing up a 100-pounder and Rhodes arranged for the women and children to shelter some times for several days and nights at a stretch down the Kimberley and De Beers mines. Labram was killed by a stray Boer shell. Kimberley was eventually relieved by General John French. Rhodes left his house Groote Schuur on the Cape when his health finally failed and returned to his cottage at Muizenburg to die there in 1902 before the war ended in the same year.

The Town of Kimberley

The Boer and diggers' names for the Colesberg party's find did not survive long under England's dignified Victorian administration and on 5th June 1873, a proclamation announced: The encampment and town heretofore known as De Beers New Rush the Colesberg Kopje No. 2, or Vooruitzigt, shall henceforth be and be described as the town of Kimberley (Fig. 3.11). The Earl of Kimberley was at the time the British Secretary for the Colonies.

Four years later, the novelist Anthony Trollope visited the diggings and wrote of Kimberley: 'I cannot say that Kimberley is an alluring town – perhaps as little so as any town that I have ever visited. . . . The town is built of corrugated iron. It is probably the most hideous that has yet come to man's hands. . . . It is difficult to conceive the existence of a town in which every plank used has to be dragged 500 miles (800 km) by oxen; but such has been the case at Kimberley.

Another visitor said that the first view was of a white sheen of tents along the ridge. The only regular road was the main street. The rest were paths between the tents and tin houses that diggers moved wherever they wished. In 1968, a huge rubbish dump was examined in Kimberley and found to contain early beer bottles from six different bottling factories and also large numbers of caviar jars. The owner of the dump was selling 'claims' to those interested in looking for relics of old Kimberley.

The camp around the old De Beers mine near by soon fused into Kimberley, and later houses first straggled along and then extended along the track to

Fig. 3.12. *The Auction Mart and Claim Office in old Kimberley. Mine workings can be seen in the far background, left.*

Fig. 3.13. *The shacks were built close to the mines, the sorting areas and the dumps. This is Kimberley, probably in the 1880s.*

Dutoitspan, about 2 miles (3.2 km) away, until the two settlements became one (Fig. 3.4).

Kimberley is high, being on the plateau of South Africa, about 4,000 ft (1,220 m) above sea-level, and is today a flourishing town in a semi-desert, but still retains much of its old mining atmosphere. Town buildings extend almost to the edge of the exhausted Big Hole. The big holes of the other mines are security areas because the mines are still in production.

Some of the old timber and corrugated iron buildings still exist. If an old building is demolished, one of the few remaining licenced diggers will usually obtain the right to work the site which he will proceed to do in the traditional manner of the pioneers, even in the middle of the bustling traffic, often making rewarding finds.

One of the finest of the old buildings being preserved is the headquarters of De Beers Consolidated Mines, who have resisted the temptation to have a modern steel and concrete block in its place (Fig. 3.15). Kimberley always remained a very English town until recent times when a big railway depot was set up and the Afrikaaner population rapidly increased.

The Kimberley Big Hole is today surrounded by a remarkable museum devoted to old Kimberley and the history of diamond digging. Many of Kimberley's old houses and shops have been moved and re-erected in the Open Mine

Fig. 3.14. *Jam of ox wagons at Kimberley in 1880–85, after bringing supplies across the desert.*

Fig. 3.15. *De Beers Consolidated Mines still occupy, in Stockdale Street, one of Kimberley's oldest buildings. Even the early atmosphere is still preserved.*

Museum, fully stocked and in some cases animated. Large new buildings house transport vehicles, mining equipment, etc. It includes Kimberley's first house, a tiny timbered building brought from the coast by ox wagon, a bar – the 'Diggers' Rest', dealers' offices, grocers', pharmacists', clothing stores, a brewery, even a church. The first major earth movements around the Hole occurred from 1975 to 1976, when 1,500,000 tons of rock fell in; and a drainage tunnel was completed in 1977.

The Wesselton and Premier Mines

On the edge of Kimberley is another pipe mine about 2 miles (3·2 km) south-east of Dutoitspan. It was discovered in December 1891, on the farm Bena-audheidsfontein, and was named the Wesselton. It is still very actively mined.

Finding of the Wesselton pipe sparked off another search for kimberlite, as blue and yellow ground were named, but by 1898, after many unpayable kimberlite areas had been located, most prospectors decided that no more big finds were likely. That was the year, however, that an ex-bricklayer named Thomas Cullinan, who had made a small fortune building, decided to go prospecting in the Pretoria area a long way from Kimberley. He met a man who had picked up a 3-carat diamond on a farm, and on looking around, he noticed

Fig. 3.16.   *A sketch showing the part of the Premier mine where the Cullinan diamond was found. It appeared in an article by G. F. Kunz in the* Century Magazine *in 1909.*

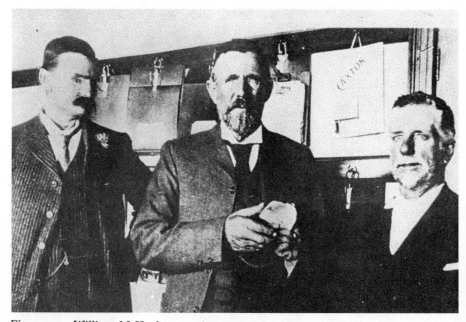

Fig. 3.17.   *William McHardy, general manager of the Premier Mine in 1905, holding the Cullinan diamond, the largest ever found. On the left of the picture is Sir Thomas Cullinan and on the right 'Daddy' Wells, surface manager, who found the stone.*

a kopje (hill) like those he had seen in the Kimberley area. The farm, Elands-fontein, was about twenty miles north-east of Pretoria.

Cullinan tried to buy the farm, but the farmer, an old Boer named Joachim Prinsloo, refused to sell because he had already been driven out of two farms, Madderfontein where gold had been struck, and another where diamonds had been found. This time Prinsloo was determined not to move as he was apparently uninterested in money. Cullinan had to wait until Prinsloo died, which was not long afterwards, until he was able to buy the farm for £52,000 from the old man's daughter.

In 1903, the kopje was identified as the mouth of a pipe that was the biggest known up to that time, the giant Premier mine. It was 2,900 ft long by 1,400 wide (884 × 427 m) and there were 3,570 claims on it, each 31 ft (9·5 m) square. The size of it gave Rhodes' partner, Alfred Beit, a severe shock, as he believed it could undermine the Rhodes empire. Eventually, however, it came under the control of De Beers Consolidated Mines.

It was here that the biggest diamond of all time was found on 25th January 1905, by the surface manager, F. G. S. Wells, projecting from a mine wall. It was named the Cullinan, after the owner of the mine, and weighed 3,106 metric carats, being about 24 oz (680 g) in weight. It was cut into 105 stones, the biggest of which are still the two biggest polished diamonds in the world (Figs. 3.17 and 17.10 and Appendix 2). Two very large pipe mines were subsequently found in Africa, the Williamson in Tanzania, and Orapa in Botswana, and are referred to elsewhere in this book.

Diamonds on the Beaches

The country where most of the world's gem diamonds are discovered today is a strip of wild, bare sandy coast running northwards from the mouth of the Orange River in the former German territory of South West Africa (Fig. 3.18) to the Republic of Angola in the north. South West Africa sits astride the Tropic of Capricorn and is bordered by the Atlantic Ocean in the west and Botswana in the east. To the north-east is a curious panhandle or corridor to the Zambezi river where Zambia, Rhodesia, and Botswana also meet. The coastal strip is part of the Namib desert, which takes up a fifth of the country and has the highest sand dunes in the world. It has a harsh landscape with no surface water and only scrubby vegetation at certain times of the year although herds of gemsbok and springbok cross it in the summer. Between the Namib and the Kalahari desert to the east is wooded steppe and savannah, but even this is waterless on the surface. No perennial river exists in the diamond area of the country. The Orange River, although the southern border, belongs entirely to South Africa.

In 1863 or 1864, a Hottentot chief, David Christiaan, gave a mineral conces-sion to De Pass, Spence and Company of Cape Town, covering a strip of coast 20 miles (32 km) wide extending from Angra Pequene, named by the Portuguese who first landed there. Working through the Pomona Syndicate, the company mined lead for a time, but found the operation unprofitable and gave it up.*

---

* The facts of this historical background are based on research by Frank Beresford, of Con-solidated Diamond Mines of South West Africa.

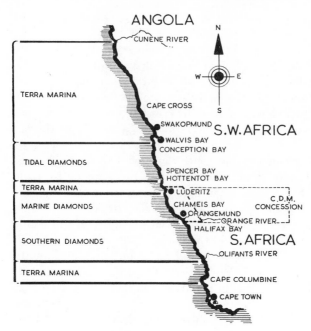

Fig. 3.18. *The coast of South West Africa, where over 80 per cent of the diamonds found are of gem quality. There are deposits under the sands on the beaches and also in the sea, where the concessions are shown on the map.*

About 1882–3, a German explorer named Lüderitz landed at Angra Pequene and went there to Bethanic, where the Hottentot chief lived. With the assistance of a missionary as go-between, Lüderitz managed to buy the coastal strip from the Orange River to latitude 26°N, probably by bartering goods. No one knows why he felt impelled to do so. Later, fearful of having his land taken back, he applied to the Cape Colony for protection, but the government there was not interested, so he made contact with the German 'Iron Chancellor', Prince von Bismarck (1815–98), who sent down a gunboat and declared the area a German Protectorate in 1884. Lüderitz was drowned trying to prove that the Orange River was navigable in a small boat. His territorial rights, including mining rights, were taken over by the Deutsche Koloniale Gesellschaft, a government-controlled company. Subsequently Angra Pequene was renamed Luderitz.*

The Germans built a railway from Luderitz which was at times blocked by 'walking sands' – drifts built up by the wind. One day in 1908, a coloured man, Zacharias Lewala, who had worked previously for De Beers in Kimberley, was shovelling sand near Kolmanskop, when he saw some crystals that he recognized as diamonds. They were shown to a railway official, August Stauch, who persuaded the German Colonial Company to grant him claims in the area. This started such a rush that within four months of the first find, the whole area north of Pomona had been pegged.

Soon it was discovered that diamonds occurred in a strip of coast from Marmosa to Conception nearly 300 miles (480 km) long and from 2 to 12 (3·2 to 19·2 km) wide. So rich was the ground in some parts that diamonds lay on the surface, where winds had blown the sands away. In the Idatal Valley bottom,

---

* Information communicated in 1968 by Willi Weiss, of Luderitz, German diamond miner at the beginning of the century.

Fig. 3.19. *During the early days of the century, the German mining companies employed labourers to crawl along the coastal sands to look for diamonds near Luderitz.*

Fig. 3.20. *Camel transport at the police post and water hole at Bogenvels in 1912 after the area had been declared Sperrgebeit – forbidden territory.*

Fig. 3.21 *Some buildings in Kolman-skop, where the Germans found diamonds in 1908, are still standing although filled with sand; the place is a ghost town. The Namib desert has the highest sand dunes of any desert.*

Fig. 3.22 *The first train to run between Elizabeth Bay and Bogenvels in about 1912.*

The Ernest Oppenheimer Bridge over the Orange River, that connects South Africa with the diamond-bearing coastal desert of Namibia (South West Africa).

However sophisticated the mining technique, human labour has to be introduced at some point. These alluvial terraces are in Sierra Leone.

There are a few independent licensed diggers still working the old claims. This washing pan at Gong Gong, near Barkly West, by the Vaal River, is still in use.

Prospecting has always been, and still is, essential to diamond mining. Here a prospector takes a sample of gravel from a stream at Mai Munene, a diamond area in Zaire.

the Germans employed African labourers to crawl on their hands and knees in a line to pick up the crystals, as shown in Fig. 3.19. In six years, the area yielded about £9,000,000 worth of diamonds (Fig. 3.20 and 3.21).

In September 1908, soon after the rush, the German Government decreed the area *Sperrgebeit* – forbidden territory – which meant that from the north of the Orange River to latitude 26°, and inland for 62·5 miles (100 km) from the Atlantic Ocean, no general prospecting was allowed by anyone except the Deutsche Diamanten Gesellschaft. In 1909, a marketing company, Diamond Regie, was formed, based in Berlin. (In fact, coastal diamonds occur from about 5 miles (8 km) north of the river mouth.)

Mining all but stopped when war was declared in 1914. A year later the German administration was overthrown and the South African Government took control, allowing restricted mining by nine German companies, who did well until 1920, when a slump in demand began to affect production. At this point, Ernest Oppenheimer, who was later to become the chairman of De Beers, Negotiated with the companies, which resulted in the formation of Consolidated Diamond Mines of South West Africa Ltd, in the same year.

Alexander Bay Diamonds

As early as 1884, a German geologist Dr. H. Pohle had a small shaft sunk beside the ancient Orange River '. . . in order to examine the sedimentary layers, hoping to make some discovery, it might be diamonds, or gold in the sand'·

Fig. 3.23.   *After Consolidated Diamond Mines took over they introduced more mechanical means of stripping the sand from beaches. This was at Elizabeth Bay.*

This was in a report to Lüderitz who had bought the territory. He found nothing.

Fifty years later a German prospector, F. W. Martens, recovered a few diamonds in the extreme south of the *Sperrgebiet* near Alexander Bay, at the mouth of the Orange River, and was followed by two other prospectors who dug inspection pits on the farm Sandkrall on the north bank of the river and found nothing, although they were only about seventy yards from rich deposits located later. In 1925, Jack Carstens found a lime-cemented diamondiferous shingle under the 'pebbly area on the commonage south of Port Nolloth'. His father, a storekeeper, was also an agent for Reuters and the news was quickly spread abroad which brought many prospecting parties to the 180 mile (288 km) stretch of Namaqualand coastline.

A digger from the Bloemhof workings, Robert Kennedy, finding nothing at Alexander Bay, returned to Port Nolloth and took a swim on the way at a place called The Cliffs. Looking up, he spotted a gravel run in the cliffs and within a week had found fourteen diamonds of about half a carat each. That was in January 1926. In August, a party comprising two lawyers and two schoolmasters from Springbok saw a diamond stuck in the wall of a new school building being erected at Kleinzee Farm and within a month had taken 500 carats from the farm. The next discovery was at Buchenberg, near the mouth of the Orange River, where Solomon Rabinowitz found 334 diamonds among oyster shells.

The H.M. Association

The biggest strike came in October 1926, when a Luderitzbucht syndicate pegged claims at lower levels in Alexander Bay. Called Caplan's syndicate, it subsequently bought higher level claims, also for £15, from a police sergeant

Fig. 3.24. *Dr. Hans Merensky with Dr. Ernst Reuning in the Caplan syndicate's territory at Alexander Bay which Merensky bought with two financial backers: Reuning only got a contract.*

Fig. 3.25. *Digging along the river line in the Caplan area by the H.M. Association, set up by Dr. Merensky.*

Fig. 3.26. *An unprepossessing spot at first sight, this is the oldest shingle deposit at Alexander Bay where over 400 carats of diamonds were recovered from twelve loads of gravel.*

called Van Wyk. M. Caplan was a storekeeper in Steinkopf. At this point, a brilliant German geologist named Dr. Hans Merensky, arrived hurriedly on the scene, having heard news of the discovery while in his homeland (Fig. 3.24). With him were Dr. Ernst Reuning, Dr. I. B. Celliers, and J. J. Buschau. Merensky held the theory that the diamonds in the area had a submarine origin and their association with the fossilized oyster line at The Cliffs confirmed it to him. The Caplan syndicate allowed Merensky to see the higher claims and, as soon as he had confirmed that there was an oyster line, he asked Dr. Reuning to try to buy out the syndicate. Reuning succeeded for a price of £17,500 and, while Merensky was away in Cape Town trying to raise money, sent him a cable saying that six days of operation would more than cover the £17,500 required. Alas, the cable never reached Merensky who, having failed in Cape Town, found two backers in Johannesburg – H. Ohlthaver and Sir Julius Jeppe – who took 25 per cent each, leaving Merensky with 50 per cent of what was called the H.M. Association. This provided enough to pay the cost of the claim and provide £12,500 working capital. There was no formal agreement, merely an entry in a minute book.* The hapless Reuning only got a contract providing him with £150 a month and £5,000 'should the contemplated venture prove to be of great magnitude', instead of the third share to which he considered himself entitled.

After surreptitious prospecting by Merensky and Reuning, Merensky applied for the whole area to be leased to the H.M. Association instead of being opened to other prospectors as well, but Cape law was that a discoverer could only

---

* Communication from the Anglo-American Corporation of Johannesburg.

Fig. 3.27. *The first shaft which was sunk through the sand on a marine terrace to the diamond-bearing gravels, on what is now the rich C.D.M. concession in Namibia (South West Africa).*

Fig. 3.28. *A deep cut into diamond-bearing gravels on the Kleinzee farm in Namaqualand immediately south of Buffels River in Merensky's time. The diggings are now exhausted and the town of Kleinzee stands near the spot. De Beers mine the Kleinzee annex on the north bank. They also mine, or have mining rights, on most of the other farms to the south, and northwards to the State Diggings which are immediately south of the Orange River.*

stake twenty 30 by 30 ft (9·14 m by 9·14 m) claims and an owner, if one existed, up to fifty claims; after that, digging ceased until the area was formally proclaimed a diggings. Merensky protested to the South African Prime Minister General Hertzog and the opposition leader General Smuts, but in vain because on 22nd February 1927, the government prohibited all further prospecting for diamonds on all Crown land and farms on which mineral rights were reserved for the Crown in Namaqualand. The declaration referring to Crown land cut the ground from under Merensky's feet. One exception was made, of the Kleinzee farm, on which the H.M. Association was allowed one claim, to the utter disgust of Merensky (Fig. 3.28). Subsequently five claims designated Reuning, Caplan (Fig. 3.26), Papert, Gelb and Kennedy, were allowed. They were at levels of from 15 to 89 ft (4·5 to 27 m) above sea level in Alexander Bay.

In the meantime a number of unscrupulous adventurers invaded the desert shore and H.M. Association had to fill in their prospecting holes to disguise the spots where diamonds had been found. Much more serious from the prospectors' point of view was that the government began to take a strong commercial interest in all their activities by passing the Precious Stones Bill in November 1927, which enabled it to set up the State Alluvial Diggings and also gave it, for the first time, a share in prospecting finds as well as control of all mining activities in Namaqualand. Obviously Merensky's huge prospecting parcel of 12,353·5 carats, was of more interest than the usual prospector's find of five or so carats, being valued at £151,948 at the time. (A 1976 estimate was £1,482,420.) The Precious Stones Act persuaded Merensky to appoint Consolidated Diamond Mines of South West Africa, controlled by Ernest Oppenheimer, as his Association's technical advisers.

The State Alluvial Diggings

The government at first demanded that the H.M. Association should not mine more than £600,000 of diamonds a year and then changed the conditions to allow hand-picking only, without a limit. This meant that the miners could use no washing plant or machinery of any kind. Nevertheless, the Association miners, to beat the claim jumpers who were causing serious losses, set to work with a will and in two months had recovered 300,000 carats by 'hand picking' (which allowed sieving) from the shore. The Caplan claim alone produced 41,189·25 carats in six days! But this activity did not help the Association because the government now refused the release of the diamonds for sale and, furthermore, took over the diggings for the State as they were worked out.

In the meantime, control of the H.M. Association had changed. In February 1927, just a year after the original prohibitions in Namaqualand, the prospecting parcel had been examined in the Cape Town offices of the Diamond Board for South Africa by Ernest Oppenheimer, at Merensky's invitation. Oppenheimer realized immediately that the sizes and qualities of the stones were uniquely high and would cause immense problems for other mines in a new industry that had already over-produced by about 4,000,000 carats in a year following the finds in Lichtenberg. So he decided that, to bring Namaqualand

Fig. 3.29. *The town of Kleinzee, built in the desert by the sea in Namaqualand.*

production under control, he would have to acquire the H.M. Association, with its claims and production, for the companies with which he was involved and others who believed in stabilizing mining by equating production and consumption. In 1928–9, the Oppenheimer companies, Barnato Brothers, and Sir Abe Bailey's group, acquired a 74 per cent holding in the H.M. Association, which prompted Oppenheimer to remark of Merensky after the crucial meeting, 'It isn't often a man comes to a meeting without six pence in his pocket and leaves it owning a million.'

New mines, government attempts at control, and the normal high risks of mining ventures were being coped with moderately successfully by a syndicate of producers and sellers, but the world depression of 1929, followed by the Wall Street crash, put an intolerable strain on their financial resources. The effect on the H.M. Association was to put it into voluntary liquidation in October after a sales agreement had been concluded with Oppenheimer, who later transferred the agreement to the newly-formed Diamond Corporation, to take over stocks valued at £3,200,000. The benefit to the Corporation was blocked by the government, however, which refused to let the diamonds be transferred to banks as security for loans to pay the Corporation's debts. The seriousness of the situation was highlighted by the Diamond Corporation sales which dropped from £12,000,000 worth in 1929 to £3,000,000 in 1930 and little over £2,000,000 in 1932. In 1933, after a government enquiry, the Diamond Producers Association was formed to provide quotas for all producers, including the State Alluvial Diggings, as well as a single channel for sales of rough. Their operations are described in Chapter Seven.

Ironically, the 'hand-picked' diamonds from the five H.M. Associations claims were not sold for fourteen years. The S.A. government allowed them to be sent to London in 1937 and in 1939 a proportion was sent to the New York Fair for display. When war broke out later that year, the whole consignment was taken to Bermuda and not sold there until 1942.

The State Alluvial Diggings in the north of Namaqualand below the Orange River proved to be a profitable operation because, in the 1930s, their prospectors discovered that Merensky had just missed the part of the oyster line richest in diamonds.*

The Oyster Line

Merensky's name is associated with his discovery of the connection between diamonds and oyster fossils. After one of his prospectors had reported finding some diamonds among fossilized oyster shells, Merensky told the diggers to follow the trail of oyster shells and they turned up some superb stones. The diggings became known as 'the oyster line', a line parallel to the sea below which oysters used to breed.

The line was in fact associated with a ledge or terrace where diamonds were trapped. News of the discovery led to wild rumours that diamonds had been found in oysters, like pearls!

* Most of the information about Dr. Merensky was provided by John Rudd, Director of De Beers Industrial Diamond Division.

Fig. 3.30. *Oranjemund – the town built by Consolidated Diamond Mines in the desert coastal strip of Namibia (South West Africa).*

The many disputes over rights led to a government survey which distinguished six formations towards the sea:

1. The oyster line.
2. The extension of the oyster line.
3. The operculum (another shell fish) bed line.
4. The pebbly limestone line.
5. An area near the Orange River consisting of river gravel instead of shingle like the others.
6. The Buchenberg area.

Terraces Farther North of the River

Soon after news of the Alexander Bay discoveries reached them, Consolidated Diamond Mines began to prospect for similar lines north of the Orange River in their own territory. There were greater difficulties owing to the much thicker overburden of sand, but by mid-1928, they had traced the main terraces for a considerable distance up the coast. Today these diggings are still the richest of all for gem diamonds (Fig. 3.23).

It was discovered later that there were double deposits at the mouth of the Orange River where sea and river deposits overlaid each other.

Further prospecting provided an estimate in 1930 that there were more than 2,500,000 carats of diamonds in the strip of land from the Orange river mouth 25 miles (40 km) northwards, but the excitement was short-lived because production had to be suspended between 1931 and 1935 during the world trade depression.

Oranjemund Founded

Mining was restarted in 1935 and C.D.M., by then mining the whole coast from their headquarters in Luderitz, gradually moved their main operations to the south. It was decided to build a town in the desert at the southern end of the concession, just by the mouth of the river, which gave the town its name, Oranjemund. In 1943, C.D.M. moved and now the town, shown in Fig. 3.30, has grown so much that it houses about 2,500 Europeans and about 3,500 Africans, mostly from Ovamboland. It is completely isolated from the outside world, not only by its remote position surrounded by sand, but by the all-enveloping security precautions, yet many people like the isolation and insularity so much that they have spent decades of their lives happily in the town. Improved security measures in the diamond security area itself made it possible to discontinue much of the rigorous control of the town from October 1975 and allow more freedom of movement to the inhabitants. (The same applied to Kleinzee (Fig. 3.29), a similar security-controlled diamond township in the diamond concessions south of the Orange River.)

There is a town centre with shops and a power station that is the largest diesel plant in southern Africa, fed by fuel oil delivered twice yearly by oil tankers and pumped through a 2 mile (3·2 km) undersea pipeline. There is a hospital, infant schools, a golf course and a sailing lake in some old diamond diggings. In 1951, the building of the Ernest Oppenheimer bridge over the river brought Oranjemund a little more into touch with the outside world.

Fig. 3.31. *Gravels being panned on the banks of the river Sewa in Sierra Leone to recover alluvial diamonds, which are in gravels only 4–5 (1·2–1·5 m) below the surface.*

Other Discoveries in Africa

When diamonds were picked out of the gravels of the Kiminina River near the Mai Munene waterfall in 1910, it was little suspected that they would lead to the discovery of the world's biggest source of diamonds. The diamond field was in the Belgian Congo and was so large that it extended into the neighbouring country of Angola, which was then held by the Portuguese. The estimated size of the fields, which comprise many ancient river beds, is 150,000 square miles (approx. 384,000 sq. km).

The concession for mining in the Belgian Congo was awarded to the Société Internationale Forestrière et Minière du Congo (Forminière), but there have been changes since the granting of independence in 1960 and the civil war that followed. These were two centres of organised mining, around Tshikapa in Western Kasai and Bakwanga in Eastern Kasai, both now in Zaire. The first, where there were 37 separate diamond areas, is currently mined by individual diggers who sell to buying offices (and by illegal ones who smuggle diamonds to Brazzaville). The other, and by far the richest, in the Bakwanga area, is now mined by the Société Minière de Bakwanga, of which 80 per cent is owned by the government.

The Angola fields were mined by the Companhia de Diamantes de Angola (Diamag), but this has changed, too, since the civil war and establishment of a Marxist regime. Only one of the pipes there, Camutue, is worked economically (see Appendix 5).

An interesting story of the earlier Congo workings illustrates the richness of the fields, which produce mainly industrial diamonds.

A curious mining official washed some of the gravel from the trommels used to cover paths in the city. He found that they had a content of 20 to 25 carats of large diamonds per cubic metre! Because of the number of large diamonds

Fig. 3.32.   *Alluvial mining in the Sewa River in the Wando and Gorama Chiefdoms of Sierra Leone. The river is dammed, as seen on the left, to divert it and allow the gravels on its bed to be picked over. (The man in the foreground is not looking for diamonds, but having a bath!)*

rejected, it was decided to instal a crusher to reduce all the large rejected material and to repass it through the recovery plant. Any large diamonds are therefore crushed.

The diamond fields of the Gold Coast, now Ghana, were discovered in 1919, when Sir Albert Kitson picked up a crystal at Abomoso near the Birim River. An important source of better quality in Sierra Leone gravels was found after a geological survey had located two diamonds in quartz gravels on the bank of the Gbobora River. Consolidated African Selection Trust were granted prospecting rights and found further rich fields. (Fig. 3.31.)

The alluvial diamond areas of Guinea, formerly French Guinea, are an extension of the same fields.

A pipe three times the size of the Premier was found in Tanganyika (now Tanzania) and named the Williamson after its discoverer and owner (Fig. 6.2). It produced about 500,000 carats a year, about half being of gem quality but is being worked out. Some of the stones are pinkish or pink in colour and one of these, of 54 carats in the rough, was cut to 26·60 carat and presented in a brooch to Princess Elizabeth, now the Queen, when she was married.

There are also alluvial deposits in Tanzania, found originally in 1910 south of Lake Victoria, but not worked until 1925.

In the 1950s, a large pipe of 44·2 acres (17·9 hectares) was found about 100 miles (160 km) north-west of Kimberley by A. T. Fincham (Fig. 6.1). The Finsch pipe is now South Africa's largest producer; about 3,000,000 carats a year are taken from it.

Mining in Botswana

One of the pipes at Orapa in Botswana is the second largest in the world with a surface area of 273 acres (110·6 hectares) against the 361 acres (146 hectares) of the largest, the Mwadui (Williamson) mine in Tanzania. The Orapa pipe was prospected by sinking pits on a grid system with 250 ft (76·2 m) sides to a depth of 40 ft (12·2 m) to estimate the immediate recovery prospects. Then fewer deeper holes were driven to 80 ft (24·4 m) to estimate first reserves. Still fewer pits down to 120 ft (36·6 m) indicated the second reserves. As the 40 ft level is removed during mining, the process of sinking pits is repeated. Mining is planned to produce an average size of stone to satisfy the demand of the market. As it is being open-cast worked, the pipe is being benched in the kimberlite itself, not in the surrounding country rock like the Finsch pipe (see Fig. 4.35), because it is uneconomic to incur capital cost by removing non-diamondiferous rock at this stage.

A few miles away at Letlhakane there are two more pipes, very close together and one larger than the other, that are worked together. Although production is less than a fifth of Orapa's, the ratio of gem to industrial stones is more than 40 per cent, compared with 15 per cent at Orapa. The Letlhakane (pronounced Let-lah-kah-nay) pipes are eluvial pipes; that is, the material from the top of the original pipes was not scattered far by the elements, but remained on the top of the pipes and in the surrounding area. In 1977, therefore, the area surrounding the pipes and including them was being mined as an alluvial operation. When this has been completed, the pipes will be open-pit mined.

Production from a third pipe, Jwaneng, will start in 1982 and produce 3,500,000 carats yearly, rising to 6,000 000 in the mid 1980s.

Pipes in Lesotho

What has been called the most 'glamorous' pipe of all is at Letseng-La-Terai, 10,000 ft (3,050 m) above sea level in Lesotho, the land-locked country formerly called Basutoland. The pipe is only expected to be mined for five years, until about 1982, but will probably produce some very large diamonds.

Prospecting indicated that Lesotho had seventeen pipes, twenty-one blows (or dyke enlargements) and over 200 dykes, probably more kimberlites to the square mile than any other country in the world. A diamondiferous pipe at Kao was the world's sixth biggest before Orapa was discovered. Colonel Jack Scott originally prospected the country by sampling streams for ilmenites and garnets and his team discovered every pipe, except for one which had fed its heavy minerals into the same stream as another pipe.

Letseng-La-Terai first came into the news with the finding of the 601-carat Lesotho Brown diamond in 1967, when the area was being mined by independent and some illegal diggers. About 1968, Rio Tinto Zinc (R.T.Z.) gained an option to mine there. They discovered that the overburden had been well mixed by the independent diggers which made accurate sampling impossible, so they drove an adit into the pipe from the hillside to take underground samples, but found them insufficiently payable. From 1973, De Beers held the option and after further sampling, decided to take it up. Keith Whitelock, one of the original prospectors, joined them from R.T.Z. as mines manager.

Diamonds up to 1,500 Carats

R.T.Z. had categorized the kimberlite into eight main groups. De Beers have isolated one type of kimberlite, known as K6 after the R.T.Z. nomenclature which forms a sort of core within the main pipe (there are actually two pipes at Letseng) and is thought to have a high proportion of very large diamonds. To recover these, the plant treats much larger pieces of kimberlite than is usual before crushing. There are two special X-ray sorting machines designed to deal with this material, from +25 mm to +60 mm, which could contain diamonds between about 120 and 1,500 carats! Smaller stones are recovered in another section of the plant. Some stones are of collection colour, but many are brown. In 1977, after only a month or so in production, about 8 per cent of the stones recovered were over 10 carats, the largest having been 82, with several in the 30- to 50-carat range. Large stones have hexagonal pitting, which seems to be typical.

The overburden was such a mixture of yellow ground, gravel and peat that it has been stockpiled. The original 601-carat stone was found in the top of the pipe near one side, having presumably been carried to this alluvial area from the K6 by natural drainage, which also carried other stones beyond the edge of the pipe to form an eluvial deposit. Under about 3 to 6 ft (1–2 m) of yellow ground, there is a particularly soft blue ground to about 40 ft (12 m), which presents some recovery problems. After that the blue ground becomes harder and harder with increasing depth.

Fig. 3.33   *The Mir pipe in Russia after work had begun stripping off the overburden.*

The most recently sampled pipe in Africa, in the Kingdom of Swaziland, has not proved rich enough to be mined economically.

Deposits in Other Countries

There are diamonds of good quality in some rivers of Guyana, formerly British Guiana, in difficult and remote terrain, which are recovered by 'pork-knockers' using relatively primitive methods. Venezuela, also in South America, produces diamonds which often have a greenish coating although the colour inside may be fine.

Borneo, a very old source, and Indonesia still mine some stones. There is a little production in Australia, although there are a number of areas in which diamonds have been found, most of them in New South Wales. One of the earliest was around Copetown, where twinned stones difficult to work were found and which was worked out by 1894. De Beers are currently prospecting in the Kimberley area of Western Australia. They are also prospecting

96

Fig. 3.34. *The town of Mirny in Yakutia, U.S.S.R., built for workers at the diamond mine as it was about 1969.*

in Canada in the St. Lawrence River area. There are isolated small occurrences in the U.S.A. – the most recent find was along the Colorado–Wyoming border. A deposit at Marfreesboro, Arkansas, was mined until 1919. There are deposits at Chang-te, Hunan, in south central China; in Liaoning province in the north-east; and possibly in the Kweichow and Shantung provinces.

Deposits in Russia

Some gem diamonds are found in gold placer deposits on the west flank of the Ural Mountains in Russia, but when prospectors explored the region it became evident that there were no pipes. From 1938, systematic prospecting was carried out in the vast territory between the Yenisei and Lena Rivers in Siberia, because geologists had declared it to be a similar platform zone to the diamondiferous regions of Africa and India.

In 1947, a big expedition was set up to explore central and eastern Siberia and a year later the first diamonds were found in the upper reaches of the Nizhnyaya Tunguska River. Many geological parties were sent into the basins of the rivers, into the Siberian forests, and through the mountain ranges, where the summers are hot and wet and the winter temperatures are rarely above −40°C. Alluvial deposits were found in several areas including the bed of the Vilyui River, but no pipes.

After the discovery of pyrope garnets in 1953 indicating the presence of diamonds, prospecting was concentrated in the same neighbourhood, which led to the finding of the first kimberlite pipe in the upper Markha River during the following year by a woman mineralogist from Leningrad, L. A. Popugayeva. The pipe was named Zarnitza (Dawn).

In the years from 1954, about 400 pipes and seams were located, but only about one in forty or so was diamondiferous. The richest pipe is the Mir (Peace) in the basin of the Lesser Batuobiya tributary to the Vilyui. The Mir pipe is oval in section, about 437 by 656 yd (400 by 600 m) in size at the top and over 1,094 yd (1,000 m) deep with sides that slope at between 60 and 75° (Fig. 3.33).

Enormous mining problems have been overcome because the soil is permanently frozen to as deep as 380 yds (350 m) and only the top 3 to 6 ft (1–2 m) thaw in the summer. The permafrost affects alluvial as well as pipe deposits because the gravels are cemented with ice even in summer. A big self-contained mining town has been built around what was an original tented community of miners and construction workers around the Mir pipe. The town is known as Mirny and is said to depend for all its power needs on an arctic atomic power station (Fig. 3.34). As soon as production at the mines became significant, a diamond laboratory was set up and also the first of several large diamond-cutting works was built at Svedtlovsk.

Second to the Mir in size is the Udachnaya (Success) pipe, discovered also in 1954, but on the Arctic Circle, about 300 miles (480 km) to the north of the Mir, in the basin of the Daaldyn tributary of the Markha River. Mining began in 1969, following plans by the Yukatulmaz, the diamond trust set up in 1957 to plan the industry. In 1959, another diamond pipe was located near the Mir and named the Sputnik. Two years after that there was another pipe find about 300 miles (480 km) north of Mirny on the Arctic Circle, which was named Aikhal (Glory). Rich deposits have been located even farther into the Arctic Circle at Anabar Tundra.

There are six central treatment plants in operation and little over 20 per cent of production is said to be of gem quality, nearly all exported to the West. The largest diamond reported weighed 166 carats and was unearthed by a prospector near Mirny in 1968. U.S.S.R. diamond production is not disclosed, following the usual communist practice of controlling all information, but was believed to be in the neighbourhood of 1,600,000 carats of gem diamonds and 6,400,000 carats of industrials in 1968. In 1977 the total output was estimated to be 12,000,000 carats a year of which about 80 per cent were industrial.

Only three mines are believed to be operated commercially at the present time: Mir, Aikhal, and Udachnaya, plus a low volume output from the Urals placers. Synthetic diamond for industrial use is produced in plants at Kiev, Leningrad, Moscow, Yerevan, and Tashkent and the output is put very approximately at 8,000,000 carats a year.

REFERENCES

The Diamond News and S. A. Jeweller, Kimberley. Various issues
The Gemmologist, London. Various issues.
Indiaqua (Industrial Diamond Quarterly) Nos 12, 13 (1976).
Optima, Johannesburg. Various issues.
Graves and Guineas, by J. T. McNish (Cape Town, 1969).
Visits to mines: By courtesy of De Beers Consolidated Mines, Anglo-American Corporation, Debswana, Consolidated Diamond Mines of South West Africa, Soguinex, and others.

Discovery of the huge Orapa pipe in Botswana was a triumph of scientific prospecting, plus knowledge and inspiration. This aerial view was taken by the author in 1968.

Sampling is an extra important activity when mining is geared to demand for particular sizes and qualities. Pits for sampling are drilled and liners inserted, as shown here, or dug.

The recovery plant at Letseng-la-Terai in Lesotho, at the highest diamond mine in the world, also called the most glamorous because of the large diamonds expected from it.

Blasting is often part of open pit as well as underground mining, when the mine is a pipe. Here a fuse line is being laid by Debswana workers in Botswana.

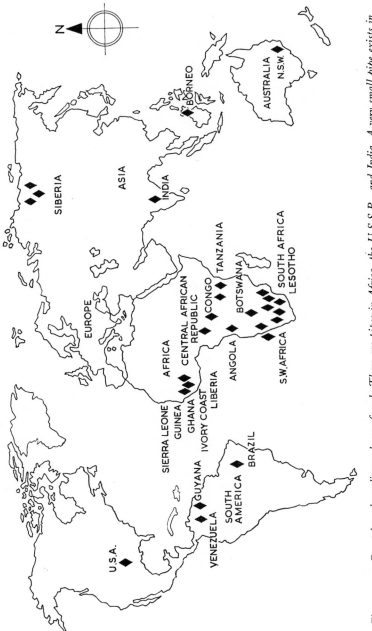

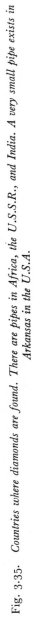

Fig. 3·35. *Countries where diamonds are found. There are pipes in Africa, the U.S.S.R., and India. A very small pipe exists in Arkansas in the U.S.A.*

CHAPTER FOUR

Mining and Recovery Methods

Early diamond diggers in South Africa introduced some basic methods of recovery that have changed only in scale and sophistication in modern days.

At the river diggings, pits were dug down to the gravels which were extracted by pick and shovel (Fig. 4.1). On dry days, gravel was sifted immediately by a man with a round sieve, like an ordinary garden sieve. The sieve had a large mesh so that it retained only pebbles over about an inch across, which after inspection were thrown away. Diamonds were unlikely to be of this size, but any that were could easily be seen and recovered.

What passed through the sieve was sifted through a finer sieve to get rid of the sand. Any diamonds the size of sand were not worth recovering. The fraction left – the 'middlings' – was taken to the river to be washed in a fine sieve to remove any remaining fine silt and dirt, and the remainder was searched for diamonds. The procedure was not possible on wet days, so the whole of the material dug up was washed while being sieved.

The Long Tom

Australian diggers introduced a form of washer used for alluvial gold which also did some sorting and was known as the long tom. It was a long sloping trough with riffles (small pieces of wood) nailed transversely across it from one end to the other. (Fig. 4.2.) The gravel was dumped on the higher end and washed down by a stream of water from buckets or a pump. Small and light material including sand was washed down over the riffles, and so were some of the larger lightweight elements, but diamonds were trapped with other heavy minerals.

To speed the process, larger stones and pebbles were raked off the long tom and thrown away. The gravel concentrate from the riffles went straight to the sorting table.

The Cradle

The next development, also introduced by gold miners, was probably the cradle, a double wooden box with handles that was stood on flat ground or rock. It was constructed so that the handles rocked the upper part, comprising three sieves from coarse to fine. One is shown in Fig. 4.3. Mud and gravel from the river was poured into the top, coarse sieve and the cradle rocked while water was poured in. After the mud had gone, the contents of the coarse sieve were emptied on the sorting table and, as it could contain larger diamonds, 'loud indeed were the shouts of acclamation and universal was the adjournment to the liquor tent when a diamond was found in this receptacle', according to a contemporary writer. The contents of the middling and fine sieves were then emptied on

Fig. 4.1.   *Digging a prospecting pit at the corner of a claim to determine the depth of the layer of diamondiferous gravel.*

opposite ends of the sorting bench and sorted. Sieves were constructed from available materials, the simplest being empty gin crates.

The Yankee Baby

A gold digger named J. L. Babe who went to South Africa in 1865, before the Vaal River diamonds were found, as a representative of the Winchester Repeating Rifle Co., joined diggers on the Vaal as related earlier. He decided

Fig. 4.2. *The Long Tom, introduced to South Africa by Australian diggers, has a very long history. This picture shows it in use; it comes from* Re de Metallica *by Georgius Agricola, published in 1550.*

that current methods were inefficient and, in his own words, 'I then invented a machine which has been universally copied, and which the miners christened the "Yankee baby"; and one man could sift with this machine as much in ten hours as four could do with the common sifter.'

By selling the machine and by using it himself on the diggings, J. L. Babe was so successful that he was able to retire to America in 1873. The baby comprised two sieves, one above the other. The main one was in a large rectangular frame hung from four rawhide thongs or light chains from four posts planted in the ground. It was fed through a smaller sieve about 2 ft (61 cm) square with a mesh that allowed through it stones up to about $\frac{1}{2}$ in. (13 mm) across. The total effect was that the larger material was discarded at one end of the baby and the fine tailings underneath. Off the other end came the middlings, which were then washed and sorted. Babe had his machine made in Colesberg. Fig. 4.4 shows a rocking screen made at some later date.

Washing could be carried out before or after screening, depending upon the deposit – how much fine material or earth was in it – and upon the availability and cost of water.

The Trommel
The baby was superseded on many diggings by the cylinder or trommel. Wire

Fig. 4.3. *Diggers on the banks of the Vaal river in the early days. On the left two boxes are being used as a rocking sieve where gravel is also washed. In the centre and on the right are picking tables.*

Fig. 4.4. *A form of rocking cradle to separate smaller pebbles including diamonds from larger ones.*

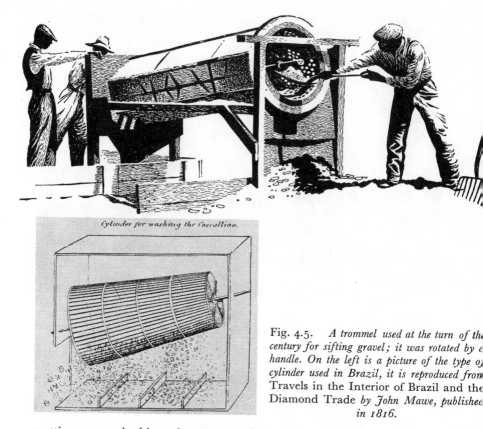

Fig. 4.5. *A trommel used at the turn of the century for sifting gravel; it was rotated by a handle. On the left is a picture of the type of cylinder used in Brazil, it is reproduced from* Travels in the Interior of Brazil and the Diamond Trade *by John Mawe, published in 1816.*

netting or punched iron sheet was used to make a cylinder several feet long. The cylinder was revolved on an axle by a handle and could be sealed with a lid at each end. It was partly filled with gravel that had already been screened and rotated while immersed in a trough of water, if possible. As it provided some security and saved labour, it was popular with diggers. Two versions are shown in Fig. 4.5.

Concentrating in Water

Water was used as a means of concentrating the heavier fraction of the gravels. The term concentrating means separating the material of higher relative density. This heavier fraction of gravel is called the concentrate, and obviously most concentrates can be further concentrated.

The sieving method introduced into the diamond fields was already known to gold miners and is still in use in various parts of the world by both gold and diamond miners.

Deposit that has been screened and washed is emptied in a convenient quantity into a sieve, which is about 30 in (76 cm) across and has a bottom of fine mesh. The sieve is held in a tub of water or in the river, where it is sharply twisted one way then the other a few times and then moved more gently up and down in a jigging motion. The actions are repeated until the lighter gravels come to the top of the sieve and the heavier ones are concentrated in the middle at the bottom. Sieves were, and still are by independent diggers, used in twos and threes to grade concentrate, dividing it into two or three groups for picking. The digger uses a large metal 'washer' between each pair of sieves so that the heavier and smaller elements from the centre of the upper sieve are passed through to the lower one (Fig. 4.6).

The sieve is lifted out of the water and taken to the picking table where it is deftly turned over and the contents dumped on the table like a child making a mud pie. When the sieve is lifted off, the gravel is left, shining wet, in the shape of a large flat cake. The picker examines the stones on the top in the middle of the pile, and picks out any diamond crystals. Then, to make sure that no diamonds have remained in the rest of the gravel, he goes through the 'cake' of gravel, a slice at a time (Fig. 4.7).

To do this, he uses a home-made tool, usually a triangular piece of iron or aluminium about 6 in long by 3 in or less wide (152 × 76 mm). With the tool, he cuts off a section of the gravel and spreads it across the sorting table, examining the multicoloured concentrate for diamonds. Then he sweeps this layer on to the ground and takes another section of the heap until it has gone.

The Picking Table

The picking table was at first nothing more than the top of a packing case standing on a heap of gravel at which the digger crouched, sat or knelt. Then packing cases were made into rough tables, perhaps covered by sacking and with strips nailed along three sides to prevent gravel from rolling off (Fig. 4.8). Iron sheet from an old enamelled advertisement or flattened tin containers was nailed on the top and the table top sloped so that water did not pour over the digger's knees when gravel was tipped on to the table in front of him. More enterprising diggers made their tables into booths with top and canvas sides to give shade for sorting.

Fig. 4.6. *Coarse and fine sieves used together to trap two grades of concentrate.*

Fig. 4.7. *A sieve, twisted in water to bring diamonds to the centre of a pile of concentrate, has here been upturned to empty its contents on the picking table, with heaviest material at the top in the centre.*

Fig. 4.8. *A picking table during the early days of the river diggings in South Africa.*

Exactly the same methods are used by individual diggers today, although the sieve may be a little different. In Guyana, for example, a cone-shaped pan, like a metal dustbin top, is used instead of a sieve. At Nooitgedacht, on the Vaal River banks, the method has not changed at all.

In the later days of the river diggings, rotary washing pans were introduced. They had been developed at the dry diggings as described on the following pages. Hand-operated rotary washing pans are also still in use today on individual claims.

Mining at the Dry Diggings

When the dry diggings were first discovered, they were thought to be the same kind of deposits as the river ones and the same methods of recovery were employed. It was naturally supposed that the deposits were of only limited depth, and claims were allowed next to each other, just like those by the rivers.

By the time that the 'New Rush' (now the Kimberley Big Hole) was found in 1871, it was known that deposits went down to a considerable depth, so it was decided that each claim would contribute a 7½ ft strip (2·3 m) which would not be worked for the general benefit. This resulted in a series of roadways 15 ft (4·6 m) wide and 45 ft (13·7 m) apart. The idea was practicable at first, but as

Fig. 4.9. *Chains of labourers working in the west side of the De Beers mine when it was still worked by open cast methods.*

Fig. 4.10.   *Rotary pans being used in the early days at the Kimberley mine. The ground was first taken to a puddling trough to convert it to mud.*

Fig. 4.11.   *The Kimberley mine in 1872 when roads left between claims were beginning to crumble at the edges.*

soon as the claims were dug deeply with almost vertical sides, the roads began to fall in. The whole area was weathered yellow ground, which became very friable as it weathered even further after exposure to the air.

The ground being mined was dug with picks and shovels and loaded into sacks, which were carried by labourers up steps cut in the side of the claim and emptied by the side of the road (Fig. 4.9). The sacks were taken to the edge of the mine and the ground broken up, screened and sorted there. Some claims had sloping ramps up which hand trucks of ground were pushed.

As the mine grew deeper, a crude system of benches evolved, each claim having terraces up to the road. The ground was thrown up to each by labourers until it reached the road as many as five levels higher. Then diggers started hauling up ground in buckets by driving posts with pulleys and ropes into the roads. Scotch carts (Fig. 2.18), which could be tipped up, were used to take the ground from the roads to the edge of the Big Hole, but animals fell into the claims and had to be slaughtered. Some diggers tried to bridge crumbled roads 'at enormous expense'. Views of the Big Hole can be seen in Figs. 4.10 to 4.20.

Haulage Systems at Kimberley

By 1872, the roads had become unsafe for use and after two years they had disappeared altogether. Aerial gear was then devised for bringing yellow ground from each separate claim to the surface at the edge of the mine.

Fig. 4.12   *Another view of Kimberley when the 'roads' were beginning to collapse. The buckets in the foreground were lowered to be filled with ground. In the background can be seen dumps on the edge of the Big Hole and staging being built.*

Fig. 4.13. *The Big Hole in 1877. Note the ladder leaning on the centre block and the staging on the right. Near the top, about quarter of the way across the picture from the left, is the runway of a trolley system, perhaps the one in Fig. 4.19.*

Fig. 4.14. *Another view of the Kimberley mine, taken between 1872 and 1878. Some claims on the far right have hardly been worked below surface level.*

Fig. 4.15. *Staging in several tiers round the edge of the Kimberley mine in 1878 to hold the cables up which hide and metal buckets of ore were drawn. It was like a giant cobweb.*

Fig. 4.16.   *The ground was spread around the Hole to allow it to become more friable. It was washed there too.*

Fig. 4.17.   *The top edge of the Kimberley mine in 1878 showing whims turned by horses to draw up the buckets of ore.*

Fig. 4.18. More elaborate cable systems with trolleys running on wires replaced some of the earlier buckets.

Fig. 4.19. There was also a 'passenger service' from the edge of the Hole to nearer the bottom.

Substantial wooden staging was built around the edge of the mine, most of it on three levels – ground, 8 ft (2·4 m) high, and 16 ft (4·9 m) high. From these thousands of standing wires stretched to the claims below. Buckets made of hide or metal were drawn up and down by natives operating windlasses. Fig. 4.15, taken in 1878, shows the stagings, which continued in use until the claims were about 80 ft (24·4 m) deep.

Whims, large horizontal drums driven by horses trotting in circles (Fig. 4.17), or whips, in which the horses trotted backwards and forwards to raise or let down containers, replaced the windlasses. Eventually these were replaced in their turn by steam engines with winding drums.

The ropes and buckets were replaced by iron or steel cables and large steel bucket-shaped bins. A still later arrangement was a trolley which ran on the cables. The trolley was a frame with four wheels carrying a container. (Fig. 4.18). Aerial gear for extracting blue ground was in use at the Jagersfontein mine as late as the beginning of the twentieth century.

Yellow to Blue Ground

Ground from the top of the pipe was kimberlite converted to yellow ground by the weathering agencies of oxygen from the air and occasional percolating water. It could be broken up quite easily by pulverizing it, using shovels and clubs called 'beaters'. The broken ground was shovelled into rectangular hand sieves with $\frac{1}{4}$ in (6·5 mm) holes in them. What passed through the holes was thrown away and what remained went to the picking tables. These crude recovery methods by the early diggers not only raised choking dust, but were so inefficient that in recent times the piles of discarded tailings have been found to be quite rich when re-worked, as many as three times, in recent years by improved recovery methods.

At first water was very short for washing except in the rainy season as the area was semi-desert. No one knew at this time that there was fossil water some distance below the surface that would eventually cause serious flooding problems in some mines, particularly the Wesselton, because of the shortage of pumps and their inefficiency.

When diggers reached a depth of about 80 ft (24·4 m) in the Kimberley mine they found that the ground changed colour to blue and became hard. There was consternation among the ex-alluvial gold miners who decided it was bedrock and the end of the diamond deposit. A number of diggers sold their claims but the more stubborn stayed and discovered that there were still diamonds in the blue ground, but the new kind of ground posed its own problems because of its hardness. New methods of recovery were necessary.

Larger lumps of yellow ground had been pulverized by shovels and beaters to break it up. This was not a practical method with freshly-mined blue ground, so it was temporarily stored in huge boxes built around the mine until it could be taken by Scotch carts to the 'floors' farther away to be laid out to weather.

The Rotary Pan

By about 1875, hand-driven rotary washing pans had come into use. The inventor may have been a J. Mackay. The rotary washing pan was simple in concept, but its exact operating principles were not fully understood and were

Fig. 4.20.   *The head of the cable system shown in Fig. 4.18.*

being studied by the Diamond Research Laboratory in Johannesburg as late as the 1970s.

In its more developed form, the washing pan was an annular container, 4 ft (1·2 m) across and about 9 in (23 cm) deep. In the central hole was a vertical axle on which four arms in the form of a cross were pivoted. From the arms rows of knives extended downwards into the pan, like rakes, as shown in the modern version in Fig. 5.5.

The ground was shovelled into the annular pan, which was filled with water. The rakes were turned by winding a handle, with the result that the water and gravels were swilled round (Fig. 4.21). Water flowed over the inner edge, taking with it the lighter materials held in suspension in the muddy water, or 'puddle' as it was called. Diamonds and other heavy minerals settled to the bottom. After each load, the pan was emptied for picking over.

Rotary washing pans are still used in Kimberley and elsewhere. The modern version is power-driven and much larger. The puddle is a thick muddy liquid or decomposed kimberlite and water with a specific gravity kept at about 1·15 to 1·25. The strange fact is that lumps of kimberlite with a specific gravity of 2·7 float *upwards* and over the central weir. In some parts of Africa, rotary pans containing only clear water are used to float fractions which would sink in still water.

Rotary pans could deal with blue ground if it were sufficiently pulverized, but that involved much more labour. Some unknown digger introduced the cylinder

Fig. 4.21.   *The original form of washing pan, which floated off most of the lighter material and caused diamonds and other heavy material to settle in the bottom.*

Fig. 4.22.   *Washing pans at the pipe mines in the early days operated by horse whims and later by steam.*

Fig. 4.23. *The tractor on the right of the picture is of the type used to winch up the buckets of kimberlite. The other is a much more primitive type: they are both in a museum in Rhodesia.*

or trommel from the river diggings and, in an improved form, it soon became an almost essential adjunct to the rotary washing machine. The cylinder was mounted at an angle of about ten degrees and had small holes in it at the higher end grading to larger ones at the lower end. As the trommel was rotated, water streamed on top of it from a perforated water pipe above. Broken blue ground was shovelled into the higher end and the finer particles and mud fell through the finer mesh on to a table with a sloping trough leading to the rotary pan. Stones and larger lumps of blue ground fell on to another table under the lower half of the cylinder and were swept away by sorters 'with watchful eyes for diamonds', as one observer put it. The largest lumps passed straight through the trommel and were taken back to depositing sites for further exposure to the air and more beating.

Mining Blue Ground

It was noticed that lumps of blue ground thrown aside began to break up. The blue ground from the upper workings was therefore spread out over large areas around the mine where it took about three months to disintegrate (Fig. 4.25). The most favourable conditions for weathering were alternate very dry and heavy rain periods. When the weather did not help, the blue ground was broken into smaller lumps by gangs of labourers using the backs of shovels or mallets and at times it was artificially watered. Even convicts were employed on these tasks. Various other ideas were tried, such as watering and crushing with steam tractors, and raking with the use of steam winches. A Mr. Cowan spent large sums of money experimenting with steam, to no avail. By now the blue ground was spread out on floors for miles around the various camps.

Blasting was also used in the mines to release and break up the blue ground and the cost of gunpowder was estimated at £100,000 a year in the last two years of open-cast working. When the workings reached about 420 ft (128 m) in depth, new hazards made the problems of the floors seem puny by comparison.

Crumbling Sides

The surrounding country rock near the surface of pipes was so soft that the sides of all the pipes in Kimberley were continuously crumbling. The reef fell into the holes more rapidly than it could be cleared away. By 1882, three tons of debris had to be removed to extract one ton of blue ground from the Kimberley Mine. At the De Beers Mine, after miners had seen what had happened at the Kimberley Mine, an attempt was made to cut back the sides, but this proved almost impossible by the methods then available. At Dutoitspan, a rim of blue ground was left as a kind of protecting wall, but one day all the walls collapsed, luckily when the mine was almost empty of workers.

Even visits to the mines were hazardous in the early days. Mud from the rotary pans was taken by endless bucket chain and ejected over screens. The more solid portion was deposited as tailings on the spot or taken by trucks elsewhere. This looked solid, but many an unwary visitor went to walk on a trailings dump and sank to his knees, waist, or even his neck!

The De Beers Mine was closed in 1908 and re-opened fifty-five years later in

Fig. 4.24. *A five-year operation, during the 1960s and 1970s, terraced the top of De Beers mine to stop overburden from falling in. About 25,000,000 tons of rock were moved.*

Fig. 4.25. *The French Company's washing plant at Kimberley before the turn of the century. In the background are the 'floors' where blue ground was spread out to be broken down by the weather.*

Fig. 4.26. *The Kimberley Central Company sunk a mine shaft in the interior of the Kimberley pipe, which was the first attempt to mine diamonds from underground.*

1963. Reef problems recurred and caused problems even when mining underground. In 1960–70 the sides were successfully cut back in terraces to eliminate further falls of reef into the hole (Fig. 4.24). The mine is still in production and nearly 140,000 carats of diamonds were extracted from it in 1975.

Underground Mining

On the suggestion of a contractor, Edward Jones, about 1883, it was decided to attempt to mine the Kimberley hole by sinking a shaft. There was insufficient money to sink a shaft from outside, so Mr. Jones developed one from inside, through the rubble on the top of the blue ground. It proved practicable, and several other shafts were sunk in other parts of the mine (Fig. 4.26).

After the Kimberley Mine came under control of Cecil Rhodes, sufficient capital was provided to sink a shaft from outside the pipe and underground workings had reached a depth of 3,601 ft (1,098 m) when operations ended in 1914.

The first system of underground working was a form of pillar-and-stall mining. Eventually, the blue ground became honeycombed with chambers and the pillars began to collapse under the pressure of rubble above. The mine was evacuated and a fresh start had to be made.

The next method, known as the Gouldie system, involved cutting chambers in a staggered plan so that the top of the blue ground formed a kind of hump underneath the overburden, which was supported at the sides like an arch, thus relieving the pressure.

Fig. 4.27. *De Beers directors photographed in September 1891. At the back are William H. Craven, Gardner F. Williams, and Ludwig Breitmeyer and in the front, John Morrogh, Francis Oats, B. I. Barnato, Charles E. Nind, and Woolf Joel.*

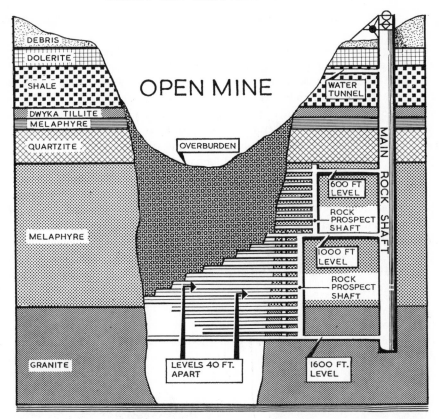

Fig. 4.28. *Principle of chambering in a pipe mine. The blue ground is the white area.*

As any pipe is mined from underground, the overburden of shale and rubble mixed with blue ground, gradually descends in the pipe as seen from the surface. The overburden causes pressure on the underground workings, of course, and it is important to prevent any more reef falling into the ever-deepening hole.

The Gouldie system became impractical in the Big Hole of Kimberley at greater depths owing to the various other systems being worked on adjacent claims regardless of safety.

Chambering

After 1887, when the De Beers Mining Company was formed, the General Manager, Gardner Williams (Fig. 4.27), developed about 1890 a uniform mining system for the whole mine known as chambering. Haulage levels were established at 600, 1,000, and 1,600 ft (183, 305 and 488 m) down from the main rock shaft which was itself sunk through the country rock by the side of the diamond pipe (Fig. 4.28).

The main shaft is normally one of two shafts which are sunk about 1,000 ft (305 m) from the edge of a pipe. It is mainly for haulage and the other is for ventilation also. Main shafts of mines are rectangular in section and have five compartments, with cages for taking miners up and down and skips for bringing ore to the surface.

Every 40 ft (12·2 m) down, chambering levels were established, and at each chambering level a series of parallel tunnels was driven across the pipe to the other side. These tunnels are the 'chambers'. They are 40 ft (12·2 m) high and 12 ft (3·7 m) wide with 10 ft (3·1 m) wide 'pillars' between them. The chambers on the level below are staggered, so that they are beneath the pillars on the level above. The corners of a chamber roof are blasted over a certain length so that the pillar above breaks up and collapses into the chamber, from where it is loaded into cars and taken away for haulage to the surface.

Mining is carried out first from the ends of the top series of tunnels, working from the centre outwards and gradually working backwards as the tunnels fill with rubble from above. As the tunnels fill on one level, mining begins on the next level below, and so on until mining is going on at several different levels, each being in advance of the one below.

Eight tons (8·2 tonnes) per shift can be removed by chambering, but it requires a large labour force and the Wesselton mine was the last to employ it (Fig. 4.29).

Block Caving

After a De Beers official had seen a method known as block caving in use in other mining operations in Canada and the U.S.A., it was decided to try it on an easily accessible block of unmined blue ground in the Bultfontein Mine. It was

Fig. 4.29.   *Loading blue ground into a hand truck after chambering.*

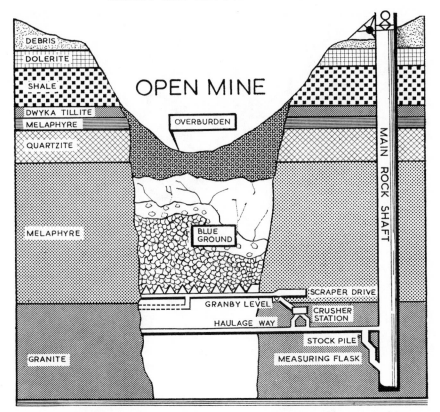

Fig. 4.30. *Principle of block caving where the blue ground (shown white) is undermined and breaks up to fall into draw points.*

so successful that in 1955 a decision was made to change over generally to block caving. Jagersfontein was the first mine to be completely converted, in 1958, and now all the Kimberley pipes are worked in this way.

Block caving reduced considerably the number of levels and shafts and the labour needs, and lends itself to continuous working and mechanization. It is also much safer for the miners and greatly reduces the pilfering of diamonds. It has been found that blue ground fractures more easily as depth increases, which favours block caving and makes chambering less practical.

In block caving, a mine level is established at a depth which may be 400 to 600 ft (122–183 m) below the top of the blue ground in the pipe, according to local conditions. A haulage tunnel for electric locos is driven right round the pipe and about 30 ft (9 m) away from it in the country rock surrounding the pipe. At intervals around the haulage level, short shafts – called raises – are driven upwards. From these, a series of parallel tunnels – scraper drifts – is driven across the pipe at 45 ft (13·7 m) intervals. At the end of each scraper drift a chamber is cut to house a winch and tackle. Finally another tunnel is cut round the pipe again, connecting each winch chamber to the next (Fig. 4.30).

The scraper drifts are lined with concrete, leaving square openings – draw points –alternatively on each side of a tunnel at intervals of about 11 ft (3·4 m)

Fig. 4.31. *The actual stirrup that draws the blue ground through the scraper drift. On the right and left can be seen a draw points through which broken blue ground has come from the pipe.*

Fig. 4.32. (below) *Winch drawing blue ground through a scraper drift in the Bultfontein pipe.*

(Fig. 4.31). Through these openings, blue ground is removed to form funnels in the blue ground of the pipe above. The entire area of blue ground above the funnels is then mined out to a height of about 7 ft (2 m) to form a huge cave.

The roof of the cave begins to break up under the pressure of the blue ground and overburden gradually being squeezed down the pipe by its own weight. Blue ground flakes off the roof of the cave and fills the funnels and draw points to the scraper drifts, until the entire cave is filled with broken ground, which helps to support the roof. The ground that comes through the draw points into the scraper drifts is extracted by large stirrup-shaped scrapers that are hauled by chains back and forth through each drift by electric-powered winches (Fig. 4.32). The blue ground scraped through each drift drops directly through a hopper into trucks, which take it to an underground crushing plant. From there it is hauled by electric locomotive to skips, which take it to the surface.

New Levels Established

Caving and drawing off continue at a calculated rate and eventually the roof of the cave breaks through to the overburden on top of the pipe. This occurs when about 60 to 70 per cent of the blue ground has been drawn off. The drawing off continues until the waste overburden has descended the 400 to 600 ft (122–183 m) down the pipe and begins to appear at the draw points. Before then, however, a new level has been established 400 to 600 ft (122–183 m) below for the next block caving operation.

Fig. 4.33.   *Granby trucks used for taking blue ground to the underground crushing plant at the Premier Mine.*

Fig. 4.34.   *The Finsch pipe from the air. It is being worked by open cast methods. The treatment plant is in the foreground. The pipe is at Lime Acres.*

Block Caving in Use

The first scraper drift level at Jagersfontein was at 1,870 ft (570 m), 400 ft (122 m) below the top of the blue ground in the pipe.

When Bultfontein was converted, it was connected to Dutoitspan underground, since the pipes are adjacent. The same haulage system is employed for both mines and the production is delivered to the same hoisting shaft at Bultfontein. This underground tramming system similar to that in Fig. 4.33 is 1,900 ft (579 m) below ground and 2,220 ft (677 m) long. Dutoitspan is mined in two sections owing to an unpayable volume of blue ground between them.

The main hoisting shaft at Bulfontein was renovated when the two mines were connected underground and was fitted with 13 ton (13·2 tonne) automatic express skips which deliver blue ground to the surface, after which it is taken by conveyor-belt to the central treatment plant.

Currently all the Kimberley mines except the Big Hole, which is exhausted, have underground workings. They number four – Bultfontein, Dutoitspan, Wesselton, and De Beers. The Premier, near Pretoria, is mined by a combination method. Jagersfontein was also mined from underground, but is now closed, and the nearby re-opened Koffiefontein Mine, also in the Orange Free State, was block-cave mined from 1977.

All other known pipes are open-cast mined at present.

Modern Open-cast Mining

All pipe mines are first worked from the top by what is known as the open-cast method. Once it was haphazard; now it is systematic. Before mining proper is begun, the pipe is very thoroughly sampled by geologists, to plot its payability, using a sampling recovery plant on the spot.

The Finsch pipe is a good example of the present open-cast method of mining. All excavation is mechanized. Because it is easier to excavate in straight lines, the worked shape is a polygon, as may be seen in Fig. 4.34. Excavation of yellow ground is deepest in the middle and proceeds in a way to produce a spiral road out of the mine, up and down which trucks are driven to remove the deposit.

The pipe itself is about 44 acres (17·9 ha) in extent and will be open-cast mined for several years, although the removal rate of ground at the end of 1968 was 27,000 loads of rock and 18,000 loads of yellow ground (a load is 10 cu ft (0·283 cu m) *in situ*) by electric shovels and 35 ton (35·6 tonne) dumper trucks working twenty-four hours a day.

The top of the pipe lay under about 16 ft (4·9 m) of ironstone rubbish and a further 13 ft (4 m) of mixed kimberlite and ironstone known locally as the 'contact zone'. Sampling has shown that the yellow ground becomes less weathered with depth until at about 300 ft (91·4 m) it is unaltered blue ground. It is fairly uniform in appearance and carries inclusions of amygdaloidal lava, diabase, shale, and mudstone, as well as the usual accessory minerals. The sides of the pipe are roughly vertical for about 1,000 ft (305 m) down. By 1975 the mine was producing about 2,500,000 carats a year from something less than 3,000,000 tons (3,048,000 tonnes) of ore. Mining was being carried out between the 407 ft (124 m) to the 525 ft (160 m) levels with the kimberlite becoming increasingly hard with greater depth.

While removing yellow ground, the sides of country rock are cut back in steps to remove the risk of rubbish falling in, as happened during all the early open-cast workings. This also improves conditions for the time when underground working is resorted to. All the earlier pipes now being worked from underground have, on top of the blue ground a heavy layer of reef which increases the pressure on the workings below.

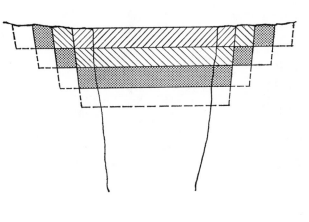

Fig. 4.35. *Economics of open cast mining. As further material from the surrounding country rock has to be removed to prevent its falling in, there comes a point when it is more economical to mine underground. The shaded portions indicate the successively greater amounts of reef to yellow ground that have to be removed. Four stages are shown. The first has two 'squares' of reef outside the pipe, the second four, the third (tinted) six, and the fourth (dotted outline) eight.*

The economics of open-cast mining depend on the ratio of country rock to kimberlite being removed. The deeper the hole, the higher the ratio of country rock to kimberlite, as shown in Fig. 4.35, and the lower the diamond load ratio. The steeper the repose angle of the walls can be made, the more economic the mine from this point of view.

The Finsch mine will be lowered to a depth of about 900 ft (275 m) before working starts from underground.

Benching

A method of mining which is partly open-cast and partly underground is carried out at the Premier Mine in the Transvaal, where it was introduced in 1945 when the mine was reopened after it had been shut at the end of open-cast working to a depth of 610 ft (186 m).

The Premier pipe is elliptical at the mouth, about 2,800 by 1,400 ft (853 by 427 m) and in the centre of the upper regions is a huge block of quartzite which divides it into two down to over 1,000 ft (305 m). The block is believed to have fallen into the kimberlite from the side of a hill while the kimberlite was still plastic. In the 1970s, work began to remove this floating reef by blasting.

The blue ground is blasted in a series of benches in each half of the pipe and falls into cones made in the blue ground below to a grizzly level and ore passes to haulage ways on the 1,060 ft (323 m) level. The kimberlite is crushed to under 6 in (153 mm) pieces below ground before being hauled to the surface. Benching is also known as slot mining (Fig. 4.36).

Fig. 4.36. *The Premier mine where a combination of surface and underground methods called benching is used.*

Fig. 4.37. *Removing sand by scrapers and bull-dozers on the beaches of South West Africa on the Consolidated Diamond Mines concession. Similar methods are used south of the Orange River at Kleinzee Annex and Dreyers Pan.*

Modern Alluvial Mining

The most efficient methods of alluvial mining are those of Consolidated Diamond Mines of South West Africa Limited, along the coast of South West Africa northwards for about fifty miles from the mouth of the Orange River to Affenruchen (Fig. 3.18). The diamonds are between 80 and 90 per cent gem quality and recovery is said to be almost 100 per cent efficient. The diamond deposits lie on a narrow bedrock parallel to the coast. The most fully developed strips have four wave-cut shelves – called terraces – where diamondiferous gravels are trapped. The shelves were caused by wave action and left when the sea advanced or retreated over long periods of time.

It is assumed that the diamonds came down the Orange River because the distribution along the coast drops in a typical curve from the river mouth northwards up the coast. The diamonds were carried in the sea by wind-driven currents and thrown up on the beaches by wave action.

Gravel and conglomerate containing diamonds is covered with marine sand and sandstone, and in some places by compacted red sand and calcrete, which is rather like a soft natural limestone concrete. Over this is a layer of sand that may be as deep as 40 ft (12·2 m).

The major part of mining is in fact a gigantic earth-moving operation. The sand has to be stripped off before the gravels are reached. Mining is carried out by opening the sides of prospection trenches (see page 165), where the over-burden is thinnest, driven at right angles to the coast.

The first mechanization of overburden removal was to use bucket excavators, which could move 80 to 100 tons (81·3–102 tonnes) of sand an hour. The sand was discharged into mule-drawn trucks to be taken away. After the Second World War, Sherman tanks, with their gun turrets removed, were employed as tractors, and after 1954, diesel-driven scrapers with huge pneumatic tyres were introduced. The smaller scrapers work in pairs with a pusher crawler tractor. The biggest scrapers, which can remove sand at the rate of 15,890 cu. ft (450 cu. m) an hour, need two bulldozers in tandem to push them while scraping up the sand (Fig. 4.37).

After the primary and secondary sand and soil overburden have been removed, the exposed terraces of gravel are loaded, by means of excavators or front end loaders, into rear dump trucks, which will carry 25 tons (25·4 tonnes) each.

The gravels were transported to one of the eighteen permanent field screening

Fig. 4.38. *The sand has been removed in the middle distance and piled in the far distance. The scraper has piled up diamond-bearing gravels on the left* (upper left to centre of picture). *In the foreground, the bedrock is being cleaned to remove any remaining gravel.*

Fig. 4.39. *Potholes in the bedrock trap heavy materials, including diamond, and have to be cleared by hand. Final clearing is done by a small brush, being used top left.*

plants sited along the coast where oversize and undersize material was rejected by vibrating grizzlies and screens and the remainder, amounting to about 20 per cent of the gravels, taken by diesel loco-drawn trucks along a coastal railway or by road transport, to a central treatment plant.

In some areas, the diamonds are found in a hard, compacted conglomerate which has to be drilled and blasted. It is stockpiled, and when convenient crushed to release the diamonds, after which it is treated in the normal way.

From 1970, the field screening plants were replaced by four recovery plants each with a heavy media separator, to which gravels are taken by dumper trucks. Concentrate, amounting to about 1 per cent of the gravels treated, is taken from these recovery plants by locked trucks to the central treatment plant. The field screening plants used to send on about 10 per cent as concentrate.

The sizes of the small and large material discarded depend on the locality of the working and the size of the diamonds likely to be recovered.

The terrace thicknesses vary from about 12 in (30·5 cm) to 12 ft (3·7 m). Where the depth is less than 3 ft (91 cm), the gravels are bulldozed into piles. When deeper, the gravels are removed by excavators into dumpers.

As the bedrock is so uneven, as may be seen in Fig. 4.39, the potholes and gullies have to be emptied by hand and most of the African labour force is engaged on this job. The usual method is to break up any hard material by compressed-air drills and to use shovels to throw the gravel on to a conveyor belt set up on the spot.

Final cleaning of the bedrock is by using small bristle brushes (one may be seen in Fig. 4.39) to sweep out gravel. Vacuum extractors called Vacuveyors (Fig. 4.40) were developed to reduce the labour of sweeping, but they are no longer in use and Poclain trench diggers (Fig. 4.41) are employed to clear suitable deep gullies. The potholes and gullies worn by the sea in the fairly soft schist bedrock are in some places 10 ft (3 m) or more deep. Diamonds tend to concentrate in these or on or near a footwall, i.e. the foot of one of the wave-cut shelves in the bedrock.

Mining around Kleinzee

To the immediate south of the Orange River in Namaqualand are the State Alluvial Diggings and below them De Beers have mining rights on nearly all the farms farther down the coast to, and well beyond, the Buffels River, which is dry for most of the year. Immediately south of the river, the original rich Kleinzee diggings have long been worked out and are the site of the present mining town of the same name (Fig. 3.29). Since the diamonds came down the river and were deposited on the beaches, the river's estuary must have moved to the north because tides take the deposits northwards.

To the north two areas are being worked, Kleinzee Annex and Dreyer's Pan. Some distance south down the coast, mining began on the Koingnaas farm in 1978. North beyond Dreyer's Pan are two more coastal farms with known reserves, Tweepad and Oubeep, one farther inland, Karee Doorne Vlei, and another much farther inland called Langhoogt.

At Kleinzee Annex, some of the bedrock is over 80 ft (25 m) under the sand, but on the most northerly farm, Oubeep, it is so near the surface that prospectors

Fig. 4.40.   *A suction hose called the Vacuveyor or bedrock cleaner was used at one time to empty potholes of sand and gravel.*

Fig. 4.41.   *A Poclain trench digger, used to clear deep gullies and also to make prospecting trenches and to load sample boxes.*

had to drag out desert plants with an improvised harrow before stripping the overburden.

When an area is being mined, white lines are painted on the bedrock to show weekly progress for bonus payments to be estimated, or red lines for prospected areas, before the overburden is replaced.

Prospecting and Sampling

To make reasonable accurate estimates of how payable an area is likely to be, trenches are cut as described earlier in this chapter and boxes filled with the sand and gravels as trenching proceeds, each box being labelled to identify the area from which the contents were recovered.

When the circumstances are suitable, a row of large holes is drilled to the bedrock and samples taken out at all levels by an auger drill which loads each on to a dump truck. This piles them ready for labelling before they are taken away to the sample plant. Williams drills, used in Namaqualand, can sink holes down to 120 ft (36·5 m). After a hole is made, it is lined with mild steel tubes by a casing puller, a small derrick on a truck. At the top of a hole, 54 in (137 cm) tubes are used and as the hole becomes deeper, the tube diameters are reduced in steps to 34 in (86 cm). See Fig. 4.42.

Over each prospect hole a miniature head gear is erected so that a man can be lowered to the bottom to clear the cemented gravels on the bedrock by hand by filling a bucket which is hoisted to the surface by an electric winch. Sometimes the conglomerate is so hard it has to be blasted.

Fig. 4.42.   *Williams auger drill in Namaqualand. The auger (one is in use and there are spares in front of the drill) lifts a sample of the sand which is then taken away by the front end loader on the left.*

Fig. 4.43. *Rows of prospecting holes, first made by the drill in Fig. 4.42 and lined with steel casings, which have been taken into the gravels and are being sampled using a small crane and a bucket. One man is working underground.*

Because of the amount of prospecting carried out, there are two sample plants, the box sample plant for trench samples and the prospect sample plant for samples taken out of the auger drill holes.

Marine Diamond Mining

It had been known from near the beginning of the century that diamonds were to be found on the coastal desert strip, the C.D.M. concession referred to earlier. Prospectors discovered diamond-bearing gravels extending under beaches between present high and low tide marks. It was, however, very difficult to mine these areas because of flooding, so they were left.

There was much speculation on whether diamonds would be found under the sea. It was argued that the diamonds in the beaches came down the Orange River and were taken up the coast by the sea, and therefore some diamonds must have been trapped in potholes *en route*. Some geologists see no reason why diamondiferous pipes should not have been formed under the sea; but coastal diamonds, in Africa at least, are related by distribution to rivers flowing into the Atlantic.

The interest in undersea diamonds of an American oil man, S. V. Collins, was aroused after he had bid (unsuccessfully) for laying an underwater pipeline for delivering oil from tankers to the C.D.M. town in the desert, Oranjemund.

In 1962, he obtained a mining concession for a 170 mile (272 km) strip off the coast from the Orange River to Luderitz, and formed the Marine Diamond Corporation to mine it. An expensive operation was launched to prospect the sea-bed and several special vessels built to bring up diamonds by a vacuum sweeping technique that was developed.

Fig. 4.44.   *One of the earlier recovery barges.* Barge 77 *was wrecked in 1963 and* Colpontoon
turned turtle later, killing seven men. It was later beached and refitted.

Fig. 4.45.   Pomona, *the recovery barge for undersea diamonds, at work off the coast of South
West Africa. The suction dredges are over the front of the barge on the left. The structure at the
back contains the living quarters and on top is a helicopter landing platform.*

Diamonds were recovered but were costing more to recover than they were worth. In 1963 and 1965 De Beers concluded agreements with the Marine Diamond Corporation for C.D.M. to take part in the sea-mining operation and to transfer C.D.M.'s tidal strip concession to the Marine Diamond Corporation.

The prospecting vessel *Rockeater* (Fig. 6.10), fitted with undersea drills, was used to plot payable areas of sea-bed. Contour maps were prepared showing the average diamond content. After Sammy Collins's experience with several barges, one of which was wrecked and another beached, the 300-feet long *Pomona*, shown in Fig. 4.45, was built and commissioned. *Pomona* worked continuously night and day with two shifts of workers living on board while a third shift was on leave. It was serviced by a number of other vessels, several aircraft and two helicopters.

When in use, *Pomona* was towed to areas where *Rockeater* had found the gravels to be payable. It was exactly located by radar beamed on fixed reflectors along the shore. It was then anchored by long lines from the stern and by long lines to anchors on each side to the bow in Y-formation. The rear anchor lines were kept taut by the barge's propellors and the lines are gradually let out so that the barge moved forwards.

At the same time, the forward anchor lines were shortened on the port and then on the starboard side alternately, so that as the barge moved forward it also swept slowly across the area.

Over the front were four vacuum tubes (Fig. 4.46), two large ones ahead, followed by two smaller ones to pick up anything left by the main tubes. The vacuum tubes later had large flared-out steel heads, in each of which were water nozzles and a suction head. The action was to employ water jets to blow away the overburden of sand and silt and then, when the head had settled through it to the gravel or bedrock, to suck up the gravel into the barge.

An added complication was the frequent heavy swell along the coast which could cause the barge to move up and down as much as 30 ft (9 m). The suction

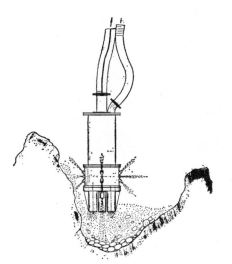

Fig. 4.46. *The head of one type of suction dredge used from* Pomona. *Water jets remove sand and silt and suction draws up gravel including any diamonds.*

Fig. 4.47. *Mining in the tidal strip by building dams before removing overburden. Two of the series of dams seen on the far left have been worked out and allowed to flood.*

dredges still had to be kept stationary in the sea-bed, and this was achieved by a system of cables holding the tubes at one end and counterweights at the other.

The gravel was drawn into the barge with a considerable amount of sea-water which was largely removed by dewatering cyclones and delivered back into the sea. Normal methods of concentration of gravels were used until the last stage, when an adaption of the old-timer's jig concentrated diamonds on the top of a pile of wet gravel on a picking table below decks. Other methods are unsuitable because of the movement of the barge. It was eventually decided that the known reserves of diamonds under the sea were insufficient to justify so costly a mining operation, and the barge *Pomona* and its support vessels were sold in the early 1970s.

Tidal Mining

The problem of mining in the tidal area was that of building dams that would withstand the sea long enough for the area to be mined. Coffer dams, or paddocks, as shown in Fig. 4.47, were bulldozed from the sand, in various shapes, some reinforced with tarpaulins and sheets of vinyl.

Some lasted a few days, others only a few hours. The secret of making them endure longer was discovered almost by accident. It was a question of extending the front wall in a certain way. As a later method, the front wall of a series of

Fig. 4.48. *A gang searching the remaining gravel after most of it has been removed from the paddock to the treatment plant.*

paddocks was made continuous, about half-way between high and low tides. It was about 40 ft (12 m) thick and high enough to cope with swells of 30 ft (9 m). Walls in some places had to be made up to 100 ft (30·5 m) thick. Special concrete blocks were found effective for constructing coffer dams.

Water was pumped out if necessary and the area was mined in the same way as the beaches above the high water mark. As each dam was mined out, work was started on the next, while another adjacent was being prepared. Behind the line of working the sea gradually reclaimed the dams as can be seen in Figs. 4.47 and 4.48.

Separate foreshore mining as described was successful but was nevertheless suspended on a full scale in 1971 because the diamonds recovered were of a type already in full supply. Some foreshore mining was resumed in 1973 but by new methods allowing it to be combined with mining above the high tide mark.

It had been intended to mine the lower half of the beach separately as it presented a much bigger task in holding back the sea. Consolidated Diamond Mines are still continuing with their exploitation of and research into diamond deposits under the sea and along the foreshore, however; and a system of skew prism walls has been developed to permit mining of the beach down to the low water mark.

REFERENCES

The South African Diamond Fields, by J. L. Babe (New York, 1872).
Early Diamond Days, by Oswald Doughty (London, 1963).
Incwadi Yami, by J. W. Matthews (Kimberley, 1792).
De Beers Consolidated Mines Limited Annual Reports.
Publications of the mining companies.
'Some Account of Diamond Winning Practices in Southern Africa', by R. J. Adamson (*Industrial Diamond Review*).
Symposium: Modern Practices in Diamond Mining in Southern Africa. The South African Institute of Mining and Metallurgy, Johannesburg, 1961.
Science and Technology of Industrial Diamonds Vol. 2. Edited by John Burls (London, 1967).
Visits to certain mines.

CHAPTER FIVE

Extracting Diamonds

The discovery of pipes and amalgamation of mining interests meant bigger scale operations and eventual separation of the operations into two sections, (1) mining kimberlite, and (2) treating it to recover diamonds from it.

Until efficient mechanical crushers were generally introduced in this century, blue ground was still spread out on the surface to weather (Fig. 4.25). In the 1890s De Beers hired from the government 1,000 convicts to break it up with picks and hammers. Later, steam harrows were introduced to plough over the floors. It was found that the deeper the level from which the blue ground came, the longer it took to disintegrate, at this time from nine to twelve months. Some blue kimberlite, called hard blue or hardbank, did not weather and was picked off the floors and crushed by a mechanical crusher. After the blue ground had disintegrated, it was thoroughly wetted and taken away to be washed and sieved. Today, primary crushing is normally carried out underground as a final stage of mining before delivery of the ore to the treatment plant.

Just before the end of the nineteenth century, concentration of the heavy minerals including diamond was carried out by a machine that had replaced hand-jigging and was known locally as a pulsator.

The disintegrated blue ground was delivered on top of a bed of 'bullets' on a sieve in water which was given a rapid pulsating movement. The heavier elements of the deposit gradually descended between the bullets to the bottom and the lighter ones were floated to the top, where they were carried by the water over the edge of the sieve to waste. The heavier fraction containing diamonds fell through the bottom of the sieve. (The pulsator method is still in use today in an improved form for concentrating sand containing tiny diamonds, which is released when kimberlite is crushed).

Diamonds were picked by hand from the resulting concentrate by teams of trained workers.

Grease Table Invented

About 1896, F. B. Kirsten, an employee of De Beers, discovered that diamonds in the concentrate were non-wettable and stuck to grease, while all the other minerals were washed over it. G. F. Labram, chief engineer of the company, devised a sloping table with five steps to take advantage of this fact. The top was covered with a layer of about a quarter of an inch of axle grease. A stream of water carrying the concentrate passed down the table and the grease trapped any diamonds in it (Fig. 5.1).

The grease table was introduced as the last stage of processing before hand sorting and reduced considerably the labour of sorting and the risk of stones being stolen.

Treatment Plants

Today large mining concerns set up treatment plants to deal with kimberlite or gravels from one or more sources. A treatment plant subjects material fed into it to a series of concentrating processes until everything but diamonds has been rejected. The main principles employed are washing, sorting gravels by size, and sorting gravels by gravity, after which the diamonds are extracted by a technical process. Finally, there is a hand-sorting.

Fig. 5.1. *Most diamonds cannot be wetted, neither can grease. If diamond-bearing concentrate is sluiced over a sloping and vibrating table covered with grease, diamonds stick to the grease and the rest of the material is carried off the bottom of the table as waste. Some concentrate has to be given a previous treatment to make the diamonds non-wettable.*

In South West Africa, in Namaqualand, and in Kimberley for the deep mines, large central treatment plants have been established. They differ from each other in certain ways because alluvial diamonds are being recovered from loose gravels in which Nature has already partly concentrated them, and pipe diamonds from solid kimberlite in which they are dispersed. Also, treatment plants at different mines and diggings have to be adapted to local conditions.

Here, therefore, the principal machines employed will be described. How they may be linked to form plants may be seen in Fig. 5.2 and Fig. 5.13, which

In the flow sheet, gravels go through tube mills (3) and over vibrating screens (4 and 6) to heavy media separators (7, 12 and 17). After removal of magnetic material (21), the resulting concentrate is sized in trommels (22 and 25) between which are grinding mills (23) before the final extraction of diamonds.

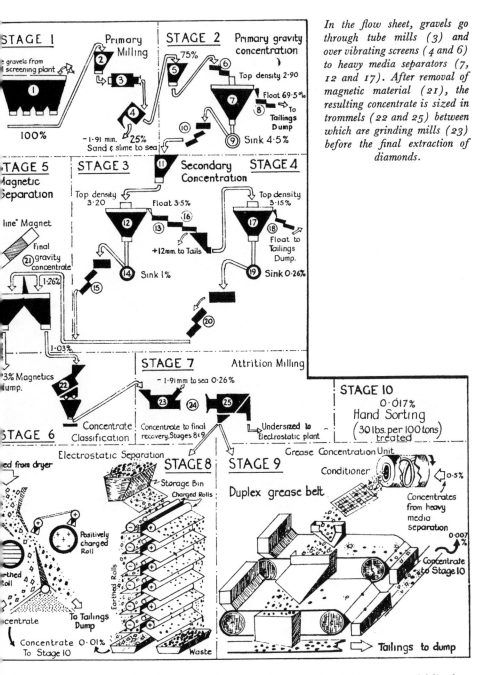

Fig. 5.2. *Diagrammatic flow sheet of the old extraction process at Consolidated Diamond Mines' central treatment plant.*

show the original C.D.M. and present Orapa plants diagramatically. Fig. 5.3 shows the Kimberley Central Treatment Plant.

Crushing and Milling

The first stage is often to crush the rock or conglomerate in which the diamonds are held. This has to be done with care to avoid crushing the diamonds themselves as they are released. Crushing is, of course, omitted when the diamonds are in loose shingle.

For some deposits, milling is more effective than crushing. Milling comprises putting the diamondiferous material in large rotating drums with water and rocks so that the material is gradually broken down to release the crystals.

Fig. 5.3. *The central treatment plant at Kimberley which extracts diamonds from the pipe mines. The waste material – the tailings – is dumped near the plant as seen in the foreground.*

Scrubbing is a similar but less violent process employed when an alluvial deposit is bound by hard clay. The deposit is tumbled over with water in large drums. This also has a washing action, of course.

Washing and Screening

Washing is an important process to remove fine material. It is usually combined with another process, such as screening. Screening is simply passing the gravels or crushed rock through a screen of known size. The material that passes through or does not pass through may be the rejected tailings, according to the size of the mesh chosen (Fig. 5.4).

Fig. 5.4. *Part of the screening and washing section of a treatment plant. From some screens the fraction that passes over is waste and from others the fraction that passes through is waste.*

Fig. 5.5. *A modern washing pan whose paddles rotate broken blue ground in a slurry. The blue ground floats over the central weir and the concentrate containing diamonds is extracted from the bottom.*

The coarsest screen is merely a row of widely spaced, strong steel bars, known as a grizzly, to separate large lumps of rock that need to be crushed before entering a plant. The finest screen is employed to let through only water and the finest sand. Such screens are of woven stainless steel wire or of slotted plastic material.

Sometimes the gravels being concentrated contain a high proportion of a material that can be extracted by a process specially introduced for the purpose. For example, in mines where there is a high proportion of ironstone, the gravel is fed to a moving belt which passes under a powerful electro-magnet. The gravels, including ironstone, affected by magnetism, can be made to fall off the end of the belt in a different trajectory to a waste chute.

Sometimes the gravels contain a high proportion of shells and other soft limestone. This is often best removed by ball-milling, the material being passed through rotating drums containing water and pebbles, to break up the shells into fine material and reject them as slime. Ball-milling is used to clean diamond surfaces as well as to break up friable material.

The most important process of concentration is by gravity. The principal machine is the rotary washing pan, in the form described on page 114, but still in use in larger, power-driven versions today. The general mode of operation has not changed (Fig. 5.5).

The rotary washing pans at Kimberley extract one ton of concentrate for every 50 tons (50·8 tonnes) of tailings swept over the weir. The concentrate is extracted continuously from the bottom of each pan by an Archimedean screw extractor, which avoids having to stop and empty the pan.

Heavy Media Separator

In 1950, heavy media separation cones were installed at several plants. This kind of separator uses a slurry – a heavy liquid. The slurry is fine ferro-silicon powder suspended in water to give it a density of 2·7 to 3·1. The density can be accurately controlled to the figure required by automatic means.

At C.D.M., in South West Africa, the separators are cone-shaped tanks 12 feet across at the top containing slurry with an S.G. controlled to 2·9. About 95 per cent of the ore fed into the top of the cone has a density less than this and floats over the rim of the tank as tailings. The material with a density over 3·2 which includes diamonds, sinks to the bottom of the cone and is removed up a pipe by an air lift (Fig. 5.6).

The concentrate from the heavy media separator is taken to a smaller secondary heavy media separator containing slurry with a density of 3·25 which provides an even smaller concentrate before final extraction of diamonds.

Another form of heavy media separator employs a kind of paddle wheel to raise the concentrate that has settled to the bottom of the slurry inside it.

The Hydro-cyclone

The hydro-cyclone is a later means of concentrating gravels. It employs the same principle as the heavy media separator, but is more efficient. The principle is shown in Fig. 5.7. The ferro-silicon slurry is continuously circulated and closely controlled to an exact specific gravity. A centrifuge effect is employed by

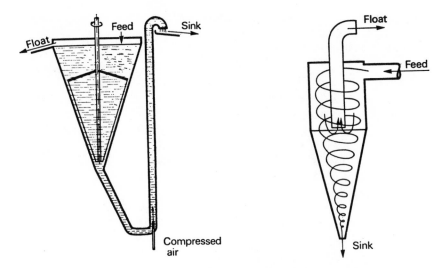

Fig. 5.6. *Principle of the heavy media separator. Gravels or broken blue ground is fed into the top. Light materials float off the top of the heavy liquid in the separator and heavier ones including diamonds sink to the bottom and are extracted.* Fig. 5.7. (right) *Principle of the hydro-cyclone. Gravel and broken blue ground fed in from the side are centrifuged, when the heavy faction sinks and the lighter one is extracted from the top.*

feeding in the concentrate and ore so that the heavier fraction moves to the outside and down the conical tank, and the light fraction comes to the middle and is forced upwards where it is floated off.

Greased Surface Concentrators

The grease table separator mentioned on page 141, was developed and became the principal method of final recovery until recent times. The early sloping grease table was developed into a heavy aluminium plate with several steps across it, vibrated rapidly from side to side by an electro-magnetic motor. Concentrate is passed rapidly down the grease tables with plenty of water.

Most of the diamonds are trapped in a band very near the top of the grease-covered table. The stream of gangue (the rest of the concentrate) tumbling over them tends to push them firmly into the grease. At intervals, the process is stopped and the grease scraped off with a knife. It is put into wire baskets which are placed in a boiler to melt away the grease (Fig. 5.8).

The diamonds are finally hand sorted to remove the small amount of salse (other materials including apatite, garnet, calcite, quartz, etc.) that gets through even the grease process, and are finally boiled in hydrochloric and sulphuric acid (or hydrofluoric acid) to clean them before they go to the Diamond Producers' Association for sorting and valuation.

The Grease Belt

The Diamond Research Laboratory designed an improved form of grease

Fig. 5.8. *After the grease on a grease table has trapped diamonds it is scraped off and put into drums. The grease is boiled off to leave the diamonds and other material that might have been trapped.*

surface concentrator which replaced the table at the main Central Treatment Plants until the X-ray sorter arrived. It employs a grease belt about 3 ft (91 cm) wide running over two rollers as shown in Fig. 5.9. The advantage is that the belts do not have to be stopped at short intervals like the grease table, to remove grease and diamonds and to resurface it with grease. The grease is applied automatically and also scraped off automatically, with any adhering diamonds.

The concentrate, with a strong flow of water, is fed across the belt, which is mounted so that it tilts sideways. Diamonds trapped by the grease are taken across the flow of concentrate by the movement of the belt and scraped off by a heated scraper blade as the belt goes round the end roller, as shown in Figs. 5.2 and 5.9.

Earlier grease belts were mounted in pairs, one below the other, so that any diamonds washed over the first were trapped by the second. It was found that the system was so efficient that the second belt was unnecessary. A further development was a very much larger single belt, the middle section of which was vibrated to encourage the diamonds to stick to the grease. One of these was installed at the Finsch treatment plant.

Conditioning Treatment

Not all diamonds are unwettable and stick to grease. Those from the marine terraces of South West Africa behaved in the same way as the gangue, and were washed over grease. The source of the trouble was a molecular thick salt coating on the crystals. It was found that a pre-treatment of the concentrate by fish acid oil and caustic soda made the diamond non-wettable and therefore able to stick to grease, but left the gangue unaffected.

Coatings of other kinds on diamonds from pipe mines sometimes have the same effect and make conditioning of the concentrate necessary before grease tables or belts can be used for final recovery. Diamonds from the Finsch and from the Williamson pipe mines need conditioning. The Tusilo plant in Angola is another with a conditioning plant.

The chemical reagent now most used is maize acid oil with caustic soda to saponify it, but there are other soap solutions that will cause the chemical action desired.

Fig. 5.9. *The grease belt largely superseded grease tables. The diamond-bearing concentrate is sluiced across the moving grease belt, which traps diamonds and carries them to the end (fore-ground) where a heated knife scrapes them off. At the other end of the endless belt, fresh grease is applied automatically. Originally two belts were used to make sure all diamonds were trapped, as shown in stage nine, Fig. 5.2, but one belt only has been found highly effective.*

Recovery of Small Diamonds

As diamond prices rise, so the recovery of smaller and smaller diamonds becomes economical. The small ones which are economically not worth recovering are sieved out and end as tailings. After certain periods of time, therefore, tailing dumps become worth re-treating to recover diamonds thrown away at earlier times.

It was known that recovery of small crystals was not economically possible by grease belt, even after treating the concentrate with a reagent, because so much of the small gangue was made non-wettable too and stuck to the belt. The solution found was to put the small concentrate through an attrition mill, which gradually ground down all the minerals except diamond into a slime. This method is applied to concentrates that have passed over the grease table or belt and are known to contain untrapped small diamonds.

Electrostatic Separation

Before the grease belt and preconditioning of concentrate was introduced at the alluvial mines in S.W.A. and Namaqualand, the principal method of final recovery was electrostatic sorting. It was developed from 1947 by the Diamond Research Laboratory, and became the basic system at most alluvial mines in Africa, but it was also used at certain pipe mines for the recovery of small diamonds below 10 mesh (about 0·066 in/1·65 mm).

The concentrate was divided into four sizes and then passed through pebble mills to make sure that the surface of gravels and diamonds were well polished. The fine fraction (under $\frac{1}{4}$ in/6.4 mm) went through a drying kiln and on to a high voltage electrostatic separation plant. This plant comprises a series of horizontal rollers in vertical columns. The rollers on one side are earthed and those on the other are positively charged. On each side is a series of chutes, leaving a clear passage between the vertical banks of rollers, as shown in Fig. 5.2.

Diamonds are electrical insulators, so when a stream of hot, dry, diamondiferous gravel is allowed to fall between the rollers, the diamonds fall straight down, while the gravels become charged and attracted towards the positively-charged rollers, which deflect them down tailing chutes.

Skin Flotation Recovery

Very small stones, micro-diamonds, are separated from the equally fine concentrate by placing the concentrate in the bottom of a Pyrex beaker and boiling it in concentrated hydrochloric acid, diluted with about three times the volume of water. Careful decanting and stirring causes the tiny diamonds to rise to the top and form a 'raft' on the top of the liquid held by surface tension, from which they may be skimmed off.

X-ray Separation

In 1958, the Russians stated that they had developed a separation technique for their new mines in Yakutia. It was based on the fact that most diamonds – perhaps all from certain sources – fluoresce when irradiated by X-rays, whereas nearly all accompanying minerals in a concentrate do not. The concentrate is

Fig. 5.10. *A Sortex X-ray separation unit at a pipe mine. It delivers diamonds and some concentrate to sealed units for fine sorting by hand.*

fed into the recovery machine and passes in a stream in the dark under an X-ray beam. Any diamond lights up, which triggers a photo-electric cell causing a gate to open and deflect the diamond into a separate chute.

X-ray sorting machines have been developed by Gunsons Sortex Limited of London, based on machines they had developed for sorting agricultural seeds. These have been installed at all the major mines (Fig. 5.10).

In the simplest system, a V-belt feeds the concentrate under an X-ray beam. When any diamond fluoresces, a photomultiplier tube causes an air jet to deflect the stone into a separate chute, as shown diagramatically in Fig. 5.11.

Modern Sortex machines employ a broad belt to carry a large amount of concentrate through at a high rate, a battery of X-ray tubes and photo-cells being directed at the end of the belt to fluoresce and remove any diamonds. Machines are normally two-stage with two such belts. Nevertheless a fair amount of tailings get through with the diamonds and final sorting has to be by hand. However, the machines are fast, efficient, and secure. Other minerals that fluoresce can sometimes be eliminated, by initial milling to wash out calcite, for example, or by a colour filter over the photomultiplier.

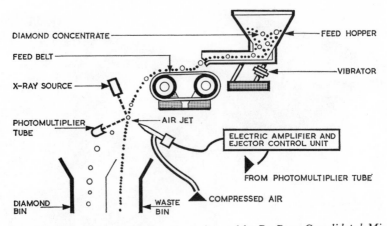

Fig. 5.11. *Principle of the X-ray separation units used by De Beers Consolidated Mines. Any diamond will fluoresce under X-rays and this light triggers an air jet that blows the diamond into a collection chute.*

Unusual Methods of Recovery

C.A.S.T. (Consolidated African Selection Trust Ltd) have an unusual technique for final recovery of diamonds under 0·08 in (2 mm) in size at their plant in Akwatia, Ghana. The concentrate is added to ten parts of caustic soda and heated in an electric furnace to 1,202°F (650°C) for forty-five minutes. This eliminates the waste minerals. A similar method of low temperature fusion is used to clean fine diamond concentrates from the Finsch Mine.

Small diamonds are recovered from concentrate at the Bakwanga Mine in Zaire by another unusual method. They are floated in a solution of lead sulphanimate, which has a specific gravity of 3·6, while heavier minerals such as silicon sink. The solution has to be kept at a temperature of 212°F (100°C). When the diamonds and lighter elements have been separated, they are placed in a similar solution with an S.G. of 3·3 so that this time the diamonds sink and the lighter elements are floated off.

Optical Separation

The Diamond Research Laboratory's X-ray separator has features in common with the optical separator the Laboratory developed from 1957. The object of the optical separator is, however, to provide a check on the tailings from the grease and electrostatic machines, to see how many diamonds, if any, have got through. The optical separator, besides indicating the general efficiency of a process, also quickly identifies a faulty separating machine.

The machine carries tailings from a plant by belt under a beam of light in the dark. A diamond reflects some light and operates a photomultiplier which causes a gate to deflect the stone to a separate outlet. The rest of the gravel, being dark, does not operate the photocell.

The optical separator is also employed in the industrial diamond sorting rooms in Kimberley. By using light filters, industrial diamonds may be rapidly sorted into groups of different colour (Fig. 5.12).

Fig. 5.12. *Optical separation units, which are similar in principle to X-ray units.*

Magneto-hydrostatic Separation

A prototype magneto-hydrostatic separation unit for final sorting was developed during 1975 by the De Beers Diamond Research Centre, and a production version appeared in 1976. Information about the process had not been disclosed during the first half of 1978, when this edition was going to press, because it was still under development.

Ultra-violet Separation

Type IIa diamonds (see page 410) are valuable as heat sinks in miniature electronic devices and a method has been devised for sorting them rapidly from bulk stocks of diamond. Type IIa stones transmit ultra-violet light and the remaining ones, the large majority, do not. The separator photographs diamonds spread on a grid in ultra-violet light. The Type IIa stones are identified on the resulting film and extracted from the grid by a mechanism linked to it.

Ratios of Diamond to Waste

At Consolidated Diamond Mines in South West Africa, the terrace gravels that are mined are crushed and screened, the fine part being discarded, which reduces the volume by about 40 per cent. Milling reduces them by another 3 per cent. From this material, 1 per cent of concentrate is extracted which milling reduces by 30 per cent. Grease belts reduce the concentrate to one part in 120, X-ray separators reduce it still more and final hand sorting separates the diamonds. Overall the reduction in volume is from about 35,000,000 parts of gravel to one of diamond.

At treatment plants for the pipe mines, the ratio is not as high. The Premier

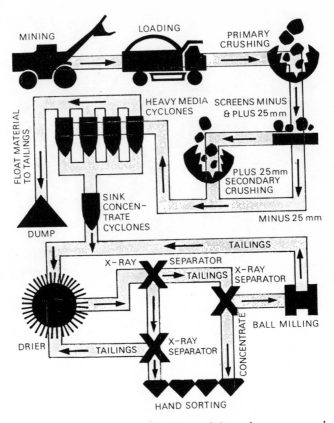

Fig. 5.13. *Simplified flow diagram of the modern recovery and treatment plant at the Debswana mines at Orapa.*

plant reduces about 10,000,000 parts of Kimberlite to one of diamond and that at Kimberley about 20,000,000 to one. Rotary washing pans at Kimberley reduce the input by fifty to one. Heavy media cyclones make a further concentration of one part in seven and treatment in X-ray separators followed by grease belts concentrate still further to about one part in 17,000. The final concentrate for hand sorting contains about one-fifth diamonds.

Fig. 5.14 shows a day's recovery from the C.D.M. plant. Over 80 per cent of the rough is gem quality.

Testing Recovery Efficiency

When the proportion of diamond to ore is in the neighbourhood of 20,000,000 to one, as is quite common, the loss of very few diamonds by the recovery process makes all the difference between profit and loss. In 1954, the Metallurgical Department of the Anglo-American Corporation of South Africa, devised a relatively simple system of testing a whole plant during one cycle of its operation.

They took some test diamonds and drilled small blind holes in them. The holes were loaded with radio-active cobalt-60 and sealed with Canadian balsam. The heavier cobalt and lighter balsam kept the specific gravity of the diamond at 3·5.

Fig. 5.14. *One day's output of diamonds from Consolidated Diamond Mines of South West Africa. About 90 per cent are of gem quality and the total is about 5,600 carats.*

The diamonds were introduced into the ore and tracked through the plant with scintillometers.

More commonly used now are octahedra made of a zinc-aluminium alloy to an S.G. of 3·5 and irradiated in a nuclear pile to make them radio-active. Most mines employ this technique for measuring the efficiency of their recovery process. Some use natural green diamonds that are recovered by eye. In certain plants, the radio-active isotope is recirculated automatically and causes an alarm to sound if it fails to do so.

REFERENCES

Occurrence, Mining, and Recovery of Diamonds, by Dr. A. A. Linari-Linholm (De Beers Consolidated Mines, London 1969).
Private communications and visits to treatment plants.

CHAPTER SIX

Prospecting Methods

The old-time prospector's favourite expression was, 'Gold is where you find it.' It was originally true, perhaps, of every mineral. Certainly the first diamonds in any country were found by chance. Any discovery drew other seekers to the area. From this, a sound prospecting philosophy arose: work outwards from known mineral deposits.

In India, Brazil, Russia, Africa, South America, Borneo, Australia, and other places where diamonds occur, someone originally picked up an unusual pebble that was subsequently identified as diamond – sometime later a rush began. Early finds were near the gravels of river beds, so prospectors naturally followed river banks and beds as they explored outwards from the original discovery.

Some of the earliest mining areas were probably wet diggings in the beds and banks of active rivers. Dry diggings were inland and often in semi-desert areas. It became apparent that these were the beds of rivers that had dried up thousands, or even millions of years ago. Although the gravel of the original find was probably exposed, prospectors naturally tried to discover the original course of the river, if it had become covered with rocks and soil, by sinking inspection pits.

It became evident during digging and recovery that diamonds were almost invariably accompanied by other heavy minerals, including garnets, ilmenites, zircons, and chrome diopsides. As the accompanying minerals were much more plentiful than diamonds, it was easier to search first for them. These red, green, and yellowish minerals are generally known as diamond indicators or indicator minerals. The Russians in recent times have named them *sputniki*, as they are little 'artificial satellites' to diamond deposits.

A mine is, of course, a wasting asset. Any miner or mining company is anxious to stay in business. Prospecting therefore becomes inseparable from mining.

Traditional Prospecting

In the old days, the prospector was usually an independent adventurer who was looking for any kind of mineral that would be rewarding. With his pick and shovel strapped to a mule's pack, he could cover all kinds of terrain, but he depended upon diamonds and other minerals being on the surface or not very deep below it. After finding a deposit, he would work it out to raise money to set off on the next trip – if he did not make the fortune that was always waiting around the corner.

In the early diamond digging days of South Africa, it was common for several diggers to form themselves into a party with a single prospector to guide them. Very few indeed of these prospectors knew much about systematic prospecting however, as even the source of diamonds was unknown. The discovery of kimberlite pipes bringing them from deep in the earth provided the prospector

Fig. 6.1. *A. T. Fincham, the prospector who found the diamond pipe afterwards called the Finsch in South Africa. In 1963 he sold his rights in it to De Beers for £2,250,000.*

with a new objective, to find areas of kimberlite, which in its decomposed form on or near the surface, he could recognize.

Yellow ground usually held more moisture than the surrounding sandy ground. Also it covered a roughly circular area which might be slightly above or below the level of the surrounding country. When a little lower, it sometimes became a *pan* – to use the Boer name for a pond on a farm. Areas of yellow ground that were small flat hills, perhaps only a few feet high, were known as *kopjes*, also in the Afrikaaner's tongue. Because of the higher moisture content of the yellow ground, there was sometimes more vegetation on a kopje of yellow ground than there was surrounding it, or on other kopjes.

There is an artificial obstacle today to prospecting in most countries where diamonds have been found. Either to do so is illegal and a right only of the state, or the prospector has to obtain a licence, which is not always readily granted. A. T. Fincham, who discovered a huge 44 acres (17·8 ha) pipe in the semi-desert Postmasburg area about 100 miles (160 km) north-east of Kimberley. He sold his rights in 1963 to De Beers for £2,250,000 and the diggings became the Finsch Mine, named after Fincham and his partner, E. Schwabel. See Figs. 6.1 and 4.34.

Scientific Prospecting

Earlier in the century, especially where industrially significant minerals were being sought, geologists had taken a hand in prospecting decisions. They studied the nature of deposits, the geology of the area, and the mechanics of transportation. They tried to deduce the locations of original sources, or to discover other areas where similar deposits might be found. This is a long way from the 'gold is where you find it' approach.

One of the geologists to apply such methods to diamond prospecting was Dr. John T. Williamson, a Canadian who had worked on the Rand in South Africa for a time and became interested in diamonds. (Fig. 6.2.) He theorized the location of the pipe from which alluvial diamonds in Tanganyika (now Tanzania) originated. After nine years of prospecting, he discovered it in 1942–3 at Mwadui, about 90 miles (144 km) from Lake Victoria. The pipe was about four times bigger than the Premier Mine, near Pretoria, the biggest then known in Africa. (See Appendix 5.)

Modern Prospecting

Pack-saddle mules and donkeys are still used for prospecting by individuals and even larger concerns when they are the best way of covering the terrain. Since geologists have controlled the bigger prospecting operations, however, the pack-animal has been superseded by the internal combustion engine and the lone prospector by teams of university-trained geologists as in the massive search mounted by the Russians to find pipes in Yakutia.

De Beers have their own prospecting company for diamonds that operates in a number of countries where prospecting rights have been obtained and are considered worth exploiting. One country where the search is becoming more intense is Canada. Kimberlite has been found in a number of areas including Kirkland Lake in western Ontario, which seems most promising. Systematic prospecting is also being carried out in Australia.

In 1968 De Beers Prospecting Unit was exceptionally successful when it located a number of new kimberlite pipes, some diamondiferous, in Botswana (formerly Bechuanaland) by scientific methods.

An operation like this starts at headquarters in Johannesburg, where a

Fig. 6.2. *Dr. John Thorburn Williamson who found the big Williamson pipe in Tanganyika in 1942–3 after prospecting for many years. He set up his own company to mine it. After his death it was acquired by De Beers and the Tanzanian government. It is now known as the Mwadui pipe.*

geological study is made of the country. The places where diamonds have already been found are plotted on a map. Attempts are made to correlate the finds in order to make an informed guess about the situation of major diamond deposits. It is decided for one reason or another to concentrate on certain areas and the logistics of the operation are planned.

Although there is an apparent whimsicality in the distribution of all minerals, and of diamonds in particular, major diamond deposits seem to occur in areas remote from civilization. For desert areas, aircraft and desert vehicles are employed by the prospecting unit, using aerial photographs and geophysical detection devices.

Prospecting in the Kalahari

In Botswana, De Beers Prospecting Unit is operating in the Kalahari Desert, the great infertile tract covering about 20,000 sq miles (51,800 sq km) between the Orange River and the Zambesi and inhabited mainly by a thin sprinkling of Bushmen. The first problem was knowing where to start, because seeking a pipe under a great overburden of sand without a very strong indication of its presence, would be a highly uneconomic proposition.

The discovery of the first diamondiferous pipe, known as AK1, is an excellent example of the combination of geological knowledge and deduction, hunch, hard work, and luck. The first pipe in Botswana had been found by the unit in 1965, in Bakgatla tribal territory beyond Mochudi in the bush, only a few hours' travel from the capital, Gaborone. It was about 400 ft (122 m) in diameter, but unfortunately contained no diamonds. There was no surface indication – no depression or hump – and the top of the kimberlite was 20 to 25 ft (6·1–7·6 m) below an overburden of ferruginous gravel and sand.

To find the pipe, now known as the Orapa pipe, Dr. Gavin Lamont, the geologist in charge of the field operation, employed a blanket sampling method which was made possible by some acute observation. It was known that colonies of termites (white ants) had inhabited the desert for thousands of years. To live, they had to tunnel down to the strata bordering the water table, which could be as deep as 300 ft (92 m), for mud to provide the humidity for the small fungi that grow in the galleries of the ant-hills and provide food for the colony. While tunnelling, they bring to the surface debris that provides samples of the ground through which they have bored. Traces of gold have been found in ant-hills and it is possible that the ancient Egyptians discovered their gold mines by this observation. Gold was found by the same prospecting methods in Rhodesia in the 1960s. As colonies of billions and billions of ants over the centuries grew and died, their huge ant-hills were destroyed by the elements to help form the top surface of the desert. The surface today therefore contains samples of the material brought up by the ants from depths up to about 300 ft (92 m).

If kimberlite were below the surface there should be indicators including pyropes (garnets) and ilmenites, on top. The indicators are found as small broken and worn crystals within $\frac{1}{4}$ in (6·4 mm) of or on the surface, where they have been exposed by wind.

Sampling consists of taking surface samples and counting the number of indicator minerals in the sample. The number rises very significantly over a

Fig. 6.3. (below) *Ant hole in the Kalahari desert. Billions of billions of ants bring to the surface material including garnets, ilmenites, and even very rarely small diamonds.* Fig. 6.4. (right) *The top of a large ant-hill: the prospecting truck behind is standing on part that has broken down. Material in the ant-hill from underground becomes the surface as the ant-hill breaks up.*

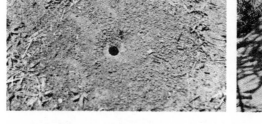

pipe, from say, less than a dozen to thousands. Fig. 6.3 shows a new ant hole from which ants are still bringing up indicator minerals and, on extremely rare occasions, small diamonds. Fig. 6·5 illustrates the size of the pyropes and ilmenites.

Reconnaisance sampling is carried out systematically by setting up a camp in the bush in the area to be tested. A base line is established by cutting down any vegetation in the way, mostly thorn bushes, and driving trucks through to form a wide path. The trucks also take samples as they go. From this, a grid is set out by pacing out the area using a measuring wheel and marker posts. Base lines are about 35 ft (10·5 m) apart and are pegged at 40 in (1 m) intervals.

At every ten to fifteen paces on the grid a sample of the top layer of sand – the deflation layer – is taken with a small scoop and transferred to a container known as a soil splitter, which retains only half of the sample to reduce the amount to be treated. When 10 to 15 lb (4·5–6·8 kg) has been collected, the sample is sealed and marked with an identification number and returned to camp, where the heavy minerals are separated by sieving in water in the traditional way and by obtaining a concentrate using bromoform as a heavy liquid. The sieving is to eliminate the sand and very small heavy minerals that may have been transported by wind and would confuse the sampling. The concentrate is examined under a microscope and the brownish-black, manganese-rich ilmenites and pale orange to red pyropes are extracted and counted.

Reconnaissance teams comprise a number of trained workers (one is seen with his scoop and soil splitter in Fig. 6.6) under a geologist. A team can cover 10 sq. miles (25.9 sq. km) a day, and since teams usually work in threes, as a field unit, they can sample 30 sq. miles (77·7 sq. km) a day. A reconnaissance field unit can cover the astonishingly large area of 450 sq miles (1,165·5 sq km) a month, which includes about three moves. The unit is supplied from a base, but field units in the Kalahari desert have small bonuses in the occasional finds of ostrich eggs, which being the size of about two dozen hens' eggs, make enormous omelets, and even the discovery occasionally of truffles!

The diamond company C.A.S.T. had found diamonds in the north-east of Botswana, in river terraces that were only about 6 in (15 cm) of gravel. The deposits were not workable. This was another traditional starting point in Botswana for Dr. Lamont – diamonds are where you find them. He carried out sampling operations upstream to the end of the valley where the river had its source, and found a few diamonds, including a 2½-carat white crystal, but no indication of the origin of the deposit.

The diamonds in a river-bed must have come from a pipe, yet there was no pipe anywhere near the source of the river. The only conclusion he could come to was that the present river source was not the original one. At this point, geological knowledge and inspiration led him to the theory that the ridge where the present river had its source was relatively recent in geological terms; it was a warp in the Earth that at some time in the past had risen across the old river, cutting it in two and sending the original head flowing in the opposite direction.

He tried to determine the area where the decapitated position of the river lay, by the sampling methods described. Within a year he had found several pipes including the major AK1, which is over five times the size of the Finsch Mine in area (Fig. 6.7).

The full code name for the pipe is 2125AK1. For sampling purposes the areas between lines of latitude and longitude are divided into four, called A, B, C and D. The first kimberlite pipe (K1) found in area A between latitude 21–22° and longitude 25–26° was therefore coded 2125AK1, or AK1 for short. It is in the Orapa area near Letlhakane about 210 miles (336 km) from Gaborone, in country

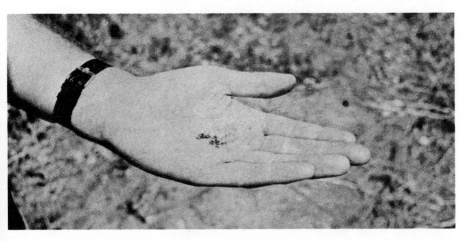

Fig. 6.5.   *Garnets and ilmenites found on the surface of the desert sand.*

explored by David Livingstone. The nearest railhead is 176 miles (282 km) away (Fig. 6.8).

By great good fortune the full depth of Kalahari Desert sand ends in an escarpment about 30 to 50 ft (9–15·2 m) high only a mile or so from the pipe. If the 5,000 ft (1,524 m) pipe had been covered by this thickness of sand, it would probably not have been found. After Dr. Lamont received an excited message about the garnets and ilmenites from the field geologist, Manfred Marx – 'We're up to 1,200 and still counting' – a more concentrated survey operation was set up to determine the limits of the pipe.

The next stage was to determine payability. A sampling plant larger than the whole recovery plant at most mines was set up on the spot to sample the ground taken from inspecting pits sunk in different parts of the pipe. When this work was completed under the supervision of geologists from the Diamond Research Laboratory, Johannesburg, the mine was handed over to the miners for open-cast working.

From the air, the area of the pipe could be recognized by a difference in colour of the vegetation which springs up after the rains. The country rock in the area

Fig. 6.6. *One of a team of men who takes samples from the surface with spade and soil-splitter so that the number of indicator minerals – garnets and ilmenites – can be counted.*

Fig. 6.7. *Dr. Gavin Lamont and Mr. Manfred Marx at the site where they discovered the big diamond pipe in Orapa, on the edge of the Kalahari desert, after covering hundreds of square miles of country.*

is basalt and there is a capping of calcrete (a limestone conglomerate) to a depth of about 15 ft (4.6 m) over the top of the pipe. The calcrete removed has been laid near by as an airstrip.

Subsequent sampling proved that two other pipes about 25 miles (40 km) to the south-east of Orapa were payable having fewer but higher quality stones and in late 1976 a mine there called Letlhakane was commissioned (see page 94). Still another pipe, Jwaneng (see page 95), was found in the south of Botswana in 1973. It is large but covered with 164 ft (50 m) of overburden and a large diameter drilling programme was carried out in 1975 to determine the grade. Small pipes bearing diamonds were also found in the same year near Beit Bridge in Rhodesia and in Dokolwayo area in the north-east of Swaziland. (See Appendix 5.)

The Russians have not published details of their prospecting methods, but they undoubtedly rest on the same basic principles.

Sampling

Prospecting is sampling on a very broad basis. As deposits are found, sampling becomes more precise to determine the limits of the deposits. Then it is even more exactly controlled, to plot the average densities of diamond to discover the richest area to exploit first.

The traditional method of sampling, by sinking a square-shaped inspection pit until the diamondiferous gravel is reached, is still employed. The gravel is extracted and washed and the diamond recovered related to the volume of overburden and gravel, or just the gravel, to give a concentration figure.

One method for sampling beaches is to use Benoto drills (Fig. 6.9). One of these will drill down to about 100 ft (30·5 m) by means of a steel caisson about 34 in (86 cm) in diameter. The sample is pulled up through the middle of the caisson by a grab.

In suitable terrain, sampling has been speeded up by the use of the sampling auger, which screws its way into the ground and lifts out a sample. It is mounted on an auger wagon that can be quickly moved to an area and will surface samples from depths of 10, 15, 20 and 25 ft (3, 4·6, 6·1 and 7·6 m) within a few

Fig. 6.8. *The pilot treatment plant set up at the Orapa diamond pipe in central Botswana to treat about 275 tons a day. The pipe, developed by De Beers, came into full operation in 1971 and now produces about 2,500,000 carats a year.*

Fig. 6.9. *Foreshore prospecting by Consolidated Diamond Mines of South West Africa. A Benoto drill is in action accompanied by a front-end loader on the right.*

minutes. It will produce more samples in a day than a party of twenty diggers in a month. (See pages 134 and 135.)

At the marine terraces above the high-tide mark along the coast of South West Africa and along the coast of Namaqualand, initial prospecting is carried out by sinking a series of boreholes to find the depth of overburden, the depth of the gravel, and the contours of the bedrock. A conventional jumper type well drill or an auger drill is used. The holes are drilled in rows at right angles to the coast line.

When a deposit is found to be workable, a trench 39 in (1 m) wide at the top of the gravel is dug, also at right angles to the coast. It may be any distance from a few hundred yards to over 5·5 miles (3,000 m) in length. The trench is divided into lengths which contain 3·3 cu. yd (2½ cu m) of gravel. The contents of each such zone are separately trommeled and jigged and the concentration sorted by hand. From the figures, the diamond deposit concentration can be plotted. Inspection trenches are sunk about 545 yd (500 m) apart and mining comprises opening out the trenches from each side.

Sampling deposits under the sea of the South West African coast is carried out by basically the same method of drilling, except that it is very much more difficult. A special prospecting ship *Rockeater* was equipped for drilling under water and bringing up samples showing the depth of overburden and gravel and whether there are diamonds, is shown in Fig. 6.10. Underwater drilling outlined extensive deposits that were too deep at 246 to 590·5 ft (75 to 180 m) to prospect,

Fig.6 .10. Rockeater, *the diamond prospecting vessel under contract to De Beers which is equipped to search for diamond deposits on the sea bed off the South West African coast.*

so special sampling equipment was developed to test the gravels during 1974–5 using a different vessel, *Ontginner*.

Yellow ground and blue ground are sampled in the same way as gravels. When a new pipe is discovered, the method of sinking a pit through the overburden to the yellow ground is identical to sinking one through overburden to a gravel deposit. Within a pipe, a load of blue ground is removed and sampled.

The problem in diamond sampling is that assaying in the way that most mineral deposits are estimated is impossible, because of the way in which alluvial diamonds become concentrated. Bulk sampling has to be resorted to. The same is true of underground sampling in pipe deposits. There are frequently parts of a diamondiferous pipe where there are few or no diamonds. Another difficulty is that the weight of diamonds recovered is insufficient information to estimate the value of a deposit. So much depends on the size and quality of individual stones that they have to be individually examined to make an estimate of real value.

A further problem is that the treatment plant on larger operations, where 25 to 30 tons (25·4–30·5 tonnes) of blue ground are being sampled at a time, has to be thoroughly cleaned through after every sampling, an operation that may take many hours.

REFERENCES

Private communications.
Travel with De Beers Prospecting Unit.

CHAPTER SEVEN

How the Market Operates

It has been found that control of the diamond market to keep prices as stable as possible suits all concerned, the primary producers, the governments of the mining countries, the diamond market, the jewellery trade, and the consumers. The policy appears to be as much benefit to the communist government of the U.S.S.R., as to the various shades of capitalist and socialist governments in Europe and Africa. In the U.S.A., where there is a strong antipathy to monopolies, control existing in the diamond market has been under attack from time to time, but no better method has been suggested.

When Cecil Rhodes gained control of the diamond fields in Kimberley, he directed some energy towards stabilizing the prices paid for stones, being keenly aware that overproduction in a market that was slow to expand and was sensitive to any recession or depression of trade in general would have a severe effect on the mines and miners. It was he who laid down the dictum of equating the supply to the demand.

It was immediately successful because De Beers Consolidated Mines received an average of 18s. 8¾d. a carat in 1889, while in 1890 when consolidation of the four mines of De Beers, Kimberley, Dutoitspan and Bultfontein, was practically complete, they received 32s. 6¾d. a carat.

Barney Barnato's Bucket

As well as wanting to prevent price-cutting of rough diamonds, Rhodes needed capital to buy more Kimberley Central shares. He invited Barnato among other prominent merchants to his board room to inspect about 220,000 carats of rough laid out in 160 piles sorted into different qualities. No-one had seen before such a sight. Rhodes said the value was in the neighbourhood of £500,000, but he would not sell under £700,000. An argument developed and Rhodes withdrew.

At last the merchants agreed amongst themselves to pay the price and split the collection, with the largest part going to Barnato Brothers. Rhodes was called and the merchants told him that they had agreed with reluctance to his price. He urged them not to resell quickly, which would upset the market, and then, to their astonishment, lifted one end of the table so that all the stones cascaded into a concealed bucket the other end.

'I've always wanted to see a bucketful of diamonds', Rhodes said to Barney, and suggested they walk to Barnato Brothers' office carrying it between them. Barnato instantly guessed the reason for the dramatic gesture, as it would take at least six weeks to re-sort the stones which would keep them off the market, but could not resist the theatrical walk suggested by Rhodes. When the stones were eventually sold by the merchants, the market prices had risen and Rhodes

Fig. 7.1. *The late Sir Ernest Oppenheimer, who, with others, created Consolidated Diamond Mines. He became Chairman of De Beers Consolidated Mines in 1929.*

was proved right, but Barnato was still blind to the dangers of large quantities of stones being dumped on the market. The time was just before the battle began between Rhodes and Barnato for control of Kimberley Central.

Rhodes dominated the African industry for about thirty years until he died in 1902. By coincidence this was the year in which a young man named Ernest Oppenheimer, later Sir Ernest, arrived in Kimberley as a diamond buyer for A. Dunkelsbuhler and Co., of Hatton Garden, and began an extraordinary career that led to his domination of the world's diamond industry.

After Rhodes had managed to consolidate various diamond interests into De Beers Consolidated Mines in 1888, a serious attempt was made by a syndicate of diamond merchants in Kimberley and London to establish a sound marketing policy. It was largely successful until it was disturbed by finds and rapidly increasing production from the Belgian Congo, Angola, and German South West Africa and elsewhere. Problems of financing the new producers also arose.

Sir Ernest Oppenheimer had, in 1917, set up the Anglo-American Corporation to exploit the gold fields in the far east Rand. In 1921, he gained control of the South West African deposits and formed Consolidated Diamond Mines of South West Africa, through Anglo-American.

By means of C.D.M. he became a director of De Beers and was appointed chairman in 1929, ironically just as the world had moved into the most serious depression it had known, when the diamond syndicate had big financial problems and the total collapse of the diamond market seemed inevitable.

For a long time, he had favoured a single sales channel for diamonds. To this end, he formed the Diamond Corporation, which with other producers became responsible for a stability that has persisted to the present time.

Cycle of Slumps

The diamond trade was subject to slumps on average once every eight years* and the situation was aggravated in the middle 1920s by the discovery of deposits of high quality diamonds at the Lichtenburg alluvial fields, the Namaqualand coastal deposits, and in the German South West African coastal strip. Kimberley, because of the cost of the deep workings, could not compete with the new sources and prices were falling.

During the world depression in the early 1930s, the demand for diamonds almost came to a halt. Conditions were so bad that, in the first half of 1933, De Beers could not even sell diamonds worth £600,000 to cover their bare running expenses. They were forced to close down all the mines, and in 1934 Kimberley was described by a visitor as 'almost a ghost city and a most depressing place with numerous empty villas, houses and shops'.

As a result of these ruinous conditions, Oppenheimer was able to persuade other producers in all countries that the only way to cushion the trade against the cycle of boom and slump was to control production and to regulate sales

* Many studies have been made into rhythmic and cyclic waves in commodity prices. The main ones appear to be 54 years (Kondratieff); 18·3 years (Juglar); 9.22 years (Inglar) and 3½ to 4 years (Kitchin).

Fig. 7.2. *Harry Oppenheimer, who became chairman of De Beers Consolidated Mines after his father's death. With Sir Philip Oppenheimer, head of the Central Selling Organization in London, he continues the policy of international cooperation.*

through one channel. He was able to bring producers together to form, with the co-operation of the government, the Diamond Producers' Association.

After the death of Sir Ernest, in 1957, his son Harry Oppenheimer (Fig. 7.2) continued the same policy with as much success as his father and Cecil Rhodes before him, despite the complications of political change and new deposits that have been found in the U.S.S.R.

Diamond Producers' Association

The Diamond Producers' Association formulates policy and sets quotas. It comprises the principle producers in the De Beers group in South and South West Africa; the Diamond Corporation, which is a De Beers subsidiary; and the South African Government, which is a producer because it owns the State Diggings in Namaqualand. The Association makes marketing agreements with outside producers through the Diamond Corporation.

Central Selling Organization

In 1934, the Diamond Trading Company was formed to carry out the actual selling of diamonds. This and the D.P.A. became the nucleus of what is called The Central Selling Organization, a group of marketing companies through which all the principal diamond producers sell diamonds on a co-operative basis.

All diamonds that the C.S.O. handles are first sent by the mines to the D.P.A. offices in Johannesburg or to the Diamond Corporation offices in London. They are divided into two groups – gem and industrial – each of which is sold through different organizations.

The Sights

The gem diamonds are sold, via the Diamond Purchasing and Trading Company, to the Diamond Trading Company, which sorts them into individual parcels to be offered to invited buyers ten times a year at sales known as sights. About 80 per cent of the world's gem diamonds pass through this system. Nearly all the rough stones pass through London, but some allocations are sold through sights in Johannesburg, South Africa, and Lucerne, Switzerland.

The parcels of rough are made up as near as possible to the requirements of each individual buyer. The buyer states the quantities, shapes, and sizes he requires. He is given the full range of good s but cannot make his own selections. Each diamond is examined at least twice before arriving at its final valuation, and, while prices are fixed and there is no element of bargaining, should a mistake occur in valuation, it will be rectified.

The dealers who are allowed to buy direct, number about 220. They are cutters and a few merchants from a number of countries (Fig. 7.3). If a buyer does not want the full range of goods, he still has to buy the whole parcel. He will then have to sell subsequently, if he can, the stones he does not want.

The Syndicate Broker

Because the D.T.C. limits the number of its clients who are invited to sights, many cutters all over the world have to depend upon other channels of trade for for their supplies of rough. If, however, one of these considers himself important

Fig. 7.3. *Buyers at the sights in London examine the contents of a parcel of diamonds. The only question is that of correct valuation.*

enough to be given the chance to buy direct he will first approach one of the firms or individuals who specialize in the process of obtaining a sight. There are eight such firms and individuals, the two largest being I. Hennig & Co. Ltd., and Bonas & Co. Ltd.

The broker will represent his client's case to the C.S.O. for a decision. Currently, De Beers do not have to seek customers, so the broker has to convince D.T.C. officials that his client is not only sound financially and in his commercial integrity, and will handle the goods in accordance with De Beers' policy, but is likely to play an important role in the industry.

If the client becomes a regular buyer, the broker will then look after such matters as applying for sights as they are announced, which has to be done each time as an invitation to attend is not automatic, informing him of changes in assortments and prices, and so on. In other words, the task of the syndicate broker is to bring buyer and seller together. He represents both and is normally paid a commision of 1 per cent by his client. (Brokers not broking between the D.T.C. and clients normally charge 2 per cent.)

Buyers attending sights sort their parcels into rough stones they want to keep and those they want to sell, if they are cutters. If they are rough dealers, they break down their parcels into different categories for their own customers.

Some idea of the value of original parcels offered at sights may be gained by the fact that the annual value of all sales of rough by the C.S.O. is about U.S. $1,000,000,000 a year, of which, say, $800,000,000 is for gem diamonds (the actual figure is no longer disclosed). This is sold to about 220 customers at ten sights a year, which gives an average of over $360,000 a parcel per customer. Not all buyers have ten sights, however, but parcels have a minimum value which in 1977 was $150,000. Diamonds are sold at sights for payment in a currency named by the C.S.O. Originally this was pounds sterling. Currently it is U.S. dollars, although British sight holders pay in Sterling, invoiced at the rate of exchange of the day of sale. Sales of rough diamonds, gem and industrial, are shown in dollar values in Fig. 7.4.

All rough gem diamonds eventually find their way through various channels, if not direct, to the cutting trade. Some difficult stones such as coated crystals and those with signs of strain in the crystal (seen by examining it between crossed polaroids as described on page 407), may 'stick' for a long time before a purchaser willing to take a chance is found.

How Prices are Controlled

The Central Selling Organization's policy is not to force unwanted parcels of stones on buyers, but, when demand is good, parcels are always accepted, although the contents may not be just what the buyers prefer. If buyers in general become reluctant to take goods they cannot sell, the C.S.O. will stock-pile stones to defend its prices.

During the 1960s, demand expanded so that the opposite situation existed and buyers at the sights were able to resell at increasing prices. The C.S.O. makes occasional overall increases in the price of rough, usually by small amounts averaging up to 5 per cent. Different qualities and sizes are altered differently in price according to supply and demand. In 1970, world demand fell and the C.S.O. had to stockpile. A similar situation occurred during the world recession that was at its peak in 1975, when not only did the C.S.O. stockpile diamonds, but increased the selling prices so that the trade would not suffer from the effects of inflation by a fall in real value.

To this end, the price of rough was raised by 17 per cent at the December 1977 sight. At the beginning of 1978 however, speculative trading in rough escalated rapidly and high premiums were being paid over C.S.O. prices for stockpiling. To damp down the demand, the C.S.O. announced that it might apply a surcharge at any sight. The first, of 40 per cent, was applied at the March 1978 sight, then one of 25 per cent.

If demand falls badly, the Diamond Producers' Association can allocate sales quotas to each of its producing members and also instruct the Diamond

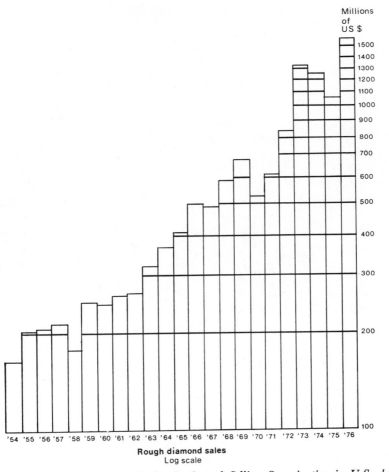

Fig. 7.4. *Sale of rough diamonds by the Central Selling Organization in U.S. dollars.*

Corporation to limit its purchases from producers who have agreements with the D.P.A. There have been two occasions since the discoveries of diamonds in South African when a trade depression has closed mines. The recession of 1958 was dealt with by temporary stockpiling by the C.S.O., while the producers continued on the same scales of mining.

Because the system of control is broad, temporary market fluctuations are ignored and there are occasions when the Diamond Trading Company is selling above open market prices and sometimes below. When diamonds are sold, a percentage of the price is retained by the Central Selling Organization to cover handling and marketing, and the rest goes back to the mines. As the C.S.O.'s expenses vary according to the stocks they have to hold, there are times when their funds build up and they make extra payments to the producers.

The C.S.O. has built up a financial reserve fund from about 1950. Later De Beers Investment Trust acted as an additional reserve fund and at present there is a series of four that can back the C.S.O. with funds amounting to hundreds of millions of pounds sterling.

Fig. 7.5. *Diamond dealers outside the Buying Office in Kimberley in the early 1870s.*

Reorganization of the C.S.O.

Many newly independent African states objected to trading with companies operating from South Africa and much reorganization of the Central Selling Organization was necessary in 1963. Buying operations in certain countries were transferred to the Diamond Corporation.

The Russians made an agreement in 1959 with De Beers to market Russian diamonds through the C.S.O., but because of the Soviet trade boycott of South Africa, the contract was not renewed, and alternative arrangements for marketing were made in 1963. The arrangements allow the Russians to follow the price pattern established by the C.S.O.

Buying Offices

The C.S.O. has set up buying offices in a number of diamond-producing African countries that do not supply directly through C.S.O. channels. These are backed up by agreements that may just call for the provision of technical advice or go as far as requiring the C.S.O. to finance and carry out full scale prospecting for diamonds.

Some offices were set up to help combat illicit digging, smuggling, and general lawlessness on the diamond fields. For example, in the early 1950s, thousands of ex-gold miners from Guinea joined other illicit diamond diggers in Sierra Leone. The Sierra Leone government lost large sums of money from smuggling, so formed an alluvial diamond mining scheme with licensed diggers and invited the C.S.O. to set up a buying organization. The C.S.O. guaranteed to buy all diamonds offered by diggers and dealers, which raised the generally lower local prices to world levels. The two, and later three, buying offices and travelling diamond valuators purchased over $400,000,000 worth during the first fourteen years of operation.

Similar problems occurred in the Belgian Congo after the civil war, when part of it became Zaire. The new government invited the C.S.O. to establish a buying office in Tshikapa, in the diamond producing area some 400 miles (640 km) from the capital, Kinshasa. Monrovia in Liberia was at one time perhaps the biggest diamond smuggling centre. The government largely solved the problem by inviting the C.S.O. to run a diamond appraisal office, which now values all the problem stones for export so that the full duty can be levied on them.

Sales outside the C.S.O.

Of the 20 per cent of the world's diamonds the C.S.O. does not handle, the most important supply is from Ghana, where a government Diamond Marketing Board grades, values, and prices (mostly industrial) rough and sells to licensed buyers.

The C.S.O. buys in a number of countries that have no specific agreement with them. These include the Central African Republic, the Ivory Coast and Guinea; the South American states of Guyana, Venezuela, and Brazil; and India. Part of the Sierra Leone Selection Trust supply goes outside the C.S.O. offices to specific buyers.

Thus with D.P.A. members and countries with separate agreements supplying rough through C.S.O. channels, countries with buying and similar offices, and buying activities in the remaining important markets by C.S.O. licensed buyers, the C.S.O. is able to penetrate the world market thoroughly and keep it stable.

Fig. 7.5.   *A licensed buyer, Mr. Jack Young, shown some stones found by diggers in Lesotho. He will weigh and study them if he decides to make an offer.*

The only supplies completely outside control are the unrecorded, but probably fairly large, numbers of stones still found and sold illegally in many producing countries which find their ways to cutting centres.

Licensed Buyers

From the earliest days, diggers had no access to markets and had to rely upon traders to sell the stones they found. Soon a new 'race' of traders appeared, the diamond buyers (Fig. 7.5). Some animosity quite naturally grew up between sellers and buyers and at times diamond buyers were accused of illicit buying, that was, buying diamonds that had been obtained illegally by claim jumping or stealing. At this time diggers had to obtain licences to operate their claims from the government, which then turned to the control of diamond buyers by restricting them in the Kimberley fields to demarcated areas of Kimberley and the adjacent village of Beaconsfield between the Du Toit's Pan and Bultfontein mines. They also had to keep records of the weights, prices and sellers of the stones they bought.

Among early diamond buyers were immigrants from central Europe who were skilful at the art of dealing. For some reason they became known as 'Peruvians' by the diggers. One of the first to become rich was J. B. Robinson, a sour man, born in the Karroo, who acquired a knighthood and was later sued for fraud. Another was Alfred Beit, a tiny German Jew who earned the friendship of the diggers by his habit of leaving a bag of silver on his counter and asking them to take what they were owed and to leave the change. A third, who made the biggest impact, was Barney Barnato, whose story was told in Chapter Three.

There are licensed diamond buyers today, some on the staff of De Beers Consolidated Mines in Kimberley, where their names appear on brass plates outside the main offices, and on the staff of the C.S.O.

The licensed buyer has an exciting life. He has to be born with a gamblers' streak as well as to acquire a deep knowledge of diamonds. He must create a private information network among diggers and their friends to relay swiftly to him news of important finds. He will make personal judgements of the value of rough diamonds that can run into tens of thousands of pounds and will pay cash on such hunches, without knowing what other buyers have bid. Licensed buyers are shown in Figs. 7.5 and 14.12.

Industrial Diamonds

Industrial diamonds are bought by the Diamond Corporation from South Africa and elsewhere and marketed via De Beers Industrial Diamond Division Ltd. There are no quota arrangements for industrials, but prices are fixed with the buyers. The marketing companies do hold stocks when the market falls, however, to keep prices steady.

Synthetic diamonds from the manufacturing plants in the Irish Republic and South Africa are marketed through a subsidiary of the industrial companies, Industrial Grit Distributors Limited.

The Clubs and Bourses

The diamond wholesale trade, which distributes both rough and polished stones to buyers all over the world, is a very ancient market organized in the form of

Fig. 7.6. *The bustling Diamond Bourse in Antwerp, where buyers, sellers, and brokers study stones in natural daylight from long windows. This Bourse, which has been renovated since the picture was taken, is one of four diamond exchanges in Antwerp, the busiest diamond trading centre for polished stones.*

Clubs and Bourses in the main diamond cities including Antwerp, New York, Tel Aviv, London, Amsterdam, and elsewhere. The Diamond Club is mainly for dealing in rough and the Diamond Bourse for dealing in polished stones. Each has a huge room with tall windows facing away from the sun with rectangular tables and benches under them. Small groups of dealers at the tables mull over and examine stones. Others stand or wander in groups talking about diamonds and the trade (Figs 7.6 and 7.7).

A Diamond Club or a Diamond Bourse – there is one of each in Hatton Garden – will be a member of the World Federation of Diamond Bourses, which sees that its rules are consistent and strictly applied. For example, a member who is made bankrupt automatically loses his membership and is only allowed back if it is considered that he has made reasonable arrangements to pay his debts. If a member is disbarred, his name is circulated (on green slips) to affiliated Clubs and Bourses all over the world and posted on their notice-boards.

The strict exclusion of possible defaulters is essential because the trade depends upon credit and mutual trust.

Buyers and sellers sit opposite each other like chess players and, after the stones have been studied, cautious bargaining is begun and a price is reached. If the seller is a broker, the stones are sealed by the man who has made the offer.

The diamond paper holding the actual stones is an 'envelope' folded in a particular way (see Appendix 3), often with a translucent pale-blue lining paper for brilliant-cut diamonds and an opaque black one for rose-cut diamonds. The broker transmits the offer to the original seller and, whether it is accepted or not, only the potential buyer may break his own seal. Payment is made on a fixed day, also verbally agreed. After the deal is made, the sealed package is taken to the Diamond Club or Bourse office where it is officially weighed and placed inside a sealed envelope with a note of the weight inside and the date and the weight written on the outside.

Any disputes are brought before a Board of Arbitrators, when a small fee is deposited by the claimant. Any member who fails to abide by a final decision is disbarred, but there is usually a right of appeal.

Of course, not all diamonds are sold in this way. Some are sold direct much like other commodities, singly and in larger quantities. Many larger diamond dealers have offices in which they transact business, but parcels and particularly single stones are always being passed through different hands by the traditional channel and a dealer looking for, say, a stone to match another, or one of particular size and shape, will probably go to a Diamond Club or Diamond Bourse to locate it.

The Jewellery Trade

Most diamonds pass to jewellery manufacturers or designers and through the retail trade to the public. Unfortunately, very few members of the public and even some jewellers do not appreciate the fact that every diamond differs in quality and that there is a wide range in price for stones of the same size but different whiteness, clarity, and quality of cutting. As with other commodities,

Fig. 7.7.   *Polished stones being checked for weight at the new Diamond Bourse at Tel Aviv in Israel.*

unless fraud is intended, one generally gets the value one pays for, although a salesman's 'puffs' may appear to upgrade the quality.

Expressing Quality

The basic elements of quality have been cleverly publicised by De Beers under the name 'the Four Cs'. Three of them refer to quality. They are *Clarity*, *Colour* and *Cut*. Of these, the first two have most affect on price, except when the cut is very bad.

The word clarity was chosen not just because it began with C but because it is a much better word than purity for the jeweller to use. By saying a diamond is pure or perfect implies that others are impure or imperfect, whereas a stone of different clarity or colour is really one created in a slightly different way by Nature. The inclusions that lower the clarity of a diamond are commonly called carbon spots. They are actually nothing of the kind. Most are small fissures caused during the natural growth of the stone, or small pieces of the original minerals with which the diamond grew – Nature's fingerprints and 'hallmarks' of its genuineness.

Colour seems the most difficult of the quality factors to judge, since it requires entirely subjective decisions. In this sense, colour means the exact tint of white would normally be called white. Even white is not right, because the finest colour is transparent and colourless. The finest colour used to be described as 'of first water', which means as pure as clear, limpid stream water. (Stones tinged with yellow were called by-water or bye.) In practice, clarity is more difficult.

The accuracy of cutting affects quality because a brilliant-cut stone must be correctly proportioned and finely polished to provide maximum brilliance. A stone of poorer colour or clarity is often cut to less perfect proportion to retain maximum weight, and therefore more value, than it would otherwise have.

Price of Diamonds

The fourth of the four Cs is *Carat Weight*. This obviously affects price. Most people know that the price of diamonds goes up as the weight goes up and also as the quality goes up. What is not usually realized is that the *price per carat* increases.

In practice this favours those who want a large show of diamonds rather than a single stone in a ring or other jewellery. For example, four diamonds each weighing a quarter of a carat each have a larger superficial area than one diamond weighing 1 carat. If they were of exactly the same quality as the 1-carat stone, they would still be much lower priced because the price per carat of quarter-carat stones is much lower than the price per carat of 1-carat stones.

It also explains why diamonds are good supporting stones for rings with coloured main stones. The price of the coloured stone will probably be much the same per carat within fairly wide limits of weight, so a large one will not be too expensive. A number of small diamonds around it will give a good show of diamonds at a relatively low price.

Large diamonds have great intrinsic beauty if effectively cut, but they are being found much less frequently. There is no doubt that smaller gem diamonds are coming from most of the world's diamond sources and that designers and manufacturers of jewellery will have to use smaller stones increasingly in their jewellery as the years go by.

The Myth of the 'Concrete Coast'

From time to time the myth of great hoards of diamonds being held back to keep up prices is recirculated. The implication is that the price is artificially inflated and liable to sudden drop. Like most myths, it has an element of truth. It appears in many forms, one of the most delightful being the belief that many square miles of desert along the Skeleton Coast of South West Africa are concreted over and guarded by the forces of Nature as well as security men to stop anyone from picking up the billions of pounds worth of diamonds that lie there on the sand. Tales are told of bleached bones in the desert and shipwrecks of those who tried to reach the treasure. There is still, however, a wrecked plane in the desert not far from Oranjemund, which crashed during take-off when a previous employee tried to remove a cache of diamonds he had built up over the years.

The truth is that early in the century, diamonds did lie on the sand of the desert, as described in Chapter Three, and many fortunes were made by Ger-

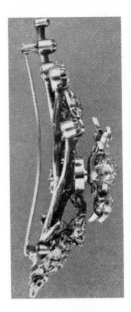

Fig. 7.8. *A tremblant jewel of about 1860. The central piece is mounted on a coil spring as shown on the right. The piece was in Landsberg & Son (Antiques) of London.*

mans who at that time occupied the area. The area is still a restricted diamond concession. It is also true that during the great depression of the 1930s, De Beers Consolidated Mines had to hoard about 10,000,000 carats of diamonds in milk cans because they could not sell them. In the 1960s, however, world demand began to outstrip supply. Old mines were being reopened and new ones worked twenty-four hours a day to keep pace with demand and keep the price of diamond from rising too high. For example, Koffiefontein, near the Reit River, was reopened in 1977 and is now the most modern mine in Africa, hydraulic tools having replaced the usual pneumatic ones. Underground working began in 1977–78 and the open-cast operation will be phased out by 1981.

Display

It is not the purpose of this book to refer to windows and shop display directly, but there are some fundamentals of lighting that must be considered for the most effective display of diamonds. The diamond is at its best when it is lit by one point-source of white artificial light in not too bright general surroundings and it is moved. The brilliance and flashes of fire are then most evident. It has been truly said that diamonds were designed for candle light. Candle light is unfortunately yellowish in colour but the flicker makes diamonds scintillate. Diamonds look worse in fluorescent lighting (although rubies can look better). The colour balance of the fluorescent tube may be reasonably accurate in relation to daylight, but the length of the tube and the low intensity of the light reduce the brilliance and fire of the stone.

White tungsten lights of high intensity are much better for window and shop display. Low voltage spot lights run off a transformer system are as effective and generate less heat. Halogen bulbs are very good because the light is white and of very high intensity.

Movement makes the diamond flash with the colours of the rainbow. Some window displays are kept vibrating by passing traffic, and this effect should not be eliminated as far as diamonds are concerned. It is sometimes impractical or tasteless to have a moving display in a jeweller's shop, although there are satisfactory ways of tackling the problem. Jewellery has occasionally been made over very many years with the diamonds mounted on fine springs so that they vibrate and flash in wear (Fig. 7.8).

The Diamond Room

A special diamond room for selling diamonds in a retail shop should be darkened and lit artifically in the way just described. The table or counter may have a low power magnifier mounted on it for the customer's use. Diagrams to explain the four Cs are useful and, of course, pictures of mining and other aids which give customers confidence in diamonds.

The jeweller himself may use the same room for grading and pricing his stock and also for buying from brokers and dealers. In that case, it should have a window facing away from the sun and a table under it with white blotting paper on it for judging colour. The window may be kept curtained when the room is used for selling.

There is no anomaly in using daylight to grade a stone to discover which stones are best in artificial light, where they are principally worn.

Some jewellers possess special diamond microscopes for grading and light boxes for evaluating colour when daylight is not available. The diamond room is where such instruments may be displayed as well as used by the jeweller for grading his stock.

In the U.S.A., and in West Germany, instruments are sometimes used to show customers features of diamonds, that is, as a selling aid. In Germany, particularly, diamond grading equipment plus a certificate showing successful completion of a course in grading are publicized by certain retailers to establish themselves quickly as 'diamond experts' and to gain public confidence.

Principles of Selling

There are two schools of thought about the principles of selling diamonds, either loose or in jewellery, when the diamond is important. One says that it is wrong to go into detail about the diamond, as it will only confuse the customer, who is buying jewellery for a purely emotional reason. The other is that it is important to give the customer the basic facts because he or she will then be more likely to buy diamonds of higher quality, which is better for the customer as well as for the jeweller.

The truth probably lies in another direction, that there are two broad groups of customer, those who buy mainly for emotional reasons and those who buy mainly for practical ones. The more first group buy because the diamond or jewellery is a symbol of what they want for themselves or for the person to whom it is being given. It may represent an emotional occasion such as an engagement, anniversary, birth of a child, and so on, or success in business or some other enterprise. The more practical people buy as an 'investment', a hedge against misfortune, a gift to ensure certain favours or services, or because a certain social occasion needs important jewellery to create an impression.

Often there is an element of both the emotional and the practical in purchase. A man may be buying diamond jewellery for his wife. She is concerned mainly with the emotional possession of a lovely piece of jewellery, but there is the practical element of whether it is suitable for wearing on all or just some occasions. Her husband is concerned in a practical way about whether or not he is spending his money wisely and also with the emotional need for his own success to be displayed to others through the richness or good taste of the jewellery his wife wears.

The salesman's problem is to isolate the person who is most likely to make the final decision and to adjust his attitudes to whether the emotional or the practical attitudes are uppermost during the sale.

What is normally common to both extremes of customer, and to all the shades in between, is a need for reassurance about the knowledge and competence of the salesman and the reputation of the shop. These are matters of training and experience in the case of the salesman, and of fair trading, courteous efficient service, reassurance through window display, and above all, recommendation by other customers, in the case of the shop.

CHAPTER EIGHT

Sorting Rough Diamonds

Before diamonds are sold by the mines they have to be given prices. The first step in valuation is to sort them into different grades of usefulness or desirability. A gem diamond is subject to sorting or grading many times during its existence. It is sorted by the miners, by the Diamond Trading Company, by the cutter, by the jewellery manufacturer, and by the retailer. An industrial stone is sorted only in its early life.

Generally the word sorting is applied to rough, which are divided into groups with similar commercial characteristics. The word grading is usually applied to polished stones, which are separated into much finer degrees of quality. An early sorting office in Kimberley is shown in Fig. 8.1.

It is important to remember that sorting and grading are carried out for commercial reasons. If the market changes, a stone that previously fitted one category might be transferred to another.

Another basic fact is that different categories of sorting and grading are

Fig. 8.1.   *Two diamond sorters in Kimberley's earlier days working on piles of rough with the aid of sieves to grade crystals into size groups.*

man-made. Nature provides a continuous band of (1) sizes, (2) shapes, (3) colours, and (4) varieties of inclusion. Any group of any of these four characteristics will merge into an adjoining group. Consequently, there will always be disputed borderline cases.

Sorting Rough at the Mines

Gem mining, and particularly diamond mining, is different from almost all other forms of mining for minerals because the end product is, and always has been, sorted by hand into a very large number of categories. In other mining activities, such as for gold, there are usually mechanical, chemical, or metallurgical processes followed by automatic grading or refining into standard purities. Because of the very great variety in which diamonds occur, they are handled as individual commodities from the moment they are discovered. Except for the very small and imperfect material, every stone is given a classification and value before it is marketed.

Sorting begins at the diggings or mine. In small outfits, the digger himself classifies the stones he finds, merely by deciding how much money he expects to get from a diamond buyer. He may know nothing of sorting, not even enough to argue with the buyer, but the buyer will have a knowledge of sorting and be able to 'make a price' in competition with other buyers.

Larger mines will do a certain amount of sorting to arrive at values. They may only divide rough stones into gem and industrial, or separate into a dozen or so classifications.

Classifications vary a lot from mine to mine, and depend on the categories at the sorting offices described in detail later. In general, a mine's classifications will include good quality crystals, known as close goods, probably categories depending upon irregular crystallization, on spotted stones, on colour, and perhaps on categories of size. Very small crystals that pass through a fine sieve are separated and known as sand.

Central Sorting Office

The main channels for the distribution of gem diamond rough were described in Chapter Seven. There are many others, including one for gem diamonds from the Russian mines, and a Tanzanian government sorting office in London for pricing and sale of stones from the Williamson and other mines to the Diamond Trading Company.

Parcels of stones from the mines in the Republic of South Africa and from South West Africa, each normally containing a month's production, are sent to a Central Sorting Office in Kimberley. Parcels from each mine are kept separate in order to preserve the identity of the mine. The diamonds are cleaned in acid, weighed, and counted.

The initial sorting is into broad gem and industrial categories. The two groups go to separate sorting offices in Johannesburg.

Some stones, although satisfactory in other respects, are too small for making into gems. Others are so awkwardly shaped or twinned or of such bad colour or bad quality that they have to be categorized as industrial. There are always

Fig. 8.2.   *Rough diamond of gem quality being sorted into size, shape, quality, and colour at the London offices of De Beers Central Selling Organization before being valued and offered to buyers at the monthly sights.*

borderline cases and commercial demand determines whether these are pre-served as gems or are consumed as industrials.

During the sorting of the gem crystals another group appears, known as near-gem, which may be sold to Industrial Distributors, in London, for eventual sorting into the top industrial grades. This group contains crystals of marginal colour and quality (clarity) which go to either the gem or industrial market, according to which is paying the best prices.

Gem Rough Sorters

Sorters are highly trained men and women who are able to identify, almost instantly, subtle differences in crystals. The sorters sit at benches in a purpose-built tower block at Kimberley under south-facing windows the length of very long rooms. The benches are covered with fresh white paper. When the diamonds reach London they are resorted in similarly arranged rooms, but under windows facing north, in the Diamond Trading Company's office in London, near Hatton Garden (Fig. 8.2). In London there is an extra problem of the short daylight hours in winter months during which diamonds can be sorted.

Sizes and Smalls

First of all, gem rough is divided into two broad categories of size. One group, known as sizes, are all crystals weighing over a certain amount, which depends on the market. Usually it is about a carat. At the time of writing, sizes are stones over 2 carats. Rough under this weight is known as smalls. Separate groups of sorters deal with sizes and with smalls. Sizes are sorted into a greater number of categories because of their higher values.

Sorting Sizes

Sizes are divided into about eleven different size groups, by sieving, not by weighing. These are distributed to sorters for separating into groups of different crystal forms, colours, and qualities. Categories of sorting have been changed from time to time in relation to demand. The basic ones are given here for completeness although at times certain categories are telescoped into each other.

Sorters first deal with the shapes of crystals (Fig. 8.3). These are, in descending order of value:

1. *Stones:* Unbroken crystals of regular formation.
2. *Shapes:* Unbroken crystals of less regularity.
3. *Cleavages:* Irregularly-shaped or broken crystals.
4. *Macles:** Twinned crystals of roughly triangular shape.
5. *Flats:* Diamond crystals of irregular shape with flat parallel sides like pieces of broken glass.

Brilliant-cut gems can be fashioned from all except the last category. Those made from suitable *macles* tend to be shallow, however. Baguettes and other small cuts are made from *flats*.

While he deals with rough by shape, the sorter is also making divisions into quality, which is the name used by sorters for clarity. When he receives his pile of crystals, he first goes through it and picks out the pure regular octahedra known as *stones*. Then he picks out any other unbroken octahedra which may be irregular in form and have varying degrees of inclusion. Any pure ones will be irregular in form and, unless very distorted, will go into his first pile of *stones*. The remainder, including those with fairly obvious inclusions which are called spotted goods, will become his pile of *shapes*. At the time of writing stones, shapes and cleavages (next page) are all grouped together in single parcels.

* Spelt macle or maccle.

The next class, *cleavages*, is normally the biggest. The crystals in it are not all cleavages in a crystallographic sense, as they include all diamonds that were imperfectly formed or were fractured, as well as those that were split along a cleavage plane at some stage of their existence. *Cleavages* can contain very large stones of the very highest quality. For example, the Cullinan would have been graded as a *cleavage* had it reached the sorting rooms. *Cleavages* range in form from near *stones* or *shapes* with distorted or broken faces to irregular lumps of diamond with no recognizable crystallographic features.

The next category of *macles*, is easily identifiable. The macle is a rotation twinned octahedron with a triangular form and usually a seam as explained in Chapter Seventeen. It is usually quite flat but often thick enough for cutting into a brilliant.

The final category of *flats* covers tabular crystals too thin for making brilliants. As this is being written, *flats* and *macles* are also lumped together at the Central Sorting Office.

The sorter now goes back to his groups of *stones* and removes from them all the crystals that have a definitely lower value. These include frosted crystals, which have one or more faces with a ground glass appearance. The difficulty with them is that they are harder to grade accurately. Oxidized stones were once removed, but are no longer. These have an orange tinge, as they contain iron oxide, and are usually from alluvial deposits. Finally, brown tinted stones are separated. Greens, which are very pale, used to be separated but are now left in the main categories. Figs. 8.4 and 8.5 show a variety of rough diamonds.

Sorting for Quality

Now the sorter returns to the remaining stones to divide them into groups of different qualities. It is not as simple as it seems, because what he is really doing is to separate them according to their value to a cutter. For example, an octahedral crystal with a heavy inclusion near one point of the octahedron will be as good as a clean crystal because the corners are bruted away during cutting, but one with an inclusion near the centre will be of low value because so much material will be lost during cutting. A substantial amount may be lost from an octahedron when a central flaw has to be sawn out. Each inclusion, according to size and darkness, as well as position, and each feather or cleavage mark within the stone, as well as any twinning, has to be examined carefully to determine the quality.

The sorter picks up the crystal between thumb and first finger and twists it in all directions by a kind of rolling action while examining it closely, and places it in a grading category. A 6X hand lens is often used to study the inclusions. Breathing on the stone to dull its natural lustre sometimes helps to see into it.

Ten grades of quality are employed for crystals, numbered from 1–10. For *stones* and *shapes*, only the first five – although this may be extended to seven if demand is strong – are regarded as the gem group. The remainder, from 5, 6 or 7 to 10 are the near-gem quality and merge into industrials. For *cleavage, macles,* and *flats* the gem group normally spans qualities from 1–4, but this may also be extended to seven when the market is lively.

Stone

Irregular shape

Cleavage

Fig. 8.3. *Categories of shape into which larger gem rough is sorted. The more ideal forms are shown in the drawings and actual examples in the photographs. Some groups have been telescoped. Mêlée (stones under about a carat) are sorted into fewer shapes and qualities.*

Macle

Flat

Stone

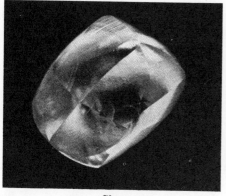

Shape

Macle

Cleavage

Flat

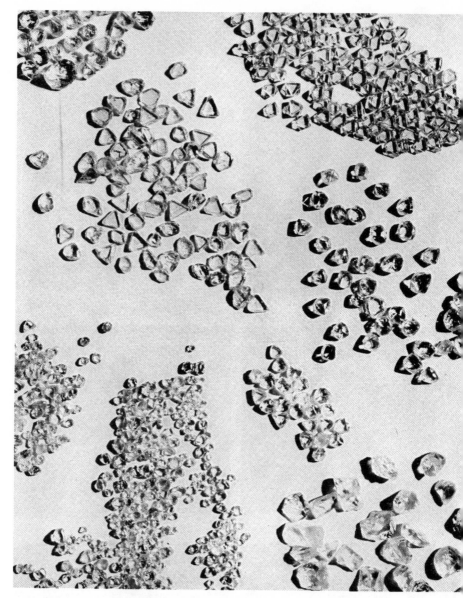

Fig. 8.4. *Some sorted rough. Top right is a pile of stones, all well-formed octahedra. Macles can be seen in the second pile down on the left. At bottom right there are cleavages.*

The sorter starts with what appear to be the cleanest stones and works down the scale of qualities making a row of piles of different sized crystals for each quality. As a fairly general guide, quality 1 is clean; 2 has a few small spots or a white spot near the edge; 3 has a larger single white spot or a crack near the edge; 5 has quite heavy inclusions, cracks or spots.

Fig. 8.5.   *Gem and industrial rough. At top left is a macle and beside it an octahedron. The large darker stone in the centre is irregular (and Type II material). The tongs hold a form of star twin which is useless as gem material.*

Sorting for Colour

Next he deals with colour. Browns have already been separated. He removes any full-bodied yellow stones known as golden fancies, and any other full-bodied colours, such as the very rare deep blues, pinks, and ambers, which are called fancies. Numbers of large golden fancies come from the Dutoitspan Mine. When they are under 2·5 carats, they are classified as industrials and when over, as gems.

The remaining crystals will be varying tints of white, from the extremely rare true blue-white down to pale yellow. Colours are divided into ten categories named 1st, 2nd, 3rd, and so on to 10th. A crystal from 1st to 6th colour (or to 7th according to the state of the market) is in the gem group provided that it is also in the correct purity quality. Crystals below the first six or seven colour categories are the near-gem group and considered as industrials.

Shapes of first colour and quality used to be called ex. collection, i.e. extra collection. Such crystals are, of course, very rare. Stones of second colour and purity were called collection. The remaining colours were numbered from one to eight and the next two at the bottom of the scale were named Capes and Second Capes, which are spotted yellow stones.

Having dealt with *stones* the sorter starts on the other categories and divides them into groups according to their colour and degree of spottiness. Generally the lower the quality of the stones, the smaller the number of other grades into which they are divided.

Yellow stones are sorted into qualities and grades of colour. Brown ones are sorted into qualities and five grades of colour: (1) Finest light brown, (2) Fine light brown, (3) Light brown, (4) Brown, (5) Dark brown.

Sorting Smalls or Sawables

The smaller crystals are similarly divided into types of crystals. The categories are:

1. *Stones:* Same as larger *stones* and *shapes.*
2. *Chips:* Same as larger *cleavages.*
3. *Macles* and *flats.*

There are many variations in the details of sorting which change from time to time.

The Sorting Bench

As mentioned earlier, the sorter receives his *stones* in size groups. He retains these and at the end of a sorting session has in front of him, on the white paper covered bench, 'grids' of piles with the largest and finest crystals at the top left and the poorest and smallest at the bottom right, as shown in Fig. 8.2. Each rectangle of piles is made for a single colour. Each vertical row contains crystals of the same quality and each row to the right is of a lower quality. In each horizontal row are stones of the same size group. Sizes are in descending order from the top.

Normally there are six colour categories and each of these six rectangles could contain up to five vertical rows of purity and say eleven horizontal rows of five sizes. A much simpler system is used for *cleavages* and *macles* and *flats* and a still simpler one for mêlée.

Formula for Valuation

When the crystals have been sorted, an official known as the Chief Valuator examines them and puts a price on them. This is obviously a task that calls for a very high degree of judgement and considerable experience. As a starting-point for evaluation, the various diamond producers have agreed amongst themselves a formula by which the basic value of a particular classification of diamonds can be calculated, for guidance. After arriving at a basic figure, the valuator adjusts it according to his assessment of what recovery of polished stone is possible from a particular crystal, i.e. how much flaws and their positions will influence the cutting. In practice, price books based on the formula are used up to 10 carats and stones are sorted against a sample parcel, but the valuator deals individually with stones of over 10 carats.

It is not easy to price a diamond crystal for the colour it will be when cut because the colour in diamonds is not always uniform. A crystal of poor quality may be improved by removing the small area which is the only part poorly coloured, and was previously suffusing the stone. A diamond crystal may be coated with a 'skin' of bad colour and be of excellent colour inside. Colour may also occur in spots or layers; some octahedra have colour only in the corners or along the edges.

Another of the difficulties of the valuator of rough diamonds is that the colour of a crystal 'improves' in relation to how much is lost in cutting. A good octahedron from which a high recovery is possible will 'improve' less than a poorly formed stone from which the recovery is lower. The phenomenon of colour saturation is well known. A deeply coloured liquid in a narrow bottle will look quite pale. Glass which is, say, dark red, will appear white if powdered small enough.

Gem Crystal Sorting by the D.T.C.

After sorting, diamonds are sold by the Diamond Producers Association, to the Diamond Trading Company (D.T.C.) and sent to their sorting office in London, where they are joined by crystals coming from many other sources. In London, the whole process of sorting is repeated in even more detail for repricing and preparation of parcels of stones to suit particular buyers. At times the D.T.C. has sorted crystals into more than 2,500 categories.

The D.T.C. Sorting Office retains parcels of selected stones in each classification for use as standards of quality and colour. From time to time, sorted crystals are compared with the standard to make sure that there is no drift in quality and that different sorters are applying the same standards. A similar system is applied in Kimberley.

Weighing Rough

When all the diamond crystals have been re-sorted, the Diamond Trading Company mixes those of the same categories from different sources, and at this point they are weighed. Up to this stage they have been divided only into general weight categories, except for stones above about 15 carat, which are sold separately. Normally, crystals are counted into groups of a hundred of approximately the same size and weight together. For example, a hundred stones might be offered as weighing 100 carats. Not every stone would weigh exactly a carat. Some might be 0·9 carat and others 1·1 carat.

Weighing is always carried out to one-tenth of a carat and shown to one place of decimals thus: 3·4 ct., 14·7 ct., 8·0 ct., 0·9 ct. After diamonds are polished, the trade weighs them to a hundredth of a carat, shown thus: 0·34 ct., 2·06 ct. 3·10 ct., and so on.

Sorting Industrials

Near-gem* crystals are sorted into three categories of crystals:

1. *Stones.*
2. *Shapes* (which include macles).
3. *Cleavages.*

These categories include crystals down to a certain size, separated by passing them through a wire sieve. They are divided themselves also by sieves into two categories of size. Near-gem crystals are then graded for quality and for colour.

In sorting for quality, different criteria apply than for gem sorting. For example, good points (corners) on an octahedron are more important than internal flaws, unless the flaws are very bad, because the corners are used as cutting tools.

There are three grades of colour in the *stone* and *shape* categories: Grey yellow, and brown; and three in the *cleavages*: Grey, coloured, and brown.

Diamonds that are not near-gem are classified into *drilling* and *boart*. Drilling also includes the small stones rejected from the near-gem categories. It is used for mounting in the heads of rock drills and sold in sieving sizes. There are four main categories: (1) Drill rounds, (2) Cast setting (for use when metal is cast round the diamonds), (3) Mixed drilling (very small stones), and (4) Dust.

Crushing boart is the lowest quality of diamond of any kind. It varies enormously in its appearance and characteristics. It can be a hard black cokey mass, sugary and greeny-yellow like Congo boart, or black in large broken octahedra crystals like much mine boart.

Automatic Sorting

From about 1966 some semi-automatic and automatic methods of sorting were introduced by the D.T.C. to prepare parcels for the 'sights'. They cover sieving shape sorting, colour sorting, sizing (weighing), and counting. Sieving is a broad classification into smalls (under 2 ct. approx.) and sizes (over 2 ct.) and then division into further weight categories. A sieving machine is simply a range of sieves clamped to a vibrating frame. Colour sorting into two broad categories is carried out rapidly by a specially-developed Sortex machine working on the principle described on page 151 and employing colour filters. Rough gem diamonds from 1·81 carat upwards are sized into weight groups spanning one carat intervals, i.e. from 1·81 to 2·80, from 2·81 to 3·80 and so on. The subdivisions below 1·81 carat are smaller. The automatic weighing and counting system developed by the D.T.C. employs thirty automatic weighing machines controlled by two computers.

Automatic shape sorting is still in the development stage and comprises a television camera, associated with computers programmed to recognize stones, shapes, cleavages and flats, which is linked to a feeder and sorter.

* Called 'Industrial Serie' in 1978 for marketing reasons.

After inspection pits have been dug in a row and sampled, a trench is opened up, preparatory to alluvial mining. A Poclain digger works on this one in Namaqualand.

Deep potholes, that contained diamonds, in the worked-out bedrock that was under up to 80ft. (25m.) of sand at the Kleinzee Annex in Namaqualand, south of the Orange River.

Wall-throwing—creating a sand wall to make a paddock that will last long enough to mine out an area in the tidal strip in the diamond territory being worked by C.D.M. in Namibia.

The area inside a paddock along the tidal strip is pumped out and the over-burden removed before it can be stripped of the diamondiferous gravels, which go to the treatment plant.

CHAPTER NINE

The History of Diamond Cutting

There was little or no incentive to polish and shape diamonds during the centuries that they were regarded as talismans. Those set in rings were usually natural octahedra and perhaps, in many cases, glassies with flat, highly reflective faces. The Indian lapidary work *Agastimata*, probably written in the fourteenth century, is the earliest record of the fact that diamonds can be finished by using other diamonds, but the author gave a warning that a diamond polished on a wheel would lose its magical powers.

To grind diamond with the use of a wheel or mill requires diamond powder, so presumably the first discovery was that diamond pieces could be pulverized into a fine dust. This invention was attributed by Robert de Berquen (writing in 1661) to his ancestor Louis de Berquen in 1476, an untrue statement that has persisted for centuries.

Grinding, Cleaving and Cutting

Grinding and polishing diamond with diamond dust is a slow but reasonably flexible process because many different shapes or patterns of facets are possible. The diamond grinding wheel called the scaife was in use in the fourteenth century and if diamonds were ground before its introduction, the operation was probably carried out in the same way as other gemstones were ground at an early date, as shown in Fig. 9.1 from the book of Presbyter Theophilus of about the tenth century. A table facet was rubbed on gems other than diamond by using a sandstone, a lead table, and finally a goat skin with brick dust moistened by saliva.

Fig. 9.1. *A gem polisher, shown in a book by Presbyter Theophilus, produced in about the tenth century.*

Fig. 9.2. *Coat of arms of an early Nuremberg diamond polisher – scaife, tang and diamonds are easily recognizable. Date unknown.*

'Diamantslijper'

De ruwe diamant, hoe duister,
Ontfangt in 't slijpen al zijn luister.
Die rein van water valt, en groot
Van lichchaam, noemt men een kleenood.

Fig. 9.3. *The earliest known pictures*
of diamond polishing are obviously,
because of the style, copied from a com-
mon source. This was said to be
Staendebuch *by Jost Amman of*
Nuremberg, 1568, though the originals
have not been traced. The top illustra-
tion has a Dutch text and appeared in
Menschelyke Beezigheeden
('Human Trades'), published in
Haarlem, 1695.

The text reads:
'Diamond-cutter'
'The rough diamond, however
    dark,
Receives in polishing all its lustre.
Those of pure water, and large
Of body, are called a gem.'

The lower comes from a different
Dutch text which may well be as old.
It has been calculated that the woman
turning the wheel has to produce nearly
$\frac{1}{4}$ of a horsepower when the scaife is
under load. In later pictures, the
woman is sometimes assisted by a child.

This engraving has been attributed to
Jan Luiken, made in Holland about
1700. The text reads:
'The Diamond-polisher'
'These are drops from one source,
    the final poem just begun.'
'Man likes being elegant,
With diamond stone, or ruby,
So that his wealth can be praised.
It would be better if he started
    correctly,
By first shining like the sun,
That will be another beauty.'

De Diamantslyper.

t Syn Dropies uit een Bron, Die eindlicht, noch begon.

De Mens wil gaaren cierlyck syn,
Door Diamantsteen, of Robyn,
Op dat zyn Rykdom zy gepreesen:
'twas beeter dat hy 't recht begon,
Om eens te blincken als de Son,
Dat sal een and're Schoonheid weesen.

Cleaving is a very much more rapid method of shaping a diamond but is exceptionally limiting because only octahedral faces and forms can be produced. Although the first diamonds used in jewellery were 'point-cut' (Fig. 1.7), they were probably produced not by cleaving but by grinding and polishing the octahedral faces of a crystal at a slight angle. It is impossible to grind them flat as they are too hard. In any case, the art of cleaving was probably unknown at this early date. The first reference to cleaving appears to have been made by Tavernier when writing of tabular crystals found in the Indian Raolconda mines. He commented that Indians were more skilful than Europeans at cleaving.

A major step in diamond shaping was the invention of bruting, usually described in the past simply as cutting (hence 'cutting and polishing' described the whole operation), which probably occurred in the late fourteenth or early fifteenth century. In bruting, a whole piece of diamond set in a stick, instead of diamond powder, was used as a tool to shape another diamond, also set in a stick (Fig. 9.7), before faceting it.

Sawing is a specialized form of grinding used to divide diamond crystals and probably followed bruting as a manufacturing method.

Origins in Venice

It is surmised from examining existing records that the polishing of diamond facets in Europe originated in Venice some time after 1330. From Venice the art spread to Bruges, in Flanders, and then to Paris. In the fifteenth century it appeared in other towns, notably Antwerp. A report of a court case of 1465, involving the Dukes of Burgundy, refers to four diamond polishers from Bruges, described as *diamantslypers*, who were called as expert witnesses. Guillebert de Metz, in his description of Paris of 1477, refers to the district of La Courarie as the home of the workers of diamonds and other stones. A diamond worker named Herman, a Flemish name, is mentioned.

There is a record of a Wouter Pauwels, *diamantslyper*, in Antwerp in 1482 and of diamond polishers in Lyons in 1497. In a bankruptcy case at Augsburg in 1538 it was reported that a diamond of 11·5 carats had been reduced to 5 carats after being worked on. This strongly suggests that the diamond had been bruted before being facetted by grinding and polishing.

The earliest reference to cutting, presumably bruting, is in 1550 in Antwerp as a document of this date includes the name *diamantsnyder*. *Slypen* appears to have meant grinding and polishing and *snyden* to have meant cutting, i.e. bruting. A guild charter was granted in 1582 to diamanten robynsnyden in Antwerp. A Nuremberg polisher's coat of arms is shown in Fig. 9.2. The date is unknown. Nuremberg flourished as an early centre of clock, watch and jewellery making at the same time as the nearby town of Augsburg.

There are, however, several earlier references to shaped diamonds. In 1420, the Duke of Burgundy owned 'un dyamant taillé à plusieurs faces' and 'un bon dyamant taillé à quatre quarrés en façon de losange'.

Trade Routes and Cutting Centres

There were two main overland trade routes by which diamonds from the Indian mines reached Venice through the Mediterranean. The southern one was from

Fig. 9.4.　*A sketch of 1874 showing the stretch of canal in Amsterdam where Coster's factory was situated. It was here that the Koh-i-Nur was recut in thirty-eight days; the scaives were driven by steam engines.*

Bombay and the ports of Malabar by sea to Aden and then overland to Ethiopia and Egypt and to Cairo and Alexandria. The northern route was from the gem trading centre of Ormus to Arabia (Aleppo), Persia, Armenia, and Turkey (see Fig. 1.5).

When the Portuguese discovered the direct sea route to India, Antwerp grew rapidly as a diamond centre, being supplied with rough through Lisbon as well as Venice, which had supplied alone until then. Venice still remained an important supplier of rough, particularly to Flanders, throughout the sixteenth century and continued as a more important finishing centre than Antwerp in the first half of the seventeenth century. A population of 186 diamond cutters worked in Venice in 1636.

In 1585, there were Spanish attacks on Antwerp and many craftsmen fled elsewhere. Some diamond cutters settled in Amsterdam, where Willem Vermaet was cutting in 1586, and there is a marriage entry dated 1589 of a diamond cutter, Pieter Goos, who had apparently come from Antwerp. A large section of the Amsterdam trade appeared to have moved from Lisbon after 1579, however, when the Inquisition gained power in Portugal.

It was because of religious persecution in the latter part of the sixteenth century in a number of countries including Spain, Portugal, Germany, and Poland, that many craftsmen including a large number of Jews took their skills elsewhere. Many found homes in the Netherlands, where there was no barrier to them until they tried to join a craft guild. As diamond cutting was relatively

Fig. 9.5.

⬦ *Diamond Mining Countries*   ⬠ *Cutting Centres*   ⬤ *Principal Markets*

1. Angola
2. Botswana
3. Brazil
4. Central African Republic
5. Ghana
6. India
7. Indonesia
8. Ivory Coast
9. Lesotho
10. Liberia
11. Sierra Leone
12. South Africa
13. South West Africa
14. Tanzania
15. USSR
16. Venezuela
17. Zaire

18. America (including Puerto Rico)
19. Belgium
20. Brazil
21. France
22. Holland
23. Hong Kong
24. India
25. Israel
26. South Africa
27. USSR
28. West Germany

29. America
30. Australia
31. Brazil
32. Canada
33. France
34. Great Britain
35. Italy
36. Japan
37. South Africa
38. Spain
39. West Germany

From a booklet: The Central Selling Organization and the Diamond Industry.

new as a craft, they had no guild, so the immigrants were attracted to diamond cutting. During the eighteenth century there was an attempt to form a guild that excluded Jews.

Near the beginning of the seventeenth century, the Dutch began buying rough direct from India and by mid-century had taken most of the trade from the Portuguese. By the end of the century, Amsterdam had become established as the main centre for the supply of rough and Antwerp as the cutting centre.

Lisbon was a cutting centre at an early date after the Portuguese began trading directly with India and it was perhaps around the same time that cutting centres were established in Spain, at Valencia, Barcelona, and Madrid.

Late in the seventeenth century London emerged as an important cutting centre, ranking third after Amsterdam and Antwerp. The British were gaining strong interests in India and the discovery of diamond deposits in Brazil in the eighteenth century, which were under the control of the Portuguese who had close links with the British, helped not only Lisbon but London as a trading centre for rough. Amsterdam flourished and reached its peak in the eighteenth century as a cutting centre, while Antwerp declined. It was in the eighteenth century that trading in rough became much more separated from cutting and, in the nineteenth century, the South African discoveries accelerated the separation of the two activities, and the influence of London as a market.

London became and has remained the centre of supply of rough. The principal cutting centres today are in Belgium (Antwerp), India (Bombay), Israel (Tel Aviv), South Africa (Johannesburg, Kimberley, Cape Town), the U.S.A. (New York), Puerto Rico (San Juan, etc.) West Germany (Idar-Oberstein, Hanau), the U.K. (London, Brighton Holland (Amsterdam), France (St. Cloud, in Jura), Portugal (Lisbon), and Sierra Leone. The U.S.S.R. has a big and still growing cutting industry at Sverdlovsk in the Urals, and perhaps at Peterhof, near Leningrad, and Kolyvanskaya, in the Altai.

There are also cutters working in Australia, Brazil, Japan, Guyana, Italy, Venezuela, Tanzania, Indonesia, and some other Eastern countries. Each centre tends to specialize in a particular class of work. For example, Antwerp handles cleavages, macles, and chips; stones and shapes tend to go to the U.S.A.; and Amsterdam, Israel, and West Germany all specialize in mêleé (small stones). India also cuts 'smalls'.

Cellini's Description
The first known description of diamond cutting (bruting) and polishing was given in 1568 by the celebrated Italian goldsmith, Benvenuto Cellini, who wrote:

'One diamond is rubbed against another until by mutual abrasion both take a form which the skilled polisher wishes to achieve. With the powder which falls from the diamond the last operation for the completion of the cut is made. For this purpose the stones are fixed into small lead or tin cups, and with a special clamping device, held against a steel wheel which is provided with oil and diamond dust. This wheel must have the thickness of a finger and the size of the palm of the hand; it must consist of the finest well-hardened steel and be fixed to a mill-stone so that through the rotation of the latter it also comes into rapid movement. At the same time 4 to 6 diamonds can be attached to the wheel. A weight placed on the clamping device can increase the friction of the stone against the moving wheel. In this way, the polishing is completed.'

Cellini's description could have been written today. In almost any diamond workshop in any part of the world will be found solder dops in which the stone is held as it is polished on the top surface of the horizontal scaife. Today's scaife is larger, however.

Cellini did not describe how the scaife was driven, but it was undoubtedly by hand. In 1604, A. Boetius De Boot described and illustrated a treadle-driven horizontal shaft with a point at the end, treated with diamond dust, for gem engraving, but early diamond polishing scaifes appear to have been driven by hand, despite the invention of a horse-driven diamond mill, claimed as early as 1550 by a Nuremberg man, H. Lobsinger. The earliest known drawings of

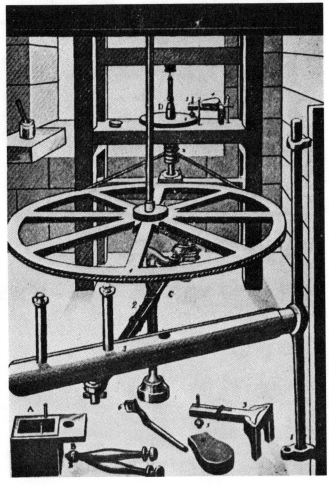

Fig. 9.6. *Diamond polisher's equipment shown in A. Felibien's book of 1676. The beam across the picture is moved to and fro by the handles to turn the large wheel and drive the scaife under the window. In the foreground left are the tools used for cleaving and bruting and on the right a tang, a weight and, centre, a spanner. On the shelf, left background, is a pestle and mortar for making diamond powder.*

Fig. 9.7. *The bruter (cutter) at work, from Mawe's book of 1823. The box receives powder produced. On the right is a charcoal fire to soften the cement for fixing diamonds in the sticks. This method is also used to produce a notch or kerf (Fig. 9.11) for the cleaving blade.*

Fig. 9.8. *Joseph Asscher cleaving the huge Cullinan diamond on 10th February 1907. Special tools were made for the task.*

diamond workers, made in Holland in 1965, show a lever that was hand-driven (Figs. 9.3 and 9.6).

Horse-drive became general in the first quarter of the nineteenth century. By mid-nineteenth century, the Industrial Revolution was responsible for the introduction of steam engines into diamond factories to drive a number of scaifes through shafts and belts. In this century, the coming of electric power resulted in scaifes being driven by individual electric motors. They are always driven anti-clockwise.

Fig. 9.9.   *Charles M. Field with the first diamond cutting machine which he patented in 1876*
He was the shop foreman to Henry D. Morse, who introduced diamond cutting into America in
1861.

Incidentally, some diamond factories are still set up with the polishers sitting at long benches with their backs to the light. This is a tradition carried over from the days of hand-drive when the flywheel took up most of the room.

Polisher's Equipment

The earliest reliable record of a diamond polisher's equipment is that published in 1676, by A. Felibien, a French architect. One of his illustrations (Fig. 9.6) shows the scaife and the dop tang (a kind of very squat three-legged stool) on the far bench. The diamond to be polished was fixed in a solder dop and was fitted to the tang to provide one of the legs. The polisher sat with his back to the window at the far end. The scaife was driven by the big cartwheel type of flywheel, turned by a crank attached to the thick horizontal arm in the foreground. The upright handles were grasped by an assistant (usually one of the polisher's family) to move the arm backwards and forwards.

Cleaving Diamond

On the left at the bottom of the drawing are a cleaver's box and lying beside it, two holders, or cleaver's sticks. The origin of cleaving is unknown. De Boot believed a cleaver could split a diamond with his fingernail and a certain amount of know-how! The diamond is cleaved with a blade and a mallet as described in Chapter Eleven (Figs. 11.7 to 11.10).

Cleaving has not changed from the early days until now, either in its technique or in the tools employed. The mystery clung to it longer than other fabricating

Fig. 9.10. *A polishing bench in John Mawe's book with a weighted tang being used on the scaife (spelt skive in the book) and another with its diamond being inspected. On the left is a pestle and mortar for making diamond dust and beside it glasses of olive oil and diamond powder.*

Fig. 9.11. *Diamond polishing equipment in mid-nineteenth century. The scaife spindles are running in blocks of the hard wood, lignum vitae (as in Fig. 9.10). Top right is a tang with dop fitted and right a tang showing the tail. The brazier in the centre was to melt the solder in the dop, which holds the diamond being polished and is like an acorn in its cup.*

practices, largely because nothing was known of crystallography, and the diamond cleaver developed his own rules-of-thumb.

Even J. Mawe in 1823 referred to the fact that cleavers kept their art a secret. Despite this, the English physicist, Robert Boyle, had given a correct explanation of octahedral cleaving in relation to the diamond cutters' grain in 1672 in his *Essay about the Origine and Virtue of Gems*. (He also mentioned trigons – triangular pits – on octahedral faces.)

Bruting (Cutting) Diamonds

The process of rounding the corners of a diamond is known as bruting. In the past it was a form of hand grinding carried out with the same tools as cleaving. A stone called a sharp, cemented in the end of one stick, was used to rub the corners off a stone cemented in the other stick, by holding one stick in each hand as shown in Fig. 9.7, which is taken from Mawe's treatise. The vigorous rubbing action was carried on over the cleaving box to catch the chips of diamond.

Very considerable force was needed when bruting by hand and the crystals could be only approximately rounded. The two vertical steel pegs that can be seen projecting upwards from the edge of the cleaver's box in Fig. 11.10 are to give purchase when bruting. The bruter wore leather gloves but still suffered from damage to his hands.

The old method of bruting by hand over the cleaver's box persisted until the end of the nineteenth century. In 1891, D. Rodrigues took out a British patent for a bruting machine driven by power, and it was his type of machines that eventually came into use. Grodzinski recorded having seen a machine-bruted diamond made in 1826, however.

Diamond Powder

Chips and other pieces of diamond unsuitable for making into gems were crushed into powder with pestle and mortar, which may be seen in Fig. 9.6 on the small table on the left beside the bench in the window. It was necessary to hammer the pestle to break up larger diamond chips.

Producing diamond dust for grinding and polishing by this method is surprisingly efficient. The dust will pass through present-day commercial sieves. Over nine-tenths of the powder is under one micron (under a fifty-thousandth of an inch) and the largest grains are only about twenty microns. Unsieved powder is still used today by diamond polishers, although many now use graded synthetic diamond powder. Diamond is the only material that can be polished by ungraded powder. Industrial users prefer to have it sieved and graded, because any larger grains in a powder will scratch metals being polished. See also pages 391 to 392.

Fig. 9.12. *Another polisher's workshop of later nineteenth century. The pins at the ends of the bars fixed on the benches (left) are to prevent tangs from being swept off the rotating scaifes. The tang is placed between the pins.*

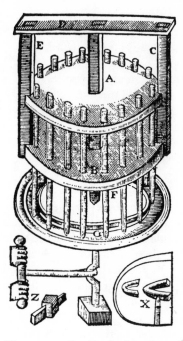

Fig. 9.13. *A solder dop which was in use until 1975. It is identical to those used centuries ago and still in use today. The copper stalk is bent to achieve the correct facet angle.*

Fig. 9.14. *De Boot's invention of 1604 for polishing sixteen diamonds at the same time.*

Tang and Dop

The tang and dop for grinding and polishing are seen in more detail in the foreground on the right in Felibien's drawing (Fig. 9.6). The tang is, in modern engineer's language, the tool holder. When using metal-cutting lathes, the operator always held the tool by hand until Maudslay invented the fixed tool holder (saddle) at the beginning of the nineteenth century, yet the fixed tool holder for diamond cutting was in use from the fifteenth century (Fig. 9.10).

The dop which held the diamond was originally a cup on a thick copper stalk, and often still is today. The diamond to be cut is fixed in a fairly large bulk of plumber's solder in the cup. (Fig. 9.13.) The solder was softened in a gas flame and the diamond embedded in it, the only part exposed being that to be ground and polished. The solder was worked, while soft, into a cone shape, with the diamond at the point, by a worker known as a vesteller. He used his thumb on the hot solder to smooth it, and consequently developed a really tough skin because the solder melts at about 420°F (215°C). There are still a few vestellers in the diamond cutting trade. Originally a coke brazier was used. (Fig. 9.11.)

A weight was sometimes placed on top of the tang, as mentioned by Cellini, to increase the grinding pressure. Such a weight is seen in the foreground of the illustration Fig. 9.6, with the spanner used for tightening the clamp for the dop. An early workshop is shown in Fig. 9.12.

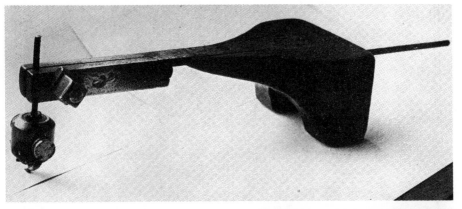

Fig. 9.15. *A tang which was in use until 1975. It is no different from one used a century ago except for the dop it holds.* (right) *A larger picture of the dop which is used to hold the diamond table up to polish the bezel facets. The stalk is bent to achieve the required facet angle.*

Mechanical Dops

In the second half of the twentieth century, the mechanical dop employing clamps instead of solder to hold the diamond became more common, and quadrants to set the angles were incorporated in some tangs. De Boot had suggested such quadrant devices, and also showed an invention of his own for polishing sixteen diamonds at the same time, in his book of 1604 (Fig. 9.14).

The clamp of the mechanical dop allows the stone to be turned easily and quickly to position it for grinding another facet, whereas turning a stone in a solder dop is a lengthy performance, but the advantages are not all on one side. It is easier to lose a stone from a mechanical dop and also the stone becomes hotter because air does not conduct away the heat generated by polishing as quickly as solder does.

Today, for small stones, there are automatic dops which change their positions to grind facets semi-automatically. One version will place forty-eight facets on the girdle of a diamond without attention in about two minutes. The traditional methods are always used for larger and more important stones, however.

Sawing Diamonds

Sawing was used to remove flawed parts, which it is impossible or uneconomic to

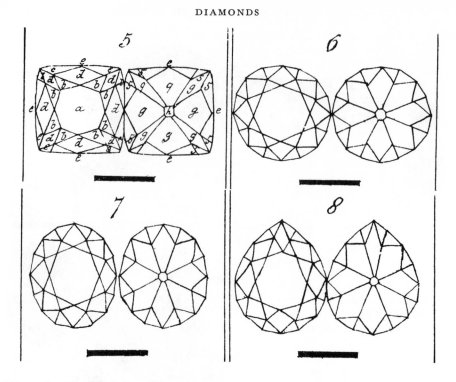

Fig. 9.16. *Illustration from* Treatise on Diamonds and Pearls *by David Jeffries, 1750, which are described as:* 5 – a square; 6 – a round; 7 – an oval; 8 – a drop. *Each is shown with the crown on the left and pavilion on the right; depths are shown by the horizontal bars underneath.*

remove by cleaving, or to reduce the size of a crystal. John Mawe described the saw in 1823. 'It was', he wrote, 'made of a fine wire of brass or iron, attached to the two ends of a piece of cane or whalebone, the teeth being formed by the particles of diamond powder, which became embedded in the wire, as soon as it is applied to the line.'

The bow saw was the ancient Chinese tool for sawing jade using crushed garnet as an abrasive. The line referred to by Mawe was a notch cut in the edge of a stone by rubbing with a sharp – as when preparing a stone for cleaving (Fig. 11.8). The notch or kerf was filled with oil and diamond dust.

The sawing direction seems always to have been 'in the cube plane', as when cutting off the point of an octahedron to form a table stone. The process was very laborious and it is recorded that it took a year to cut the 410-carat Regent Diamond in half. Mawe wrote, 'If the stone be large, the labour of eight to ten months is sometimes required to complete the operation.'

Circular saws for cutting gems were referred to by Felibien in 1676, the saw blade being vertical as modern practice, but it was apparently not until much later, about 1900, that the method was applied to diamonds.

L. Claremont wrote in 1906, 'There is in use in Amsterdam an instrument in the form of a circular saw, for the purpose of dividing diamonds. It consists of a small, thin metal disc, with an edge prepared with diamond powder. . . .

With this machine it is possible to cut through a diamond in any direction. The process, however, sometimes takes as long as two or three weeks.'

Claremont was wrong about being able to saw in any direction. It is impossible to saw in an octahedral direction because the diamond will cleave instead. Diamond was at first always sawn in the cubic direction and it was not until the 1930s that it was sawn in the dodecahedral direction as well. Today, sawing is the usual practice with octahedral crystals. Banks of sawing machines are tended by a single sawyer.

Centuries ago, diamond polishers used to carry round with them their scaifes, and tangs and dops, and set them up where they worked. Even today there are highly-skilled polishers who will only use their own scaifes and not those supplied by the firm for which they work. There is still very much individuality about these craftsmen, who are temperamental and still regard their craft as a highly personal art.

Effect of Different Diamonds

After the discovery of the diamond fields in Africa, the craft of cutting and polishing expanded considerably and skills were extended to include knowledge of the attributes and disadvantages of stones from different mines. For example, those from the Jagersfontein mine were regarded as 'brittle'. They were not often sawn for this reason and were bruted (cut) with care, using olive oil as a lubricant. Special attention was required when mounting 'Jagers' in solder drops because the stone could crack if overheated and quenched in water. Instead, the dop was cooled in wet sand, taking care not to touch the diamond with the sand. Wesselton rough had a reputation for greyness. Sometimes the polished stone remained greyish, with a loss of brilliance; at others the greyness was like a 'skin' and the stone was yellowish inside.

When cutters and polishers were faced with important, expensive or large stones and decisions had to be made about the best way to saw or cleave it, a technique for making plaster casts from clay moulds was developed so that the casts could be sawn and filed in various ways to discover the most effective means of treatment.

REFERENCES

Gemmarum et Lapidum Historia, by A. Boetius de Boot (1604).
Essay about the Origin and Virtue of Gems, by R. Boyle (London, 1672).
Treatises on Goldsmithing and Sculpture, by Benvenuto Cellini (Florence, 1568).
A History of Jewellery 1100–1870, by Joan Evans (London, 1953).
Des Principes de l'Architecture, de la Sculpture, de la Peinture et des Autres Arts qui en Dependent, by A. Felibien (Paris, 1676).
Diamond Technology, by P. Grodzinski (London, 2nd ed., 1953).
The History of Diamond Production and the Diamond Trade, by Godehard Lenzen (London, 1970).
Treatise on Diamond and Precious Stones, by J. Mawe (London, 2nd ed., 1823).
Industrial Diamond Review. 'Special Supplement on History of Diamond Polishing', by Grodzinski and Feldhaus (London, 1953).

CHAPTER TEN

The History of Cuts

About 1490, Bartolomeo de Pasti wrote a book of commerce which referred to two types of diamond, *diamanti*, which were shipped to Antwerp, and *diamanti in punto*, which went to Lisbon and Paris. *Diamanti* were no doubt rough sent for cutting. *Diamanti in punto* were pointed stones, which may have been octahedral rough called glassies or point-cut stones.

The Point Cut
Pointed diamonds in old jewellery have angles appreciably below those of the natural octahedron and must have been fashioned into point cuts. The point cut is believed to be the earliest diamond cut (Fig. 1.7). Macles – flat, triangular octahedral twins with specular faces top and bottom – were also set in jewellery.

Pointed stones appeared in diamond jewellery of the Middle Ages, and remained popular into the Renaissance period. The first true cut for diamond was the table cut, introduced into Europe some time before 1538, perhaps with the invention of bruting, but maybe earlier if the flat table facet was produced by grinding.

The Table Cut
The table cut was an octahedron with its top point flattened to a square facet called the table, as shown in Fig. 1.8. Sometimes the lower point was also ground to make a smaller facet, the collet or culet. Many early table stones had a facet on the bottom about half the size of the table facet on the top and were known as Indian-cut as they came from the Orient. Most were re-cut in Europe. The table cut was produced by bruting and polishing.

Cutting was dominated by the table stone throughout the sixteenth century and into the beginning of the seventeenth, because classical influences remained and the golden mean of Pythagoras, who mingled geometry with magic, was exemplified by the cut. Although the golden mean was the ratio 1:1·618, it was based on the square; the table stone from the top presented one square within another. Many coloured stones were also table cut for what seemed to be the same reasons.

Point stones were still common during the period, but they were gradually being re-cut as table stones. De Boot of Bruges, writing in 1600, described in detail the procedure for manufacturing a table-cut stone out of a pointed stone.

The Rose Cut
A rose-cut stone has a flat back and a domed and faceted front. The form may be as old as the table cut because the Koh-i-Nûr, which was cut no later than

The larger pipe at Letseng-la-Terai in late 1977, after it had begun full production. One area of kimberlite within the kimberlitic body is expected to produce very large diamonds.

Pomona, the suction dredging barge that worked the sea bed, but unprofitably, off the coast of Namibia for some years. The top of the living quarters is a helicopter landing platform.

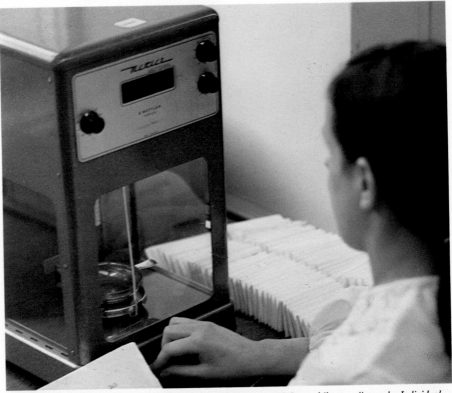

The Diamond Trading Company grades and weighs 80 per cent of the world's gem diamonds. Individual weighing (as above) has been joined by computer-controlled automatic methods.

Some diggers selling to the Diamond Buying Office in Tshikapa, Zaire, are casual about what they use as weights; matchsticks and crown bottle tops are employed.

530, was a form of rose cut, as was the Great Mogul (Fig. 10.1). Cellini described, in 1568, methods of cutting the rose and faceted stones as well as table-ut and pointed stones.

The shape of the original diamond crystal largely determines the shape into which it will be cut. The rose was found to be more suitable for flatter and thinner rough. The name of the 'modern' rose cut, from the seventeenth century, derived from the fact that it is supposed to look like an opening rose bud. It can show considerable life, but is invariably deficient in fire.

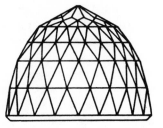

Fig. 10.1. *The Great Mogul diamond, from the Kollur Mines in India, which is said to have weighed $787\frac{1}{2}$ carats in the rough and 280 carats when cut.*

Rose-like cuts were already in wide use in the first half of the fifteenth century. They were of various shapes, triangular being the most common, with each face divided into three facets. The term rosette stood for an early arrangement of diamonds of pear-shaped outline arranged in a circle like petals of a flower.

Both Amsterdam and Antwerp specialized in rose cuts, particularly in the eighteenth and nineteenth centuries. The Dutch rose is more pointed than most other rose cuts. The facets are in groups of six, the upper or central ones being known as the crown or star facets, and the surrounding outer groups of six, the teeth. The height is usually half the diameter of the stone and the diameter of the base of the crown about three-quarters of the diameter. The base of the crown is usually three-fifths of the total height from the base (Fig. 10.6).

The Antwerp rose, also called the Brabant rose, was not as common as the Dutch rose. It is not as high and the base is more steeply inclined, while the crown is less so (Fig. 10.6).

Most rose-cut diamonds were round, but some were of oval and pear-shaped outline. There were, of course, other variations of the rose in the arrangement of the facets. The double rose had some popularity in the nineteenth century and the earlier part of this century for ear-rings and watch-chain pendants before the wrist watch became popular. The stone is faceted in a dome on both sides. The double rose cut is old, because at least two historic diamonds, the Florentine and the Sancy, were cut in this way.

Diamonds faceted all over, called briolettes, pendeloques and beads, are a form of rose cutting. Both are shown in Fig. 10.8. They were often pierced along their lengths for use as earrings or beads and sometimes through the tops, when used as a pendant.

Faceted Octahedra

The table stone lent itself to modification by adding facets. The first elaboration was to grind and polish the four edges of the table and the pavilion to provide

four extra narrow facets on the top and four on the bottom to improve brillianc
and lustre. This modification is shown in Fig. 10.3. Further modifications int
more complex pattern of facets were similarly possible by grinding facets o
edges, as shown in the same illustration.

It seems likely that from about 1500 to about 1650, the table cut was the mos
popular, but there were point-cut stones in use, too, although many were bein
re-cut to table stones and, for the more ashionable wearer, some table cut
were being modified by adding extra facets. Modifications were also being mad
to the outline of the stone, when seen in plan, by rounding the corners b
bruting before faceting, and later by rounding the sides. Up to this time, th
octahedral origin of the cut stone was clearly discernible. Although the outlin
was changed, the angles of the table and the pavilion to the girdle remaine
not very different from those of the original crystal, about 55°.

Early inventories refer to diamonds 'taille à facettes', but what was mean
were what we call rose-cut stones. For example, the necklace worn by Marie d
Medici for her wedding in 1600 included six table-cut diamonds and two rose
cut (taille à facettes). But when Charles, Prince of Wales, went to Spain in
1623, he borrowed a hat band mounted with gold buttons in which were se
eight 'four-square Table Dyamonds, two flower-square Table Dyamonds cu
with fawcettes, two large poynted dyamonds, one faire Hart Dyamond and
three tryangle Dyamonds'. The table diamonds with facets were presumably
something like the old single cut.

The Old Single Cut

Professor Joan Evans in her book *History of Jewellery 1100–1870* writes tha
diamonds 'taille en seige' were introduced between 1640 and 1645. Diamond
'cut into sixteen' presumably refers to the old single cut similar to that shown in
Fig. 10.3. These were the simple pre-brilliant shapes based on the octahedra
crystal.

Logical addition of facets led to the rounded single cut, English star and
square cuts and other variations.

The Mazarin Cut

One of the early faceted cuts has become known as the Mazarin cut, having
been named after Cardinal Mazarin of France (1602–61), who was one o
Tavernier's best customers. His diamonds included the famous Sancy and the
Mirror of Portugal. He left them in his Will to the French Crown on condition
that they were to be known as The Mazarin Diamonds (see Chapter Twenty).

The cut was cushion-shaped in outline with seventeen facets above the girdle,
including the table, and seventeen facets below, including the culet. The cut was
not invented by the Cardinal, but was, according to H. Tillander, introduced
before his era, in about 1620 (Fig. 10.3). Mr Tillander says the cut is rare and,
as far as he has discovered, is not included in the Mazarin diamonds, most of
which were table-cut.

Early cuts had a large culet, by modern standards, as it was needed as a
reflecting facet to increase brilliance. In the early twentieth century, the lower

art of the stone, the pavilion, was made shallower to improve internal reflec-
on and more or less eliminate the culet.

The various versions of faceted cuts may have evolved into what became
nown as the brilliant cut, but this is in doubt.

The Brilliant Cut

There was no single inventor of the brilliant cut although it is often credited to a
eventeenth-century Venetian lapidary named Vincenzio (or Vicenzo) Perruzzi,
bout 1700. One faceted cut is named after him. Research by H. Tillander has
hown that the Perruzzi family came from Florence and that there is no record
f a member named Vincenzio.

Faceted diamonds based on the octahedron with rounded corners or cushion
utlines, as well as the more modern conical shapes with round outlines, were all
alled brilliant-cut diamonds and referred to colloquially as brilliants.

An increase in the cutting of brilliants occurred about mid-seventeenth
century, and the eighteenth saw a spate of re-cutting to modernize old cuts. This
vas partly due to the awakening of interest in technical innovation and partly
lue to the waning interest in the invariable classical form of the table stone.
Rough stones were often rounded by the immensely laborious process of hand
ruting if they were of octahedral form. Many cutters, however, according to
Tillander, found that rough of approximately rhombic dodecahedral form lent
tself naturally to the fashioning of brilliant-cut stones. As there were insufficient
rystals of dodecahedral shape, someone named Perruzzi may have invented a
imilar design from octahedral rough.

The discovery of the Brazilian deposits gave great impetus to the brilliant cut
n a form known as the triple cut, shown in Fig. 10.4, and today usually referred
o as old-mine cut. The girdle outline is cushion-shaped and there are thirty-
hree facets on the crown and twenty-five on the pavilion, making fifty-eight in
ll, the same as the modern brilliant. Another name for these stones is old-
niners.

Even as late as 1750, the English jeweller David Jeffries thought the
rilliant cut to be a whim of fashion and that the rose cut would outlive it,
ut over the next two centuries large numbers of old roses were re-cut to
rilliant form with 'dreadful sacrifice of weight', as C. W. King put it in
870. Some cuts illustrated by Jeffries are shown in Fig. 9.16.

Smaller and less valuable stones were double cut instead of being triple cut.
The double cut was an older style with a square table and sixteen other facets
n the top with duplicate facets on the bottom, except that the culet was much
maller than the table, making a total of thirty-four. There was an English
louble-cut brilliant that had the triangular corner facets reversed so that the
able became octagonal and the centre of an eight-rayed star, while the pavilion
emained similar to that of the double cut except for the loss of four corner
acets (Fig. 10.3).

The outline of the girdle of a stone depended much more on the form of the
crystal before it was cut in earlier days than today because the problems of
manufacture were greater. Most girdle outlines became cushion-shaped, as
lready mentioned, but some were almost or quite round and others of rounded

triangular shape, when the facets were grouped in threes instead of fours. Other crystals lent themselves to the manufacture of oval or pear-shaped brilliants.

Most historical diamonds were cut in modifications of the brilliant form, although the original cut of some was different. The retention of weight has been an important consideration when cutting or re-cutting, however, so that the full brilliance has not always been achieved.

In the nineteenth century, more rounded brilliants appeared and with these and cushion shapes, English cutters tended to make thinner girdles than Dutch cutters, an indication of origin. The thin girdles have often become chipped. Round brilliants of the time, with small tables and large culets by modern standards and greater overall depth to the stone, are known in England as Victorian cut.

The Modern Brilliant Cut

The modern brilliant cut came about with the publication of the ideal dimensions in a theoretical treatise on the subject by Marcel Tolkowsky in 1914. The angles of the pavilion to the girdle and the angle of the crown had been largely determined by the octahedral crystal angles although some cutters particularly in New York, U.S.A., had previously been experimenting and discovered that they could increase brilliance by reducing these angles.

Making brilliants to Tolkowsky's ideal cut involved much more work on the rough material and encouraged the introduction of machine bruting to round the crystals and machine sawing to shape material. Not all brilliant cut-diamonds were cut to the ideal proportions by any means, but Tolkowsky's work had a very important influence on the cutting of larger and higher quality material. Lower quality rough was cut to retain maximum weight, as it is today.

The brilliant cut with the round girdle became almost universal. The culet was small, but still very noticeable through the table, and the facets below the girdle reached about half-way down the pavilion, as shown in Fig. 10.4. After the Second World War, there were further small modifications. The lower girdle facets became gradually longer some extending to eight-tenths the distance down the pavilion, and the table tended to become larger, resulting in a shallower crown.

A modern form of the ideal cut is shown in Fig. 10.2. The names of the facets of the brilliant originate from cutting procedures and can be quite complex, particularly of those around the girdle, which have been simplified to upper and lower girdle facets in the diagram.

Variations of the Brilliant Cut

The brilliant cut is applied to shapes other than the conical or standard brilliant. They include the boat-shaped marquise or navette cut, the pear-shaped pendeloque cut, the oval brilliant cut, and the heart-shaped brilliant cut. They are shown in Fig. 10.5.

It has been pointed out that for a gem such as diamond, depending for some of its beauty on colour dispersion, the number of facets should be increased with the size of stone. S. Rosch suggested that no facets should be longer than

·118 in (3 mm) or shorter than 0·019 in. ($\frac{1}{2}$ mm), from which it follows that stones of over 10 carats should have more than fifty-eight facets, and those of under $\frac{1}{8}$-carat (about twelve points) should have fewer facets to give maximum brilliance.

In fact most small stones today are made as eight-cuts (single-cuts), or Swiss-cuts, with fewer facets as shown in Fig. 10.7. For larger stones there are several modifications of the brilliant cut with more facets, including the Jubilee with eighty-eight, the King with eighty-six, and the Cairo star cut with seventy-four, as shown in Fig. 10.5.

Faceted Girdles

The girdle of a brilliant-cut diamond is normally left in its bruted state, which is matt, so that it reflects very little light internally. The loss is very small if the girdle is of normal width. A few cutters concerned with high quality do facet or polish the girdles of stones, however. Louis H. Roselar in the U.S.A. placed forty small facets around the girdle. A. Monnickendam in England polishes the girdle in a circle without facets by a special technique.

Patents on faceted girdles have now expired and some other cutters add them to the standard brilliant-cut. In one version, known as the Royal 144, forty extra facets are placed on the girdle, and forty-eight more, as a 'wreath' of extra cross, skill and kite facets on the pavilion near the girdle. These are claimed to add to the stone's brilliance, but can hardly do so. Small facets are today often cut very rapidly by automatic processes.

Girdles of polished stones that are not round, including pendeloque, emerald, and square cuts, are ground and polished. The girdle of marquise stones can be bruted or ground and polished.

Step and Square Cuts

A step or trap cut may have pointed or bevelled corners. When such cuts are bevelled, they are often called emerald cuts (Fig. 10.8). Diamonds cut thus naturally lose brilliance and lustre because the cuts are not ideal from the point of view of beauty. The proportions of both can vary from square or almost square to a long oblong, depending on the shape of the original crystal. Steps cuts are often made from octahedra that are elongated in one direction. When the shape is very elongated in relation to its width, the cut stone is called a baguette after the long French loaf, shown in Fig. 10.7.

It is possible that the earliest baguette diamonds were produced in India by cleavage in a dodecahedral direction from an octahedral crystal to give long, boat-shaped chips.

The most common fault in an emerald or square-cut stone is a window, a facet through which one can see, looking at the stone from the table. The number of steps is unimportant, but to avoid windows, the pavilion facets should be cut at greater than the critical angle of 24° 26'. This is sometimes difficult, if not impossible, particularly with the end pavilion facets of an elongated octahedron crystal.

As the pavilion of a step or square-cut stone is deeper than that of a brilliant-cut stone, the crown should be shallower, in order to make the overall depth about the same as an equivalent brilliant. Brilliance is lost when a stone is over deep. A rule of thumb is that the width of the bottom pavilion facets should together be about equal to the width of the table.

Similar considerations apply to diamonds cut in triangle, kite, and other shapes, but when such shapes are favoured it is often because of particular shape and flatness of the rough, so that it is difficult or impossible to apply sound optical principles to the cut.

Brilliant Square Cut

The fact that square and emerald-cut diamonds lose so much in brilliance, fire and scintillation compared with round brilliant-cut stones does not often compensate for the extra weight retained by the square or emerald cut. With this in mind, and the call by jewellery designers for a brilliant square cut, a Johannesburg cutter and polisher, Basil Watermeyer achieved in 1971, after many years of experiment, the most brilliant square cut so far.

Called the Barion cut, combining his wife's name Marion with his initial, it has twenty-five facets on the crown and twenty-nine on the pavilion, a total of sixty-two, as shown in Fig. 10.9. There are half-moon facets just below the girdle (which is polished) on each side. This enables an emerald-cut pavilion to be superimposed on a modified brilliant-cut pavilion.

The design provides more scintillation than a normal step cut because, when the stone is tilted, the steps on the crown break up the reflections from the pavilion to provide a fountain-like pattern. The fire is equivalent to that of a round brilliant cut, although weight retention from the rough is much higher; the design avoids the lumpy appearance that causes a dark centre.

Other Modern Cuts

Among other cuts employed in modern times are two designed for macles, the 48-facet troidia, devised by Edouard Sirakiar in Belgium, and the new trilliant developed by Asscher's Diamant Maatschappij in Amsterdam, Holland, which has forty-four facets and a polished girdle (Fig. 10.10). P. Lancon of Geneva, Switzerland, developed a star-shaped cut (Fig. 10.11) and another Belgian cutter and polisher has managed to produce many shapes including the horse's head shown in Fig. 10.12.

In 1960, a London cutter, A. Nagy, introduced an unusual and economic cut for flat crystals to give a large superficial area of diamond. It was at first called the Princess cut and is now the profile cut. The shape, shown in Fig. 10.8, is based on a cut originally developed for diamond tools used for dressing grinding wheels. It comprises a series of V-grooves on the back of the stone at the angle shown in the diagram. The cut is lively, but lacks fire.

Diamond Cuts

The various ways in which diamonds can be shaped and faceted may be divided into four main groups, each containing variations on a basic cut. They are listed in the following table.

BRILLIANT CUT

Possible Chronological Development

Point cut (corrected octahedron with 8 polished faces)
Many fancy shapes
Table cut (9 to 10 facets)
Tablet cut
English square cut (17 + 13 = 30 facets)
Mazarin cut and variations
(17 + 17 = 34 facets)
Perruzzi cut (33 + 25 = 58 facets)
Rounded single cut (9 + 9 = 18 facets)

English star cut (17 + 9 = 26 facets)
Old mine or cushion cut (33 + 25 = 58 facets) and variations with same number of more facets
Old European round brilliant cut (33 + 25 = 58 facets)
English round cut brilliant cut (33 + 25 = 58 facets)
Full cut or modern brilliant cut (33 + 25 = 58 facets)

Note: *Only the full brilliant cut, under chronological development, is now made. It outnumbers all other cuts by a vast majority.*

Variations on the Brilliant Cut with more Facets

Jubilee or twentieth century cut (40 + 40 = 80 facets)
King cut (49 + 37 = 86 facets)
Cairo Star cut (74 facets)

Magna cut (61 + 41 = 102 facets)
Royal 144 (33 + 73 + 48 on girdle = 154 facets)

Note: *There are many other cuts with more facets but few are used. The Royal 144 is the only one for smaller stones.*

Modern Shaped Variations of the Brilliant Cut

Oval brilliant cut (33 + 25 = 58 facets)
Marquise or navette cut (33 + 25 = 58 facets)
Heart-shaped brilliant cut (37 + 28 = 65 facets)

Troida cut (48 facets)
Barion cut (35 + 29 = 62 facets)
Pendeloque or pear-shaped brilliant cut (33 + 25 = 58 facets)
Trilliant cut (25 + 19 = 44 facets)

Note: *33 + 25 = 58 facets, etc., means that there are 33 facets on the top of the stone, and 25 under it, totalling 58. Both table and culet (although sometimes a point) are counted as facets.*

Round Cuts for Small Stones

Single or eight cut (9 + 9 = 18 facets)
Swiss cut (17 + 17 = 34 facets)

French cut (9 + 9 = 18 facets)
Split brilliant (21 + 21 = 42 facets)

ROSE CUT

Triangular rose
Full Dutch rose or Holland rose (24 + 1 = 25 facets)
Double-Dutch rose or Double Holland rose (36 + 1 = 37 facets)
Pear-shaped rose (24 + 1 = 25 facets)
Boat-shaped rose (24 + 1 = 25 facets)

Double rose (24 + 24 = 48 facets
Half brilliant (33 + 1 = 34 facets)
Twelve-facet rose, Antwerp-rose or Brabant rose (12 + 1 = 13 facets)
Six-facet rose (6 + 1 = 7 facets)
Three-facet rose (3 + 1 = 4 facets)

Note: *Larger rose cuts are not now made except perhaps for a special purpose such as restoration of a piece of antique jewellery, but many roses up to 30 or 40 points still come from Amsterdam.*

STEP CUT

Emerald cut (square or oblong in shape with truncated corners)

Square cut or bevel cut (square in shape with pointed corners)

Baguette (long oblong with pointed corners)

Tapered baguette

Spade baguette or bullet cut

Pentagon

Triangle

Kite

Hexagon

Long hexagon

Octagon

Long octagon

Trapeze

Lozenge

Trap brilliant and many others, mainly for smaller diamonds used as surrounds

Note: *The numbers of facets are not given for step-cut stones because they vary with the size of the stone. Larger emerald cuts are relatively common, but most step cuts are for smaller, thinner rough.*

BEAD CUT

Bead   Briolette   Rondelle   Note: *All are rare.*

Miscellaneous: Princess or profile cut.

Principles of Diamond Design: Lustre

As the most prized diamonds are colourless, their beauty depends entirely upon their optical properties other than colour – high refractive index, high degree of clarity, colour dispersion, reflectivity, and lustre. To make the most of optical effects, the designer is obviously confined by optical laws.

The quality of light reflected from the surface of a material is known as its lustre. In diamond, this quality is unique and is known as adamantine lustre. The only other gems approaching it in lustre are zircon and demantoid garnet.

Lustre depends not only on the light reflected from the surface, but on rays that have been partly absorbed before being reflected back. Materials of high transparency, such as diamond and glass, would not be expected to be very reflective, and most are not, but diamond is an exception. The surface will reflect about 17 per cent of the light falling directly on it, compared with about 5 per cent of light falling on a transparent paste (glass) gem.

Changing intensities of light reflected are important in lustre. If a diamond were cut out of a flat plate and seen by a stationary observer in motionless surroundings, it would appear to have little lustre. Cut in rose or brilliant style and seen in moving candlelight, it would have a high lustre.

Reflection and Life

Lustre plays only a small part in the total optical effect because the other 83 per cent of light falling on the front of a gem passes into it. The objective of the design is to make sure that such light is not lost through the back and sides, but is reflected internally and sent back to the eyes of the viewer. The most important factor to him is the critical angle of diamond, the angle at which total internal reflection of light occurs. It depends upon the refractive index and for diamond is 24° 26'.

PARTS AND FACETS OF THE BRILLIANT CUT

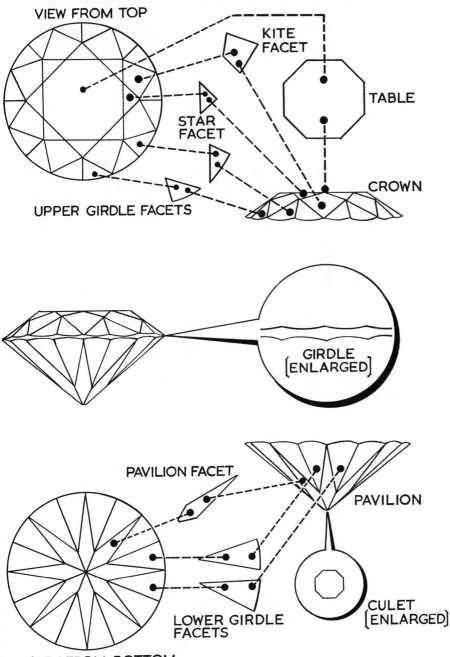

VIEW FROM TOP

KITE FACET

TABLE

STAR FACET

CROWN

UPPER GIRDLE FACETS

GIRDLE [ENLARGED]

PAVILION FACET

PAVILION

LOWER GIRDLE FACETS

CULET [ENLARGED]

VIEW FROM BOTTOM

Fig. 10.2.   *Parts of the brilliant cut diamond. The names of the facets have been simplified from the old cutters' terms and are generally accepied.*

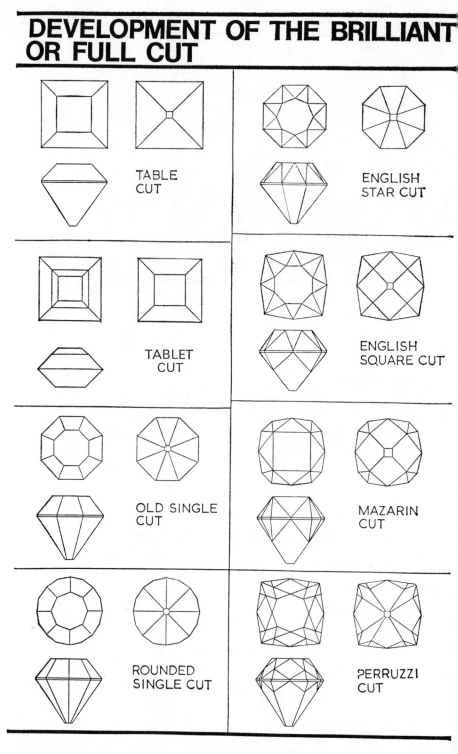

TABLE CUT

ENGLISH STAR CUT

TABLET CUT

ENGLISH SQUARE CUT

OLD SINGLE CUT

MAZARIN CUT

ROUNDED SINGLE CUT

PERRUZZI CUT

Fig. 10.3.

DEVELOPMENT OF THE BRILLIANT OR FULL CUT

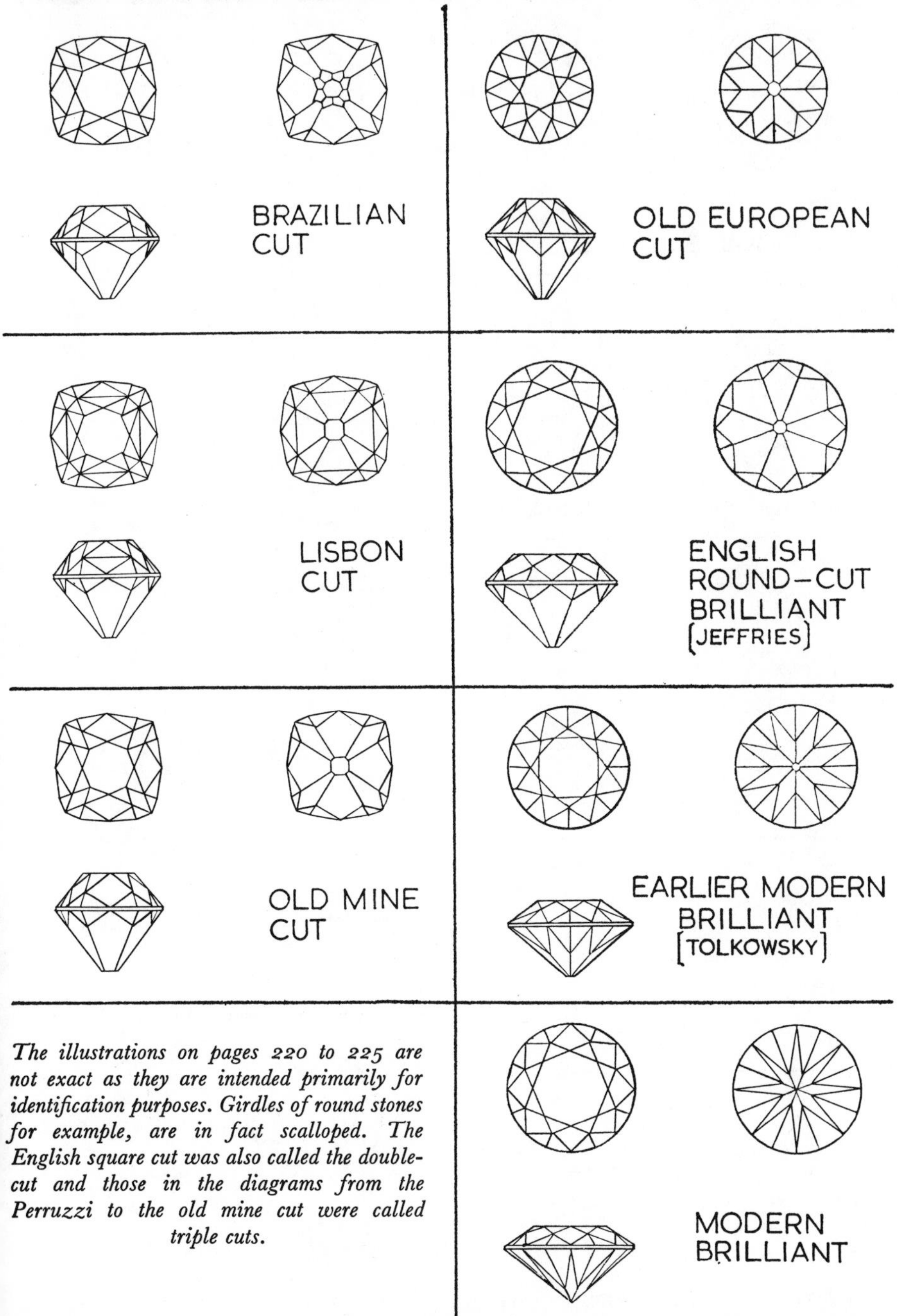

BRAZILIAN CUT

OLD EUROPEAN CUT

LISBON CUT

ENGLISH ROUND–CUT BRILLIANT [JEFFRIES]

OLD MINE CUT

EARLIER MODERN BRILLIANT [TOLKOWSKY]

The illustrations on pages 220 to 225 are not exact as they are intended primarily for identification purposes. Girdles of round stones for example, are in fact scalloped. The English square cut was also called the double-cut and those in the diagrams from the Perruzzi to the old mine cut were called triple cuts.

MODERN BRILLIANT

Fig. 10.4.

SOME VARIATIONS OF THE BRILLIANT CUT

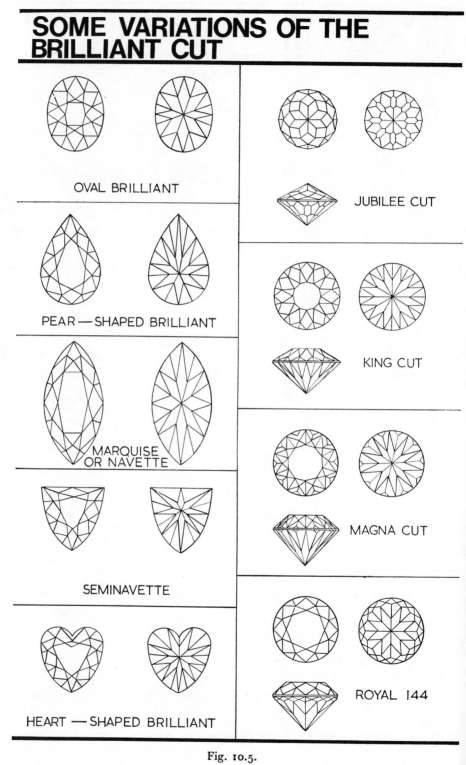

OVAL BRILLIANT

PEAR — SHAPED BRILLIANT

MARQUISE OR NAVETTE

SEMINAVETTE

HEART — SHAPED BRILLIANT

JUBILEE CUT

KING CUT

MAGNA CUT

ROYAL 144

Fig. 10.5.

ROSE CUTS

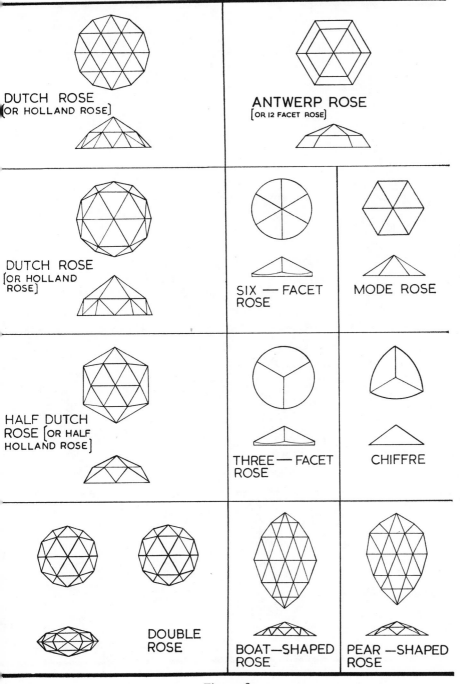

Fig. 10.6.

223

CUTS FOR SMALL STONES

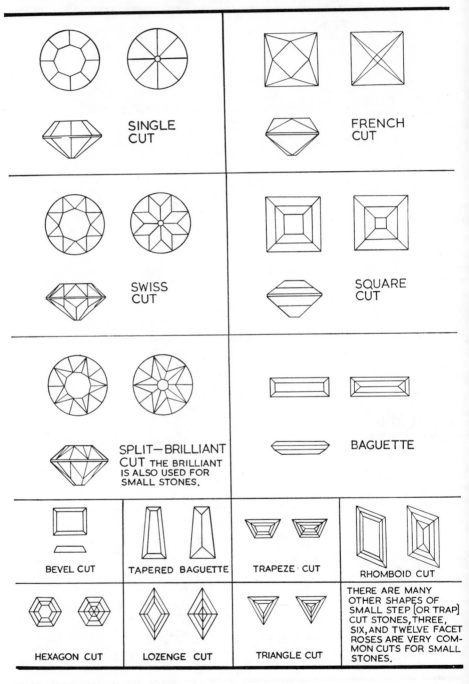

SINGLE CUT

FRENCH CUT

SWISS CUT

SQUARE CUT

SPLIT—BRILLIANT CUT THE BRILLIANT IS ALSO USED FOR SMALL STONES.

BAGUETTE

BEVEL CUT

TAPERED BAGUETTE

TRAPEZE · CUT

RHOMBOID CUT

HEXAGON CUT

LOZENGE CUT

TRIANGLE CUT

THERE ARE MANY OTHER SHAPES OF SMALL STEP [OR TRAP] CUT STONES, THREE, SIX, AND TWELVE FACET ROSES ARE VERY COMMON CUTS FOR SMALL STONES.

Fig. 10.7.   *The single-cut is also called the eight cut.*

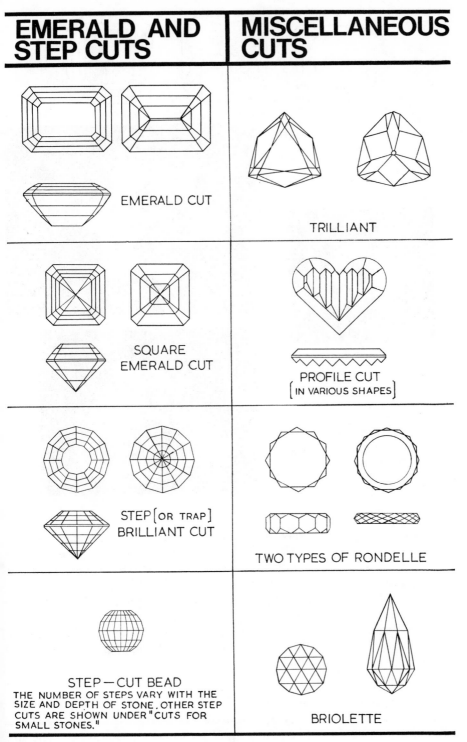

EMERALD AND STEP CUTS	MISCELLANEOUS CUTS
EMERALD CUT	TRILLIANT
SQUARE EMERALD CUT	PROFILE CUT [IN VARIOUS SHAPES]
STEP [OR TRAP] BRILLIANT CUT	TWO TYPES OF RONDELLE
STEP—CUT BEAD THE NUMBER OF STEPS VARY WITH THE SIZE AND DEPTH OF STONE. OTHER STEP CUTS ARE SHOWN UNDER "CUTS FOR SMALL STONES."	BRIOLETTE

Fig. 10.8.

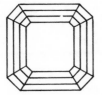
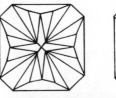

Fig. 10.9. (above)   *The Barion cut, designed to improve the brilliance of square and rectangular stones.*

Fig. 10.10 (above)   *The brilliant cut for triangular rough, developed by Asscher's of Amsterdam.*

Fig. 10.11. (above right)   *Star-haped cut developed by P. Lancon in Switzerland.*

Fig. 10.12. (right)   *A Belgian cutter can produce many shapes, such as this horse's head, weighing 6·50 carats.*

In a cut diamond designed with angles to take fullest advantage of total internal reflection, the back facets will act like mirrors inside the stone and most light entering the stone from the front will therefore be reflected back out of the front, to give maximum life to the stone (Fig. 10.13).

This quality of returning the maximum amount of light from the stone to the eye – from the surface lustre and from internal reflection – is known as 'life'. Accurate design and cut alone will not guarantee maximum life for a diamond, however, because if the stone is flawed or coloured some light will be lost by absorption.

Dispersion and Fire: Scintillation
The fire of a gem is the display of spectrum colours (and scintillation) caused by its refracting white light before returning it to the eye (Fig. 10.14). The fire depends therefore on the dispersive power of the material – diamond has one of

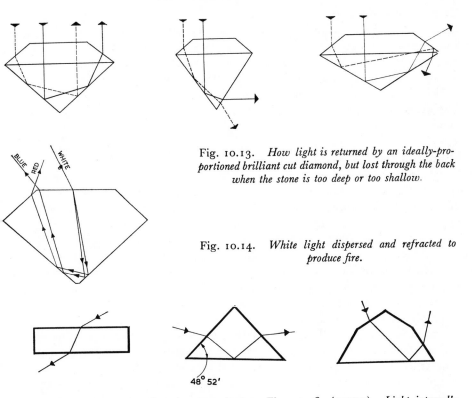

Fig. 10.13. *How light is returned by an ideally-pro-portioned brilliant cut diamond, but lost through the back when the stone is too deep or too shallow.*

Fig. 10.14. *White light dispersed and refracted to produce fire.*

Fig. 10.15. *Light passing through a portrait stone.* Fig. 10.16. (centre) *Light internally reflected from the back of a theoretical rose-cut stone.* Fig. 10.17. *Light internally reflected more towards the front of a rose-cut stone.*

the highest among gems – the amount by which light entering the stone is refracted, and the length of the path of the dispersed beam. Like lustre, fire is enhanced by movement of the stone. As more fire is gained by more refraction, some light will be lost to the viewer as fire is increased, so that the maximum life and maximum fire cannot be achieved at the same time.

There is another optical quality of diamond that does not receive as much attention as the others. It is the scintillation or amount of sparkle, which is the number, intensity and frequency of flashes of white and coloured light.

Brilliance: a Total Effect

By far the most efficient and popular cut for diamond is called the 'brilliant' because of its ability to achieve maximum brilliance. Brilliance has never been exactly defined. As it is used in a general way, it should cover all the visual properties which have been concentrated, in the last two paragraphs, into the terms 'life' and 'fire'. We can therefore say that the brilliance of a stone depends upon the optimum combination of its life and fire. If the two qualities could be quantified, brilliance would be at a maximum when life × fire was at a maximum. A stone with high brilliancy has what can be described as a 'hard' or 'sharp' appearance.

Brilliance and Colour

One would expect that the whiter a stone the greater the brilliance possible, and that is true, although many people who handle diamonds maintain that good coloured yellow brilliant-cut stones are more brilliant than white ones. The reason appears to be an optical illusion similar to that which makes many vehicle drivers believe that yellow headlights are better in foggy conditions. The illusion is caused by an association in the brain between bright light and the colour of the sun.

Diamond Design: the Rose Cut

A natural portrait diamond has two parallel surfaces. Light striking one will be refracted and pass through the other, being refracted again as shown in Fig. 10.15. It will therefore be possible to see clearly through the stone. If the top is angled and the bottom left flat as in Fig. 10.16, the result is the basic rose cut.

It can be shown by simple geometry that if each lower angle is twice the critical angle, i.e. 48° 52', the rose cut is excellent for reflecting all light back through the front, i.e. it has excellent life. However, this simple solution has a big disadvantage owing to the fact that the light leaves the stone at the same angle as it enters. It is not refracted and therefore no fire results.

To obtain some fire from rose cuts, it is necessary to 'break' the angles, as shown in Fig. 10.17, so that light entering at one angle leaves at another angle, and provides a small display of spectrum colour, although at the expense of life. Fundamentally, the rose cut is wrong, and is rarely if ever cut at steep enough angles because it is much better to use suitable material for brilliant cuts.

The Brilliant Cut

Turn the rose cut upside down and it becomes the basic brilliant cut in Fig. 10.18. By calculation it can be shown that for light entering the top to be reflected out again as shown, the angle of the facet causing the first reflection must be more than 48° 52' and that for the facet causing the second must be less than 42° 43', which is impossible in a symmetrical stone, so a compromise has to be found.

It was calculated by Marcel Tolkowsky in 1919 that the best compromise angle is 40° 45' as it provides the greatest refraction, and therefore most vivid fire, with least loss of life, i.e. the greatest brilliance. A greater angle would give better reflection but would not compensate for the loss of fire.

Although most light is reflected back as shown by ray 1, in the basic cone-shaped brilliant cut of Fig. 10.19, some can still be lost round the edges as shown by ray 2. The loss can be corrected by inclined facets which refract the light instead of reflecting it (and also increase dispersion) as shown in Fig. 10.19. Tolkowsky calculated the best angle for these bezel facets to be 34° 30'.

As twice reflected oblique rays may be lost at the edge of the bezel, small facets need to be added at an angle of about 42° to refract them. These are the half facets or halves, also called the upper girdle facets. Similarly, facets about 2° steeper than the pavilion, said Tolkowsky, should be added near the girdle at the back to avoid losses from light which might be reflected from the facets round the bezel. They are the halves on the pavilion, or lower girdle facets.

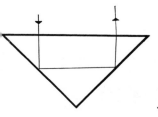

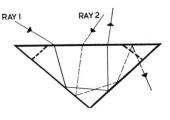

Fig. 10.18. *Light entering and internally reflected out of a theoretical brilliant-cut stone.* Fig. 10.19. (right) *Light that might escape from the edges is allowed to escape from the front if the edges are bevelled.*

Other facets are normally added around the table of the stone, known as the star facets, at about 15° to the horizontal. They tend to decrease the light leakage through the back and improve the distribution of light. They decrease dispersion, however, but compensate by increasing the number of rays that are dispersed.

Certain other basic conditions are required for maximum brilliance from a brilliant-cut diamond. They are: maximum clarity and no trace of colour in the stone, absolute symmetry in the placing of facets which must be an even number around the stone, and the highest quality of polishing.

European and American Cuts

Many other suggestions and calculations over the years have modified Tolkowsky's. Among them, Johnson and Rösch calculated in 1926, by graphical methods, the angles for maximum brilliance with light at right angles to the table. They were never accepted by the trade, perhaps because of the low brilliance from side angles and the thick crown which reduced the spread for the weight.

From 1940, Dr. W. F. Eppler calculated three sets of figures for different sizes of diamonds. His 'practical fine cut' has become the most acceptable for higher quality stones in Germany. The proportions are shown in Fig. 10.22.

The main apparent difference between Tolkowsky's calculations and later ones are in the size and the depth of the table. Americans have adhered to the earlier figures. Tolkowsky-proportioned diamonds are sometimes, therefore, said to be American-cut. Eppler-proportioned brilliants have been called European-cut.

In 1970 the Scandinavian countries published a standard proposal for Europe, known as Scan. D.N., giving standards of nomenclature and grading. It suggests ideal proportions with a slightly larger table than most other 'ideal' cuts.

	Tolkowsky	Johnson & Rösch	Eppler	Scan. D.N.
Diameter of girdle	100%	100%	100%	100%
Diameter of table	53%	56·1%	56%	57·5%
Thickness of crown	16·2%	19·2%	14·4%	14·6%
Thickness of pavilion	43·1%	43·1%	43·2%	43·1%
Depth, table to culet*	59·3%	62·3%	57·7%	57·7%
Angle of crown facets	34° 30′	41°5′	33° 10′	34° 30′
Angle of pavilion facets	40° 45′	38° 40′	40° 50′	40° 45′

* To this must be added the 1 to 3% for the girdle (*a* in the diagrams) to give total depth.

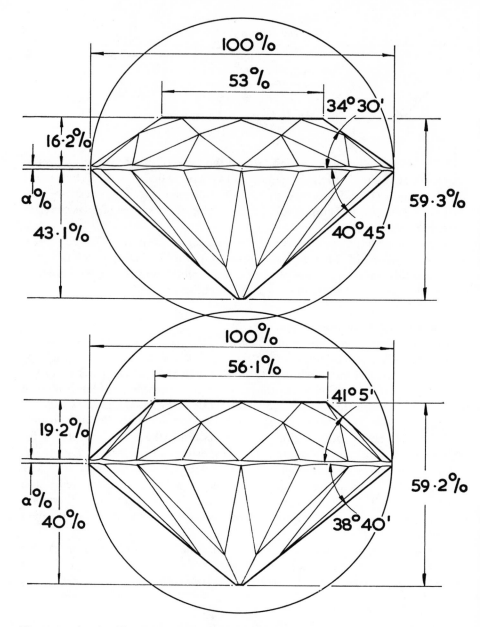

Fig. 10.20. (top)   *The ideal brilliant cut, according to Tolkowsky, on which is based the modern American ideal cut.*

Fig 10.21. (bottom)   *The Johnson and Rösch proportions, which provide a deep crown and stone.*

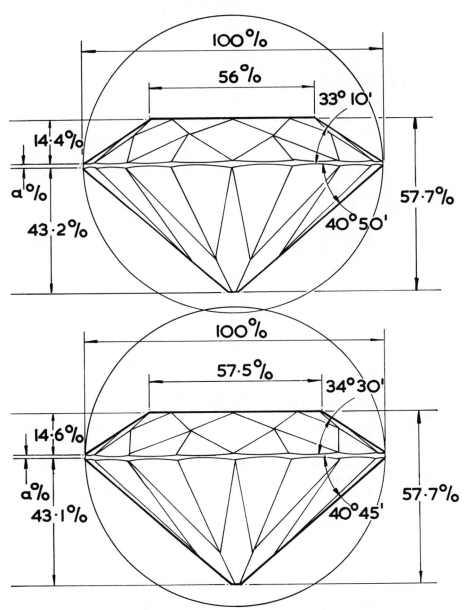

Fig. 10.22. *Proportions of the Eppler fine cut, regarded as the European cut.*
Fig. 10.23. (bottom) *Angles for the brilliant cut in the Scandinavian standard, Scan.D.N.*

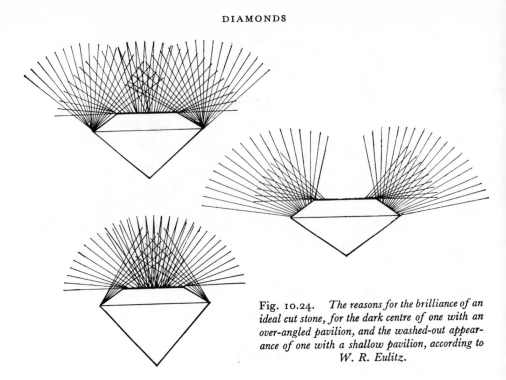

Fig. 10.24. *The reasons for the brilliance of an ideal cut stone, for the dark centre of one with an over-angled pavilion, and the washed-out appearance of one with a shallow pavilion, according to W. R. Eulitz.*

more in accordance with cutting practice and derived from the Eppler fine cut (Fig. 10.22). The figures were empirical, being based on the examination of a large number of polished stones selected for their outstanding brilliance by H. Tillander.

For comparison, the relative proportions as percentages of the diameter of the stone and degrees in the case of angles are given on page 229.

In 1970, Dr. Shigemasa Suzuki proposed a 'double dispersion' design which, although mainly intended to enhance cut stones of lower R.I., provided for diamond and its simulants. Five years later Bruce L. Harding suggested that calculations should take into account the fact that the viewer's head blocks direct rays to the stone and offered several sets of figures.

Modified Tolkowsky proportions and some other theoretical ones are shown in Figs. 10.20 and 10.21. Fig. 10.23 shows the proportions in Scan. D.N.

A study by Dr. W. R. Eulitz has emphasized the need for reasonable accuracy in the pavilion angles particularly. He calculated the angles of emergent rays of light for three different brilliants with pavilion angles of 35°, 41°, and 48°. The results are shown in Fig. 10.24.

The top illustration with a pavilion angle of 41° is of a good brilliant cut. When the angle is too shallow, as on the right, there is a blank area in the middle of the stone which makes it dark and results in what is known as a fish-eye (see also Fig. 14.5). When the pavilion angle is too great and the stone is deep, as on the left, the bezel reflections are poor and the stone has little or no fire (see also Fig. 14.6).

In practice, even high quality diamonds are not always cut to precise angles for a variety of reasons. The crown angles will be found to vary from 29° to 35°

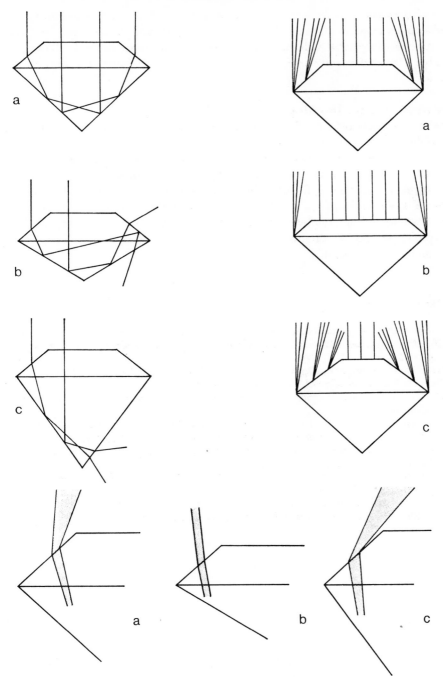

Fig. 10.25. *The main features of a brilliant-cut stone summarized.* (left a and b) *Loss of light through wrong pavilion angles.* (right a and b) *Life reduces and fire increases as the table becomes smaller.* (c) *A spread stone.* (bottom) *Effect of crown angles on fire; (c) has much fire but loses life. The best compromise is (a) in each case.*

233

in whole stones and from 29° to 30° in sawn stones. It is not even necessary to be absolutely exact in all the dimensions, and a difference of, say, 5 per cent in the diameter of the table will make no appreciable difference to the brilliance. The table diameter is measured from opposite corners of facets, not between two sides.

Variation from the Ideal

When the proportions of a brilliant-cut stone are far from ideal, there are almost invariably good reasons for this. A cutter can concentrate on:

1. Obtaining the maximum weight of cut stone from the crystal, or
2. Arriving at the ideal proportions for maximum quality of cut.

In each case he is influenced by the price likely to be obtained for the cut stone. If the crystal itself is not of the highest quality in colour and clarity, the cutter may well try to obtain the maximum weight to optimize his profit. If the crystal is of high quality, he will try for more ideal proportions. Frequently a compromise is sought.

REFERENCES

Precious Stones, by Max Bauer (Reprint edition, London, 1970).
The History of Diamond Production and the Diamond Trade, by Godehard Lenzen (London, 1970).
Handbook of Diamond Grading, by Verena Pagel-Theisen. (W. Germany, 1973.)
Diamond Design, by Marcel Tolkowsky (London, 1919).
'A New Design for Brilliance Plus Dispersion' by Shigemasa Suzuki, Tokyo. *Australian Gemnologist*, May, 1970.
'Faceting Limits', by Bruce L. Harding. *Gems and Gemology*, Vol. XV. No. 3, 1975.
Figures given in *Zentralblatt für Mineralogie* by Dr. W. Fr. Eppler (1940).
'Faceted Gemstones: Cutting for Maximum Brilliance', by O. Le M. Knight. *The Journal of Gemmology*, London, Jan. 1960.
'The Optics of Brilliant-Cut Diamonds', by W. R. Eulitz. *Gems & Gemology*, Los Angeles, Vol. XII. No. 9, 1968.
Lecture to Fellows of the Gemmological Association of Great Britain, by H. Tillander of Helsinki (London, April 1965) and private communication.

CHAPTER ELEVEN

Diamond Manufacture

Only diamond will cut diamond and the problem involved has been dramatized by likening it to sharpening a pencil with a piece of wood. The diamond cutter and polisher is known in the trade as a diamond manufacturer, because he manufactures polished goods from rough goods, but the only true manufacturer of diamonds is the maker of synthetic diamonds. Diamond cutting can mean almost any diamond manufacturing process and is not a very appropriate term. Here it will be used in a general sense and avoided for particular operations in favour of the following terms:

Cleaving: Splitting a diamond along a cleavage plane.
Sawing: Dividing a crystal by diamond saw.
Bruting: Removing part of a crystal by rubbing with another crystal.
Grinding: Making a flat surface by the abrasive action of a rotating wheel or lap prepared with diamond powder.
Polishing: Preparation of the final high-quality surface by a similar method to grinding.

The Designer
The designer in a diamond factory – he has different names in different places or none at all – has perhaps the most important task of all. Usually the owner of a cutting works is also the chief designer. He studies each diamond and decides how it should be cut to produce the optimum value in polished form. With clean regular octahedra this is relatively simple. With large irregular stones without crystal faces, it can be very difficult. In extreme cases, as with the Cullinan, the crystal may be studied for weeks before a decision is made. The grain against which to polish is easily determined once the stone is cleaved or sawn.

The designer has to bear in mind the weight of the rough and its quality. Into how many polished diamonds should it be cut? Usually this is the minimum number, because the price per carat rises steeply with the size. Should the polished stones be cut to exact angles, or would cutting them to gain maximum weight per polished stone at a lower carat price produce more profit? What is the demand at the moment for different sizes and qualities of polished goods? Any decisions are affected by this important consideration. Whether lower qualities of rough are made into gemstones or tool tips is determined very largely by demand.

During his preparatory examination, the designer has also to consider the crystal classification – whether the rough is a stone, a shape, a cleavage, a macle or a flat – whether or not it is coated, and the actual shape of the crystal. The

235

Fig. 11.1.   *How a brilliant cut is spread to gain weight and increase diameter which results in an overdepth pavilion. A stone can be cut with correct angles, as here, but with a correct depth of pavilion and a table which is too shallow.*   Fig. 11.2. (right)   *How a brilliant can be cut from a macle.*

shape will determine how the crystal can be cut and what shape it will be when cut.

A simple example is that a well-shaped octahedron will be fashioned into one brilliant cut stone if small and two if larger, but an elongated octahedron may be cut into a brilliant-cut oval or marquise or an emerald-cut diamond, if of high quality. A large irregular stone might be divided to make polished stones of different cuts.

The cut is the shape of the finished diamond and the pattern of its facets. The brilliant-cut is the standard for diamond and all others are lumped together under the name of fancy cuts.

The Make

The nearness of the finished brilliant cut to the ideal proportions (see page 228) is known as its make. A stone which is near the ideal is said to be of good make or fine make. One that has been cut to gain in weight, to spread the diameter so that it weighs less than it should, is out of round, has the pavilion out of centre, has too thick a girdle, or has facets at incorrect angles, is of poor or bad make.

The diamond cutter works to the market. If he is cutting medium and lower quality goods, he will make the best return he can on his rough, which often means cutting to recover as much weight as possible while producing an acceptable make. The commonest way of doing so is to increase the diameter of the stone by sacrificing some crown height and adding to the width of the table. An octahedron is sawn in half through the girdle (see Fig. 11.12), and each half may become a spread stone. The amount of weight gained by spreading the stone instead of cutting it to ideal proportions is shown in Fig. 11.1. As much as 10 per cent can be saved in this way.

Even high quality goods are sometimes spread, especially when spreading takes the stone over a carat or another favoured unit in weight. Thus a cutter can offer a carat stone, say, at considerably less than an 80-pointer which would have resulted had the proportions been nearer ideal.

Increasing pavilion angles also costs weight. A thick girdle will add a considerable percentage to the weight. Considerable weight, in fact, can be saved by leaving a stone thick.

Macles that are cut in brilliant style are often too thin to provide the full depth without too much loss of material. Weight is therefore made up by increasing the girdle width and the culet size, as well as by spreading the table (Fig. 11.2).

Thin macles and flats are made into baguettes and other cuts that are thin.

Fig. 11.3. *Marking a stone with Indian ink to show how it is to be sawn.*

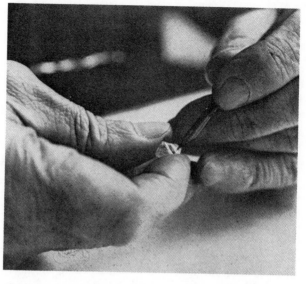

When the rough is too flattened to be made into a reasonable brilliant-cut yet too thick to be wasted on minor cuts, it is made into a pear-shaped or marquise-cut diamond, in which the pavilions may be much shallower than the brilliant-cut gems.

Reducing Flaws

With all these possibilities in mind, the diamond designer first studies the stone from outside. For example, he will decide where the girdle of the cut stone should be. The thinnest side will then become the table and the thickest side will become the bottom. It is preferable to keep inclusions to the top, as any in the bottom will be reflected several times and therefore appear even worse than they are.

Then, having made a first decision, he examines the stone carefully inside, usually rolling it between thumb and first finger and looking inside through an $8 \times$ or $10 \times$ hand lens. The designer then imagines himself to be inside the stone, decides just where the flaws are, which must be removed, and which may be left in the polished stone. Again the decision is often a nice balance to produce an optimum value.

The internal examination may determine whether a fancy cut would be more satisfactory than a brilliant one and what the make should be. Some diamond designers will examine a stone in polarized light to discover the strain in it from the extinction pattern (Fig. 18.15). This will isolate the stones which would be risky to saw or cut in any other way.

Before a final decision is made, the rough is often 'opened' from various angles, by grinding facets or even cleaving thin pieces off opposite faces. These windows enable the interior to be studied much more accurately.

Finally, the designer must decide on the method of manufacture. The three general methods in fact determine the broad commercial classifications of rough, as shown over:

1. *Makeables:* Whole stones which are ground without preliminary work. (macles, cleavages, chips, etc.).
2. *Sawn:* (Stones, shapes, mêlée, chips, smalls, etc.).
3. *Cleaved:* (Cleavages, macles, chips, etc.).

Having made his decisions, the designer takes a pen and Indian ink and marks the crystal with fine lines to show where it is to be sawn or where it is to be cleaved. A good operator will divide the Indian ink line down the centre when sawing or cleaving a precisely-marked stone. It is usually only necessary to mark whole stones with a dot to show the position of the table (Fig. 11.3).

Grain

The diamond cutter relates all his work to what he calls the grain of the diamond; thus he 'saws grain' and polishes 'against the grain'. The grain is represented by the lines forming a triangle seen on octahedral faces (Fig. 11.4), the straight lines on dodecahedral faces (Fig. 11.5), and those in a 'cross' on cube faces, represented in Fig. 11.6 as the top of an octahedral crystal, where the lines on the octahedral faces show the directions of grain on the cube face. The faces are also shown diagramatically in Fig. 11.28. The grain is related to the crystal axes and structure (see Chapter Eighteen) and exists inside the crystal, too, where sometimes it can be seen through a lens or microscope as fine parallel lines.

Fig. 11.6. (right) *Grain from the cube direction of an octahedron.*

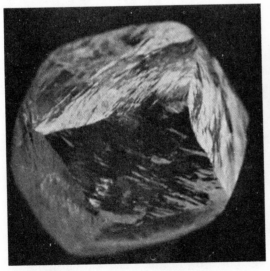

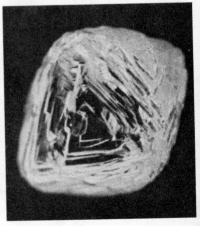

Fig. 11.5. *Grain on dodecahedral faces.*   Fig. 11.4. *Grain on an octahedral face.*

Cleaving

The cleaver in cutter's parlance, follows the grain. That is, he cleaves in an octahedral direction, which is parallel to any of the faces when the crystal itself is an octahedron. In any shape of crystal there are four directions of cleaving (Fig. 11.7). Cleaving a rhombic dodecahedral crystal truncates a three-pointed corner.

The cleaver has several special sticks about eight inches long and a cleaver's box. Even today these are often the personal possessions of the cleaver. The box is fixed to the bench. It is rectangular and also has hollows to hold loose crystals as shown in Fig. 11.8 and 11.9.

CLEAVED
OCTAHEDRON

Fig. 11.7. (above) *The part of an octahedron removed by cleaving. Each of the eight faces can be cleaved off i.e. there are four cleaving directions.*

Fig. 11.8. *Rubbing a kerf before cleaving. The actual kerf is shown on the right. The box catches the powder that results.*

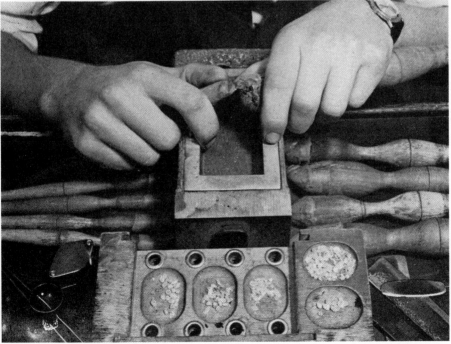

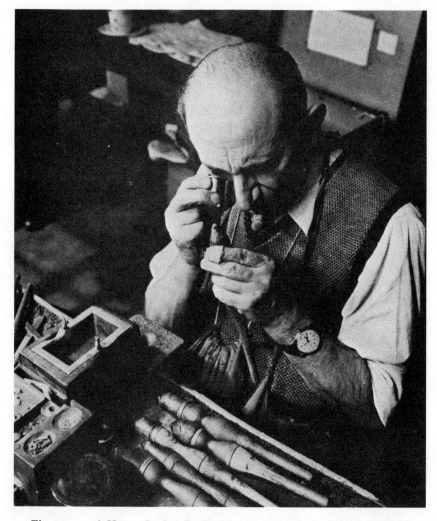

Fig. 11.9. *A Hatton Garden, London, cleaver studies the kerf before cleaving.*

The diamond to be cleaved is cemented to the end of one of the special sticks with a cleaver cement, which may vary a lot in composition but is basically a mixture of shellac and resin with brick dust, finely powdered glass or similar material. (One old recipe for diamond cement includes a glass of 'good' brandy or rum!) The cement of course must be slightly elastic as the diamond has to be parted without flying out of the cement.

Another diamond is cemented into the end of another stick. This stone is usually a chip with a cleavage edge and is used to make a nick called a kerf in the edge of the diamond to be cleaved, as shown in Fig. 11.8. The cleaver rubs one diamond against the other (Fig. 11.8) so that the kerf is produced on the Indian ink line made by the designer. The chippings removed fall in the box.

Next, the stick holding the diamond to be cleaved is fixed upright in a tapered

240

hole in the bench or cleaver's box. The cleaver rests a special knife-blade in the kerf and gives the blade a sharp tap with the handle end of a cleaver's stick. Some use a short iron bar. The stone will split along the cleavage plane. The cleaving action is shown in Fig. 11.10. The knife is a rather thick steel blade about 4 in by 2 in (10 × 5 cm) in size. The edge is thin but not sharp and rests in the kerf without touching the bottom so that it acts like a wedge. The slightly curved sides are polished for a short distance from the cutting edge.

A cleaver needs a knowledge of diamond structure (grain directions), a good eye and a steady hand. He also needs an even temperament because so much depends on that simple little action of tapping the blade. It is possible to shatter a very valuable crystal by bad cleaving. Cleaving is so exacting that at one time it was commonplace to send stones to a group of specialist cleavers in Amsterdam.

Cleaving may be useful for opening a window in a stone, removing a flaw, or reducing a large crystal to smaller pieces. It was commonly used for making rose cuts, which have flat backs. As it can be carried out only in four directions, it is of no help in splitting an octahedron in two for the manufacture of brilliant-cut diamonds. This cut has to be made parallel to the cube face, as indicated in Fig. 11.12.

Cleaving has a place in making industrial diamond tools. One example is to cleave irregular rough in four directions to make octahedra which are then polished by a tumbling process. These artificially-made octahedra are used for setting in the crowns of drills.

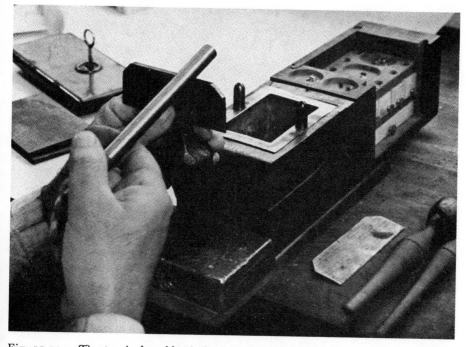

Fig. 11.10. *The stone is cleaved by placing a special blade in the kerf and tapping it with a rod.*

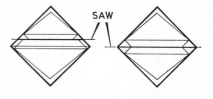

TWO BRILLIANTS FROM ONE
OCTAHEDRON- TWO METHODS

Fig. 11.12. *Two ways of sawing an octa-hedron to produce two brilliants. The first is known as a bishop's head.*

Fig. 11.11. *A particularly fine octahedron sawn in two by A. Monnickendam Ltd to make two emerald cut stones of identical weight.*

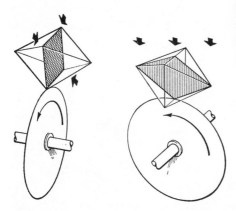

Fig. 11.14. *Flaw sawn out of the middle of an octahedron. The slightly curved lines are the saw marks and the straight lines at right angles to them are grain.*

Fig. 11.13. (left) *Sawing in a cube plane (four point) from a corner and sawing in a dodecahedron plane (two point) from an edge.*

Sawing

The sawyer 'saws grain'; that is, he cuts in a non-cleaving direction. There are two normal directions of sawing, one in the cube direction and the other in the dodecahedral, to use the crystallographer's terms. The sawyer calls these four-point sawing and two-point sawing. The first is through or parallel to an imaginary plane through the four points of the octahedron. The second is through or parallel to an imaginary plane through two points of the octahedron. Fig. 11.13 should make this clear. It is almost impossible to saw diamonds in another direction, even if only a few degrees different.

When a medium sized or larger octahedral crystal classified as a stone is being sawn, it is usual to divide it across the natural girdle in the manner shown in Fig. 11.12, so that it will produce two brilliant-cut stones of approximately equal size, or sometimes, when it is more economic, two of different size, called a

Fig. 11.15   *Banks of sawing machines in the works of A. Monnickendam Ltd at Brighton,*
England. One man attends to a bank of machines.

Fig. 11.16.   *Adjusting a machine to saw an octahedral crystal in a cube plane. The Indian ink*
mark made by the designer can be seen. On the right edge is a long screw that acts as a stop. It is
adjusted so that the diamond is cut in a number of stages.

bishop's head (Fig. 11.12). The wastage occasioned by manufacturing from the awkward shapes that were the only ones possible to produce by cleaving, is largely eliminated by sawing (Fig. 11.15 and 11.16).

Sawing is also employed to remove flaws. Fig. 11.14 shows how the centre of an octahedron containing a bad feather can be sawn out, leaving two pieces to be shaped into brilliant-cut stones. Windows are usually polished on the girdles of rough crystals before sawing, in order to locate any flaws, spots, and naats.

Diamonds are sawn in a machine by a very thin disc made from a special bronze. The diameter of the disc is between 3 and 4 in (7·5–10 cm) and the thickness only 0·024 to 0·014 in (0·06 to 0·15 mm). A driving belt turns the sawing blade at speeds from 4,500 to 6,500 revolutions a minute, as needed.

The blade, which has a central hole with two or four slots to prevent it from dishing, is clamped between two thick flanges (Fig. 11.17) in the machine. When mounted, it is made to cut true to within half a thousandth of an inch by running the machine and holding the edge of sharp chisel (usually made from a hacksaw blade) to the edge of the wheel. Sometimes a new wheel will have some side whip. This is eliminated by massaging the sides of the blade with a hardwood stick, working outwards towards the rim.

Next, a new blade has to be dressed with the diamond powder which is responsible for the cutting action. Any diamond powder will have grains lying in all directions, from hardest to softest. Therefore, there will always be some grains in a hard direction that will cut a diamond in a soft direction.

Diamond powder of less than 325 mesh, under about 0·04-mm. or 0·0016-inch grain size, is prepared by moistening it with a few drops of olive oil until it becomes a paste and letting it stand for at least two days. From ten to twenty drops of oil to a carat of powder is the right proportion. Some paste is applied to the surface of a hardened steel roller (Fig. 11.18) and the roller held by hand against the rotating disc, as shown in Fig. 11.19. The roller is moved slowly from side to side across the edge of the disc and sometimes the sawyer will slow down the disc by braking it with his thumb. The sawing disc will rotate the roller and diamond powder will be forced into the pores of the metal disc edge.

A small kerf (Fig. 11.7) is generally made to start the sawing. A modern technique is to cut the kerf more accurately by laser.

The diamond to be sawn is mounted in a holder at the end of an arm of the machine so that the diamond rests on the top of the sawing disc, as shown in Fig. 11.20. The diamond is held by a clamp or by a cement of plaster of Paris and fish glue in a dop. The holder can be adjusted to any position to present the diamond at the correct angle to the sawing disc.

The pressure of the diamond against the edge of the disc is provided by gravity but is adjustable because different stones need different pressures. A weight at the end of the arm provides the pressure (Fig. 11.20) and there is also an adjustable stop, to be seen about half way along the arm in the same figure. This stop is adjusted progressively to control the depth of cut. It also prevents the stone dropping after it is sawn through.

To start a cut, the diamond is mounted so that it is sawn across a diagonal (if in the four-point sawing direction), but is set a few degrees off the grain so that it will be on the grain when the cut reaches the centre of the stone, and therefore

Fig. 11.17. *The phosphor bronze wheel, in its spindle, used for sawing.*

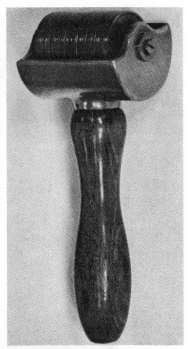

Fig. 11.18. *The roller used to apply diamond dust in oil to the edge of the sawing wheel.*

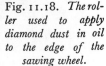

Fig. 11.19. *Applying diamond powder to the edge of the wheel.*

the greatest bulk. This is necessary because of the swinging action of the arm holding the diamond. The marks of sawing across a diagonal are shown in Fig. 11.14. Occasionally part of the sawn surface looks as if it has been polished.

A wide blade is sometimes used to start the cut and a thinner one after the cut has been established. At the half-way stage, through the widest part of the stone, the blade is usually recharged.

Sawing wears down the diameter of discs, which means the rate of revolutions has to be increased to keep the cutting speed the same. A single disc will cut about half a dozen 1-carat stones before becoming too small for further use.

The sawyer keeps a very close watch on stones being sawn, examining them from time to time with a lens. He normally looks after a bank of sawing machines. He has particularly to watch for any changes of hardness through an area of different crystallization. These naats sometimes have rope formation or spider's web formation in a stone and will turn the blade and spoil the cut.

If a naat is met by the blade, sometimes it can be sawn by changing the direction of rotation, which is done by crossing the driving belt. Sometimes a naat will drop out after being approached from different directions by the saw blade. At others it will have to be broken out. A similar technique is used to avoid splitting when a blade runs into a natural cleavage in the crystal. Sometimes the blade will wander towards an easy direction, i.e. towards a cleavage plane. When this happens, the sawyer turns the stone round and begins a cut from the opposite side.

Special diamond-impregnated sintered bronze discs have been developed to overcome many of the problems of sawing through naats, but most diamond factories stick to the old methods. With increased demand and competition however, there is a slow process of change.

Sawing is still a very slow operation compared with cleaving. To saw through a quarter-of-a-carat octahedron takes about forty minutes. A carat stone may take from well over two hours to a day according to the difficulty of sawing. If an attempt is made to speed up the sawing process by applying more weight to the stone, a dished cut is likely to result – one surface being convex, the other concave. Australian stones are so full of naats that they cannot be sawn.

It takes about a tenth of a carat of diamond powder to saw through a one carat stone and the loss in weight of the crystal which is sawn is about 3 per cent of its weight.

Bruting

The bruter works on sawn, cleaved, or whole stones. He shapes them into circular outlines in such a way that he removes what flats he can and yet retains as much as possible of the original crystal.

The lathe or bruting machine is like a small wood-working lathe and will not only produce a round girdle on a stone but can be used to make a flat surface such as the table of a brilliant. The tables of gem diamonds are normally produced by grinding, but bruting is used for the tables of industrial die stones.

The diamond to be bruted is cemented into a dop which is mounted in the chuck of the bruting machine (Fig. 11.21). Another diamond, selected as the

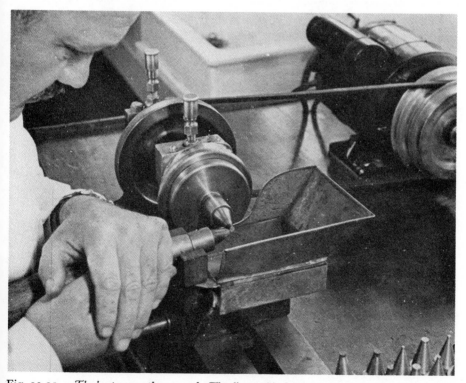

Fig. 11.21.   *The bruter or cutler at work. The diamond is fixed to a dop that is rotated at 800 to 1000 r.p.m. The cutter has a wooden stick with a similar diamond dop screwed on the end as a tool.*

cutting-tool tip, is cemented to a similar dop at the end of a stick about 2 ft (61 cm) long. The bruter holds this stick under his arm and applies the diamond at the end of it to the diamond which is rotated in the lathe. There is a holder for the stick at the front of the lathe and also a pan to catch the diamond dust and chips, as may be seen from Fig. 11.21.

The diamond being bruted has to be centralized so that the minimum amount of chips are removed to make it round. For example, if one corner projects more than the others, more of this will have to be removed otherwise there will be excessive wastage. It is also necessary at times to bring flaws or inclusions in a stone to an eccentric position so that these are removed in an early part of the bruting operation. The bruter has to obtain more 'rondist' on the side where the flaws are, i.e. a wider girdle there. In Fig. 11.21, the diamond being bruted is cemented in the conically-shaped dop in the bruting machine. This dop screws into a circular plate which is so designed that tapping the edge with a stick or mallet will move it out of centre. After a flaw has been removed, tapping the opposite side of the chuck will bring it back to the central position.

The bruter – still frequently called the cutter in many workshops – has to be very skilful in making sure that he ends with a round diamond and not an oval one when engaged in such operations. The bruter, like all diamond workers, has at all times to keep losses as low as possible, and will often brute a stone so that there is a small part of the original skin – natural surface of the crystal – left. It indicates that he has extracted the maximum possible diameter from the

Fig. 11.22. *Vesteller mounting a diamond in a solder dop ready for polishing facets on it. A ga*
flame is used here and a piece of metal instead of the vesteller's thumb.

Fig. 11.23. *Polisher's benches at the Monnickendam works where traditional methods are still employed to cut high quality stones.*

crystal. Such an indication, known as a natural or a naif (Fig. 13.31), is not infrequently seen on the girdle of a polished stone. One natural is most commonly seen on a stone but, if the rough is particularly symmetrical, two could be seen on a two-point stone, three on a three-point stone and four on a four-point stone. (See Fig. 11.28.)

Usually the diamond used as the tool is one of those to be bruted. The corners are used progressively to remove the corners of the stone in the lathe. A glance at Fig. 11.21 again will show that the dops in the end of the stick and in the machine chuck are identical, so that it is only necessary to unscrew and interchange them. A sharp edge of a piece of diamond is also used for cutting, as is a macle, said to be particularly suitable.

The bruter's service is needed again during the grinding and polishing stage.

Grinding and Polishing

The final stage in the preparation of a gem diamond is to grind the facets and to

Fig. 11.24. *Three diamonds being polished at the same time in mechanical dops. All the tangs are weighted. The scaife is of the traditional pattern. In the foreground, left, is the kind of folding lens favoured by diamond polishers.*

polish them. Although grinding and polishing are carried out by an almost identical operation, they are separated because the first is a coarser process than the second.

The equipment comprises a power-driven horizontal grinding wheel, the scaife, and a holder for the diamond, the tang (Fig. 11.23). A few works still employ solder dops, as described in Chapter Nine, but the great majority have changed to mechanical dops, some are shown in Figs. 11.25 and 11.26. The diamond is held in a clamp which is screwed tight to hold it in the position required. Whether a solder or a mechanical dop is employed, it has a copper stem, which can be bent to obtain the exact angle needed to grind a particular facet.

The Scaife

The scaife is made of a cast-iron disc from 10 to 12 in (25–30 cm) in diametre and about 1 in (25 mm) thick when new. The thickness is reduced as the surface is from time to time trimmed to get rid of grooves caused by the grinding process. Through the centre of the traditional scaife is a steel axle with pointed ends, so that the whole is like a big top, as shown in Figs. 11.23 and 11.24.

The points of the axle run in conical holes to two *lignum vitae* or other hardwood blocks, above and below the scaife and are lubricated with tallow or grease. Since 1940, some scaifes have been made without top axles, as can be seen in

Fig. 11.25. The scaife is driven by a belt or directly by an electric motor at a speed of about 2,500 r.p.m. It is mounted in a bench so that the bench surface is approximately at the same level as the surface of the scaife. Also mounted on the bench are two pegs or stops. These are placed so that the tang is held in position with the diamond resting on the scaife and is not swept aside by its rotation. One of the pins rests against the side of the tang itself and the other against a rod projecting from the back of the tang like a tail.

The scaife has to run absolutely true and free of vibration for accurate diamond grinding and polishing. It is balanced by small lead weights, held underneath in a groove near the spindle by a thin cord wound round. The cast iron surface is turned in a lathe and lapped to be as flat as possible. Then it is scored as shown in Fig. 11.26 to retain diamond paste. The scoring is done by hand with a stick of the hard material, silicon carbide.

Diamond paste is made with diamond ground in a pestle and mortar and mixed with a few drops of olive oil in the same way as described for sawing. There is not the same necessity to grade the diamond powder accurately when cutting diamond as there is when cutting softer materials by diamond powder. Diamond polishers often have their own 'formulae' for making paste, using the white of an egg, spittle, detergent, and other such media. The paste is applied with the thumb, as a rule.

The scaife surface is usually divided into three areas by the polisher (Fig. 11.27).

Fig. 11.25. *A modern scaife with ball-bearing mounting instead of a top pivot, in use in Belgium. The mechanical dop is also of modern adjustable design.*

Fig. 11.27. *The three rings on the scaive can be seen here. The inner one is for testing, the centre one for grinding, and the outer one for polishing.*

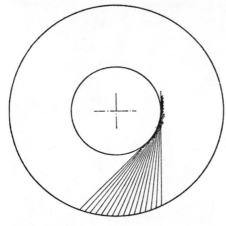

Fig. 11.26. *Scoring a scaife to hold diamond paste.*

1. The testing ring, used to find the correct starting point of a facet, by judgement and some trial and error. It is usually prepared with dry diamond powder.
2. The running ring (also called the loopkring) on which the facet is ground to size.
3. The polishing ring (also known as the soetkring) for polishing the facets to as perfect as possible surfaces by removing the grooves – the running lines – caused by grinding.

The testing ring and running ring are towards the centre and the polishing ring, which has the biggest area, towards the edge of the scaife. The polisher will gradually 'use up' the surface of the scaife, abandoning a grinding or polishing ring as it ceases to cut or produce a good finish. A good polisher will use a scaife for six to eight weeks before the surface needs renewal. Paste is worked into the surfaces by actually polishing a facet.

A polisher will usually grind from two or four diamonds at the same time on a scaife, but in some works even more.

Four-, Three- and Two-point Stones

The diamond polisher has to decide upon a plan of action before he starts work on a stone. This will first of all depend upon relation of the crystal structure to the final brilliant-cut. The polisher puts it another way; how he cuts the stone will depend upon whether it is a four-pointer, a three-pointer, or a two-pointer. These expressions are explained in relation to structure in Fig. 11.28. A three-pointer stone is also called a was – pronounced 'vaas'.

To the polisher, a four-point stone is one in which the table originally had four corners. It may be a whole stone or part of a sawn octahedron. The saw marks across the table indicate that it is a four-point stone and also indicate the direction to the grain.

A three-point stone has a table which was originally an octahedron face with three corners. It may be a whole stone, a macle, or a cleaved stone as in Fig. 11.28.

A two-point stone has a table in a rhombic dodecahedral direction, that is, it is along one of the straight edges of an octahedral crystal and therefore has only two corners. It will almost certainly be a stone sawn in this direction.

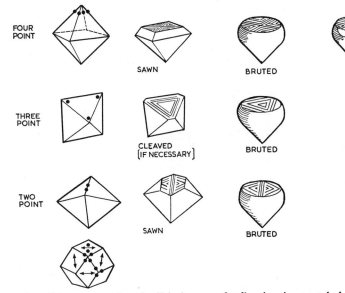

Fig. 11.28   *Diamond cutter's and polisher's names for directions in an octahedral and* (bottom) *a dodecahedral stone.*

253

The three possibilities and the directions of grain are shown in the three illustrations. The polisher would not only look for sawing lines but also at grain lines on any naturals left by the bruter to establish the best direction for grinding and polishing. When he has established the possible directions, he will try them on the testing ring to discover which polishes best. Although two opposite directions are equally possible, usually one polishes much better than the other.

Practical Cutting

The best indication to the polisher that the direction is good is the sound. A diamond that is running well makes little sound, like a faint ringing note. The more off the best grain direction, the louder the sound, although very occasionally a stone will produce quite a loud note when it is running well.

The facet surface is also an important indication. The more the stone is forced by running in an unsatisfactory direction, the less perfect the finish. Forcing with the grain will make the facet greyish and even tear the scaife and the facet surface.

Often a lead weight is placed on the tang to obtain the best grinding pressure, but increasing the pressure or speed indefinitely does not produce faster and faster cutting. There is a point when the facet begins to burn or graphitize.

Each facet is made at the correct angle by studying the tang upside down and by bending the copper stalk of the dop holding the diamond and by turning it in its clamp when necessary.

A quite exceptional degree of accuracy is achieved by diamond polishers measuring by eye alone. Once the basic facets are put on, they work by aligning edges and reflections of edges. P. Grodzinski measured the angles between facets on a brilliant-cut stone and found them to be within a few minutes of a degree.

Compass of the Tang

As diamonds can only be ground in certain directions, the diamond grinder and

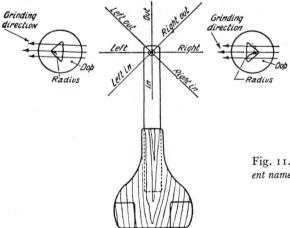

Fig. 11.29. *One of a number of different names used by polishers to describe the direction of cutting.*

polisher uses a jargon of his own to describe the direction of cutting once the stone is adjusted in the dop in a tang. It is a kind of compass direction, as shown in Fig. 11.29, which is the simplest of several notations. The tang is 'read' by taking it off the anti-clockwise running scaife and holding it with the diamond pointing to the eyes. The stone can now be turned so that the point of a facet being cut is left out, right, or whichever direction is appropriate. The actual directions in which brilliant facets are cut is shown in Fig. 11.34.

Modern diamond-bonded wheels used for cutting diamonds for diamond tools have not been found suitable for polishing gems as they do not give the high finish obtainable by using the traditional scaife.

In practice, making brilliant cuts from bruted stones is not divided strictly into grinding and polishing, but into cross-cutting and brillianteering.

Work of the Cross-Cutter

The cross-cutter puts on the first eighteen facets. These are the table, the culet, four corners and four bezels on the top, and four corners and four pavilions on the bottom. The order in which this is done differs from factory to factory, but a common sequence is shown in Fig. 11.32 to 11.33.

The table is ground first. The next step is to grind the first facet. This is most important and critical of the whole process, because the entire symmetry, life fire and ultimate quality of the final gem depends upon the accuracy with which this facet is ground.

The first facet is normally a corner at the top of the stone, which should be at the correct angle to the plane through the girdle. It is also extremely important to grind the facet to the right size. Although the cross-cutter will use a gauge, much depends upon the accuracy of his judgement and his skill and experience.

When satisfied, he will grind the corner opposite, and then the third and fourth (Fig. 11.32). He then proceeds to polish the bottom facets. It is of the greatest importance that these facets are at an angle of not more than 41° and not less than 40° in order to obtain the maximum brilliance. They must meet in a point (which will become the culet) in the exact centre of the diamond.

The bottom facets must be perfectly aligned under the top facets to obtain a perfectly even girdle. Also if one facet either on the top or bottom is not the same depth in the girdle this will give the appearance of a seesaw edge. If the angles of the bottom facets are over 41° the diamond will have a blackish appearance in the centre. If the angles are under 40° the stone will appear 'watery' and the girdle will be reflected through the table.

There are now four facets on the bottom of the stone and four facets on the top. Viewed through the table, the culet should be in the exact centre of the now square table. The cross-worker examines a reflection of the bottom facets in the table. It should be quite square and of a certain size.

Four more facets are now cut on the top of the stone, usually in sequence opposite each other. There are now eight, which are known as the eights (Fig. 11.32). The sizes of the facets must be accurately ground so that when completed they are all the same size and make the table a perfect octagon.

The stone now has eight facets on the top and four on the bottom. It is turned

Fig. 11.30. *Actual pictures of rough, marked, sawn, bruted blocked, and finished brilliant-cut diamond by Baumgold Bros. of New York, U.S.A.*

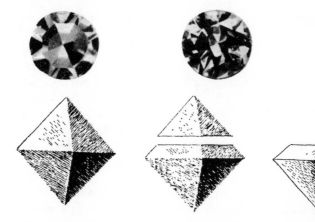

Fig. 11.31. *An octahedral crystal in the rough, sawn (centre) sawn as a bishop's head and (right) with the lower half bruted.*

Fig. 11.32. *Work of the cross-cutter. The table of the stone is ground first, then a top facet (on the left-hand diagram). The eights have been completed in the centre. The illustration on the right has the sixteen main facets plus the table and culet.*

Fig. 11.33. *The brillianteerer puts on the remaining facets either in groups or in sequence.*

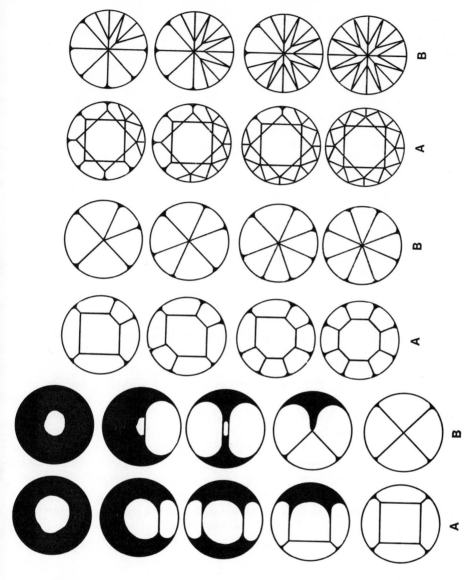

Fig. 11.34. More detailed stages in bruting and polishing the crown (A) and pavilion (B). The sequences follow in each column from the top.

257

over again and four more facets, called the pavilions, added to the bottom by grinding on the edges of the four original facets as shown in Fig. 11.32. At this stage the stone has eight facets and culet at the bottom and eight facets and table at the top.

Rondisting

Before further grinding or polishing, the stone is returned to the bruter for further work on the girdle which is now thinner and can be made perfectly round in an operation called rondisting.

Polishing

The cross-cutter has the stone back to polish the facets he has ground. He does this on the outer polishing ring on the scaife. Grinding leaves a series of curved grooves on facets which have to be removed before the adamantine polish is achieved, but it usually takes only a few seconds to polish a facet, by swinging the dop quickly in an arc to and fro across the polishing ring. Each facet is polished in sequence and examined frequently under a magnifying eyeglass to make sure that the polishing is effective and even.

The Work of the Brillianteerer

Brillianteering is the final stage in making a brilliant-cut diamond by adding the remaining twenty-four facets to the top or crown and the remaining sixteen facets to the bottom or pavilion.

Starting on the top of the stone, the brillianteerer will place and polish a star-facet as accurately as he can. This is a key operation and demands a high degree of skill and judgement because the facet is cut quickly and has to be inspected every few seconds to make sure that the angle of the dop is exact.

The star-facets are those surrounding the table so as to form an eight-pointed star. Each is placed at the junction of the edge between two eights with the table, as shown at top of col. 5, Fig. 11.34. It is ground so that it extends half-way down the edge of the eights. It is usual with mechanical dops, in which the diamond can easily be adjusted, to complete all the star-facets before grinding the rest of the facets in sequence on the top of the stone. With solder dops, to avoid too much work moving the diamond, it was usual to complete what polishers call a set,

Fig. 11.35. *The extremely simple gauge used by most diamond polishers to make sure that the pavilion angle to the girdle is as required.*

Fig. 11.36. *The actual grinding and polishing directions in four-point, three–point, and two-point stones.*

which comprises two stars and four girdle facets as shown in the illustration in Fig. 11.37.

The upper girdle facets, also known as halves, number 16 and each connects the outer point of a star-facet to a point on the girdle midway between the eights, as can be seen in the top diagram of Fig. 10.2. After a set is finished, the original eight has become a kite-shape and is sometimes known as a kite facet. (See Fig. 10.2.)

The stone is next turned over to complete the bottom facets. All sixteen of these are halves or lower girdle facets, around the girdle. At one time they were cut to form points about half-way down the edges between eights, but the modern fashion is to make these facets much longer. In most makes today, they extend about thirteen-sixteenths (about 80 per cent) of the distance from girdle to culet, with the exception of when a stone is flat in the bottom because the facets are at an angle less than 40°.

Closed Culets

On earlier made stones it was the practice to leave a relatively large culet. Today the culet is frequently missing, which illustrates the extreme skill of the

Fig. 11.37. *Facets are placed in sets like this when using a solder dop, today usually on top grade stones only. With mechanical dops, facets of the same kind are placed in sequence.*

Fig. 11.38. Two sets of Piermatic automatic diamond-polishing machines at work. The Piermatic polishes forty-eight of the fifty-eight facets on a brilliant-cut diamond. It reduces skilled labour, assists quality control and shortens the production cycle. At first it was used only on small diamonds, but is increasingly being used for those of carat size.

260

cutter. It is best to have a very small culet, however, as it has a practical function. It minimises damage to the point. A sharp point or short edge, called a closed culet, is more easily fractured. Too large a culet can be too readily seen through the table, marring the brilliance.

Final Finishing

Top quality diamonds are given a final check visually and 'repair' work, known as making-over, carried out if necessary. This comprises polishing very tiny facets (that are not visible to the naked eye and do not affect the quality of make) to remove any remaining minute defects.

Modern polished diamonds are sometimes given an acid bath after cutting to remove any oil and debris that have entered any tiny fractures and cleavages that reach the surface of the stone. Acidizing can have an important effect on quality and there are specialists in the process.

Automatic Diamond Polishing

Diamond polishing is expensive, requiring considerable human skill and long periods of time, but the cost represents only about 10 per cent of the value of the raw material, unlike most other manufacturing processes. This fact and the high cost of rough diamonds has inhibited research into more efficient methods of production. From the early 1970s, however, automatic polishing machines have been produced by Professor Y. Yarnitsky of the Technion's Faculty of Mechanical Engineering, in Israel, and by De Beers' subsidiary company of Piermatic Machines Ltd, in London, for polishing mêlée and smaller rough

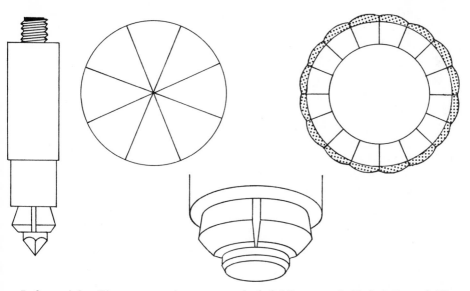

Left to right. Fig. 11.39. *A press pot or chuck, holding a partly blocked diamond.* Fig. 11.40. *The first eight facets on the bottom.* Fig. 11.41. *A press pot holding a diamond with its rounded table bevelled.* Fig. 11.42. *The top of a diamond with sixteen facets which will become the upper girdle facets. The press pot (shown dotted) is also faceted so that it can control the next stage.*

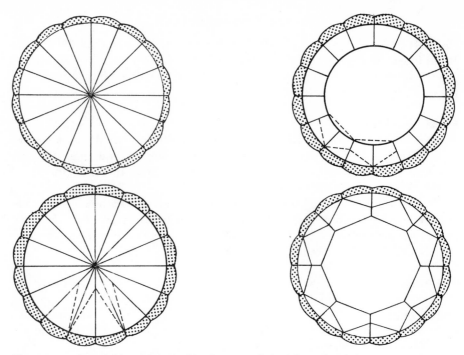

Fig. 11.43. (top left)   *How the kite facets are derived from the 16 facets around the bezel.*
(bottom) The completed crown.
Fig. 11.44. (top right)   *The 16 facets on the bottom. (bottom) How the lower girdle facets*
are derived. The final pavilion is not shown.

diamonds. About 2,200 Piermatic machines were in use in Israel, Belgium, and other countries at the end of 1976 and more were being commissioned daily. Customers are supplied with production units of forty machines with ancillary equipment. Training in the use of a machine takes less than half the time of learning a hand skill.

Professor Yarmitsky's device is a special dop, controlled electronically, four of which work round a scaife, the diamonds being held in special jigs. He has also developed a rondist polishing machine for polishing the girdles of stones.

The Piermatic machines also process four stones to a scaife, but the whole machine is integrated (Fig. 11.38). The success of the system (like all batch and mass production units) depends upon a certain uniformity of the input material. Diamonds have therefore to be bruted and then divided into size groups to fit into appropriate press pots – like drill chucks – which are held in the polishing machine (Fig. 11.39). For the first process, blocking, they are mounted with the pavilion projecting from the press pot. The machine will now automatically put on eight facets at $41\frac{3}{4}°$ using two grain positions (Fig. 11.40), after initial lining up by eye. Contact of the metal press pot with the iron scaife completes an electronic circuit to start a new facet. The object of this first process is to remove the bulk of the stone.

The next stage is polishing the top, for which the stone is set the other way up in another press pot, around which is an adjustable contact ring. The diamond is first bevelled on the edge of the round table (Fig. 11.41) to avoid damaging the scaife. It is then set up in a projector to align it and set the metal contact ring to the polishing depth for the half facets, which are at $36\frac{1}{2}°$. The holder is refitted to the machine, which will put on these sixteen upper bezel facets using four grain positions. Use of the ring as a contact causes the press pot itself to be cut with the diamond, as shown shaded in Fig. 11.42, to the facet angles.

A short-circuiting piece is now inserted between the ring and the press pot so the press pot itself again acts as the contact when it touches the scaife. The machine will now add the eight cut that provides the kite facets, finding the grain and facet position automatically, although the angle may have to be adjusted manually owing to slight variations in the stones. Two kite facets are shown partly finished and dotted in Fig. 11.43 to indicate where they are placed. When the scaife reaches the point of the kite it touches the metal press pot, shown shaded in the diagrams, and the machine lifts the holder and turns it to start on the next facet.

The bottom is completed in a third press pot, using the same methods as used for the top. The sixteen halves, which become the lower girdle facets, are completed using the $41\frac{3}{4}°$ angle (Fig. 11.44). Then the eight cut (pavilion facets, Fig. 11.44) are made. As they are only $\frac{3}{4}°$ different from the lower girdle facets, they need accurate setting of the press pot with the aid of a projector. The operation on the bottom of the stone decides the thickness of the girdle.

As the machine cuts to consistently accurate angles, the stones it produces cannot be 'swindled' to make the shape irregular and increase the weight, although girdles can be thickened. It will be seen from the illustrations that the facets are put on in a different sequence from those put on by hand.

Standardization of bruted rough into size groups is necessary, as already stated. Normally a stationary stone is held against the one to be bruted, which is revolved in a sort of lathe. The process has been additionally mechanized by rotating both stones, which are held in the machine tool and controlled by calibrated instruments. One operator can attend five such bruting machines.

Automatic polishing has made such a big impact on the industry that, in 1977, it was estimated that up to 20 per cent of mêlée that was exported had been polished automatically. By the following year, some plants were polishing stones of up to one carat automatically. Marketing and servicing of Piermatic machines, research and development have now been taken over from De Beers by Bonas Machine Tools Ltd.

REFERENCES

Basic Notes of Diamond Polishing, by Jules J. Canes (S. Africa, 1964).
Diamond Technology, by P. Grodzinski (London, 1953).
'Diamonds are Different', paper by D. M. Rainier, Diamond Research Laboratory (Johannesburg, 1968).
Personal communications from diamond manufacturers.

CHAPTER TWELVE

Grading Polished Stones for Colour

Grading a cut stone for colour means deciding the amount by which it deviates from the whitest possible (truly colourless) i.e., how much off-colour it is. Nature provides a continuous darkening in the tints from white to yellow, from white to brown, from white to green, and (in the industrial category) from white to grey. There are no natural divisions in any of these groups. Divisions are determined by demand and the ability of the human eye to separate one tint from an adjacent one that is very slightly lighter or darker.

The white to yellow group, the most important and largest in gem diamonds, may be divided into, say, three categories, or fifty. Many people will be able to grade a pile of cut stones into three colour groups, but very few indeed will be able to separate them into fifty that gradually increase in yellowish tinge. Everybody, however, will have the same difficulty with stones that fall between two adjacent groups, and this will always be so.

Picking Prices
In the colour categories of any commercial firm there are always some stones that could arguably be graded higher or lower. That is why firms that work on broader divisions of colour and quality impose a higher price per carat on a customer who wants to pick out stones himself from a category instead of accepting what he is offered.

The picking price is between the price for the particular category and that for the next higher category. Of course, a customer electing to pay a picking price must know what he is doing. He could pick a stone that merges into the next lower category and thus pay too much for it.

Conditions for Grading
Since a body, or fundamental, colour of a diamond must be judged in white light, it follows that the white light must not be reflected from coloured surfaces in a room. The ideal room for judging colour should therefore have dead-white walls. Also the stones must be seen against a dead-white background. White paper or white blotting-paper is normally used, but white paint is used in grading instruments and white plastics materials are also suitable, provided that they are not strongly fluorescent.

A second, and very important consideration is that any fluorescence in the stone must be suppressed. A visible blue fluorescence can be caused in a yellowish diamond when ultra-violet light, which is invisible, falls on it. If the diamond is examined in sunlight, even reflected light, which contains ultra-violet light, the blue fluorescence will tend to cancel the yellowish body colour because the colours are nearly complementary, and the stone will appear to be whiter than it is. These stones are often mistakenly called 'blue-white'. Similarly a stone that fluoresces yellow will appear worse in white light containing ultra-violet.

It is therefore important to grade stones in white light that is relatively free of ultra-violet and the orthodox method is to use daylight from a north-facing window in the northern hemisphere and from a south-facing one in the southern, i.e. with one's back to the sun. Morning and evening light have an excess of red because of refraction through the atmosphere when the sun is low. Also there must be sufficient intensity of light. These restrictions mean that in the winter in London, for example, it is only possible to grade between the hours of about 10 a.m. and 2 p.m.

Standard Lighting

To provide a standard light for colour grading and to eliminate the nuisance of being only able to grade during a few hours of daylight, the Gemological Institute of America introduced the Diamondlite. A standard artificial white light free of ultra-violet and equivalent to north daylight, is contained in a metal box with an open front. The inside of the box is painted dead-white. This eliminates reflections from surroundings and also limits the confusing effects of dispersion of colour, enabling the stone under test to be compared with master stones. The instrument also incorporates an ultra-violet tube for detecting fluorescence in diamonds and a magnifier for examining small stones. The

Fig. 12.1. *The Koloriscop, a specially-designed standard light box for judging the whiteness of diamonds. A stone can just be seen in the tray. Fig. 13.3 shows a desk light for grading diamonds made by System Eickhorst. It contains an ultra-violet light in the top for checking fluorescence.*

265

Americans provide a special colour-grading lamp for use in conjunction with their diamond-grading microscope.

A standard light box for diamond colour-grading is also made in Europe under patents held by Dr E. Gübelin, of Switzerland. It is called the Koloriscop (Fig. 12.1) and has a stronger source of light than the G.I.A. version, which makes it more convenient for use in daylight. System Eickhorst of Germany make this and also a desk version with a built-in ultra-violet light also (Fig. 13.3.).

Each instrument has the important advantage of providing a standard light in which to judge colour, but it must be remembered that diamonds are rarely seen in such ideal conditions in wear because there is some ultra-violet in most daylight.

Judging Colour in Daylight

The stone should be removed from its paper packet, especially if this has a blue lining paper, which is intended to 'improve' the colour.

The most convenient method of judging the colour of loose polished diamonds in daylight is that traditionally used by diamond sorters. The only 'equipment' required is a piece of white paper. It must be white or slightly grey, but it should have no tinge of colour. Comparison of different sheets of 'white' paper will soon show that the whiteness varies as much as the whiteness of diamond. Special

Fig. 12.2. *Diamonds placed table down in fluted white paper so that the colours may be judged by looking through the sides of the pavilions.*

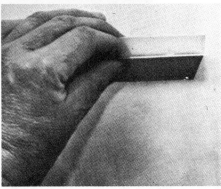

Fig. 12.3. *A thin V-shaped card which is effective for colour judgement.*

paper is available from trade sources, but there is no problem in finding ordinary blotting paper suitable for all but the finest grading.

It is difficult to judge the body colour of a polished diamond by looking at the table of the stone because the spectrum colours caused by fire confuse the eye. The stone must be examined through the side of the pavilion.

Cut the paper into a rectangle measuring 3 by 4 in (10 × 13 cm) and fold it into a concertina shape as shown in Fig. 12.2. A diamond for grading is placed in a fold with the table down on the side nearest the grader so that the colour of the side of the pavilion may be seen. (Stones are similarly examined in the standard light boxes previously described, being placed in a groove in a metal or plastic holder.) The folded paper is held or placed on a table, so that light from the north falls on it. A small piece of selected thin white card with a single fold, such as that marketed in West Germany for the purpose, is also very effective for grading when used as shown in Fig. 12.3.

The best way to gauge the colour of a stone is to compare it with a similar one of known colour grade, a comparison stone. It should be reasonably easy after some practice to decide which of the two stones has a lighter tint or whether they are nearly the same. Using one or more standard stones for colour grading is the safest method because then one's judgement does not vary much.

Professional diamond graders do not constantly use standard stones, however, because they become quick and accurate without them. Nevertheless, even the most skilled grader can experience a drift in colour judgement, especially after a long grading session, and he will from time to time make a comparison with one or more stones that have been agreed as standard colours by his company.

Very few diamonds are truly colourless and the professional grader can distinguish a range of extremely faint tinges of colour in stones that to anyone else are all absolutely colourless. Practice enables most people to start seeing yellow tinges; that is, when the stone begins to 'draw colour'. Few notice the very slight brown tinges and often it is only the skilled grader who is able to see at once the slight green tinges. In polished stone grading, faint tinges of brown are usually treated as comparable depths of yellow because scales are based on ranges from white to yellow. Sometimes breathing on a stone, to dull it momentarily, helps in colour judgement.

Learning to Grade

Stones that just begin to draw colour are the mental standard used by anyone, including the skilled grader, when not using a standard stone by which to judge. If a stone is placed by itself – without a comparison stone – in the paper concertina, the first thing to determine is whether it draws colour, whether it has any body colour at all, even the very, very faintest tinge. Anyone judging stones must know the grade of the stone in which he personally can just see a tinge of colour.

The way to begin is to examine as many stones as possible and compare them with each other and with stones that have already been reliably graded. Then take a single polished stone, study it in the folded paper and determine whether it draws colour. Then make the following decisions.

No draw :	Decide if the colour is	Fine White
	or	White.
Just draws :	Decide if the colour is	Commercial White
	or	Top Silver Cape.
Obviously draws :	Decide if the colour is	Silver Cape
	or	one of the lower categories.

The grading shown above is one of the scales used in the U.K. It does not matter what names, numbers, or letters are used, the principle of grading without standard stones is the same. For example Top Crystal is the key colour that just draws in the Scandinavian standard colour grading scale.

Comparison Stones

Without doubt, the use of standard comparison stones is the most reliable method of grading. It is essential to most people when grading the top range of colour. One comparison stone is better than none. The colour grade chosen should be determined by the purpose of grading. Suppose a retailer wants to buy loose stones only above White grading. His standard stone should be the lowest colour that would still be accepted as White, that is, on the borderline between White and Commercial White. It will then do the duty of two comparison stones because any stone as good or better in colour is White or better, and any stone that is worse in colour is below White. Three standard stones is a practical number to carry on one's person and five or seven are nearer the ideal. The stones should be selected so that they are one, two, or more steps apart in the colour scale, according to the accuracy needed (See frontispiece).

In use, the stones are placed in a standard viewing box or the folded paper concertina in grade order with about an inch between each. The stone under test is moved from gap to gap until it is seen to fit into the colour graduation, when it can, of course, be given a category.

G.I.A. and C.I.B.J.O. Standard Stones

The use of standard stones is in fact universal amongst professional graders, although they may not refer to them on every occasion. The G.I.A. uses them and the practice has been considerably extended by the member nations of C.I.B.J.O.* A master set is deposited in a non-commercial independent laboratory in each country for laboratory use and duplicate sets are available to those who wish to purchase them.

The depth of colour of a stone depends upon its bulk. If, say, a Silver Cape stone is recut to a quarter of its weight, it will improve in colour to Top Silver Cape or better. This also applies to diamonds in groups. If two diamonds are being compared for colour, they should not be placed so close as to touch each other because the stone with the stronger colour will tend to suffuse the other and make it appear poorer than it is. This effect is particularly apparent in a parcel of stones which may appear all to be of the same colour. When the stones are separated, some of much better or much worse colour may be found 'hidden' in the parcel. When the value is high, it is always wise to spread the stones to see if there is a big variation in colour.

* International Confederation of Jewellery, Silverware, Diamonds, Pearls and Stones.

Another problem for cutters and dealers who buy stones in quantity is that stones of better or worse colour become 'hidden' in a parcel or pile of stones because of colour saturation. It is only possible to check such a parcel by examining the stones one by one away from the others.

Grading Mounted Stones

It is impossible to grade mounted diamonds accurately because the setting and any surrounding stones affect the colour and also because one often has to look at the table where spectrum colours can confuse the eye.

When the setting is yellow gold, the diamond inevitably reflects or transmits some yellow from the metal. A fine stone is therefore depreciated by mounting it in yellow gold. Platinum is by far the best metal for mounts as it is not only white but much more hard wearing than gold. In the past, and currently with fine stones, it was normal practice to make the mount itself out of platinum whatever the rest of the ring or other jewel was made of. More weight, and therefore cost, of platinum is needed, however, so white gold is often substituted for it today and well designed claws of white gold are usually quite satisfactory. One compromise is to have platinum claws on white gold.

When a diamond is mounted close to a blue stone, suffusion causes its colour to 'improve'. That is one reason why blue sapphires surrounded by diamonds are so popular. Diamonds set with red, yellow, brown, or green stones, naturally tend to suffer as far as their colour is concerned. If daylight is being used, it is best to use a comparison stone held in a prong type holder beside the ring (Fig. 12.4 or 12.5).

Traditional Colour Grading Terms

Names used in colour grading fall into three main categories: those based on the names of mines or areas from which the bulk of such rough originated, such as Wesselton and Cape; those used by the cutters, such as Fine White and Commercial White; and those based on neutral numbers and letters. A traditional scale of colour grades is given on the next page.

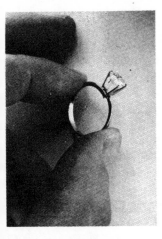

Fig. 12.5. *One form of clip holder is ring shaped and useful for visualizing a stone when set.*

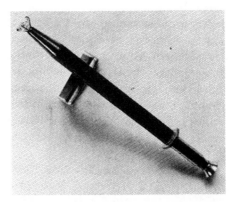

Fig. 12.4. *A prong holder is useful for comparing a loose stone of known colour against one of unknown colour set in a ring.*

1. Jager
2. River
3. Blue Wesselton
   (or Top Wesselton)
4. Wesselton
5. Top Crystal
6. Crystal
7. Top Silver Cape
8. Silver Cape
9. Cape
10. Very Light Yellow
11. Very Light Brown
12. Light Yellow
13. Light Brown
14. Yellow
15. Brown
16. Dark Yellow
17. Dark Brown
18. Very Dark Yellow
19. Very Dark Brown

Small stones
face up
colourless

All stones
face up
colourless

In lay terms, all of these from River to about Cape are shades of White. Without guidance and practice, the layman would see no colour in the first nine grades. Large or small stones in the first five or six grades will face up without colour. That is, only a skilled eye is likely to detect a trace of colour when the diamond is seen from the front. Small stones in the next grades down to Silver Cape will also face up colourless, but larger ones will show a tinge of colour to the trained eye. (See frontispiece.) Mounted stones below that grade will become increasingly evidently coloured, even to the untrained eye.

It remains a fact, of course, that stones in the top grades cannot be accurately classified even by the most skilled sorter, if they are mounted.

'Blue-White'

Jager, number one in the traditional colour scale, is abnormal and is usually omitted from current scales. It refers to a particular type of white stone from the Jagersfontein Mine that is very slightly bluish, usually owing to its strong blue fluorescence. The term blue-white arose from such stones. Jagers are very few indeed and it is incorrect to call other stones blue-white. The term has been much abused. There were even firms in the USA that called their lowest grade blue-white! It is probably true to say that 99 per cent of the diamonds that used to be sold retail as blue-white were not only *not* blue-white, but are not even in the top five colour grades.

In the Code of Trading issued by the National Association of Goldsmiths of Great Britain and Ireland, Rule 40 states: 'It is an unfair trade practice to use the term "blue-white", or any other term, expression, or representation of similar import, as descriptive of any diamond which under daylight or its equivalent, shows any colour other than a trace of blue.'

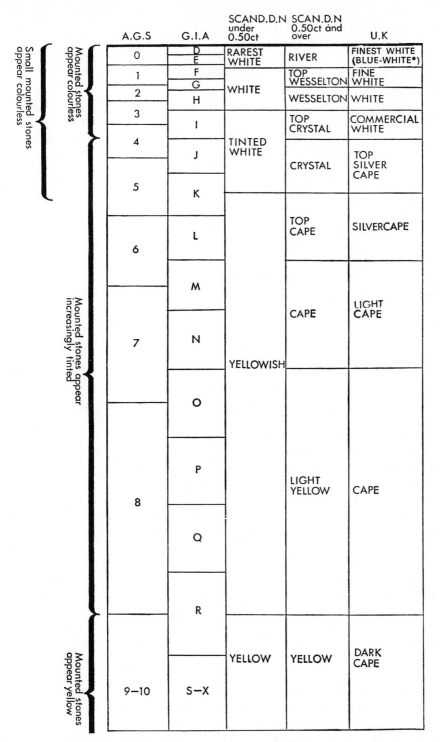

	A.G.S	G.I.A	SCAND.D.N under 0.50ct	SCAN.D.N 0.50ct and over	U.K
Small mounted stones appear colourless / Mounted stones appear colourless	0	D / E	RAREST WHITE	RIVER	FINEST WHITE (BLUE-WHITE*)
	1	F	WHITE	TOP WESSELTON	FINE WHITE
	2	G / H		WESSELTON	WHITE
	3	I	TINTED WHITE	TOP CRYSTAL	COMMERCIAL WHITE
	4	J		CRYSTAL	TOP SILVER CAPE
	5	K		TOP CAPE	SILVERCAPE
Mounted stones appear increasingly tinted	6	L	YELLOWISH		
		M		CAPE	LIGHT CAPE
	7	N			
		O		LIGHT YELLOW	CAPE
	8	P			
		Q			
		R			
Mounted stones appear yellow	9–10	S–X	YELLOW	YELLOW	DARK CAPE

Fig. 12.6. *Approximate comparison scales of colour. Blue-white is marked with an asterisk because it truly applies to the rare Jager colour but is commonly and incorrectly used for exceptionally white stones all over the world. See facing page.*

This is identical to Rule 28 in Rules for the Jewelry Industry published by the Federal Trade Commission in the U.S.A. from which it was derived. Members of the American Gem Society are forbidden use of the term 'blue-white' in advertising because the term has been misused so widely.

'Over-Blue' Diamonds

Other diamonds with strong blue fluorescence that can be seen in daylight usually come or came from the Premier or the Williamson Mines. If the body colour of the stone is White or better, the colour may appear milky blue or clear blue. If the body of the stone is yellowish, the blue fluorescence may give the stone an oily bluish appearance. Such stones are known as 'Premiers'.

False White Stones

If a stone has blue fluorescence and a tinted yellow body colour, the colours being complementary may cancel each other so that in some conditions the stone appears white. The experienced grader will recognize such stones because their colour grade appears to vary in different light intensities. A white light free of ultra-violet will disclose the true body colour, and an ultra-violet lamp the fluorescence.

Scan. D.N.

In 1970, the Scandinavian countries (Denmark, Finland, Norway, and Sweden) issued their Scandinavian Diamond Nomenclature and Grading Standards, known as Scan. D.N., in seven languages. The standards contain definitions, colour standards, clarity standards in great detail, and standards of cut. Colours are defined in terms of readings by a special German colour photometer, originally developed for the textile trade but modified for work on diamonds. Colours are named from the traditional scale but with different names for small stones because there is no commercial reason for grading them so accurately. The colour scales, shown with the American official scales and a British one for comparison, are illustrated in Fig. 12.6. The American scales, referred to again later, are also based on readings of a different instrument, a colorimeter, which is no longer made.

Ranges of Grade

Colour grading systems for polished diamonds vary considerably even among cutters and dealers in the same country, but very gradually a broad degree of standardization is emerging through the activities of certain professional gem organizations, related instructional classes, and international trading in diamonds.

For the individual business, the grading scale used must depend on the class of goods bought or sold. A cutter who polishes only a certain quality of goods has no need of an elaborate system extending far beyond the quality of the roughs he buys. One who deals only in low qualities requires three or four broad categories. One who deals in top goods must have more fine classifications, but they need extend only over the top end of the colour scale. Few firms employ more than a dozen classifications.

Some concerns use the traditional named colours, but many have devised systems of their own which are too numerous and confusing to detail.

Practice in the Trade

In the cutting trade certain terms have become generally accepted although exact interpretations of what is meant by them may vary, and there are also variations in some of the expressions. They are:

Blue-White
Finest White
Fine White
White
Commercial White

Top Silver Cape	Finest Light Brown
Silver Cape	Fine Light Brown
Light Cape	
Cape	Light Brown
Dark Cape	Dark Brown

Where this scale fits in relation to the traditional scale depends entirely on the interpretation of the manufacturer or dealer. How it should fit into other scales is shown in Fig. 12.6.

The position of the brown grades shows approximately where they stand in price. Very light brown in the traditional scale has been upgraded to Finest or Fine Light Brown and made roughly equivalent to yellow tints. Very light tints of brown are less easily seen than those of yellow, especially with the stone face-up. There are bigger steps in the lower end of the scale.

Commercial considerations must affect any such scale since it exists for commercial purposes, i.e. it determines the price. The U.K. has always been a very big market for the middle qualities of stones because of the diamond engagement ring tradition, hence a compression of the scale into the middle range by dealers. In any case, it is pointless usually to attempt fine grading for colour or other considerations for stones under about half a carat.

Commercial Scales

Many commercial scales are based on numbers or letters of the alphabet, which is reasonable, but even so have become confusing because of upgrading, so that a scale that originally began with A may now begin with AAA, and one that originally started at 1 or 0 may now start at 000. The reason may be the quite legitimate expansion of the firm's business into a higher grade than it previously dealt in, so that its best now becomes its second or third best and other categories are added without upsetting the existing ones.

One of the best known individual letter system is that of the British firm of A. Monnickendam Limited because it exports most of its production and deals in top qualities. For colour, the scale is AA, A, AAB, AB, B, BC, C, D, which covers the top of the traditional colour scale down to Silver Cape. Figures are used for purity grades. What is most important is the consistency in grading that they have maintained.

Some diamond dealers have their own grading systems but sell according to the particular systems and standards employed by their individual customers, so that a stone may be sold as a certain grade to one person and at another grade to another person, although the price will remain the same. The merchant will probably have a third grade for his office standard.

One fact is certain, that if say Fine White stones are bought from a dozen firms, their colours may actually range over several grades in the colour scale. The reason is not because of dishonesty in trading. It is mainly because each category must spread over a range of colour, and, particularly in lower grades, some firms use broader colour scales than others. Also, there is no universally accepted grading scale, and each firm has its own standard. The judging of colour is in any case a personal, subjective judgement and some people are better able to do it than others. The instruments in use for measuring colour are by no means perfect.

Measuring Fluorescence

The influence of fluorescence, particularly blue fluorescence, on grading has become recognized since the first edition of this book, when probably only the G.I.A. in the U.S.A. noted its influence on diamond certificates. Its importance is now generally accepted and its intensity, as well as its presence, is sometimes measured and noted. The intensity is measured in the same way as body colour; by comparison with a set of standard stones, perhaps five or six, in this case selected by their increased blue fluorescence under long-wave ultra-violet irradiation. Currently there is no agreed scale of fluorescence, but the Belgian Hoog Raad Voor Diamant (H.R.D.) certificate gives a fluorescence figure (see Appendix Six).

American Standards

The term Commercial White has been very much abused by applying it, particularly in the U.S.A., to goods of lower quality and therefore the American Gem Society forbids its use if it misleads the public.

The Americans were first to move towards a universal colour standard. There are in fact two scales in use. One is technically based on the A.G.S. colorimeter, an instrument which was available only to American Gem Society members. The A.G.S. system has eleven grades from Colourless to Yellow designated as 0, 1, 2, 3, 4, 5, 6, 7, 8, 9, 10. The steps are broader than in the traditional scale.

The other U.S.A. standard is that devised by the Gemological Institute of America in which the steps are smaller than in the traditional scale and are indicated from colourless to yellow as: D, E, F, G, H, I, J, K, L, M, N, O, P, Q, R, S, T, U, V, W, X. The top grade was coded as D to avoid any confusion with the various A, B and C systems employed by dealers. The bottom end goes beyond colours normally encountered in the gem diamonds, which end at Q or R.

The G.I.A. encourages use of its system by courses of training for members, by designing and selling colour grading instruments, and by running two Gem Trade Laboratories which will grade diamonds and issue certificates. One is in New York and the other in Los Angeles.

Members of the trade (at a trade fee) and members of the public (at a retail fee) may have stones graded. There is also a lower fee for diamond students. A certificate is issued for the stone giving not only colour grade but weight, measurements, shape and cut, fluorescence, purity grade, proportion grade (i.e. percentage variation from ideal cut), and details of flaws in finish.

Problems of Standardization

Despite these meritorious efforts to standardize colour grading, the problem remained unsolved largely because there were four problems in one, each of which had to be tackled separately.

They are: (1) Standardizing the terminology, (2) Standardizing the conditions under which stones are graded, (3) Standardizing the comparison stones,

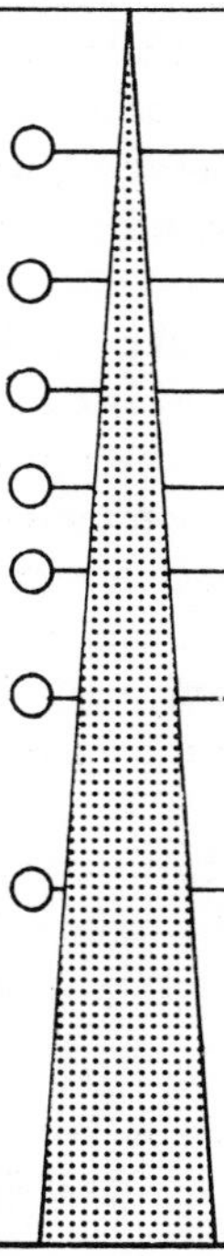

MASTER STONES	CIBJO INTERNATIONAL COLOUR GRADING SCALE	OTHER TERMINOLOGY	
		GIA	SCAND.D.N.
	EXCEPTIONAL WHITE +	D	RIVER
	EXCEPTIONAL WHITE	E	
	RARE WHITE +	F	TOP WESSELTON
	RARE WHITE	G	
	WHITE	H	WESSELTON
	SLIGHTLY TINTED WHITE	I J	
	TINTED WHITE	K	
		L	
	TINTED COLOUR	M	
		R	

Fig. 12.7.   *The C.I.B.J.O. international colour grading scale follows the G.I.A. scale in the white stones with broader groupings for the tinted stones. The wedge shape on the left represents depth of coloration, and shows where the C.I.B.J.O. master stones are located. The G.I.A. uses master stones just below the top of a grade instead of on the borderline.*

i.e., the named colours, and (4) Overcoming the forces of conservatism and th
economic circumstances that perpetuate present systems.

On the other hand, there are some diamond cutters and dealers who handl
diamonds in large numbers, dividing them into parcels of broad ranges of middl
qualities, who have a genuine grievance. They say that, owing to the propagand
about grading, their customers complain about individual stones in a parcel
Their prices, however, have been determined by economic rapid and broa
grading. If stones were sold with individual gradings, the prices would be mucl
higher.

The solution will probably come about through operation of the market i
such a way that the trade in all countries is forced to accept a common system
just as cutters have to accept basic grading of rough diamonds from the mines

C.I.B.J.O. Colour Grades and Grading

Since the four problems above were set out in the first edition of this book, the
international organization C.I.B.J.O., of which there were thirteen members i
1976 – Austria, Belgium, Britain, Denmark, France, Finland, Germany
Holland, Italy, Norway, Spain, Sweden, and Switzerland – has taken a big ste
towards solving them. Nomenclatures for colour grading and purity grading (se
next chapter) were agreed and, between 1975 and 1977, the colour grading wa
accepted by all member nations as well as the International Diamond Manu
facturers Association and the World Federation of Diamond Bourses.

Sets of colour graded stones were agreed amongst them, checked inde
pendently for consistency by Dr. E. Gübelin's laboratory in Switzerland and th
Gemological Institute of America's laboratories, and issued to laboratories i
each member country. These laboratories are independent of any commercia
undertaking and, using their master sets of C.I.B.J.O. colour graded stone
under controlled lighting conditions with standardized equipment, will issu
warranties as to the colour (and purity) of any diamonds submitted. Th
warranties are not transferable; the object of this is to avoid or minimize illega
switching of stones and warranties.

The C.I.B.J.O. colour grades are entirely consistent with the G.I.A.'s colou
grading system as shown in Fig. 12.7. As with most other systems, the bands ar
narrower in the better and therefore more valuable colours. Some of the name
are different from those previously current. They are:

Exceptional White Plus	To be judged in white light with a
Exceptional White	colour temperature of 5,000°K
Rare White Plus	(8,540°F/4727°C).
Rare White	
White	
Slightly Tinted White	
Tinted White	
Tinted Colour	

Tinted stones include brownish and greenish stones as well as yellowish.
There is one further grade for deeply coloured stones:
Fancy Diamond.

C.I.B.J.O. Comparison Stones

One object of the C.I.B.J.O. system is to provide a graded stone or graded set to anyone who wishes to buy it. The master set and any duplicates supplied comprise stones of the lowest acceptable colour for that grade. This means that the standard stones number seven, as shown in Fig. 12.7. Using a standard stone of the lowest colour for the grade has the considerable advantage that any stone compared with it that is better, must be in the same grade or better; and any stone that is worse, must be in a lower grade or worse. Alternatively, a stone that fits for colour between two comparison stones is positively in the category of the lower comparison stone.

The C.I.B.J.O. grades were selected deliberately to correlate positively with G.I.A. grades. The comparisons are also shown in Fig. 12.7. There is no

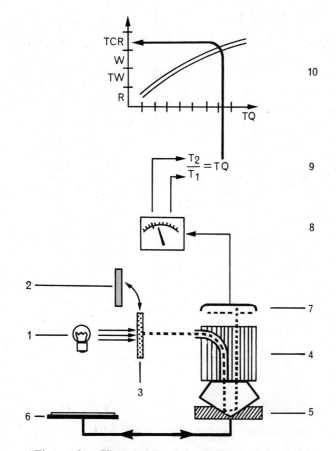

Fig. 12.8. *The principle of the Eickhorst diamond photomaster: 1: light source; 2: monochromatic filter (blue); 3: monochromatic filter (yellow); 4: fibre optics; 5: diamond holder; 6: calibration standard 'white'; 7: photo cell; 8: readout meter; 9: transmission quotient (TQ); 10: calibration curve to read off colour grade from TQ (in this case, Top Crystal).*

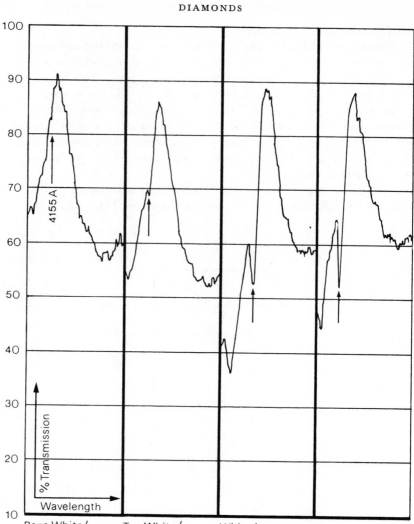

100

90

80

70

4155 A

60

50

40

30

% Transmission

20

Wavelength

10

Rare White/   Top White/   White/   Top Crystal/
   Top White   White   Top Crystal   Crystal

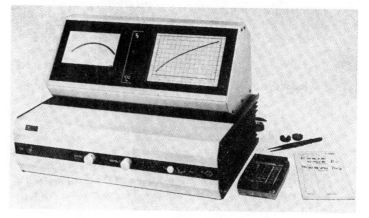

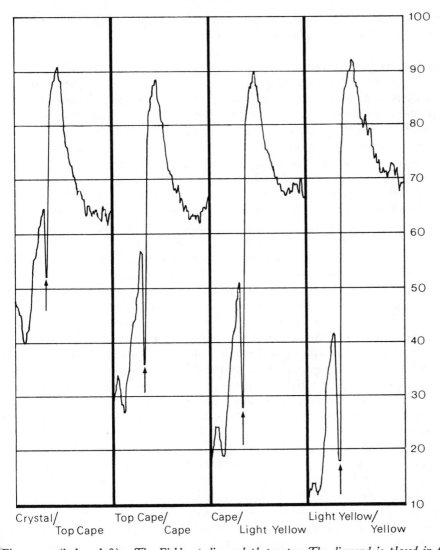

Crystal/   Top Cape/   Cape/   Light Yellow/
    Top Cape   Cape   Light Yellow   Yellow

Fig. 12.9. (below left) *The Eickhorst diamond photometer. The diamond is placed in the retracting holder, seen on the right projecting from the instrument. The instrument scale on the left is used to make comparisons of transmission factors. That on the right is a graph (which can be changed) to relate the transmission quotient to the grading scale being used.*

Figs. 12.10 and 12.11. (above left and above) *The eight diagrams show the 4155 Ångstrom absorption of diamonds (indicated by an arrow) in various grades using the Scan. D.N. scale. Note that the White/Top Crystal and Top Crystal/Crystal are so near that each must be Top Crystal in grade.*

separate grading for smaller stones, but it is recommended that C.I.B.J.O. grades should not apply to stones below 0·5 carat.

Grading by Instrument

Grading by eye, whether using master stones or not, is subjective, and attempts have been made to remove the element of human judgement. Those that have been successful to some degree have depended upon an observation made by B. W. Anderson in 1963 that, in Cape Series diamonds, the amount of yellowness of the stone was proportional to the absorption in the 4155 Å system in the spectrum. The relationship is shown in the graphs in Figs. 12.10 and 12.11, provided by M. Eickhorst of Hamburg, West Germany.

The first relatively practical instrument was devised by Robert M. Shipley, founder of the American Gem Society, and used for establishing the datum lines of the A.G.S. diamond colour grading scale, but was not suitable for general use. In recent years, Eickhorst designed a more practical diamond photmeter (Fig. 12.9), of which a number have been sold to diamond dealers. The diamond to be graded is inserted in a holder and drawn into the instrument. The instrument is zeroed on a standard white and then the 'transmission factor' of the stone is measured, by passing light through a yellow filter into the table of the stone and collecting the amount that is reflected and refracted back out of the stone. The amount is measured by a photo-cell and a meter. The same procedure is carried out with light through a blue filter corresponding to light at around 4155 Å. One figure divided by the other gives a transmission quotient (TQ), which can be related to a graph, prepared for the particular grading system being used, in order to read off the grade. (Figs. 12.10 and 11). Using transmission factors enables stones of varying cut and purity to be compared for colour.

The diamond photometer is designed specifically for white to yellowish stones and will give false readings for brownish ones. In principle, however, there is no reason why the characteristic 5040 Å line of absorption for Brown Series stones should not be measured in the same way. Fluorescence of a stone in certain lights can make a seeming difference of grade, a variation of apparent colour that used in the past to be called a 'false colour'. The fluorescence of a stone should be measured and noted separately, since the object of grading is to evaluate the body colour of the stone; the machine ignores fluorescence. Sensitivity of the diamond photometer is claimed to be about three times more than expert judgement by using comparison stones.

A more precise reflectance photo-spectrometer for measuring the characteristic absorption of Cape Series diamonds has been developed by Diamond Grading Laboratories, London, in conjunction with Carl Zeiss of West Germany.

The instrument is zeroed on a standard white (the accepted white of magnesium oxide) and absorption measurements of a stone under test recorded at three absorption lines: (a) 4120, (b) 4152, and (c) 4200 Å, which bridge the peak. By using an established formula ($\log a + \log b - 2 \log c$) on the results, a figure is arrived at which represents the yellowness in units from 0 to 10,000. Units can be converted into any established colour scale; for example, 0 to 50 covers what was known as Blue-White in the trade, 51 to 350 represents Top Fine White, and so on. The main absorption line has been found usually at 4152 Å, but can vary. The spread of readings and location of the main absorption zone compensate and are claimed to provide very accurate results.

Instruments are objective and claimed to be more accurate than human graders as well as de-skilling the task of grading. They are not accepted in the diamond trade however, except by a few, because of their cost, the time they absorb compared with human colour graders, and the fact that they are not yet practicable for commercial use by diamond manufacturers and dealers, who still prefer the eminently portable lens and tongs.

CHAPTER THIRTEEN

Grading Polished Stones for Clarity (Purity)

The clarity or purity of a polished diamond affects its quality and therefore its price, because any inclusion, cleavage, crack, or other natural feature inside or defect on the surface will interfere with the passage of light through the stone and affect its brilliance or appearance to some extent. Even normally invisible defects, such as twinning, can act as light sinks, absorbing some of the light entering the stone. The term clarity is preferred to purity, because purity suggests there are only two types of diamond, pure and impure.

Grades of Clarity

Diamonds are graded according to the degree of clarity, the finest being called flawless, clean, pure, perfect, or similar name. There are other names for levels of decreasing clarity.

Diamonds which just fail to be of the highest clarity are internationally referred to by dealers as VVS. This originally meant very, very slightly imperfect. The word imperfect is unsuitable when referring to natural inclusions and by general agreement among the leading trade and gemmological organizations of most countries the meaning has been replaced by very, very small inclusion.

Next down the scale of clarity is VS, meaning very small inclusions, then SI, small inclusions. After that, clarity grades are called First piqué, Second piqué, and so on. *Piqué* is French for pricked, referring to the inclusions. It is often written as PK.

Some cutters and dealers have lower grades which they call Spotted and which may also contain two or more categories. A number have a bottom category which they find profitable to cut and sell although it does not fit into their normal scale of clarity. These goods they call Rejection.

As with colour, scales of clarity vary in different countries and from cutter to cutter. They also depend upon the class of goods being graded. Owing to the steeper rise in price according to quality, top quality stones will obviously be graded on a much finer clarity scale than stones that are of lower quality in clarity and colour.

Equipment for Grading

Very little equipment is needed for grading diamonds. As with colour, however, a refined instrument is also available for those who prefer more sophisticated methods. The basic tools of the grader are a pair of diamond tongs, a piece of chamois leather, and a good hand lens of 10 × magnification. (Fig. 13.1.)At times, a shaded spot lamp is also required.

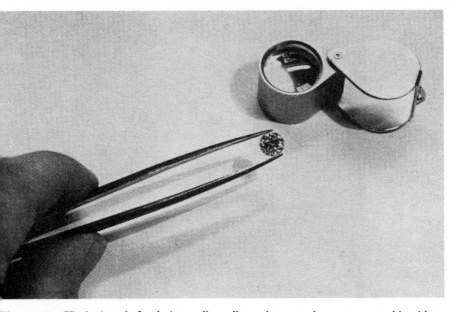

Fig. 13.1.   *The basic tools for clarity grading: diamond tongs and a 10× corrected hand lens.*

Cleaning Stones

It is easy to be misled by specks of dirt and tiny hairs on the surface of a diamond if one is not a professional grader. It is therefore essential to clean a stone before attempting to grade it for clarity.

The grader should wipe the stone with a small piece of clean chamois leather and afterwards it should not be fingered, but handled only with stone tongs. Some graders dip stones in surgical alcohol (even methylated spirit) or carbon tetrachloride before wiping them with a chamois leather, to make sure they are absolutely clean. A camel hair paint brush is also useful for removing dust.

Standard Magnification

Since it is relatively easy to find inclusions or other features in most diamonds with a sufficiently high-powered microscope, and clarity grading is for commercial purposes only, the degree of magnification must be specified. This is internationally agreed to be by a 10× magnifying lens, which has been corrected for chromatic and spherical aberration. The magnification should not be greater, or the stone might be downgraded. Neither should the magnification be lower, otherwise the stone might wrongly be upgraded.

It is also essential that a stone be examined under adequate illumination and by a trained eye. The traditional way of grading for clarity is to use a 10× hand lens (most top graders seem to prefer the Zeiss) in daylight against a corrected white paper background. Grading can be done efficiently also by artificial light, preferably using a heavily-shaded spot lamp as shown in Fig. 13.2.

Fig. 13.2 *How the stone should be held in relation to the shaded lamp, so that inclusions can be seen. Stones can also be clarity graded, of course, in suitable daylight.*

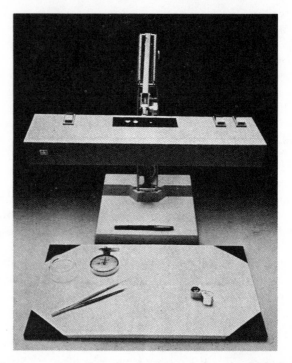

Fig. 13.3. *A bench-type diamond grading lamp that is intended for both colour and purity grading. It has also an ultra-violet lamp on top facing upwards, with a shield (not shown), for gauging the fluorescence of stones. Made by Eickhorst Systems.*

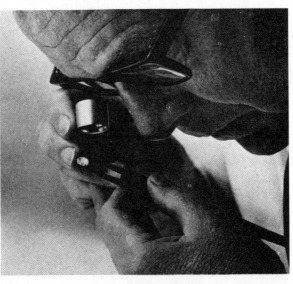

Fig. 13.4. There are many effective ways of holding the stone and lens, but the lens must always be near the eye and the hands touching to hold the stone steady and adjust the focus. Here is one way and another is shown in Fig. 13.5 below, taken at the Tel Aviv Diamond Bourse. Still another method is shown in Fig. 14.17.

Diamond Tongs

The usual stone tongs employed by most gemmologists are too coarse for holding diamonds. Special diamond tongs with fine non-slip tips are available. They are blunter than watchmakers' tweezers, have fine milling inside the tips, and usually are not so strongly sprung. Some tongs incorporate slides to hold the stone in the clamped position, but usually these will be found less convenient as skill in handling improves.

Most people hold the stone in tongs in the left hand and the lens in the right hand. It is therefore most convenient to be able to pick up the diamond left-handed, but many people find it easier to pick up a stone with the tongs in the right hand and then transfer them to the left. A stone is most conveniently picked up by tongs if it is standing on its table on a firm surface. Picked up from the paper, it is likely to be held out of square and may fly from the tongs. The tips of the tongs should be just past the centre line of the stone.

Stones should be examined in a comfortable position where there is no danger of losing a stone if it is accidentally dropped.

A lamp, if used, should have an opaque shade and should be positioned in front of the grader as shown in Fig. 13.2. The stone may be held so that light from the side of the lamp reaches it. This provides almost dark field illumination and sometimes makes it easier to find inclusions. At other times, a sheet of white paper under the diamond provides part-transmitted light which may prove to be better.

Focusing the Diamond

To keep the stone in focus, rest a finger of the hand holding the lens on the other hand so that both hands are steady together, and stretching or relaxing the finger will provide fine focusing. The method is shown in the illustration, Fig. 13.4 and an alternative in 13.5.

One method of examining a stone internally, is to look into it from the pavilion side. Inclusions will often be reflected a dozen or many more times by facets, which increases the chances considerably of finding them. Having noted any that show up through the pavilion, turn the stone over and examine it systematically through the table, first searching the volume under the table and then going round the volume under the other facets clockwise to make sure none of the stone is missed.

Afterwards – or before, if this is preferred – a similarly systematic study of the surface of the stone, both above and below the girdle and around the girdle itself, should be made. Turn the stone so that light is reflected from the surfaces of the facets, which will show up any naats, polishing lines, missing or extra facets, or damage.

It will be necessary to put down the stone and pick it up again after turning it about 90° in order to make sure that no inclusions or other features were concealed by the tongs. Several rotations will also be necessary when examining the girdle.

The Gemolite Microscope

The Gemological Institute of America advises the clarity grading of diamonds by a binocular microscope magnifying to ten times, preferably with dark field illumination. It supplies such a microscope, rather confusingly named the Gemolite, which provides either dark field or light field illumination and has a special universal holder for the stone (Fig. 13.6).

There is wide field binocular magnification and also a zoom lens, so that a particular inclusion, say, may be examined at a higher magnification. The Gemolite is an excellent instrument and makes the mechanics of grading much easier, but it is expensive in the U.K., and is, of course, not portable. Japanese and German instruments for grading have also been placed on the market.

A standard grading light is available for attachment to the Gemolite so that clarity and colour grading may be carried out with the aid of the instrument.

The zoom feature has led to a practice in certain places of noting the location of very small inclusions at 50 × magnification and then seeing if they can be found by 10 × magnification. Not all the trade accepts this practice.

A Basic Grading System

Anyone, particularly a retailer, handling diamonds, should acquire the habit of looking at them, whether set or unset, with the naked eye to see if inclusions

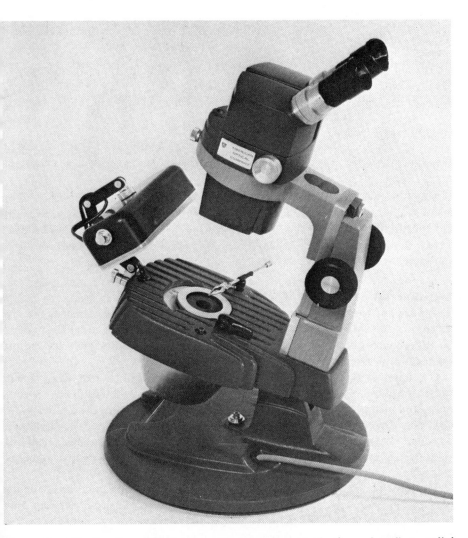

Fig. 13.6.   *The Gemolite, an effective 10 × binocular microscope for diamond grading supplied by the Gemological Institute of America. The diamond is held in the removable clip seen on the stage, under which is dark field illumination. Over the stage is a colour grading lamp. A zoom lens is incorporated and there are other fittings including a special eyepiece for proportion grading.*

are visible. It is very easy *not* to see inclusions unless the act of looking for them is deliberate.

This first inspection by naked eye is the first act of grading into an upper or a lower class. When inclusions can be seen by the naked eye, the stone falls into the piqué grades or below.

The beginner can look at grading in this way:

Top Grades: Flawless, VVS, and VS can only be identified with a 10 × lens. If there is any mark under the table, it must be very inconspicuous.

Middle Grade: SI can be identified with a watchmakers' eyeglass.

Lower Grades: Piqué and spotted stones can be identified with practice by the naked eye, but should be graded through a lens, each lower grade becoming more obvious.

Dark-coloured spots downgrade a stone more than light-coloured ones. A spot in the pavilion will often be reflected several times in a stone and this will downgrade it more than a spot in the crown which is not multiplied by reflection.

Unfair Descriptions

There are some expressions that are regarded as unethical in grading polished diamonds, because they are misleading. They include eye-clean, commercially perfect, and 'our very best quality'.

'Clean' is a term commonly used in the U.K. and exception is not normally taken to it. It was so abused in the U.S.A., however, that it has been prohibited as a clarity description of diamond by the American Gem Society. The Federal Trade Commission in the U.S.A. allows its use only if the diamond meets the Commission's definition of perfect.

Commercial Grading

There are not as many different grading systems for clarity or purity as there are for colour, but there are many different interpretations of the scales that do exist by different cutters and dealers, and many different names for scales using numbers and letters.

If a diamond is bought from a reputable dealer, it will be a certain price per carat. If another diamond of the same size and quality is bought from another reputable dealer, the price will be in the same region. Comparison of how the different dealers describe the stones may reveal a considerable difference however. One stone might well be described as 'Fine white, clean', and the other as 'Commercial white, slight piqué'. There is no universally accepted standard of grading.

The same problem occurs with clarity as with colour grading, i.e. that Nature does not provide convenient steps into which one can classify inclusions. For example, a spot under the table would grade the stone lower than one at the edge, but suppose the spot is between the table and the edge, at what point is the stone downgraded? The grader is always having to make borderline decisions like this, and the more divisions into grades the more borderline cases occur.

It is obvious therefore that disputable classifications occur and that within any category there are better and less good qualities, so that a picking price is usually charged as described on page 264.

Grading Scales

The N.A.G.* Code of Trading requires a stone described as Internally Flawless to be completely transparent and free from internal inclusions when examined by a skilled observer with normal or corrected to normal vision in daylight or its equivalent with a $10 \times$ lens corrected for chromatic and spherical aberration. To be claimed as Flawless it must also be free from surface marks.

The broad scale of clarity used by the Gemological Institute of America is given below and compared with one commonly employed in the U.K. In most gem diamond classes in Europe, the American scale or a version of it is used, but the diamond trade employs its own grading systems.

The Scandinavians have included in their recommended scale a grade between Flawless and VVS to accommodate stones with slight marks on the surface only that can be made Flawless. The grade is called Internally Flawless, and has been included below.

The C.I.B.J.O., in its *Rules of Application for the Diamond Trade,* adopts the same principle but goes further and makes Internally Flawless the top grade. This means that external marks, such as chips, scatches, faulty cut, blemishes and additional facets, are disregarded in the purity grading. The term 'purity' is used by the C.I.B.J.O. instead of clarity.

* National Association of Goldsmiths, London, E.C.2.

A Scale Commonly Used in the U.K.	Scandinavian Diamond Nomenclature	Gemological Institute of America Scale	C.I.B.J.O. Scale
Flawless (clean)	FL	FL	
	IF (Internally Flawless)		IF
VVS	VVS_1	VVS_1	VVS_1
	VVS_2	VVS_2	VVS_2
VS	VS_1	VS_1	VS
	VS_2	VS_2	
SI	SI_1	SI_1	SI
	SI_2	SI_2	
1st Piqué	1st Piqué	I_1 (Imperfect)	P_1
2nd Piqué			
3rd Piqué	2nd Piqué	I_2	P_2
Spotted	3rd Piqué	I_3	P_3
Heavy Spotted			
Rejection			

Fig. 13.7.   *Four main purity, or clarity, grading systems. They are more consistent than colour grading systems, but differences exist in interpretation.*

The Americans and Scandinavians have divided each of the VVS, VS, and SI grades into two for larger stones, of over half a carat. It is very difficult to grade small stones into such fine categories, and also rather fruitless as far as price is concerned. As the size increases, however, from about half a carat upwards it becomes less and less difficult to make these finer gradings.

In general, grading of such accuracy is only necessary with larger stones of higher quality and value. Even then, the market is likely to operate more powerfully as an influence on price of exceptional goods than the grading system, to judge by the range of price asked for and obtained in private and auction sales. The main grading systems are shown in Fig. 13.7. The G.I.A.'s was the first to be universally applied, as was the G.I.A. colour scale.

Grading Examples

Examples of inclusions and blemishes in polished diamonds and how they are graded in Figs. 13.8 to 13.34 refer to stones of half a carat and over.

Clarity grading depends upon:
1. Size, position and brightness of inclusions within the stone.
2. Surface damage.
3. Imperfections of make more conveniently considered under clarity.

The third category requires some explanation, because make – the nearness of the cutting to the ideal proportions – is a separate consideration when estimating the quality of a cut stone. Sometimes a cutter will add a very tiny extra facet (Fig. 13.8) at a junction of facets to remove a tiny part of the original crystal skin or a tiny flaw in the crystal. The facet will not affect the make, because it makes no difference to main angles or proportions. Very small extra facets do not down-grade the diamond in the clarity scale, although larger ones do so.

The size of the polished diamond must also be considered when grading for clarity. It is obviously a waste of time grading small diamonds with great accuracy because there is not enough price difference to make it worth while. It must never be forgotten that the purpose of all grading is commercial. Generally, stones below 0·50 carat will be graded into fewer classifications than larger ones.

Criteria for Grading

Some examples of the maximum allowable blemishes are shown below as a

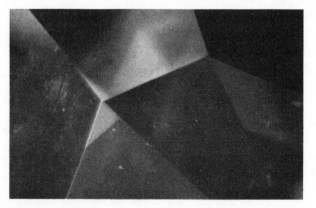

Fig. 13.8. *Very small extra facet on the front of a stone, the result of removing a tiny blemish. It does not down-grade the stone.*

general guide. The descriptions in the first edition were in line with the teaching of grading at Sir John Cass College, London. In this edition, they have been relaxed to some extent to come more into line with commercial practice.

The position, as well as the size and brightness of an inclusion, is important in grading. As a general rule, an inclusion of a given size and brightness will downgrade a diamond less and less as it appears in the following positions:

1. Under the table.
2. Under a star facet.
3. Under any other crown facet, except when near the girdle.
4. Near the girdle.
5. Seen only, or only clearly from the pavilion side.

For definitions of sizes of inclusions and grading, see Appendix 6.

Maximum Allowable Blemishes Only Just Visible with 10 × Lens

Flawless	Internal growth lines that show no colour from the front of the stone. Minor natural (skin left after bruting) on girdle. Minor roughness of girdle. Very small extra facet not visible from front which does not flatten girdle.
IF (Internally Flawless)	As above with the addition of minor nicks or pits not in the table, girdle roughness, and slight facet abrasion, all of which may be removed by simple diamond polishing.

Very difficult to find with 10 × Lens

VVS	Internal very tiny spot or group of externally small spots outside the table. Very tiny colourless crystal. Tiny feather not visible from the top of the stone. Tiny feather. Externally, minor naturals on the girdle, minor pits and scratches not in the table. Slightly rough facet edges. Slight bearding of the girdle not visible from the front. Very slight abrasion of the culet. Slightly larger extra facet.

Difficult to find with 10 × Lens

VS	Internal growth lines that show slight colour from the front. Small cleavages. Small colourless crystals. Group of pinpoints. Small cracks. Surface scratches. Indented naturals on the girdle. Some general abrasion. Bearding of girdle. Abraded culet. Slightly larger extra facet.

Just Visible with Watchmaker's Eyeglass

SI	Groups of pinpoints. Fissure under a facet edge. Colourless crystals. Dark crystal or small crystals. Small cracks or cleavages. Slight cloudy areas. Rough culet. Nick in girdle. Slightly larger extra facet.

Only Just Visible to the Naked Eye

| 1st Piqué | Slight visible cloud (fluorescent) under table. Dark crystal. Colourless reflecting crystal under table. Cleavage visible from the front. Small cracks from girdle. Externally, small indentation of table. Rough girdle. Larger extra facets. |

More Easily Visible to Naked Eye

| 2nd to 3rd Piqué | Internal butterfly not under table. Groups of dark spots under table. Dark cloud under table. Feather under table. Longish coloured cleavage not under table. Externally more scratches and abrasion. More abraded culet. Larger extra facets. |

Easily Visible to Naked Eye

| Spotted | Internal butterfly under table. Fair sized dark inclusion or group of spots under table. Coloured cleavage reaching under table. Cloudy areas reaching under table. Externally, scratch on table, more abrasion. Larger indented naturals. |

Very Easily Visible to Naked Eye

| Heavy Spotted | Internal large or very numerous dark spots under table. Large areas of colourless crystals under table. Coloured cleavage under table. Externally, deeper scratches on table. Broken culet. Natural near girdle. Flat on girdle. Large extra facets. |

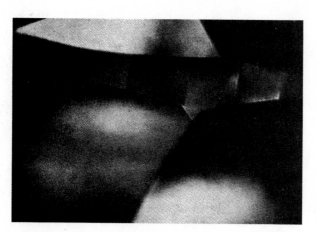

Fig. 13.9. *A very small extra facet under a faceted girdle, magnified fifty-five times. It is not a blemish.*

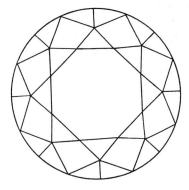

Flawless

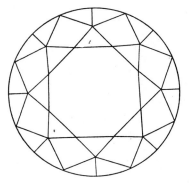

VVS 1

VVS 1

Fig. 13.10. to 13.26. *Examples of clarity grading. Where there are two grades given, the first is in line with current commercial practice while the second is that given in the first edition.*

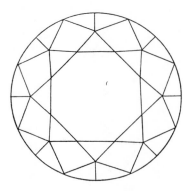

VSS 1–VVS 2

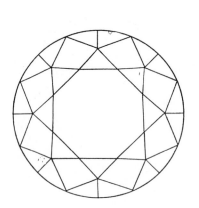

VVS 1–VVS 2

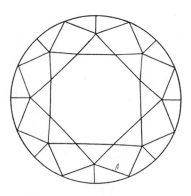

VVS 2–VS 1

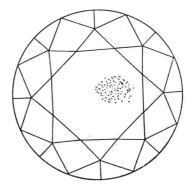

VS 1–VS 2

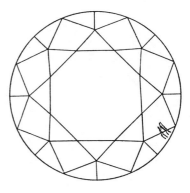

VS 1–VS 2

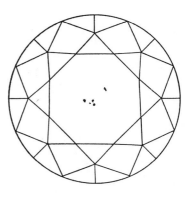

VS 2–SI

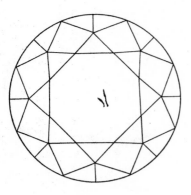

SI–1st piqué

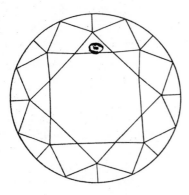

SI–1st piqué

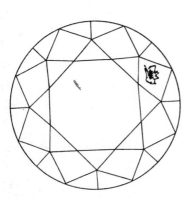

SI–2nd piqué

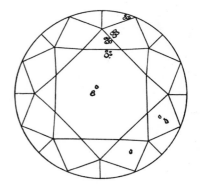

SI–2nd piqué

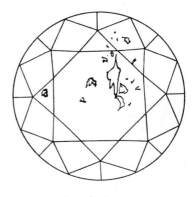

1st–3rd piqué

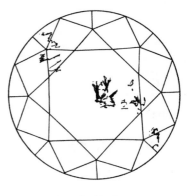

1st–3rd piqué

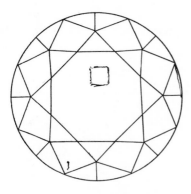

2nd–3rd piqué

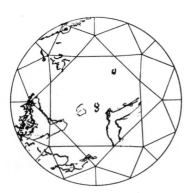

3rd piqué–Spotted

3rd piqué–Spotted

3rd piqué–Heavy spotted

3rd piqué–Heavy spotted

3rd piqué–Heavy spotted

Rejection

Rejection

Rejection

Scan. D.N. and C.I.B.J.O. Scales

The grading scale detailed in pages 289 to 292 is one that was (and still is) taught in the U.K. to students entering the Gemmological Association's examinations for the Gem Diamond Diploma certificate; but it will be changed when the C.I.B.J.O. scale comes into general use. Several European cutters and dealers have pointed out to the author that this scale is more severe than those in general use commercially. Some have made a point of the high level of their grading by complying generally with the scale in the first edition. It has therefore been broadened, as explained on page 293.

As this edition goes to press, C.I.B.J.O. have not published their limiting cases, but they may well be very similar to those already published in Scan. D.N. (Fig 13.29 to 13.34). The G.I.A. system is currently the most used in the world; it is taught not only in the U.S.A. but also in several other countries. The G.I.A. does not however publish its grading system, except to students and graduates of its courses. The following diagrams are offered, therefore, as from the Scandanavian standards, which may well be in line with the C.I.B.J.O. scale when it is agreed upon. Copies of the Scan. D.N. diagrams can be obtained from the Gemmological Association of Great Britain, St Dunstan's House, Carey Lane, London E.C.2.

Internal features		External features	
.	Pinpoint.	N	Minor natural.
∴	Group of pinpoints.		
•	Dark spot.	N	Natural.
∴.	Group of dark spots.		
	Cloud of tiny pinpoints.	N	Indented natural.
	Group of colourless crystals	∨	Girdle nick.
	Colourless crystal.		
	Cleavages around colourless crystal.		Minor girdle roughness.
	Group of dark inclusions.		Girdle roughness.
	Dark inclusion.		Group of small pits.
	Dark inclusion, surrounded by cloud.	•	Pit or cavity.
	Small cleavage.		Scratch.
	Larger cleavage.		Polishing lines.
	Girdle cleavage, surrounded by cloud.	*	Percussion figure.
			Growth line.
	Girdle fringes.	∇EF	Extra facet.
	Growth or twin line.		Rough culet.
			Abraded culet.

301

F

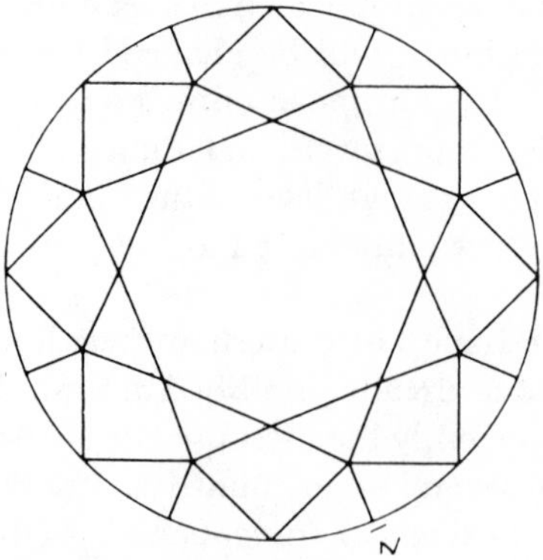

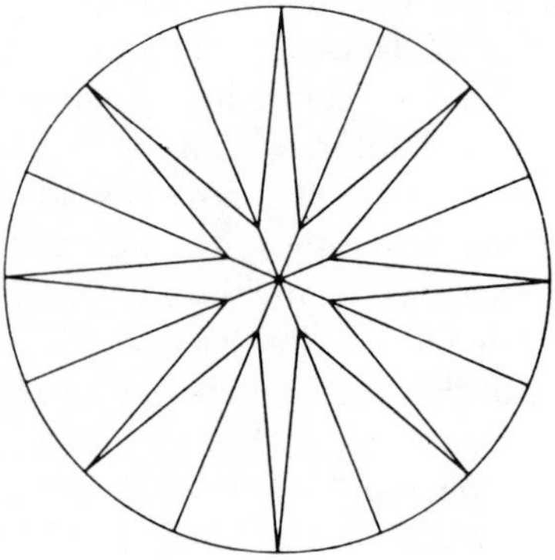

A minor natural.

IF

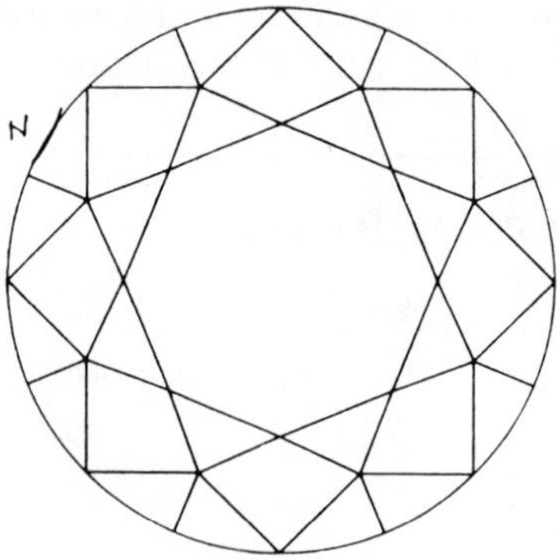

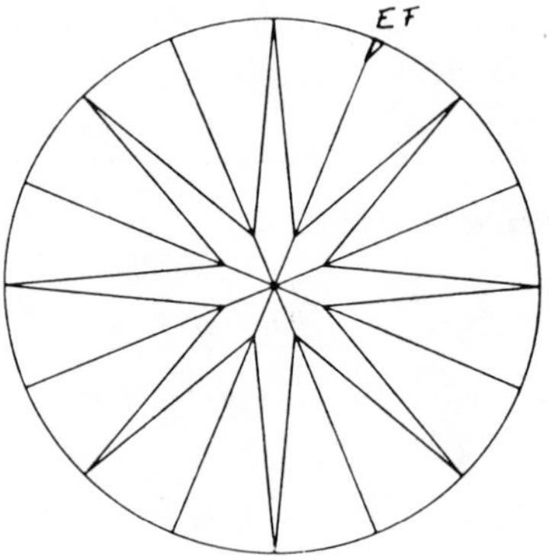

A natural and a minor extra facet.

IF

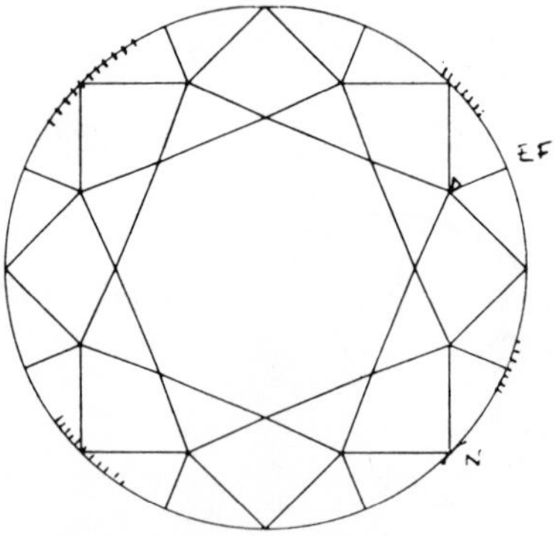

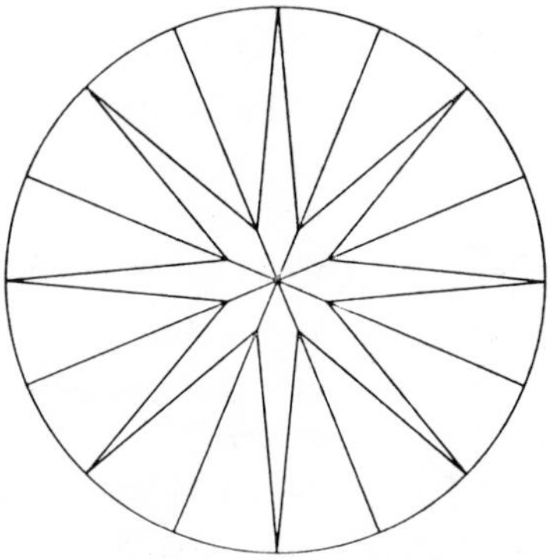

A natural, girdle roughness and a minor extra facet.

Fig. 13.29. to 13.34. *Examples of stones graded according to the Scan. D.N. scale. These, and the symbols on page 301, are published by kind permission of Herbert Tillander, Chairman, and other members of the Scandinavian Diamond Nomenclature Committee, Helsinki, Finland.*

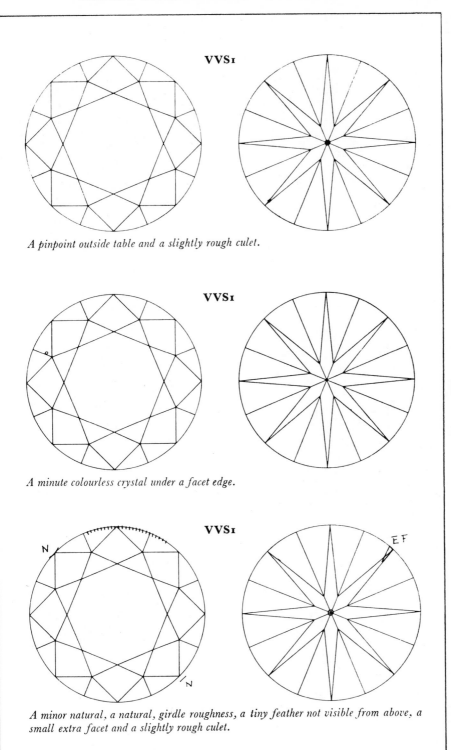

VVS1

A pinpoint outside table and a slightly rough culet.

VVS1

A minute colourless crystal under a facet edge.

VVS1

A minor natural, a natural, girdle roughness, a tiny feather not visible from above, a small extra facet and a slightly rough culet.

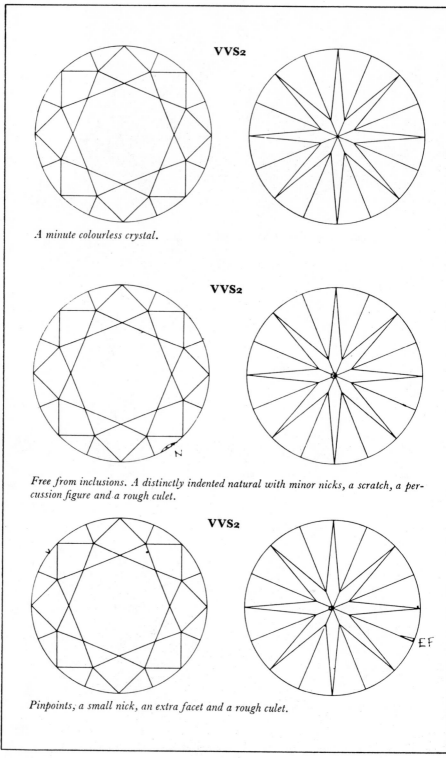

VVS₂

A minute colourless crystal.

VVS₂

Free from inclusions. A distinctly indented natural with minor nicks, a scratch, a percussion figure and a rough culet.

VVS₂

Pinpoints, a small nick, an extra facet and a rough culet.

VS1

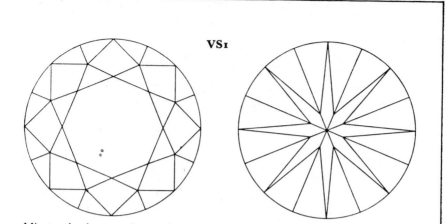

Minute colourless crystals very close to table surface.

VS1

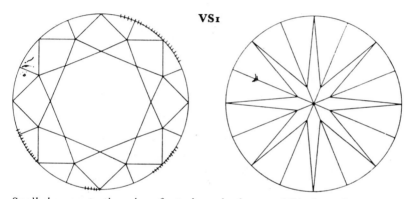

Small cleavages partly under a facet edge and only some visible from above, a minor colourless crystal and areas of girdle roughness.

VS2

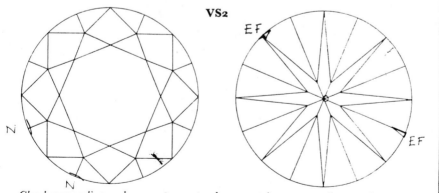

Cloud surrounding a cleavage, two naturals, a scratch, two extra facets and a rough culet.

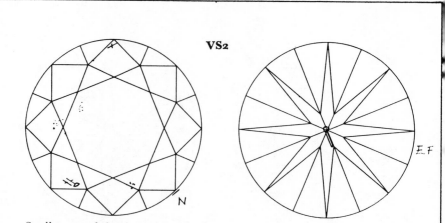

VS2

Small groups of pinpoints, minor colourless crystal, a minor natural, scratches, an extra facet and a rough culet.

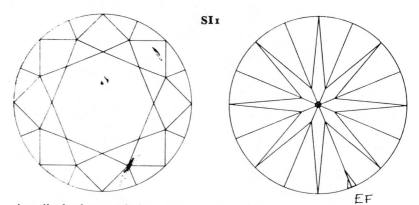

SI1

A small colourless crystal, cleavages (one of these reflects and another is surrounded by a small cloud), extra facets and a rough culet.

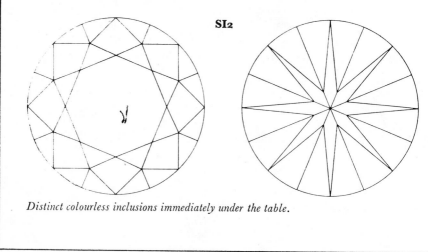

SI2

Distinct colourless inclusions immediately under the table.

P1

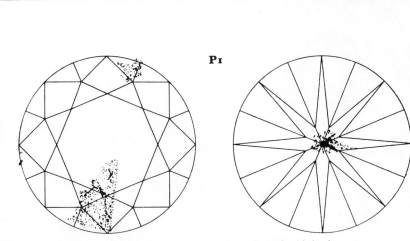

Large cleavages, a reflecting cleavage near culet and an abraided culet.

P2

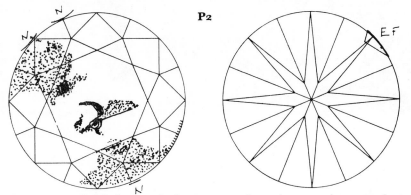

Colourless and dark inclusions, cloudy areas, naturals, a minor natural, an extra facet and girdle roughness.

P3

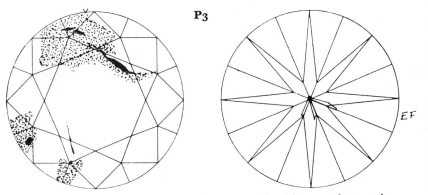

Dark inclusions, colour-filled cleavages, clouds, a girdle nick, extra facets and an abraided culet.

Fig. 13.35. *A feather* (top right) *and butterfly* (above, centre), *as seen through a 10 × lens.*

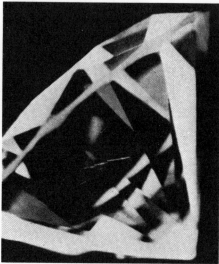

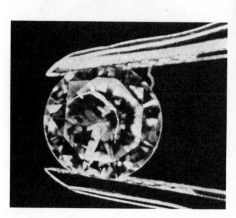

Fig. 13.36 *Crack under the table.*

Fig. 13.37. *Cracks inside the pavilion.*

'Carbon Spots'

An inclusion that diminishes quality may vary from the tiniest spot which is black or white and only just possible to find with a 10 × lens, to masses of coke-like inclusions and cleavages that can instantly be seen with the naked eye.

For fine grading of top quality larger stones, it is very important to study inclusions by light from the sides of the stone to give a dark field effect or to use if possible proper dark field illumination, otherwise it is impossible to know whether some inclusions are transparent or opaque. All look black if light is passed through the stone (transmitted light). From this fact arose the incorrect belief that all inclusions were black 'carbon spots'. Very few, if any, are carbon and only a few are truly black.

Types of Internal Blemishes

Inclusions and other blemishes usually fall into the following categories:

1. *Solid inclusion,* which may be black or white and vary from a pin point to a large mass.
2. *Bubble,* which is transparent and roundish and may be very tiny to fairly 'large'. (Actually a transparent inclusion, probably of olivine, see page 387.)

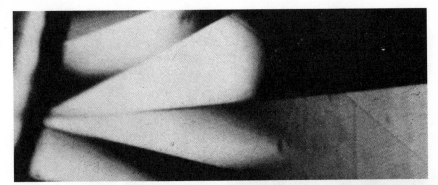

Fig. 13.38. *Naats showing as a result of polishing.*

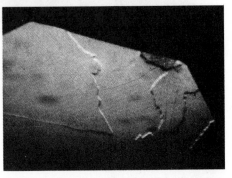

Fig. 13.39. *Naats on the surface of a polish-ed stone.*

3. *Cloud,* which is a group of very tiny transparent bubbles or inclusions too small to be seen individually but gives a clouded appearance.

4. *Cleavage, feather* or *glets* (the Dutch name), a cleavage crack that looks like a feather when viewed flat on (Fig. 13.35).

5. *Butterfly,* an inclusion with cleavage cracks around it, that from some directions look like the wings of a butterfly (Fig. 13 35).

6. *Crack,* a fracture in a non-cleavage direction (Fig. 13.36 and 13.37).

7. *Graining,* twinning which although usually visible externally may also be visible if internal as phantom parallel lines (Fig. 13.45). Very occasionally these are a different colour from the rest of the diamond (Fig. 13.45). They also occur as dark banding. (See page 383.) Graining, seen only through the pavilion and not whitish, coloured or reflecting, does not downgrade the clarity.

8. *Growth line,* an internal jagged line which can be seen to have fine serrations under higher magnification. (See page 383.)

9. *Fringe,* series of radial cracks penetrating into the stone from the girdle.

10. *Bearded girdle,* like a fringe, but finer and caused by bad cutting; actually a fault of make (Fig. 13.40).

11. *Fezels,* shallow, white, whispy inclusions in a twinning plane, similar to those in Fig. 17.53.

External Features

For a diamond to be regarded as flawless, it must be free of external blemishes as well as being clean internally. There is one exception to this rule. As already mentioned, a small natural on the girdle is not regarded as an external flaw

Fig. 13.40. *Bearding around a girdle which may be slight enough to be almost invisible, or fairly obvious.*

except by some graders when the girdle is polished. It does not cause loss in brilliancy if it does not flatten the girdle and is no wider than the girdle.

The main external blemishes are:

1. *Scratches.*
2. *Chips* and *nicks.*
3. *Pits* or *cavities.*
4. *Flats* on the girdle.
5. *Naats* on the surface. Raised surface features (Fig. 13.39).
6. *Polishing lines.* (Fig. 13.44.)
7. *Burn marks* caused during polishing (Fig. 13.44).
8. *Naturals* or *naif* (the Dutch name) near the girdle (Figs. 13.41 to 13.42).
9. *Rough girdle.*
10. *Rough or broken culet.*
11. *Twinning lines* or *naat.* External line or parallel lines (Fig. 13.38) caused by polishing over a twinned area.

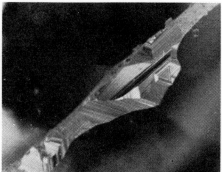

Fig. 13.41. *Natural on a girdle large enough to be a blemish.* Right: *Magnified view of a large natural.*

Surface Damage on Cut Diamonds

Abrasions and scratches on the surfaces of cut diamonds are caused by contact with other diamonds. Under a lens, the defects look like white lines. Although a scratch on a facet may appear straight and sharp, magnification will show the edges to be rough. Normally such scratches are very shallow. Sometimes the edges of facets have become abraded by rough contact with other diamonds and may also be nicked. The culet may also be damaged by abrasion or by chipping.

As carrying two or more cut stones loose in a diamond paper causes the damage described, the stones are often referred to as 'paper worn' or 'paper marked'. Cut stones should always be carried in separate papers. If they are small, several can be carried between a folded piece of lint in the paper. Using lint is a sensible protection for all valuable stones.

Chips usually occur on girdles, but may be seen on facet edges. They are often conchoidal fractures caused by light blows. Impact from a hard pointed article can cause cleavage marks on the surface of a stone. These marks are normally square or hexagonal (according to whether the piece removed was in the direction of the cubic or dodecahedral plane). Damage to a stone caused by

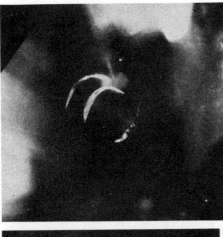

Fig. 13.43. *One fault of make is damage to the surface, caused during polishing. Usually this is a burn mark, but here, on a Russian stone, the result is similar to a ring crack. The stone weighs 0·30 ct.*

Fig. 13.42. *Exceptionally large natural on the pavilion.*

Fig. 13.44. *Polishing lines on a facet.*

impact usually shows signs of both fracture and cleavage, which occur together in a roughly stepped formation.

A fissure in the surface of a stone will have been caused by a cleavage crack extending to the surface.

Naats usually show as pits in the surface. A pit, or in more extreme cases, a cavity, may have been caused by a naat being pulled out of the surface while polishing. A naat on the surface will stand up as a slightly raised plane with straight edges because of its different hardness when the stone was being polished. (Fig. 13.39), just like a knot in a piece of sandpapered wood.

Other Surface Features

Polishing lines are seen as a series of close parallel lines on the surface of a facet and may be the result of a facet having been ground and by accident not polished, by careless polishing, or by the facet having been forced by trying to grind it in a hard direction, i.e. with the grain. (Fig. 13.44.) One result in this case will be burn marks but it can cause cracks, as in Fig. 13.43.

Bearded girdles are strictly internal faults, but are sometimes included with the external ones because they are, like most external faults, induced in some way. They are in fact caused by over zealous bruting during the manufacturing process, which causes a series of fine hair-like cracks extending a short distance radially into the stone from the girdle, as shown in Fig. 13.40. Such fuzzy girdles also lack the normal waxy finish because bruting has been carried out too rapidly.

A girdle can be rough, lacking its waxiness, but not bearded, which is a minor feature. Bearding is usually only part way round a girdle. It can be so fine that it is difficult to detect, or fairly obvious. There is no excuse for bearding in high purity stones because sufficient care should have been taken in manufacture. The Gemological Institute of America reports one instance of bearding having been removed by making the girdle <-shaped. The same profile was introduced subsequently for a form of polished girdle.

Fig. 13.45 *Two examples of graining, photographed at the G.I.A.'s Santa Monica gem laboratory. The prominent ones on the left look like polishing lines, but extend across facet edges and are therefore grain lines. The grain lines in the 1.22 ct diamond below are very unusual because they are purple in colour.*

Figs. 13.46 and 13.47. *Laser-treated diamonds. The lower picture shows a drill hole that is reflected a number of times.*

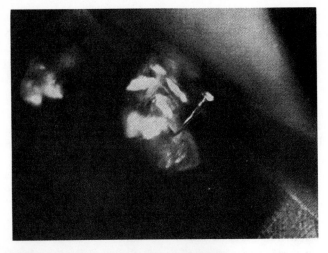

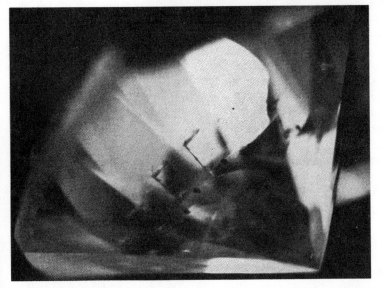

Laser Treatment

The first experiments of drilling holes in diamond by laser beams were made to improve manufacture of diamond wire-drawing dies. In 1972 the unpublicized fact became known that one concern was drilling into dark and coloured inclusions in diamond and leaching out the inclusions to make them light in colour, thus upgrading the quality of the stone. M. Lorie and Perlman Bros, of Antwerp, claim to have been originators of the process. There is still secrecy about the techniques employed, but it is known that holes can be drilled in diamond by using a carefully pulsed beam from a YAG (yttrium aluminate) laser and that the hole produced ranges in diameter from about 0·001 to 0·0001 in (0·025 to 0·0025 mm). At first, depth seemed to be limited to about 0·16 in (4 mm), but was soon increased considerably.

At first laser holes were rough, but soon became much smoother as techniques improved. Also in earlier lasered stones there are sometimes two or three 'shots' at an inclusion, whereas in later ones there is usually only one.

The present technique is to mount the diamond in a ball-jointed chuck that can be adjusted for angle with micrometer precision. The laser, or solid state optimal maser, is aligned with the aid of an optical microscope under from 50 to 100 × magnification so that the beam enters at right angles to a facet in order to reach the inclusion. If it enters at an angle, focusing is more difficult because of refraction. Depths and diameters of holes can be preset, and the process takes half an hour or more. Currently firms in Antwerp, Tel Aviv and London are offering the service, the cost being about £20 to £30 a stone.

Drill holes are made from a facet on the crown or pavilion, through the table, or through the girdle, whichever is more convenient to reach the inclusion with least penetration and obtrusiveness. When the inclusion is reached, it is leached out by acid fumes under vacuum, according to one report; others suggest that a liquid is injected to reduce the blackness by altering the optical relationships in the stone, and a third theory is that the black inclusions are graphitic carbon which is converted to carbon dioxide gas when the inclusion is opened to the atmosphere.

Laser holes in polished diamonds can usually be seen quite clearly from the side, using a 10 × lens, by turning the stone in tweezers so that light reflects from the facet where the hole is. A tendency to funnelling can be seen in some laser holes and another not uncommon feature is one or more slightly enlarged places along the drill hole, like elbow joints, where presumably the laser has been stopped and restarted. (Figs. 13.46 to 13.49.)

Rough (unpolished) stones are sometimes drilled by laser and are much more difficult to detect as having been treated.

After being worn in jewellery for some time, the laser holes in diamonds can become filled with dirt and are more easily seen under a lens. It was reported in the U.S.A. in 1972 that some concerns treating stones had managed to fill the holes with colourless epoxy resin, presumably by using a vacuum process.

One, two or three laser holes are encountered in single stones; very occasionally there are more. The Gemological Institute of America's New York Laboratory received one stone just under a carat in weight with as many as ten laser holes, one of which had failed to reach its target. Another 'drilled' stone had a laser hole that looked like barbed wire. Examined under polarized light, the hole was seen to have passed through an area of great strain. The G.I.A.'s Los Angeles Laboratory about the same time received a diamond that appeared at first sight to have about a dozen laser holes. Closer examination revealed that some did not reach the surface and those that did were not aimed at inclusions; the 'drill holes' were in fact included crystals probably of peridot and pyrope. The same Laboratory reported in 1974 an exceptionally long and narrow drill hole that went through one inclusion about halfway down from the table and on into another at a greater depth. The hole was parallel-sided but rather rough-walled, particularly at the greater depth.

In general only lower quality diamonds are so treated and certainly, in a few of the earlier treated stones, the 'cure' was worse than the fault. Manufacturers who handle stones with butterflies or other dark inclusions in the middle of

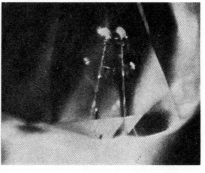

Fig. 13.48 and 13.49. *More laser-drilled diamonds. An 'elbow joint' (*right*) mirrored in an adjacent facet. (*left*) Several 'knuckle joints' magnified 120 times, it shows.*

octahedral rough normally saw out a slice as shown in Fig. 11.14, leaving two small ends for diamonds, the slice being of low value for boart. A few treat the rough by laser drilling and leaching to produce two much larger by bishop's head sawing (Fig. 11.12). The larger stone will be of much lower quality, but the two would still be worth more than two more perfect small stones.

Laser drilling in order to modify inclusions caused a dispute in the trade. One Association took the view that the process was akin to other manufacturing processes which meant that it was not necessary to disclose the fact that a diamond had been laser treated. Gemmological associations, among others, took the opposite point of view and in the C.I.B.J.O. *Rules of Application to the Diamond Trade* is a requirement that such stones must be designated as 'stones with artificially modified inclusions'.

Grading Lasered Stones

Grading for clarity or purity is carried out as if the drill hole and remaining 'inclusion' were natural, disregarding what the original grading may have been. Since the object of treating stones is to increase the value, the grade will have been improved. Incidentally, a laser hole on the surface that has been temporarily 'lost' when looking through a lens or microscope can sometimes be 'found' again by running the point of a needle over the surface of the facet.

REFERENCES

Diamanten-Fibel, by Verena Theisen (Essen, 1968). English edition, *Handbook of Diamond Grading,* 1973.

can. D.N. Diamond Nomenclature and Grading Standards. (Helsinki, Finland, 1969).

Rules of Application to the Diamond Trade, C.I.B.J.O. (Berne, Switzerland, 1975).

CHAPTER FOURTEEN

Grading Polished Diamonds for Cut Weighing and Weight Estimating

Brilliant-cut Proportions

An accurately proportioned stone, (Figs. 10.20, 10.22 and 10.23) will attract the highest price per carat. When the diamond is cut to gain weight, or spread to make it look larger than it is, it may be too deep or too shallow above or below the girdle, or the table may be too wide in proportion to the total diameter of the stone. The price per carat will be lower.

At the bottom of the price scale are the badly-cut stones, which may be unsymmetrical, out-of-round, have irregular tables, or misplaced facets, the table out of square, the culet not central, too large a culet, etc. Some examples are shown in Figs. 14.1 and 14.2. Visual inspection of the outside of the diamond with a 10 × lens will instantly show whether a stone is really badly cut and often examination with the naked eye is sufficient.

The Make

Some cutters stake their reputations on always guaranteeing a good make, i.e. they always stick to certain proportions. Makes vary considerably and it is possible to identify the origin of some brilliant cuts by their make. The diamond trade all over the world estimates the quality of the make of a stone simply by eye, using a lens.

If the stone is unmounted, it is easy to examine for proportion. If mounted, a little guesswork is inevitable as damage or bad cutting could be concealed by the claws or mounting, but it is still relatively easy to estimate the quality of the make, unlike estimating clarity and colour.

The general proportions of a brilliant-cut stone are based on the full diameter across the girdle. From this can be estimated (1) The diameter of the table as a percentage of the full diameter, (2) The height of the crown, (3) The depth of the pavilion, and (4) The thickness of the girdle. These proportions are listed exactly in Chapter Ten. Some commercial variations are given in Appendix Six.

Spread Table

When the table is spread, i.e. made too large in relation to the diameter of the stone, the thickness of the crown is necessarily reduced, as indicated in Fig. 14.1, although the angles may well remain absolutely correct. A shallow crown and wide table mean smaller crown facets and less display of prismatic colours because the crown facets are mostly responsible for such fire. Although a shallow table may suggest that the cutter has lost weight, in fact he has gained it, by

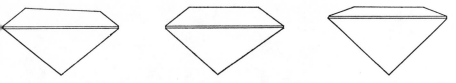

Fig. 14.1. *Sloping table; out-of-centre culet; and overdepth pavilion with correct angles; thin crown (spread stone).*

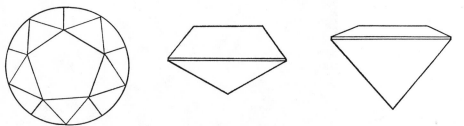

Fig. 14.2. *Asymetrical cutting; crown deep with shallow pavilion; and pavilion overdepth with wrong angles; thin crown. Stones that are out-of-round are not uncommon also.*

making the diamond of larger diameter than would be possible with ideal proportions (Fig. 11.1).

When the crown is thin, the pavilion appears to be over-depth, but in relation to the diameter of the stone, it is quite likely to be reasonably correct. An over-deep pavilion is caused by the pavilion angles being made too great, more than the ideal of about 40° and nearer the 55° of a natural octahedral crystal.

A simple way of gauging the table size in relation to the diameter of the stone has been suggested. The table with the star facets comprises two squares superimposed on each other at 90° as shown in Fig. 14.3. It is said that, if the sides are square, the table is about 60 per cent, and if they are concave or convex, the table is less than or greater than 60 per cent. This is only true, however, if the bezel facets reach half way up the bezel.

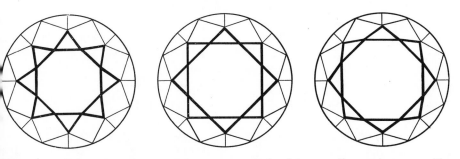

Fig. 14.3. *If the star facets reach half way across the bezel* (centre diagram) *a stone with a 60 per cent table appears as shown. Those with smaller and larger tables are as on the left and right.*

Fig. 14.5. *Fisheye stone with shallow pavilion.*

Fig. 14.6. *Dark-centred or lumpy stone with an over-angled pavilion.*

Judging Pavilion Depths

To be able to judge by eye whether or not the pavilion of a stone is over or under depth is not difficult to acquire with practice because it can be done by using reflections in the table, looking direct at the table.

In the centre of the table of a correctly-proportioned stone, viewed by eye or through a lens, it should be possible to see a bright image of the table, caused by reflections from the pavilion facets. The depth of the pavilion of this stone is just about 43 per cent of the diameter of the diamond. If the table is about the correct proportion the reflection of it (Fig. 14.4) should be from a third to a half the width of the table itself.

Fig. 14.5 illustrates a diamond which is too shallow below the girdle. A ircular reflection will be seen near the edges of the table. It is a reflection of the irdle of the stone and in the diamond trade is known as a fisheye, or cod's eye.

If the pavilion is too deep, the stone is known as lumpy. In such stones, there re large black reflections in the centre of the table as shown in Fig. 14.6, and he stones are described in the trade as dark-centred or black-centred. The deeper the pavilion over the ideal 40 per cent, the blacker will be this reflection.

acet Proportions

Next look at the pavilion from the side. Modern practice is for the lower girdle acets to be made long, to the proportions shown in Fig. 10.4. When the round orilliant-cut was introduced before the First World War and until after the Second World War, the lower bezel facets were usually no more than half the ength of the pavilion, as shown in Fig. 10.4.

Girdle and Culet

The girdle should not be knife-edged, which encourages chipping, in its thinnest parts, neither should it be too thick. (Figs. 14.7 and 14.8). Practice makes estimation of girdle proportion relatively simple. Ideal proportions for different izes of stones used in the U.S.A., are given on page 321. One cannot measure these without an optical instrument, and there is little point in doing so vhen judgement by eye is effective. The girdle should be as shown in Fig. 10.20, and the thickness is about the same for stones from about fifteen points up, nowever big. It should, of course, be even all round and not thicker one side than he other.

There may be small naturals on the girdle, but these are not considered as cutting flaws unless they extend over a facet.

The culet should also be examined directly or through the table if it is not accessible. Too big a culet mars the appearance of the modern brilliant cut from he front. A closed culet, i.e. where the pavilion comes to a point, is likely to lead o breakage of the point, which also mars the appearance. The ideal is for the culet to be just identifiable as having a very, very small facet. On old styles of make, it was common for the culet to be large.

Fig. 14.7. *A very thick girdle, made to save weight.*

Polish

All the facets should be highly polished. Colour interference, like oil on a puddle of rain, can sometimes be noticed under a lens on a well-finished facet. Very occasionally a stone is seen where the brillianteerer has missed finishing a facet. (Fig. 14.9.) The facets should also be correctly shaped.

Occasionally extra facets are added to remove a poor part or damaged part of the crystal. When extra facets are relatively large, they downgrade the make, but when very small they are acceptable as already noted.

The ProportionScope

In 1967, the Gemological Institute of America introduced an optical comparator for rapid checking of the proportions of a brilliant. It is called the Proportion-Scope and will handle stones from about 0·18 to 1·30 and from about 1·21 to over 8 carats on one or other of its two screens. A magnified shadow of the stone is thrown on a line diagram of the correct proportions on the screen, as shown in Fig. 14.10. The diamond is held in a jig that can easily be manoeuvred, by means of a zoom, so that its shadow fits the appropriate diagram.

The ideal proportions are modified from the earlier Tolkowsky figures. Some tolerances are permitted, for example, the correct table proportion is 53 per cent, but tables from 53 to 57 per cent are allowed. Similarly although 16·2 per cent is considered ideal for the height of the crown, the range acceptable is 15·1 to 16·5. For the pavilion depth, ideal 43·1, a figure between 42·9 and 43·3 is permitted before quality and thereafter prices begin to suffer.

It is notable that a stone cut to acceptable European proportions would be downgraded by the Proportionscope.

The G.I.A. gives these percentages of stone diameter as reasonable for the girdle:

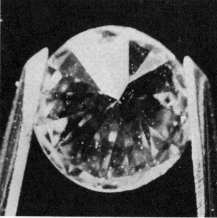

Fig. 14.8. *A thin girdle which is liable to chipping.*

Fig. 14.9. *Some lower girdle facets have been missed when cutting this stone.*

Up to 0·40 carat	.	.	.	up to 3·00 per cent.
0·41 to 0·80 carat	.	.	.	2·0 to 2·5 per cent.
0·81 to 1·50 carat	.	.	.	1·5 to 1·75 per cent.
1·51 to 3·00 carat	.	.	.	1·25 to 1·75 per cent.
3·10 carats upwards	.	.	.	1·0 to 1·5 per cent.

More convenient to use is a special eye-piece with the ProportionScope diagram, which can be inserted in the Gemolite microscope. The light from the base is screened by a ground glass 'slide' and the stone clamped in a holder held magnetically to the microscope stage so that it can be moved to centre it. Both American systems require a power point and are not portable, so the Japanese have introduced a hand-held pocket instrument, the Topcon diamond proportion hand scope, that can be used in any reasonable light and has a fitting for single stone mounted rings as well as loose stones. It has Scan. D.N. proportions,

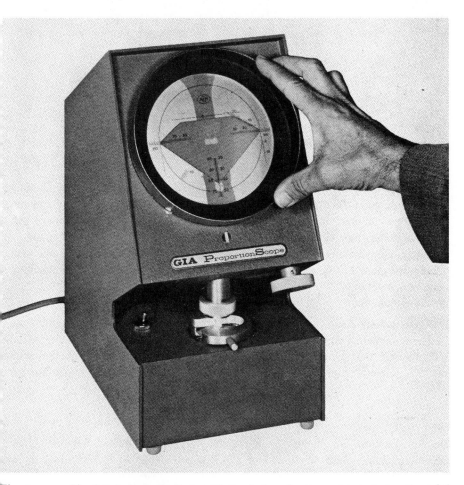

Fig. 14.10. *The G.I.A. ProportionScope with the shadow of a diamond under test on the scaled screen.*

as compared with Tolkowsky proportions on the American instruments. Th
ranges are: ProportionScope, 0·18 to 8·00 ct; Gemolite *de luxe*, 0·10 to 5·50 c
(non *de luxe*, 0·25 to 1·80 ct); Topcon, 0·25 to 2·00 ct.

Make and Price

Up to now the quality of cut has been the least important factor in decidin
price, compared with the weight, colour and clarity. The importance of goo
proportion in relation to price per carat depends to a considerable extent on th
market. In some countries, more than others, buyers are very conscious of mak
in larger fine diamonds. Good make has a much bigger influence on the price c
top-quality stones than on lower-quality ones in any market.

The U.S.A. has the most proportion-conscious market, with the result tha
top quality Tolkowsky stones have dominated in price. From about 1975
however, similar stones of about three-quarters of a carat and above, but c
European cut with more spread tables, have equalled them in price owing t
the strong European demand. Indeed, it has been reported that some America
cut stones have been recut in Europe because they were considered 'old
fashioned'.

It is difficult to state exactly what the relationship is. If a stone of fine qualit
is cut correctly, and another of equal quality and weight is cut to poor pro
portions, with a deep pavilion and thin crown, say, the price difference could b
calculated by estimating the weight that would be lost by recutting the poorl
made stone, then mentally repricing it at the lower price per carat, becaus
of its reduced weight, and adding the cost of cutting. This estimated valu
could be as low as 60 per cent of that of the well-made stone of the same to
quality.

As a very general rule of thumb, it can be said that the price of a stone of ver
fine colour, which is flawless and of excellent make, would fall to about 90 pe
cent if the cut were just good, i.e. if some of the proportions were just off th
ideal, causing the stone to lose some brilliance. If the cut were only fair, as fo
example when the table is too large, the price could be down to 80 per cent. A
poorly-cut stone which is lumpy or a fisheye, would bring the price down to 6
per cent or less.

Weights of Diamond

The previous chapters plus the first part of this one have described the estimatio
of three factors in gauging the value of a diamond, the colour, the clarity, and th
cut. The fourth, the carat weight, is the final factor, and is often the mos
important.

Early Measures

One of the first owners of the Koh-i-Nûr diamond, Sultan Barbar, gave it
weight as about eight *mishkals* and described the *mishkal* as equalling 40 *ratis*
Other records give different values for the *rati*. The Indians had another weigh
between the two, the *mangeli*, which seems to have been much nearer the *rat*
than the *mishkal*.

Air lifts on the Sewa River in Sierra Leone, part of the alluvial mining operation two miles south of the confluence. Diamond areas extend to the north-east into Guinea.

In the larger plants, the process is continuous and the various parts are linked by conveyor belts. An alluvial plant may have to serve a large area.

Panning, coffer dams, and air lifts, which are used for transporting diamond-bearing gravels from the Bafi River bed here, in Sierra Leone, to a more convenient place for concentration.

Before the days of standardized weights, merchants had to rely on natural objects that were fairly common. Dried seeds were most favoured for small weights, especially if they did not much vary in weight from seed to seed. The dried grain of wheat, simply known as the grain, was common, and so was the dried seed of the Carob tree, called the carat.

The Grain

The grain was employed at an early time for measuring the weight of pearls and also of diamonds. It was lighter than the carat, and is now considered to be 50 milligrams or ¼ metric carat. The grain became the unit of comparison between the Avoirdupois general system of weights and the Troy system for precious metals in the United Kingdom. One ounce Troy is 480 grains and one ounce Avdp. equals 437½ grains. A gram equals 15.432349 grains.

Grains are not now a legal weight for gemstones in the U.K., but the pearl trade still refers to weights in grains and the diamond trade occasionally refers to grains as a general indication of size, in the expressions a grainer, a three-grainer, a six-grainer and so on, for diamonds of about 0·25, 0·75, and 1·50 carat and so on.

The Carat Weight

Diamonds (and other gemstones) are normally measured by the very old unit of weight, the carat. In the U.K. in 1969 it became illegal to describe gemstones' weights in anything but metric carats. The carat weight was originally the seed of a tree that is common in the Middle East, the locust tree or Carob tree

Fig. 14.11. *Carob beans and their seeds, originally used as 'carat' weights.*

Fig. **14.12.** *Mr. Trevor Urry, a South African licenced diamond buyer, using portable scales in his Maseru office.* See also Fig. 7.7.

(*Ceratonia Siliqua*). Its fruit is an almost black bean (Fig. 14.11). Inside the pod is a sweet syrup and many small seeds. The ancient pearl merchants of the Middle East discovered that the seeds when dried were exceedingly uniform in weight and adopted them as units of weight for pearls.

The word carat comes from the Greek name for the tree, *keration*, meaning little horn, which its bean pod resembles. Incidentally, it was the syrup from these locust beans that John the Baptist probably ate in the Wilderness, not the flying grasshoppers called locusts.

As commerce in gems increased, various countries standardized the carat in relation to their own units of weight, which varied. A London carat was therefore different from a Venice carat and both were different from a Madras carat. Early in the twentieth century, various countries agreed to accept an international standard metric carat, which was one-fifth or 0·2 of a gram, and to express weights in decimals instead of the old fractions of 64ths, when a weight was shown as, say, $12\frac{36}{64}$ carat. This is the system used for diamonds and other gems.

The weight of a polished diamond of one and a quarter carats is expressed as: 1·25 ct. When a stone is less than a carat the weight is shown correctly in this way: 0·25 ct, 0·30 ct, 0·05 ct. To avoid confusion, a zero should be placed before the point and two digits are always shown after it. It is common practice to call the hundredths 'points' so the three weights just given are referred to as twenty-five points, thirty points, and five points (see Appendix Six).

When polished stones are much smaller than a carat in weight, they are commonly referred to as so many to the carat, instead of being so many points each. Since there are always small variations from stone to stone, it is more

Fig. 14.13. *Chemical balance used by jewellers for weighing gems.*

Fig. 14.15 *A portable balance for weighing diamonds which requires no external power source.*

Fig. 14.14. *The Oertling diamond balance.*

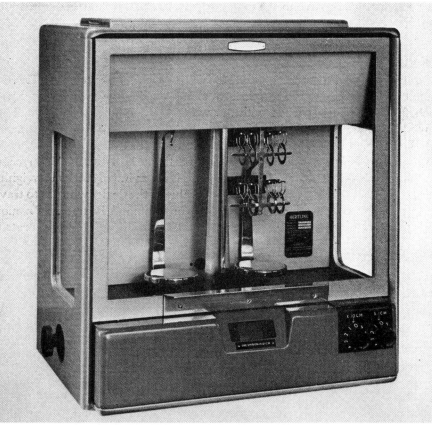

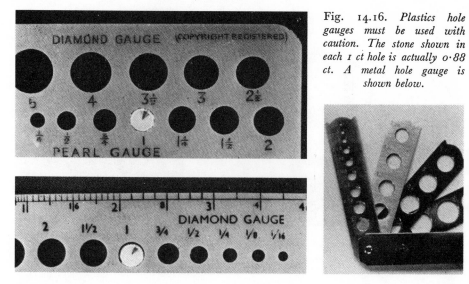

Fig. 14.16. *Plastics hole gauges must be used with caution. The stone shown in each 1 ct hole is actually 0·88 ct. A metal hole gauge is shown below.*

accurate to refer to a parcel of small stones in the first way. Polished stones may therefore be, say, five to the carat, or even as small as four hundred to the carat.

Weighing Loose Stones

The only problem in weighing loose stones today is that of accuracy. The traditional diamond scales are a simple form of pan balance as shown in Fig. 14.12, which folds up and is packed with the weights in a small wooden box. They are used by holding them by hand in the air or by mounting them on the opened box. Such scales have been in use for centuries and are still used today by merchants in many parts of the world and particularly by diamond buyers at the mines, where accuracy in weighing crystals is not as important as in weighing polished stones. Diamond scales are of most value to the dealer who has to travel to places where there is no Diamond Club or Diamond Bourse and a more accurate balance is not available. With them, it is very difficult to be accurate to 0·01 carat.

Many jewellers and gemmologists employ a simple chemical balance of the type shown in Fig. 14.13 for weighing gems. With great care it is possible to be accurate to about a point.

Diamond merchants use a more sophisticated balance which can be operated from outside its enclosing case and indicates the points on an illuminated scale. An example is the Oertling diamond balance in Fig. 14.14. The stone is placed in the left-hand pan. If it is less than a carat, the weight is shown on the illuminated scale in the centre of the base. If it is between 1 and 100 carats, the extra units are added by weights that are dropped on the beam by an outside control, or added to, the right-hand pan. The scales indicate to 0·01 carat and are easily zeroed. A simpler one-pan balance is shown in Fig. 14.15.

Fig. 14.17. *One plate from a diamond sieve is in the foreground. Sieve plates fit into a barrel.*
See Fig. 8.1.

The Mettler diamond balance is one of the most sophisticated, needing no weights.

Estimating Weight by Hole Gauge

When a diamond is mounted, there are problems in making an accurate evaluation of its weight. The only way is to measure the stone, visually inspect it for proportion, and make an estimate of its weight from its dimensions. The simple diamond hole gauge (Fig. 14.16) is most commonly employed for this purpose to give an instant reading of the weight. In the hands of extremely few highly experienced jewellers it is surprisingly accurate. In the hands of most people, it is frequently as much as 20 per cent wrong.

For brilliant-cut diamonds, the gauge holes correspond to the diameters of ideally-cut diamonds of increasing weights. The gauge takes no account of the fact that some diamonds are lumpy and that others are fisheyes. Allowance has to be made from experience. It is often difficult, owing to the setting of a stone, to make an accurate gauging, i.e. to match the hole exactly to the outside diameter of the diamond.

The hole gauge has its uses as a rough guide, but valuations of costly stones should never be made on its evidence alone. A high quality diamond may be worth £2,000 a carat, which is £20 a point. With a ring gauge one can be 20 points out, a difference in the valuation of more than £400 if the estimate of weight is too high, and much more than £400 if the estimation of weight is too low, because the price per carat varies with the size of the stone.

The Sieve

A form of hole gauge, a steel plate with a grid of accurate holes in it, is used by

Fig. 14.18. *A version of the Moe gauge for mounted diamonds.*

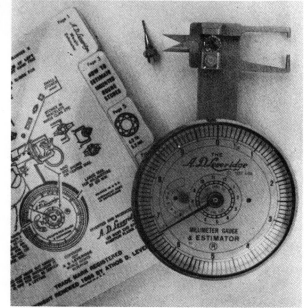

Fig. 14.19. *The Leveridge gauge and tables for mounted stones. A loose stone is between two of the jaws. The pointed piece is to fit to the caliper jaws for deep set stones.*

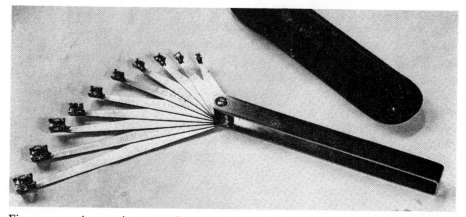

Fig. 14.20. *A comparison gauge for mounted stones. Brilliant cut synthetic spinels are made to the dimensions of different weights of diamond.*

diamond manufacturers and dealers for sorting quantities of polished stones. It is used as a sieve in conjunction with other gauges with smaller and larger holes, to divide stones into plus and minus size (and therefore weight) groups (Fig. 14.17).

The Moe Gauge

A simple caliper gauge, known as the Moe gauge, is made to take into account the depth as well as the diameter of a diamond of which the weight is being estimated (Fig. 14.18). After these dimensions have been taken, a table is referred to and the weight obtained. The Moe gauge is a big improvement on the ring gauge, but some models available are not easy to read accurately as the scale is stamped in the metal for cheapness, which nullifies some of the advantage. It is possible to estimate weights within, say, 5 per cent using a well-made Moe gauge, or closer with experience. The tables are easier to use than those for the Leveridge gauge.

The Leveridge Gauge

One of the more accurate diamond gauges is the A. D. Leveridge mm diamond gauge and estimator, invented in 1937 by an American of that name and now made for his company in Switzerland. The gauge, shown in Fig. 14.19, is a precision instrument and shows sizes in millimetres on a dial. It has jaws to measure the dimensions of stones in almost every type of setting likely to be encountered. The tables provided with the gauge are calculated for diamonds of almost all cuts. Moreover, they can also be used for other gems by a simple calculation to allow for the different specific gravities.

The tables provided are calculated for mêlée of 0·25 carat down to 0·02 ct. brilliant cut, and from 30 to 240 stones a carat eight-cut, both of which are gauged for diameter only. For larger brilliant-cut stones from 17 points to 7·50 carats, there are tables by diameter, each with a series of depths for stones with thick and thin girdles. Similar tables are provided for other cuts. It is possible to gauge within about 2 per cent of the true weight of larger stones and also to make allowance for out-of-round stones. Other tables give weights for gauged marquise, pear, emerald, and square cuts, even baguettes.

More accurate gauges of other makes measuring to 0·01 mm are also available.

An unusual gauge shows actual colourless brilliant-cut synthetic spinels of equivalent diamond weights, for direct comparison with diamonds that are set and perhaps cannot be gauged another way (Fig. 14.20). It is particularly useful for demonstrating the visual appearance of a diamond of a particular weight without the problem of obtaining the diamond.

Weight by Calculation

P. Grodzinski suggested a formula that gives the weight of a brilliant-cut diamond in relation to its diameter (d) in millimetres to an accuracy of 5 per cent.

$$\left(\frac{d}{6\cdot42}\right)^3 = \text{weight in carats.}$$

B. W. Anderson gives a more accurate formula that includes depth, for the use of those with a millimetre gauge but no tables. Measure the diameter (d) and height (h) in *centimetres* and:

$$6hd^2 = \text{weight in carats.}$$

Leveridge also gives a formula, for larger round brilliant cuts over ·47 in (12 mm) in diameter, that takes into account the height (h) as well as the radius (r) in millimetres:

$$0\cdot0245\ hr^2 = \text{weight in carats.}$$

APPROXIMATE SIZES OF BRILLIANT-CUT DIAMONDS

Average diameter in mm	Weight of brilliant in carats	Average height in mm
1·38	0·01	0·78
1·74	0·02	0·98
2·37	0·05	1·33
2·98	0·10	1·67
4·04	0·25	2·26
5·09	0·50	2·85
5·83	0·75	3·27
6·42	1·00	3·60
6·91	1·25	3·88
7·35	1·50	4·12
7·74	1·75	4·33
8·09	2·00	4·54
8·71	2·50	4·88
9·25	3·00	5·19
9·76	3·50	5·47
10·19	4·00	5·72
10·60	4·50	5·95
10·98	5·00	6·16
11·33	5·50	6·37
11·67	6·00	6·55

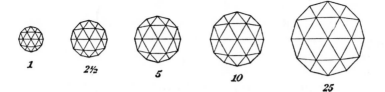

Fig. 14.21. *Approximate sizes of Dutch rose cut diamonds.*

The table opposite is based on one calculated by P. Grodzinski. The diameters and depths are shown to two places of decimals as, in practice, it just possible to estimate to a tenth of a millimetre with a good millimetre dial gauge. Grodzinski's formula for diameter only, tends to exaggerate the weights of larger stones.

SIZES AND WEIGHTS OF MÊLÉE

Eight-Cut		Brilliant-Cut	
Stones per carat	Diameter in mm.	Stones per carat	Weight in carat
240	0·9	—	—
200	1·0	—	—
155	1·1	—	—
125	1·2	—	—
100	1·3	—	—
85	1·4	100	0·01
73	1·5	80	—
58	1·6	60	—
48	1·7	50	0·02
40	1·8	40	—
33	1·9	36	—
30	2·0	33	0·03 +
	2·1	29	—
	2·2	25	0·04
	2·3	22	—
	2·4	20	0·05
	2·5	18	—
	2·6	16	0·06
	2·7	14	0·07
	2·8	12	0·08
	2·9	11	0·09
	3·0		0·10
	3·1		0·11
	3·2		0·12 +
	3·3		0·14
	3·4		0·15
	3·5		0·16
	3·6		0·17
	3·7		0·18
	3·8		0·20
	3·9		0·22
	4·0		0·25

BRILLIANT CUT DIAMOND DIAMETERS

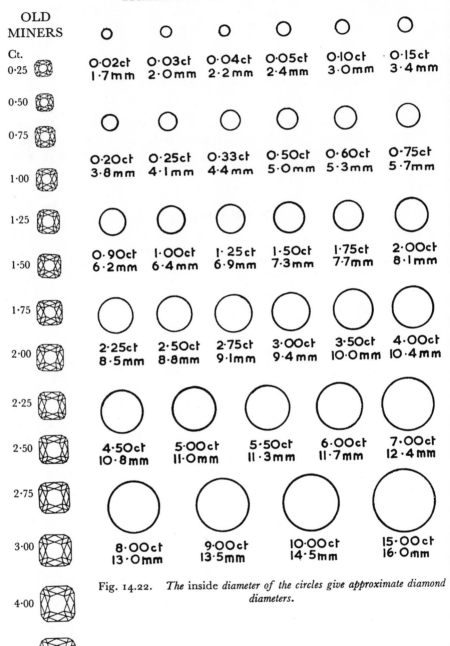

OLD MINERS						
Ct. 0·25	0·02ct 1·7mm	0·03ct 2·0mm	0·04ct 2·2mm	0·05ct 2·4mm	0·10ct 3·0mm	0·15ct 3·4mm
0·50						
0·75	0·20ct 3·8mm	0·25ct 4·1mm	0·33ct 4·4mm	0·50ct 5·0mm	0·60ct 5·3mm	0·75ct 5·7mm
1·00						
1·25	0·90ct 6·2mm	1·00ct 6·4mm	1·25ct 6·9mm	1·50ct 7·3mm	1·75ct 7·7mm	2·00ct 8·1mm
1·50						
1·75	2·25ct 8·5mm	2·50ct 8·8mm	2·75ct 9·1mm	3·00ct 9·4mm	3·50ct 10·0mm	4·00ct 10·4mm
2·00						
2·25	4·50ct 10·8mm	5·00ct 11·0mm	5·50ct 11·3mm	6·00ct 11·7mm	7·00ct 12·4mm	
2·50						
2·75	8·00ct 13·0mm	9·00ct 13·5mm	10·00ct 14·5mm	15·00ct 16·0mm		
3·00						

Fig. 14.22. *The inside diameter of the circles give approximate diamond diameters.*

Fig. 14.23. *Approximate sizes of old mine cut stones*

SIZES IN CARATS

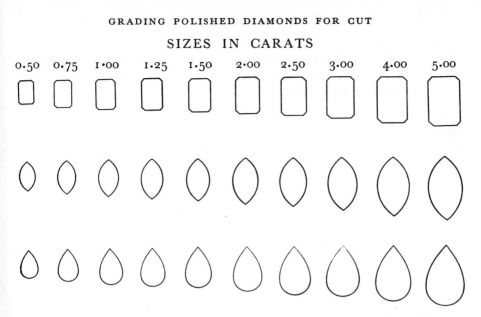

Fig. 14.24. *Approximate sizes of emerald, marquise, and pear-shaped diamonds.*

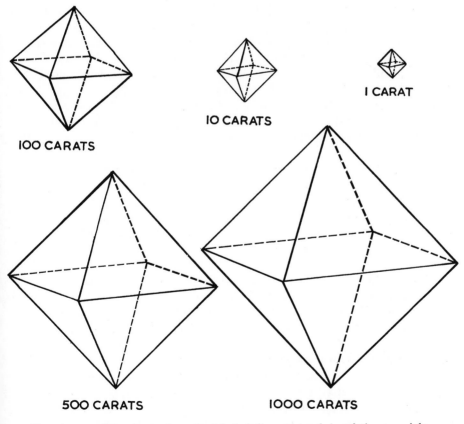

Fig. 14.25. *Approximate sizes of octahedral diamond rough in relation to weight.*

Small Diamonds

Small diamonds of below about ·08 in (2 mm) diameter (30 per carat) are often eight-cut instead of brilliant cut when the quality is lower. The weights of these can be calculated by Grodzinski's formula with 5 per cent added.

Weight of Rough

B. W. Anderson gives a formula for estimating the weight of octahedral diamond crystals which is useful to prospectors and buyers in the field with only a milli- metre gauge available. If the side(s) of a regular octahedron is measured in centimetres:

$$8·29s^3 = \text{weight in carats.}$$

Sizes and Weights

Approximate sizes of various cuts of stone and of octahedral crystals are given in Figs. 14.21 to 14.25.

Tolerances in Marketing

Because diamonds are cut and polished individually, and the cost of the material is so high, they are not made in groups of sizes like most other goods and a dealer may have stocks of diamonds weighing, for example: 0·90, 0·91, 0·93, 0·94, 0·96, 0·98, 1·01, 1·02, 1·04, 1·07, 1·08 and 2·02 carats. As the unit of a carat has a special attraction and he has a demand for carat stones, he will supply them within a stated tolerance which is visually acceptable. The tolerance varies with different dealers and manufacturers. The buyer pays according to the actual weight, of course, and knows exactly what he is getting when buying individual stones, but not necessarily with a parcel, of which he will know the number of stones and the total weight, but not necessarily the spread of weight. One Antwerp dealer quotes these ranges:

Quarter carat	.	.	.	0·25 to 0·28
Third carat	.	.	.	0·29 to 0·37
Half carat	.	.	.	0·45 to 0·54
Carat	.	.	.	0·95 to 1·29
One and a half	.	.	.	1·45 to 1·65
Two carats	.	.	.	1·96 to 2·25

Dealers in higher quality stones would have closer tolerances because they work in smaller price brackets. The tolerance for a 1 carat stone in these circum- stances could be 0·98 to 1·05. With the very highest quality stones, there can be a price premium if the stone is not one or two points below the carat figure.

Equipment for Diamond Setting

Special equipment for grading and sorting has already been mentioned, such as sieves. Other specialized items are available from such firms as R. Rubin and Son in Antwerp. For example, Fig. 14.26 illustrates a washing cup for cleaning diamonds in alcohol. To be examined effectively for clarity, stones must

Fig. 14.26. *A pot to hold alcohol and diamonds in a sieve for cleaning before grading them for clarity.*

obviously be clinically clean. Carbon tetrachloride is also effective, but evaporates more rapidly.

Scoops, like small metal dust-pans, are essential when dealing with quantities of stones. A dimpled and grooved sorting tray or sectionalized box is of considerable assistance for counting and sorting.

Diamond parcel papers or briefcas (the specially folded papers in which the diamonds are carried) are needed, with parcel paper boxes to hold them in an office, and parcel paper wallets to hold them in the pocket. Some dealers line their papers (see Appendix 3 for illustration) with other thin transparent papers, called 'flutes', to enhance the colour of the stones. Flutes can be obtained in pale blue for top colour white stones, in extra white for light brown goods, pale blue for Cape stones, dark blue for Indian and Far East use, broken white for silver Cape and light brown qualities of diamonds, yellow-white for brown and yellow goods, and black for rose-cut diamonds. For carrying expensive stones, a folded piece of lint is often placed between the flute and the paper.

REFERENCES

'Diamond Proportion Grading and the New ProportionScope', by Richard T. Liddicoat, Jr. *Gems and Gemology*, Spring 1967 (G.I.A., Los Angeles).

CHAPTER FIFTEEN

Prices of Diamonds: Valuations

A general rule for pricing rough diamond used by merchants for many centuries, and probably introduced to Europe by Tavernier, is not valid today. David Jeffries wrote in 1750: 'The . . . rule is that the proportional increase, or value of diamonds, is as the square of their weight, whether rough or manufactured.'

He went on to explain that a parcel of rough of various qualities, all suitable for cutting, would be priced at so much a carat for the whole parcel. Price of the individual crystals could then be worked out from the rule. For example, suppose the average price were £200 a carat (Jeffries suggested £2 a carat!). A 2 carat crystal would therefore be priced at £200 times the square of the weight, i.e. (£200 × 2²) = £800, which is £400 per carat. A 3 carat crystal would be worth (£200 × 3²) = £1,800, which is £600 a carat.

Another 'rule', proposed by Schrauff and quoted by Dr. K. Schlossmacher in 1962, provides a multiplication factor that increases at a lower rate and arrives at a less exaggerated figure compared with today's prices. It is:

$$\text{Price} = \text{carat price} \times \frac{\textit{carat weight of stone}}{2} \times (\text{carat weight} + 2).$$

Today, the price of 80 per cent of the world's rough is related to a much more complex formula (see page 92), so the old rule has only very general application.

Prices More than Doubled by Cutting

When a stone is manufactured, at least half the weight is lost, so this, apart from costs of cutting immediately at least doubles the price of a polished stone compared with the rough crystal from which it was made. As a very general rule, then, it can be said that, if the 2 carat rough in the example of the previous paragraph were cut, it would produce a 1 carat diamond of approximate value £800, which is £800 a carat compared with £400 a carat for the rough. When cut, the 3 carat stone would be worth about £1,200 a carat according to the squaring rule.

Because mining and recovery methods have improved, fewer large diamonds are being found, modern cuts reduce the percentage of recovery from crystals, more poorly-shaped crystals are cut, demand has changed, and many other things have changed since Jeffries' days: this included, in 1968, a different pattern of pricing rough by the Diamond Trading Company, with the effect that the prices of lower qualities and smaller stones were increased substantially.

Quality and Price

The figures opposite are for polished stones of low and high quality for the year 1972, and were supplied by diamond manufacturers in the U.K. and Belgium.

EXTRA WHITE FLAWLESS

Carat weight	0.50	1.00	1.50	2.00	2.50	3.00
Price per ct	1300	5560	6500	7780	8060	10000
Price per stone	650	5560	9750	15520	20150	30000
Squaring rule	*1390*	*5560*	*12510*	*22240*	*35000*	*50000*
Scrauff's rule		*5560*	*14595*	*22240*	*31275*	*41700*

TINTED WHITE VVS2

Carat weight	0.50	1.00	1.50	2.00	2.50	3.00
Price per ct	430	750	1140	1470	1640	1950
Price per stone	215	750	1710	2940	4100	5851
Squaring rule	*188*	*750*	*1688*	*3000*	*4688*	*6750*
Scrauff's rule		*750*	*1969*	*3000*	*4219*	*5625*

Below each of the actual figures has been inserted in italics the price calculated by the squaring rule and by Shrauff's rule. The 'rules' give much too high prices for higher qualities, but are of some help in lower ones.

The price of diamonds, since they are controlled from source, follows reasonably predictable trends, so that it is possible to chart prices. A cutter's prices depend upon the price he pays for his rough, his overheads and other costs, and the usual business considerations. He is able then to compile a price list at which to sell various sizes and qualities. This may be different from a similar list produced by another cutter. It is sometimes forgotten by retailers that there is not an absolutely fixed price for diamonds. Cutters compete with each other like other merchants in price and quality.

A Method of Estimating

If one is a buyer of diamonds or diamond jewellery, or a valuer, it is necessary to be able to arrive at reasonably accurate prices, often over a very wide range of goods. Anyone not handling diamonds so regularly that he has a mental picture of the price structure, can adopt the method to be described. Its rules are three:

1. Weigh the stone or make an accurate estimation of weight by a gauge, preferably a Leveridge gauge.
2. Evaluate the quality of the stone as explained elsewhere in this book (by colour, clarity, and cut).
3. Refer to a chart of prices.

The chart of prices is the usual stumbling block. There are some diamond merchants who issue lists to their customers. A current price list obviously can be made the basis of a chart. Some trade associations from time to time provide members with average prices for different qualities of stones. Actual buying and selling provides the most useful information of all.

There are obviously many ways of compiling a personal chart of prices for reference because there are four variables – weight, colour, clarity and cut. Weight is the most important and must have its own columns. Cut may be omitted and all prices assumed to be of good cut, mental allowance being made for lower qualities of cut. Colour and quality have to be separated to some

PRICE PER CARAT

	0·25	0·50	0·75	1·00	1·25	1·50	2·00
Exceptional White	£	£	£	£	£	£	£
Flawless	—	—	—	—	—	—	—
VVS	—	—	—	—	—	—	—
VS	—	—	—	—	—	—	—
1st PK	—	—	—	—	—	—	—
White							
Flawless	—	—	—	—	—	—	—
VVS	—	—	—	—	—	—	—
VS	—	—	—	—	—	—	—
1st PK	—	—	—	—	—	—	—
Slightly Tinted							
Flawless	—	—	—	—	—	—	—
VVS	—	—	—	—	—	—	—
VS	—	—	—	—	—	—	—
1st PK	—	—	—	—	—	—	—

Fig. 15.1.   *A means of keeping a note of known prices and extrapolating them.*

extent but can be grouped, so that one arrives at a chart with weights along one co-ordinate and quality along the other, as in Fig. 15.1.

The steps in weight and the closeness of grading depends upon the uses to which the chart is to be put and the market in which the user is operating. Some users may need only the middle grades on a broad scale, others require fine differences in top-quality stones only. It is fairly obvious that the higher the quality, the finer the shades of difference in price between different weights and qualities.

Having drawn out the columns of the chart in a pocket notebook, the prices can be filled in in the appropriate places when they are discovered. Obviously there will be variations, but a pattern will begin to emerge and it will be possible to estimate missing ones by extrapolation. Also any excessively high (or low) price will at once show up for what it is because it does not fit into the grid.

A modern way to tackle the problem, adopted by one diamond graduate from London, is to derive a formula from the information and use it to programme a pocket computer.

Prices of stones over, say, 2 carats, are more subject to fluctuation of price because the demand is more variable, whereas stones of, say, under a carat are bought in quantity by jewellery manufacturers which tends to keep prices more stable. The chart will therefore be a more accurate guide on lower weights.

Milling in rotating drums, as seen here at Letseng-la-Terai, is sometimes a convenient part of the extraction of diamonds by grinding down and washing away softer materials.

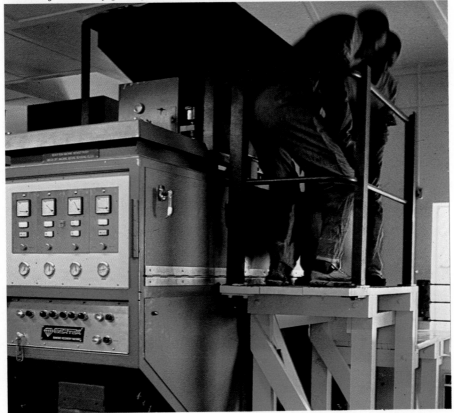

X-ray final extraction is common at the larger plants. This Sortex machine is one of several at the computer-controlled Consolidated Diamond Mines plant in Namibia.

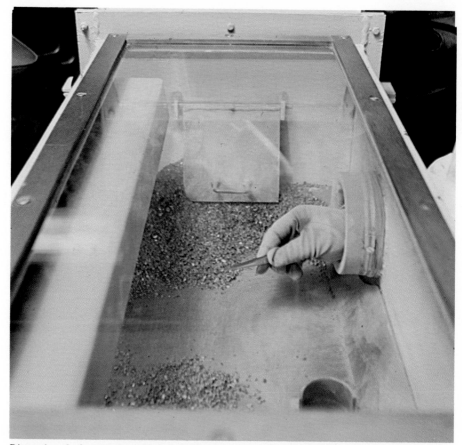

Diamonds and other concentrate from the x-ray extractors are delivered to sealed units such as this, in Lesotho, where sorters with sealed-in gloves direct the diamonds into a separate chute.

A range of stones of different colours from a day's production at Consolidated Diamond Mines in the Namib desert along the coastal strip of South West Africa.

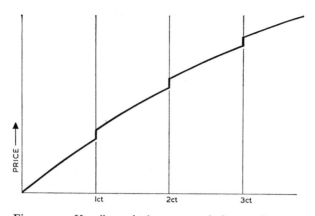

Fig. 15.2. *How diamond prices per carat rise in steps. For stones of exceptional quality, there is sometimes an additional premium.*

Prices per Carat

The prices in the chart are given in prices per carat, which is the normal way of indicating price in the diamond trade. For example, a parcel containing a stone may be marked '0·55 ct £600 pc.' This means a price of 55/100 × £600 = £330 for the stone. A few dealers mark parcels with the actual price in such a way: '0·55 ct. £330 for the stone'.

Using the grid in Fig. 15.1, then, one must remember that £400 under the column 0·25 ct does *not* mean that a quarter-carat stone of that quality is valued at £400. It is valued at £400 *per carat*, or £100 for the stone.

Market Fluctuations

The chart should be kept up to date because prices keep creeping upwards. The major price changes come when there is an increase in the price of rough or the selling pattern is changed. If De Beers announce increases according to size or quality amounting to 5 per cent, that does not mean all prices in the chart can be increased by 5 per cent. The increase is an average one to cutters, and is most likely to increase the price of some qualities of goods at the expense of other qualities or sizes.

It should also be noted that there may be 'humps' in the grid caused by demands for particular sizes and qualities. At a particular time, for example, there may be very strong demand for stones around twenty points which causes a price hump at this level.

There are price humps at carat levels also, known as carat premiums, which are an artificial feature of demand caused by the 'magic' of owning a diamond of 1 carat, 2, 3, 4 carats or whatever it may be, rather than one of just under a carat, just under two carats, etc. The graph in Fig.15.2 shows how the price jumps at each carat level and also applies to a lesser extent in quarter carat, and half-carat steps. The factor is a nuisance in the market and was for some years aggravated by an extensive advertising campaign to the public in several countries which illustrated diamonds in these steps of size.

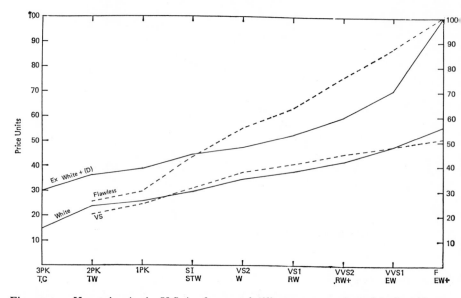

Fig. 15.3. *How prices in the U.S.A. of 1 carat brilliant-cut stones changed in the mid 1970s with purity (solid lines) and colour (dotted lines). Note the greater difference between these two aspects of quality on higher quality stones (top lines). In 1977–1978, colour became a very important factor in world sales (see Fig 15.4). The colours, TC to EW+, are C.I.B.J.O. grades (see Fig. 12.7).*

As polished stones increase in size, they do not continue to increase in price at the same rate. Buyers become fewer and less willing to pay the increased rate per carat. The price increase per carat therefore becomes less and less as the size increases until it levels off. The levelling in price was at about 10 carats in 1975.

Ultimately a polished stone could become so big that no buyer could afford or want to afford it. Crystals of this size are only cut for special purposes or people. Ordinarily, large crystals are cut into a number of stones of sizes that provide the optimum increase in value.

Premium Prices

Special top quality diamonds of one carat or over sometimes command extra premium prices, i.e. above the cutter's normal price for such a stone. The premium depends upon demand and will fluctuate with the market and state of the economy. Normally such a stone will be Flawless or Internally Flawless and not lower than Rare White in colour; also a lower weight tolerance will not be acceptable, i.e. a carat stone will have to be one carat or over. Premium prices vary from about 5 to 30 per cent over the 'list' prices.

Influence of Quality on Price

Colour and clarity have roughly the same influence on price, but the actual amount depends on public taste. In most countries there is a stronger demand

340

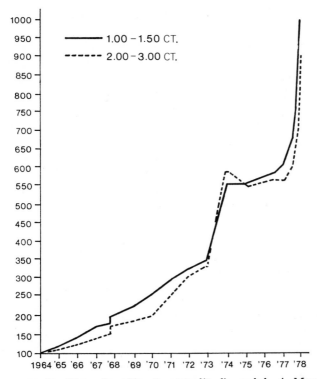

Fig. 15.4. *Increases in selling prices of investment quality diamonds by A. Monnickendam Ltd. over the period 1964 to 1978. They refer to White and better polished brilliant cuts from Flawless to Pique grades. The steep rise from 1977 to 1978 was caused partly by increased demand for fine colours. Over the same year, the average price rise of all diamonds was considerably less, at about 40 per cent, but still high. 100 is taken as the base price in 1964.*

for better colours, with clarity a secondary consideration. In others, the public prefers a stone to be flawless even if the colour suffers a little.

It is difficult to show the influence of make or accuracy of cutting on value in the same way because make can be improved by re-cutting, but colour can not; neither usually, can clarity. A fine quality stone may fall only to 80 per cent of its value through poor cutting, if it can be recut without losing much material. Another factor is that a top-quality stone is not likely to be badly cut, but a low-quality one could have been 'swindled' to gain maximum weight.

These factors have prompted the Scandinavians to suggest a special category of grading for stones that are flawless except for superficial defects in finish, that can be removed by repolishing with the removal only of a very small amount of material, and C.I.B.J.O. to accept it.

Diamonds and Investment
In general it is the policy of those whose actions determine the prices of diamonds to keep these prices as stable as possible. A free market in diamond would destroy its stability of price. If it is regarded as a currency, its purchasing power has

probably remained steadier than that of any other currency, including gold. Certainly it has remained more stable than any of the paper currencies.

The implications of keeping the average price of diamo stable is rarelynds fully realized, even by the trade. A stable average price means that as the cost of living goes up, so does the average price of diamonds. It means too, that diamonds, regarded as a currency, will purchase about the same now as they did last year, five years ago, or twenty years ago.

It means that if a diamond would have purchased a plot of land fifty years ago, it should still buy the same plot of land today, all else being equal. Compare this with the real value in purchasing power of most countries' paper money which has plummeted in almost every country in the world.

Comparison of diamonds with gold as currency also shows a more realistic situation for the diamond. Gold prices have been manipulated because they are still tied to the values of paper currencies, and because international settlements are still made by gold bullion.

Portability and Durability

Diamonds regarded as a currency have not only remained more stable than other currencies, but have the same advantages in that they are portable and durable and can be exchanged all over the world for the local currency or for goods. In addition, they have a high intrinsic value, unlike paper money or other demonetized currency.

If there were only one quality of diamond as there is only one quality of pound notes, the validity of what has just been written would be easily appreciated. In fact there are thousands of qualities of diamond and wide variations of carat price in relation to the size of a stone. The average price per carat of diamond is somewhere among extremes of price in various direction.

It is human nature to seek the best, rarest, most beautiful, and to pay for it with effort, or money (the result of effort), despite what some theorists would like us to believe. Therefore, rarer stones – those of top quality and larger size – are more sought after than smaller ones of poorer quality. The result is that larger stones of higher quality are of much higher price than smaller, low-quality ones. As the size increases or the quality improves, so does the rate of increase of price. Furthermore, the difference increases with time. This indicates that high-quality larger stones, within limits, are more likely to be a profitable investment.

Prices and Inflation

Since the average price remains approximately in step with the cost of living, it follows that prices of low-quality diamonds must go down in purchasing power.

This can be expressed in another way. The average price of diamonds is advanced roughly in step with world inflation, which was advancing at say 3 to 5 per cent a year when the first edition was published. The purchasing power of money therefore goes down at about the same rate as the average increase in diamond prices. In practice the D.T.C. does not make a blanket increase in rough prices but applies different increases to different classes of stones to provide an average increase of 3, 5, 7, 10, or even 15 per cent or whatever it might be. In the past, the higher quality and larger stones were usually increased most in price because they were most in demand.

The rate of world inflation has increased rapidly in recent years and there have been regular increases in prices of rough diamonds to keep pace. One result was that demand dropped off for the higher-priced top quality and larger stones and increased for the lower quality and smaller stones. Because of this changing pattern, the Diamond Trading Company took steps in 1977 to bring the bottom and top ends in quality closer together in price by substantially increasing the prices of rough diamonds of smaller sizes (melée) and of lower qualities through all sizes. In some cases, the increase after cutting amounted to as much as 25 per cent.

The change in the assortments in parcels at the 'sights' was such that cutters took some time to adjust their prices to achieve stability again. It modifies the statement earlier that higher quality, larger stones are the better 'investment', but only in degree and probably over the short term.

Prices in U.S. Dollars

Another important factor in 'investment' depends upon the currency in which the D.T.C. sells rough diamonds. In the past it was in pounds sterling, but with Sterling weak some years ago, it was changed to U.S. dollars. This means that whenever there is a price rise (rough diamond prices are never reduced), the price is adjusted to the currency of the country concerned. It also means that if that country's currency falls or rises in value in relation to the dollar, diamond prices go up or down accordingly, and as far as cutters' selling prices are concerned, usually immediately. It has been said that buying diamonds is like buying dollars.

Best Sizes and Qualities

It is now possible to answer the question, 'Are diamonds a good investment?' The answer is, 'Yes, if they are of high quality and are large enough.' In practice this means the best stones to invest in are from about 0.50 to 3 carats in weight and of White, S.I. quality or better. Larger stones may appreciate more but are sometimes more difficult to sell. In fact, there are some who say that the best stones to buy are ½ to 2 carats, for this reason. It depends on where they are likely to be sold.

Being able readily to sell is an important factor in investment. A good investment of any kind may turn out to be a poor one if it is not possible to turn it into cash in an emergency.

Another factor in some countries, including the U.K., is liability to value added tax (on purchase), capital gains tax and capital transfer tax.

Medium Qualities and Investment

In retail shops, the question 'Is it a good investment?' is often asked by a customer who is interested in buying diamond-set jewellery. Jewellery should never be bought as an investment, only for its beauty, but the customer must be answered and the answer could in this case be given in terms of purchasing power.

'A woman was left a fine solitaire diamond ring which became her favourite possession. One day, however, she fell for a £8,000 sports car. The dealer persuaded her to part with her ring, which he decided to keep for himself in exchange for the sports car. In five years' time, the woman took back the sports car to sell it and found it to be worth £1,800. But the ring, now being worn by the dealer's wife, would still have purchased a brand new sports car.'

The point is that diamonds will hold their value against currency and withstand devaluation, inflation, runs on currency, and the uncertainties caused by unstable government. Stocks and shares which often produce substantial profits, are not as stable as they can tumble in value overnight. They cannot be transferred elsewhere or cashed easily. Their value is in most cases utterly dependent on the actions of the government and the economy concerned. But diamonds have lasting value.

To some extent, diamond production, and therefore diamond prices are also dependent on government, but the actions of a single government are not so effective in upsetting values because of the international marketing arrangements. For example, prices have remained relatively unaffected by the 'wind of change' in Africa, when African governments took over, the revolution in the Congo, various pressures on the South African Government, big pipe finds in the U.S.S.R., and the manufacture of synthetic diamonds.

If diamond prices can withstand such upheavals, they can probably withstand anything except a disastrous world recession or a return to the free-for-all days. From about mid-1977, extreme pressures from the market were forcing a return to the days of boom and slump. Stockpiling of rough as a hedge against depreciating paper money reached alarming proportions and pushed up prices to 60 to 70 per cent over those charged by the Diamond Trading Company. The D.T.C. imposed a surcharge – the first was 40 per cent in early 1978 – at sights to force cutters and other buyers to disgorge stockpiles and end the speculative spiral. As this edition went to press, the surcharges were beginning to have the effect intended.

True Investment Values

It must never be forgotten that the value of gem diamonds depends entirely on the value of them in jewellery. It would be very dangerous if the stability of the market were threatened by currency speculators and diamond investment operators with no interest in jewellery, but powerful enough to influence prices, as has happened in the art world. Diamonds are not a substitute for investment of other kinds, but more a supplementary investment with special aspects of security.

Diamonds alone should be regarded as long-term investment, to which the normal criteria of buying at the right price and time from the right person, etc, apply. Diamond jewellery is normally bought for emotional reasons; but, at least, the value of the diamond content will appreciate with time.

Diamonds as a 'Hedge'

It is better to talk of diamonds as a 'hedge' instead of as an 'investment'. To hedge is to reduce a risk by making an opposite speculation. Because every possible effort is made to resist falling diamond prices, the 'investor' in diamonds stands to lose less (as well as gain less) than the investor in other commodities, stocks and shares. Diamonds are a hedge against the falling value of money and against the extreme variations in the value of stocks, shares and commodities. A study of diamond prices during the world depression of 1929 to 1932 shows that they dropped about 50 per cent on the commodity market compared with the price of gold (with an all-important monetary role), at the same time as shares in general on the New York stock market dropped in price by about 70 per cent. At that time control of the diamond market was rudimentary compared with today, and it suggests that gold was a better investment. Gold, however, has its own problems, one of which *is* its monetary role, putting it at the mercy of politicians; the huge monetary gold stocks were, in 1975, sufficient to keep the world's jewellery industries going without further mining for thirty years.

Diamond Investment Companies

Many companies have sprung up all over the world for the sole purpose of selling loose diamonds for investment. The majority know little about diamonds; they buy stones from the manufacturers and sell them at inflated prices to the public. Some are fraudulent in their claims. It is very easy to delude a laymen over the quality of a stone because he has no way of assessing it himself. If he is sold the stone in a sealed transparent box, as is a common practice, with an injunction not to break the seal otherwise the 'guarantee' to repurchase will be invalidated, there is no means of a genuine grader being able to assess the stone with any accuracy. Such stones are usually supplied with certificates filled in by the seller, which is obviously not satisfactory, or by a so-called 'independent' laboratory; one of which at least will provide 'official' certificates, at a price, in response to a telephone call describing the stone! The C.I.B.J.O. scheme for providing warranties issued by truly independent laboratories after careful examination of stones, combined with the already existing G.I.A. certification, should improve the situation by giving better protection to the consumer, but no one yet has found a solution to certificate switching, when a certificate for an expensive stone is switched to another similar but lower-priced stone. If both are sealed in transparent boxes, switching is made very much easier.

There is no established market for the layman who wishes to sell loose diamonds. This also helps the dubious diamond investment companies and is a hindrance to the few that sell at reasonable prices. Those that contract to buy back from their customers usually have to purchase the stones themselves for resale. When many customers want to sell, it is not a good time to buy for resale. These conditions occurred in several countries in 1976–7 and put a number of diamond investment companies out of business. A factor often ignored or not understood by the lay buyer is that, in most countries, he will have to pay value added tax, currently 15 per cent on diamonds in the U.K., which effectively he will have to deduct when he comes to sell to a dealer. Some dealers deposit stones for their customers in the Channel Islands to avoid V.A.T., so the customer probably never knows just what he bought – until he comes to sell it.

Price Structures

The layman is generally ignorant of the fact that all wealth originates in producing things and trading in them. Agriculture, mining for materials to manufacture into articles people need or want, and distributing them to people who require them, all of these activities create increased money values. Every merchant must make a profit on a transaction to stay in business – to pay his employees and his overheads after replacing the item he has sold.

The diamond merchant and the jeweller, like every other trader, has to make a profit on every transaction. Yet a surprisingly high number of customers imagine that they can sell back diamonds and diamond jewellery at the same prices as they paid. Even if it is explained that the trader cannot afford to lose his profit, they fail to see that he has to make one on the buying transaction as well as the original selling transaction. This applies right along the line and accounts for the value of everything.

A diamond is worth nothing if picked up in the desert by a native tribesman with no access to the civilized world. It is worth more to someone who knows it only as a pretty pebble and wants it for an ornament or a toy and is therefore prepared to exchange it for a tin of tobacco. It is worth more still to someone who has discovered that it can be used for inscribing other stones, or to someone who covets it because no one else has one. A price structure is beginning to emerge.

There is the first cost of finding the place where diamonds occur, then in mining them, in carrying out manufacturing processes, and last but not least in distributing them to the people who want or need them. At each transaction there must be a profit to pay for staff, buildings, equipment and other items. If there were no profits in industry and commerce, there would be no money to buy the products of industry and commerce. In the process, various non-producers, notably governments, but also lawyers, doctors and others, take large parts of the profits in return for services which, however valuable, do not add to the wealth of the country, but do add to costs and therefore prices.

In the case of diamonds, the first cost is for prospecting and mining. It is high because of the low rate of recovery. The government in whose territory the mines are situated usually takes a percentage of the value; for example, the South African Government receives 15 per cent of the value of exported diamond rough. Some governments take a profit at source.

Price Margins

At the sights, when De Beers sell rough to about 250 selected dealers and cutters, sales are negotiated through authorized brokers who receive a fee of 1 per cent. Some goods that are in demand elsewhere are sold by dealers who may add from 5 to 10 per cent brokerage. In 1969, cutters and dealers were buying rough at an average price of about £100 a carat. Less than half the rough was recovered as polished goods, so the average price of these was about £250 a carat.

After that, the jewellery manufacturer has to mark-up his products about 25 per cent, to pay his craftsmen's wages and his overheads. In the U.K., at the last stage of retailing diamond jewellery the government steps in and demands a part of the value in tax, before the retailer can legally sell the jewellery. The retailer has therefore to add his own mark-up and the government's (which can be the higher).

Mark-up is usually confused with net profit in the public mind, and often in the minds of otherwise highly intelligent people. From mark-up a gross profit results, out of which, rent, wages, insurance, taxes, rates, etc., have to be paid, leaving the individual trader with, he hopes, enough to live on.

Synthetic Diamonds and Prices

The question is often asked, 'Won't diamond prices fall if gem diamonds are made in the factory?' The answer is that natural gem diamond prices are *not* likely to be affected by synthetic gem diamonds if they are made commercially in quantity.

The reason for the price of natural stones not being affected – or perhaps even being enhanced – arises from two factors. The first has already been referred to – human nature, which demands the best of the natural gems. (In the jewellers' shops of Gorky Street in Moscow, people queue for diamond jewellery, which is produced in some quantity since the big diamond finds in Russia, so the kind of economy makes no difference.) The second factor is the ability to distinguish between natural and synthetic gems. Its importance is not fully realized even by many people in the gem trade.

While it is possible to prove categorically that this stone is natural and that one is synthetic, a price difference will remain between them.

The less perfect a gem material, the more likely will be opportunities for finding some difference between the natural and the synthetic. Diamond is such a perfect mineral and is very occasionally so pure that the eventual polished synthetic gem diamond, may prove to be difficult to identify, but early tests on the first gem diamonds synthesised in 1970 suggest that positive identification will not be difficult if undertaken by a properly-equipped gem laboratory.

The whole of the gem jewellery trade affected by synthetic stones depends utterly on the ultimate deterrent of a gemmological laboratory's ability to detect synthetic stones to prevent them from being sold as natural. It can only be ignorance that makes a number of important jewellers selling expensive gems indifferent even to the existence of an efficient laboratory.

Making a Valuation

Appraisal of diamonds and diamond jewellery can be carried out more accurately than of coloured gemstones and jewellery. The reason is two-fold.

1. Diamond prices are relatively stable and price changes are notified.
2. Standards of quality are universally acknowledged and the quality of a stone can be ascertained.

The value in cash of anything, however, depends upon the circumstances of the sale. When an appraisal is given, therefore, it is assumed that the price quoted would be that obtainable on an open market. Nevertheless it is still necessary to know which market would be involved. In the U.K. there are three general groups of sale.

347

1. *For probate.* The price the articles would fetch, if sold on the open market at the time of death of the deceased.

2. *For resale.* A valuation for resale may be higher than for probate because it is assumed that the owner can wait for the best market conditions. It is also assumed that the item will be sold in isolation, whereas when items, other than special pieces, are sold for probate they are usually offered as a single lot.

3. *For insurance.* When a customer wants a valuation for insurance, he is asking what the replacement value of the jewellery or diamond would be at that time to him. In other words, he wants an estimated retail price for an identical new article.

One more form of 'valuation' is probably peculiar to the jewellery trade and causes considerable damage to honest reputations and generates much bad feeling. It is initiated by a customer who buys an article from one shop and then goes to another shop for valuation as reassurance that the price paid in the first shop was fair.

A jeweller asked to price new goods should make it quite clear that he is valuing for insurance. He should be very cautious if he is asked to make an offer. To be offered new goods for sale is always suspicious when so much jewellery is being stolen.

Unfortunately there are a few unscrupulous traders in all countries who will deliberately undervalue goods bought from their competitors in order to discredit competitors, a practice called 'poisoning' in the trade. A retailer faced with a customer who bought from him an article that has been poisoned by a competitor should offer the customer the full price of an identical article bought at the lower price quoted by the competitor.

There are simple people about who think that if they buy a diamond today for, say £1,000, they can sell it tomorrow for the same price, yet do not expect to do the same with a motor-car. A buyer of a diamond will have to wait until any rise in value swallows the original retailer's margin and the selling margin before he can even get his money back.

Some retailers, quite legitimately, offer to buy back diamond jewellery at a future date against the sale of a more expensive article. They will often make a loss in buying because the original price included purchase tax, but they are prepared to lose some profit to keep the customer.

Methodical Appraisal

In the U.K. the engagement ring tradition ensures large sales of diamond rings. If a trader knows this kind of stock, it is not difficult for him to make a quick valuation which is usually quite accurate. The reason is that such rings fall only in a fairly narrow band of quality. Large numbers of diamonds set in them, for example, are Top Silver Cape, second piqué. As soon as the size is known, the insurance value is quickly estimated. After estimating the price of the diamond, the value of the jewellery in which it is set is arrived at in stages. The mental process is as follows:

1. Gauge (or weigh) diamond and calculate price.
2. Add estimated cost of mount.
3. Add retail margin.

When the diamond is sizeable and of higher quality, a more sophisticated approach is necessary. The principle is to obtain the weight of the stone, to ascertain its quality, and to refer to a current table of prices, as explained earlier in this chapter. Accurate weight estimation is extremely important.

Valuation of Other Cuts and Small Stones

Valuations for resale or probate of fancy cuts is a more difficult task as the factor of ready saleability has to be taken into account. In this case, a fancy cut can depreciate the price of a stone or jewellery. For example, some earlier emerald-cut stones are almost unsaleable except for re-cutting. This gives the clue to estimating the value of unfashionable and old cuts of stone, including old mine-cut and Victorian-cut stones, of which there are many still in existence.

As a general rule, all fancy-cut stones (except, perhaps, small ones) will be worth less than round-cut ones of the same weight. Of the different cuts, emerald- and square-cut will be lowest in price and marquise highest, with ovals, pear-shapes and hearts somewhere in between, probably in that order. An emerald-cut stone priced in 1976 was as low as half the carat price of a brilliant-cut stone of the same weight and quality.

Very small brilliant-cut stones, from about 6 or 7 points, actually increase in value as their weights decrease because of the high labour content. For example, a 0.01 ct stone would be 45 to 50 per cent more per carat than a 0.06 ct stone. Also quality, unless noticeably low, does not affect the price very much.

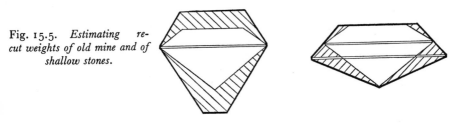

Fig. 15.5. *Estimating re-cut weights of old mine and of shallow stones.*

Valuing Stones of Old-fashioned Cut

To estimate the value of an old mine or similar cut, gauge or weigh the stone, then estimate how much weight could be recovered if it were re-cut as a modern brilliant. The estimating process is as follows:

1. Gauge (or weigh) diamond.
2. Estimate weight if re-cut in brilliant style (usually from 40 to 60 per cent).
3. Calculate price of brilliant cut.
4. Deduct price of re-cutting.

The same principle of estimating the re-cut value and deducting the cutting charges may be employed with all badly cut stones.

If a Leveridge or Moe gauge with tables is available, estimating recut sizes is simple. Decide whether the stone is over or under depth. If over, take the smallest diameter and look it up in the table against a normal depth and if under, take the height with normal diameter. Each will give an approximate recut weight (Fig. 15.5).

Re-cutting prices depend upon the size of the diamond and are charged at a rate per carat, but naturally vary according to any difficulties encountered. It must be emphasized that this is for re-cutting an already polished stone. Cutting rough obviously costs much more.

Rose-cut diamonds pose a different question for valuation as only the larger ones are suitable for re-cutting as brilliants. The loss in weight in this case will be very much more. There is, however, a small demand in the antique jewellery trade for rose-cuts for replacement of lost stones. Prices offered are below the equivalent prices of brilliants, but it is impossible to give a guide because demand fluctuates considerably.

Keeping Records

In the diamond trade, there are some remarkably dedicated dealers in special stones who claim to be able to recognize every stone that has passed through their hands in a lifetime of trading. For those not blessed with such visual memories, it is necessary to keep records. If accurately completed, a certificate or warranty is such a record, or course. Here is a suggested list of items that

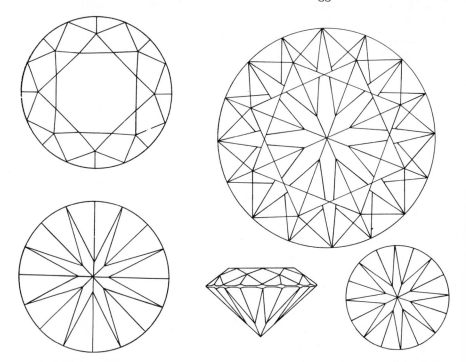

Fig. 15.6. (left) *Diagrams for recording inclusions and* (right) *an alternative if a more accurate record is required. The table reflections are used for more accurate location. This system was devised by the Diamond Grading Laboratories Ltd, London.*

could be recorded, together with diagrams for recording in ink specially recognizable inclusions or marks and other peculiarities. It is obviously possible to do with less information, depending upon the purpose of the record:

Shape	Proportions (in % of girdle diameter)
Cut	Total depth
Weight in carats	Table diameter
Clarity grade	Crown depth
Colour grade	Pavilion depth
Fluorescence	Description of girdle
Diameter (min. and max.) or other dimensions	Finish
Depth	External blemishes

The outline diagrams can show the facet outlines, as is normal, or show reflections as well, as used by a diamond grading laboratory in London and shown also in Fig. 15.6, to pinpoint the location of inclusions more accurately. Anyone wishing to use symbols systematically for different types of inclusions and damage could not do better than to follow the system originated for the Scan. D.N. clarity diagrams. They are logical and easy to remember and reproduce. Some are shown on page 301.

REFERENCE

A treatise on Diamonds and Pearls; in which their Importance is considered; and plain rules and exhibited for ascertaining the value of both; also the true method of manufacturing diamonds, by Richard Jeffries, Jeweller (London 1750).
The Economics of the Israeli Diamond Industry, by Michael Szenberg (New York, 1973).

CHAPTER SIXTEEN

Origin and Geological Distribution

All diamonds were found in the gravels or conglomerates of active or extinct rivers until about a century ago when they were discovered in great pipes or plugs of rock that penetrate deeply into the Earth. It was supposed that the rock, subsequently called kimberlite, was solidified lava and the tapered pipes of it were the roots of extinct volcanoes. The supposition is now known to be incorrect. Kimberlite pipes are not in fact simple funnels that go down to the mantle under the earth's crust. They are more like forked carrots – great cavities filled with kimberlite – that were fed from a number of narrow vents. See Figs. 16.1, 16.2 and Appendix 5.

Any diamonds are closely contained in the kimberlite rock, but are not attached to it. As single diamond crystals are found with faces bounding all sides, they did not grow attached to a matrix like many gem crystals such as beryl and quartz.

Eclogite the Parent Rock?

For the first part of the twentieth century, it was suggested that the birthplace of diamond was the rock eclogite. Professor T. G. Bonney's pronouncement that diamond crystallized in it, made this ultra-basic rock world famous. He supposed that the rock was disrupted to release the diamonds, which became accidental inclusions in kimberlite. Some diamonds had been found in eclogite, which is a constituent of kimberlite. Eclogite is a rock that may occur as boulders in pipes. In the Roberts Victory mine, the eclogite is an aggregate of green pyroxene, red garnet, bluish kyanite and white mica, which is very pretty when slabbed and polished, and is considered as a border-line case between igneous and metamorphic rocks. Small outcrops are found in the oldest Pre-Cambrian rocks of the Scottish Highlands, Norway and elsewhere.

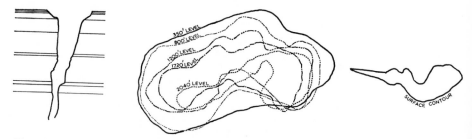

Fig. 16.1. *Examples of a diamond pipe in section, contours of a pipe at different depths, and the surface contour of a fissure. See also Appendix 5.*

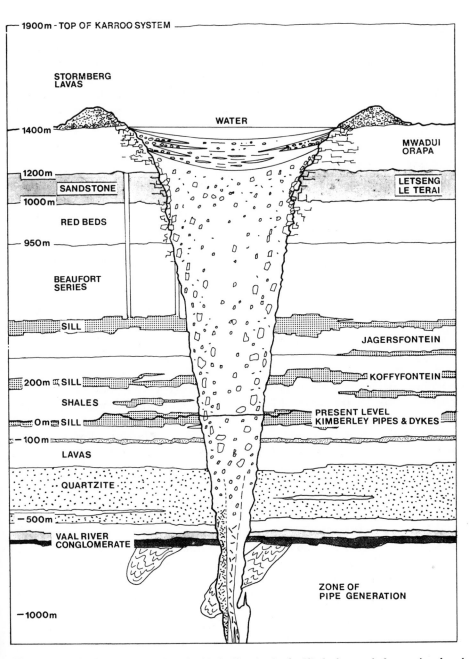

Fig. 16.2. *Diagrammatic section of a kimberlite pipe in the Kimberly area before erosion, based on a model by J. B. Hawthorne, Chief Geologist of De Beers Consolidated Mines, Kimberley. There are eluvial and alluvial deposits of diamonds on and around the Mwadui, Grapa and Letseng pipes because the surrounding terrain had not been eroded like that in the Kimberley area, from which diamonds were carried long distances by the elements.*

Current Theory

It is still uncertain how diamonds originated; they were certainly formed much deeper on the earth than any other gemstone. The magma – the mother liquid in which they were formed – appears to have originated more than 120 miles (about 200 km) down, but diamonds were probably not themselves formed at the source. Most diamonds are found in continental areas with a history of long periods of geographical stability.

Theories of Genesis

Current theories about the genesis of diamond depend to some extent upon analyses of the kimberlite that brings it to the surface. Kimberlite, as one earth scientist put it, 'provides a window' to the Earth's upper mantle (Fig. 16.3), because it contains samples of minerals in the mantle. Certain visible inclusions in diamond are similar and therefore came from the same source, as did minute droplets of the mother magma that have been detected in diamond.

If diamond begins, at least, to crystallise in conditions of heat and pressure when it is thermodynamically stable, it is likely that it was formed at depths of 95 miles (150 km) or more. The interval between the pipe and diamond formation is unknown. Some scientists think that diamonds crystallised first, but perhaps most take the opposite view.

It is possible that fluids rich in water and carbon dioxide and also in sulphides of iron, nickel, copper, and cobalt, played an important part in diamond's genesis, but how is in considerable doubt. Some workers believe in a solid state transition from graphite (in the same way as almost all synthetic diamonds are made). Others argue that a carbonaceous fluid or gas was the source.

One theory is that diamond seeds were formed in pools of liquid in the Earth's crust and grew by deposition of carbon atoms on their surfaces from carbon dioxide (reduction of CO and CO_2) or the oxidation of methane gas (as some synthetic diamonds have been grown experimentally), but not necessarily in the same place. These gases also provided the pressure to drive the kimberlite to the surface.

It is clear that diamond-bearing rock – kimberlite – is not lava, as lava erupts at a temperature of 1800 to 2100° F (1,000–1,200° C) and any diamonds in it would vaporize. Some kimberlite has been found to contain pieces of coal and log and even human bones that must have dropped at least a mile down from the surface. It is inconceivable, therefore, that the kimberlite came to the Earth's surface as lava.

Syngenetic inclusions in diamond (those formed at the same time) point to its association with eclogite since one of the constituent of eclogite was mostly transformed into pyrope garnet, which is also found as a diamond inclusion. Pyrope is coloured by chromium which is characteristic of rocks from deep in the Earth. Other chrome minerals found as diamond inclusions indicating its deep origin are chrome diopside, chrome enstatite, and chrome spinel. A further fact, pointed out by Dr. E. Gübelin, is that olivines found in diamonds contain traces of chromium, but olivines found in kimberlite do not, which suggests that

OCEAN & CRUST ABOUT 12KM

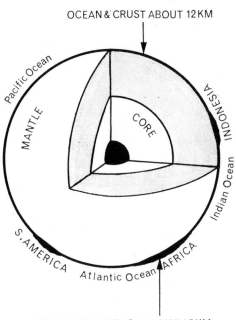

Fig. 16.3. *The interior of the Earth. On the outside is a crust, which is granitic under the continental masses and basaltic under the oceans. The mantle (shown dotted) goes down to about 1800 miles (2900 km) below the surface and is of peridotite, probably containing pure olivine and eclogite (a dense form of basalt). The outer core (shown white) is liquid iron and the inner core (shown black) is of solid iron.*

CONTINENTAL CRUST ABOUT 35KM

diamonds cannot have originated in kimberlite. One of the most remarkable inclusions is the sulphide mineral pyrrhotite, because it may have been the mineral that released the carbon from carbon dioxide to provide the raw material for the genesis of diamond.

Formed from Methane?

Some Russian research workers into synthetic diamond believe that methane was the mother material of diamond, not carbon dioxide (Co_2). Methane (CH_4) is marsh gas, the simplest of all the hydrocarbons. Methane may have been decomposed in the magma at a high temperature and pressure. When the magma cooled to a suitable temperature, it is suggested that, in some instances, the pressure also might have been favourable to the formation of diamond. In any case, the temperature would have been very much lower than those currently used for diamond synthesis. Dr. J. J. Gurney has calculated that the garnet peridotites in Kimberley pipes stabilized at 1700 to 1800°F (940–980°C).

Graphite is thought to be an unlikely candidate for the mother material since it is unlikely to be a constituent of the magma at the temperatures and pressures which have been indicated by the presence of the inclusions.

The Possible Course of Events

To sum up, it seems that diamonds crystallized from carbon over long periods of time in great reservoirs of molten magma in certain favourable parts of the Earth's mantle of peridotite. Various accompanying minerals possibly crystallized also in the same magma, which, perhaps while in a plastic or semi-plastic state, was driven upwards by explosive pressures of gasses from great depths, to

355

pierce the Earth's crust in a multitude of relatively small fissures and pipes, and to solidify.

On the way, the magma became altered by chemical change and also picked up many other rocks and minerals, to become kimberlite. During this forceful process, constituent minerals were released, some were broken or altered and retrapped or suffered other changes.

Although most irregular diamonds were so formed, diamonds that are broken, chipped or cleaved when mined must have been damaged *en route*. A. F. Williams records the finding of a large diamond, shaped like a man's finger, in the De Beers mine. It was in two separate pieces with cleaved surfaces that fitted exactly together. Yet the two pieces had been recovered in two quite distinct parts of the pipe which were mined separately.

Pipes are referred to as primary sources of diamond, but are not truly so, because the diamond was transported from its original source deep in the Earth.

The current theories were broadly anticipated in 1897 by Sir William Crookes who described kimberlite as, 'a geological plum-pudding of heterogeneous character, agreeing, however, in one particular. The appearance of shale and fragments of other rocks shows that the melange has suffered no great heat in its present condition, and that it has been erupted from great depths by the agency of water vapour or some similar gas.'

Kimberlite Pipes

In geological terms, kimberlites are dykes that are vertical or nearly vertical. Some dykes are as long as 53 miles (48 km) says Dr. J. J. Gurney, an authority on South African kimberlites. Enlargements of dykes near the surface are called 'blows' and in some conditions these take the cone-shaped form called 'pipes', of various sizes. Sills of kimberlite are very rare. A sill is a sheet-like body of rock that lies broadly parallel with the strata whereas dykes cut across the strata.

Kimberlite containing diamonds, according to Dr. Gurney, 'have a very restricted geological setting'. They are in, or at the edge of, areas of greatest stability and were always formed at least 500,000,000 years after the Earth's crust. The map (Fig. 16.4) shows that kimberlite occurrences in southern Africa spread over an enormous area roughly oval in shape. Kimberley appears to be the central diamond area because the farther from Kimberley in any direction – west to South West Africa, east to the Orange Free State and Lesotho – the fewer the diamonds in any deposit. This may also be true to the north in Botswana, but it is difficult to be certain owing to the overlying Kalahari Desert sand and deposits of calcrete. Nine major pipes and about fifty minor occurrences have been mined in the top semi-oval area indicated on the map.

The huge carrot-like kimberlite pipes are sometimes found more or less level with the surface, but some still project about it forming a flat kopje and others had weathered into a shallow depression, like the Premier and Wesselton when they were discovered. The original height of pipes when extruded through the surface was about 2,600 ft (800 m) above sea level according to some geologists, although J. B. Hawthorne, De Beers' chief geologist, has put them as nearer 4,875 ft (1,500 m), the original surface of the Karroo being about 4,550 ft (1,400 m) as shown in Fig. 16.2.

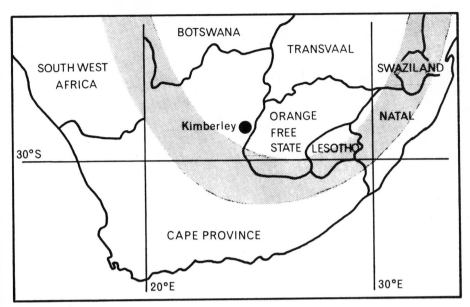

Fig. 16.4 *A map showing where all kimberlite pipes in southern Africa, containing economic quantities of diamonds, are to be found (top enclosed area); where some contain diamonds worth mining (shaded area); and where none contain diamonds (outside shaded area). It was devised by Dr. J. J. Gurney of the Council for Scientific and Industrial Research of South Africa.*

The pipe area usually decreases with depth and eventually becomes a number of fissures. This may occur several thousands of feet down. Pipes are not normally uniform in section as they often have hollows or protuberances in the sides. They vary considerably in size. The smaller ones are under 100 ft (30·5 m) across. The largest in Africa are the 360·5 acre (146 ha) Williamson mine in Tanzania, the 273·1 acre (110·6 ha) Orapa mine in Botswana, and the 79·5 acre (32·2 ha) Premier Mine in Pretoria, Republic of South Africa. (See Appendix Five.) Although they may be very long, as mentioned earlier, dykes – and fissures – can be only a few inches wide.

It is estimated that there are about 900 pipes and fissures located in Southern Africa, alone. There are many in the South West Africa (Namibia), but not one is diamondiferous although the very many diamonds found along the Sperrgebiet coast must have come from pipes. There is another group of pipes south of them in South African territory. This group is also not diamondiferous and in fact is not truly kimberlitic. To the south of the rich pipes in Kimberley are other groups that are very poor in diamonds. Some of the fissure deposits in South Africa are still worked privately for diamonds.

Ages of Deposits
Most known alluvial deposits are young in geological terms simply because kimberlite is easily eroded by the forces of nature. As shown below, the ages of known diamond deposits span thousands of millions of years, from the Wit-

watersrand gold placer deposits (see page 364) to the geologically recent South West African alluvial deposits along the coast.

				million years
Witwatersrand conglomerates	.	.	.	2600
Premier mine		.	.	1700
West African kimberlites		.	.	1100
Brazilian conglomerates		.	.	1000
Indian conglomerates		.	.	500
Mir pipe, U.S.S.R.		.	.	400
Roberts Victor pipe*		.	.	106
Dutoitspan pipe*		.	.	87
Tanzanian kimberlites		.	.	60
South West Africa coast alluvials		.	Recent times	

In view of these figures, Dr. Gurney says that it is not easy to confirm the statements of some geologists that kimberlites were more often produced in recent geological time.

Kimberlite

Kimberlite is related in origin to peridotite and to eclogite. It varies very considerably in composition and in general appearance from pipe to pipe and even in the same pipe. Sometimes it is a very finely granular and compact material. At others it is an assemblage of huge boulders of different rocks, sometimes feet across. When it contains diamonds, the diamonds also vary in crystal habit, colour, quality, and in other ways, from pipe to pipe.

The colour changes with depth. In the Finsch pipe, for instance, the yellow ground becomes progressively less weathered with depth, changing gradually to blue ground, until at about 300 ft (90 m) down, the kimberlite is hard and unaltered. The weathering of kimberlite into blue ground and yellow ground is fairly consistent throughout pipes in a wide area because the climate controls the rate of oxidation.

In the deposits of the Siberian plateau in the U.S.S.R. the weather prevents oxidation, so there is no yellow ground and, in at least one place in South Africa, Reit Fonteins in Gordonia in the Cape, blue ground has not weathered into yellow ground.

There is a third form of kimberlite named hardebank by the diggers because it did not disintegrate even when exposed to the elements for fifty years or more. Hardebank appears to be a form of kimberlite that cooled rapidly when it formed. It is found in parts of some pipes where blue ground grades into hardebank, as can be readily seen by the change in colour, but there is no definite line of contact between the two forms of kimberlite. It is most evident in the small fissure and dyke formations of a number of small mines in South Africa.

* Pipes in the Kimberley area are generally around 100,000,000 years old.

Composition of Kimberlite

Although the composition of kimberlite varies from mine to mine, the most abundant of the primary minerals forming it is olivine, a mineral that is subject to many alterations, one of which is to serpentine. Other minerals are ilmenite, phlogopite, perovskite, magnetite, and apatite. There are also traces of nickel. Nickel was one of the first catalysts used in making synthetic diamond.

Secondary minerals in kimberlite may include serpentine, calcite, chlorite, talc, magnetite, limonite, siderite, phlogopite, perovskite, amphibole, haematite, leucoxene and pyrites. The principal minerals that may have been transported in the rock are pyrope garnet, chrome diopside, chrome spinel, enstatite, ilmenite, magnetite, rutile, hornblende, augite, and of course diamond.

Among diamonds that occur in pipes are perfectly formed crystals only a fraction of a millimetre in size, which have to be recovered by special techniques. The presence of micro-diamonds suggests that kimberlite includes the magma in which diamonds were originally formed.

Some kimberlite also carries shales, sandstones, conglomerates, etc., which are accidental inclusions and are probably from the country rock surrounding the pipe. There are reports of very strange inclusions, including coal, fossilized branches of wood, old blackened ostrich eggs, and human skeletons, including a headless one, the head having been discovered 50 ft (15 m) away at half the depth. A whole undamaged ant-hill was also found about 50 ft (15 m) below the surface of one pipe.

'Cape Rubies' and 'Tanganyika Rubies'

Garnets are usually scattered throughout the kimberlite and vary in size from specks to crystals about 0·5 in (13 mm) across, although occasionally large pieces occur over 6 in (15 cm) across. In the earlier days of diamond digging in the Cape, diggers used to sell the many garnets they recovered with diamonds as 'Cape rubies'. Those from Tanzania are still mis-called 'Tanganyika rubies'.

Nodules of chrome diopside often occur in a shell of kimberlite in the kimberlite mass. This also happens to garnets, olivines, and other minerals, too. In a number of mines there are occurrences of large numbers of these nodules packed together ranging in size from marbles to cannon balls and cemented together by decomposed kimberlite.

Mica and Iron Ores

Phlogopite is a form of mica and appears commonly in kimberlite both as a primary mineral and a transported one. It occurs in sizes up to 6 in (15·2 cm). The flash of smaller mica inclusions is readily seen in a lump of kimberlite. Often the phlogopite crystals are like the pages of a book buried in the kimberlite. Biotite is another form of mica, but is much less common in kimberlite.

Magnetite is a magnetic iron ore commonly found in masses of small cubic or octahedral crystals, when it has been transported, but it also occurs as scattered particles when the olivine has broken down to serpentine. It is easily extracted from crushed blue ground by magnets. It is opaque and black to pale brown. Some of it occurs in large lumps corroded round the outside.

Ilmenite, another iron ore, is found in kimberlite in large corroded lumps, and also scattered through the rock in small opaque specks.

Zircon, Corundum and Other Minerals

Zircon is quite common in kimberlite and, being dense, is recovered in the concentrate of other heavy minerals including diamond. The zircon crystals are almost invariably broken and irregular. Corundum – ruby and sapphire – also turns up in the concentrate, but in quite good crystals because it is hard and tough enough to survive attrition.

Apatite is found in specks and rarely in larger crystals or broken lumps of crystal. Calcite is a common constituent impregnating kimberlite and is also found as very large included nodules, sometimes 2 ft (60 cm) across. It also appears in well-formed crystals.

Graphite and Quartz

Graphite, which might be thought a common constituent of kimberlite, is rare. Impure graphite in large nodules has been very occasionally found.

Although kimberlite containing quartz and chalcedony is very rare, when it does occur, it is rich in quartz. At least this appears to be true of the South African mines. Some Brazilian diamonds are said to contain quartz as inclusions. The presence of quartz in kimberlite has not yet been satisfactorily explained, but silicated water was responsible in the specimens from South Africa.

Concentration of Heavy Minerals

If blue ground is crushed, many of the minerals it contains are released as separate pieces or crystals, which can be concentrated into a different density group. The average specific gravity of blue ground is around 2·8, but many of the constituent minerals are much denser. These include magnetite at 5·0, zircon about 4·7, ilmenite 4·5, rutile 4·2, garnet about 4·0, corundum 4·0, spinel 3·6, diamond 3·5, epidote 3·3, olivine 3·3, and apatite 3·2.

Diamond Yields from Pipe Mines

The deeper a pipe mine is mined, the smaller the yield of diamonds, and the smaller average size of diamond. In South Africa, for example, the Bultfontein mine yielded 0·42 carats a load (1,600 lb/3,500 kg of blue ground) at the upper levels and 0·31 at about the 1,000 ft (305 m) level.

The decrease in yield was particularly sudden in the Premier mine. Only 0·19 carats per load was recovered from the ground between 410 and 510 ft (125–155 m) levels, but the blue ground at the top gave from 0·80 to 1·29 carats a load. This suggests that the very top of the mine which was eroded away by weathering may have been very rich indeed. Over 27,000,000 carats came from the first 500 ft (150 m) of blue ground so it is probable that very much more than this amount was eroded away.

It would appear that yield decreases with depth. Certainly a number of mines have ceased to pay as they were worked deeper. Occasionally, as happened with the Premier, an intruding sill increases the yield temporarily. Not all geologists accept this as a rule, however.

360

Diamonds from underground in pipe mines probably account for much less than 10 per cent of all those mined. It is difficult to estimate how much diamond is produced from both open-cast and deep working of pipes, but it may be in the region of 20 per cent of the world total, which means that about 80 per cent comes from alluvial sources, although the Russian pipe mines have probably altered the proportion.

Alluvial Deposits

It is assumed that all alluvial diamonds were released from pipes or similar extrusions. The pipes must have been upstream of the river beds where diamonds are found, although river courses may have changed, perhaps very considerably, over millions of years. It is possible that pipes occur under what is now the sea bed, although none has been discovered.

The original kimberlite at the tops of pipes undoubtedly weathered very rapidly compared with other rocks, to free any treasury of diamonds it may have contained. Weathering takes place at all times, but it was much more violent millions of years ago during long periods of torrential rains and greater extremes of heat and cold. Diamonds and other minerals and rocks released would have been carried quickly away by rushing waters.

Water carried the diamond-bearing gravels and other detritus short or long distances, sometimes hundreds of miles towards and even into the sea, before depositing the gravels as beds or terraces (Fig. 16.5).

Formation of Terraces

Rocks are broken up by contraction and expansion, the daylight and winter/summer temperature variations causing cracks between the mineral grains, and are then washed away by rains. They are also eroded by chemical processes when acted upon by water, carbon dioxide, and oxygen.

A river will build terraces as a result of several natural processes. It may be fast flowing and therefore able to carry much detritus. If it reaches a plain, it is slowed down and has to deposit the detritus; it may then flood, and the deposited detritus spreads over the 'flood-plain'. At a later stage, the river may have to cut its way through the flood plain to form a new channel, possibly at a lower level. Excessive rainfall may increase the volume of river water and consequently the detritus carried, but again this may be deposited on a flood plain when the water volume is reduced. Terrace formation may follow infrequent changes in water level or water course.

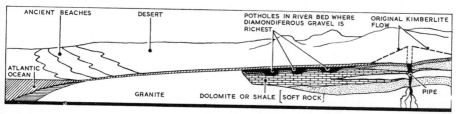

Fig. 16.5. *How diamonds were carried from the heads of pipes down rivers to the sea.*

When a river reaches the sea its flow may be checked and the detritus load is deposited. This may lead to scouring of the river bed farther upstream coupled with the erosion of the flood plain and the formation of terraces of silt sand and gravel. Sudden storms may increase the flow of water and the river may straighten a tortuous course leaving the remnants of former flood plains as terraces (Fig. 16.6).

Marine Terraces

If the finer and larger diamonds both north and south of the Orange River were in fact at the tops of pipes, many of the best stones were carried to alluvial deposits. Certainly the alluvial deposits along the South West African coast have produced the greatest number of fine gem crystals and continue to do so.

So much diamondiferous gravel was brought down to the sea on this south west African coast that huge quantities were deposited in the sea itself. The Orange and other rivers would have been torrents when this happened. Now they are dried out for most of the year.

A longshore current up the coast, caused by the prevailing SSW wind, took the gravels up the coast for distances of over 100 miles (160 km). The action of the tides and waves tended to concentrate diamonds in areas at the edge of the sea in beaches. Over a long period of time, the sea advanced and receded a number of times, leaving four wave-cut rock platforms, each with a deposit of diamondiferous gravel just like a modern shingle beach except that it is covered with sand, the depth of which varies on different parts of the coast from 1 ft (30 cm) or so to as much as 80 ft (25 m); (Fig. 16·7).

These marine terraces overlaid the river terraces near the northern bank of the Orange River mouth. The gravel include pebbles of various agates, and

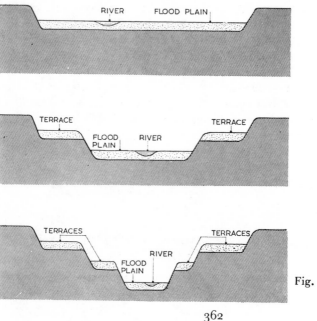

Fig. 16.6. *How a river forms terraces.*

other forms of quartz, including jasper, that are attractive when tumble-polished.

In areas farther north up the coast, near Luderitz, high winds that still today cause walking sands (moving drifts), concentrated diamonds in old valleys and blew the sand away so that millions of pounds worth of fine stones were left exposed in this wild inhospitable area for anyone to find and pick up. At the beginning of the century, most of them were found and picked up by prospectors from Germany.

Diamondiferous Gravels

Alluvial gravels are usually in a well-defined band – although not a strata – of boulders from local sources mixed with small pebbles. The pebbles are mainly of chert, quartz, quartzite, jasper, chalcedony, and banded ironstone. There is usually fine silt, rather than sand with the pebbles. The gravels may be any distance from a few inches to many feet below the surface, and in bands of thickness from a few inches to several feet.

Marine terraces have layers of boulders, pebbles and grit, all rounded by the action of the sea, which often lie on a bedrock of shale, covered by sand. The range of sizes is greater than in alluvial deposits. There is sand with the gravels, as well as on top of them, and often oyster and mussel shells. The pebbles are mainly of quartz with some banded ironstone. Pebbles of chalcedony, epidote, feldspar, garnet, and jasper are also found.

Diamonds are still found in the beds of some very active, torrential rivers, such as some in Guyana, South America, where pockets in the bedrock trap diamonds and other heavy minerals. The conditions are presumably similar in some ways to what those in the alluvial fields of Africa were many thousands of years ago.

Water-worn Crystals

In alluvial sources, the forces of Nature have acted as a sorting plant. As diamonds are relatively heavy, they tend to sift to the bottom of layers of sand

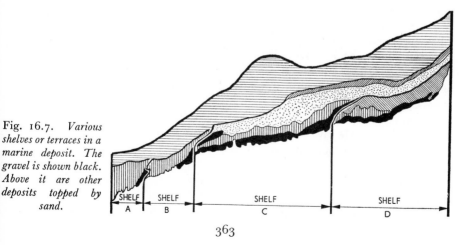

Fig. 16.7. *Various shelves or terraces in a marine deposit. The gravel is shown black. Above it are other deposits topped by sand.*

SHELF A   SHELF B   SHELF C   SHELF D

and gravel during movement. Also larger diamonds settle more rapidly than small ones. The small crystals were therefore more likely to have been carried on towards the sea and carried there more rapidly so that they suffered much less from wear. Any small crystals that travelled slowly for one reason or another would have become water-worn, through being jostled for aeons of time in the gravels. The same action must have broken up flawed and previously fractured stones and spilt up porous crystalline diamonds. This may be why there is a very high proportion of gem diamonds along the South West Africa coast.

Some years ago, the Diamond Research Laboratory carried out experiments to discover the durability of different qualities of diamond that were jostled among pebbles. They put into a ball mill – a drum containing many steel balls and water – some heavy gravels from the diamond mines in South West Africa, six gem quality diamonds from the same source and six diamonds of boart quality from Bakwanga in Zaire. The diamonds were the same size as the heavy gravels. The mill was rotated for 950 hours and every hour it was stopped, emptied, the fine material removed through a screen, and recharged. After only seven hours, all the industrial diamonds from Zaire had disappeared, but after 950 hours the S.W.A. diamonds had lost only 0·01 per cent of their weight.

Sharp-edged octahedral crystals (glassies) are found in alluvial deposits, such as those in Sierra Leone, that are probably a long way from the original pipes, yet the crystals show no evidence of wear during their long journey with river detritus. It is possible that sharp-edged diamonds are found in all alluvial diggings. Perhaps they travelled originally with much softer materials. It is unlikely that they were ever jostled together. Diamonds will wear each other quickly, as dealers who carry cut stones together in gem parcels soon find out.

Other Sources of Diamond

In the Witwatersrand in South Africa, diamonds are found in a conglomerate that is older than the kimberlite pipes. Another place where they occur is in hard conglomerates, almost like concrete, in dry diggings and also in marine deposits, but the conglomerates are in these cases merely gravel that has become concreted through natural action after the gravels were laid.

A few diamonds are found in gold mines. In 1968, it was stated that those from South Africa's gold mines totalled thirty-eight and all were then in museums. They all appear to be ordinary Type I crystals, but are greenish in colour. After studying them, the Diamond Research Laboratory at Johannesburg decided that they must have suffered irradiation by charged particles and at some stage of their existence became annealed at a temperature of not more than 932°F (500°C).

Dr. A. A. Linari-Linholm claims the cause to be the presence of uranium in some of the reefs. He says a few hundred of diamonds have been found there, but the present gold recovery methods by which the reef is crushed to a fine powder also mean the end of any such diamonds, especially those of poorer quality.

Diamonds are found in association with alluvial gold and other heavy minerals such as sapphire, topaz, tourmaline, and cassiterite (a tin mineral), not because they had similar origins but because being dense and more chemically nert than common minerals that form rocks, they were brought together by the action of ancient rivers. Diamonds are found occasionally in the tailings of tin dredgers on Phuket Island and at Phangnga in Thailand. They are also found in alluvial deposits in New South Wales, Australia, associated with gold, cassiterite and gem quality sapphire.

REFERENCES

Internal World of Gemstones, by E. Gübelin (Zürich, 1974).
International Diamond Annual, 1970.
The Genesis of the Diamond, by Alpheus F. Williams (London, 1932).
'The Parent Rock of the Diamond in South Africa', by T. G. Bonney. *Geological Magazine*, 1899. p. 309.
'The Genesis of Diamond Deposits', by George C. Kennedy and Bert E. Nodlie. *Economic Geology*, August 1968.
Physics and Chemistry of the Earth – 9. Papers presented at the first International Diamond Conference on Kimberlites Cape Town, 1973. (Oxford, 1975.)

CHAPTER SEVENTEEN

Diamond Crystals

The Octahedron (111)

The octahedron is the normal habit of diamond, although from some sources another form of crystals may be more common. The most regular crystals have flat, smooth faces and straight edges and are known in the trade as glassies (Fig. 17.1). They come from various mines, both pipe and alluvial. Some Russian crystals are even 'glassier' than those from Sierra Leone, and sharper at the edges.

Glassies in general tend to draw colour, i.e. they do not include the finest whites, which usually are in other crystallizations including worn octahedra. When the colour of a gem diamond is poorer, the clarity often tends to be better, according to sorters, and there is a good proportion of high clarity stones among glassies.

Glassies are commonly distorted by one or two faces not having developed to the same extent as the others, probably because the face was starved during crystallation. The face of an octahedron becomes smaller in area as it grows. The underdeveloped face is therefore larger than the others, as shown in Fig. 17.2. Sometimes the flattening is so extreme that the crystals become tabular (see later). Distorted octahedra are shown in Fig. 17.11.

Octahedra with rounded edges and corners are the most common of this form of diamond crystal and are found in many different sources, both pipe and alluvial. Examined from the side, the edges will be seen as curved or humped, as shown in Fig. 17.3. Again, few such crystals are perfect so that the opposite

Fig. 17.1. *A glassie.*

Fig. 17.2. *Developed* (left and right) *and undeveloped* (centre) *faces of an octahedron.*

366

Fig. 17.3.   *Rounded octahedral crystal containing a naat (interpenetrant twin crystal).*

Fig. 17.4.   *A cubic crystal.*

pairs of faces are rarely equidistant. The faces are usually domed, sometimes have traces of other possible crystal forms and invariably have trigon markings even if these are not immediately evident.

Some have grooved instead of rounded edges. (See negative crystals, later.)

The Hexahedron or Cube (100)

Cubic crystals are relatively common, but are almost entirely confined to low quality (industrial) stones. Cubes of chrome yellow colour are occasionally found in gem quality. The edges of cubes are usually rounded and not as square as shown in Fig. 17.4, and may sometimes be fairly clearly defined as dodecahedral faces (Fig 18.8). Faces are frequently domed. They are never smooth but are covered with growth or etch features. These may be terraced steps aligned to the edges of the cube, or pyramidal depressions aligned with the diagonals across faces.

Sometimes a pyramidal depression occurs in the centre of a face. (See negative crystals, later.)

Isolated cube faces occur frequently on crystals of combined form in gem as well as industrial qualities.

The Rhombic Dodecahedron (110)

As the edges of an octahedron (1 1 1) become more developed, as seen in Fig. 18.4, the rhombic dodecahedron (110) crystal appears. It can also derive from the (111) edge of the cube developing (study Fig. 18.8). In each case the original octahedron or cube faces become smaller and smaller and eventually disappear. (Fig. 17.6.)

True dodecahedron crystals are rare (Fig. 17.5), but crystals of intermediate form tending towards spheres are common. These often have hexakis hexahedroid* faces. One is shown in Fig. 17.7. The dodecahedron edges are nearly always sharper than the octahedron edges.

* As many forms of crystal have rounded sides and edges, the suffix 'oid' is sometimes used to describe these, as suggested by J. R. Sutton in *Diamond* (1928). Hence octahedroid, dodecahedroid, and hexahedroid (rounded cubic form), etc.

Fig. 17.5.   *Rhombic dodecahedral crystal.*   Fig. 17.6.   *Combination   dodecahedral   and octahedral form.*

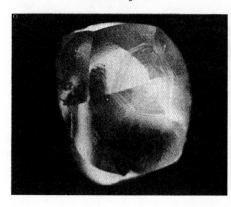

Fig. 17.7. (right)   *A combination form. The rhombic dodecahedral face at the top has a seam across it, which is the beginning of a tetrakis hexahedron.*

Crystals of near dodecahedron form occur not infrequently in yellow colours and are often of high clarity. As the colour denies their use as gemstones, they are much sought after for industrial use in wire drawing and are known as die stones. A hole is drilled through a die stone and is employed to reduce and control the diameter of wire during its manufacture. It is obvious that purity of the crystal is important in die stones. The direction in which a die stone is drilled affects its wear because hardness is directional. If a die stone is drilled at right angles to a (111) face, the hole will eventually wear triangular. If it is drilled at right angles to a (100) face, it will wear square.

The Tetrakis Hexahedron
A dodecahedral face can be recognized by its rhomb or boat shape and occurs commonly in crystals or mixed form. There is often a fine ridge or seam across the short diagonal, which is the beginning of the formation of a tetrakis hexahedron (Fig. 17.7.). A tetrakis hexahedron is like a cube with a four-sided pyramid on each face and is rare, if it exists, in a pure form. (See Fig. 17.4.)

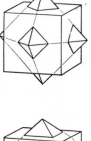

CUBE AND
OCTAHEDRON

CUBE AND
DODECAHEDRON

ig. 17.8. *An apparent tetrahedral diamond f about 0·50 ct and* (below) *its relationship to the octahedron.*

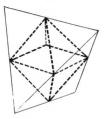

DODECAHEDRON AND
OCTAHEDRON

Fig. 17.9. *Relationship of the three basic shapes of diamond crystal.*

Triakis and Hexakis Octahedra

Triakis and hexakis octahedra also probably do not occur as whole crystals, but the forms are quite common as faces on octahedroid and dodecahedroid crystals.

The Tetrahedron

Sutton says the tetrahedral form 'is not frequent, and even then probably illusory. Its symmetry always is either masked by curvature or it is in combination with some other form.' He reported that an excellent tetrahedron with plane faces was recovered at Wesselton, but examination showed every face to be leavage. A. F. Williams wrote, 'in all the years I have examined diamond, I have never found a diamond having the form of a tetrahedron'.

It is probable that the true tetrahedral diamond crystal does not exist. The nearest approach to tetrahedral form is probably the distorted octahedron, an example of which with curved faces is shown in Fig. 17.8. Tetrahedral crystals of certain minerals show pyro-electricity and also piezo-electricity. That is, they develop positive and negative polarity when heated and also when squeezed. A tetrahedral diamond crystal should show similar effects.

Irregular Crystals

Crystals of no form or a hardly recognizable one, are the most common of all. There is no recognizable exterior form, but when the crystal directions have been

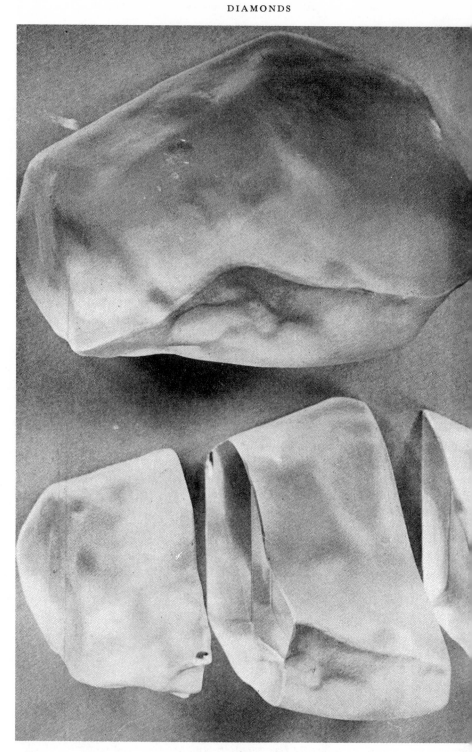

Fig. 17.10.   *The 3,106 carat irregular Cullinan, shown full size, and (below) how it wa*
first cleaved.

identified the gem cutter can often make a high recovery. Some have one or more cleavage faces. The famous Cullinan was such a stone and was cleaved into workable sizes and shapes as shown in Fig. 17.10.

Shapeless industrial stones are sometimes cleaved into octahedra and polished all over by a tumbling process, which makes them more useful for setting in tools and drills. Except to the experienced eye, which recognizes a peculiarity on the surface lustre, these rounded octahedra look like natural ones.

Tabular Habit

Very thin crystals occur when parallel faces on an octahedron are hardly developed while the others are very strongly developed. Usually such crystals are hexagonal in outline as if a slice were taken out of the octahedron parallel to the undeveloped faces (Fig. 17.11). Sometimes one face is hexagonal and the other triangular. Those of cuttable thickness are known as flats. The thicknesses of tabular crystals varies considerably from crystal to crystal. Some are as thin as a post card. In the past, such crystals have been used to glaze miniature paintings and are called portrait stones or lasques. Today they are very occasionally cut square or rectangular and fitted as 'glasses' in very expensive watches. They are, of course, scratchproof. (Synthetic colourless sapphire is commonly used for scratchless watch crystals.)

Cushion, Bolster and Round Crystals

Combinations of forms based on octahedral and dodecahedral crystals are sometimes of flattened cushion form. Not infrequently the crystal is elongated or of bolster form. Usually there are some recognizable faces. Sometimes crystals are almost perfectly round (Fig. 17.64). (Round stones known as ballas are not single crystals.)

Cushion and bolster-shaped crystals often have smooth rounded faces, some of recognizable form, such as octahedra, triakis and hexakis octahedra, and rhombic dodecahedra (Fig. 17.12 to 17.14).

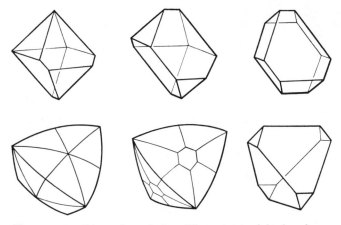

Fig. 17.11. *Distorted octahedra. That at top right has become tabular.*

Dog's Tooth and Nail Crystals

The extreme rhombic dodecahedral forms with certain faces over-developed become long thin crystals which are curved slightly and have one end blunt and the other pointed, like a dog's tooth (Fig. 17.13). Very occasionally there is a head at the blunt end, giving the crystal the appearance of a horse-shoe nail.

Multiple Crystals

Diamonds are commonly found which are two or more crystals joined together. They can be large or small crystals, of various crystal form or more, and can be locked together in various ways, some more intimately than others. The extremes are two crystals (twins) and masses of tiny crystals (aggregates).

Fig. 17.13. (below)   *Dog's-tooth crystal.*

Fig. 17.12.   *A cushion-shaped stone.*

DISTORTED HEXAKIS OCTAHEDRON

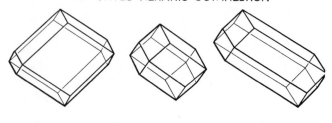

Fig.   17.14.   *Other forms of distorted crystals.*

DISTORTED   DODECAHEDRA

Twinning

True twinning occurs when a material of crystal structure has changed the orientation of its structure during growth. This naturally changes the outward forms of the crystal. It also alters physical properties, particularly the hardness.

The result of a change in orientation of the atomic structure is a composite or double crystal, with some of its edges and/or faces parallel, but others reversed. Twin crystals are of two types, and interpenetrant and contact. Both are common in diamond.

Interpenetrant Twins

An interpenetrant twin occurs when two crystals appear to have grown within the same space but with different crystal orientations. One appears to penetrate the other (Fig. 17.15).

Occasionally a diamond is found to contain another diamond crystal which is of quite separate formation; the inside one is an included crystal and not an interpenetrant twin and the atomic structures of the containing and the included crystal in this case are entirely separate. There are usually strain cracks in the large crystal around the smaller one.

An interpenetrant octahedral twin is shown in Fig. 17.17. A corner of one crystal can be seen poking through an octahedral face of the other. Interpenetrant twins occur occasionally in octahedra and also in cubes (Fig. 17.20).

Interpenetrant tetrahedra twins are found on rare occasions. They have a centre of symmetry, unlike the tetrahedron, thus falling within the most symmetrical crystal class, 32. The crystals are eight-pointed, as shown in Fig. 17.21

Star Twins

Extremely rare is the dodecahedron interpenetrant twin, which is star-shaped with six points alternatively above and below the central plane (Fig. 17.19). About fifteen miles from Virginia in the Orange Free State, South Africa, is a

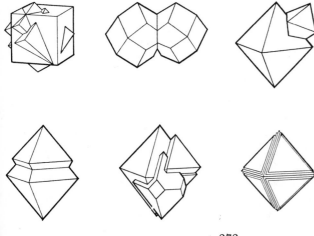

Fig. 17.15. *Forms of twinning in diamond.* Top row: *interpenetrant cubes, contact twin dodecahedra, and interpenetrant octahedra.* Bottom row, left and centre: *parallel growth in octahedra and* (right) *lamellar twinning in an octahedron.*

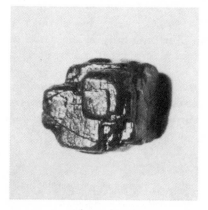

Fig. 17.16. (top).   *Twin cubic diamonds.*

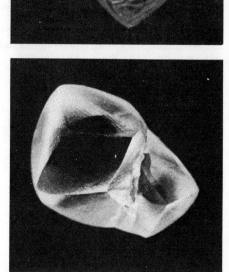

Fig. 17.17. (top right) *Twin octahedra. Note
the trigons.*

Fig. 17.18. (right)   *Twin dodecahedra.*

small mine which produced an exceptional number of star-shaped diamonds and the company working it was called Star Diamonds (Pty) Ltd. Most stones were of very good colour.

Star twins of various mixed forms also occur. Two are shown in Figs. 17.21 and 17.23. Stars can also occur through contact twinning as indicated later. Another form of star is the result of cyclical twinning and is extremely rare. There are apparently six points, but one will be found to comprise two smaller points.

Contact Twins

Contact twins are like crystals that have grown side by side, but with different orientation. One part of the crystal appears to have been rotated through 180° around an axis – the twinning axis. It can also be regarded as being rotated on a plane. Another name is in fact rotation twins.

If rotation occurs through 180° on a cube (100) plane of an octahedral crystal, another octahedral crystal will grow on it parallel to the original one, as shown in Fig. 17.30. The twinning crystals will have their axes and faces parallel to

374

Fig. 17.19.   *The sketches show other forms of diamond twins. The tetrahedral twin on the right is shown also in Fig. 17.21, and the star in the centre below in Fig. 17.25. The lower sketches are development forms of the diamonds shown in Fig. 17.22.*

Fig. 17.20.   *Interpenetrant twin cubic crystals.*

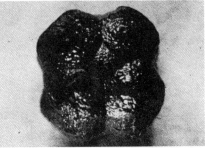

Fig. 17.22.   *This form occurs occasionally, sometimes with flat faces* (top) *or more rounded faces* (above).

Fig. 17.21.   *Interpenetrant twin tetrahedra.*

Fig. 17.23.   *A form of star twin.*

Fig. 17.24. *A botryoidal form of diamond in the Smithsonian Institution, Washington D.C. (actual size).*

Fig. 17.25. *A twin of the form shown in Fig. 17.19. top right.*

Fig. 17.26. *Worn surfaces of a strange twin.*

Fig. 17.27. *Side view of a complex macle.*

Fig. 17.28. *Extremely rare mixed twin.*

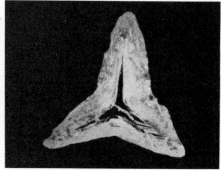

Fig. 17.29. *Extremely rare star form, presumably heavily etched.*

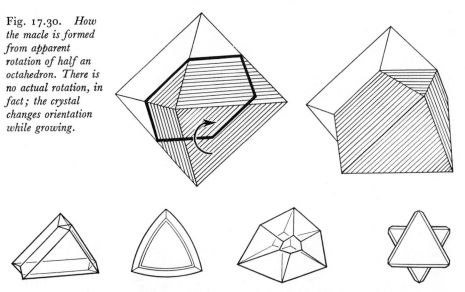

Fig. 17.30. *How the macle is formed from apparent rotation of half an octahedron. There is no actual rotation, in fact; the crystal changes orientation while growing.*

Fig. 17.31. *Forms of macle. From the left: with re-entrant angles, triangle, with hexakis hexahedral faces, and partly rotated to form a star.*

each other, but will not usually be of the same size. Often, too, they are displaced as shown in Fig. 17.15.

Contact twins of this type often comprise more than two individuals and are known as parallel growths. Some parallel growths are truly so, as in alum, but true parallel growth is not common in diamond. The twinning crystals are usually only approximately parallel. Diamond aggregates of approximate parallel growth occur frequently.

Macles

Contact twins occur very commonly in diamond with one crystal rotated through 180° on an octahedral plane. This, unlike rotation on a cube plane, radically alters the appearance of the crystal. The change is so unexpected it is difficult to visualize without the help of a model and has in fact been made the basis of a puzzle. Fig. 17.30 attempts to show how such a twin occurs.

The resulting twinned octahedron is universally known as a macle or maccle (French for twin) in the diamond trade. The plane of rotation of a macle is a hexagon, as shown in Fig. 17.30. The resultant twin crystal is triangular and tends to be tabular in habit. Macles often have a re-entrant angle, as shown in Figs. 8.3 and 17.31, which is an indication that the crystal is definitely a twin and not an untwinned tabular crystal, known as a flat.

The twinning or composition plane is usually called the seam in the diamond trade. It is rarely a flat plane, which introduces problems for the diamond cutter. The majority of macles also seem to be flawed at the edges by feathery lines running inwards from and at right angles to the edges, parallel to dodecahedron faces, as shown in Fig. 17.35. When the faces are flat they are often highly specular.

377

Triangles

Macles also occur with rounded faces, sometimes showing triakis or hexakis octahedroid features. The rounded faces form sharp points to the crystals, masking the re-entrant angles, and the crystals are usually called triangles. Careful examination will usually indicate whether or not these triangles are twinned. Many have large feathers or cracks in them. One is shown in Fig. 17.35.

Sometimes crystals are found in which the two parts of the macle appear to have slipped or moved slightly in relation to each other, towards one of the edges. On other occasions, the rotation has been through a little less than 180°. Very rarely, half of the macle rotates to produce a crystal of six-pointed star shape. (Fig. 17.31.)

Macled cubes have been reported from Brazil. A macled tetrahedron, if such exists, would be identical in shape to an octahedron.

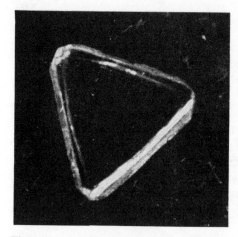

Fig. 17.32. *A flat transparent macle from the C.D.M. mines.*

Fig. 17.33. *Side view of the stone in Fig. 17.32.*

Fig. 17.34. *A particularly fat macle from the C.D.M. mines.*

Fig. 17.35. *Macles and triangles are commonly flawed in the centre like this example.*

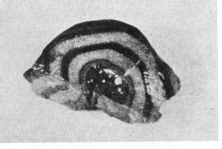

Fig. 17.36. *Banded growth in a well-formed octahedral crystal. Occasionally the banding is very obvious as the quality of the diamond is different in the alternate bands or layers.* (Below) *A more irregular form tending towards hailstone boart, see Fig. 17.61.*

Repeated and False Twinning

Twinning on a plane can reverse repeatedly. This gives rise to a series of crystal layers, or lamellae, of different orientation, each being rotated by 180° in relation to the next layer. The lamellae may be quite thick or extremely thin. Such polysynthetic twinning or lamellar twinning, as it is also known, is common in diamond. Banded growth is sometimes lamellar (Fig. 17.36).

Lines and ruts caused during growth or by etching through the corrosive forces of nature during a long period of time can be like parallel twinning in appearance and are then known as false twinning.

Crystal Aggregates

The growth of several diamond crystals together as an aggregate is common. There may be only two, three, four or so crystals locked together, or as many as hundreds. The sizes may be large or minute.

Again, the aggregate may be irregular, with no relationship between the orientation of the crystals, or regular, when different axes, edges, or faces are parallel to each other. Diamond aggregates are nearly always irregular. Many are formed of large masses of small crystals in haphazard order.

If there are no outward faces or edges to define separate crystals, a mass may still be made up of thousands of tiny crystals of diamond of different orientation, but the mass is then more a cryptocrystalline mass than a crystal aggregate.

Growth in Layers

It has been revealed by X-ray diffraction topographs that diamond grew in nature by a series of concentric layers of atoms on the octahedral (111) faces. Inclusions obviously interrupted this ideal situation. There may also be a few or many dislocations in the crystal lattice. Normal growth, therefore, favours the octahedral crystal. The banded growth in Fig. 17.36 seems to bear this out.

Similar studies have shown that rounded dodecahedral diamonds were originally sharp-edged octahedrons and, at some time during their history, the

379

edges of the octahedron were dissolved parallel to the (110) directions (see Fig. 17.9).

Growth Features

The growth of diamond occurs in layers. Crystal faces are often marked by lines which, on examination, are seen to be shallow steps or terraces. They are usually close to and parallel to the edges of octahedron faces. Sometimes the triangular terraces appear on an octahedron face in repeated flakes or lamellae. On other crystals there may be more prominent pyramids. Stepped crystal development of this type on a cube face is square. The striations on dodecahedral faces are parallel to the long axis. These and the lines on other faces are one outward expression of what the cutter calls grain.

Shallow depressions such as trigons in the octahedral faces and the squares in cubic crystals are similar phenomena. All are believed to be growth features. Accelerated growth produces an elevated projection and decelerated growth produces a depression which is orientated oppositely to the face.

Secondary face development occasionally results in hexagonal terraces near the centre of an octahedron face as shown in Figs. 17.6 and 17.7, although the crystals have developed almost into dodecahedral form.

Negative Crystals

Some octahedral crystals have quite deep grooves along the edges, because these were negatively developed, and even holes in the corners. They are sometimes referred to as negative crystals (Fig. 17.38). A similar growth occurs with cubes, when four-sided hollow pyramids appear on the faces. The corners of the hollow pyramids point to the sides of the crystal, and the sides of the hollows may be terraced in steps – in the form called a hopper or skeleton cube – may be columnar and straight, or basin-shaped (Fig. 17.37).

Negative growth is believed to be caused when conditions of growth favour the edges rather than the faces of a crystal or faces rather than edges (Fig. 17.38).

Fig. 17.37. (right and lower right) *A hopper cube or skeleton cube.*

Fig. 17.38. (below) *So-called negative growth, causing grooves along the edges.*

Trigons

Almost every, if not every, natural octahedral face has triangular markings on it, known as trigons. Some trigons are easily recognizable by the naked eye and a face with visible trigons probably invariably has thousands of faint ones as well, when viewed under high magnification. Some may be as shallow as ten Ångstrom units. The triangles are equilateral with straight edges (Fig. 17.39). They are orientated oppositely to the face – their corners point to the edges of the face – and they are always aligned strictly with each other.

Trigons appear to be of at least three types – pyramidal pits which go down to a sharp point, pyramidal pits with flat bottoms, and flat-bottomed pits with steep almost vertical sides.

Professor S. Tolansky, after making a special study of diamond surfaces by his multiple beam interferometry methods, examined one portrait stone which had no apparent trigons on its surfaces. Under an effective magnification of 500,000 ×, he found well over a million shallow trigons on each of the two sides. The area of each side was only about 0·15 sq. in (1 sq. cm).

Etch Features

By etching diamond with a hot oxidizing agent, Tolansky has produced surface features on various faces. These are triangular on octahedron faces, boat-shaped

Fig. 17.39.　*Trigons on an octadedral face. They are orientated in an opposite direction to the face.*

Fig. 17.40. *Continued etching of an octahedral face cause the triangular pits to overlap and appear to be rectangular.*

on dodecahedron faces, and square in outline on cube faces. All are orientated with the face. The etched triangles of an octahedron face are aligned with the edges of the face, for example, compared with natural trigons which are orientated in an opposite direction. As etching proceeds, in each case the edges of the pits become curved. They afford clear evidence, he says, that in each crystal, growth has been preceded by a layer formation, the layers being parallel to the octahedron faces (Fig. 17.40).

On the other hand, in 1958 Frauk and Puttick produced trigons orientated like natural ones by placing diamonds in fused kimberlite and a decade later two Indian scientists, named Patel, did the same by using a carbon arc.

Fracture and Cleavage
It is because growth of the diamond has proceeded in places parallel to the octahedral planes that diamond will cleave in these planes, leaving flat faces. Diamond is often found in nature with one or more cleaved faces. It will also fracture in other directions and again diamonds are found in nature with concoidal fractures which show a shell-like rippled form. There is often a combination of these.

A cleaved surface is extremely flat by ordinary standards. It may vary by less than a millionth of an inch in unevenness. Although the octahedral cleavage of diamond is said to be perfect, however, it is very rarely so when examined by interferometric methods. The cleaved surface when highly magnified is often found to be broken in almost conchoidal form. It has been shown by Tolansky that this is the characteristic cleavage of the most common diamond, Type I.

On the other hand, the cleavage of Type II stones is almost perfect. There are almost flat regions separated by steps which are only a few Ångstrom units high. It has been suggested that Type II stones consist of a mosaic of separate 'blocks' each being of a more perfect crystalline unit than Type I. This would perhaps account for the steps.

There is also possible dodecahedral cleavage in diamond, since this direction gives the next looser bonding of the atomic planes. Some of the chips used in early Indian jewellery are said to be dodecahedral.

Twinning, Naats and Graining

Diamond is commonly twinned internally, part of the material having grown with an opposite crystal orientation, a mirror image. This poses problems for the cutter and polisher as the hard directions of the twinned part are opposite to those of the rest of the stone. The manufacturer calls such an area a *naat*, after the Dutch word for knot, comparing it to a knot in wood. A *naat* can turn the sawyer's blade or make a cleavage impossible. It can cause a line, parallel lines, or very slightly raised areas of various shapes, on the surface of a polished diamond (Figs. 13.38 and 13.39). Very occasionally a small *naat* will be torn out of a surface while grinding, causing a hole. Twinning lines on polished stones, also called 'graining', can be single or several parallel lines. As they are natural, they should be distinguished from polishing lines caused by the process of manufacture. Polishing lines vary from facet to facet, but the continuous lines of graining will cross from facet to facet, changing direction as they do so, or will change direction on a facet. (See Fig. 18.14.)

Graining includes the growth lines sometimes seen inside a diamond. These are the result of different phases of growth of the stone, which are seen as fine toothed lines or as phantom lines under magnification. They are usually the same colour as the rest of the stone but very rarely are more yellowish or brownish, in which case they affect commercial grading.

Another form of graining has been described by Robert Crowningshield, director of the Gemological Institute of America's laboratory in New York. In a number of high quality diamonds, he discovered graining that was misty and appeared as dark lines or bands sometimes running in more than one direction. They were visible even to the unaided eye in some instances. Such stones fluoresced with an intense yellowish-green and phosphoresced for a long time afterwards, whereas stones with 'normal' phantom grain lines fluoresced blue without phosphorescing. Crowningshield also reported that the misty graining cannot be seen in the rough material, so that a cutter could buy an apparently flawless rough stone only to find that the resultant polished stone had to be graded VVS because of the visible dark grain.

Fig. 17.41. *A face has been cleaved off this octahedron to show the 'coating'.*

Coated Crystals

Many diamond crystals are coated when mined. The surface is more opaque than and often a different colour from the material inside. The name is a misnomer because the coating is inferior quality diamond near the surface. The depth of coating varies considerably, from very thin to a substantial part of the stone.

Coated stones come from various mines and the Congo provides a high proportion of industrial quality. An example with an octahedral face cleaved off it, is shown in Fig. 17.41. The nature of the coating gives an indication of the area where the crystal was found.

At times a coating of bad colour conceals diamond of magnificent gem colour and quality. This is particularly true of certain Brazilian stones which appear, when mined, to be light green to brown, according to the thickness of the coat, but can be collection colour once the coat is removed. On the other hand, some are brown stones all through. Venezuelan stones sometimes have a shiny coat of sea-green colour under which the diamond is of top quality.

Under a coating may be a diamond of fine quality but fancy colour. A. Monnickendam refers to a stone of about 5 carats in the rough, which was 'coated with a dirty-looking layer of skin'. When cut it proved to be a magnificent ruby red. He also points out that coated stones are not necessarily the same or better under the coating. They can be worse. Octahedra from Namaqualand may appear whitish in the rough and Silver Cape in colour when cut and are a source of worry to master cutters. They do not appear to be coated, but 'one infers that they have a transparent coat of such a nature that the yellowish tint in the stone is neutralized'.

Close examination of a coating will show it to be part of the diamond which contains many small inclusions which make the coating, or appear to make it, a different colour from the rest of the stone. Under the microscope, the inclusions are often like many small flakes of foreign material close to the surface, and the coating colour may be grey, greenish, brown or black. The surface may be shiny or dull, frosted or drusy.

When examined by X-ray diffraction topography, coated diamonds show a transition from a normal growth of a crystal facet to one of a fibrous nature with inclusions of micron-sized foreign particles. The division between modes of growth is often abrupt.

Green coatings are believed to be 'skins' of induced colour caused by the crystals having been in the vicinity of radio-active materials such as uranium.

It is normally a highly speculative financial operation to buy a coated crystal which has not been opened. Opening comprises polishing windows (facets) opposite each other, through the coating. Then some appraisal of the purity and colour may be made. The coating that remains will still prevent close judgement of colour, however. Sometimes, when stones are octahedra, opposite faces are cleaved off to open the stone.

Accidental Coatings

On very rare occasions a cut diamond acquires a coating by accident that depreciates its colour. One such case was reported by Robert Crowningshield, Director of the G.I.A. Gem Trade Laboratory in New York, in 1966. An engagement ring with a stone of less than half a carat had become gradually yellow over eighteen months. Examination showed a brownish-yellowish coating that would not wash off. After treatment with hot acid, the original fine white colour was restored. The coating was apparently caused by the local iron-rich water.

Skin

Cutters sometimes refer to a skin on octahedral faces. This is in fact a physical effect caused by sudden changes in hardness when the direction of grinding is changed, as described on page 406.

Inclusions in Diamonds

Dark inclusions in diamond were for generations called 'carbon spots', although it is now known that amorphous carbon does not occur as inclusions. One reason was that the hardness and value of diamond made if difficult or uneconomic to remove inclusions for identification. The high refractive index and the fact that inclusions were distorted into unfamiliar shapes made recognition under a microscope difficult. Relatively recent research by Dr. W. Eppler of West Germany and by Russian mineralogists using X-ray crystallographic techniques has identified the larger inclusions and given a guide to the genesis and provenance of diamonds.

A distinction must be made in this book between the classification of diamond inclusions for grading, as dealt with in Chapters Eight and Thirteen (when any internal feature such as a cleavage fissure is regarded as an inclusion and the mineralogical nature of the inclusion is irrelevant) and the classification for gemmological reasons, when their nature can prove an identifying factor and perhaps indicate also the country and area of origin. Diamond inclusions can also prove the natural origin of the stone, but have not been employed for this as no synthetic gem diamond is as yet on the market. A broad classification of

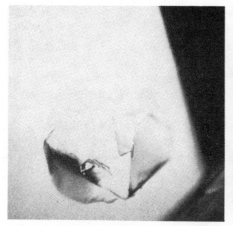

Fig. 17.42. *A glassie octahadron included in a glassie.*

Fig. 17.43. *Partially included diamond in diamond. (× 6)*

Fig. 17.44. *Purple garnets in a diamond from the Finsch mine. (× 80)*

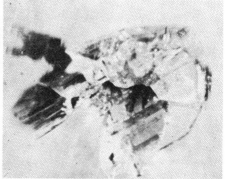

Fig. 17.45. *Inclusion of diopside in a sawn diamond slice. (× 14)*

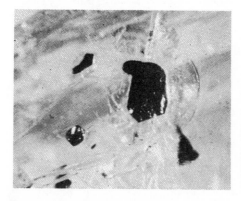

Fig. 17.46. *Globular-shaped chrome-spinel inclusions; the large one is exposed. (× 10)*

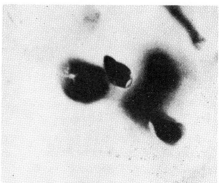

Fig. 17.47. *Isometric, well-faceted magnetite inclusion. (× 64)*

All inclusions shown on this page are syngenetic. Photographs by J. W. Harris of University College, London, except Fig. 17.42.

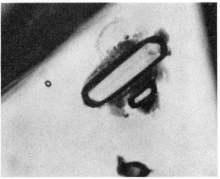

Fig. 17.48. *Group of various guest crystals (well developed diamonds and garnets as well as resorbed olivines and diopsides) forming an interesting assembly of the diamond's paragenesis. All are twin formations of the host.*

Fig. 17.49. *Pair of pseudo tetragonal olivine crystals that settled on an octahedral face lying parallel to the edge of the octahedral face. Olivine crystals are of syngenetic origin with diamond.*

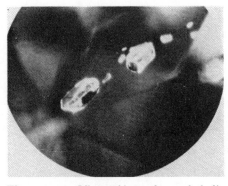

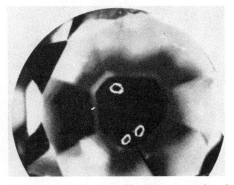

Fig. 17.50. *Idiomorphic partly-resorbed olivine crystals aligned parallel to a former edge of an octahedron face of the host diamond when it was still in the juvenile phase.*

Fig. 17.51. *Very small olivine crystals of well-formed shapes.*

Photographs by E. Gübelin, Geneva.

Fig. 17.52. *Straight flat cleavage fissure running diagonally through table of a brilliant-cut diamond. Such a fissure forms a zone of weakness in the host, easily causing its breakage.*

Fig. 17.53. *Irregular tension cracks diverging from a common centre. Such cracks are very dangerous for the diamond as they may cause it to break easily.*

387

Fig. 17.54. *Two powdered goethite inclusions (probably pseudomorphs)* (× 25)

Fig. 17.55. (above) *Graphite platelet inclusions that lie in octahedral planes.* (× 25)

Fig. 17.56. (left) *Rosette form of pentlandite and pyrrhotite inclusions. Rosette fractures are caused by the different relative expansion rates of the sulphides and diamond during the diamond's ascent in the kimberlite.* (× 25)

All these inclusions are epigenetic, formed subsequent to the diamond host. Photographs by J. W. Harris.

inclusions is: (1) protogenetic – already existing minerals incorporated in a gem during its genesis, (2) syngenetic – material formed at the same time as the gem and included in it because the host grew more rapidly, and (3) epigenetic – materials formed or included in a gem at some time after its genesis. All three occur in diamond but syngenetic inclusions are by far the most common in a large variety of minerals.

Known protogenetic inclusions are earlier existing diamonds around which host diamonds have formed. This is evident from the fact that some included diamonds are fractured, an example being an octahedron with a broken point.

Olivine is a common syngenetic inclusion (Figs. 17.48 to 51). The included crystals are usually transparent and of an elongated form with rounded edges which caused them to be mistaken for bubbles or zircons (which do not occur in diamond). The elongated crystals are aligned along the octahedral directions in the stone and when extremely numerous and submicroscopic in size probably form the mists, particularly those sometimes seen in the form of a cross within a stone, according to Dr. E. Gübelin, who has made a special study of gem inclusions. A few olivine inclusions may be faintly green, but none have the deep green of the olivine formed in kimberlite. Garnet is another commonly encountered inclusion and is occasionally seen exposed to the surface of a polished stone (Fig. 17.44), as the inclusion is often quite large. The garnets range in colour from yellow to brown, orange and red, and from pink to violet and purple. Most are red pyropes. Red to brown and black chrome spinel occurs frequently in diamonds from some areas like the previous two minerals as individual crystals or in groups. Diamond is another fairly frequent syngenetic inclusion (Fig. 17.43), as are the green chrome diopside and the almost identically appearing green chrome enstatite. More syngenetic inclusions that have been identified are pyrrhotite, pentlandite and pyrite – all sulphide minerals – as well as ilmenite, rutile, coesite (silica), bronzite and spinel.

Some syngenetic inclusions suffered pseudomorphic changes to become such minerals as serpentine, biotite, phlogopite and chlorite; and thus became epigenetic inclusions. Occasionally the micaceous minerals of phlogopite and chlorite are seen split into leaves like partly-open books.

Other epigenetic inclusions are caused by minerals in solution penetrating the stone from outside through cleavages and fissures. Various iron oxides penetrated stones in this way. Oxidized diamonds are relatively common and sometimes polished stones are seen with oxidized fissures, the reddish-brown colour of which tints the stone. Other minerals introduced in this way include rutile, calcite, hematite, goethite, quartz (see page 360), pyrrhotite, pentlandite, kaolinite, sellaite, and xenotime, according to Dr. Gübelin.

One more epigenetic mineral that is not uncommon occurs by a different process. It is graphite, which can arise in stressed areas of diamond as the result of some of the host diamond being converted to graphite. Fig. 17.53 shows the kind of cracks where graphite inclusions may be formed, and Fig. 17.55 an inclusion. It is also seen on the surface of other inclusions such as garnets.

If it becomes necessary to identify natural diamond by its inclusions, the presence of the chrome inclusions will probably be the main diagnostic feature, plus typical cleavage fissure where they occur, as shown in Fig. 17.53.

Fig. 17.57. (right) *A 620·15 ct diamond from Sierra Leone, bought from Selection Trust by Lazare Kaplan & Sons Inc., New York, U.S.A. in 1970. It is one of the world's largest diamonds but is not of gem quality.*

Fig. 17.58. (below) *Micro-diamonds from the Premier Mine. (×30)*

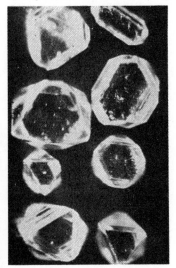

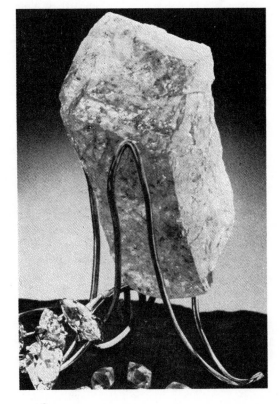

Fig. 17.59. (left)   *The Amsterdam Black diamond of 33·74 ct, 0·943 in (23·96) mm long, with 145 facets; it belongs to D. Drukker & Zn. N.V.*

Fig. 17.60 (above)   *An octahedron of 3 ct, with a part-developed rhombic-dodecahedral face, coloured brown in the points.*

Colours

Diamonds are found in a much wider range of colours than is commonly supposed – yellowish, brownish, greyish, and greenish being the most common. The colour is often distributed unevenly; for example, an octahedron may be whitish in the middle and coloured at the points (Fig. 17.60). Yellows are very rarely a bright canary; more often they have a muddy appearance or greenish cast. Browns can be attractively golden or cinnamon, but are generally an uninteresting reddish-brown, ashen or blackish. The most favoured fancy gem colours are probably emerald-green, red, sapphire-blue, pink, orange, violet-blue, pale blue, canary, the more attractive browns, and the more attractive greens, such as apple-green. Orange stones can be so unattractive that they are called 'sick' in some cutting circles. All colours can occur in different intensities.

Black diamonds are that colour because of their very large number of very small or sub-microscopic black inclusions which absorb nearly all the light falling on the stone. They are usually translucent to very strong light and often have grey spots in them. The surface of most of them becomes pitted when polished, although the author has seen one, belonging to one of the staff of Gustave Katz (the Johannesburg cutters and polishers), that had a good polish. There was no opportunity of examining it under high magnification. Black diamonds do not have the rarity and high values attributed to them in fiction, although there are at least two famous and therefore highly valued black diamonds, one of which is shown in Fig. 1.18. One large black diamond was cut in 1974–5 and named the Amsterdam. It weighed 55·85 carats in the rough and cost only about $6 a carat. The owners, the Amsterdam cutters and polishers, D. Drukker & Zn., began to cleave it for industrial use and found that it was exceptionally hard as well as being absolutely black and opaque. They therefore decided to cut it into a 33·74 pear shape with 145 facets, which turned out to be a laborious task. It was found somewhere in South Africa and has been certified by gemmologist Dr. Peter Zwaan as a natural diamond with a specific gravity of 3·513 (Fig. 17.59).

Micro-diamonds

There is a minimum size to diamonds recovered from mines because of the high cost of extracting small ones. The minimum size has become lower and lower over the years as the demand and average price received has risen, recovery methods have been improved, and it has become economic to work over old tailings. There still remain very large numbers of very small diamonds, however, known as micro-diamonds, which are of grit size and very much too expensive to extract and use as grit; but thousands of carats, representing many millions of tiny diamonds, have been extracted for scientific research purposes. They follow the same general crystal patterns as the larger stones, being octahedra, macles, dodecahedra (but more perfect ones), interpenetrant twins and so on. Some are of gem quality; many are of irregular shape and inferior quality. A surprisingly high percentage of micro-diamonds are Type II (see Chapter Eighteen), suggesting that many diamonds were formed of this purer type of material and became coated with the less pure Type I diamond as they grew in size. (Fig 17.58).

Diamond Grit and Powder

The use of diamond grit and powder has been referred to in the chapter on gem diamond manufacture. Here, for the sake of completeness, its production is described. It has a very wide role in modern industry, which consumes perhaps 5 tons (5·1 tonnes) of natural grit a year as well as about the same amount or even more of synthetic diamond grit. The sources of natural grit are pieces of diamond remaining from diamond-shaping processes and inferior industrial diamond (crushing boart). In earlier times chips were crushed by hand using a pestle and mortar or, as described by Leonardo da Vinci in 1485, wrapped in a sheet of lead which was folded repeatedly and was beaten with a hammer.

The grit was recovered by melting the lead and skimming off the scum, which was cleaned in strong acids. The pestle and mortar method continues into this century, but the mortar is provided with a seal around the pestle to prevent loss of powder, the pestle being hammered for about ten minutes with a mallet while the mortar rests on a soft pad. There are sealed pestles and mortars operated mechanically and also ball mills for making powder. A ball mill comprises a closed metal tube containing a large hard metal ball which is thrown from one end to the other alternately as the tube is rotated about a cross axis. The powder is cleaned with hydrofluoric acid and even the powerfully corrosive action of that mixture of hydrochloric and sulphuric acid when hot will not dull the sharp edges of the diamond particles.

Grading by Sedimentation

'Grading' was once a rather casual procedure, being no more scientific than waiting to see the glint disappear as the powder was reduced, turning the pestle in the mortar to gauge the 'feel' of the grit, and testing small samples by rubbing them between thumb and forefinger. A modern sealed pestle and mortar will reduce 90 per cent of the diamond to grit of no more than two microns*, with a maximum of twenty microns for the remainder, in ten minutes.

* A micron is 0·001 mm or 0·00004 in.

The size of the largest particles is very important in metal finishing as it determines the polishing limitations of the powder. The larger particles cause scratching, so a systematic method of grading was devised some years ago. The powder was thoroughly mixed with olive oil in a jar and allowed to stand for five minutes. The mixture was then poured into another jar, stirred, and left for ten minutes. The process was repeated several times at increasing intervals until the oil was clear. In each jar was left grit of decreasing particle size. For example, an engineering handbook of the 1940s listed these grades of diamond dust: No. 1, 10 mins; No. 2, 30 mins; No. 3, 1 hour; No. 4, 2 hrs; No. 5, 10 hrs; No. 6, until oil is clear. Powder can be and is graded also in other liquids such as water and alcohol.

Sieves for Powder

Currently powder is initially graded by passing it through fine mesh wire sieves with standardized hole sizes, referred to by the number of wires (therefore openings) to the linear inch or in some cases centimetre. U.S. mesh sizes have been most used today, grit being available from 16/20 mesh through 20/30, 30/40 and so on to the finest, 400/500, covering seventeen groups. Synthetic grits usually start at 20/25 for the coarsest size. With each sieve now being formed in a single sheet with square or round holes, the European standard of grading by average micron size, is rapidly being adopted. The price of synthetic grit fell sharply when the patents ran out and is now much cheaper than that of natural grit, which is difficult to obtain.

Centrifuging and Elutriation

The finer powders are still separated by suspension in a liquid, but two other processes are also used to speed production. One is centrifuging, in which the liquid containing the powder is spun rapidly so that the larger particles are transferred to the walls while the smaller ones remain in the liquid. The other is elutriation, in which the diamond powder, made into a slurry with gelatine solution, is introduced into a stream of water being forced up a pipe. The finer particles are carried upwards and extracted. Elutriators can be connected in series to extract different grades of powder.

Grading for Shape

Since the 1960s, powder has been graded according to shape as well as size. The shape considerably affects the efficiency for different applications. The main groups are blocky, needle-like, and rounded. The Diamond Research Laboratory in Johannesburg has developed a triangular sloping table (like the open top of a grand piano) which vibrates and sorts particles into shape groups as they race across it. There is also a sorting procedure to eliminate 'partials' that are weak.

Synthetic grits can be produced within limits to specification, covering their shape, size, strength, thermal stability, self-sharpening ability, etc., to suit their particular use. Some are supplied coated with nickel or one of the metal alloys to simplify the task of bonding them to the abrasive holder.

Industrial Crystals

Although this book is primarily concerned with gem diamonds, a brief classification of industrial stones is included for completeness. The borderline between classification of whole crystals as gems or as industrials depends upon their quality and the economic circumstances at the time.

Normally about 80 per cent of production is for industrial use. The diamonds are consumed, eventually disappearing. Of the remaining 20 per cent used as gems, over half the weight is lost in cutting, so somewhat less than 10 per cent of all diamonds are not consumed.

Stones considered to be industrial are those that do not meet the current demand for gems in quality, or are too small, badly crystallized, crypto-crystalline, or awkwardly twinned from the cutter's point of view (Fig. 17.42). A stone may be almost perfect as a crystal and flawless in purity, but if it is of yellow or brown colour unsuitable for gem use, it becomes an industrial (Fig. 17.60). Similarly, a fine octahedral crystal of collection colour may be classified as industrial because it has bad inclusions.

All diamonds can be classified into the following general groups:

1. Gem diamonds.
2. Industrial stones,
     (a) shaped diamonds, (b) rough diamonds.
3. Diamond boart.

The most preferred gem crystals are those of good octahedral shape which are as pure and white as possible. The most preferred shapes of crystal for shaped diamonds for industrial use are the dodecahedron and similar rounded crystals, as well as the octahedron. The purity must be as high as possible, but the colour is not so critical, although hardness or durability appear to be related to colour (page 406).

Shaped diamonds include die-stones, which are drilled with a shaped hole for wire manufacture, shaped tips for metal-cutting and finishing tools, tips of hardness indenters for measuring hardness, record player needles, truing diamonds for shaping grinding wheels and tips of rock drills.

Octahedra are better for tools used for truing grinding wheels. Triangles are also classified separately for industrial use, particularly tool-tips.

The second class of industrial stones under 2b above, is that of irregular crystals used for glaziers' diamonds, stone saws, rock drill bits, etc.

Boart

Boart is the name given to minutely and randomly crystallized, and usually yellowish-green or grey to black, masses of diamond which are extremely hard and, when crushed, are valuable as an abrasive. The name is also used in a more general way at the mines where 'mine boart' is exceptionally low quality rough fit only for crushing. Boart is also made synthetically. The name is derived from an old French name for 'bastard'.

Hailstone boart is of particular interest as it is different from other types, being made up of alternate layers of diamond and a grey to black cement-like material in appearance. The diamond comprises shells of clouded material and the other substance is like a porous paste. When the outer layer is diamond, the

Fig. 17.61. *Hail-stone boart, cut across the middle to show the layers.*

shape is octahedroid or dodecahedroid; when it is paste, the boart is shapeless. The core is either diamond or the other material (Fig. 17.61).

Diamond material known as ballas or shot boart has a spherical form, and ranges in colour from milky white to steely grey (Figs. 17.62 and 17.63). It does not show crystalline faces or edges, appears to have no definite lines of cleavage, and does not have inclusions like common boart. The ball shape derives from a stalk-like formation of diamond crystals i.e. polycrystalline diamond with

Fig. 17.62. *A large well-formed ballas of 3·75 ct.*

Fig. 17.63. *Twin ballas.*

Fig. 17.64. *Sometimes a single diamond crystal develops almost to a ball shape, but is not, of course, a ballas. The example shown weighs 1·40 ct.*

crystalites in (110) radial directions. The random directions of greatest hardness give it great durability. It is an intermediate form between carbonado and true diamond.

Carbonado or Carbons

Carbons are a crypto-crystalline material composed of diamond graphite, and amorphous carbon – diamond in various transitional stages, in fact. They are commonly called carbonado, the Brazilian name. Carbonado occurs in some quantity and in sizes weighing as much as several ounces in the States of Bahia and Minas Gerais, in Brazil. They were first discovered in 1843 in the gravels of the River José in Bahia; the biggest found weighed 31·67 carats. The specific gravity is from about 3·20 to 3·47; carbonado over about 3·40 is regarded of being better quality.

Some South African forms of carbonado have acquired special names such as 'framesite', which has larger than usual grain and is usually very impure, and 'stewartite', which contains some magnetite and is magnetic. C. Jeynes points out that the natural carbonado can be regarded as a ceramic, being similar to a modern sintered aggregate like diamond powder and metal.

REFERENCES

The Genesis of the Diamond, by Alpheus F. Williams (London, 1932).
Diamond, by J. R. Sutton (London, 1928).
Microstructures of Diamond Surfaces, by S. Tolansky (London, 1955).
Industrial Diamond Review 'The Recognition of Diamond Inclusions', by J. W. Harris (Sept. and Oct. 1968).
Internal World of Gemstones, by E. Gübelin (Zurich, 1974).

CHAPTER EIGHTEEN

Physical Properties of Diamond

Chemically, diamond is carbon in an exceptionally pure form. The only foreign element commonly present is nitrogen, which may amount to as much as 0·2 per cent. Any other foreign elements will be only parts in a million.

The carbon atom is unique in having four electrons in an outer shell which can hold up to eight. It therefore occupies a position half-way between the electro-positive and electro-negative elements, yet is not chemically neutral. Two carbon atoms can link together by sharing an electron from one, which fills a hole in the shell of the other. As there are four electrons and four holes to each atom, each atom can link with four others; i.e. it has a valency of four.

Such bonds are called covalent and can hold atoms together so that they form geometrical structures known as atomic crystals. The lattices are always strong and rigid and the resulting substances are hard solids with high melting-points. The most exceptional atomic crystal is that of diamond; it has the following structural form:

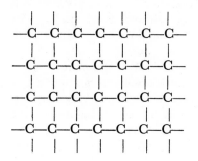

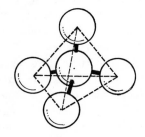

Fig. 18.1. *Tetrahedral bonds of the carbon atoms.*

Single molecules of such substances do not exist. Diamond can therefore be described as a giant saturated molecule of carbon.

The four bonds to each atom are not of course flat, as in the structural formula shown, but are at 109·5° to each other as shown in Fig. 18.1. Each atom is at the geometric centre of four others which are at the corners of an imaginary tetrahedron. Every bond is the same, 1·544 angstrom units long.

The linking of a number of carbon atoms in this way into a three dimensional diamond lattice can be seen in Fig. 18.3. One layer is shown shaded to draw attention to the puckered hexagonal rings of atoms that result from the structure. This is in fact one octahedral direction in the crystal, the others being in the planes of a tetrahedron, as shown in Fig. 17.8.

In graphite, the only other crystalline form of carbon, the atoms form also

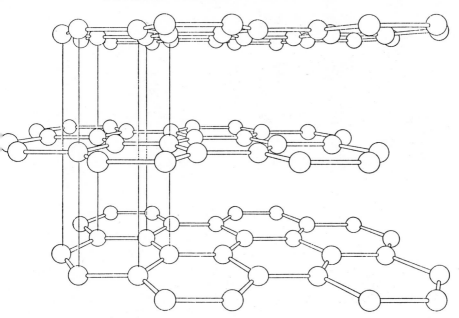

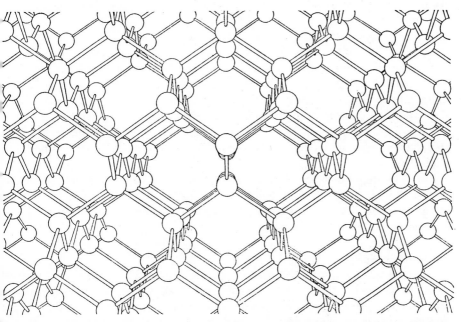

Fig. 18.2.   *Graphite atoms are bonded in layers with weak links between the layers. The top drawing shows a rather dramatic view; but the sketch is still highly representational. Below is a similarly imaginative view from inside a diamond crystal.*

397

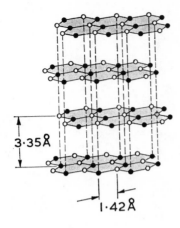

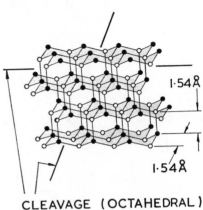

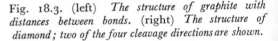

CLEAVAGE (OCTAHEDRAL)
DIRECTIONS

Fig. 18.3. (left) *The structure of graphite with distances between bonds.* (right) *The structure of diamond; two of the four cleavage directions are shown.*

into hexagonal rings, but the rings are flat and in thin plates or scales as shown in Figs. 18.2 and 18.3. Within a scale or layer, the atoms are closely linked with atomic bonds of 1·42 ångstrom units – more powerful even than diamond. Atomic forces between the layers are feeble, however, the bond being 3·35 ångstrom units, and they sheer easily, giving the substance a greasy feel.

The melting-point of graphite is in the region of 3,500° C (6,330° F) and that of diamond is thought to be as high as 3,700° C (6,690° F) owing to its atomic structure. Behaviour under heat is described in Chapter Nineteen.

As there are no free electrons or holes in a perfect diamond crystal lattice, diamond has high resistance to the passage of electricity. Graphite, owing to the loose bonding between scales, has free electrons which provide the ability to pass an electric current. The lattice of diamond is exceptionally strong, which results in its extreme hardness and resistance to deformation, but it is not particularly dense.

Many other physical properties can be related to the atomic lattice of diamond. The very high thermal conductivity, for example. The high refractivity of light is probably due to the long chains of carbon atoms that extend in all directions.

Crystallography

Most minerals are crystalline, having regular internal structures, but not all form into single crystals, in which the external form reflects the internal lattice. Sometimes the substance is made up of many zones that have crystallized, but in different directions to each other, so that the whole is crystalline and without external form. Diamonds occur both in single crystals and also in formless crystalline masses.

398

Crystals are divided into seven main systems of symmetry and diamond falls into most symmetrical of them, the cubic, also called the regular or iso-metric system. As well as these systems it is possible to build up thirty-two crystal classes in ascending order of symmetry. The cubic system, being the most symmetrical, includes the last five classes, from 28 to 32.

It has not been definitely established whether diamond belongs in the most symmetrical, Class 32, or in the next down, Class 31. Investigations of its atomic lattice by X-ray techniques appear to favour Class 32, the most perfect. If diamond should belong to Class 31, another form of crystal is possible, the tetrahedron, which does not have a centre of symmetry.

The possible forms in Class 32 are as follows and are shown in ideal shapes in Fig. 18.4.

Hexahedron, or cube	6 faces	(100)
Octahedron	8 faces	(111)
Rhombic dodecahedron	12 faces	(110)
Tetrakis hexahedron	24 faces	
Icositetrahedron	24 faces	
Triakis octahedron	24 faces	
Hexakis octahedron	48 faces	

In the diagrams, crystal axes are shown, from which faces are identified. A face is often indicated by a kind of shorthand indicating the axes which the face intercepts and known as the Miller indices. With brackets these indices indicate the whole form, as included in the list above. A plane in any shape of diamond can be identified by its crystal name, as shown in Figs. 18.7 and 18.8.

It is conventional in crystallography to represent a crystal by a space lattice that is a model of the unit cells of the same shape that make up the crystal. A cubic crystal is thus shown as an assemblage of skeleton cubelets. The basic unit of diamond is not a single, but a double cell. It is represented by two inter-penetrating face-centred cubes, as shown in Fig. 18.5. Perhaps a simpler way of visualising it is as a face-centred cube (with atoms in the corners and centres of the faces). Inside this are four other atoms located at the centres of four of the eight smaller cubes that make up the cell.

Crystal Dynamics

It must not be thought that crystal lattices are formal structures of hard balls of atoms joined by rod-like forces, as suggested by models and the diagrams here. It is true that atoms appear to behave like spheres in contact, but they are better imagined as closely jammed together, and in movement.

Dame Kathleen Lonsdale has described the image in these words: 'The space lattice is quite imaginary; there is no actual framework. The atomic model is quite imaginary; the crystal is much more like a quivering jelly full of vibrating pips.' In diamond, vibration is considerable even at room temperature, and at over 700°C (1290°F) becomes so violent that the atoms jump into the more stable atomic arrangement of graphite.

Trace Elements

Although relatively so pure, diamond usually includes a few atoms of other elements in its lattice. Among these are nitrogen, aluminium and boron, which

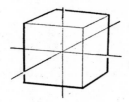

CUBE

TETRAHEDRON

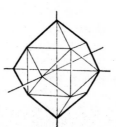

OCTAHEDRON

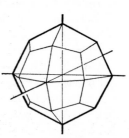

RHOMBIC DODECAHEDRON

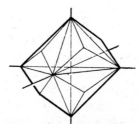

TETRAKIS-HEXAHEDRON

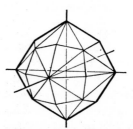

ICOSITETRAHEDRON

TRIAKIS-OCTAHEDRON
(or TRIS-OCTAHEDRON)

HEXAKIS-OCTAHEDRON
(or HEX-OCTAHEDRON)

Possible forms of diamond crystal, with crystal axes

Fig. 18.4. *Ideal possible forms of diamond crystal. The natural habit is the octahedron.*

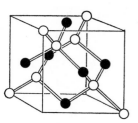

UNIT CELL

Fig. 18.5. *Unit cell of diamond*

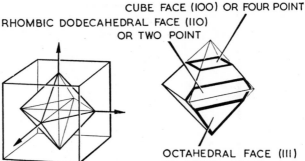

CUBE FACE (100) OR FOUR POINT

RHOMBIC DODECAHEDRAL FACE (110) OR TWO POINT

OCTAHEDRAL FACE (111) OR THREE POINT

Fig. 18.6. (left) *Relation of octahedron crystal axes to cube crystal axes.* Fig. 18.7. (right) *Different faces or directions in an octahedral crystal.*

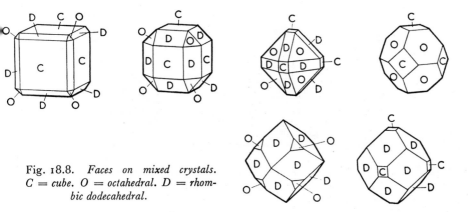

Fig. 18.8. *Faces on mixed crystals. C = cube. O = octahedral. D = rhombic dodecahedral.*

have decisive effects on the physical properties, as explained later, of silicon, calcium, iron, copper, magnesium, barium, chromium, silver, titanium, strontium, sodium, and even lead. Diamonds from different areas include different trace elements.

Without foreign atoms, the structure could be perfect, like that in Fig. 18.3, all through, but foreign atoms have different bonding which upsets the regular arrangement. The result is a mosaic structure of crystallites which are staggered or warped like bricks in a badly-constructed wall. They can even be in spiral formation.

Cleavage

When a crystal model of diamond is viewed from certain directions, the atoms are seen to be in layers. These directions are the cubic, the octahedral, and the rhombic dodecahedral. It will also be noticed that the density of the bonds between atoms is higher between layers in certain directions than between layers in others. In the octahedral direction, there are alternate layers with more and fewer bonds, i.e. every other layer is less strongly bonded.

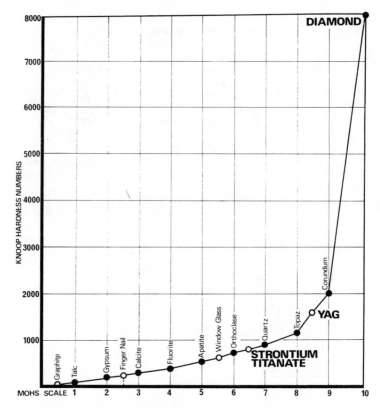

Fig. 18.9. *Various materials compared on the Knoop indentation hardness scale with Mohs' equal interval scratch hardness scale along the horizontal co-ordinate.*

A layer with more bonds is shown shaded in Fig. 18.3. It has three to every one in the same area of the next layer. When diamond is cleaved in an octahedral direction, it splits between two such closely bonded layers breaking only one bond in each tetrahedral group, so that the resulting cleaved surfaces are 'perfect'. Although octahedral cleavage is usually the most common, Sir C. V. Raman has reported finding rare dodecahedral and even cubic cleavage on some very small pieces of diamond.

Valency bonds per unit area are also a general indication of hardness in different directions experienced by the cutter when grinding and polishing diamond.

Hardness

Hardness is difficult to define in an absolute sense. Hardness scales depend on the relative hardness of one substance in relation to others. One of the earliest scales, devised by the mineralogist Mohs, was 'scratch hardness' based on the fact that any mineral in a numbered scale will scratch those of lower numbers and be scratched by those of higher numbers:

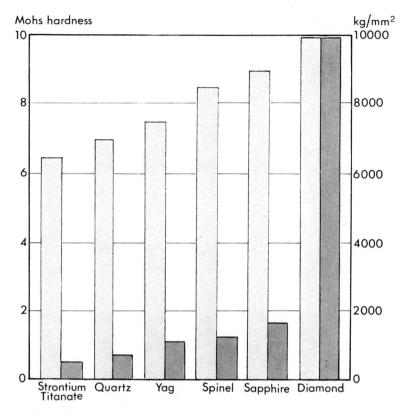

Fig. 18.10. *Indentation values using C. A. Brook's pentagonal indenter (dark shading and right-hand scale) compared with Mohs' scale (light shading and left-hand scale).*

1. talc; 2. gypsum; 3. calcite; 4. fluorspar; 5. apatite; 6. feldspar; 7. quartz; 8. topaz; 9. corundum; 10. diamond.

On the scale, a fingernail would be about $2\frac{1}{2}$ and a steel file about $6\frac{1}{2}$. The scale is by no means linear. For example, the hardness gap between 9 and 10 is much greater than that between 1 and 9. There are no natural minerals in the gap from 9 to 10, only manufactured hard materials such as the carbides of tungsten, silicon, and boron.

Another comparison is to measure the power of penetration of another hard material under pressure. In his book *Diamonds* (1909), Sir William Crookes described a test he carried out. 'The intense hardness of the diamond can be illustrated by the following experiment. On the flattened apex of a conical block of steel place a diamond, and upon it bring down a second cone of steel. On forcing together the two steel cones by hydraulic pressure, the stone is squeezed into the steel blocks without injuring it in the slightest degree. In an experiment I made at Kimberley the pressure gauge showed 60 atmospheres, the piston being 3·2 in diameter, the absolute pressure was 3·16 tons, equivalent on a diamond of 12 sq mm surface to 170 tons per square in. of diamond.'

Hardness tests are influenced by the anisotropy of the material, i.e. the

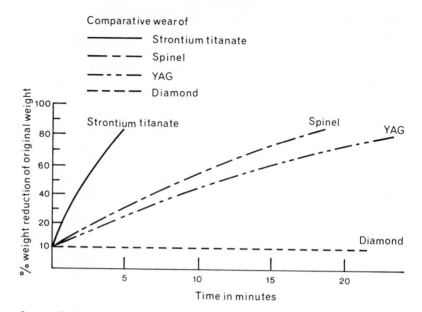

Fig. 18.11. *Rates of wear of diamond and some imitations, measured by C. Levitt using fluid energy mill tests. The weight reduction of the diamond was hardly detectable after twenty-five minutes in the mill.*

tendency of its physical properties – in this case hardness – to vary from one crystal direction to another on the same crystal face. Mohs was aware of this fact.

Although the word 'hardness' has many interpretations, it can broadly be classified into resistance to scratching, abrasion and denting. The original Brinell hardness test uses a steel ball, and the Rockwell test a cone, which is pressed into the surface and the impression measured to record hardness. Such tests are not suitable for gem minerals – the Vickers and Knoop tests employ pyramidal and rhombohedral diamond indenters which are better for minerals other than diamond. C. A. Brookes and a team at Exeter University's Engineering Department developed a five-sided diamond indenter in the 1970s that largely offsets the anisotropic effects and can be used on diamond itself (Fig. 18.10).

Dr. Brooks was unable to obtain a single indentation on diamond with a Vickers indenter, but up to 20 with a Knoop. The pentagonal indenter, however gave an average indentation hardness of 10,000 for diamond compared with 2,200 for the nearest gem material, sapphire. Spinel was graded at 1,700 to 1,730, Y.A.G. (yttrium aluminate) at 1,550 and strontium titanate at from 460 to 615 according to direction. If diamond be considered as 10 on Mohs' scale, the ratios for the other minerals are sapphire just over 2, spinel and Y.A.G. half way between 1 and 2, and strontium titanate about $\frac{1}{2}$.

Abrasion tests are usually carried out by applying a miniature grinding wheel treated with diamond powder to a specimen for a given time and measuring the amount of material removed. Using such methods, Mrs. E. M. Wilks, of Oxford University's Clarendon Laboratory, showed that there is no simple relationship between wear by abrasion and Mohs' scratch tests. Dr. Wilks found that Y.A.G. wears 2,000 to 3,000 times more readily than diamond when both are measured in their hardest directions. Sapphire wears 5,000 times more readily than diamond, spinel 20,000 times, and strontium titanate 250,000 times, all in their hardest directions.

A third series of tests in the 1970s was made by the Diamond Research Laboratory in Johannesburg by a team headed by Dr. C. Levitt, using a fluid energy mill that they had developed to measure abrasion rates. Blocks of specimen minerals were tumbled to produce spheres, if possible, the weights being measured at intervals and the losses taken as a measure of resistance to abrasion. After twenty-five minutes, there was no detectable difference in the weights of diamond samples, but diamond substitutes tested showed substantial reductions in weight as shown in Fig. 18.11.

Polishing Gems

When gems and most other materials are polished, the surface is not abraded, but is made to flow. It is locally melted on the high spots so that the polished surface becomes a series of flakes that have flowed. The surface layer is in a vitreous amorphous state about 0·0001 mm (0·00004 in) deep, rather like a coating of varnish that is harder than the original surface, and is called a Beilby layer after its discoverer. An experienced lapidary can feel when the surface slips as he is polishing a gem. It is said that, to obtain the best surface when re-polishing a gem other than diamond, the original polished layer should first be removed by grinding it away.

Diamond is believed not to behave in this way. The surface is abraded and does not form a Beilby layer. The abrasion of diamond is still little understood despite the long history of cutting. Dr. M. Seal has experimented with rubbing one diamond very slowly (at a rate of 1 cm a second) against another. This produced wear and a debris that did not appear to be diamond; it was of hexagonal structure. He thinks that diamond grinding is not entirely a mechanical or thermal process but may be linked with conversion of diamond to another substance.

Directional Hardness

Diamond is not isotropic in hardness. The relative hardness in different directions has been studied by E. M. Wilks and J. Wilks, who give this order from softest to hardest:

1. Dodecahedron parallel to crystal axis.
2. Cube parallel to crystal axis.
3. Octahedron towards dodecahedron.
4. Octahedron towards cube.
5. Dodecahedron 90° to axis.
6. Cube 45° to axis.

The difference in hardness from hardest to softest varies from something under ten times to as much as 100 times. The only two really practical grinding (polishing) directions are the first two, which are shown diagrammatically in Fig. 18.12.

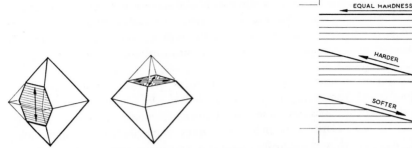

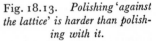

Fig. 18.12. *Possible grinding directions in an octahedral crystal on the dodecahedral and cube faces. The true octahedral face cannot be ground. Here the grinding face is shown tilted, in a direction that permits grinding.*

Fig. 18.13. *Polishing 'against the lattice' is harder than polishing with it.*

The third 'softest' direction, on the octahedral face or was, is very difficult to grind and perhaps impossible on the true (111) face. Cutters always lift the point of the face slightly so that the face is tilted towards the dodecahedral direction (Fig. 18.12).

Fig. 18.14 shows the polished cube face of a gem diamond by phase contrast photography. Superimposed over the polish lines are rectilinear patterns. Such a picture is unique for any polished diamond, according to E. M. Wilks, and is more marked on poorer quality diamonds.

Although opposite grinding directions on dodecahedral and cube faces should theoretically be of equal abrasion hardness, the polisher will usually find one way very much harder than the opposite. This difference has also been investigated by Wilks and Wilks, who found it was caused by crystal faces being out of alignment with the atomic lattice. On one diamond a difference of three times the hardness was found in opposite directions. Misorientation of the face in relation to the crystal lattice may be only a few minutes of a degree or as much as two or more degrees. The difference in hardness arises from polishing 'against the lattice' as in Fig. 18.13, a kind of 'ratchet' effect.

For the four-fold hardness symmetry of the cube face to be evident, the face must be at least within thirty minutes of the true crystallographic plane. An octahedral face, which has three-fold hardness symmetry, is very much more sensitive to accurate orientation, and because of this, is believed by some cutters to have a hard skin. The real reason is that slight misorientation of the face to the crystal lattice can make the change in hardness very abrupt when turning the stone on the scaive.

Four-point corners of natural octahedral crystals are used as industrial cutting tools. These are softer when reground and the reason is that the cutter cannot grind an octahedral face and has to tilt the stone very slightly in a dodecahedral, i.e. a softer, direction.

Hardness and Colour

The tilt of the natural surface of a diamond in relation to its crystal lattice, is related to the colour of the crystal. In white crystals, the surfaces may be aligned or misaligned with the true octahedron faces without bias in a particular direction. Brown stones, on the other hand, tend to have faces slightly tilted towards the cube plane. Yellow stones tend to have relatively larger tilts towards the dodecahedral plane. As brown stones incline towards a harder direction than yellow ones, they stand up to wear better than yellow ones.

Density and Optical Properties

The specific gravity of diamond is very constant and is usually given as 3·52. The exact figure depends upon the impurities in the stone and Anderson confirms a range of densities from 3·514 to 3·518 previously arrived at by Crookes as accurate for larger stones of good quality. Carbonado may have a density as low as 2·9 dependent upon the impurities it contains.

Measurements made in the U.S.S.R. give an average of 3·51532 to 3·51542 for Type I diamonds and 3·51501 to 3·51511 for Type II, the spread of S.G. being due to lattice faults and not tolerance in measurement. If the S.G. is calculated from the lattice constant at 25°C (77°F), the temperature at which the measurements were made, the theoretical value for diamond's S.G. is 3·51525.

As diamond is optically isotropic, it is normally considered to be singly refracting, but the presence of two types of material causes bi-refringence in many stones. Between crossed polaroids such stones show anomalous double-refraction (Fig. 18.15). Anomalous D.R. also occurs in crystals under strain and some cutters determine whether a stone may safely be cut by examining the extinction patterns.

A difference may be seen between the anomalous D.R. in stones that are predominantly Type I, when the interference colours are patchy, and predominantly Type II, when they are striated.

Fig. 18.14 *Polished lines (diagonal) and rectilinear grain pattern on a cube face.*

Fig. 18.15. *Anomalous double refraction in a brown diamond.*

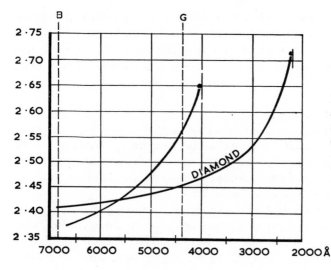

Fig. 18.16. *Refractive index of diamond for different wavelengths of light. The actual figures for red (6563 Å) and green light (5461 Å) are 2·4099 and 2·4237. The other line shows the R.I. of strontium titanate.*

The refractive index of diamond, generally given as 2·42, is more accurately 2·4175 in sodium light and is the highest of all natural gemstones. Dispersion between the B and G Fraunhofer lines, i.e. the difference in refractive index over the visible spectrum, is 0·044. The figure is low in relation to diamond's refractive index, despite the usual statement that diamond has a 'high' dispersion. If the curve for refractive indices is plotted from the deep red to the ultra-violet, it will be found flatter in the visible range, which accounts for the relatively low dispersion from B to G (Fig. 18.16).

Transparency and lustre were dealt with in Chapter Ten.

Type Classification

In 1934, a study by R. Robertson, J. J. Fox, and A. E. Martin showed that diamonds fell broadly into two categories, which they called Type one and Type two. They showed sharp differences in their transparency to ultra-violet light and in their infra-red absorption spectra. Type I diamonds absorbed ultra-violet strongly after about 3,300 Å and showed absorption bands at 7·8, 8.3, and 9·1 μ in the infra-red. Type II stones did not absorb ultra-violet light until about 2,200 Å and showed no absorption bands in the infra-red.

Further research pinpointed other differences which can be summarized as shown in the table opposite.

Birefringence

It was thought that only about one in a thousand diamonds was Type II, but investigation of large numbers of stones by Tolansky has shown that almost all diamonds incorporate both Type I and Type II material. In any diamond it is usually Type I or Type II that predominates, which determines the final classification.

Diamonds comprising both materials exhibit anomalous birefringence (anomalous because diamond is isotropic) because of lattice distortion and dislocations. Birefringence is also caused by inclusions and precipitates, and by stress through damage – in fact, the tiny ring cracks on diamond surfaces suggest that no diamond with its original surfaces is likely to be free from stress and therefore from birefringence.

Crystal Habit and Type

Type II diamonds are the purer and approximate more to the ideal diamond crystallographically. Type I stones are less pure and much more common. J. F. H. Custers has pointed out that nearly all larger diamonds are Type II. They include the biggest ever found, the Cullinan. Almost all large diamonds do not have a definite crystal form. The Cullinan, for example, was a cleavage.

It appeared that, when diamonds were formed, certain impurities were necessary in the crystal structure to cause crystallization into a definite form and that these impurities also gave rise to physical property defects. Stones of good crystal form, such as octahedra, are therefore certain to be Type I. Type II stones tend not to show symmetrical crystal faces, and this is perhaps why they include larger stones not restricted in growth by crystal form.

Stones containing both types of material, in layers or mosaics, are under physical as well as optical strain which may explain why many fractured crystals are recovered from mines.

Nitrogen in the Structure

The impurity that causes diamond to divide into two types was found in 1959 by W. Kaiser and W. Bond to be nitrogen. Type I diamonds can be broadly defined as those with nitrogen in their structure and Type II diamonds as those without.

Nitrogen has a valency of five compared with carbon's four, which means that the presence of nitrogen alone would free electrons and make the diamond conduct electricity. Almost all diamonds contain some aluminium atoms, however, which have a valency of three and mop up free electrons, so that current cannot pass.

	Type I	*Type II*
Infra-red absorption	Between 8 and 10 μ Bands at 4 to 5 μ	None between 8 and 10 μ Bands at 4 to 5 μ
Ultra-violet absorption	Complete beyond 3,400 Å	Type IIa complete beyond 2,250 Å
X-ray diffraction	Shows extra spots and streaks	Normal
Birefringence	Present	Absent (but see page 408)
Photoconductivity	Poor	Good
Thermal conductivity	Very good	Extremely good
Electrical conductivity	None	Very few IIb are semi-conductors
Luminescence	Present	Present with differences
Cleavage	Relatively uneven	Relatively perfect

Type IIb Diamonds

Custers proposed in 1952 and 1959 that Type II stones should be divided into Type IIa and Type IIb on the basis of differences in luminescence and photo-conductivity. Type IIb stones are a very small proportion of Type II, possibly about one in a thousand. Unlike other diamonds, they are electrical semi-con-ducters, i.e. they are neither good conductors nor good insulators. The reason is the presence of boron (which like aluminium has a valency of three) and the absence of nitrogen. The missing bonds (holes) in the lattice permit the passage of electrons.

Type IIb includes all natural blue stones, the main current source of which is the Premier Mine. The famous Hope blue diamond is also Type IIb and this almost certainly came from the old Kollur Mine in India.

Types and Colour

Nitrogen and aluminium in the lattice of a diamond are responsible for many of the optical properties of diamond. When the concentration of nitrogen is low (in the order of one part in a million) and the nitrogen atoms are dispersed through the crystal lattice, the diamond absorbs light in the blue region. This upsets the colour balance and results in a yellowish body colour. Greater con-centrations of nitrogen introduce a green tinge.

All Type I diamonds contain relatively substantial amounts of nitrogen and it would therefore appear that none could be of gem colour, which is contrary to the facts. The explanation was discovered by scientific workers at the Diamond Research Laboratory in Johannesburg. If the concentration of nitrogen is greater than one part in 1,000, the nitrogen atoms will have migrated in most cases into local concentrations of platelets, as shown in the electron microscope picture, Fig. 18.17. They are more stable thermo-dynamically in this form.

Nitrogen atoms dispersed at random throughout a crystal require a long and stable period of high pressure and temperature to detach themselves from where they are anchored and gradually move through the carbon atom lattice towards other nitrogen atoms to form platelets. Such conditions presumably existed for

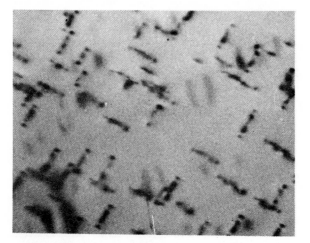

Fig. 18.17. *Nitrogen plate-lets in the atomic lattice of Type Ia diamond, photo-graphed by the Diamond Re-search Laboratory, Johannes-burg.*

millions of years during diamond formation deep in the Earth.

When nitrogen is concentrated in platelets, it has a different effect on light. Instead of absorbing in the blue part of the visible band, giving the stone a yellow to green colour, the absorption is shifted into the ultra-violet. Visible light is therefore unaffected, and the stone can have a white body colour, up to the finest gem colour according to the absorption of the particular stone.

Some natural Type I stones contain only dispersed nitrogen, but they are few in number, about one in 1,000. They were given the designation Type Ib by Diamond Research Laboratory workers in 1965. Type Ib stones are paramagnetic.

Type IIa stones contain no appreciable nitrogen and are usually dark to lightish brown in colour; although a few, like the Cullinan, are of fine gem colour. Most large ones seem to be formless. The colour is caused by an 'absorption tail' in the blue part of the spectrum, perhaps caused by unconverted graphitic regions in the stone.

Synthetic Diamonds

Because synthetic diamonds are made in a relatively short time and do not remain at high temperatures and pressures for long periods of time, there is no opportunity for any nitrogen atoms trapped in the lattice to migrate into groups, Consequently synthetic diamonds are normally Type Ib, of a yellowish to green colour, and paramagnetic. If nitrogen is specifically excluded during growth, synthetic diamonds become Type II and are colourless.

Summary of Types

All diamonds can be divided into the following categories, but many are mixtures of categories merging into each other:

Type Ia: Diamonds containing nitrogen in fairly significant quantities as an impurity up to 0·1% in which the nitrogen appears to have segregated into platelets in the crystal. They comprise the majority of natural diamonds.

Type Ib: Diamonds containing nitrogen as an impurity which is dispersed through the crystal. They are thought to comprise about 0·1% of Type I natural stones; almost all synthetic stones are Type Ib.

Type IIa: Diamonds without significant nitrogen in the crystal lattice. They are rare in nature and have enhanced optical and thermal properties.

Type IIb: Diamonds thought to have boron as an impurity. A very small proportion of Type II, they are therefore extremely rare. They have semi-conductor properties and are usually blue in colour.

Type III: Diamonds with a hexagonal instead of a cubic crystal structure, found in meteorites and made synthetically. Also called Lonsdaleite after Kathleen Lonsdale.

Note: The approximate proportions of quantity apply to larger stones mined. Research by Tolansky and others has shown Type II stones to be much more common among micro-diamonds normally rejected by the mines.

Photographic Method of Separation

If there is occasion to separate Type I from Type II stones, a simple method is immersion-contact photography. A camera is not needed. The diamonds are placed on photographic paper in water and exposed for a few seconds to short-wave ultra-violet light for a short time, using a short-wave ultra-violet lamp with a Chance No. 7 (OXY) filter over the lamp and exposing in the dark. If printing paper is used and afterwards developed, the Type II stones, which transmit ultra-violet light, appear dark and the other white against the black background.

Spectra of Diamonds

When examined by a spectroscope, most diamonds are found to have characteristic absorption spectra. The predominant band is in the violet at 4155 Å, and, according to Anderson, is the 'arrow head' of a series of less powerful bands (Figs. 18.18 and 18.20). Nitrogen in the lattice (probably configurations of three N atoms) is responsible for this 4155 system, which causes light absorption mainly in the ultra-violet region but encroaches on the blue end of the visible spectrum, thus affecting the body colour of the stone.

If the 4155 system is entirely absent, the diamond is of the very finest quality in whiteness. If it is present, but only very faintly, then the diamond is a top White, but just misses being of the finest colour. As the 4155 system becomes more evident, so the diamond becomes more yellow – from White, to Commercial White, Top Silver Cape, Silver Cape, Cape, and so on. Anderson has shown that the intensity and width of the main band increases in step with the depth of colour and that other bands appear as the colour deepens.

Cape and Brown Series

Diamonds with the spectrum just described are Type Ia and are called Cape series stones.

Some diamonds have another characteristic spectrum based on a line at 5040 Å, also visually the hinge of a series of bands with mirror-image symmetry (Figs. 18.18 and 18.20). These are diamonds known as the brown series, which have body colours in increasing shades of brown to amber and also a greenish colour. They include stones with a relatively large amount of dispersed nitrogen and fewer platelets, i.e. Type Ia, which merge into Type Ib.

When the colour of a diamond has been altered artificially by irradiation (see Chapter Nineteen), the structural damage to the atomic lattice causes a colour change that is also detectable in the spectrum. The most diagnostic line is at 5940 line in the yellow. It is narrow and not easy to detect, but G. R. Crowningshield and B. W. Anderson have both seen it in large numbers of treated golden yellow stones. The 5940 line does occur in nature, but is very rare indeed.

Using the Spectroscope

The hand spectroscope usually favoured by gemmologists can be employed with light reflected off or transmitted through the stone. It is difficult to transmit light through a brilliant-cut diamond, so the best way is to hold the stone sideways in a clip or by a blob of plasticine so that light is transmitted through the girdle.

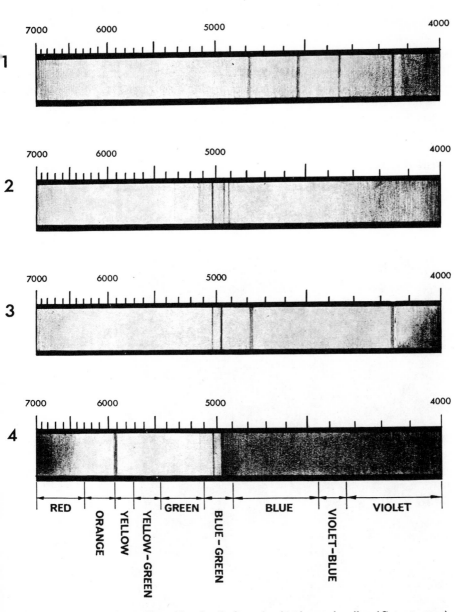

Fig. 18.18. *Spectra of some diamonds, after R. Crowningshield. 1, pale yellow (Cape spectrum);*
2, brown; 3, treated yellow, yellow-green, light brown, and some blue; 4, treated yellow-brown,
yellow, and black. The red of the spectrum is shown on the left in the traditional manner employed
by gemmologists in the U.K.

As the principal lines are in the blue end of the spectrum Anderson suggests making them more visible by using light which has passed through a flask of blue copper sulphate solution (Fig. 18.19).

Spectral Lines in Diamond

It is possible to see only a few of the lines in a diamond's spectrum by means of a hand spectroscope. To see more, a suitable spectrophotometer and low temperatures are needed, which is outside the scope of this book, but there are some hints on page 417. However, a fuller list of lines found in diamonds follows, with stronger lines in bold and weaker ones in brackets.

Natural colours

Cape Series: **4780**, 4650, 4510, 4350, 4230, **4155**, 4015, 3900
Brown Series: (5370), **5040**, (4980)
Yellow-Brown: 5760, 5690, 5640, 5580, 5500, 5480, 5230, 4935, 4800, 4600

Fig. 18.19. *Examining the spectrum of a diamond with spectroscope on the top of a microscope without the ocular. Light passed through a flask of copper sulphate solution is passed also through the diamond on the stage. The gemmologist is Basil Anderson, founder and former director of the Gem Testing Laboratory in London, the first in the world.*

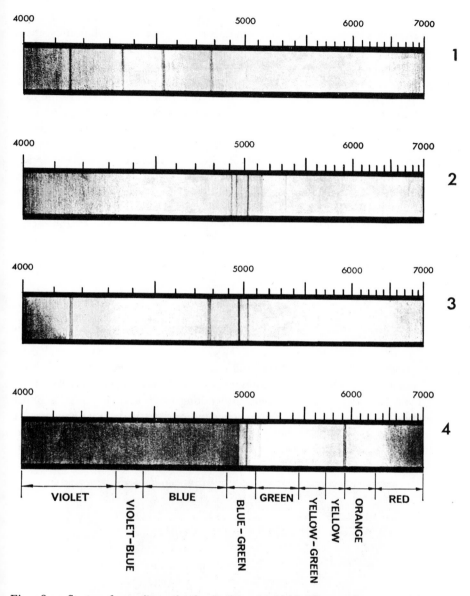

Fig. 18.20 *Spectra of some diamonds after R. Crowningshield. They are the same as those shown in Fig. 18.18, but with the violet on the left in the current scientific mode, as employed by gemmologists in the U.S.A.*

Artificial colours

Green: **7410**, **5040**, 4980, 4650, 4510, 4350, 4230, 4155
Yellow: **5940**, 5040, **4980**, 4780, 4650, 4510, 4350, 4230, 4155
Brown: (7410), 5940, **5040**, **4980**, 4780, 4650, 4510, 4350, 4230, 4155

Luminescence under Ultra-violet Light

Luminescence is the visible glow of light produced in certain substances when rubbed, scratched, subjected to chemical change, or irradiated in some way by invisible electromagnetic radiations, such as sunlight, ultra-violet rays, cathode rays, and X-rays. The gemmologist is most concerned with fluorescence, when the substance glows when irradiated, and phosphorescence, any after-glow when shielded from the source of radiation.

In gemmology an ultra-violet lamp providing long wave (3660 Å) and short wave (2537 Å) emissions by a switch is normally used (Fig. 18.21). Some diamonds fluoresce under long-wave u.v. but very few do so, and those weakly, under short wave at normal temperatures. The most common fluorescence is blue or mauve, ranging from bright sky blue to weak and rather dark violet. Other colours are green, yellow, and orange. Intensities of fluorescence vary widely from stone to stone (Figs. 18.22 to 18.24 and Plate). Quite often the glow is patchy or in bands and may vary in relation to the crystal face. One curious and rare effect is an inclusion that fluoresces (Fig. 18.23).

Anderson pointed out in 1943 that there are three main groups of fluorescent colours:

1. Blue. The most common, Cape series stones with the 4155 absorption band system.
2. Yellow-green. Less common Brown series stones with the 5040 absorption band system.
3. Yellow. Mostly industrial quality stones, but including true canary yellow diamonds with no visible absorption bands at normal temperatures.

Some pink diamonds from India fluoresce and phosphoresce with a strong orange colour. The Hope blue diamond has a red fluorescence. Most natural blue (Type IIb) diamonds are inert under long-wave u.v., but give a bluish after-glow. They do give a blue fluorescence under short-wave u.v., however. In general, Type II stones do not fluoresce; but the famous Sancy Diamond, according to E. A. Jobbins of the Institute of Geological Sciences, London,

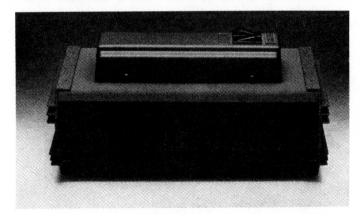

Fig. 18.21. *One of the commercial ultra-violet lamps providing long and short wave for gem testing.*

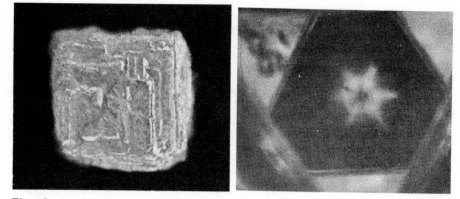

Fig. 18.22. *Fluorescent cubic crystal, photo-graphed under an ordinary 'daylight' fluorescent tube.*   Fig. 18.23. *Long-wave ultra-violet fluores-cence of a misty inclusion in a rough diamond.* (R. Webster)

although Type II, has the unusual reactions of fluorescing a distinct yellow under short-wave u.v. with no phosphorescence, and fluorescing a pale salmon-pink under long wave, with very noticeable greenish-yellow phosphorescence.

Blue to mauve fluorescing diamonds will phosphoresce in shades of yellow and green when the source of u.v. is cut off, which is diagnostic for diamond. A simple method of checking the after-glow is explained in Chapter Twenty.

Luminescence in diamond is largely controlled by two impurities in the crystal lattice – nitrogen and boron – and whether they have aggregated very closely together or are dispersed. Luminescence can be examined with a spectroscope in the same way as other light. When this is done, the fluorescent absorption system will be seen as an exact mirror image of the normal absorption system.

Cold Improves Lines and Fluorescence

The sharpness of the absorption bands in diamond, and also the intensity of the fluorescence and phosphorescence, depends upon temperature. At room temper-ture, as when generally examined by the gemmologist, they are broad and poorly defined. The physicist studies them at temperatures near that of liquid nitrogen (80°K or −315°F, −193°C) when they are sharply resolved. A practical way of improving visual examination by hand spectroscope without elaborate equip-ment is suggested by Anderson. Obtain a block of solid carbon dioxide (dry ice) and, handling it with rubber gloves and non-heat conducting utensils, stand the diamond being examined on a piece of it, which will reduce the stone's tempera-ture to about −70°C (−94°F). The rest of the dry ice can be kept for a time in a large vacuum flask. The diamond will have to be wiped from time to time to remove the hoar frost. Fortunately dry ice does not fluoresce. Temperature changes from, say, summer to winter, have no noticeable effect on spectra.

When examining the fluorescence of a diamond with a hand spectroscope, the slit should be opened quite wide. The mirror image of the 4155 Å system – if seen – is, of course, diagnostic of diamond.

Fluorescence and Body Colour

The ultra-violet light in sunlight will cause some diamonds to fluoresce blue in daylight, and some have an after-glow in darkness, but this effect is slight and has been exaggerated in past reports. Usually the fluorescence cannot be separated by the eye, and when blue, will mask any yellow tinge in a stone. A diamond may therefore appear to be of a higher quality in colour when seen in sunlight or light from the direction of the sun, even if masked by clouds. The same applies in any artificial light that contains a high proportion of ultra-violet. The blue fluorescence of a few stones is evident to the naked eye in daylight and gives the stone a bluish milky, or even oily, appearance. These are the over-blues, also known as Premiers. There are also a few stones that have a yellow-green fluorescence strong enough just to be evident in daylight that gives the diamond the colour of Vaseline.

Identification Records

Robert Webster has suggested a practical application for the unpredictable response of diamonds to long-wave ultra-violet in the identification of jewellery set with many diamonds. If the fluorescing jewellery is photographed, a picture similar to that in Fig. 18.24 is obtained. The picture is unique and even an otherwise identical piece would give a different pattern. The jewellery is first photographed in white light and then in filtered ultra-violet light with an Ilford Q or Wratten 2B filter over the camera lens.

Fluorescence and Impact Strength

It has been discovered that colourless diamonds that do not fluoresce can withstand most compression, but are lower in impact strength than diamonds that exhibit green or yellow fluorescence. This fact has an industrial value because the latter stones are best used in drilling crowns used in fractured and broken rock.

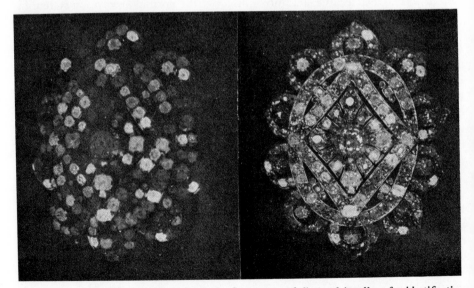

Fig. 18.24.   *A means of photographing the fluorescence of diamond jewellery for identification purposes, suggested by R. Webster.*

418

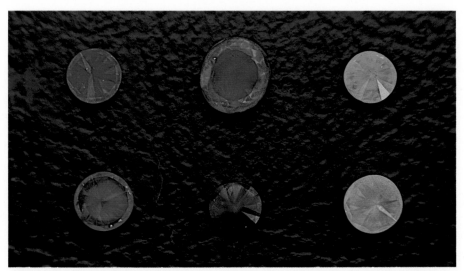

Fluorescent polished diamonds under long-wave ultra-violet emission. Those fluorescing blue can cause trouble when grading for colour, especially in sunlight.

Gordon's diopside (one of the pyroxene family) with diamond inter-growth, an unusual combination photographed by Dr. J. W. Harris, of Edinburgh University.

An unusual pattern of inclusions in an octahedral diamond crystal, photographed by Dr. J. W. Harris.

A collection of small industrial quality rough diamonds, each with different fluorescent features, photographed under long-wave ultra-violet light by the author.

Other Luminescent Effects

Diamonds under X-rays will usually show the most consistent luminescent effect, a rather uniform bluish white glow, caused by a broad emission system based around 4500 Å approximately. Cathode rays give most brilliant fluorescent effects and some diamonds glow different colours on different faces.

A diamond made to fluoresce blue under ultra-violet light will phosphoresce yellow-green at the same time, but the yellow-green will be masked by the strong blue emission. If the ultra-violet light is cut off, the stone will have yellow-green after-glow because the blue emission remains 'frozen' in the stone. It may later be released by heating the stone to about 200°C (392°F), when it will glow blue. This effect is called thermo-phosphorescence.

Diamond will luminesce if rubbed, exhibiting triboluminescence. C. F. Kunz stated that the luminescence could be produced by rubbing the stone on various materials including wood, wool and certain metals. He found that it was most evident when the diamond was rubbed on wood across the grain!

Conduction of Heat

Diamonds feel cold to the touch because of their high thermal conductivity, which is the highest of any known material. Diamond conducts heat so rapidly that it can be plunged red hot into liquid nitrogen without being harmed, whereas most non-metallic minerals would shatter. Its high thermal conductivity is a principal reason why diamond is such an effective material for tipping tools.

The thermal conductivity of diamonds depends upon waves called phonons through the lattice, which means that lattice defects affect it. At room temperature, Type I diamonds are more than twice as conductive of heat than copper, and Type IIa more than six times. Maximum thermal conductivity for diamond occurs at −190°C (−310°F), when Type I stones are nearly three times and Type IIa stones nearly five times more conductive than they are at room temperature. Type IIa stones are in demand therefore as heat sinks to conduct heat away from delicate apparatus, as in electronic components carrying heavy currents. The thermal expansion of diamond is extremely low, being almost zero at 39°C (102°F). In general it is about 80 per cent that of invar, the nickel steel used for the pendulum rods of high precision clocks.

Electrical Behaviour

Although Type I stones and Type IIa stones are classed generally as extremely good insulators, there are a few Type IIa stones with lower resistances, nearer Type IIb. Diamond is exceptional in conducting heat and resisting electricity. Usually heat and electrical conductivity go together.

Type IIb stones can be used as p-type transistors, but the conductivity varies from stone to stone. The semi-conductors silicon and germanium have the same form of crystal structure as diamond.

Diamonds are photoconductive, retaining their high resistivity only in the dark and in light with no ultra-violet content. When ultra-violet light falls on them, their resistance drops. Type IIb stones are photoconductive to gamma rays. When gamma rays fall on such a crystal any current of electricity through it is amplified, so it may be used like a geiger tube, for counting radiation.

If a D.C. voltage is applied across a Type IIb stone, at first the current will be small, perhaps a few milliamps. After a few minutes, it will rise to several ampères and the stone will become red hot and eventually vaporize if the current is not cut off. This does not seem to occur if A.C. current is used, but the diamond scintillates with blue light.

Other Physical Characteristics

Diamond is unique or exceptional in several other characteristics beside those examined already in this chapter, among them being its elasticity, compressibility, and frictional properties. The springiness, or elasticity, of a material is proportional to the load applied to it. The deflection is proportional to the load and is known as Young's modulus. The larger this figure, the stiffer the material. Rubber has a modulus of about 1,000; for wood, it is about 2,000,000, steel about 3,000,000, corundum (sapphire) 60,000,000, and diamond 170,000,000. Elasticity has a relationship to surface tension, the behaviour of a surface like an elastic skin, which is measured in force (dynes) per square centimetre. For water this is about 77, steel and other structural materials around 1,000, and diamond 5,400. Compressibility is also concerned with elasticity. Diamond is the least compressible of all known materials.

Friction and Hardness

Diamond has a low frictional resistance to sliding. The coefficient of friction* for diamond on diamond is between 0·05 and 0·10, compared with dry wood 0·25 to 0·50, steel (unlubricated) 0·58, and 0·04 for the very low friction plastics material P.T.F.E. (polytetrafluorethylene). In air, the friction of diamond is the same, whether or not it is degreased, just cleaned, or covered in oil or grease (as also with graphite at 0·10), which may be a reason why rose diamonds, apart from their durability, were used so successfully in the eighteenth century as endstones (end bearings) of the balance wheels of watches. Moreover the coefficient of friction decreases and then levels off as the load increases, a benefit of diamond styli for long playing discs. The fourth factor is the relationship of friction to crystal orientation. As might be expected, the friction is higher in directions of better abrasion (polishing directions). The friction of a diamond stylus can be as much as eight times greater in a soft direction, with correspondingly greater wear, compared with a hard direction. On an octahedral face, friction is lowest of all and is the same in all directions. Friction is important in industrial applications, but another factor sometimes overrides it, the fact that iron will combine with diamond. This means that diamond is not the best material for cutting ferrous metals at high speeds, when much heat is generated, although it is for most non-ferrous materials. A synthetic mineral known as cubic boron nitride has been developed for cutting steels at high speeds. Although not as hard as diamond, it wears less in such applications.

*Ratio between the force needed to cause slipping and that to maintain it.

REFERENCES

Gem Testing, by B. W. Anderson (London, 1964).
Physical Properties of Diamond, edited by R. Berman (Oxford, 1965).
Properties of Diamond, Industrial Diamond Information Bureau leaflet, undated.
De Beers Industrial Diamond Conference, London, 1977.

CHAPTER NINETEEN

Synthetic Diamonds: Artificial Coloration

In 1673, the English physicist, Robert Boyle (1627–91), discovered that diamond disappeared in acrid vapours when heated to a high temperature and some years later a diamond was caused to vanish at a public demonstration in Florence by heating it with a burning glass. In 1772, Antoine Lavoisier (1743–94) showed the vapours to be carbon dioxide and we now know that diamond begins to burn and convert to carbon monoxide and dioxide in air at a temperature between about 700–900°C (1290–1650°F) depending on the quality of the stone.

Diamond was shown to consist only of carbon by the English chemist Smithson Tennant (1761–1815) in 1797, when he burned a stone in oxygen enclosed in a vessel made of gold. The weight of the carbon in the carbon dioxide that resulted corresponded exactly with the weight of the original diamond.

Diamond jewellery accidentally dropped into a fire or overheated during repair by the jeweller's blowtorch, usually suffers superficial damage which shows as dulling or clouding of the polished surfaces to a leaden colour. Repolishing usually restores the finish. In extremely hot fires, as for example may occur after an air crash, some stones may be damaged beyond repair.

Soldering Diamond Jewellery

The traditional and usually effective means of avoiding damage to a stone set in jewellery being hard gold soldered is first to coat the diamond with a paste made of boracic acid powder and water. This dries as a coating that will prevent air from reaching the stone. As no oxygen can reach the stone, it cannot therefore burn and will stand a much higher temperature without damage. Diamond jewellery is only repaired with the stones in place when it is uneconomic to unset and reset them, as would be done with more valuable stones.

The modern way to avoid damage is to use resistance or microwave welding, which is so rapid that a negligible amount of heat travels through the metal and reaches the stone when altering the size of the shank, and even when replacing a claw with the stone in position, if microwave welding is employed.

Conversion to Graphite

Diamond heated in the absence of oxygen, such as in a vacuum or in an inert atmosphere, will not burn and will eventually convert to graphite. The process begins to take place at between 800°–1700°C (1470 and 3090°F), depending on the quality of the diamond. At first only a thin layer of the surface is affected. At a temperature of approximately 1700°C (3090°F), a second process begins and conversion to graphite is rapid and right through the stone, which eventually disintegrates into a pile of graphite powder.

Diamonds can be damaged or converted to graphite by forms of heating other than a fire or furnace, such as intense radioactivity and by passing a current of electricity through a stone that is a semi-conductor. Too rapid cutting or attempting to cut in a hard direction will also cause some conversion (burning), which appears as areas of small dark spots. It is more common on whole stones than on sawn stones. Diamond powder collecting on the clamps of mechanical dops will also at times cause abrasion and even burning of the stone during polishing because the high frequency vibration causes the clamps to act as ultrasonic drills.

Diamond is a thermodynamically unstable form of carbon at normal temperature and pressure. In simple terms, the rate of transition of diamond to graphite at room temperature is zero. At a temperature around 1700°C (3090°F) transition is rapid – taking only a few minutes.

Attempts to Make Diamond

For centuries, interested experimenters in alchemy or natural history tried to make diamond without knowing it to be carbon. The information that diamonds were discovered in river gravels gave no hint of their composition, but it was certainly known to some at the beginning of the nineteenth century that carbonaceous materials, heat and pressure, were needed to produce diamonds. It was from that time that some attempts at synthesizing can be regarded as scientific.

When diamonds were found in pipes around 1870, the kimberlite was regarded as the magma in which the diamonds were formed and a number of efforts were made by amateurs and scientists to produce diamonds from melts of kimberlite.

Meteoric Diamonds

In 1880, diamonds were detected in a nickel-iron meteorite that had fallen in Siberia. In 1893, meteoric iron from the giant crater of Canyon Diablo in Arizona, U.S.A., was also found to contain them. In both, the proportion of diamond to meteorite was much higher than the proportion of diamond to kimberlite in pipes. These discoveries gave fresh ideas to would-be diamond makers.

There are two diametrically opposed theories about the origin of diamonds in meteorites. The first is that they were formed from carbon by the heat of the meteorite after it passed through the Earth's atmosphere and the shock of the impact. The other is that they were already contained in the meteorite, because some studies suggest that meteoric diamonds were formed under static high pressure.

The Canyon Diablo meteorite iron contains polycrystalline cubes of diamond and also cubo-octahedra. Some of the diamond is of hexagonal crystallographic structure. As the Canyon Diablo region contains graphite and the microdiamonds were found in the iron round the rim, it seems likely that the shock and heat of impact of the giant meteorite formed diamonds in the crater.

Studies of meteoric diamonds led Professor S. Tolansky to speculate that the moon may be a source of diamond. Russian astronomers have calculated that about 22 lb (10 kg) of diamonds fall on Earth in meteorites every year.

Transition of Graphite to Diamond

Despite the disarming similarity between crystalline carbon as graphite and as diamond, changing the stable graphite into the unstable diamond proved far from easy.

Graphite is a hexagonal structure of carbon in flat hexagonal rings in planes, with loose bonds between planes, which give it its soft, flaky texture. Diamond is a cubic structure or puckered hexagonal rings with no loose bonds. Graphite's more open structure gives it a density of 2·2 grammes a cubic centimetre. Diamond is denser, weighing 3·5 grammes per c.c.

The problem is to squeeze the graphite until its hexagonal rings of carbon atoms become puckered and take up the smaller cubic atomic structure, and then to prevent the atoms from springing back to the hexagonal structure of graphite after the pressure is removed. High temperature is applied during the squeeze to keep the atoms moving to that they will be encouraged to take up the new bonds.

The two structures are shown in Figs. 18.2 and 18.3.

Notorious Attempts to Make Diamond

Some earlier diamond-makers were more concerned with making money. One was Henri Lemoine of Paris, who began a series of experiments in 1905. He managed to obtain an interview in London with Sir Julius Wernher, the South African financier who founded Wernher, Beit and Co., and who was also a life governor of De Beers Consolidated Mines, to ask for financial backing. He claimed to be able to make gem diamonds on a commercial scale by a secret process which he offered Sir Julius in exchange for royalty payments on the diamonds he made.

Lemoine persuaded Sir Julius to visit a laboratory he had hired in London to carry out a demonstration. He prepared certain ingredients in a crucible which he put in an electric furnace for half an hour. Then he withdrew it, stirred the contents, and produced twenty-five small, well crystallized diamonds of good colour. Sir Julius advanced enough money for Lemoine to set up a laboratory in Paris, where for three years he continued experiments, sending sample diamonds at intervals to Sir Julius.

Eventually even Sir Julius became suspicious, especially as there was no difference between Lemoine's 'synthetic diamonds' and crystals recovered from the Jagersfontein mine in the Orange Free State. After an investigation, Lemoine was charged with fraud and arrested. He was tried and sentenced to six years' imprisonment.

A much more mysterious affair took place as late as 1952, when a large group of West German scientists under Dr Herman Meincke, claimed to have synthesized diamond. A series of tests in the presence of two solicitors produced twenty small stones of up to 2·8 mg (0·0006 ct.) each. They were real diamonds, but were fractures of crystals exactly similar to industrial boart. In a further test attended by the public prosecutor and three detectives, crystals were produced but they were not diamond. Legal action followed.

Early Synthesis Experiments: Hannay

One of the first serious attempts was in 1823 by V. Kazarin, founder of Kharkov University in Russia, who made some carbonaceous crystals that resembled diamond, according to Mendeleer, the inventor of the periodic table of elements, who examined them.

Most interesting of the early attempts was made by a Scotsman called James Ballantyne Hannay, a Glasgow chemist (1855–1931), who had been searching for a solvent for alkali metals such as sodium and potassium. He found that even an inert substance like paraffin would decompose when heated under pressure with hydrogen gas and one of the alkali metals. The hydrogen combined with the metal and the carbon from the paraffin was freed. This gave him the idea that carbon could be made to re-crystallize as diamond.

To obtain the high pressure necessary, he had thick coiled tubes of wrought iron made by the same methods as gun barrels but open only at one end. A tube was filled with the reaction material and sealed with a blacksmith's weld. It was then placed in a large reverbatory furnace for several hours.

After a long series of eighty experiments, only three were successful. In most cases the tubes exploded or leaked. On several occasions, the furnace was wrecked. In the three successful experiments, he used a 4 mg (0·00014 oz) of lithium and a mixture of 10 per cent rectified bone oil and 90 per cent paraffin spirit. After being fired, the tubes were found to contain much gas, a little liquid, and a smooth mass of solid material covering the walls. Pulverizing the mass yielded some tiny transparent crystals.

Hannay decided these were diamonds and submitted some to M. H. N. Story-Maskelyne, F.R.S., Keeper of Minerals at the British Museum, who announced in a letter to *The Times* on 20th February 1880, that there was no doubt that Hannay had produced diamonds. Later that year, Hannay presented a detailed paper to the Royal Society.

Of all the early claimants to have synthesized diamonds, J. B. Hannay was unique because his material still exists, but attempts to repeat his experiments have failed.

In 1943, the crystallographers F. A. Bannister and Kathleen Lonsdale borrowed the twelve surviving Hannay crystals from the British Museum and submitted them to X-ray diffraction tests not available to Hannay. They found that eleven were diamonds, but one was not. Michael Seal reported in 1962 that on examination of the specks by electron microscope, he found traces of silica on the surfaces. Hannay was known to have mixed grains of silica with his carbon.

R. B. Angel of the Department of Mineralogy, British Museum, found no evidence by electron spin resonance studies that the specks were synthetic and S. Tolansky from surface studies concluded that they were natural. More evidence for the same view came in 1975 when A. T. Collins of the Physics Department of Kings College, London, employed still another testing technique which he had developed, measuring their cathodoluminescence. A beam of electrons from a hot tungsten filament is accelerated by voltage (typically 50 kv.) and focused on to a diamond, which releases some of the energy as visible light.

The colour of the luminescence is characteristic of the diamond, but more accurate analysis is possible by use of a spectrometer. In most cases the spectrometer will separate natural diamonds, which luminesce predominantly blue, from synthetic ones, which are never predominantly blue. Dr. Collins found that Hannay's crystals were natural diamonds.

Of the three theories: that Hannay planted the diamonds; that one of his workmen did so in fear of more explosions; and that his starting materials were contaminated by diamond fragments, the last is most likely according to E. P. Flint, who studied Hannay's character and methods.

Moissan's Experiments

About ten years after Hannay's work, F. F. Henri Moissan (1852–1907) carried out a large number of experiments in France. The discovery of tiny diamonds in the Canyon Diablo meteorite suggested to him that, if he selected a metal that would expand on solidifying, an outer skin would be formed as it cooled and extremely high pressures would be produced at the centre. This should produce temperatures and pressures sufficient to form diamond from carbon.

He examined the solubility of carbon in the metals aluminium, chromium, iron, magnesium, manganese, platinum, silver and uranium, and also in silicon. His most successful results were when dissolving carbon in pure iron in a carbon crucible in an electric furnace. The molten mass of iron with absorbed carbon was plunged into water to form a rigid crust, then allowed to cool in air. Afterwards he found that cooling in molten lead was more effective. After the whole was solidified, it was placed in an acid bath and slowly eaten away to release any crystals it contained.

The particles that resulted were found by Moissan to scratch ruby, and to have a specific gravity of between 3 and 3·5. He examined them under the microscope and also measured the amount of carbon dioxide they gave off when burned in oxygen. As a result he pronounced them to be diamond.

Moissan's reports to the Académie des Sciences in 1893 and 1894 caused considerable controversy and many attempts were made by others to reproduce his experiments. In England, Sir William Crookes produced the required pressures by exploding cordite in closed steel tubes and claimed to have produced diamonds. Sir Charles Parsons, also in England, reported to the Royal Society in 1918 that he had repeated both Hannay's and Moissan's experiments with improved apparatus and had also employed some ingenious techniques of his own. He had no success with Hannay's apparatus but claimed it with Moissan's method. Later he withdrew this claim.

M. Seal and A. R. Bobrowsky have repeated Moissan's work in recent times and submitted the particles produced to X-ray tests. They followed Moissan's own instructions with success in four of twelve runs, producing about twenty crystals in each of the four. The crystals, examined through a microscope and photographed resembled Moissan's published drawings and in some the similarity was quite striking.

Submitted to individual X-ray diffraction tests by special techniques, crystals tested turned out to be of silicon carbide, amorphous material or alumina. Seal concluded that, although Moissan was well aware of the presence of these materials, 'it is tempting to suggest that Moissan's product was also silicon carbide or alumina'.

First Repeatable Synthesis: A.S.E.A.

Unqualified success was not achieved until 1953, when the Swedish company Allmana Avenska, Elektriska Aktiebolaget, known as A.S.E.A., made crystals of under ·04 in (1 mm) in size under the direction of B. von Platen. A.S.E.A. apparently thought they were the only concern working seriously on the problem and their intention was to make gem quality stones. It seems that they did not realize the potential of the industrial market. Consequently, they did not announce their success until 1955, when the Americans had also had success.

The Swedish technique employed pressures of between 80,000 and 90,000 atmospheres at a maximum temperature of about 2760° C (5000° F). The major problem is generating the high pressures because even a vessel made of carboloy (tungsten carbide cemented with cobalt), which has the highest compressive strength, will fail at about 65,000 atmospheres. It was found, however, that pressures much above the yield point can be maintained if the vessel is surrounded by massive supports.

The supports have to be arranged so that the pressure increases towards the centre. This was done by using six four-sided pyramids arranged with their points together in the form of a cube. The points were removed to form a hollow spherical chamber of about 24·4 cu. in (400 cu. cm). If the area outside is, say, fifteen times greater than the area of the chamber inside, pressure per square centimetre applied on the outside will be magnified fifteen times inside. In the Swedish experiments an outside pressure of about 5,800 atmospheres was boosted to about 97,000 atmospheres.

Pressure was applied to the six pyramids by six pistons and the whole assembly was placed in a tube about 22 in (53 cm) in diameter strengthened with steel bands. Water was pumped into the tube until its pressure was 5,800 atmospheres. This forced the pistons and pyramids together.

In the hollow centre was placed a hollow sphere of soapstone containing thermite; in this was another hollow sphere of tantalum, and in the centre of this sphere a reagent, comprising iron carbide and graphite. Thermite is a mixture of magnesium and barium peroxide, which produces a very high temperature when ignited. The 0·16 in (5 mm) thick shell of soapstone was to insulate the thermite from a copper holder in which the whole sample was contained, as it was ignited electrically. The diameter of the whole sample was about 0·28 in (7 mm).

After cooling, the sample was removed and cut in half. Diamonds were found in the centre of the iron carbide. Later, electrical means of heating and metal-graphite mixtures were found more effective. A factory was set up at Robertfors, in the north of Sweden, manufacturing industrial diamond at a rate which had reached about two million carats a year in 1964.

In 1967 A.S.E.A. made an agreement with De Beers, referred to later.

American Synthesis: G.E.

Experiments were meanwhile being conducted by the company General Electric in the U.S.A., using similar principles of boosting pressure and dissolving carbon in molten metals. At first they used a mixture of iron sulphide and heated it while in contact with carbon and tantalum metal. Tantalum was found to act as a catalyst. Subsequently it was discovered that nickel and cobalt were satisfactory catalysts, as was iron.

G.E.'s first experiment produced smaller amounts of diamonds than the A.S.E.A., method, but in 1955 they were able to announce that they had made synthetic diamonds and were able to repeat the process so that commercial production of synthetic diamond was possible. They were, of course, unaware of the work that had been successful in Sweden owing to the secrecy of A.S.E.A. G.E. applied for, and obtained, world patents.

The theoretical basis of the success rested on the work of Nobel Prize winner, P. W. Bridgman, and the group mainly responsible for the practical synthesis comprised Francis Bundy, H. Tracy Hall, Herbert Stroud, and Robert Wentorf. Their largest crystals weighed about one thousandth of a carat and were not more than ·04 in (1 mm) long.

It was discovered by G.E. that the mineral pyrophyllite had a unique property that was valuable for diamond synthesis. Pyrophyllite is a soft, slate-like material. It is a hydrous aluminium silicate which is in the same family as the material used for slate pencils, as talc, and as the steatite or soapstone used in the Swedish method. When subjected to extreme pressures, its melting point rises from 1360° to 2720°C (2400° to 4800°F).

The Practice Apparatus

The success of the G.E. production depends to a great extent on a high-pressure apparatus known as the belt, which is versatile and will stand up to much abuse as well as being simple and having a good capacity. The belt is a ring made of tungsten carbide. The hole in the centre is shaped to form a cylinder which is flared at each end. Two tapered pistons are driven into the opposite ends of the central hole as shown in Fig. 19.1. Pressure is applied to the pistons by a large hydraulic press.

To make diamond, a short cylinder of pyrophyllite is filled with the reaction material – graphite or other form of carbon, with tantalum or nickel – and placed in the hole in the belt. Pressure is then applied and a current of electricity passed through the centre to provide the temperature. The pyrophyllite acts as a gasket to seal the gaps. It flows under very high pressure and allows the pistons to advance and compress the carbon and metal.

The pyrophyllite also prevents leakage of current and heat when the electrical current is passed through. Pressures employed are over 100,000 atmospheres (about 1,500,000 lb a square inch) and temperatures over 2000°C (3630°F), with transient peaks in the range of 3000°C (5430°F). Diamonds are recovered by using acids on the hard black mass of material that results. The belt was one of the designs of Bridgman and Tracy Hall. Another method used in diamond production is a tetrahedral structure of hydraulic rams employing tetrahedrally-shaped pieces of pyrophyllite to hold the carbon and metal (Fig. 19.8).

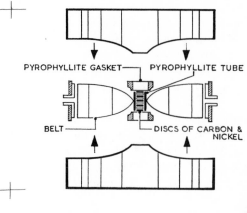

PYROPHYLLITE GASKET — PYROPHYLLITE TUBE

BELT — — DISCS OF CARBON & NICKEL

Fig. 19.1. *Principle of diamond synthesis using the belt (a tungsten carbide ring) between the jaws of a hydraulic press. An electrical current produces the heat.*

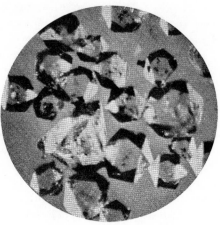

Fig. 19.2. *Some synthetic diamond crystals. They are magnified, being only of grit size.*

South African Success: De Beers

In 1959, De Beers Consolidated Mines announced that they also had evolved a commercial process for making diamond. The decision to carry out research was made in 1955 within a month of the G.E. announcement, in co-operation with the Belgian Congo mining company the Société Minière du Becéka. Becéka produced most of the world's natural industrial diamond grit until disturbances occurred in the Congo after the granting of independence.

The successful De Beers team was J. H. Custers, H. B. Dyer, B. W. Senior, and P. T. Wedepohl, of the Adamant Research Laboratory, Johannesburg. By coincidence, the first South African synthetic diamonds were made on the same day in September 1958, as the lifting of a secrecy order imposed by the U.S. Government on the G.E. method.

The South African team also used a belt system, developed from work published by Bridgman and others, and their first diamond was 0·02 by 0·01 in (0·4 by 0·25 mm) and comprised six equal sized particles closely cemented together. Continuous production was next achieved and a patent applied for. Later, there was a patent dispute between G.E. and De Beers which was eventually settled to the advantage of both.

A synthetic diamond factory, Ultra High Pressure Units, was set up at Springs, in the Johannesburg area, with seventy-five high-voltage presses. The pyrophyllite cylinders in which the diamonds are made are about $2\frac{1}{2}$ by $\frac{3}{4}$ in

(63 by 19 mm) with tapered rings over each end as shown in Fig. 19.1. They are electrical insulators and expand during the process. The reaction material comprises a series of alternate discs of carbon and nickel. The operating cycle is short.

The nickel discs melt, expand, and percolate the carbon discs, on the edges of which diamonds form. The masses of hard material removed from the presses go to a chemical cleaning section where they are crushed and boiled in various acid baths which dissolve non-diamond materials. Diamonds recovered, a substantial amount per cycle, are cleaned, dried and sent to the sorting department (Fig. 19.2).

Sorting into sizes is carried out through a cascade of six or seven vibrating sieves. The upper one traps the largest grit and the lower ones successively smaller sizes.

Sorting into different shapes is done by an ingenious electrically vibrated sorting table designed by Diamond Abrasive Products. The table is triangular and fixed at a sloping angle. Along one side is a series of twelve to fourteen traps like 'billiard table' pockets. From the opposite corner a glass container feeds diamond particles on to the surface. These swarm over the table like demented ants and finish in one or other of the pockets. Blocky particles move in a downward direction and needle-shaped ones in an upwards direction.

The particles are marked in about twenty-five categories of size and shape for industrial abrasive uses. In 1963 Ultra High Pressure Units opened a synthetic diamond factory in Shannon, Eire, and in 1967 an agreement was made with the Swedish concern A.S.E.A. to combine production.

The price of synthetic grit was at first nearly twice as much as natural grit, but by 1965, had fallen below that of natural grit. Synthetic grit will not do all that natural will and each has its industrial applications. World production in 1969 was estimated to be 40 million carats of synthetic grit compared with 44 million carats of all natural diamonds.

Mechanism of Synthesis

Experiment showed that substances containing carbon could be converted to diamond at prolonged pressure of 110 to 120 kilobars (1,600,000 to 1,750,000 lb per sq. in) and temperatures of about $3000°K$ (about $5970°F/3300°C$). If the carbon is heated for a very short time, in the range of several ten-thousandths of a second, by passing a current of electricity through it, the temperature required drops by about $300°C$ ($572°F$) and the pressure has to be increased by about 10 kbar (about 15,000 lb sq. in). Such results enabled Dr. Berman and Prof. Simon to plot a graphite/diagram equilibrium line, at Oxford in 1955. Such a diagram (Fig. 19.3) shows the pressure and temperature conditions in which graphite will be converted to diamond. The area below the curve (the dotted part of it is extrapolated) represents graphite and that above it diamond.

If a catalyst is used, diamond can be synthesized at the lower temperatures and pressures shown on the graph referred to. A catalyst is a substance that changes the rate of a process without being subject to change itself. The best catalysts for diamond production are the Group VIII metals (i.e. iron, cobalt, nickel, and the platinum group) of which iron and nickel have been most

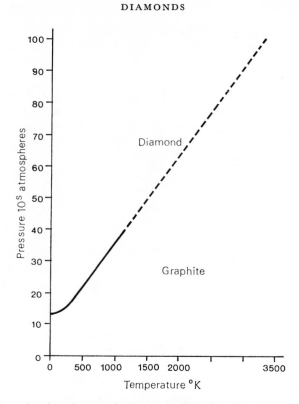

Fig. 19.3. *A carbon phase graph. Diamond will be formed in areas of temperature and pressure above the curve; below it the result will be graphite. 1,000 atmospheres is about 15,000 lb per sq. in. Degrees Kelvin are absolute temperatures, i.e. 273° above Celsius or centigrade. Berman and Simon were the first to produce such a diagram in 1955.*

successful, plus some other metals such as manganese and tantalum, and a few compounds.

It has been found that pure carbon cannot be turned into diamond and that some types of carbon and graphite are not easily convertible. Substances that graphitize readily, and also well-structured graphite, seem to assist in the formation of diamond. Diamonds made from well-structured graphite reflect this in their own structures.

Direct Synthesis by Explosion

Attempts have continued to be made to synthesize diamond directly from graphite, despite the success of the static pressure/temperature techniques which have become commonplace. In 1959, J. van Tilburg took out a patent for a method using explosives, and interested N. V. Asscher, the famous diamond cutters. About the same time, work was going on along similar lines in Poulter Laboratory of the Stanford Research Institute in the U.S.A.

De Carli and Jamieson achieved the first proven diamond synthesis in 1961 when they generated a pressure of about 300 kbar for about a microsecond and made some tiny particles of carbonado containing rhombohedroid crystals of diamond, said to be like those found in some meteorites. For raw material, they used what is called rhombohedral graphite and compressed it along a particular axis known as the c-axis. Very tiny particles of diamond were also produced by Trueb in 1971 by shock compression, using a pressure range of 250 to 450 kbar for 10 to 30 microseconds, which produced a temperature of 1100°C (2010°F). The platelets were found to comprise aggregates of cubic crystals, the largest only about a ten-thousandth of a millimetre (see Figs. 19.4 and 19.5).

If a cast-iron metal block with carbon inclusions is compression-shocked, the metal cools the inclusions and tends to prevent any diamonds that are formed from reverting to graphite after the pressure wave has passed. A patent for such a process was granted in 1966 to Cowan, Dunnington and Holtzman, of Du Pont de Neymours and Co. It employs pressures of above 1·5 lb per sq. in and produces partly hexagonal type diamond, which is typical of conditions of very high pressure with relatively low temperature (Fig. 19.4).

Explosion-synthesized diamonds are normally polycrystalline and are therefore very hard, like carbonado, but are coarser and contain a high proportion of metallic inclusions.

Growing from Seed Crystals

It occurred to some experimenters that a gas containing carbon might be used for growing diamonds on small diamond 'seeds' instead of trying to convert carbon or graphite. Perhaps the first to try – unsuccessfully – was W. Bowlton in 1911. The theory was that, if the diamond seed were held at the appropriate conditions of heat and pressure (much lower than for synthesis), a supersaturated carbonaceous gas around it would give off carbon atoms that would attach themselves to the diamond lattice.

A number of attempts to grow diamond were made with varying success and in 1950, a patent was granted to William G. Eversole, of Union Carbide's Linde Division, for a process of growing diamond powder in methane (marsh gas) and similar hydrocarbons. A similar method had been discovered two years earlier by B. V. Derjaguin and B. V. Spitzin in the U.S.S.R., using carbon tetraiodine gas 1100°C (1830°F). The free carbon atoms attach themselves to the diamond surface to extend the crystal lattice in a kind of 'bricklaying' process, but

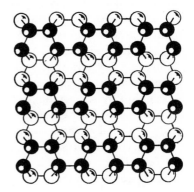

Fig. 19.4. *Structure of hexagonal diamond.*

graphite nuclei also tend to form in the gas and become deposited on the seed crystal. Fortunately the carbon atoms favour the diamond; nevertheless the growing process has to be interrupted from time to time to clean off accumulated carbon. This is done in hydrogen at a pressure of 750,000 to 3,000,000 lb per sq. in.

The Russians found that by employing more than five four-hours cycles they could increase the weight of diamond powder by 9·5 per cent. In the 1970s, B. V. Derjaguin and D. B. Fedoseev devised processes for growing larger crystals at much higher rates without appreciable graphite forming by pulsing the heat. One such process produces threads or whiskers of diamond that lengthen at a remarkable rate and then thicken so that they become spherical or almost polyhedral in shape. This is quite different from the production of so-called 'carbon fibres' in the U.K. which comprise threads of graphite crystallized into its immensely strong chains of carbon atoms (see Fig. 18.2) by graphitizing rayon or synthetic polymer filaments.

A diffusion method of 'building' with free carbon atoms was employed to create the world's first synthetic gem diamonds. (See page 437.)

Diffusion growth results in diamond with a lattice dimension about 1 per cent smaller than that of natural diamond, i.e. of slightly greater specific gravity. The film of new diamond therefore grows under compression, which might account for the fact that growth rate slows considerably after the initial stages.

Improvement of Gem Diamond Colour
Dennis Elwell pointed out, in 1977, that the most interesting fact from the gemmologist's point of view was the colour change from grey to off-white or light blue that occurred after several depositions of film and cleaning cycles. This might be used to enhance the appearance of natural polished diamonds of poor colour, although it did not yet appear possible (in 1977) to deposit diamond layers uniformly on relatively large stones.

In November 1977, however, a more direct method was reported in *Nature* by R. M. Chernko, R. E. Tuft and H. M. Strong of General Electric, who annealed Type Ib diamonds at 2000°K and 60,000 atmos. for thirty minutes, when the stones became partly Type Ia with an appreciably paler yellow colour, reduced absorption spectrum and weaker paramagnetism.

Features of Synthetic Crystals
G.E. in America have released certain information about the growth of crystals in their process and a number of research workers have studied De Beers as well as G.E. diamonds.

Diamond crystals produced synthetically are often more regular than those found in nature. The irregularities of natural crystals are probably the result of constriction by surrounding rocks when they grew and lack of carbon in the solution. Laboratory experiments suggest that natural diamonds may have been partly dissolved after their original formation.

When synthetic crystals are grown at the lowest possible range of temperatures and pressures, the cube is the most common crystal form. Growth occurs in roughly square-shaped layers parallel to the cube faces. The layers start in the

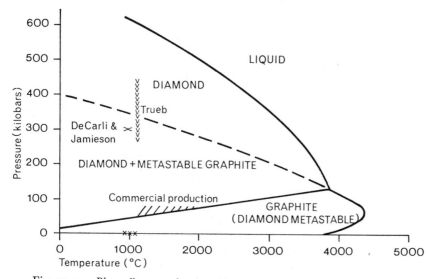

Fig. 19.5. *Phase diagram of carbon (devised by D. Elwell after Bundy and others) showing some of the regions of experiment referred to in the text. A kilobar is 1,000 atmospheres or approximately 15,000 lb per sq. in. De Carli and Jamieson (1961) and Trueb (1971) used shock comparison techniques.*

centre of the faces and creep outwards so that each face is smooth but in a series of very fine steps towards the raised centre. Natural cubes are rough on the surface and pitted.

At higher temperatures and pressures, octahedra are formed. These, too, grow layer by layer, but on the octahedral faces. The layers in this case are of triangular form. If the temperature is maintained, the crystal grows to a certain point and then begins to dissolve. The surfaces become etched with small pits, which are triangular on octahedral faces. The pitting is similar to that produced by etching natural or synthetic crystals in molten potassium nitrate. Octahedral faces, however, being more perfect crystallographically, are more resistant to attack than other faces such as cubic and dodecahedral.

Dodecahedral crystals rarely occur in synthetic production although forms of them are common in nature. The reason is thought to be that dodecahedra are formed by part dissolving of another form of crystal. The many variations of natural dodecahedra may occur because crystals have been submitted for millions of years to attrition by natural forces. On the other hand, synthetics made with nickel and some chromium as a catalyst tend to be cubic or cube-octahedral, and other catalysts, including niobium and copper, result in a high proportion of octahedral crystals.

Rate of Growth

Diamond crystals grow rapidly when produced by the belt method. A rate of about 0·33 mm (0.12 in) per second has been calculated. Growth at lower temperatures is slower and at higher ones much more rapid so that masses of small crystals are formed. The latter conditions will produce the synthetic equivalent of carbonado, a porous mass of variously orientated tiny crystals.

The slower the growth, the better quality the crystal.

Twinning occurs in synthetic crystals as it does in natural ones, and macles can be grown in different thicknesses and lengths.

Some research is concentrated on producing stones large enough for use in tools and drill crowns. There are also many possible applications in electronics for pure gem crystals.

Colour of Synthetics

Colour is, of course, of major importance in gem diamonds but not of direct significance in industrial ones. It has been found that variations in temperature and pressure during manufacture affect the colour of synthetics. As might be expected, black is common at the lower temperatures of diamond formation. As the temperature is raised, so the colour 'improves' through shades of green and yellow towards weaker colours.

The colour is also affected by interstitial nitrogen. The colours mentioned are not the only ones that can be produced to order. Shades of grey and blue, as well as of yellow and green are possible. Larger crystals can be made nearly opaque with the intensity of coloration.

Inclusions and Substitution Atoms

Inclusions occur frequently, especially when the crystals are rapidly grown. When growth is slower, inclusions tend to take up positions related to crystal

Fig. 19.6. *Synthetic industrial diamond on the pole of a magnet.*

axes. Nickel used to be found up to 10 per cent, but by 1975 it had been reduced to about 4 per cent; garnet has also been identified. Synthetic diamonds usually include dispersed nitrogen and are therefore Type Ib and are paramagnetic (Fig. 19.6).

Surface Features

There are differences in the surfaces of natural and synthetic diamonds that have practical uses, one of which is in identification. Tolansky carried out extensive research on this subject. He says that the chief differences are that although trigons are very common on natural octahedral faces, they are very rare on synthetic ones. Pits are found on some octahedral faces of De Beers synthetic diamonds and are oppositely orientated to trigons, i.e. their edges are parallel to the triangular octahedral face. On the cube faces of synthetics, spiral growth patterns are sometimes seen. There is no known instance of a spiral growth

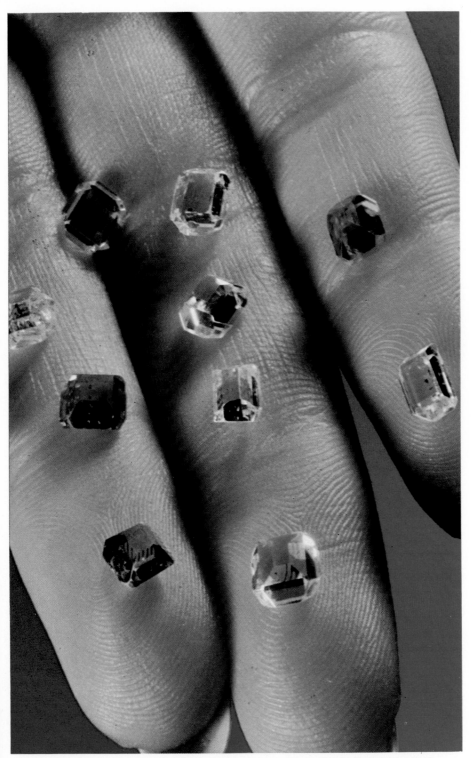

The first synthetic gem diamonds, which were of tabular habit and were made by General Electric of Schenectady, New York. Some are on show in the Smithsonian Institution, Washington.

Assortments of gem quality rough that have been sorted into sizes and qualities at the offices of the Diamond Trading Company in Charterhouse Street, in London.

on a natural cube face. One of the most striking differences is that cube faces are smooth on synthetics and always, as far as is known, very rough on natural stones.

Very occasionally a surface skin appears on G.E. synthetics. Many cleavages are found amongst synthetics. A.S.E.A. synthetics are often internally fractured in non-cleavage directions.

Types of Synthesis

The earlier successful A.S.E.A., G.E. and De Beers methods of producing synthetic diamonds by dissolving carbon in molten metals have become a very important industry carried out in the U.S.A., South Africa, the U.S.S.R., Eire, Japan, Sweden, the Netherlands, Czechoslovakia, and probably China. The plant at Shannon in Eire is shown in Fig. 19.7.

Synthetic diamonds are now grown by many very different techniques and, according to R. J. Wedlake, of De Beers Diamond Research Laboratory, Johannesburg, they are:

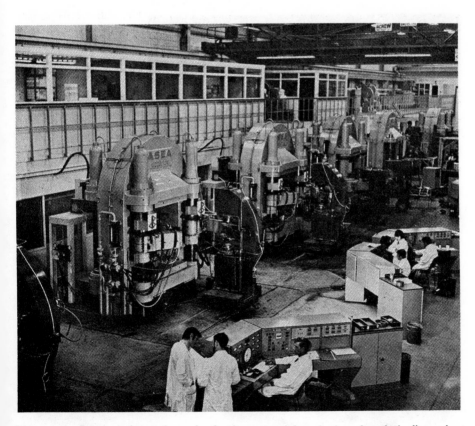

Fig. 19.7. *Presses and control consoles for the commercial production of synthetic diamonds at De Beers' plant at Shannon, Eire.*

435

(1) Growth from a molten solvent-catalyst.

(2) Shock wave synthesis.

(3) Direct transformation in the absence of a solvent.

(4) Growth from a carbon melt.

(5) Metastable synthesis from a carbonaceous gas using a diamond seed crystal.

For the first method (that commonly in use), many different types of pressure unit have been used successfully over the past ten years beside the belt, referred to earlier. They include the girdle, tetrahedral (Fig. 19.8), opposed anvil, and piston and cylinder. Over the last twenty years, the incomplete science has become a technology in which many processes are closely-kept secrets. The products are industrial grit and powder, which can, within limits, be produced to specification as shown in Fig. 19.9.

Dr. Wedlake says that the process of diamond synthesis from carbon can be regarded as a three-stage process, thus:

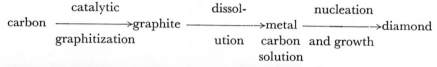

catalytic   dissol-   nucleation

carbon ——————→graphite ——————————→metal ——————————→diamond

graphitization   ution   carbon and growth

solution

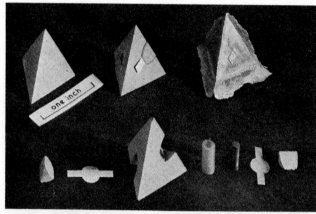

Fig. 19.8. *Principle of the Tetrahedral chamber ultra-high-pressure apparatus.* (above) *Samples of pyrophyllite tetrahedra from which the National Physical Laboratory, Teddington, England, made diamond in 1960. Along the top are a solid sample, a loaded sample and one that has been squeezed. Below are parts of the tetrahedron: a silver chloride sleeve, the carbonaceous rod and electrical contacts.*

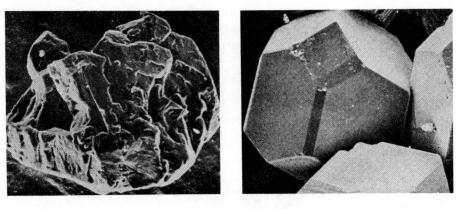

Fig. 19.9. *Synthetic diamond particles seen at very high magnification by a scanning electro microscope. That on the left is a typical friable particle, as used in resin-bonded wheels for grinding carbide tools. That on the right is a typical high-strength particle, as used in metal-bonded wheels used for sawing stone and concrete.*

At all stages the nature of the carbon-diamond surface plays an important part. Actual mechanisms involved in diamond formation are still not established, and probably await the development of high-pressure technology so that more experiments can be carried out.

Synthetic Gem Diamonds

Production of white, clear synthetic gem quality diamonds in a laboratory was first announced by General Electric in the U.S.A., in 1970. Some crystals they made weighed over a carat (Fig. 19.10). They were described as having cost many times more than gem quality rough from Africa. The men responsible were Dr. Herbert M. Strong and Dr. Robert H. Wentorf. The best crystals were classified as equal to natural rough that was white and had very small flaws and inclusions.

A special pressure chamber (Fig. 19.11) is used with the belt type of apparatus. A small mass of synthetic diamond crystals is placed in the centre of the chamber and on each side of it a bath of catalyst metal, such as iron or nickel, which becomes molten at operating so that there are free carbon atoms in the bath. The central part of the chamber is maintained at a higher temperature than the ends. More carbon is dissolved at the hot part in the centre than the cooler ends can hold in solution, so that carbon atoms wandering in the bath tend to come out of solution and crystallize at the ends. They would normally crystallize as graphite, but diamond seed crystals are provided at each end on to which the carbon atoms move slowly from the central synthetic diamond mass to the seeds at the ends until the diamond mass is used up. Rate of growth is about 2–3 mg (0·0004–0·006 ct) an hour.

The greater the difference in temperature between the centre and ends of the

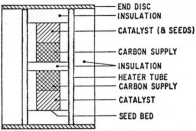

END DISC
INSULATION
CATALYST (& SEEDS)
CARBON SUPPLY
INSULATION
HEATER TUBE
CARBON SUPPLY
CATALYST
SEED BED

Fig. 19.10. *Some General Electric synthetic gem diamond crystals compared with a pencil. They are tabular in habit, being truncated octahedra with modified cube faces. Sizes are from 0·60 to 1·10 ct. An example can be seen in the Smithsonian Institution, Washington, D.C.*

Fig. 19.11. *Diagram of the pressure vessel used in synthetic gem diamond production.*

pressure chamber, the faster the seed crystals grow. Usually a difference of 28° to 33°C (50° to 60°F) is enough. Typical figures are 1427° and 1455°C (2,600° and 2,650°F). These temperatures are held for several days at a pressure of about 60,000 atmospheres. The best crystals grow at the bottom of the molten bath because dirt and stray diamond crystals float upwards and stay out of the way of the growing crystal. Impurities can be added to achieve unique features of colour, electrical properties, hardness, internal structure, and so on. Crystals first produced were tabular in habit.

Some of G.E.'s synthetic gem diamond crystals have been cut and polished by Lazare and Kaplan & Sons of New York, who reported that they behaved no differently from natural ones in the process. Three brilliant cut stones – GE1, a 1-carat white crystal that made a 0·33-carat brilliant, a pale blue and a canary yellow – as well as a crystal, were presented to the Smithsonian Institution, Washington, D.C., U.S.A., in 1971.

It was found that the elimination of nitrogen impurities allowed white crystals to be made. The inclusion of boron as an impurity turned the colour blue. Stones of either colour are semi-conductors.

Russian Synthetic Gem Diamonds

In November 1971, some time after the G.E. announcement, a startling article appeared in the Belgian journal, *Diamant*. Jos Bonroy, a Belgian sawyer, wrote that, in November 1967, he was introduced to a Russian delegation led by Professor Bakul, director of the Kiev Synthetic Diamond Research Institute, and asked if it would be possible to saw and polish stones made in the laboratory. Having seen only diamond grit, Bonroy was very sceptical; then Bakul produced some straw-coloured crystals of excellent purity and of a size and shape Bonroy had never seen before. He sawed the stones with difficulty because it was not easy to determine sawing directions and the diamond was exceptionally hard. The cutter and polisher had similar problems, but when finished, the stones looked no different from natural ones, according to Bonroy. About a dozen had become colourless, as sometimes happens with slightly tinted or coated natural diamonds.

Professor Bakul asked that the existence of the polished diamonds should be kept secret, to which Jos Bonroy agreed, 'knowing the hypersensitive diamond market would be rocked by news such as this'. In April 1971, Bonroy was invited to attend the international synthetic diamond symposium in Kiev and asked to speak on how he had been approached to saw and polish the synthetic gem diamond crystals in 1967. Afterwards, Bakul told him that the Russians considered synthetic gem diamonds much too uneconomic to produce to compete with natural ones.

Identification of Synthetic Gem Diamonds

Robert Crowningshield, director of the Eastern Division of the Gemological Institute of America, was probably the first professional gemmologist to examine the G.E. synthetic gem diamonds. He reported that the white and blue crystals were somewhat truncated octahedra with modified cube faces. The yellow stones were well-developed octahedra with one point diminished.

Under 10 × magnification they varied in quality from Flawless to Imperfect, some of the Imperfect ones having round or platey iron-nickel inclusions from the catalyst. All had fine white dust inclusions under high magnification, but this did not affect the brilliance of the flawless stones. The dark blue stones showed a whitish cross under high magnification, apparently a consequence of the dust. The near colourless stones would have been graded H to J on the G.I.A. diamond grading scale.

Crowningshield said that, while perhaps 10 per cent of natural white diamonds fluoresce under long-wave ultra-violet light (3660 Å), none of the G.E. crystals did so. However the G.E. diamonds, except for the yellow ones, did fluoresce strongly in tones of yellow and green under short-wave u.v. (2537 Å), which was diagnostic as it was rare for a natural diamond to fluoresce under short-wave u.v. Moreover, all except the yellow G.E. stones phosphoresced strongly after the u.v. source was removed and continued to do so for an abnormally long time, except for the dark blue stones. Only natural blue stones phosphoresce under short-wave u.v.

All but the yellow stones were semi-conductors, which was the object of G.E.

439

in making them. Only natural blue stones are semi-conductors. Finally, none of the synthetic gem diamonds showed any absorption lines in their spectra, whereas only natural Top White stones have no lines.

Later G.E. Synthetic Gem Diamonds

General Electric have continued to experiment with making gem quality diamonds and, in 1974, Dr. Arthur Beuche, vice-president of the division responsible for their development, presented a ring set with a brilliant-cut synthetic diamond to Lady Porter, wife of Professor Sir G. Porter, director of the Royal Institution. Subsequently, G.E. loaned a 0·28-carat round brilliant to the Royal Institution for examination by Diamond Grading Laboratories, Hatton Garden, using normal gem testing and grading methods.

The stone was cut to G.I.A. ideal proportions with a good finish. The clarity grade was SI on the Scan. D.N. scale as very many pinpoint inclusions could be seen in the heart of the stone at 10 × magnification. They were most numerous under the table. No other internal marks were noted. The colour was greyish with no trace of yellow. The stone was not of Cape Series, as shown by the absorption pattern obtained on the D.L.G. spectrophotometer compared with a Cape Series stone, in Fig. 19.12.

The stone was singly refracting under a polariscope and, when rotated, it showed a Maltese cross extinction pattern. Under short-wave ultra-violet light (2540 Å), there was slight yellowish-green fluorescence, which persisted for several minutes as a more blue-green phosphorescence after the light was removed. Unlike the crystals that Crowningshield studied, under long-wave u.v. (3660 Å) this stone had a fluorescence similar to that under short-wave, but without the following phosphorescence. A strong light blue fluorescence under X-rays (50 Kv., 19 ma.) was similar to that of natural diamonds, and persisted as light blue phosphorescence for several minutes. No absorption bands were seen with a hand-held spectroscope.

When the surface of the stone was examined by the interferometry 'finger

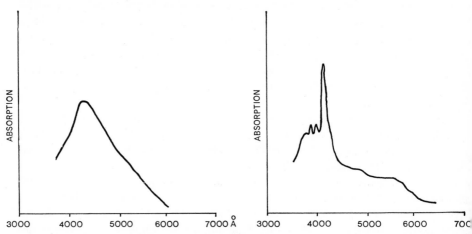

Fig. 19.12. *The absorption curves of a G.E. synthetic gem diamond* (left) *and a natural one of Cape Series, prepared by Diamond Grading Laboratory, London. The absorption axes are not necessarily comparable.*

printing' technique, few distinctive growth features could be seen although the familiar polishing lines were present, which suggests a more controlled growth than that of the natural crystal.

Fraudulent Coloration

Probably throughout the history of marketing there have been attempts to improve the appearance of gem diamonds, particularly of their colour. The most effective method depends upon the fact that mixing light of complementary colours produces white light. Thus the yellowish tinge of a Silver Cape stone may be partly neutralized by applying the complementary colour of violet. Even blue will effect an improvement. For the method to be effective, a painted stone must be yellowish to start with. Painting a grey stone will not be successful.

One of the earliest methods of the fakers was to use an indelible pencil or violet ink and to apply the colour to the culet, girdle, or pavilion of the stone. The girdle was marked by the moistened pencil, or the pavilion or part of it was dipped in the ink of coloured solution. The girdle, having a matt surface, is much easier to mark. Various dyes have also been used.

Such coatings can usually be seen with a 10 × lens because they tend to be streaky. They may be removed by water, alcohol, or a commercial jewellery cleaner.

After the Second World War, attempts were made to improve diamonds by coating them by the same methods as used for improving the light transmission of camera lenses, by vacuum sputtering of fluorides. Stones so treated are easily detected because of the purplish bloom, as seen on lenses. The coatings are durable and have to be removed by hot acid.

In the 1940s, extra thin coatings that were resistant and almost invisible were developed for making transistors. Someone thought of applying them to off-colour diamonds and by 1950 it was possible to send diamonds, like any suitable materials for electronic uses, to a treatment laboratory in the U.S.A.

By 1962, several specialist coaters were in business in the U.S.A., and traffic in fraudulently coloured stones – almost invariably larger ones of 5 carats and over – had become a menace in New York particularly. Coating lifted the price by 25 per cent and more. No easy method of detection was discovered. Chemical and X-ray methods were not effective, which left the standard technique of searching the surface of the diamond in reflected light under a microscope for local areas of coating. It has been found also that a skilled sorter cannot assign a precise colour grade to a coated stone of this type, which is a rather refined clue. No doubt some of these stones were brought to Europe and have remained undetected so far.

Detected coatings, which are often near the girdle on smaller stones are seen to be spotty, granular or splodgy, with tiny craters or burst bubbles.

The Gemological Institute of America was shown a ring with a coated stone on which it was not possible to detect the coating. Permission to unmount the stone was refused, but the whole ring was boiled in concentrated sulphuric acid, which removed the coating from the stone and revealed its true yellowish body colour. The coatings are only a fraction of a wavelength in thickness and are applied in a small area only, often concealed by the mount.

Fraudulent Coloration of Rough

Rough diamonds are occasionally fraudulently 'coloured' by burning them so that the surface begins to oxidize and turns whitish. They are removed before becoming too leaden in appearance. A yellowish stone treated in this way can appear to be a white one with a frosted surface. The Gemological Institute of America reported in 1971 that a cutter had purchased an entire parcel of stones so treated that became yellowish after cutting.

Artificial Coloration

The colour of diamonds has been altered in the course of scientific experiment and as a result it is possible to have stones treated commercially to make them green, dark yellow, golden brown, or blue, by irradiation and if necessary by subsequent heat-treatment. The practice of treating decorative and gem materials has been accepted for centuries. Huge quantities of agate are dyed; all blue and golden zircons are heat-treated; and most citrine is purple amethyst that has been turned yellow by heat treatment. It is not reprehensible to colour a diamond artificially, but it is fraudulent to sell it without disclosing the fact.

First to colour diamond by irradiation was Sir William Crookes, in experiments with radium carried out from 1904. The green tint he produced is quite attractive unless it is too dark, when it is similar to the blackish tourmaline green. It is different from the apple-green of the very rare natural green stones. According to R. Webster, a score or so radium-treated stones are known to be on the market in the U.K. They can be detected immediately by a Geiger counter or, without one, by leaving the stone overnight in contact with a photographic plate in a light-tight box and developing the plate, which will show an image of the stone (an auto-radiograph, Fig. 19.13). The amount of radioactivity is not harmful, as after treatment a diamond loses about half its radioactivity every ten minutes.

Development of nuclear reactors, particle accelerating machines, and other means of irradiation has made treatment of stones easier and also increased the research into the mechanism of colour change. Only a limited range of changes is possible. It is caused by damage to the crystal lattice of the diamond which alters the light absorption and therefore the visible colour. Partial annealing of the lattice by heat-treatment can change, but not destroy the colour.

It was not (in 1977) commercially possible to change a yellowish diamond to a white one, although it has been done in the laboratory (see page 432). By current techniques, colour is additive. The 'improvement' comes from treating, say, a Cape stone and turning it into a fancy colour.

The main techniques are as follows, but only 1 and 3 are normally employed. (1) Neutron bombardment; (2) Proton, deutron, or alpha-particle bombardment; (3) Electron bombardment; (4) Gamma irradiation; (5) Radioactive isotope bombardment, particularly by cobalt 60, but sometimes by Americium 241 powder, in which the diamond is buried by remote control for the appropriate number of hours and subsequently washed in acid. There may be other methods, but they have not been disclosed. Treatment normally turns stones green, the depth of colour depending on the length of time of treatment, which itself depends on the intensity of radiation and the weight of the stone. Time of treatment is inversely proportional to the cube root of the weight of the stone. The colour varies from a pale green to a bottle green and finally to opaque black if treatment is too prolonged.

Heat-treatment

Subsequent heat-treatment for some hours at about 500–900°C (930–1,652°F) of green irradiated diamonds changes the colour of most stones to yellow or cinnamon brown, which is generally thought to be more attractive than the green. The yellow or brown colour is not lighter than the previous green. In other words, it is still additive. It is not possible to turn a yellow stone to green, then heat-treat it to make it a lighter yellow.

Certain diamonds treated in an electron accelerator, such as a Van de Graaff

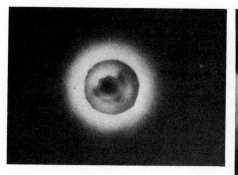

Fig. 19.13.   *Autoradiograph of a radium-treated diamond.*

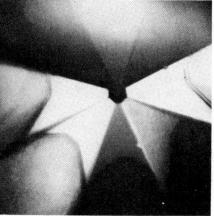

Fig. 19.14.   *'Umbrella' seen around the culet of some cyclotron-treated diamonds.*

generator, are changed to an attractive pale aquamarine colour or to a greenish-blue. Gamma irradiation will produce a bluish-green colour, but is rarely employed. The colour in both cases does not penetrate the stone and can be polished off.

In the U.S.A., commercial services for the coloration of diamonds are available. Some fine colours have been achieved, not only excellent blues, but reds and purples. The most common commercial demand is for greens and golden browns because these are cheaper to produce. Only a very small number of natural diamonds can be changed to blue, red, or purple. In the U.K. the Atomic Energy Authority will treat diamonds to change the colour, but the service is of more value to scientific workers than the trade, as it is more experimental than commercial, and the higher energy machines now installed result in less critical irradiation. Israel also has a treatment service.

The behaviour of stones under treatment depends largely on their type. All tend to turn green after neutron bombardment. Subsequent heat-treatment changes Type Ia stones to yellow or amber and Type IIa to brown with intermediate shades for intermediate types. The rare Type Ib stones will become red to purple.

Electron bombardment has the same effect on Type Ia stones, but Ib and IIa stones become blue to greenish blue. Subsequent heat-treatment has the same effect again on Type Ia stones, but those of Type Ib become red to purple and IIa become brown. These comments are only a guide since it is difficult or impossible to predict colour changes with any degree of accuracy.

A stone that is neutron bombarded is at first intensely radioactive, but the activity soon dies out. The colour goes right through the stone, because the neutrons are uncharged particles. As far as is known, it is permanent.

Diamonds treated in a cyclotron by protons, deutrons, or alpha-particles, also lose their radioactivity soon after treatment. The colour is only skin-deep because the charged particles cannot penetrate deeply. It can be polished off, but is permanent, as far as is known.

Identification

If the diamond has been cyclotron-treated through the table, a dark ring will be seen on looking down on the pavilion. If it has been treated through the pavilion, a shape like an opened umbrella will be seen on looking down through the table (Fig. 19.14). If treated through the side, there will be a zone of colour near the girdle, probably on both sides of the stone. Pile-treated and isotope-irradiated stones show no particular markings.

A conclusive test for stones that have been heat-treated to turn them amber or brown is a line at 5940 Å in the spectrum. Bands centred on 5040 will be induced because of the new colour, but the original 4155 system will still be evident if the stone was originally of Cape colour.

There are, however, still problems of identification of some artificially coloured stones without elaborate and expensive equipment for measuring electron spin.

A natural blue diamond is Type IIb, which is a semi-conductor of electricity. An artificially-coloured blue diamond will not be Type IIb and therefore will be an insulator. An obvious test therefore is to attempt to pass a current through the stone. A simple circuit, suggested by R. Webster, is to attempt to pass an a.c. current through the stone with a meter in series. A meter-reading indicates that

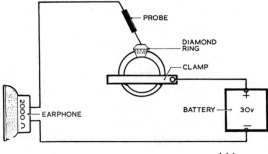

Fig. 19.15. *Circuit with earphones which will crackle if the diamond is conductive, i.e. Type II b.*

the blue diamond is natural. Alternatively the stone may be touched with a neon-indicating screwdriver while current is applied to it. Other tests are to measure the resistance with an ohmmeter, or to use a battery and earphone in a circuit and to listen for scratching when using a probe on a stone thought to be a Type IIb (Fig. 19.15).

The 'Deepdene' Diamond

The most notorious artificially-coloured diamond was the 'Deepdene', offered at Christie's sale in Geneva on 21st May 1971, and described as 'of golden-yellow colour, cushion-cut, weighing 104·52 ct with a certificate for natural colour and purity (VVS 1). This famous diamond is one of the largest of its colour and purity in the world. It ranks next to the "Tiffany" of 128·51 ct. The "Deepdene" was on loan for many years to the Philadelphia Academy of Sciences. . . .' It had been certified for colour and purity by a German gemmological institute and the University of Mainz, but before the sale Dr. E. Gübelin of Switzerland, who had previously examined the stone in his laboratory, warned Christie's that it had been artificially coloured.

Christie's conferred with the German authorities who maintained their view and the sale was allowed to go ahead with the recommendation that the stone be examined by a fourth laboratory. Van Cleef and Aspels bought it for £190,000 and it was then submitted to the London Gem Testing Laboratory where B. W. Anderson showed conclusively that Dr. Gübelin was correct in stating that the colour had been artificially induced. The money paid was returned and the stone handed back to its owner in Frankfurt.

The Deepdene was originally listed as weighing 104·88 carats, being cushion-shaped, yellow and with a Maltese cross-like inclusion, but there is no such inclusion according to Dr. Gübelin; the cross-like pattern is that seen in many diamonds of similar cut such as the Tiffany and Red Cross. There are, however, two small crystals below one of the crown facets near the girdle. The stone sold in 1971 was either another stone or the real 'Deepdene' which had been artificially improved in colour. The latter seems more likely, as otherwise there would have been a protest from the owner of the real 'Deepdene'. The few points less in weight, if the original weight was correct, could have been lost in repolishing.

Sintered Diamond

To conclude this chapter, an interesting composite diamond (reminiscent of early 'reconstructed ruby') that has been developed by De Beers, should be recorded, although it has no value as a gem and is used as a tool tip because of its toughness. Called Syndite, it comprises well-formed diamond particles of high purity sintered together into a compact mass under rigidly-controlled high temperature and pressure. The random orientation of the particles eliminates preferential cleavage planes.

CHAPTER TWENTY

Famous Diamonds

All famous diamonds are large by present-day standards. Most of them have an interesting and, in some cases, blood-stained history. The famous ones without great historical interest are always particularly large or of unusual colour or quality. There are many 'unknown' large diamonds.

Most of their histories are very difficult to disentangle because of misdescriptions, changes of name, and assumptions made by writers owing to the secrecy surrounding extremely valuable stones. The Great Mogul and the Koh-i-Nûr, for example, were claimed for many years to have been the same stone, but are now known not to be so. The Hope, on the other hand, is almost certainly part of the Blue Tavernier, stolen during the French Revolution. The Great Table, which was described and illustrated by Tavernier, may not have been a diamond at all. The shape of the crystal as illustrated by Tavernier, suggests that it is more likely to have been a ruby. On the other hand, a more recent suggestion is that it was a diamond and was subsequently cut into two now famous pink diamonds.

The Hon. Ian Balfour has researched the histories of large diamonds and a summary of his conclusions were published under the title *Famous Diamonds* by De Beers Consolidated Mines Limited. The basic historical information in this chapter relies on this and his later research, to avoid introducing information that is too controversial, but all additional information is, of course, the author's responsibility.

The Cullinan

The Cullinan's history is recent and therefore well authenticated. It weighed 3,106 carats in the rough and its fame depends on it being the biggest diamond crystal ever found, and also upon it being of exceptionally high quality and purity.

It was on 25 January 1905, that 'Daddy' Wells, the surface manager of the Premier Mine in the Transvaal, South Africa, was on an inspection tour and saw a glint in the yellow ground of a side wall of the mine (Fig. 3.17). He went to the spot and began digging with his penknife, to unearth a diamond that was $3\frac{15}{16}$ inches long and $2\frac{5}{8}$ inches high and weighed slightly over one and a third pounds (Fig. 17.10). The stone was put in the safe and the chairman of the mining company, Sir Thomas Cullinan, was informed.

The huge rough diamond was sent with the rest of the week's production by mule cart to the station to be taken to Johannesburg. Surprisingly, it became almost an embarrassment to the Premier Mining Company because, although it remained the wonder of the London diamond market for two years, no-one

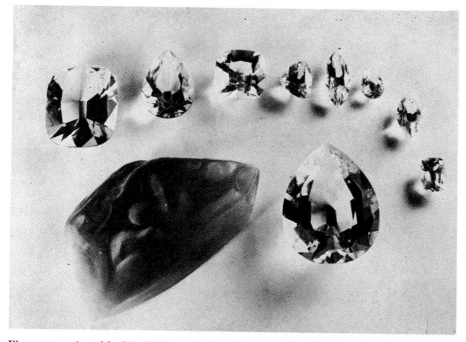

Fig. 20.1. *A model of the Cullinan rough and of some of the polished stones obtained from it. The largest is the Star of Africa (or Cullinan 1) which is not as pointed as in the model.*

wanted to buy it. In the end it was bought by the Transvaal government, at the suggestion of General Louis Botha, the Prime Minister, for £150,000, and presented to King Edward VII on his 66th birthday on 9 November 1907.

The King decided to entrust the work of cutting it to Joseph Asscher and Company of Amsterdam, who had cut the Excelsior (q.v.). The newspapers were told that the stone was being posted but, in fact, Joseph Asscher took it in his pocket over the Channel on a steamboat.

The Asschers studied the huge crystal for about six months before deciding how it could be cleaved to yield the best number and size of stones. The first cleavage yielded two pieces of about 2,000 and 1,000 carats. It was eventually divided into nine major stones, 96 small brilliant-cut stones, and nearly 10 carats of unpolished 'ends'. The recovery was 34·25 per cent, so the total weight of the cut stones was 1,063 carats.

The Star of Africa

The largest stone was the Cullinan I, or the Star of Africa, weighing 530·20 carats. It has 74 facets, and is still the largest cut diamond in the world. The Cullinan II, weighing 312·40 carats, with 66 facets, is still the second largest diamond in the world. The Cullinan I is pear-shaped and set in the Royal Sceptre, which is kept with other Crown Jewels in the Tower of London. The Cullinan II is cushion-shaped and is set in the Imperial State Crown, also among the Crown Jewels. The principal nine gem diamonds are all in the

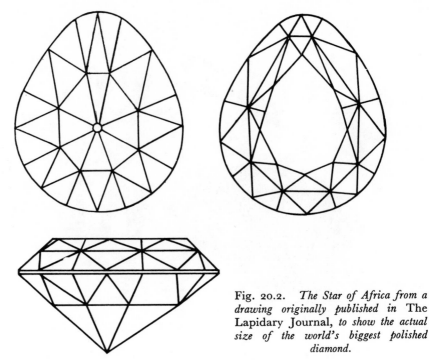

Fig. 20.2. *The Star of Africa from a drawing originally published in* The Lapidary Journal, *to show the actual size of the world's biggest polished diamond.*

Crown Jewels or in the personal possession of the British Royal Family.

After the stones were cut and polished, for which special tools had to be made, security was a problem again. Mr. Asscher announced that he was crossing to England to arrange delivery. The captain of the old Great Eastern steamer, *Cromer*, on which he travelled, said he hoped he would have the honour of carrying the Cullinan. Then Mr. Asscher said, 'You had it last week.'

When the Cullinan crystal was examined after being found, it was seen to have a natural 'skin' or 'nyf' only on one side. That, and a cleavage face, suggested that it was part of a very much larger crystal. Sir William Crookes, who had made a special study of diamond, suggested that it might be even less than half of an original octahedral crystal, but this could not have been so, because it is known today that the Cullinan is Type II material which does not form into regular crystal shapes but remains irregular.

There were several rumours of the discovery of the 'missing half' of the Cullinan in South Africa after the Premier discovery, but no facts of any substance suggest it was found, even if it ever existed.

The Braganza

The second biggest stone ever found would have been the Braganza, or King of Portugal, if its weight of 1,680 carats in the rough, or even its existence, could be proved. A stone called by this name existed, and its finding was reported by John Mawe in his book *Travels in Brazil* (1812), but may have been a pale topaz. Where it is now is not known. In a subsequent book, Mawe gave its weight as 144 carats.

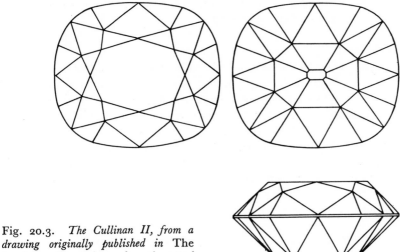

Fig. 20.3. *The Cullinan II, from a drawing originally published in* The Lapidary Journal, *to show the actual size of the world's second largest polished diamond.*

The Braganza, whatever it is or was, is thought to have been picked up in a dried-up part of the bed of the River Abaete in the Minas Gerais province of Brazil, which is famous for its precious stones, including topaz, aquamarine, touramaline, and diamond. It was claimed, with all other diamonds of over 20 carats, by the King of Portugal who at that time owned the mines. King John VI of Portugal (1816–26) had a hole drilled through the rough stone and wore it suspended around his neck on special occasions.

The largest gem diamond to be found in Brazil is the President Vargas (q.v.), of 726·60 carats.

The Excelsior

The second largest stone ever found, if the Braganza (q.v.) was not a diamond, is the Excelsior, discovered in the Jagersfontein Mine in South Africa in 1893, twelve years before the Cullinan (Fig. 2.22). An African mine worker found it in a shovelful of gravel. Like many stones from the same mine, it was of high clarity and was described as 'blue-white'. It was found on the day that the contract expired between the mining company and the London syndicate that purchased the output. The syndicate tried unsuccessfully to sell this 995·2 carat rough diamond for ten years, and then decided to send it to Asschers of Amsterdam to be cut in 1903.

It was an irregular stone with a cleavage face, shaped something like a bread roll, so a large polished stone could not be obtained from it without unacceptable wastage. Recovery was 37·5 per cent, which meant that the 21 stones that were polished weighed 373·75 carats, the largest being a marquise of 69·80 carats.

Another marquise-shaped stone of 18 carats from the Excelsior was shown by De Beers at the 1939 New York World's Fair.

The Great Mogul

The third biggest stone of gem quality, the Great Mogul was discovered in the middle of the seventeenth century in the Kollur Mine, near Golconda in Hyderabad, India. Its present whereabouts are unknown, and it may have been divided into smaller stones. It has been confused with the Darya-i-Nûr (q.v.), the Koh-i-Nûr (q.v.) and the Orloff (q.v.), but the Koh-i-Nûr existed before the Great Mogul was known and the Darya-i-Nûr was pinkish and could not have been the Great Mogul, according to V. B. Meen and A. D. Tushingham, who made a study of the Iranian Crown Jewels in 1967. There are good reasons, on the other hand, for believing that the Orloff and Great Mogul may be the same stone, both having been recorded as having a rose cut and a faint bluish tinge.

The stone was named after Shah Jehan, who built the famous tomb, the Taj Mahal in Agra, and it may have been set, like the Koh-i-Nûr, in his fabulous Peacock Throne, which still exists in the treasures of the Shah of Persia, but minus a number of its magnificent gems. Aurangzeb, Jehan's third son and successor, showed the diamond to Tavernier, who described it as looking like half an egg and referred to a flaw on the edge: (the Orloff has a surface flaw).

The rough stone is said to have weighed 907 ratis (about 793 old carats), but was only 280 old carats when seen by Tavernier, who related a story that it had been faceted so badly as a rose-cut by a Venetian, Hortensio Borgio, that the Mogul not only refused to pay him, but inflicted a huge fine. The Persians are believed to have adquired the stone after Nadir Shah sacked Delhi in 1739.

The Great Table

A pale pink stone of unusual table-cut shape was seen before 1677 in Golconda, India, by Tavernier, who called it the Great Table and said it weighed $242\frac{5}{16}$ old carats (Fig. 20.4). After that reference, nothing is known, but it may have been cut into two other stones, one the Darya-i-Nûr (q.v.) and the other the Nûr-ul-Ain.

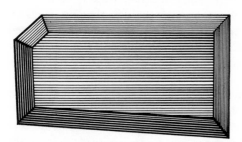

Fig. 20.4. *The Great Table, redrawn from a sketch by Tavernier to illustrate the size and appearance of the stone; Tavernier believed it to be a diamond.*

The Darya-i-Nûr

The Darya-i-Nûr is the largest and most beautiful stone in the Crown Jewels of Iran, having been taken from the Mogul's treasures when Delhi was sacked in 1739 by Persian invaders. It is flawless and quite limpid with a weight estimated to be between 175 and 195 carats in its present step-cut table form. The colour is a pale pink. The stone 'disappeared' for a long time and was 'rediscovered' by V. B. Meen and A. D. Tushingham, two Canadian gemmologists, in their study of the Crown Jewels of Iran in 1967.

The present Shah is said to have shown it to Queen Elizabeth II and Prince Philip, the Duke of Edinburgh, when they visited Iran in 1961, and wore it at his coronation in 1967. An inscription in Persian on one of the pavilion facets says: *As-Sultan Fath-Ali Shah Qajar 1250*. (1250 is 1834 A.D., when Fath Ali Shah died.)

The Darya-i-Nûr is currently set in a rectangular gold frame with other diamonds. Above it is a crown flanked with lions with ruby eyes, carrying scimitars.

Meen and Tushingham concluded from their examination that the Darya-i-Nûr was the Great Table Diamond, as described by Tavernier, which had been damaged some time before 1834 and had been recut to remove the damaged part by Fath-Ali Shah. They identified another diamond, the 60-carat brilliant-cut, Nûr-ul-Ain, as having the same quality and colour as the Darya-i-Nûr which, after experiments with a model of the Great Table, they decided could well have been the other part of the Great Table.

Of the Great Table, Tavernier wrote, in 1677, 'Being at Golconda I saw this Stone; and it was the biggest that ever I saw in my life in a Merchant's hands. It was valu'd at 500,000 Roupies, or 750,000 livres of our money: I offer'd 400,000 Roupies, but could not have it.' Professor S. Tolansky believed that this pale pink stone was a ruby (pink sapphire), because Tavernier referred to it as a stone, not a diamond, and because it probably was a crystal of tabular habit, to judge from Tavernier's diagram of the table-cut stone (Fig. 20.4). The weight of evidence now seems to be towards the pink diamond theory.

The Darya-i-Nûr, belonging to the Nawab of Dacca and reputed to be of almost square cut and about 150 carats in weight, was offered for sale in 1955. It is an Indian stone, but has no connection with the true Darya-i-Nûr.

The Koh-i-Nûr

The Koh-i-Nûr mean the 'Mountain of Light' and has the longest history of all famous diamonds, although not of diamond jewellery (Fig. 1.2). It was known to have been in the possession of the Rajahs of Malwa as long ago as 1304. When the Mogul, Sultan Babur, invaded India two centuries later, it was captured by him and remained in the hands of subsequent Mogul emperors. It is believed to have been set in the famous Peacock Throne, constructed under the commands of Shah Jehan and Aurungzeb, as one of the peacock's eyes. The other eye was the Akbar Shah diamond (q.v.).

Nadir Shah of Persia invaded North-west India in 1739, as already mentioned, and took the throne. It is related that when he first saw the diamond, he exclaimed 'Koh-i-Nûr', by which name the diamond subsequently became known. There is another story that the Persian Shah received the Mogul emperor, Mohammed Shah, knowing that the Mogul had hidden the Koh-i-Nûr in his turban. He offered to exchange turbans and the Mogul was unable to refuse.

After the death of Nadir Shah, his empire broke up, and in some way the diamond was returned to India and came into the hands of Ranjit Singh, 'the Lion of the Punjab', in 1833. It is not known how the stone arrived in India, but one story is that an Afghan soldier of Nadir Shah's bodyguard took it when the Shah was murdered and fled with the stone to Afghanistan, where ultimately he became Amir of Afghanistan. A later Amir, Shah Shuja, is supposed to have fled the country during upheavals in 1809 and to have offered the stone to the Lion of the Punjab in exchange for military help. The Lion accepted the stone, then refused his help. The stone was put in the treasure house in Lahore and when trouble broke out between the Sikhs and the British, which resulted in the Sikh wars in in the Punjab, the diamond was taken by the East India Company in partial indemnity against their losses. It was eventually presented to Queen Victoria in 1850 at a levée to mark the 250th anniversary of the founding of the East India Company by Queen Elizabeth I.

There was disappointment at the lack of brilliance of the famed diamond when it arrived in London and was put on public show at the Great Exhibition in Hyde Park in 1851, and the Queen decided to have it recut (Fig. 1.2). In 1862, the work was carried out in 38 days by Mr. Foorsanger, and Mr. J. A. Fedder, who came from the Coster cutting works in Amsterdam to repolish the stone on the premises of Garrard's, the Crown Jewellers in Panton Street, London. The original weight of the stone in the partly cut form in which it came from India was 186 carats and when recut, 108·93 carats. What it weighed in the rough is unknown.

The Queen first wore the stone in a brooch. After she died it was set in the centre of the State Crown, which was worn by Queen Alexandra, and then Queen Mary. In 1937, it was set in the front of the circlet of the Crown, below the 'Black Prince's Ruby' (a spinel), for the coronation of Queen Elizabeth, the Queen Mother. The Crown is kept with the other Crown Jewels in the Tower of London.

The Akbar Shah

The Akbar Shah diamond, supposed to have been one of the eyes of the Peacock Throne, was named after the grandfather of Shah Jehan. It was one of the stones looted from Delhi in 1739. It indicated that the Indians knew at an early time how to engrave diamonds, because it bore the names of both rulers in Arabic characters.

During the first half of the eighteenth century, it disappeared and did not turn up again until it was recognized by the inscription on it Constantinople in 1866. It had been renamed the 'Shepherd Stone', and was bought by George Blogg, an English merchant, who had it recut in London, reducing its weight from 116 carats to 71·70 carats and, of course, polishing off the inscription. In its new drop shape, it was sold to the Gaekwar of Baroda for about £35,000 in 1867.

The Orloff

The Orloff is thought to have weighed about 300 carats when it was found in the Kollur mines, near Golconda, in India, at the beginning of the seventeenth century (Fig. 20.5). It is another stone that is said to have been in the Mogul's treasure house and to have been carried off by the Persians in 1739. At one time, it was confused with the Great Mogul (q.v.) and the Darya-i-Nûr (q.v.) but the Orloff is now known to exist in the Diamond Treasury of the U.S.S.R. in Moscow. The Darya-i-Nûr is among the Iranian Crown Jewels. It may be, however, that the Orloff and Great Mogul are the same stone, both having a pale bluish tinge.

One tale told is that the Orloff was set as the eye of the god, Sri-Ranga, in a Brahmin temple at Srirangem, in Trichinopoly in Southern India; and that it was stolen by a French soldier, who had deserted after fighting in the Carnatic wars and disguised himself as a Hindu. He is said to have sold the stone to an English captain in Madras, who in turn sold it to a Persian merchant in London, who took it to Amsterdam. There, in 1774, it was sold to Prince Gregory Orloff. His object was to reinstate himself with Catherine the Great of Russia, who at one time had considered marrying him, but had been turned against him by his enemies.

His gift to her of the diamond made things worse for him. She accepted this half egg-shaped stone of exceptional quality for which the Prince paid over £100, then continued to spurn him. She had the stone set in the Imperial Sceptre, according to the story.

Fig. 20.5. *A model of the Orloff, one of the world's most historic diamonds, which is in the Diamond Treasury of the U.S.S.R.*

The Black Orloff

There is one black diamond with a history, the Black Orloff (Fig. 1.18), also, known as the Eye of Brahma. It weighed 195 old carats in the rough, 67·50 metric carats polished, and is one of the few black diamonds that did not come from Brazil, its origin having been in India. It is reputed to have been stolen from a shrine in Pondicherry, which was in French India. Eventually it came into the possession of Princess Nadia Vyegin-Orloff of Russia and more recently to that of Mr Charles F. Winson, of New York. Its value was put at £150,000.

The **Black Star of Africa** is another and larger stone, at 202 carats polished which is not from Brazil. It was shown in Tokyo in 1971 at an exhibition of, Belgian gems and valued at $1,200,000 U.S. The 55·85 carat **Amsterdam** was bought at boart price, although its cutting cost 10,000 guilders.

The Idol's Eye

There is a stone known as the Idol's Eye, which came from the Indian diggings at some time in the early seventeenth century. In 1607 it belonged to the Persian, Prince Rahab. The East India Company seized it from him in compensation for a debt he had not honoured. When the stone reappeared about three hundred years later in 1906, it was in the possession of Abdul Hamid II, Sultan of Turkey. One story is that his predecessor received it as ransom for Princess Rasheetah, whom he had abducted from the Sheikh of Kashmir.

At some point, the diamond was set in the eye of an idol in the sacred temple of Benghazi. It is a flattened pear shape, the size of a bantam's egg, and apparently is a true blue-white, being of the finest white with a light blue tint (Fig. 20.6). Its polished size is 70·20 carats and its rough size unknown. The diamond was stolen from the idol's eye by a servant and the story is that the Sultan and his first minister planned the theft to sell the diamond, with others, in France. The object was to transfer money, as the regime was tottering, but the servant double-crossed them. It sounds unlikely. In any event, the diamond was bought in 1906 by a Spanish nobleman who kept it in a London bank for several years.

In 1947, the Idol's Eye was purchased by the New York dealer, Mr. Harry Winston, who sold it privately. In 1962, Mr. Harry Levinson, a Chicago jeweller, bought it and in 1968 it came up for sale once more.

Fig. 20.6. *The Idol's Eye, as it is now set as a pendant to a diamond necklace.*

The Mazarin Diamonds

The Italian Cardinal Mazarin (1602–1661) was one of the greatest collectors of diamonds. He was one of Tavernier's best customers and owned a number of famous stones, including the Sancy (q.v.) and the Mirror of Portugal (q.v.). His position in France was extremely powerful. Louis XIV was not five years old when his father died so, during the long Regency, the Queen Mother and her minister, who was Cardinal Mazarin, shared power.

In 1649, the French Crown Jewels were pledged to the Colonels of the Swiss Regiments to pay the Swiss troops from the Cantons, who were the traditional mercenaries for the French. There were many difficulties over paying and in

1652, a year after Louis XIV had come of age and acceded to the throne, three Captains of the Three Companies succeeded in carrying off the French Crown Jewels to Geneva. Cardinal Mazarin adopted all kinds of devices to recover the jewels without success and it was not until 1665 that the debt was finally paid off and the jewels returned.

When he died, Mazarin left the Sancy and the Mirror of Portugal, together with sixteen other diamonds, to the French crown with the agreement that they were to be known as 'The Mazarin Diamonds'. It is likely that King Louis XIV owed his own great love of diamonds to the Cardinal. The Cardinal also left a spray of 50 diamonds to the Queen, and a big circular diamond, the Rose d'Angleterre which was a 14 carat rose-cut stone, to Anne of Austria. When the French Revolutionary government revalued the Mazarin diamonds in their inventory of 1791, all but one of them, number 12, were given different weights. Some, including the Sancy and Mirror of Portugal, were weighed more or less accurately, it is supposed, but it seems that the other sixteen were recut, some more than once.

The Mazarins were among the stones stolen from the Garde-Meuble during the Revolution and only five were recovered. Subsequently the Sancy turned up. All are difficult to identify positively and that in the Louvre, described as 'Mazarin No. 8', does not correspond in weight or colour with earlier descriptions, according to Lord Twining.*

The Mazarin Cut

An early diamond of cushion-shape with 17 table facets (including the table itself) and 17 pavilion facets (including the culet at the bottom) was known as the 'Mazarin cut'. According to Mr. Herbert Tillander of Helsinki,† who has carried out research on the history of cutting, the Mazarin cut was introduced around the year 1620, before the era of Cardinal Mazarin, and indeed before the English star-cut and English square-cut were introduced (see Chapter 10).

Mr. Tillander quotes a letter from a member of the French Academy to Madame de Thermes in 1644 as the source of the error. It states: 'The Cardinal has demanded a cut with 16 facets above and 16 below the girdle; he makes a triumph of this double cut.' (The table and culet were not included in the count.) The most likely possibility is that the cut was ascribed to the Cardinal because he became famous for his collection of diamonds.

The Mirror of Portugal

The Mirror of Portugal's weight in the rough is unknown. When cut, it weighed 30 carats. Its first recorded owner was Antonio de Castro, who was defeated by Philip II of Spain in his attempt to claim the throne of Portugal, which was vacant. He escaped to London with the diamonds of the Portuguese Crown, which Queen Elizabeth I accepted in return for offering to aid him. One of the diamonds was the Mirror of Portugal. Meanwhile Dom Antonio was condemned to death in his absence.

---

* *A History of the Crown Jewels of Europe* by Lord Twining, London 1960.
† Lecture to Gemmological Association of Great Britain, April 1965.

The Mirror of Portugal remained with the English Crown Jewels until the Civil War when, in 1644, Queen Henrietta Maria took some of them to France to enlist aid for the Royalist cause. Among jewels she gave as security for a loan from the Duke of Épernon was the Mirror of Portugal. She was unable to repay the loan and the Duke kept the diamond as a forfeit, later selling it to Cardinal Mazarin who left it to King Louis XIV when he died. It was stolen in 1792 with the French Crown Jewels during the Revolution and no trace of it has been found since.

The Sancy

The Sancy or Great Sancy diamond has had one of the strangest and most involved histories of all. Its original weight when found probably in India, is unknown, but when cut it was pear-shaped and weighed 55 carats. Charles the Bold, Duke of Burgundy, lost a diamond said to have been the Sancy on the battlefield in 1477, but according to Lord Twining this story was put about by someone trying to flatter the king as the possessor of the great historical diamond. Another story is that the stone he lost was the yellow Florentine.

The Sancy was named after Nicholas Harlay, Seigneur de Sancy, who was the French Ambassador in Turkey and who owned it in 1593, having bought it in Constantinople. He took it to France, and apparently the young king, Henry III, wore it on a cap with which he concealed his baldness. King Henry IV borrowed the stone from Sancy, who by then had become France's Superintendent of Finance, in order to pledge it to raise money to hire mercenary soldiers. After the stone was returned, Sancy's brother, who was Ambassador to England, sold it in 1604 to the new king of England, James I, whose inventory described it as '1 fair diamond cut in facets bought of Sancy'. It is, in fact, of fine colour and is faceted on both sides.

After his downfall in 1688, James II took refuge in St Germain, near Paris, and carried the Sancy with him, which he eventually sold to King Louis XIV of France for £25,000. During the French Revolution, the Sancy was one of the diamonds stolen from the Garde-Meuble, which was a museum as well as a furniture store.

The Great Crown Jewels Robbery

At the height of the French Revolution, some crowns and ornaments had been melted down and lesser 'frightful souvenirs of the former kings' destroyed. Precious objects that remained were put on show for the public in the Garde-Meuble. The Crown Jewels were kept in glass cases in a room on the first floor. Theirry, who was in charge of the treasury, realized that the security precautions were very poor and had the jewels placed in eight boxes which were locked in a heavy commode with a secret lock. The Sancy, the Regent, the pearls, as well as other gems, were in one box. Unset diamonds and the rest went in the other boxes. Later the Crown Jewels were placed in eleven cabinets.

After King Louis was arrested, the Minister of the Interior proposed the sale of the Crown Jewels to raise money to back the paper currency. This was on 16 August 1792. The previous year, the jewels had been valued at nearly 30,000,000 francs. On 17 September 1792, however, it was discovered that thieves had broken into the Garde-Meuble during the previous night and carried off almost all the jewels. Only about 5,000 francs' worth remained.

The theft became entangled with politics and various people, including Marie Antoinette, were accused of instigating it, so the truth has remained obscure. At the time of the robbery, a man named Sergent was in charge of the treasury, Thierry having been killed in the massacre about a fortnight earlier. Sergent was arrested and taken to the Avenue Montaigne where apparently, after his eyes were bandaged, he pointed to the foot of a tree. The ground was excavated and a large part of the Crown Jewels unearthed. Many famous stones were missing, however. The Regent was later discovered in an attic, but the Sancy, the Mirror of Portugal, the Blue Tavernier Diamond, the Côte de Bretagne, and all but five of the Mazarin diamonds were not recovered.

Of the missing diamonds, the Mirror of Portugal completely disappeared and is still missing today. The Blue Tavernier Diamond, according to Lord Twining, was eventually cut into three stones, the largest of which, weighing 44·50 carats, is believed to be what is now called the Hope (q.v.). The second biggest, at 13·75 carats, was eventually sold by the Duke of Brunswick in 1874 in Geneva for 17,000 Swiss francs; and the third, weighing 1·74 carats, was bought by a firm of Paris jewellers in 1862 and sold two years later to Edwin W. Streeter, the Bond Street jeweller of London.

The Côte de Bretagne was for a time in Hamburg, but somehow eventually came into the possession of Louis XVIII and is now in the Louvre.

The True Sancy

The Sancy turned up again many years later in 1828, when a French merchant sold it to a member of the Russian house of Demidoff, but it is said to have been identified in Spain in 1809. In 1865, it went to India, having been purchased for £20,000 by Sir Jamsetjee Jeejeebhoy, but shortly afterwards was sold to a firm of Paris jewellers and was shown at the Paris Exhibition of 1876 by a French jeweller, G. Bapst, and priced at 1,000,000 francs.

A diamond owned by the Maharaja of Patiala is said to be the Sancy but, although pear-shaped, its measurements are not in accordance with earlier records and the diamond thought most likely to be the original Sancy is that bought in 1906 by William Waldorf Astor, who became the first Viscount Astor. He bought it as a wedding present for his son, whose wife, Nancy Lady Astor, used to wear it in a tiara on state occasions. After her death in 1964, it passed to her son the 3rd Viscount Astor. It was on show in Paris in 1962 in the Ten Centuries of French Jewellery Exhibition at the Louvre.

The Regent

The Regent is a truly historic diamond of which the history is reasonably well known. When discovered in 1701 by an Indian slave in the Partial Mine on the Kistna River, near Golconda, it weighed 410 carats, and was one of the last big diamonds to be found in India.

The story of the slave has an element of romance, and is difficult to authenticate. He is supposed to have hidden the crystal in the bandages around a self-inflicted wound. He escaped and found his way to the coast where he exchanged half the value of the stone for a passage to a country where he would be free. The offer was made to an English sea captain, who accepted it and later murdered the slave to gain possession of the diamond. The story ends neatly, for the captain is supposed to have sold the diamond to an Indian merchant and squandered the proceeds on liquor, eventually to hang himself in a fit of delirium tremens and remorse.

Whatever happened, the stone was sold for £20,400 in 1702 to Thomas Pitt, Governor of Madras, and grandfather of the famous William Pitt, the British Prime Minister after whom Pittsburgh, Pennsylvania, in North America, was named. Pitt took it to England and had it cut into a cushion-shaped brilliant of 140·50 carats, which was named 'The Pitt' (Fig. 1.3).

Cutting the rough crystal took two years, much of the time being taken by the process of sawing with a wire and diamond dust. The large stone that resulted is said to be one of the finest of all large diamonds in quality, having only one small imperfection, and one of the most brilliant. Several smaller parts of the crystal were rose-cut and sold to Peter the Great of Russia.

The main stone was sold by Pitt in 1717 for £135,000 to the Duke of Orleans, Regent of France when Louis XV was a boy, and it was then renamed 'The Regent'. It was set in the crown that Louis XV wore at his coronation in 1772. Later Marie Antoinette, Queen of King Louis XVI, wore it in her jewellery.

On the night of 17 September 1792, early in the French Revolution, the French Crown Jewels were stolen (see page 456). Some of the treasures were recovered soon after the robbery, but not the Regent, which came to light fifteen months later in a hole in a beam of a Paris garret.

During the Directoire in France, the five Directors of the Committee for Public Safety had the State Jewels revalued and used them for various complicated financial transactions to pay the huge cost of maintaining fourteen armies in the field. At one stage the Adjutant-General, who was in charge of army recruitment, pawned certain diamonds, including the Regent, to a Berlin banker for 4,000,000 francs. The Regent was taken to Berlin, but later was redeemed by the French and passed to a Dutchman named Valenberghem as security for a series of loans. The Dutchman displayed the stone at receptions for his friends in Amsterdam, but, after the stone had been returned to France, admitted that only a copy had been on display. The real Regent had been worn all this time by his wife round her neck and out of sight under her bodice.

Napoleon Bonaparte had the Regent diamond set in the hilt of a sword that he carried when he was crowned Emperor of France in 1804. When he went into exile to Elba in 1814, the diamond was taken to the Château de Blois by his second wife, Marie Louise. It was returned later to the French government by her father, Francis I of Austria, however and restored to the French Crown Jewels.

In 1883, many of the French Crown Jewels were sold by auction, but several treasures were preserved, including the Regent diamond, which had been valued in 1791 at about 12,000,000 livres. The jewels that were for sale had been put on display from 20 April to 12 May and the sale took place from then until 23 May, which not only attracted jewellers from all over the world but considerably depressed the world market for diamonds and jewellery, so dealers in general were very much relieved when it was over.

In 1940 when Hitler's armies invaded Paris, the Regent was again hidden, this time in the plaster behind a white marble fireplace in the Château Chambord. It was returned to Paris after the war was over and later the Regent and the Hortensia (q.v.) were put on display in the Louvre.

The Hortensia

The Hortensia (Hydrangea) diamond, a 20-carat, five-sided stone of fine pink colour, was originally purchased by Tavernier in India and sold to Louis XIV in 1669. It was one of the stones reserved before the sale of some of the French Crown Jewels in 1883.

The Hope

The Hope is supposed to be a part of the famous Blue Tavernier Diamond found in the Kollur Mine, near Golconda in India, and brought to Europe by the French traveller and stone merchant Tavernier after he had purchased it in 1642 (Fig. 1.4). The Blue Tavernier weighed about 112 carats in the rough and was of a fine deep blue colour (it was therefore a Type IIb diamond).

In 1668, when he last returned from the East, Tavernier was presented to King Louis XIV, who wished to see his collection of stones for sale. Tavernier sold the King 22 diamonds, including the Blue, which accounted for 220,000 livres of the total bill of 897,731 livres. The stone was officially designated 'The Blue Diamond of the Crown'. It then weighed about 112 carats and had been cut, like most of the others, by Indian lapidaries to give maximum weight. Louis had it recut to bring out the brilliance and the weight was reduced to 67·50 carats.

The Blue diamond was one of those stolen during the French Revolution (q.v.) and never recovered, although one suggestion was that it was divided into three as described on page 457. At any rate a diamond of similar colour, but of 44·50 carats in weight, was offered on the London market in 1830 and was bought for £18,000 by Henry Thomas Hope, a banker and gem collector. It seems likely that this was indeed a part of the Blue diamond in the French Crown Jewels.

It was while the diamond was in the possession of the banker that it became known as the 'Hope', and acquired its gruesome reputation for bad luck. Henry Hope's son lost his fortune after he inherited the stone. In 1908, it came into the hands of Abdul Hamid, the Sultan of Turkey, who paid £80,000 for it or so it was reported.

In 1911, it was sold by Cartier's in Paris to an American widow, Mrs Edward B. McLean of Washington, and according to legend is supposed to have brought tragedy because her only child was killed in an accident, the family broke up and Mrs McLean lost her money and committed suicide. It seems likely that some of the fateful events have been telescoped by legend into the time when she owned the stone.

When her jewels were sold in 1949, the Hope was bought by Harry Winston, the New York diamond merchant. Although he did not believe in the Hope legend, apparently many of his clients did, because they would not touch it when it was shown to them. He often flew the Atlantic safely while carrying the Hope.

Harry Winston presented the Hope Diamond in 1958 to the Smithsonian Institution in Washington, where it is on show to the public with other gems. At the time it was valued at 1,000,000 dollars. It returned to France for a short spell in 1962, when it was exhibited with the Regent, the Sancy, and other famous diamonds in the Ten Centuries of French Jewellery Exhibition.

The Wittelsbach

The Wittelsbach is another of the very few big blue diamonds. It is also known as 'The Great Blue Diamond' and 'The Blue Brilliant', and is oval-shaped in cut, weighing 35·56 carats, about 9 carats less than the Hope. It is an Indian stone and was in the possession of the House of Hapsburg in Austria in 1722.

It gained its name by being part of the bridal treasure of Princess Maria Amelia of Austria, when she married into the Bavarian Royal family of Wittelsbach. However, shortly afterwards, her father-in-law, the Elector Maximilian Emmanuel, pawned it to help finance a war with Hungary. It was redeemed in 1726 by Charles VII for 543,781 florins. In 1761, it was set, with 700 other brilliant-cut stones, in the Order of the Golden Fleece, the highest Hapsburg honour.

After the First World War, the Bavarian Crown possessions were put in a special fund. In 1931, the jewel, without the Golden Fleece which hung from the bottom, was offered for sale at Christie's, but withdrawn when the bidding only reached £5,072 10s. It 'disappeared' until 1962, when it was bought by a syndicate of Belgian firms led by J. Konkommer. A value of £180,000 was placed on it, and two years later, it was sold privately in Germany for a price that was not revealed.

The Florentine

The yellow Florentine is another diamond with a mysterious history. The legend is that it was the diamond lost on the battlefield by Charles the Bold, Duke of Burgundy, when his army was routed at Granson in 1476. A Swiss soldier is supposed to have picked it up, together with a pearl in a box, and thrown it away, thinking it was a piece of glass, but on second thoughts picked it up again. Then, the story goes, he sold the stone to a priest for a florin at Montigny.

Charles the Bold's diamond is more likely to have been another, perhaps one of pyramidal shape said to have been given by Queen Mary I in 1554 to her husband Philip II of Spain, a descendant of Charles the Bold, although Lord Twining claims that it remained among the Crown Jewels of England until 1644, when Queen Henrietta Maria took her jewels to France to raise money for the Royalists during the Civil War.

It is known that the real Florentine belonged to the Medici family, which ruled Tuscany for centuries. The first authentic record of it is that of 1657, when Tavernier saw it among the Treasures of Tuscany and described it as a diamond whose colour ran into citron yellow.

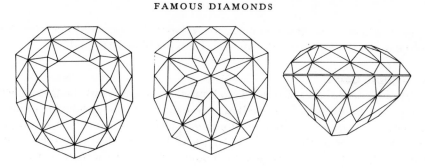

Fig. 20.7. *The Florentine, from a drawing originally published in* The Lapidary Journal, *shown actual size. Its colour was described as citron yellow.*

Through marriage, the stone passed to the Austrian Royal house in 1743 and remained in Vienna among the Austrian Crown Jewels for several generations. After the collapse of the Austrian Empire, it was taken by the Imperial family into exile. When the Germans invaded Austria during the Second World War, they carried off a diamond said to have been the Florentine, which was later reported as having been restored to Vienna by the American authorities, but this was false. The diamond probably disappeared when the last Emperor went into exile.

This stone is 137·27 carats in weight and is cut as a double rose with 126 facets, in an elongated nine-sided outline. It is possible that this is not the Florentine, but another yellow diamond once in the Hapsburg Crown, and known as the 'Austrian Yellow Brilliant'.

Other Famous Diamonds

The Arcot Diamonds

Two pear-shaped diamonds, together weighing 57·35 carats cut, were presented to Queen Charlotte, consort of King George III, by the Nawab of Arcot in 1777. After her death they were sold to the Crown Jewellers, Rundell, Bridge and Co.

In 1837, the first Marquis of Westminster bought them for £11,000; the Nassak diamond (q.v.) for £7,200, and a 32·20 brilliant for £3,500. Later the Arcot diamonds, the brilliant, and 1,421 smaller diamonds were mounted in the Westminster tiara, which was sold at Sotheby's in 1959 for the then world-record price for a piece of jewellery of £110,000.

The Brunswick Blue

A pear-shaped 13·75 carat diamond, dark blue in colour, was sold in Geneva in 1784 with some jewels that had belonged to Charles, the Duke of Brunswick. Its present whereabouts are unknown. At the end of the last century Edwin Streeter, jeweller and author, after examining it, decided that it could have been part of the Blue Tavernier or Blue Diamond of the Crown (q.v.), the other part now being the Hope (q.v.). Mr. Albert Monnickendam, the well-known

Hatton Garden cutter and polisher, has declared that it would not have been possible to recover so large a second stone from the Blue Diamond.

The Grande Condé

A light pink, pear-shaped diamond of about 50 carats, was awarded, along with an estate in Chantilly, to Louis de Bourbon, Prince of Condé, when he became a national hero after he was made commander of the French armies during the Thirty Years War at the age of 21. In 1892, it was bequeathed to the French government, with the provision that it must remain in the Musée Conde in Chantilly, where it is now on display. It is also called the Chantilly Pink.

The Dresden Green

One of the rarest diamonds in the world is the Dresden Green, because of its apple-green colour. Almond-shaped and weighing 40·70 carats, it was bought from a Dutch merchant at the Leipzig Fair in 1742 by Augustus the Strong, Elector of Saxony and King of Poland, and was displayed in the famous Green Vault under the Royal Palace in Dresden from the eighteenth century until the palace was damaged in the Second World War.

This stone and other Saxon treasures were removed to the Saxon Castle, Königstein, on the river Elbe. Afterwards they were found, confiscated, and taken to Russia by the Soviet Trophies Organisation, but the Dresden Green and other treasures have now been returned to the restored vault in Dresden for exhibition. The Vault comprises vaulted rooms decorated in green, but the name is a coincidence.

There is also a **Dresden White**, sometimes called the Saxon White, in the Green Vault. It is the largest in the collection, with a weight of 48·50 carats, and suffered the same fate of the Green during the war, being returned with it in 1945.

Fig. 20.8. *The Briolette of India: a very exceptional 90·83-carat diamond cut as a briolette. It is said to have belonged to Eleanor of Aquitaine and to have formed part of the ransom of her son, Richard I the Lionheart.*

The English Dresden

At 119·50 carats, the English Dresden was the third largest diamond to come from the Bagagem Mine in Brazil. It was found near where another famous stone, the Star of the South (q.v.), had been found four years earlier. It was named after E. H. Dresden, a London merchant, who bought it in Rio de Janeiro and had it cut by Coster of Amsterdam to a drop form of the first water, weighing 76·50 carats. Later it was bought by an English cotton merchant from Bombay, who died after a disastrous fall in cotton prices. It was sold by his executors to the Gaekwar of Baroda, Mahler Rao, who also acquired the Akbar Shah (q.v.), the Star of the South (q.v.), and the Eugenie (q.v.). After he was deposed for gross misgovernment in 1875, his diamond vanished.

The Eugenie

A fine oval-shaped brilliant cut stone of 51 carats, the Eugenie was worn in a hair ornament by Empress Catherine II of Russia. She gave it to Prince Grigory Aleksandrovich Potemkin, from whom it eventually passed to Empress Eugenie, wife of Napoleon III of France, when she wanted a diamond for a wedding present despite having the Crown Jewels to wear. After the Second Empire collapsed, the Empress fled to Chiselhurst in Kent, England, and had her jewels smuggled out of the Tuileries wrapped in newspapers, or so it is related. Later the Eugenie Diamond was sold privately to the notorious Gaekwar of Baroda, but disappeared with other famous diamonds he owned after he was deposed in 1875.

There is a cornflower blue diamond of about 31 carats, now called the **Eugenie Blue** and said to have belonged to the Empress, on show in the Smithsonian Institution, Washington D.C., USA. It is almost certainly the stone called the Blue Heart which Cartier sold in 1911 and Van Cleef showed in a pendant in 1953, according to the Hon. Ian Balfour.

The Eureka

The first stone of any consequence found in South Africa, a 21-carat crystal, found by a Boer boy near the banks of the Orange River in 1866, was named the Eureka (Fig. 2.10). In 1946, it was bought at Christie's Auction Rooms by Mr. Peter Locan, cut to weigh 10·73 carats, and set in a bangle. At The Ageless Diamond exhibition in London in 1959, it was exhibited set in a ring. De Beers Consolidated Mines bought the stone later and exhibited it in 1966 at their Diamond Pavilion in Johannesburg to mark South Africa's Diamond Centenary. It was subsequently presented by them to the South African government.

The Jahangir

A pear-shaped stone of 83 carats, the Jahangir was one of those engraved by Indian lapidaries in Persian characters with the names of the Mogul Emperors, Shah Jahangir (1569–1627) and his son Shah Jehan (1627–1658) (Fig. 1.6). A hole is drilled through the top, by means of which it is believed to have been suspended from the beak of the Mogul's famous Peacock Throne. It belonged at some time to the Maharajah of Burdwan, and then to Mr. Stavros S. Niarchos, the Greek shipowner. Mr. C. Patel now owns it.

The Jonker

A rounded crystal with a cleavage face which weighed 726 carats when it was picked up by a hitherto unlucky digger, Jacobus Jonker, in the alluvial diggings of Elandsfontein, near Pretoria, in 1934. It is considered by many who have studied it to be the finest gem diamond ever discovered.

The Diamond Corporation bought it for £70,000 and it was eventually sold to Mr Harry Winston of New York, for a figure reported to be $700,000. He had it cut into twelve perfect gems, all being emerald-cuts except for one which was marquise, which totalled 358 carats. The largest is an emerald-cut with 58 facets, which at first weighed 142·90 carats, but was subsequently recut to 125·65 carats. King Farouk of Egypt bought it, and at the time it was reputed to be valued at $1,000,000 U.S. At some time at the start his exile in 1952, he sold it to the Himalayan state of Nepal. It is now believed to be privately owned in Japan.

The fourth largest polished stone was sold in 1975 to a South American collector for £276,609.

The Jubilee

Another stone of exceptional whiteness and clarity was the Jubilee, which was made into a faultless cushion-shaped gem of 245·35 carats (Fig. 20.9). In the rough, when discovered in 1895 in the Jagersfontein Mine in South Africa, it was an irregular crystal of approximate octahedral shape weighing 650·80 carats, and was named the 'Reitz' after the President of the Orange Free State. Then it was renamed the 'Jubilee' because it was cut in 1897, Queen Victoria's diamond jubilee year. For some years the Indian industrialist, Sir Dorah Tata, owned it. Later it came into the possession of Mr. Harry Winston and was valued at £714,000. The present owner is M. Paul-Louis Weiller of Paris.

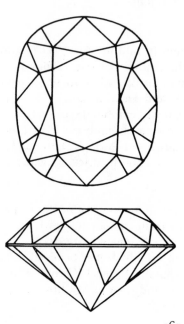

Fig. 20.9.   *The Jubilee, from a drawing originally published in* The Lapidary Journal, *showing its actual size. It is said to be of such perfect cut that it be balanced on its culet; it is also, of exceptional quality.*

Fig. 20.10.   *The Jubilee diamond, weighing 245·35 carats, as set when it was exhibited in the Diamond Pavilion of the Rand Easter Show at Johannesburg in 1966.*

The Kimberley Octahedron

A huge yellow octahedron, well-shaped but not of the best quality, was found by a crusher attendant, Mr. Abel Maretela, at the Dutoitspan mine, Kimberley, on 17 April 1974. Weighing 616 carats, it is the largest octahedron and the ninth largest rough diamond ever found. It is on display in the Old Mines Museum at the Big Hole, Kimberley. Curiously enough, 616 is the mining company's post office box number (See Fig. 1.15).

Dutoitspan is famous for the number of big yellow octahedra found there. One of 253·7 carats, found in 1964, was purchased by Mr. Harry Winston, the famous New York merchant and cutter, and presented to the Smithsonian Institution, Washington D.C., U.S.A. in memory of Sir Ernest Oppenheimer.

The Kimberley

A flawless, champagne-coloured emerald-cut diamond of 50·09 carats was recut in 1921 from a large flat stone in the Russian Crown Jewels, and again recut in 1958 by the present owners, Baumgold Brothers of New York. It is thought to have been found in the Kimberley Mine, and is called the Kimberley, but its weight in the rough is unknown.

The Lesotho Brown

A 601·3-carat diamond of gem quality but with a brownish tinge (Fig. 1.13) found in the diamond diggings at Letseng-la-Draai, near a stream that feeds the Orange River in the mountains of the independent state of Lesotho (formerly Basutoland). It was found by a woman, Mrs Ernestine Ramoboa, in 1967. She is the wife of Petrus Ramoboa, the biggest shareholder in the syndicate of four that owned the claim. The stone was bought by Mr. Eugene Seraphini, a Bloemfontein buyer, for £108,180. It was cut into 18 gems, including two emerald cuts of 71·73 and 69·67 carats, and a 40·42 carat marquise-cut, by Mr. Harry Winston.

The Matan

The Matan is a curious crystal said to weigh 367 carats and to be shaped like a smooth pear. It is thought to have been discovered in the Landak Mines near the west coast of Borneo in 1787, and to have belonged to the Rajah of Matan, but nobody has been allowed to examine it. It may be a rock crystal.

465

The Nassak

The 90-carat Nassak was first known in the temple of the Hindu God Shiva at Nassak (now spelt Nasik) about 100 miles from Bombay. It was sold to raise funds for the local rulers who were fighting the British, but fell into the hands of the East India Company in 1818, who had it valued at £30,000.

The British Crown Jewellers, Rundell, Bridge and Company, bought it and had it recut it to obtain more fire, preserving the triangular shape and sacrificing only 10 carats. The Marquise of Westminster acquired it in 1837 for setting in his dress sword, and after 1927 it was bought by Mr. Harry Winston of New York. He had it recut to a modern emerald-cut of 43·38 carats. It was sold in April 1970, to an American buyer for £500,000.

The Nepal

A pear-shaped cut stone of 79·41 carats, said to have come originally from the Golconda Mines. It remained in India and passed to the royal family of Nepal until it was sold to Mr. Harry Winston in recent years. It was exhibited at The Ageless Diamond Exhibition in London in 1959.

The Niarchos

A 426·5-carat crystal found in the Premier Mine in the Transvaal in 1954 and regarded by the late Sir Ernest Oppenheimer as having the most perfect colour of any diamond he had seen. Mr. Harry Winston bought it and had it cut into a pear-shaped stone with 144 facets weighing 128·25 carats, which cutting took 1,400 hours. It was sold to Mr. Stavros S. Nchiaros, the Greek shipowner, after whom it was named. The crystal yielded two other stones, an emerald-cut of 40 carats and a marquise of 30 carats.

The Nizam

A crystal thought to weigh 340 carats in the rough which was found in the Kollur Mine in the Golconda area and came into the possession of the Nizam of Hyderabad. Little is known of it, but it may have been cut and faceted, irregularly.

The Pasha of Egypt

An octagonal-shaped diamond with a form of brilliant-cut which is of good quality and weighs 40 carats. It was bought in 1848 by the Egyptian general Ibrahim Pasha for £28,000, and is now believed to be in England.

The Paul I

A cushioned-shaped diamond of 13·35 carats which is said to be a delicate pink in shade and very pure. It was named after Tzar Paul I, son of Catherine the Great, and is now in the Russian Treasury of Diamonds and Precious Stones. It is mounted with a foil back as the centre stone of a diamond diadem.

The Piggott or Pigot

An oval-shaped stone of fine quality, reputed to have weighed 40 carats, which was given to Lord Pigot, Governor of Madras, by an Indian Prince. Pigot brought it to England in 1775. After his death it changed hands a number of times; once, it is said, as the result of a lottery. Ali Pasha, the ruler of Albania, owned it when he was mortally wounded in a dispute in 1822 with the Sultan of Turkey. He is supposed to have told a soldier to shatter the stone before his eyes, but there is no evidence of this order having been carried out, although today the diamond is missing.

The Polar Star

A 40-carat brilliant-cut gem said to have belonged to Joseph Bonaparte, the eldest brother of Napoleon. In the 1820s, it went to Russia, and was in the family of Prince Youssoupoff for over a century. It now belongs to Lady Deterding.

The Porter-Rhodes

A stone named after the owner of the claim in the Kimberley Mine where it was found in 1880. It was a 153·5 octahedron of exceptional colour and quality. The stone was presented to Queen Victoria at Osborne House in the Isle of Wight, who at first doubted its African origin because it was thought that stones of the best colour came only from Brazil. It was exhibited in London and valued at £60,000. Later it was emerald-cut to 56·60 carats. Believed to be in India.

The President Vargas

A flat crystal of 726·6 carats found in 1938 in the alluvial gravels of the San Antonio River in Minas Gerais, Brazil, and which was named after the President. It is of the purest water except for a faint yellowish tinge on two edges. It was bought in 1939 by Mr. Harry Winston for about $600,000, who later had it cut into 23 stones. Eight were emerald-cuts. The name 'President Vargas' was adopted for the largest stone of 48·26 carats.

The Red Cross

Christies sold a polished yellow diamond of 205·07 carats at Geneva in November 1973. It was the Red Cross (Fig. 20.11), so-called because it had been presented in 1918 by the London diamond syndicate to the British Red Cross and Order of St John of Jerusalem. Most appropriately, the diamond has a pattern of inclusions which, when seen through the table, looks like a Maltese cross.

Fig. 20.11. *The Red Cross, a yellow diamond with an unusual Maltese cross inclusion, as photographed for the Christie's sale in Geneva in November 1973.*

The Shah

An Indian partly-polished stone of 88·70 carats that was engraved with three names. The first is of a native prince in the Mohammedan year 1000 (1591 A.D.), the second indicated that it was among Shah Jehan's treasures and was attached to the Peacock Throne, and the third, dated 1824, shows it belonged to the Shah of Persia, probably after the Persians robbed Delhi of its treasures in 1739. After a mob stormed the Russian Embassy in Tehran in 1829, killing the Ambassador, the Persians sent the diamond to Russia in appeasement. It is now in the Kremlin.

The Shah of Persia

Another stone carried off by the Persian Nadir Shah after the sack of Delhi in 1739 and named after him. After the First World War it is said to have been given to the Russian military expert, General Strosselky, who helped the Persians. He then took it to the U.S.A. It is a yellow cushion-shaped stone of 99·52 carats in its cut form and was mounted in a diamond pendant brooch when it was bought by Mr. Harry Winston, the New York diamond merchant, in 1957.

The Star of Este

An Indian stone of 26·16 carats and of fine quality that belonged to the Italian family of Este. Through marriage it became a part of the Austrian Royal Family's gems. The present Archduke Otto, son of the last Royal ruler of Austria, Emperor Charles I, has said that many family jewels were stolen in 1922, but did not refer specifically to the diamond. A stone of similar description was sold to King Farouk of Egypt in 1950.

The Star of Sierra Leone

The third largest rough diamond ever discovered was picked out of the separator plant at the Diminco mine at Yengema, 300 miles south-east of Freetown in Sierra Leone by the engineer in charge, Sierra Leonean Mr. E. O. Williams, on 14 February 1972, St Valentine's Day. The weight is 968·9 carats (Fig. 1.14) and it was named the Star of Sierra Leone.

The stone was offered in London for £1,000,000. Some cutters who examined it were dubious about obtaining very big stones from it, because of the inclusions. It was thought that one orange-coloured spot near the tip might be a garnet but turned out, when the stone was cut, to be iron. Mr. Harry Winston of New York bought it for an undisclosed price and managed to recover 34 per cent of the material, compared with 37 per cent for the Excelsior (q.v.). The main polished stones made were an emerald-cut of 143·20 carats (it was flawed, so was later recut to a flawless 32.52 carat stone), a pear-cut of 53·96 carats, an emerald-cut of 30·15 carats, a marquise of 27·34 carats, an emerald-cut of 23·01 carats, and a pear-cut of 22·27 carats.

There is a curious little story attached to the need for producing a number of models of the rough relatively quickly. The author was asked if he knew of someone who could mould some in hard plastics instead of having models cut in quartz or modelled in glass. By chance, his plastics-bodied car had just been damaged by another car belonging to an employee of a firm that specialized in plastics models, and who turned out to have the right knowledge for the task.

The Star of South Africa or the Dudley

This was the stone that started the South African diamond rush. It was picked up by a Griqua shepherd-boy on the farm Zendfontein near the Orange River in 1869. The story is told on page 36. The rough weighed 83·50 carats and was bought by a cutter, Louis Hond, and three associates, who fashioned it into a three-sided oval brilliant of the finest colour and lustre (Fig. 2.12). It was sold for £30,000 to the Countess of Dudley, and made into a hair ornament. It came up for sale in April 1974 and fetched £225,300.

The Star of the South

One of the two big diamonds found by a woman, a negress working in the Bagagem Mines in Brazil. She found the 261·88 carat crystal in 1853 and was rewarded by being given her freedom and a life pension. It was cut by Voorsanger of the firm of Coster, Amsterdam into an oval stone of 128·80 carats. After it was shown at the London Exhibition of 1862 and the Paris Exhibition of 1867, the Gaekwar of Baroda paid £80,000 for it. It was later sold to Rustomjee Jamsetjee of Bombay.

The Sterns

On 15 October 1973, Mr. Andrew Moraldi, a crusher attendant at the Dutoitspan Mine, Kimberley, picked up a large yellow octahedron under the crusher box under the shaft head. It weighed 223·6 carats and was bought by the Sterns Diamond Organization and by the firm of Kagan. The largest stone recovered, brilliant-cut and weighing 85·93 carats is called the Sterns Star (Fig. 20.12).

Fig. 20.12. *The 223·6-carat yellow octahedron which was picked up in the recovery plant of the Dutoitspan Mine in 1973. The Stern Star was later cut from it.*

The Stewart

A 296-carat stone found in the Vaal River diggings, South Africa, in 1872, and for a long time the biggest alluvial diamond ever discovered. A merchant named Stewart in Port Elizabeth, S.A., bought it for £6,000 and sold it for £9,000. It was slightly yellow, but cut into a fine 123-carat brilliant-cut stone. Where it is now is not known.

The Taj-e-Mah

The name means 'Crown of the Moon'. The stone is said to be of the finest colour and is rose-cut. It was taken from the Moguls by the Persians after the sack of Delhi in 1739. It and the Darya-i-Nûr (q.v.) were once set in a pair of bracelets. The 115·06 carat Taj-e-Mah is rose-cut and is among the Iranian Crown jewels.

The Tiffany

A golden-coloured diamond found in the Kimberley mine in 1878 and bought by Tiffany and Company, New York. The 287·42-carat crystal was cut in Paris into a cushion-shaped gem of 92 facets, 41 of them including the table being on top. At 128·51 carats, it is the largest golden-yellow in existence.

The Victoria

A stone of 469 carats found in the Jagersfontein Mine in 1884; it is also called 'The Imperial' and 'The Great White'. It was cut in Amsterdam into two brilliants, an oval stone of 184·50 carats, and a circular stone of 20 carats.

The Williamson

A rose-coloured stone found in the Williamson Mine, in Mwadui, Tanzania, and presented by Dr. John T. Williams to Queen Elizabeth II on her wedding in 1947. The 54·50-carat crystal was cut in London by Briefel and Lemer and became a round brilliant-cut gem of 23·60 carats. It is one of the finest in the world for its quality and unusual colour, and is mounted in a jonquil-shaped brooch.

The Woyie River

A 770-carat crystal which is probably the largest ever found in an alluvial digging. It came from the Woyie River in Sierra Leone in 1945 and was cut in London by Briefel and Lemer into thirty stones, the largest of which was an emerald-cut gem of 31·35 carats. Other large crystals have come from the same gravels, a 532-carat one in 1943 and a 249·25 carat one in 1945.

The Queen's Necklace

The notorious 'affair of the Queen's necklace', although it concerns famous diamond jewellery rather than famous diamonds, deserves to be recorded here. Marie Antoinette, Queen of Louis XVI of France, was fond of having diamonds and other gems from the Crown Jewels removed from their settings and frequently reset in different forms. Nevertheless, when the Crown Jewellers, Boehmer and Bassenge, spent most of their funds – 1,160,000 livres – to make a necklace from the finest diamonds then on the market, she refused several times to buy it.

The French Ambassador in Vienna, Cardinal Rohan, had earned Marie Antoinette's displeasure when he complained about her frivolous conduct to her mother, the Empress Maria Theresa. When he returned to Paris, he planned to become Prime Minister by currying favour in court. He met by chance an adventuress, who called herself the Countess de la Motte, and who claimed she had influence with the Queen. The Crown Jewellers had also been persuaded by her that she could persuade the Queen to buy the necklace.

In 1785 the so-called Countess told the jewellers that the Queen had agreed, but an important person was required to negotiate the price. Cardinal Rohan is said to have done this, a figure of 1,600,000 livres payable by instalments having been agreed. He was to hand over the necklace to a man described as a valet of the Queen. When, however, the jewellers asked the Queen for the first instalment of the money, she declared that she had not ordered or received the necklace.

When the whole court was assembled, the Captain of the Guard was instructed to arrest the Cardinal, who was dressed in his robes and surrounded by priests. In the trial that followed, the Cardinal was acquitted, but the Queen became very unpopular because it was thought that she had used the Countess to vent her hate on the Cardinal.

The Countess was sentenced to be branded, whipped and shut up in the Salpetrière, but later she escaped. Meanwhile the 'Count de la Motte' (presumed to have played the part of the valuer) had slipped away to England with the necklace, which was broken up and the stones sold.

The Premier Rose

Potentially famous stones are still being found and polished, one while this edition was being put to press. A 353·9 carat stone of exceptional colour and quality was picked out of mined kimberlite at 1,500 ft (460m) in the underground workings of the Premier Mine in 1978, thus being saved from being broken in the crusher. It was named the Premier Rose after Mrs Rose Mouw, who marked it for sawing and cutting. The larger of the two pieces into which it was sawn over a period of about six weeks by the firm of Mouw in Johannesburg, was about 270 carats, and the smaller about 80. These were again divided to provide five polished stones with a recovery rate of about 40-45%. The largest stone was a pear expected to weigh 120 carats.

Readers interested in celebrated diamonds are referred to *The Diamond Dictionary*, and to *Diamonds, Famous, Notable and Unique* published by the Gemological Institute of America, as well as to *Famous Diamonds* by Ian Balfour, published by De Beers Consolidated Mines Ltd.

CHAPTER TWENTY-ONE

Identification of Diamond

Examination by Eye

People who handle diamond crystals regularly and frequently can recognize them on sight. Those who handle polished diamonds as often can also recognize them without difficulty and are certain enough to pay extremely high prices without even considering an identification test. Nevertheless, even an experienced jeweller can make a mistake, especially when the stone is set.

Bad light conditions, an expensive setting for a fine simulant, a new simulant to the jeweller, having to make a judgement in a hurry or under unfavourable conditions, all can cause a temporary loss of skill in identification. A clever confidence trickster can be responsible for creating such conditions. Even without the atmosphere, the rare diamond doublet or the new simulant, zirconium oxide (also called cubic zirconium), in an old cut may deceive even a wary jeweller.

What are the characteristics that make a diamond recognizable by eye? First is its adamantine lustre. On no other material can such a high surface finish be produced. This polish, the high reflectivity and the exceptional flatness of facets produce surfaces in which undistorted reflections may be seen. By tilting a stone, a good reflection of, say, an electric light bulb or window frame, will appear in the table.

The low critical angle of diamond – 24·5° – means that a brilliant-cut stone reflects back most of the light entering from the front. It is therefore impossible to look right through a properly fashioned *modern* brilliant-cut diamond from the top and see what is below it. Only through the culet, if large enough, would anything be visible. If a loose brilliant-cut diamond is held up to the light in a pair of tongs and looked at with the naked eye from the crown side, the stone will appear black except a pinpoint of light through the culet. The less accurate the brilliant-cut, the more likely are there to be windows or areas of light, so this is also a rough check for accuracy of cut.

It is, of course, possible to look *into* a diamond. Whether the stone is set or loose, it will be noticed that it appears shallower than in fact it is, when the back facet edges are examined through the table. The cause is the high refractive index. Simulants with lower refractive indices, particularly colourless quartz, paste (glass), topaz, synthetic spinel, and white sapphire (synthetic or natural) do not foreshorten to such a marked degree.

The 'Tilt Test'

The high refractive index of diamond makes possible a simple test, even when mounted, to distinguish it quickly from simulants with lower R.I.s, such as Y.A.G. and paste. If a brilliant-cut diamond is held with its table horizontal

Fig. 21.1. *The 'tilt test' photographed by Alan Hodgkinson. Every stone is tilted away from the eye. Stones are in order of increasing refraction: Top, synthetic spinel; second row, Y.A.G. and zircon; third row, G.G.G., zirconium and strontium titanate; bottom, diamond and synthetic rutile.*

below one's eyes and tilted away from the body, it will still remain brilliant; but if this 'tilt test', as it is referred to, is carried out on brilliant-cut stones of lower R.I., such as YAG or paste, the light will appear to empty itself from the stone. i.e. there will be a dark area on the far side of the table (Fig. 21.1). The stones, the diamond in particular, must be clean at the back, to avoid light leakage. Diamond's affinity for grease means that a stone in a ring should be frequently cleaned at the back.

Transparency

The greater apparent transparency of stones other than diamond, is a strong clue to their nature when examined unset, but more care must be taken when they are set. For example, it is possible to see newsprint through a loose colourless synthetic spinel placed on a newspaper table down, but not through a diamond, as shown in Fig. 21.2. But to disguise the transparency of synthetic spinels they are often backed with a reflecting surface, which may not be apparent after they are set. so that it is impossible to see through them. The expression 'apparent transparency' is used because diamond is in fact an exceptionally transparent material as may be noted when examining a portrait stone, which is thin with parallel faces. The transparency can be deceiving.

Confusion is also possible with old cuts of diamond in which full advantage of the low critical angle was not taken in cutting. Someone who has handled only modern brilliant-cut stones may be puzzled by some old mine stones, which, when set in antique jewellery, look like old or poor paste at first sight because of their low brilliance, apparent lack of fire, and generally 'dirty' appearance. Others which have not suffered from wear and have their original sharp edges,

Fig. 21.2. *A diamond and synthetic spinel* (right) *table down on a pen line.*

and which were well polished originally, will appear to be unnaturally clear or transparent for diamonds. The large culet and the facet edges will be immediately apparent to the naked eye through the table. This results from the larger angle of the pavilion facets which allows light to escape through the back of the stone. When unset, such a stone held up to the light will let much through.

Windows are not uncommonly left by cutters wishing to preserve the weight of emerald and square-cut diamonds, so the cut stones have lower brilliance and fire and more apparent transparency. However, the lustre and other features detectable by eye will reveal them as diamonds.

Quick Guides to Identification

Diamond has much higher thermal conductivity than any other gems so that it is colder to the touch and also becomes warm more quickly, when worn. If therefore a loose stone or diamond jewellery is left to attain room temperature and then touched, it will feel quite cold. Loose stones may be picked up with tongs, also at room temperature, or the jewellery by hand, and the stone touched on the lip or other sensitive parts of the face. Paste will feel relatively warm.

Breath Test, 'Sticky' Test, Water Test

Another simple way of identifying diamond from its simulants, using thermal conductivity, is to place the suspect stone with a known diamond and to breathe on them. The mist will clear sooner from a diamond than from its simulants. Again both stones should start at room temperature.

Diamond sorters and graders often pick up the smaller loose stones with a damp finger, moistened on the lip. This cannot be done with many other stones and is a useful guide, failing a more reliable method of checking. Simulants will drop off the finger much more quickly.

There is a different 'feel' also to some stones. For example, quartz (rock crystal) is quite tacky to a finger moved lightly across it, compared with diamond and sapphire.

If the top surface of a diamond is thoroughly clean and free of grease, a drop of water on the table will remain as a globule for a long time whereas on the tables of other stones the globule will spread in a relatively short time, depending on the mineral. Another guide test, of reflectivity, is given on page 484.

Refractive Index

If a diamond, mounted or unmounted, is put in a white cup containing a highly refractive liquid, its outline will still be visible, whereas *some* stones used to simulate diamond tend to become less visible. This simple test will only prove that a stone is *not* diamond. The safest method is to place a known diamond in the liquid with the stone being examined and to compare them (Figs. 21.3 and 21.4).

Suitable liquids are monobromonaphthalene (R.I. 1·66) commonly used in

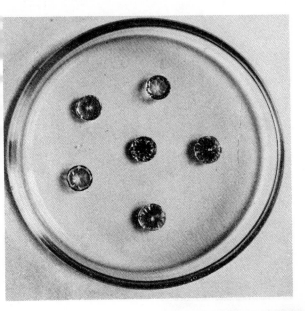

Fig. 21.3. *Stones in a cell, with diamond in the centre and, from 12 o'clock, strontium titanate (Fabulite), synthetic rutile, zircon, synthetic white spinel, and paste.*

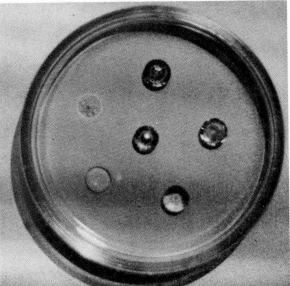

Fig. 21.4. *The cell above filled with monobromonaphthalene (R.I. 1.66). The synthetic white spinel and paste have almost disappeared and the zircon is more transparent. The diamond in the centre, as well as the strontium titanate at the top and the zircon next to it are still clearly visible. Synthetic white sapphires also tend to disappear.*

microscope work, and the standard heavy liquids methylene iodide (1·74), and bromoform (1·59). Benzene (1·50) can be used also, although lower in R.I. than the others.

If a suspect stone is immersed in a white porcelain cell, or a glass one standing on white paper, the diamonds will stand out in high relief while stones of lower R.I. will tend to disappear (Fig. 21.4). It must be noted, however, that certain substitutes including sphene, zircon, strontium titanate, yttrium aluminate

Fig. 21.5. *The print* (right) *was exposed with bromide paper under the dish of stones, the dish being empty. For the second exposure* (below), *the dish was filled with a solution of monobromonaphthalene (R.I. 1.66) to cover the stones. The phenacite (3), with an R.I. almost the same as liquid, has almost disappeared. (Photos E. Bruton).*

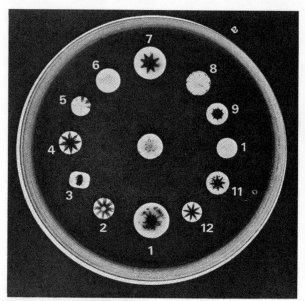

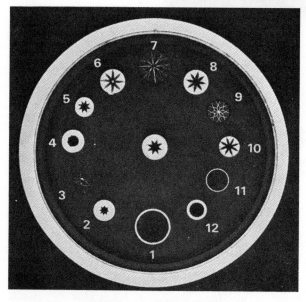

1. *Colourless sapphire (R.I. 1.76–1.77)*
2. *Zirconium oxide (Djevalite) (R.I. 2.18)*
3. *Phenacite (R.I. 1.66)*
4. *Zircon (R.I. 1.93–1.99)*
5. *Lithium niobate (R.I. 2.21–2.30)*
6. *Synthetic rutile (R.I 2.61–2.90)*
7. *Topaz (R.I. 1.62–1.63)*
8. *Strontium titanate (R.I. 2.41)*
9. *Paste (R.I. 1.63)*
10. *Dialite doublet*
11. *Synthetic spinel (R.I. 1.73)*
12. *Yttrium aluminate (Y.A.G.) (R.I. 1.83)*
The diamond (R.I. 2.42) is in the centre.

Y.A.G. and rutile have high refractive indices and will stand out in bold relief.

B. W. Anderson, has refined this test of immersion contrast by introducing a photographic technique particularly useful for unset stones, which are immersed in a liquid of known refractive index in a glass cell. The cell is placed on hard photographic bromide paper in a dark room and illuminated from above. The best method is to use light from an enlarger. The exposure has usually to be found by trial and error. The paper is afterwards developed in the usual way. (Fig. 21.5.)

The more light that has passed through a stone, the darker will be the area of the photographic print underneath it. When the stones are of higher R.I. than the liquid, as with diamond in the test already described, the borders will be white and the facet edges dark. Stones with lower R.I.s than the liquid (7 and 9 in Fig. 21.5) will show on the print with dark borders and white facet edges.

Hardness and Wear Tests

Even after many years of constant wear, cut diamonds will preserve their sharp edges and corners when most other stones will have become worn and chipped. Under a hand-lens, the edges of diamond facets will be clean and sharp. Most simulants after a few years of wear will have rolled (rounded) edges between facets.

Fractures in the edges and corners of substitutes which have been in wear some time in jewellery are quite common. Fractures can and do occur in diamonds, but they are usually on the culet or perhaps near the girdle, caused by a knock or careless setting. The nature of the fracture will indicate diamond. Typical abraded edges of diamond after many years of use are shown in Fig. 21.6.

Unfortunately it is not easy to test a suspected diamond for hardness without damage to the stone if it is not diamond. Flat polished pieces of synthetic ruby or sapphire (corundum) are available for use as hardness test plates. The girdle of the supposed diamond is drawn firmly across the surface of the corundum. If it scratches and the mark cannot be removed by rubbing it with a moistened finger, the stone is a diamond. Any suitable piece of ruby or sapphire, natural or synthetic, will do of course. No other gem material will scratch them.

Fig. 21.6. *Abraded facet edges of a diamond.*

Diamond is the only one that will 'bite'. Examine the scratch with a lens to make sure it is a scratch.

Nevertheless, a hardness test is not recommended for a diamond, especially if a fine one, as damage may ensue. For the same reason, in no circumstances should hardness pencils, files, or other hard materials be used to attempt scratching the facets, edges or any part of the surface of a polished stone believed to be a diamond. From time to time some ignorant or stupid person will test a diamond by trying to scratch some hard material with the pointed culet of the stone, or by using a file on the point of the culet. This is almost always fatal to the culet because of fracture through cleavage.

These injunctions do not apply to diamond rough. A reasonably well-forme crystal is easy for anyone to identify with some experience and practice but industrial diamond crystals in particular not infrequently appear to be anything but diamond. Some industrials could easily be mistaken for small pieces of coke. Using it to attempt to scratch a piece of synthetic ruby or sapphire is simple and effective, useful as a field test to prospectors without immediate access to a laboratory.

Accuracy of Cut

Because of its nature and value, diamond is usually cut much more accurately than other gemstones and the accurate meeting of the facet corners is one indication that the stone is a diamond. Similarly, polishing lines and scratches may be seen even on the best simulants but not on the best diamonds which they imitate.

Surface Features

Look on the polished surfaces for straight ridges or lines (Fig. 13.38) which are caused by twinning in the crystal resulting in differences of hardness and cannot be polished out. They occur only on diamond. There may also be irregularly shaped areas which appear to be slightly higher than the general surface, like shallow plateaux. They, too, occur only on diamond and are caused by naats (knots) or changes in crystal direction, and therefore hardness (Fig. 13.39).

The girdle of a brilliant-cut diamond is different in appearance from that of other stones. It has a matt, waxy appearance, caused by the fracturing process of bruting. It is not dull like ground glass, but has the shiny lustre of wax. Sometimes the girdle is bearded, having fine 'whiskers' – actually fractures – extending from it into the stone (Fig. 13.40). Such a flaw, caused by bruting too rapidly can occur only in diamond. Occasionally the girdle of a brilliant-cut diamond is polished or faceted. Girdles of most other cuts of diamond are polished.

A natural on the girdle or near it is an indication of diamond. A natural is part of the orginal crystal surface and usually looks much brighter than the girdle (Fig. 13.41). Trigons may sometimes be seen on naturals, when they are part of an original octahedral face. Lines across a natural indicate it was part of a dodecahedral face. Both indications are good proof by eye that the stone is a diamond, but there is one stimulant, yttrium aluminate (Y.A.G.), in which similar naturals are also occasionally left.

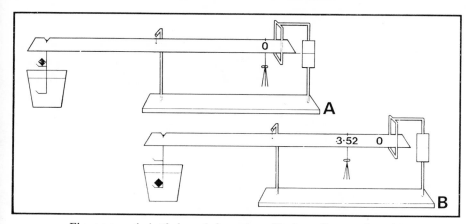

Fig. 21.7. *A simple beam balance that will give a direct reading of S.G.*

Internal Features

With a hand lens or microscope, certain internal features are diagnostic for diamond, particularly cleavage. Internal cleavages are quite common. No diamond simulants except topaz show cleavage and topaz can be eliminated for other reasons, such as its low brilliancy and lack of fire.

A cleavage (Fig. 17.52) is a split within the crystal which appears as a line edge-on and an irregular patch seen flat-on, and is often called a feather. Larger feathers are seen easily with a hand lens, but a higher powered microscope will be needed to examine smaller ones. Multiple ones are like butterflies, which is what they are called.

Specific Gravity

Specific gravity tests are impossible to apply to mounted stones, but elementary for loose ones if the apparatus supplied by Hanneman Lapidary Specialities, California, U.S.A., is employed. This is a simple beam balance that gives direct readings of S.G. (Fig. 21.7). Another, but fussier, method is to use heavy liquids. There is only one other gem similar to diamond that also compares with its relative density: sphene with an S.G. of 3·53 compared with diamond's 3·515.

Fluorescence

A spectroscope will give positive identification of diamond if the characteristic band at 4155 Å in the violet is seen. More details are given in Chapter Seventeen.

Although so variable, diamond fluorescence is a useful pointer in testing. On the other hand, the variance can be an advantage when testing a piece of jewellery set with many diamonds. If the jewellery is examined under either short or long wave ultra-violet light, no fluorescence or very even fluorescence indicates that the stones are not diamond. Uneven fluorescence as shown in Fig. 18.24 is an indication that the stones are diamond.

B. W. Anderson devised a simple test using fluorescence when he was director of the London Gem Testing Laboratory. It applies to stones that have a rather stony blue fluorescence under long-wave ultra-violet light (3660 Å). If the stone is a diamond, it will have a brief yellowish after-glow or phosphorescence. Make sure the eyes are adapted to the dark and hold the fluorescing stone in the palm

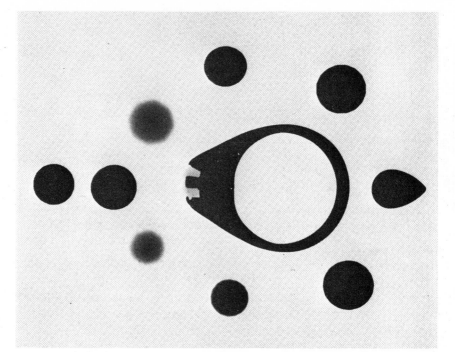

Fig. 21.8. *X-ray photograph by R. Webster showing* (left) *paste (RI 1.62), synthetic white scheelite (at 9 o'clock, then clockwise), synthetic white spinel, white zircon, yttrium aluminate (Y.A.G.), lithium niobate (Linobate–pear shaped), strontium titanite (Fabulite), synthetic rutile, and synthetic white sapphire, compared with a diamond ring in the centre.*

of one hand. Then remove it swiftly from the rays, placing the other hand over it to form a small dark chamber and applying one eye to the chamber. Only a diamond will show a yellow afterglow (which will be in step with the brightness of the blue fluorescence). Remember that not all diamonds have a blue fluorescence. The test is useful because it can be applied to mounted as well as unmounted stones. The French physicist, A. H. Becquerel (1852–1902), invented a more sophisticated way of seeing phosphorescence for those who wish to experiment. He made a stroboscope with two holes. One admitted ultra-violet light to the specimen under test; the other showed the specimen unlit.

X-ray Tests
Diamonds have bluish fluorescence under X-rays – a reliable test.

A more sophisticated test for diamond is to use its transparency to X-rays compared with substitutes, owing to the low atomic weight of carbon. If a known diamond and the suspected stone are placed on a photographic plate and exposed for a short time to X-rays, stones other than diamond will show black against the faint shadow of the diamond (Fig. 21.8). If the exposure is too long, the diamond will not show at all on the plate. Yttrium aluminate (YAG), strontium titanate, paste, and zircon are all opaque. The test is often used for court evidence. Better contrast can be obtained by burying the stones in plasticine before X-raying them. X-ray tests are used to establish the proportion of diamond to graphite and amorphous carbon and other materials in carbonado.

Fig. 21.9. *Doubling in zircon.*   Fig. 21.10. *False doubling in diamond.*

Single and Double Refraction

The refractive index of diamond is too high at 2·42 to be checked on a normal refractometer, which is limited by its contact liquid to a top reading of 1·81. (There is also a real danger of scratching the soft glass table of the instrument.) Taking a refraction reading with more elaborate instruments is not within the scope of normal testing. Refractometer tests of stones which are within the range of the instrument will, of course, separate them from diamond.

Diamond is isotropic and therefore does not cause doubling. Looking through the table with a hand lens, the edges of the back facets and the culet should appear undistorted. Some simulants, including zircon and synthetic rutile are doubly-refracting. Light rays passing through the stone are split into two, so the back facet edges doubled as shown in Fig. 21.9. It may be necessary to turn the stone through different angles and look through bezel facets instead of the table to discover doubling of the back facets because there are directions of single refraction in doubly-refracting minerals.

It is not always possible to see doubling in a doubly-refracting mineral, usually because the double refraction is too small. Use of a polarizing microscope, or polariscope will quickly reveal a stone that is doubly-refracting. Diamond does invariably exhibit anomalous double refraction, however.

Diamonds never show doubling of the back facets. It does happen rarely, however, that bad cutting of a brilliant-cut stone will cause an effect known as false doubling. An example is shown in Fig. 21.10. False doubling can quickly be recognized if its nature is appreciated. It is a series of reflections which cause an image of the culet edges, *around* another image of the same edges. True doubing is a second image which is *displaced* so that it overlaps the first one. The second effect is similar to double vision.

Another diagnostic feature of diamond of modern cut is immediately apparent to the eye – the degree of fire or play of spectrum colours. Moving a brilliant-cut diamond will result in a display of flashes of pure spectrum colours from the smaller facets around the table.

Reflectivity Tests

The high reflectivity of the surface of diamond is a quantity that can be measured to diagnose the material, if one of the relatively recent reflectivity instruments, such as 'The Jeweller's Eye' or the 'Gem Analyzer' is employed. The instrument measures light energy reflected from a facet which moves a pointer over a scale of gem names. Strictly it is a comparator and an unknown stone, if a diamond, should give the same reading as a known diamond. It works only with stones that have a good polish and have been thoroughly cleaned.

A very simple test for diamond is taught by Alan Hodgkinson in his gem identification courses. Fit a low-powered clear tungsten bulb into a table lamp and hold the stone under the lamp so that a reflection of the bulb can be seen in the table of the stone. Writing on the bulb can be clearly identified in the reflection from the table of a diamond, but with simulants it is less distinct.

The Diamond Eye

Dr. W. W. Hanneman developed, in 1978, an instrument specifically for demonstrating that simulants of diamond, nearest to it in appearance, were not diamond. Called the 'Diamond Eye', it is similar to his original reflective meter, but has more sensitivity over a narrower range and is easier to zeroise and to use. It is mainly intended to separate zirconium oxide from diamond, but the scale is also marked for Y.A.G., G.G.G., strontium titanate and, of course, diamond.

Fig. 21.11. *A new reflectivity comparator, introduced by Hanneman in 1978. It is designed to separate diamond from its nearest simulants (zirconium oxide, Y.A.G., strontium titanate and G.G.G.) quickly.*

Paste

Paste, that is, lead glass, is the most common substitute for diamond and can be surprisingly like diamond when well cut and mounted and seen in wear. The fire can be very similar. Dispersion of a typical lead glass is 0·041 compared with 0·044 for diamond.

The surface polish usually gives a clue at once to the material. As most paste is softer than the particles of quartz in dust, the facets may have become dulled or scratched and wear may show on facet edges and corners. A lens will often reveal small air bubbles and sometimes swirl clouds of bubbles in the glass.

Glass is singly refracting, so this offers no evidence in relation to diamond, but the refractive index does because, although it can vary considerably, it is usually between 1·52 and 1·68. The simplest test is by immersion (see page 475).

Paste was not considered a simulant for diamond in the eighteenth century and was worn in the highest circles set in fine jewellery, so the quality of the setting is not a guide. There are more comments on this on page 489. Pastes were often cut in shapes not seen or even possible with diamond.

Yttrium Aluminate (Y.A.G.) Diamonair

A diamond substitute that appeared in 1969 is cut from manufactured crystals of a material known as yttrium aluminate (Y.A.G.) that has no counterpart in nature. Known by gemmologists as Y.A.G., it has been given the trade name of Diamonair and became well known when Richard Burton bought an 69·42 carat pear-shaped diamond for his wife, Elizabeth Taylor, and had a duplicate of it cut in Y.A.G.

Y.A.G. is extremely transparent, nearly always free from inclusions and relatively hard (8½ on Mohs' scale). It is singly refracting and the refractive index at 1·83 is below that of diamond, as is the dispersion, at 0·028. The first stones cut from the material were not particularly successful, but after the ideal angles were calculated by the Gemological Institute of America Laboratory in New York, Y.A.G. was found to have considerable potential as a diamond simulant, and many cut stones have been sold in jewellery.

A very good polish, with a lustre approaching adamantine, can be obtained and the fire, although low, is enough to imitate diamond. The brilliance is less if the table is looked at from an angle and compared with the brilliance direct on. This 'tilt text' may provide the first clue that the stone is not a diamond, especially in subdued light (Fig. 21.1). The breath test (p. 474) is a useful check.

Diamonair is cut from pulled boules and to retain maximum weight, cutters occasionally leave a small part of the skin on the girdle which has a remarkable similarity to a natural on a diamond girdle.

The lower refractive index will distinguish it from diamond in a refractive liquid. Occasionally, curved lines similar to those in synthetic ruby, may be seen under a low-powered microscope and when inclusions do occur they are sometimes extended bubbles.

If a stone that looks like a particularly fine white diamond is loose, it can be weighed and, if it is much heavier than a diamond of its size should be, it could be Y.A.G., or strontium titanate. A possible procedure would be to make an accurate estimate of the weight if it were diamond using a Leveridge gauge, and then to obtain the actual weight on diamond scales. If the stone were gauged at a carat, it would be within a few points of this on a balance if a diamond. If Y.A.G., it would weigh about 1·28 carat and if strontium titanate, about 1·46 carat (Fig. 21.12).

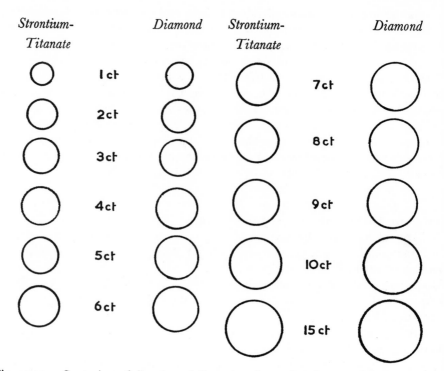

Fig. 21.12   *Comparison of diameters of diamonds and strontium titanates of the same weight.*

Strontium Titanate (Fabulite)

Another successful simulant of diamond, strontium titanate, is also entirely a product of man's ingenuity since it does not occur naturally. It has been given many trade names, the best known of which are probably Fabulite and Starilian, since it was introduced in 1953. Its main disadvantage is its relatively low hardness (6 on Mohs' scale), which results after a period of wear in rolled or blunted edges to the facets and particularly blunting of the sharp points where the facet corners meet. The low hardness also means that it will not take a really fine polish and under a hand lens it does not have the adamantine lustre of diamond, being almost greasy in appearance. In fact, the material is so difficult to cut that many stones are produced with flaws and many without the full fifty-eight facets of the brilliant-cut.

Nevertheless, brilliant-cut strontium titanate has almost the same refractive index and is nearer in appearance to high-quality diamond than yttrium aluminium garnet. It has often deceived those who do not know it or have never seen it. To anyone who handles polished diamonds, the first impression of a strontium titanate is that it is too good to be true. This arises from the dispersion, which can be quite spectacular. It is 0·200 compared with diamond's 0·044. Strontium titanate gives no doubling of the back facets, and is identical to diamond in this, but is much heavier (Fig. 21.11).

Because of its high refractive index it is not susceptible to the 'tilt-test' but will cloud longer than diamond when breathed upon. With practice, the easiest way to identify it as strontium titanate, or as not diamond, is to look through the table at the back facets. If studied carefully, these will appear quite different from those of diamond because they appear to be separated by fine white lines (the facet edges) and to be light and dark panels reminiscent of a dartboard. The 'dartboard effect' is a description attributable to Alan Hodgkinson.

Under a low-powered microscope, strontium titanate immersed in a highly refractive liquid will often show inclusions reminiscent of the rungs of a ladder. Similar markings may sometimes be seen on the surface under a lens. A. E. Farn suggests that the 'ladders' are a surface effect, not inclusions, as he has induced them by pressure with a pin. Strontium titanate does not fluoresce under ultra-violet light.

Zirconium Oxide (Djevalite)

One effective simulant of diamond is sold graded by colour and purity, like diamond. It is the man-made zirconium oxide produced under the name of 'Djevalite' by the Swiss synthetic gem company, Hrand Djevahirdjian S.A. The colours in which it is made are white to slightly tinted yellow and brown. Its R.I. of 2·18 is near enough to diamond for the stone to remain quite brilliant when tilted to various angles and, although the dispersion at 0·060 is higher than that of diamond, this is not immediately apparent. The S.G. is much higher at 5·65, so a loose stone is relatively easy to check (see page 483).

The flaws in some of the stones may trap the unwary as they are very similar to cleavage and stress cracks in diamond and, especially if the Djevalite is cut in the old style and mounted, can be deceiving. Loose stones can be checked by trying to pick them up with a moistened finger and mounted ones by the breath test, each compared with diamond. Introduced in 1977, this simulant is probably the most effective to date. A version called Phianite, containing 15 per cent yttrium oxide, has been produced in the U.S.S.R.

Synthetic Rutile

Another titanium compound, synthetic rutile, was first produced in 1948 and soon cut and sold under many different trade names, one of which was Titania, as a diamond simulant. It could be taken for a diamond of poor colour. It has a high refractive index – at 0·280 – six and a half times the dispersion of diamond, which gives it quite an exceptional display of fire. It is never without a yellowish tinge of body colour, however. The two effects produce an opalescence that might be described as a faintly 'baleful' appearance, recognizable after experience.

Very occasionally synthetic rutile has been bloomed by a cathodic sputtering method, like camera lenses. The bluish tinge is intended to improve the colour, but the yellowness remains. Synthetic rutile has extremely high double refraction which usually can be seen by doubling of the back facets, an easy test.

Synthetic Spinel and Synthetic Sapphire

Synthetic white spinel is commonly used as a diamond substitute in cheaper jewellery without intent to deceive when it is sold. The same is true of synthetic white sapphire. Both are commonly used in brilliant-cut form as small stones surrounding larger coloured stones in rings. A refractometer test will immediately establish the identity of each substitute if the table facets are unobstructed. An immersion test (page 475) is useful when a number of stones that could be diamond but are more likely to be synthetic spinel or sapphire are to be tested, particularly if they are too small, numerous, or awkward to get at because of the setting, for other tests. It is particularly useful for the numbers of small transparent colourless synthetic stones often set around a large stone in a ring, for example, to imitate diamond 'chips' of Swiss and other cuts. In older jewellery which has been repaired, it is possible that a lost diamond has been replaced by synthetic spinels or sapphires, and quick identification by the same method is valuable.

Another quick check is to examine the jewellery in short-wave ultra-violet light. If the small stones, such as baguettes, purporting to be diamonds have a blue fluorescence, they are probably synthetic spinels.

Spinel is singly refracting like diamond, but sapphire is doubly refracting and will show four extinction positions when rotated between crossed polarizers, as in a Rayner or Rutland polariscope. The doubling is often difficult to see with a hand lens. Colourless white sapphires of natural origin can also be identified.

Other Synthetics

Colourless synthetic scheelite is cut in brilliant style and could be mistaken for diamond. So is lithium niobate which is marketed under the name of Linobate. Gadolinium-gallium garnet (GGG) is another man-made stone that is cut brilliant fashion in its colourless form. It is singly refracting but very heavy.

One other natural material, sphene, is superficially like yellowish diamond, but has twice the double refraction of zircon, so should be easily recognized.
The constants of these materials are given in the table at the end of this chapter and will suggest tests on lines already described.

Zircon

A common substitute for diamond is colourless zircon, which is hard, has a high refractive index and wide dispersion, and is usually cut in brilliant or similar style. Its fire is less than that of diamond, but is sufficient to trap the laymen into thinking it diamond. The visual test for zircon is simple because of its considerable double refraction. Viewing a back facet through the table with a lens the edges of the facet will usually be seen doubled as in Fig. 21.9. Zircon has a slightly steely appearance that is a quick indication to those who recognize it.

Topaz

Colourless white topaz may occasionally be found in jewellery, particularly that originating in the East or Near East. Again a refractometer test is the easiest if it is possible. Visually, there is much less brilliance and particularly fire in both topaz and sapphire than in diamond, and natural colourless sapphire sometimes has a very slightly milky appearance.

Topaz, with a refractive index of 1·62–1·63, is doubly refracting which can be discovered by rotating it between the crossed 'nicols' of a polariscope because the doubling is not enough to be seen with a hand lens. The immersion contrast method will separate topaz from diamond as the relief in the refractive liquids mentioned is lower even than spinel (see page 475).

Rock Crystal

Much the same remarks are true of colourless quartz (rock crystal). Both topaz and quartz have such low brilliance that they should not be mistaken for diamond. Quartz has a different 'feel' from most other stones. With practice, a slight tackiness can be noticed to the fingertips or the eyelid or lip.

Doublets

Diamond doublets are uncommon, and can be deceiving. The top of the stone in invariably diamond and the pavilion may be synthetic colourless sapphire, quartz, or paste, cemented on. One would normally encounter such a stone mounted, not loose (Fig. 21.14). The quality always appears poor. A lens or microscope will usually show up bubbles in the cement layer, and immersion in methylene iodide will immediately make visible the two parts of the doublet. If the stone is moved while looking through the table facet with the naked eye, it is possible usually to see a reflection of the octagonal table in the cement layer (Fig. 21.13).

Another, but inferior, doublet that may deceive the unwary, is the garnet-topped version with a base of colourless glass. The garnet is a thin slice cemented to the base to become the table. Although the garnet is coloured, the doublet faces up colourless. The easy test is to immerse the stone in a white cup containing water. If viewed sideways, loose or mounted, the top will show up clearly.

One modern doublet is one of the best simulants of diamond. It has a base of strontium titanate to provide the fire and dispersion and a crown of synthetic white spinel or synthetic white sapphire which is relatively hard. Sapphire is, however, doubly refracting. Another version has a pavilion of strontium titanate and a crown of another man-made material that is singly-refracting and known as GGG (gadolinium-gallium garnet). All of them can be recognized by the reflection of the table edge on the cement layer (Fig. 21.16). This test is best carried out by facing the direction from which the light comes and gradually tilting the table of the stone from the horizontal towards the light. If the stone is unmounted, the two parts may be seen by immersing the stone sideways in a refractive liquid or even in water in a white cup.

Coloured Diamond Substitutes

It is more likely that a fancy-coloured diamond will be mistaken for another stone than that a coloured stone will be mistaken for a diamond. Fancy colours in diamond, except for browns and yellows, are rare.

B. W. Anderson says that natural scheelite should not be overlooked when identifying a stone as diamond. Although it is soft, it is very near diamond in appearance when set and brilliant-cut. It may be colourless, yellow, orange, or brown, all diamond colours. Testing on the girdle with a needle point will reveal its softness, and a lens should reveal doubling of the back facets, unless the

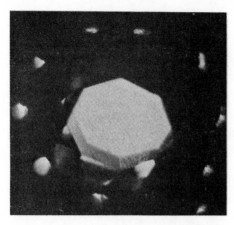

Fig. 21.13. *Reflection in the table of a diamond doublet.*

Fig. 21.14. (top right) *Diamond doublets are always close set.*

Fig. 21.15. *A diamond doublet out of its setting. The crown is diamond and the pavilion another material.*

stone is small. The specific gravity is even higher than that of strontium titanate, so a loose stone would be much too heavy for its weight if it were a diamond.

Blende can occur in transparent yellow as well as brown and orange and is cut as a specimen, although much too soft to be cut commercially as a gem for jewellery. It has a refractive index near that of diamond and is singly refracting, which gives it a diamond-like appearance. It is also called sphalerite.

The yellowish to leaf-green variety of andradite garnet known as demantoid could be mistaken for fancy diamond because of its high refractive index and its dispersion, which is more than that of diamond. Under a microscope the internal features are quite different. 'Horse tails' of fibrous material are a characteristic of demantoid.

Blue and golden zircon could possibly be mistaken for fancy diamonds, but are so characteristic in their colours that when seen a few times they should be readily recognized again. It is more likely that a diamond that has been artificially coloured blue by electron bombardment might be mistaken for a zircon or an aquamarine, if the blue is deep in colour.

Blue and yellow synthetic rutile is made and cut in Japan, but should not be mistaken for diamond if the precaution of looking for doubling is taken. Blue rutile is highly electro-conductive and could be mistaken for blue Type IIb diamond if this test is applied.

Artificially coloured diamonds and their identification are dealt with in Chapter Nineteen.

Fig. 21.16. *The reflection of the table edge that can be seen in the cement layer if a doublet is is tilted towards the light.*

Diamonds and Simulants in Jewellery

As a very general principle, diamonds are not set in cheaply-made twentieth-century gold jewellery or even in well-made twentieth-century silver jewellery, so the quality of the setting is a quick indication of whether the stone is a diamond or a simulant. On the other hand, simulants are not infrequently set in good-quality modern jewellery, so the converse is not a good guide.

With older jewellery this rule of thumb does not hold good. From early days to the twentieth century, diamonds were very commonly set in silver and during the time that paste was popular, from about 1700 to 1865, this too was set mainly in silver jewellery, often of the highest quality. In the eighteenth century, paste was not regarded as counterfeit or a simulant but was worn in the highest court circles, by such as Madame de Pompadour and the Empress Eugenie.

From Renaissance times, stones were set in several ways: the closed setting was a rim to hold the stone closely with the base enclosed; the open setting was a similar rim without a bottom; the claw setting was a circlet of claws, which may still have a closed back, to hold the stone; and the pavé (pavement) was where many small stones were set close to each other by drilling holes in the metal to fit the pavilions of the stones and raising small grains of metal around each indentation to hold the stone set in it.

Diamonds were set in open and closed settings but after about mid-sixteenth century, the claw setting came into fashion. In the eighteenth century, claw and pavé settings were most common, the first for larger and more important stones and the second for groups of smaller ones. In the nineteenth century many small diamonds were set in a form known as millegrain, in which the metal used to hold the diamonds was crenelated by drawing a hardened steel wheel round the metal. Another setting is called illusion. A small diamond is set in a larger serrated and polished plate soldered in the claws of the setting.

Paste, on the other hand, was almost invariably close-set during the eighteenth century, the edges of the setting being tightly moulded to the edges of the stones to make them airtight. The reason was to prevent tarnishing of the reflecting foil behind the stone.

Before the eighteenth century most stones, including diamonds, were close-set and foiled at the back to improve their brilliance or deepen their colours. Foiling during the Renaissance was as important an art as cutting is today. Foils of yellow, blue, red or green, were used for tinting diamonds. Another practice was to cover the back of the diamond with lamp black or coloured paint or to set the stone in a bezel painted inside and with a reflector of crystal glass cut in a square behind the stone, according to Cellini.

In reproduction jewellery, crumpling of the foil may sometimes be seen through the stone, but in well-made eighteenth-century paste jewellery, the foil is rarely visible and still remains untarnished today, so that the paste is brilliant enough to be deceiving.

The modern equivalent of foiling, commonly employed for synthetic white spinels or sapphires, is to make the back facets into true mirrors which are then given a protective coating of gilt paint and set in jewellery so that the backs are hidden.

In much early diamond jewellery, the stones have a spot of black paint or pitch applied to the culet, which appears as a black spot when viewed through the table. The black spot also appears on the pastes in the best pieces of eighteenth-century paste-jewellery, so is no guide in identification. A few modern diamonds also have the culets blackened (Fig. 21.16). The best guide is the great variety of shapes to which pastes were commonly cut. The finer paste jewellery frequently contains no circular cut stones.

Platinum became the accepted setting for diamonds at the end of the nineteenth century and a special trade of diamond mounter came into being. However, the rising price of platinum from about mid-twentieth century reduced its use considerably in favour of white gold. However, since then gold prices have risen to correspond; so platinum, despite its greater weight, is in fashion once more.

Silver persisted as a setting for diamonds in a few pieces of jewellery until the early twentieth century.

Gold settings of natural colour for diamonds of good colour degrade the whiteness of the stones but have become popular in modern times when fashion can be more influential than logic. The most satisfactory compromise for diamond rings is a white gold or platinum mount on a yellow gold shank if the whiteness of the stone is to be preserved in yellow gold.

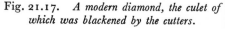
Fig. 21.17. *A modern diamond, the culet of which was blackened by the cutters.*

Fig. 21.18. *A D.G.L. photograph showing the unique growth structures and polishing lines on a facet of a 1·0 ct diamond.*

Identification for Record Purposes

Two methods of recording individual diamonds or jewellery set with diamonds for future identification have already been referred to, the fluorescent picture (page 418) and the surface topography photography showing polishing and crystal growth lines (page 407). The first is not in commercial use, but the second is, under the name of Crystalprint, by Diamond Grading Laboratories, who use a Nomarski interference facility with a research microscope. (Fig. 21.18.)

Another commercial technique was developed by the Weizmann Institute in Israel and is marketed under the name of Gemprint. A low-power helium-neon laser beam is directed on to a rotating diamond through a hole in a photographic film. Light spots reflected from facets are recorded on the film. A random pattern is produced by a diamond that has been polished by hand, which is unique to that diamond. Simulants, being machine-cut, produce more regular patterns,

Fig. 21.19. (left)   *A Gemprint of a diamond.* (right). *A Gemprint of a G.G.G.*

Fig. 21.20. *The record prin-ted in the centre of a diamond table, magnified about 1,000,000 times, and used for an identification card.*

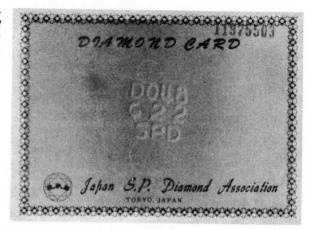

but there seem to be patterns attributable to different types of stone (Fig. 21.19.), and a number of users employ the Gemprint for identification also.

A method of 'fingerprinting' which cannot be be affected by recutting or

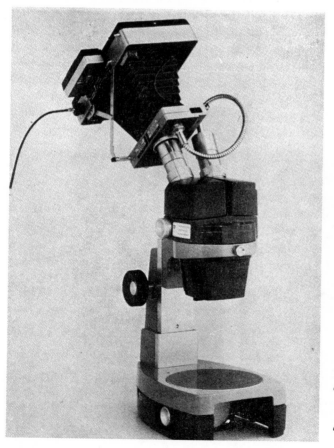

Fig. 21.21. *The spe-cial fitment for recording microscope pictures with a Polaroid camera developed by the G.I.A.*

polishing was suggested by A. R. Lang and G. S. Woods of H. H. Wills Physics Laboratory, Bristol University, in 1976. They prepared X-ray topographs showing the internal structures of rough stones which were then cut and identified by similar topographs showing internal dislocations. The system has not been put to any commercial use.

Kazumi Okuda in Japan has developed a method of printing a microdot in the centre of the table of a diamond to record it and its grade. The area of the record is about one hundred thousandth of a square millimetre and a special microscope is provided to read it (Fig. 21.20).

Finally, for recording features seen by a microscope, the Gemological Institute of America developed a fitment for the automatic light metre of a Polaroid camera to link it with one eye-piece of a binocular microscope while the camera fits over the other, so that the correct exposure is automatic (Fig. 21.21).

New tests for diamonds

Since the appearance of the second edition, new tests to distinguish diamond from its simulants have appeared. The simplest is a special diamond pen produced by the Gem Instrument Corporation of Santa Monica, California. It leaves a smooth single drop of ink on the surface of a diamond, but the spot 'beads up' on simulants. Some simulants have been coated, according to R. Crowingshield, to give a diamond response; but a mild abrasive will remove this coating.

A new instrument seems to be the most reliable yet, if it proves to be robust. It measures the thermal conductivity of the stone on a scale by means of a spring-loaded probe, which can be used on stones as small as 0·02 carats even if they are deep set. This is the Ceres diamond probe, made in the U.S.A., which gives a reading by measuring the rate of dispersal of heat after short pulses of electric current. It gives a reading on a scale marked red at one end, yellow in the middle, and green at the other end. All diamonds register in the green and all simulants register in the red: there is a substantial difference in the readings. According to Dr K. Nassau, the literature values of thermal conductivities at room temperature in watts per cm per degree K are: Diamond Type I, 10–20; Type IIa, 26; Type IIb, 15. All simulants including natural stones are about 0·3.

REFERENCES

Gem Testing, by B. W. Anderson, B.Sc., F.G.A. 7th edition (London, 1964).
Four Centuries of European Jewellery, by Ernle Bradford (London, 1967).
Antique Paste Jewellery, by M. D. S. Lewis (London, 1970).
Gems: Their Sources, Descriptions and Identification, by Robert Webster, F.G.A. 2nd edition (London, 1970).
'Diamonair: A new Diamond Substitute', by Robert Crowingshield. Jewelers' Circular Keystone (December, 1969).
'Fingerprinting Diamonds by X-ray Topography', by A. R. Lang and G. S. Woods. Industrial Diamond Review (March, 1976).
'A Test of the Ceres Diamond Probe', by Dr K. Nassau. Gems and Gemology (Winter 1978–79).

DIAMOND AND SUBSTITUTES IN APPROXIMATE ORDER OF NEARNESS IN APPEARANCE

	Hardness	Specific Gravity	Refractive Index	Double Refraction	Dispersion	Fluorescence	Transparency to X-rays
Diamond	10	3·52	2·417	none	0·044	usually dull violet to light blue l.u.v.	transparent
Zirconium oxide (Djevalite)	8	5·65	2·18	none	0·060	faint orange-brown l.u.v., yellow s.u.v.	opaque
Strontium titanate (Fabulite)	5½	5·13	2·41	none	0·200	none	opaque
Paste (typical)	5	3·74	1·63	none	0·031	usually weak bluish or inert l.u.v., stronger blue s.u.v.	opaque
Yttrium aluminate (y.a.g.) (Diamonair)	8	4·55	1·833	none	0·028	yellow l.u.v weaker s.u.v	opaque
Lithium niobate (Linobate)	5	4·64	2·21 – 2·30	0·090	0·120	none	opaque
Rutile (synthetic)	6½	4·25	2·610 – 2·900	0·287	0·300	none	opaque
Zircon	7½	4·69	1·926 – 1·985	0·59	0·039	yellow (mustard) l.u.v., weaker s.u.v.	opaque
Blende	3½	4·09	2·37	none	0·156	none	opaque
Scheelite (inc. synthetic)	5	6·0	1·920 – 1·937	0·017	0·026	none, l.u.v., bright blue s.u.v.	opaque
Spinel (synthetic)	8	3·63	1·727	none	0·020	none, l.u.v., greenish to bluish white s.u.v.	translucent
Sapphire (natural or synthetic)	9	3·99	1·760 – 1·768	0·008	0·018	none – sometimes bluish white s.u.v.	translucent
Topaz	8	3·56	1·612 – 1·622	0·010	0·014	weak yellowish or greenish l.u.v.	translucent
Quartz	7	2·65	1·544 – 1·553	0·009	0·013	none	translucent

l.u.v.: long wave ultra-violet rays. s.u.v.: short wave ultra-violet rays.
Figures in the first five columns are taken with permission from B. W. Anderson's *Gem Testing* (Heywood, London, 1964). The information in the last two columns was kindly provided by Robert Webster. There is one exception: The zirconium oxide figures come from an analysis by Dr. E. Gubelin in the German Gemmological Journal, Dec. 1976.

Glossary of Terms

A glossary covering all the trade terms used by miners, dealers, cutters, polishers, sorters and others would defeat its own object. This one therefore covers expressions not used in the text as well as others that do appear but might be tedious to look up via the index.

Acidising. Treating a diamond with acids (usually hot) to clean it after mining or after cutting, especially to remove oxides or polishing residue from surface fissures.

A.G.S. American Gem Society.

á jour. A diamond mount that exposes the pavilion to the light. Most modern mounts are of this type, unlike earlier closed settings.

American cut. A brilliant cut developed by Henry D. Morse and other American cutters and generally confirmed in the dimensions calculated by Tolkowsky near the beginning of the century. It has a higher crown and smaller table than the European cut.

American setting. An open (á jour) setting with a particularly high mount.

Baby. Diggers' slang term for a rocking sieve, invented by J. L. Babe.

Baguette. Diamond cut in the shape of a narrow bar and named after the long French loaf.

Ballas. Ball-shaped diamonds formed of extremely small intergrown crystals, therefore being very hard and having industrial uses.

Bast. A rough diamond with a frosted surface, the name originating from the Dutch name for tree bark.

Batea. The wide and shallow washing pan used by early Brazilian gold and diamond prospectors.

Baton. Another name for a baguette-cut diamond.

Beard. The tiny whiskers seen around the girdle of a brilliant-cut stone that has been cut too rapidly, hence 'bearded girdle'.

Bedrock. The solid rock under deposits of gravels, silt, sand, soil, etc.

Bezel facets. The cross-cutter makes the 4 top corner facets into 8, which become the bezel facets.

Bicycle tyre. A thick girdle.

Blackened culet. A culet that has been blackened by pitch, a practice of some earlier cutters.

Blocking. Putting on the 16 main facets, by the cross-cutter.

Blocking. Putting on the table, culet (if included), and 16 other main facets by the cross-cutter or *blocker*. Also called *lapping*.

Block carving. A current method of continuous mining of diamond pipes by blasting an underground cave in the kimberlite, the roof of which breaks up and is drawn out for crushing.

495

Blue ground. Miner's name for the unoxidized kimberlite in a pipe or other kimberlitic deposit.

Blue-white. A confusing term often wrongly applied. A blue-white stone should have a faint tinge of blue, but the description is usually intended to mean colourless, although it is applied even to stones with a tinge of yellow.

Boart. (Also spelled bort, boort, and bortz.) Very low grade diamond suitable only for crushing into diamond grit for industrial use.

Bow-tie. The dark bow-tie shape seen in the table of marquise, oval, and pear-shaped polished diamonds.

Briefca. Another name for a diamond parcel paper.

Brillianteerer. (Also spelled brilliandeur.) The craftsman responsible for the final stages of putting on and polishing the 40 facets, after the cross-cutter's work.

Bruting. Another name for cutting.

Bunch ring. A ring set with a very very tiny, part-faceted or rough diamond, so called because such rings were sold in bunches.

Burn mark. Mark caused on the surface of a polished diamond by overheating when polishing. It can be whitish and frosted or dark.

Buyer's box. A special metal box used at sights to hold several hundred parcel papers containing rough diamonds. Larger stones are offered individually.

Calibré cut. Stones cut to standard dimensions so that they are easy for manufacturers to set into standard mounts.

Cape. A broad colour-grading covering stones with a yellow tinge. The name arose from the fact that early shipments of diamonds via Cape Province were yellow compared with the shipments from Brazil.

Carbonado. Very hard and impure industrial diamond which looks like black, brown, or dark grey rock.

Carat. A unit of weight for gemstones that formerly varied from country to country, but is now standardized as a metric carat of 200 milligrams or 0·20 of a gram.

Cascalho. The Brazilian name for diamondiferous alluvial gravels.

Chambering. An earlier method of mining diamond pipes underground by making a 'chessboard' of rectangular chambers and pillars, and then mining another 'chessboard' underneath them so that the chambers were underneath the pillars. Blasting then dropped the blue ground of the pillars into the chambers below them.

Chip. Common name for a small rose- or single-cut diamond, or a small irregularly-cut one. The term is also used by sorters of rough for pieces of cleavage less than a carat.

C.I.B.J.O. International Confederation of Jewellery, Silverware, Diamonds, Pearls, and Stones.

Clatersal. Small pieces of diamond that are crushed to make powder.

Clean. A description commonly used to indicate that a diamond has no readily visible inclusions. It has been so abused that it is frowned on or banned by some professional and trade associations.

Cleavage. The tendency of diamond to split along the grain parallel to one of its octahedral faces. Also a name used for rough diamonds that have at some time in their history been cleaved from a larger stone.

Cleaver. The craftsman who cleaves a diamond into two parts by exploiting its cleavage planes.

Closed culet. The sharp point at the bottom of the pavilion of a brilliant cut, or knife edge on an emerald-cut stone.

Closed goods. An old name for good quality rough such as well-shaped octahedra.

Coating. Some rough diamonds are found with a coating that may be impure diamond or some other mineral of greenish, brownish, or blackish colour. Also the superficial green colour of rough that has been in contact with uranium is sometimes called a coating.

Collection. Name used by sorters of rough for a very white grade.

Concentrate. Dense minerals concentrated together during an extraction process while the rest of the material is rejected.

Conglomerate. Alluvial diamonds are sometimes found in conglomerate, a solid sedimentary rock comprising gravels and sediment, instead of in loose gravels.

Corners. Name given by cross-cutters to the 8 main facets, excluding table and culet; hence first corner, second corner, etc.

Crack. A fracture in a stone that is irregular; therefore usually one not in a cleavage direction.

Crown. The upper part of a polished stone above the girdle.

Cross-cutter. The craftsman who puts on or grinds and polishes the first 16 facets. Also called a *lapper.*

Cross cut. A horizontal tunnel mined across the direction of the strike.

C.S.O. The Central Selling Organization that distributes about 80 per cent of the world's rough gem diamonds.

Culet. (Also spelled collet and culette.) The very small facet on the bottom of the pavilion, parallel to the table.

Cut. The shape into which a rough stone is cut and polished. See pages 217 to 231 for diamond cuts.

Cutter or *bruter.* The craftsman who makes the rough diamond round before it is faceted.

Dark centre. The dark central area of the table seen in a stone with too deep a pavilion.

Diamond paper. Another name for a parcel paper.

Diamond parcel paper. The specially folded paper in which a diamond is or diamonds are held for carrying, or for transporting in a parcel.

Dispersion. The prismatic effect of a colourless material splitting white light into its spectrum colours.

Dop. The holder for a diamond being polished. Solder holds the diamond in a solder dop and metal jaws in a *mechanical dop.* An *automatic dop,* used mainly for small stones, puts on facets semi-automatically.

Dop mark. A small burn mark on the surface of a polished diamond caused by the overheating of the jaw of a mechanical dop.

Double rose-cut. Cut with a rose on the top and on the bottom. Also called a double rosette.

Doublet. A false gem made of two parts, the crown, or part of it, of one material and the pavilion of another.

Drag line. A polishing flaw caused by foreign material in the diamond powder, usually drawn from a surface crack in the stone.

Draw. A diamond with a tinge of yellow or another colour is said to 'draw colour'. The term is also used for the phenomenon of colour saturation. A large parcel of stones will draw more colour, i.e. will appear more deeply coloured, than a parcel of say half the number of the same stones.

Drive. A horizontal tunnel mined in the direction of the strike.

Dudley Diamond. Another name for the Star of South Africa.

Dutch bort. Not diamond boart, but an old and false name for zircons found in the South African mines.

Eight-cut. Cut for small diamonds with 8 facets on top and 8 on the bottom, plus the table and culet (if included). Equivalent to the cross-cut stage of the brilliant. Also called the *single cut.*

Eights. The first 8 main facets, apart from the table and culet, to be ground by the cross-cutter.

Ex-collection. Name used by sorters of rough for the finest, extra-white stones.

Extraction. Removal of diamonds from concentrate.

Extra facet. A small facet, in addition to those required by the cut, usually applied to remove a small blemish.

Faceted girdle. A girdle on which a series of small facets have been polished to improve the brilliance of the stone, patented by Ernest G. H. Shenck.

Face up. With the table of the stone facing the viewer.

False colour. An earlier name for a stone that seemed to change its colour in different lights, now known to be caused by the stone's fluorescence. See *Premier.*

Fancies. A fancy is an attractively coloured diamond. Colours in order of rarity are possibly: emerald green, red, sapphire blue (but always of poor colour), pink (seldom more than a tint), black (but see notes in the text), orange, canary, coffee-brown, reddish-brown, golden-brown, tints of violet, blue (the darker the rarer).

Fancy. A diamond of an attractive colour other than white suitable for gem use.

Fashioning. A general term for the operations of manufacturing a polished diamond.

Feather. A cleavage crack in a stone that resembles a feather.

Fezel. A feather-like inclusion often seen in macles, but occurring also in other stones, that is white and like a streamer.

Finish. Quality of polish, symmetry, proportions and general fashioning.

Fire. The flashing spectrum colours seen when a suitably cut diamond is moved, which is the result of its disperson.

Fisheye or *Cod's eye.* The ring of light caused by reflection of the girdle seen around the table of a shallow stone, making it appear like a baleful eye.

Flat. A grade for the shape of rough stones, i.e. those that are relatively thin, which may include parts of macles, but not whole ones which are graded separately.

Flute. A thin paper used to line a diamond parcel paper.

Footwall. The floor of a mine working.

Four-point diamond. With a cubic face as the table.

Full-cut brilliant. Correct name for a brilliant-cut diamond with 56 facets plus table and culet.

G.A. Gemmological Association of Great Britain and Northern Ireland.

Garimpeiro. Unlicensed Brazilian miner or prospector.

G.I.A. Gemological Institute of America.

Girdle. The outline edge of a polished stone, by which it is normally set.

Girdling. Another name for cutting or bruting, by which the rough stone is rounded.

Glassie. Miner's name for a regular octahedral crystal with flat, glass-like faces.

Glazing. An intermediate process of sanding between grinding and polishing used for faceting gemstones other than diamond.

Gletz. (Also spelled glets, glatts, etc.) Another name, of Dutch origin, for a feather.

Goods. For security reasons diamonds are commonly referred to as 'goods', as in 'rough goods' and 'polished goods'.

Grader. A skilled person who separates polished diamonds into sizes and quality grades by clarity, colour, and accuracy of cut.

Grain. A quarter of a metric carat, hence a grainer is a diamond of that weight, a four-grainer is a carat stone, and a six-grainer is a stone of 1·50 carats.

Grain. Cutter's and polisher's name for the visible evidence of the crystal structure of a diamond, which determines his procedure.

Growth lines. Banding sometimes seen (with difficulty) within a diamond, parallel (usually) to the octahedral faces.

Habit. The shape of crystallization favoured by a mineral. For diamond it is the octahedron.

Halves. Brillianteerer's name for the lower girdle and upper girdle facets.

Hanging wall. The roof of a mine working.

Herkimer diamond. Not a diamond, but a small, bright, double-terminated quartz crystal from Herkimer County, New York, U.S.A.

Hidden stone. Because of colour saturation in a parcel of stones, one or several of worse or better quality, are 'hidden' by the effect until separated.

Hope Collection. The Hope Diamond was only one item in the early 19th century collection of Thomas P. Hope, which included a 2½ in (65 mm) pearl, a 1½ in (35 mm) catseye, and a 45 carat flawless chrysoberyl.

I.D.B. Illicit diamond buyer.

Illusion setting. A mount for a very small diamond which is set in a reflecting plate to make it look larger.

India-cut. A clumsy form of single-cut adopted in the past by East Indian cutters but rarely seen in western markets.

Indicator mineral. A mineral such as garnet or ilmenite that may indicate the presence also of diamond. Called a 'sputnik' by Russian miners and a 'bantam' by South African diggers.

Jager. A diamond with a faint tint of blue, named after those found in the Jagersfontein mine. The blue may be due to strong blue fluorescence.

Kerf. A notch cut in a diamond with another to prepare it for cleaving.

Lasering. Drilling a diamond by laser to remove dark inclusions by acidising.

Lasque. Same as a portrait stone.

Laxey. Appearance of a diamond that is cut brilliant style, but very shallow.

Limpid. Transparent, like water.

Loose diamond. An unmounted, polished stone.

Lumpy stone. A polished diamond with an over-depth pavilion.

Lustre. Quality of a surface in reflected light. A diamond's is unique and called an 'adamantine lustre'.

Maakbar. Belgian cutter's name for a low quality rough diamond that cannot be sawn or cleaved. The Indian cutting industry specializes in them.

Macle. (Also spelled maccle.) A usually rather flat, triangular-shaped natural diamond caused by so-called spinel twinning of an octahedron.

Make. The finish or variation applied to a cut by a particular diamond manufacturer.

Makeables. Rough diamonds that can be cut and polished without preliminary sawing or cleaving.

Mangelin. An old Hindu weight for gems equal to about $1\frac{3}{8}$ carat.

Mecal. A manufacturer's term for bad diamonds.

Melange. An assortment of diamonds of different sizes larger than mêlée that may also be of mixed qualities.

Mêlée. Rough diamonds (now called *sawable*), between 0·2 and 1·4 ct; or polished diamonds brilliant-cut between about 0·20 and 0·50 ct.

Middlings. The screened-out medium-sized gravels in which diamonds are most likely to be found.

Miner's wallet. A long bag, nearly 5ft (1.5m) by 18in (45cm), formerly used by miners to carry gravel to water for screening.

Mishkal. An early Moslem weight for gems, equal to 40 ratis or 36·4 carats.

Mixed-cut. Two different cuts mixed, such as a brilliant-cut crown and step-cut pavilion.

Motichul. Hindu name for a diamond that is clear and brilliant.

Mount or *Mounting.* The part of a piece of jewellery into which a stone is set. There is a separate craft of mounter.

N.A.G. National Association of Goldsmiths, Great Britain.

Naif (Also spelled nyf, naive, and naife.) The natural surface of the unpolished diamond or what cutters and polishers call its 'skin'. A *natural* (q.v.) is a naif.

Natural. A part of the natural surface of a rough diamond left on the girdle by the cutter striving for maximum weight retention. Another name is *naif.* An indented natural is sometimes called a *bewijs* by cutters.

Navette. Another name for marquise, i.e. boat-shaped.

Near-gem. A quality of rough diamonds between gem and industrial, that could be used as either depending on demand of the markets.

Octagon work. The process of putting the 8 main facets on the top and bottom of a stone, which makes the table octagon-shaped.

Old-miner. An old mine-cut diamond. (See Fig. 10.4).

Ore pass. A vertical or sloping tunnel down which ore passes by gravity.

Open culet. A culet that is larger than normal.

Open table. Larger than normal table facet.

Open cast or *open pit*. Mining from the surface.

Opening a diamond. Polishing a window on a rough stone to see inside it.

Over-blue. A diamond that has such strong blue fluorescence that it has a milky blue appearance in daylight, masking its true body colour.

Oxidized diamond. One coated or containing iron oxide which produces an orange or reddish brown colour, removable if the colouring is on the surface or in an open fissure.

Parcel. A collection of different categories of rough diamonds made up by the D.T.C. for a client at a sight.

Pavilion. The bottom part of a polished stone below the girdle.

Pipe. A roughly funnel-shaped, approximately vertical extrusion of volcanic breccia and kimberlite that may or may not contain diamonds.

Piqué or *PK*. A term meaning a lower grade of clarity or purity.

Point. A hundredth of a carat: thus 0·72 ct is seventy-two points.

Polished girdle. A girdle that has been polished but not faceted, patented by A. Monnickendam.

Polishing lines. Grooves left by the scaive on the surface of a facet.

Portrait stone. A thin flat natural or polished diamond that has been bevelled for use as a 'glass' for a miniature portrait or as a watch 'glass'.

Premier. The name given to a stone that is more or less cloudy with a bluish tinge that changes to a yellowish or brownish shade in some lights. Such stones are found in the Premier Mine.

Puddle. The mud formed when using a mechanical washing pan which helps to float off some of the tailings.

Pure. A word used as an alternative to clean.

Quality. The degree of excellence of a diamond, measured by its weight, colour, purity or clarity, and (polished) its perfection of proportions and finish.

Rati. An Indian weight for gems equal to 0·91 carat.

Reef. The country rock surrounding a diamondiferous kimberlite.

Reflector. A brilliant-cut diamond that shows multiple reflections of an inclusion when viewed through the table.

Rejection. Term used for very spotted stones only just good enough for cutting and polishing, by apprentices for example, or if there is a market.

River. An old name for the white colour of many stones found in the river diggings.

Rondisting. Second rounding operation carried out by the bruter after a diamond has been blocked.

Rough. The name given to crystals of diamond as they are mined, i.e. before being cut. It is used as in 'rough diamonds' or just 'rough'.

Running lines. Lines on a facet made by grinding or polishing.

Sawyer. The craftsman responsible for sawing diamonds.

Sawable. Rough goods in the stone and shape categories that can be divided by sawing.

Scaife. (Also spelled scaive or scaif.) The horizontal, rotating mill or grinding wheel on which a diamond is polished.

Screening. Sieving gravels, usually with water, to eliminate large and very small stones.

Series. Rough diamonds between about 1 and 10 carats in weight.

Set. A diamond or other stone is set in a mount. (But, confusingly, a mount is also called a 'setting'.)

Shape. A rough diamond of good, untwinned crystal shape, but not good enough to be classified as a stone.

Sharp. The name given to the piece of diamond used for notching a diamond to be cleaved.

Shovel. A small stainless steel scoop used for handling large numbers of small diamonds.

Sights. The special sales held in London by the D.T.C. at which invited buyers examine the parcels of rough selected for them before purchase.

Smalls. Small rough diamonds below about 2 ct.

Snowy. An old description for a very white stone, especially a rough stone.

Sorter. A skilled person who separates rough diamonds into sizes and quality grades by shape, colour, and purity.

Specials. Rough diamonds over 10 carats each in weight.

Spotted. A term used for low purity stones, with marks visible to the naked eye, when grading them.

Spread Stone. A brilliant-cut diamond with a large table (over about 60 per cent) and thin crown.

Star facets. The 8 triangular facets around the table that make it star-shaped.

Step-cut. With rows of four-sided facets.

Stone. When used as a grading term, a diamond of good octahedral shape.

Stope. The working place where the ore (in this case diamonds) is extracted in an underground mine working.

Swindled stone. A diamond cut to retain maximum weight at the expense of accuracy of cut.

Table. The large facet on the top of the crown of a stone.

Tailings. Discarded rocks and minerals from a mining operation.

Tang. A frame or jig to which is attached a dop when polishing a diamond.

Terrace. An alluvial deposit on a flat area of a river or former river bank. Also known as a bench placer.

Three-point diamond. With an octahedral face as the table.

Treated. Description applied to a diamond that has been altered (except by normal cutting and polishing) to change its appearance, e.g. by artificial coloration or laser drilling.

Triangle. A triangular-shaped rough diamond with pointed corners that may or may not be a macle. The classification is industrial.

Trigon. A triangular growth or etch feature that occurs in large numbers on the octahedral faces of natural diamonds.

Trommel. Circular rotating drum with holes along the sides for sieving gravels.

Two-point diamond. With a dodecahedral face as the table.

Wass. A Dutch name, pronounced 'vass', for grain, an octahedral face, or a diamond cut with this face almost as the table.

Wassie. A large *cleavage* made by a *cleaver*.

Well. Another name for a dark centre in a polished stone.

Wesselton. An early colour grading term based on the kind of stones found in the Wesselton mine. A top Wesselton stone had a very very slight tinge of yellow and was placed just under a River stone.

White. An adjective used by the diamond trade to mean colourless and transparent.

Wholestone. Manufacturer's name for a stone that has not been sawn or cleaved, i.e. a two- or three-point stone.

Window. A facet polished on a diamond that has a rough or coated surface, in order to see inside it. Also a facet on a polished stone that leaks light and looks like a window when seen through the table.

THE WORLD'S LARGEST ROUGH GEM DIAMONDS

Rank	Carats	Name	Date found	Place	Cut into
1.	3,106·0	Cullinan	1905	South Africa	Cullinan I–IX; 96 others
2.	995·2	Excelsior	1893	South Africa	21 gems (largest 69·80 ct)
3.	968·9	Star of Sierra Leone	1972	Sierra Leone	143·20 ct emerald-cut + 10 others
4.	793·0	Great Mogul	1650	India	Great Mogul (280·00 ct)
5.	770·0	Woyie River	1945	Sierra Leone	30 gems (Largest 31·55 ct)
6.	726·6	Vargas	1938	Brazil	Vargas (48·26 ct) + 22 others
7.	726·0	Jonker	1934	South Africa	Jonker (125·65 ct) + 11 others
8.	650·3	Reitz	1895	South Africa	Jubilee (245·35 ct) + 1 other
9.	616·0	Kimberley Octahedron	1974	South Africa	Uncut; at Open Mine Museum
10.	609·3	Baumgold Rough	1923	South Africa	14 gems (sizes unknown)
11.	601·3	Lesotho	1967	Lesotho	17 gems (largest 70·00 ct)
12.	600·0	Goyaz	1906	Brazil	8 ct gem from 1 fragment
13.	572·3	(unnamed)	1955	South Africa	(found in Jagersfontein)
14.	532·0	(unnamed)	1943	Sierra Leone	(unknown)
15.	527·0	(unnamed)	1965	Lesotho	(unknown)
16.	516·5	Kimberley Rough	1896	South Africa	Kimberley (55·09 ct)
17.	511·3	Venter	1951	South Africa	32 gems (largest 18·00 ct)
18.	509·6	(unnamed)	1976	Sierra Leone	(unknown)
19.	469·0	Victoria 1884	1884	South Africa	Victoria 1884 (185·00 ct)
20.	455·0	Darcy Vargas	1939	Brazil	(unknown)
21.	454·0	(unnamed)	1914	South Africa	(found in Dutoitspan)
22.	434·6	Light of Peace	1969	West Africa	Zale Light of Peace (130·27 ct)
23.	434·0	De Beers	1890	South Africa	De Beers (234·50 ct)
24.	426·5	Niarchos	1954	South Africa	Niarchos (128·25 ct) + 2 others

		(ct)	Country	Year	Notes
25.	Berglen	416·3	South Africa	1924	(unknown)
26.	Broderick	412·5	South Africa	1928	(found at Barkly West)
27.	Pitt	410·0	India	1701	Regent (140·50 ct)
28.	Presidente Dutra	409·0	Brazil	1946	46 gems (largest 9·06 ct)
29.	Coromandel IV	400·7	Brazil	1941	(unknown)
30.	Arc	381·0	South Africa	1921	(found at Gong Gong)
31.	Diario de Minas Gerais	375·1	Brazil	1941	(unknown)
32.	Red Cross	375·0	South Africa	1910?	Red Cross (205 ct)
33.	Tiros I	354·0	Brazil	1938	(unknown)
34.	Premier Rose	353·9	South Africa	1978	120 ct pear (largest estimate)
35.	(unnamed)	350·0	South Africa	1951	(found in Jagersfontein)
36.	(unnamed)	346·2	Brazil	1948	(a cleavage)
37.	Nizam	340·0	India	1835	Nizam (277·00 ct)
38.	(unnamed)	338·0	Lesotho	1969	(found at Kao)
39.	Bob Grove	337·0	South Africa	1908	(found at Vaal River)
40.	Brady	330·0	South Africa	1902	(found at Vaal River)
41.	Victoria II	328·3	Brazil	1943	44 gems (largest 30·39 ct)
42.	Nooitgedacht	325·0	South Africa	1965	(found at Nooitgedacht)
43.	(unnamed)	325·0	Brazil	1948?	(unknown)
44.	Patos	324·0	Brazil	1957	(unknown)
45.	(unnamed)	315·0	South Africa	1956	(found at Nooitgedacht)

Original list by courtesy of N. W. Ayer and Son Inc., New York, U.S.A.
New information by courtesy of the Hon. Ian Balfour, London.
As far as is known, all these stones were of cutting quality. The Kaplan (620·00 ct) is the tenth biggest known, and the biggest still in rough, but is not of gem quality.

APPENDIX 2

THE WORLD'S LARGEST POLISHED GEM DIAMONDS

Rank	Carats	Name	Colour	Shape	Present owner or location
1.	530·20	Cullinan I	white	pear	British Crown Jewels – Tower of London
2.	312·40	Cullinan II	white	cushion	British Crown Jewels – Tower of London
3.	280·00	Great Mogul (?Orloff)	white	rose cut	Disappeared after 1747
4.	277·00	Nizam	white	dome	Nizam of Hyderabad – 1934
5.	245·35	Jubilee	white	cushion	Paul-Louis Weiller – Paris
6.	234·50	De Beers	yellow	(unknown)	Indian prince – about 1890
7.	205·07	Red Cross	yellow	square	Unknown – auctioned in London, 1918
8.	202·00	Black Star of Africa	black	(unknown)	Exhibited in Tokyo, 1971
9.	189·60	Orloff	white	rose-cut	Russian Diamond Treasury – Kremlin, Moscow
10.	185·00	Darya-i-Nûr (Iran)	pink	table-cut	Iranian Treasury – Teheran
11.	184·50	Victoria	white	oval	Nizam of Hyderabad – about 1885
12.	183·00	Moon	yellow	brilliant	Unknown – auctioned in London, 1942
13.	152·16	Iranian A	yellow	cushion	Iranian Treasury – Teheran
14.	150·00	Darya-i-Nûr (Dacca)	white	cushion	Nawab of Dacca – India 1959
15.	147·00	Turkey I	(unknown)	(unknown)	In Turkish regalia in 1882
16.	140·50	Regent	white	cushion	The Louvre – Paris
17.	137·27	Florentine	yellow	double rose	Disappeared after World War I
18.	136·50	Queen of Holland	blue	cushion	Indian maharajah – about 1927
19.	136·32	Unnamed	bluish	cushion	Offered in London – 1960
20.	135·45	Iranian B	yellow	cushion	Iranian Treasury – Teheran
21.	130·27	Zole Light of Peace	(unknown)	pear	Zale Corporation, U.S.A.
22.	128·50	Star of the South	white	oval	Rustomjee Jamsetjee – Bombay – about 1939
23.	128·51	Tiffany	canary	cushion	Tiffany & Co. – New York
24.	128·25	Niarchos	white	pear	Stavros P. Niarchos – Greece
25.	127·00	Portuguese	white	emerald	Smithsonian Institution – Washington

Rank	Carats	Name	Colour	Shape	Present owner or location
26.	125·65	Jonker	white	emerald	Royal Family of Nepal – 1959
27.	123·93	Iranian C	yellow	cushion	Iranian Treasury – Teheran
28.	123·00	Stewart	white	brilliant	Unknown – cut about 1875
29.	123·00	Julius Pam	white	(unknown)	Unknown – cut about 1890
30.	121·90	Iranian D	yellow	octahedron	Iranian Treasury – Teheran
31.	120·00	Moon of the Mountains	white	cushion	Disappeared after 1900
32.	120·00est.	Premier Rose	yellow	pear	Being cut – 1978
33.	118·05	Meister	yellow	cushion	W. Meister, Zürich
34.	115·06	Taj-e-Mah	white	'mogul'-cut	Iranian Treasury – Teheran
35.	115·00	Edna Star	(unknown)	emerald	Sold in New York – 1957
36.	114·28	Iranian E	yellow	cushion	Iranian Treasury – Teheran
37.	114·03	Unnamed	yellow	cushion	Sold by Christies – 1962
38.	111·59	Earth Star	brown	pear	Baumgold Bros. – New York
39.	109·26	Cross of Asia	champagne	table-cut	Unknown – exhibited about 1935
40.	108·93	Koh-i-Nûr	white	oval	British Crown Jewels – Tower of London
41.	107·46	Rojtman	yellow	cushion	Mrs. Marc Rojtman – New York – 1966
42.	107·07	Louis Cartier	white	pear	Sold in Geneva – 1958
43.	106·75	Star of Egypt	white	emerald	Unknown – shown in London Office after 1850
44.	105·54	Sol et d'Or	yellow	emerald	Exhibited in Paris
45.	104·88	Deepdene (?104·52)	yellow	cushion	Colour treated stone offered in Geneva – 1971
46.	104·15	Great Chrysanthemum	bronze	pear	Julius Cohen – New York
47.	102·00	Ashberg	yellow	cushion	Unknown – sold about 1960
48.	101·00	Hastings	(unknown)	(unknown)	Unknown since presentation to George III, 1786
49.	100·00	Jacob	white	(unknown)	Bank of India – 1956
50.	99·52	Shah of Persia	yellow	cushion	Private owner – 1965
51.	95·40	Golconda d'Or	golden	emerald	Dunklings, Jewellers, Melbourne, Australia
52.	95·38	Unnamed	yellow	square	Sold by Christies – 1973
53.	94·80	Star of the East	white	pear	Unknown since abdication of King Farouk, 1952
54.	94·40	Cullinan III	white	pear	British Crown Jewels – Tower of London
55.	90·38	Briolette of India	(unknown)	briolette	Sold in Europe – 1971
56.	88·70	Shah	white	bar	Russian Diamond Treasury – Kremlin, Moscow

Rank	Carats	Name	Colour	Shape	Present owner or location
57.	88·00	Star of Persia	yellow	cushion	Private owner – 1965
58.	86·61	Iranian VI	yellow	triangular	Iranian Treasury – Teheran
59.	86·28	Iranian VII	yellow	'Mogul'	Iranian Treasury – Teheran
60.	85·93	Sterns Star	yellow	brilliant	Sterns Organization, Johannesburg
61.	84·00	Spoonmaker's (?Turkey II)	white	pear	Was in Turkish regalia – 1882
62.	83·00	Jahangir	white	pear	C. Patel – India – 1957
63.	81·83	Unnamed	pink	oval	Sold in London – 1972
64.	79·41	Nepal	white	pear	Private owner – 1960
65.	78·96	Iranian VIII	yellow	cushion	Iranian Treasury – Teheran
66.	78·54	Archduke Joseph	white	cushion	Private owner – 1951
67.	78·54	Storewin	(unknown)	emerald	Sold in Geneva – 1962
68.	78·53	Porges	champagne	emerald	Sold in U.S.A. – 1968
69.	76·50	English Dresden	white	pear	Cursetjee Fardoonji – India – about 1939
70.	75·52	Star of Independence	(unknown)	pear	Sold to Middle East buyer – 1976
71.	75·29	Iranian IX	yellow	cushion	Iranian Treasury – Teheran
72.	75·00	Iranian X	yellow	pendeloque	Iranian Treasury – Teheran
73.	75·00	Unnamed	(unknown)	brilliant	Sold in Belgium – 1973
74.	72·84	Iranian XI	yellow	pendeloque	Iranian Treasury – Teheran
75.	72·00	Nepal Pink	pink	cushion	Reported in Napal, 1959
76.	71·73	Lesotho I	brownish	emerald	Private owner – New York
77.	71·07	Fleischman Star	canary	emerald	Sold in Paris – 1957
78.	71·70	Akbar Shah	white	drop	Gaekwar of Baroda – 1867
79.	70·20	Idol's Eye	white	cushion	Harry Levinson – Chicago
80.	69·80	(from Excelsior)	white	pear	Unknown – sold by Tiffany, 1903
81.	69·42	Taylor-Burton	white	pear	Elizabeth Taylor
82.	68·00	Tennant	yellow	(unknown)	James Tennant – 1873
83.	67·89	Transvaal	champagne	pear	Baumgold Bros. – New York
84.	67·50	Black Orloff	gun metal	cushion	Charles F. Winson – New York
85.	65·65	Iranian XII	champagne	pear	Iranian Treasury – Teheran
86.	65·60	Golden Maharaja	golden	pear	Shown in Paris – 1937
87.	64·00	Golden Pelican	yellow	emerald	E. Severy and M. Ginsberg – Antwerp – 1958

Rank	Carats	Name	Colour	Shape	Present owner or location
88.	63·60	Cullinan IV	white	square	British Crown Jewels – Tower of London
89.	62·50	Jagersfontein	white	pear	Private owner – 1954
90.	62·05	Winston	white	pear	See Louis XIV (No. 101)
91.	61·50	Golden Dawn	yellow	brilliant	Aga Khan – 1926
92.	61·50	Tigerseye	amber	brilliant	(Rough from Vaal River – 1913)
93.	60·75	Cuiaba	rose	(unknown)	(Brazilian stone)
94.	60·67	Lesotho II	brownish	emerald	Unknown – cut in New York
95.	60·40	Sancy (Patiala)	white	pear	Maharajah of Patiala – 1944
96.	60·25	Prince Edward of York	white	pear	Private owner – 1901
97.	60·00	Iranian XIII	yellow	brilliant	Iranian Treasury – Teheran
98.	60·00	Nûr-ul-Ain	pink	(unknown)	Iranian Treasury – Teheran
99.	60·00	Tai Hang Star	(unknown)	(unknown)	Cut in Johannesburg
100.	60·00	Half Regent	white	D-shape	Sold in Paris – 1933
101.	59·46	Louis XIV	white	pear	Sold as pair with Winston – 1964
102.	58·10	Christopher Black	black	(unknown)	Sold in New York – 1969
103.	57·85	Iranian XIV	yellow	brilliant	Iranian Treasury – Teheran
104.	57·15	Iranian XV	yellow	cushion	Iranian Treasury – Teheran
105.	56·60	Pam	white	brilliant	Unknown after being shown to Queen Victoria, 1892
106.	56·60	Porter-Rhodes	white	emerald	Private owner – 1939
107.	56·19	Iranian XVI	yellow	cushion	Iranian Treasury – Teheran
108.	56·00	Bickerton-Carteen	white	(unknown)	Sold in Paris – 1958
109.	55·67	Iranian XVIII	yellow	cushion	Iranian Treasury – Teheran
110.	55·09	Kimberley	champagne	emerald	Baumgold Bros. – New York
111.	55·00	Baumgold-Brilliant	white	brilliant	Private owner – 1966
112.	55·00	Sancy (Astor)	white	pear	Viscount Astor – England – 1966
113.	54·70	Byfield	(unknown)	(unknown)	Sold in New York – 1971
114.	54·58	Iranian XVIII	white	cushion	Iranian Treasury – Teheran
115.	54·35	Iranian XIX	peach	cushion	Iranian Treasury – Teheran
116.	53·96	Star of Sierra Leone	white	pear	Unknown – Cut in New York
117.	53·50	Iranian XX	yellow	cushion	Iranian Treasury – Teheran
118.	52·00	Baumgold-Brilliant	white	brilliant	Unknown buyer

Rank	Carats	Name	Colour	Shape	Present owner or location
119.	51·90	Iranian XXI	white	oval 'mogul'	Iranian Treasury – Teheran
120.	51·00	Eugenie	white	oval	Mrs. N. J. Dady – Bombay – about 1935
121.	50·53	Tri-Sakti	white	emerald	Borneo stone – Sold by Indonesian government
122.	50·28	La Favorite	white	(unknown)	Private Owner – 1934
123.	50·00	Cleveland	white	cushion	Unknown – cut in New York, 1884
124.	50·00	Grand Condé	pink	pear	Condé Museum – Chantilly
125.	50·00	Crown	honey	cushion	Russian Crown Jewels
126.	50·00	Indore Pears	(unknown)	pear	Two 50 ct stones – sold New York, 1976
127.	50·00	Baumgold Pears	bluish	pear	Two 50 ct stones – cut in New York

Original list by courtesy of N. W. Ayer & Son Inc. New York. New information from the Hon. Ian Balfour and the G.I.A.'s Diamond Dictionary.

FOLDING A DIAMOND PAPER

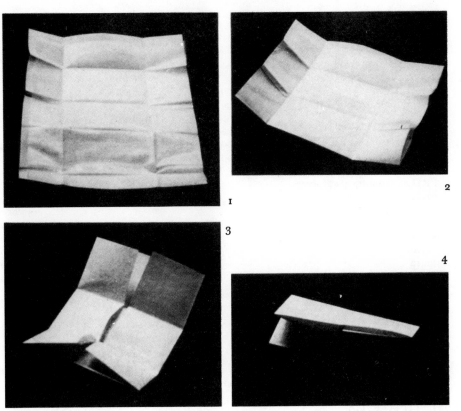

Sequence of folding a diamond parcel paper, the traditional method of carrying polished diamonds. This paper has a white lining paper. It is best to place larger diamonds in a folded piece of lint inside the paper.

APPENDIX 4

ESTIMATED WORLD PRODUCTION OF DIAMONDS, 1975 (in carats)

Country	Gem	Industrial	Total
AFRICA (large producers)			
De Beers (except as below)	2,518,000	2,061,000	4,579,000
Premier Mine	509,000	1,527,000	2,036,000
South West Africa	1,660,000	88,000	1,748,000
Zaire	1,076,000	11,734,000	12,810,000
Sierra Leone	600,000	900,000	1,500,000
Botswana	362,000	2,052,000	2,414,000
Ghana	233,000	2,095,000	2,328,000
AFRICA (smaller producers)			
Angola	—	—	460,000
Central African Rep.	—	—	339,000
Guinea	—	—	80,000
Ivory Coast	—	—	209,000
Lesotho	—	—	3,000
Liberia	—	—	406,000
Tanzania	—	—	448,000
De Beers	—	—	680,000
TOTAL AFRICA			30,004,000
U.S.S.R.			9,700,000
All mines	1,950,000	7,750,000	
SOUTH AFRICA			
Venezuela	239,000	821,000	1,060,000
Brazil	—	—	270,000
Guyana	—	—	21,000
ASIA			
India	—	—	20,000
Indonesia	—	—	15,000
TOTAL OTHERS			11,086,000
GRAND TOTAL			41,126,000

CHANGES IN TOTAL WORLD DIAMOND PRODUCTION

1970	11,349,000	40,554,000	51,904,000
1973	12,462,000	30,605,000	43,067,000
1974	12,212,000	32,310,000	44,522,000
1975	10,867,000	30,259,000	41,126,000
1976	10,320,000	29,406,000	39,726,000

Figures for industrial grit production are not available. In 1969, the estimated production was 40,000,000 carats; in 1978, it must far exceed this and also the volume of natural grit, the production of which is falling.

The figures were compiled from those calculated by Adelmo Lunghi from the records of Bureau of Mines, Washington D.C., and published in the Belgian journal *Diamant*. Acknowledgement is gratefully made to these sources.

APPENDIX 5

Shapes and Sizes of Diamond Pipes

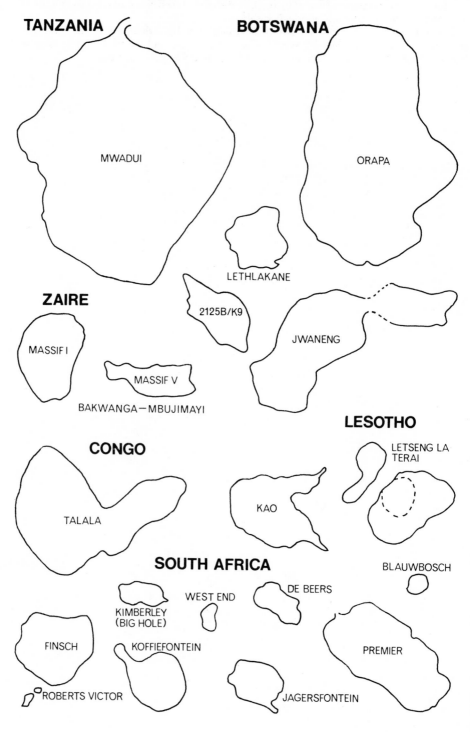

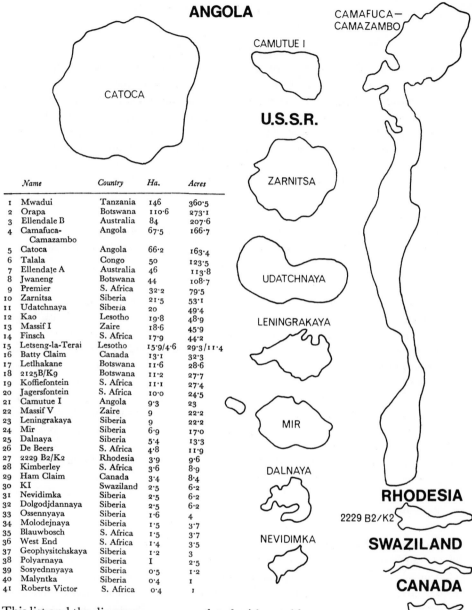

ANGOLA

CATOCA

CAMUTUE I

CAMAFUCA—
CAMAZAMBO

U.S.S.R.

ZARNITSA

UDATCHNAYA

LENINGRAKAYA

MIR

DALNAYA

RHODESIA

2229 B2/K2

NEVIDIMKA

SWAZILAND

CANADA

HAM CLAIM

BATTY
CLAIM

	Name	Country	Ha.	Acres
1	Mwadui	Tanzania	146	360·5
2	Orapa	Botswana	110·6	273·1
3	Ellendale B	Australia	84	207·6
4	Camafuca-Camazambo	Angola	67·5	166·7
5	Catoca	Angola	66·2	163·4
6	Talala	Congo	50	123·5
7	Ellendale A	Australia	46	113·8
8	Jwaneng	Botswana	44	108·7
9	Premier	S. Africa	32·2	79·5
10	Zarnitsa	Siberia	21·5	53·1
11	Udatchnaya	Siberia	20	49·4
12	Kao	Lesotho	19·8	48·9
13	Massif I	Zaire	18·6	45·9
14	Finsch	S. Africa	17·9	44·2
15	Letseng-la-Terai	Lesotho	15·9/4·6	29·3/11·4
16	Batty Claim	Canada	13·1	32·3
17	Letlhakane	Botswana	11·6	28·6
18	2125B/K9	Botswana	11·2	27·7
19	Koffiefontein	S. Africa	11·1	27·4
20	Jagersfontein	S. Africa	10·0	24·5
21	Camutue I	Angola	9·3	23
22	Massif V	Zaire	9	22·2
23	Leningrakaya	Siberia	9	22·2
24	Mir	Siberia	6·9	17·0
25	Dalnaya	Siberia	5·4	13·3
26	De Beers	S. Africa	4·8	11·9
27	2229 B2/K2	Rhodesia	3·9	9·6
28	Kimberley	S. Africa	3·6	8·9
29	Ham Claim	Canada	3·4	8·4
30	KI	Swaziland	2·5	6·2
31	Nevidimka	Siberia	2·5	6·2
32	Dolgodjdannaya	Siberia	2·5	6·2
33	Ossennyaya	Siberia	1·6	4
34	Molodejnaya	Siberia	1·5	3·7
35	Blauwbosch	S. Africa	1·5	3·7
36	West End	S. Africa	1·4	3·5
37	Geophysitchskaya	Siberia	1·2	3
38	Polyarnaya	Siberia	1	2·5
39	Sosyednnyaya	Siberia	0·5	1·2
40	Malyntka	Siberia	0·4	1
41	Roberts Victor	S. Africa	0·4	1

This list and the diagrams were completed with considerable assistance from John Martens, General Manager, Orapa Diamond Mine, Botswana, and Arthur Wilson, Editor of *The International Diamond Annual*. Not all the kimberlite pipes named are in production and it is not known if all those in Siberia are diamondiferous. There is a bigger pipe in Australia, the Fitzroy (128 ha./315·3 acres), but it is not known at this reprinting whether it is diamondiferous or not.

APPENDIX 6

Practical Grading Standards

The Hoog Raad Voor Diamant (H.R.D. – Diamond High Council), Antwerp, Belgium, which is the controlling body of the industry in Belgium and covers four diamond exchanges, the professional associations and the trades unions, has set up a diamond certification service under the control of the General Sciences and Physics division of the solid state laboratory of Antwerp University. Certain standards agreed by the H.R.D. fall in most cases into line with those of the G.I.A.* in America, R.A.L.† in West Germany, and C.I.B.J.O.‡ in European and other countries. They are summarized below:

Weight

Weight is expressed in carats to two points of decimals. If the third point is under 9, the second is rounded down; if it is 9, the second point is rounded up.

Purity

Internal characteristics only are judged. To determine the limit between IF (Internally flawless) and VVS1, a series of test stones was selected with bright pinpoint features that increased in size from 3 to 12 micron (0·003 to 0·0122 mm). It was found that the average experienced grader failed to find features below 5 micron using a 10 × loupe under normal lighting. This definition was therefore derived:

> 'A diamond is referred to as being internally flawless as long as it does not contain any internal characteristics which are better visible than the internal characteristic whose perceptible image has a circle shape having a diameter of 5 micron and a brightness of 1.'

The grade IF is retained for diamond with only structure failures, such as growth lines, twinning seams, and knot lines, but a remark is made on the certificate. Mention is also made on the certificate if important external features are evident.

Colour and Fluorescence

Colours are determined by the C.I.B.J.O. scale, corresponding to the master stones held in Paris. Corresponding colours on the G.I.A. or Scan.D.N.‡‡ scales will also be given on certificates if required. Colours that are light brown (or other non-yellowish tints) are compared with the master stones in the same way as diamonds having yellowish tints and the colour variation noted on the certificate if clearly visible. Fluorescence is graded similarly against standard test diamonds under long wave ultra-violet light.

* Gemological Institute of America
† (Reichs)-Ausschuss fur Lieferbedingungen und Gutessicherung beim DNA, or German Standards Association's (State) Committee on quality.
‡ Comité International de Bijouterie, Joaillerie, et Orfevre; also called the International Confederation of Jewellery, Silverware, Diamonds, Pearls, and Stones.
‡‡ Scandinavian Diamond Nomenclature and Grading Standards.

Proportion and Finish

Proportions are given on a certificate, but no judgement of quality is made. Commercial ranges of proportions have been published by the H.R.D., however, as follows:

Crown height to total height	10 to 16·5%
Pavilion height to total height	40·5 to 45%
Table diameter to total diameter	56 to 68%
Crown angle	30 to 37·5°
Pavilion angle	39 to 42·5°

An application for a certificate automatically involves a preliminary examination and, if this reveals that the diamond could be upgraded by removal of some blemish, it is returned for improvement before final certification.

A System of Purity Grading

Diamond Grading Laboratories Ltd, London, who have standardized colour grading by a points system (that can be converted to other systems) by using a spectro-photometer modified for use on diamonds (page 280), have attempted to standardize purity grading. The size of the defect is defined by reference to a series of circles and corresponding dots numbered from 1 to 9. They are based on the Porton graticule standard by K. R. May and increase by a factor of $\sqrt{}$.

Such a graticule is built into one eyepiece of a 10 × stereo microscope with dark field illumination. The size of an inclusion is designated by two of the numbered dots, one corresponding to its width and the other to its length. The sum of the two figures is modified by a brightness or reflectivity factor, by a second relating to the position of the defect, and by a third relating to its nature. The number of points finally arrived at is referred to a grading system. For example, 1·5 to less than 5 points relating to external marks only, is Internally Flawless; 26 to 61 is VS1; and 1000 to 2500 is 1st Piqué.

Index

Page numbers in italics refer to the illustrations

519

pipe mines—*contd.*
  distribution, South Africa, *357*
  geology of, *352–3*
  yields, 360–1
Pitt, Thomas, 458
Pitt (*later* Regent) diamond, 4, *4*, 23, 208, 457–9
pitting, hexagonal, 95
Platberg, 30
platinum mounting, 269, 490
Plato, 8
Plewman, Mr., 46
Pliny the Elder, 2, 6, 16
Pniel, 30, 41, 44, 46–7, 52
Poclain trench digger, 132, *133*
Pohle, Dr. H., 83
point-cut, 7, 197, 210
poison, diamond as, 9–10
Polar Star diamond, 467
polarised light, examination by, 33, 172, 237, 314, 407, 440
polished stones
  clarity (purity) grading, 282–315
  colour grading, 264–81
  cut grading, 316–22
  weight, 322–34
polishing and grinding *see* grinding and polishing
polishing lines, 286, 310, 312, 383, 478
Pomona, recovery barge, *136*, 137
Pomona syndicate, 79
Popugayeva, L. A., 97
Porter-Rhodes diamond, 467
portrait stones, 371, 473
powder, diamond, 205, 244, 251, 422, 431
  manufacture, 391–2
practical fine cut, 229
precious and semi-precious, origin of terms, 8–9
  classes, 9
Precious Stones Act, 87–8
Premier mine, 78–9, *78*, 94, *125*, 126, 128, *128*, 158, 272, 356–7, 360–1, 410, 446
Premier Mining Co., 446
President Vargas diamond, 449, 467
Pretorius, President, 47–8
prices, 6, 12, 21, 27, 167, 170, 178, 273–4, 282, 322
  control, 172–3, 180, 341, 344
  cutting and, 336–7
  estimating, 337–9
  investment, 341–5
  per carat, 180, 235, 264, 288, 316, 336, 338–9
  picking prices, 264, 288
  premium, 340
  rough, 336
  slumps, 169–70, 181
  stability, 341, 344
  structure, 345–6
Princess (profile) cut, 216, *225*
Prinsloo, Joachim, 79

production, worldwide, 17
properties of diamond, 18–20, 396–420
  cutting, 1, 5
  density, 407, 425, 479
  elasticity, 420
  electrical behaviour, 150, 398, 410, 419–20
  friction, 420
  hardness, 1, 2–3, 244, 246–7, 402–7
  melting point, 398
  optical, 407–19
  thermal conductivity, 398, 419, 474
proportions
  ideal, 228, 235, 290, 316–22, *318*
  misproportioned stones, *317–20*
  ProportionScope, 320–2, *321*
prospecting and sampling, 134, *134–5*, 156–66
  coastal and marine, 165–6
  Kalahari, 159–63, *160–3*
  modern, 158–9
  sampling techniques, 159–60, 164–6
  scientific, 157–8
  traditional, 156–7
Ptolemy, 23
pulsator, 141
purity *see* clarity
pyrophyllite, 427–8
pyroxene, 352
pyrrhotite, 355
Pythagoras, 210

quality, 179–80
  sorting rough for, 188–90
quartz, 360, 363, 403, 472, 474, 487
Queen's Necklace affair, 470–1

Rabinowitz, Solomon, 84
radioactive isotope bombardment, 442
radium treatment, 442
railways
  South Africa, 44, 76
  South West Africa, 80, *82*
Raleigh, Sir Walter, 16
Raman, Sir C. V., 402
Ramkheria workings, 26
Ramulkolta (Raolconda) workings, 26, 197
Rand goldfields, 72
rarity value, 11
Rawstone, Fleetwood, 56–9, 61
record-keeping, 350, 491–3
Red Cap Company (Colesberg Party), 56–9, 57
Red Cross diamond, 467
reef-fall, 118–20, 127
reflectivity tests, 481–2
refraction, 226, 228–34, 314
  double, 407, 481
  refractive index, 385, *408*, 472, 475–7
Regent (*formerly* Pitt) diamond, 4, *4*, 23, 208, 457–9
rejection clarity grade, 282, 300